CHILDREN WITH LEARNING DISABILITIES

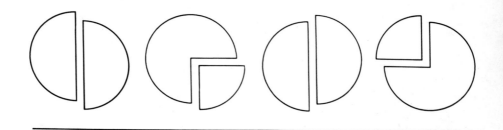

HOUGHTON   MIFFLIN   COMPANY   Boston
Atlanta   Dallas   Geneva, Illinois   Hopewell, New Jersey   Palo Alto   London

THEORIES
DIAGNOSIS
TEACHING STRATEGIES

Children with Learning Disabilities

SECOND EDITION

Janet W. Lerner
Northeastern Illinois University

To Eugene

Printed in the U.S.A.

Library of Congress Catalog Card Number: 75-26085

ISBN: 0-395-20474-7

Contents

TEACHING STRATEGIES

Foreword

The field of learning disabilities, having expanded rapidly in the past decade, has now become one of the most significant areas of special education. The efforts of parents, state departments of education, and the federal government have stimulated and promoted services for children who otherwise have been neglected.

There are many cogent reasons for this development of the field of learning disabilities. During the postwar period, special education concentrated on the expansion of services for children with previously identified disorders — the visually and auditorially handicapped, the mental deviates, the physically handicapped, the speech defective, and the emotionally disturbed. After such programs were established in public and residential schools, it was discovered that there remained many children who were physically unimpaired and intellectually normal, but who failed to perceive visually, to process auditory information, to talk, read, spell, or think adequately. A more thorough analysis of these children's behavior suggested that they had central processing dysfunctions that inhibited learning by ordinary methods. In response to these diverse problems a new discipline arose that borrowed and integrated insights from neurology, psychology, speech pathology, and remedial reading. The subjects of this new field were given various names — brain-injured children, children with perceptual handicaps, children with minimal cerebral dysfunction, and children with learning disabilities. The latter term, because it emphasizes the educational character of such disorders, has become the most acceptable for educational purposes. The field has now become sufficiently specialized to undertake the diagnosis and remediation of severe learning problems.

The first edition of *Children with Learning Disabilities* became a welcome addition to the literature. It presented the discipline from a broad point of view, without attempting to promote any single method or theory. Many teachers complained of the overly theoretical approach of much that had been written on learning disabilities, and pointed out that very little information was available on how theory is implemented. Dr. Lerner minimized that problem by emphasizing in her book the development of teaching strategies for various disabilities.

The second edition of *Children with Learning Disabilities* has retained the valuable features of the first. Dr. Lerner has revised and extended her material and she has added new concepts and practices that have been developed since the publication of the first edition.

Children with Learning Disabilities integrates theory, diagnosis, and teaching strategies into a comprehensive guide not only for regular classroom teachers and special teachers of children with learning disabilities, but also for administrators of programs, and for instructors of college courses in learning disabilities.

Samuel A. Kirk

Preface

Children who are destined to become educational discards unless their learning disabilities are recognized and alleviated are likely to be found in any typical classroom. The condition of learning disabilities is perplexing: although such children are not blind, many do not see as normal children do; although they are not deaf, many do not listen or hear normally; although they are not retarded in mental development, they do not learn. Many of these youngsters exhibit other behavioral characteristics that make them disruptive in the classroom and at home. Such children are the concern of this book.

Interest in and knowledge about the field of learning disabilities have expanded at an extremely rapid pace since the appearance of the first edition of *Children with Learning Disabilities*. Growth and change are evident in the areas of research, assessment, teaching materials, educational services provided by the schools, teacher preparation programs, legislation, parent involvement and leadership, and in the burgeoning membership of learning disabilities organizations. This revision was undertaken to incorporate these consequential changes.

Among the recent topics, issues, and concerns included in this revision are: programs for early childhood and the adolescent, new concepts of delivery systems including mainstreaming, legislation, the cross-categorical movement, the role of parents, and the administration of learning disabilities programs. In addition, the revision was updated with significant recent research and theories, as well as recent diagnostic procedures, instructional materials, and teaching strategies.

Children with Learning Disabilities is designed to provide a broad overview of the field of learning disabilities for present and prospective teachers, educational clinicians and therapists, administrators, psychologists, language pathologists, counselors, and other professionals preparing to work with the learning-disabled child. The book is also intended for regular classroom teachers who wish to better understand learning-disabled children in their classrooms, and it can serve parents by providing necessary background information. The approach of the book is eclectic, to offer the reader a comprehensive view of the field: the various theories, diagnostic procedures, and teaching methods and materials. Teachers of learning-disabled children should have an understanding of the diverse theoretical approaches to the field, knowledge of diagnostic procedures, skill in the art of clinical teaching, and familiarity with teaching techniques and materials. This book deals with each of these essential areas.

The book is organized into four major parts:

Part One is an overview of the field of learning disabilities. Chapter 1 describes the multidisciplinary nature of the field; Chapter 2 offers an historical perspective; Chapter 3 presents emerging directions; and Chapter 4 examines the contributions of medicine.

Part Two deals with the diagnostic-teaching process. Diagnosis and clinical teaching are viewed as interrelated parts of a continuous process of trying to understand a child and helping him or her learn. Diagnosis that does not lead to teaching is a dead end, while teaching without a clear purpose may be wasteful and detrimental. Diagnosis is discussed in Chapter 5, and clinical teaching is the subject of Chapter 6.

Part Three reviews the theories that provide the basis for diagnostic and teaching decisions. It also presents teaching strategies that evolve from each of the theories. The role of theory in the field of learning disabilities is discussed in Chapter 7. Sensory-motor and perceptual-motor theories are reviewed in Chapter 8. Theories of perception and memory are examined in Chapter 9. Chapter 10 discusses theories of language as they are related to learning disabilities. Cognitive development is studied in Chapter 11. Maturational, emotional, and behavioral perspectives comprise the content of Chapter 12.

Academic implications and teaching strategies based on each of the theories follow the theory section in each chapter of Part Three. Included in the teaching strategies sections are: methods for teaching motor development, perception, memory, oral language, reading, spelling, handwriting, written expression, arithmetic, reading comprehension, self-concepts, social perception, and behavior modification.

Part Four discusses the organization and management of learning disabilities programs. Chapter 13 reviews systems for delivering educational services. Chapter 14 looks at the problems of administering the learning disabilities program.

The Appendixes are designed to provide useful source and reference materials.

Children with Learning Disabilities grew out of my experiences teaching courses in learning disabilities and working with children with reading and learning problems. It has been considerably influenced by feedback from college students and teachers enrolled in courses I have taught. The most helpful source in preparing the second edition were the students in my classes at Northeastern Illinois University who alerted me to new concepts, programs, and materials and provided essential feedback. In addition, I am indebted to many authors of books and articles, to numerous speakers at conferences, to a number of educators in school districts and universities with whom I have communicated, and to colleagues at Northeastern Illinois

University, all of whom provided invaluable information and new insights. I have also been fortunate in having had the opportunity to become aware of the current scene from professionals and parents at conferences held in various communities throughout the country.

I wish to thank a number of reviewers who read the manuscript at various stages and provided helpful suggestions and criticisms: Dr. Veralee Hardin, Dr. Betty Harrison, Dr. John Junkala, and Dr. Martin Steigman. Dr. Samuel A. Kirk played a continuing role in the making of this book: as my first college instructor in special education, as a perceptive and discerning editor of the first edition of the book, and as a current stimulating and provocative scholar and writer. I acknowledge my children, Susan, Laura, and Dean for their continued support. Finally, thanks to my husband, Eugene, who provided the encouragement and faith needed to complete this work.

Janet W. Lerner

ONE

Overview of Learning Disabilities

1. Learning Disabilities: An Interdisciplinary Field

THE ENIGMA OF LEARNING DISABILITIES

There is at present a growing concern for the child with learning disabilities. The enigma of the youngster who has difficulty in learning is, however, not new. Children from all walks of life have experienced such difficulties throughout the years. Indeed, there is evidence that some of the world's most distinguished persons had unusual difficulty in certain aspects of learning.

Thomas Edison, the ingenious American inventor, was called abnormal, addled, and mentally defective. Writing in his diary that he was never able to get along at school, he recalled that he was always at the foot of his class. While his father thought of him as stupid, Edison described himself as a dunce. Auguste Rodin, the great French sculptor, was called the worst pupil in the school. Because his teachers diagnosed Rodin as uneducable, they advised his parents to put him out to work, though they doubted that he could ever make a living. Woodrow Wilson, the scholarly twenty-eighth president of the United States, did not learn his letters until he was 9 years old and did not learn to read until age 11. Relatives expressed sorrow

2

for his parents because Woodrow was so dull and backward (Thompson 1971).

Nelson Rockefeller, political leader, former governor of New York, and vice president of the United States, suffered from severe dyslexia, which kept him from achieving good grades in school. Moreover, during his political career his poor reading forced him to memorize his speeches (*Time*, September 2, 1974). Albert Einstein, the great mathematical genius, did not speak until age three. His search for words was described as laborious, and, until he was seven, he formulated each sentence, no matter how commonplace, silently with his lips before speaking it aloud. School work did not go well for young Einstein. He had little facility with arithmetic, no special ability in any other academic subject, and great difficulty with foreign languages. One teacher predicted that "nothing good" would come of him. Einstein's language disabilities persisted throughout his adult life. When he read, he heard words; writing was difficult for him; and he communicated badly through writing. In describing his thinking process, he explained that he rarely thought in words; it was only after a thought came that he tried to express it in words at a later time (Patten 1973).

These persons of eminence fortunately were able somehow to find appropriate ways of learning, and they successfully overcame their initial failures. Many youngsters with learning disabilities are not so fortunate.

Tony is one such case. His parents have long been aware that their son has severe problems in learning. As an infant, Tony was colicky and had difficulty in learning to suck. His early speech was so garbled that no one could understand him, and frequently his inability to communicate led to sudden temper tantrums. The kindergarten teacher reported that Tony was "immature"; his first-grade teacher said he "did not pay attention"; and succeeding teachers labeled him "lazy" and then "emotionally disturbed." Tony's distraught parents attempted to find the source of his learning problems to alleviate his misery and theirs. They desperately followed suggestions from many sources that led to a succession of specialists and clinics dedicated to treating such difficulties.

One clinic detected a visual problem, and as a result Tony received visual training exercises for several years. Another clinic diagnosed Tony's problem as a lack of neurological organization and instituted a lengthy series of motor exercises. An opinion of emotional disturbance at another agency led to years of psychotherapy for both Tony and his parents. A reading tutor analyzed the problem as a lack of instruction in phonics, and Tony received intensive phonics instruction for a period of time. The family pediatrician said that the boy was merely going through a stage and would grow out of it. Yet despite this wealth of diagnosis and treatment, Tony still cannot learn. He is unhappily failing in school, and, understandably, he has lost faith in himself.

The problems encountered by Tony and his parents are typical. Each specialty viewed Tony's problem from its own perspective and therefore saw only part of the picture. What was needed, instead, was a unified interdisciplinary approach to the problem of Tony's learning disabilities — a coordinated effort, with each special field contributing its expertise to the analysis and treatment of the child. A unified procedure was required to mobilize the team and coordinate the efforts of the various contributing professions.

Without a coordinated effort, each field may see the child with learning disabilities in terms of its own perspective, much as the fabled blind men of India are said to have "seen" the elephant. In the proverbial tale, one blind man felt the elephant's trunk and concluded an elephant was like a snake; another, feeling the leg, said it resembled a tree trunk; the third, feeling the tail, believed the elephant was like a rope; the fourth touched the ear and thought the elephant was like a fan; the fifth felt the tusk and likened the elephant to a spear; while the last man, feeling the side, said the elephant was like a wall. Similarly, in learning disabilities each profession sees but one part of the child; it is necessary to bring the parts together to understand the whole child.

This problem of fragmentation is noted by Bassler (1967, p. 3). Within our schools and community, we have untapped resources to help the underachieving child become an achiever. However, too many schools have failed to integrate the various professional services being used with an individual child.

> The reading consultant knows the child has a complex of reading problems; the school nurse observes a hearing problem; the speech therapist, a lisp. The school psychologist, the family doctor, the optometrist, the opthalmologist, the parents, each has a different view of the child and his constellation of problems. We have so segmented and fragmented the child, we have so atomized our approach to the educational problems, that we have lost the child in the labyrinth of professions and techniques.

An important task of the learning disabilities specialist is to integrate the various professional services. An overview of the major disciplines concerned with the learning-disabled child is presented in the next section.

DISCIPLINES CONTRIBUTING TO THE STUDY OF LEARNING DISABILITIES

The major disciplines contributing to the study of learning disabilities can be grouped in five categories: *medicine, psychology, language, education,* and *other professions.* The mingling of professions brings a multidisciplinary depth to the study of the child with learning disabilities.

MEDICINE

The medical specialties (represented by both practitioners and researchers) include pediatrics, neurology, ophthalmology, otology, psychiatry, pharmacology, endocrinology, electroencephalography, nursing, and school nursing.

Figure 1.1 Learning disabilities: an interdisciplinary field

Medical specialists are, by training and experience, cause oriented — always searching for the source or etiology of a health problem. Once the cause of an illness is determined, a cure can be prescribed. Medical specialists tend to view a learning disability as a pathological condition, and their terminology, which is frequently concerned with the cause of a learning disorder, is medical in origin. Many of the terms are adaptations of words used to describe various kinds of damage to the nervous system of the adult patient, such as a cerebral stroke. Terms such as brain impairment, cerebral insult, brain damage, brain injury, apraxia, agnosia, dyslexia, and aphasia are examples of medically oriented terminology.

PSYCHOLOGY

Important contributions to the field of learning disabilities are being made by psychologists, particularly specialists in child development and learning theory. The psychologists observe, test, evaluate, and characterize the outward behavior of children. The psychological perspective also leads to the development of views concerning the psychodynamic concomitants of learning abnormalities. Psychology has contributed such terms as perceptual disorder, impulsivity, disinhibited behavior, perseveration, and hyperkinetic activity.

Specialists in child development focus on the developmental processes of the normal child, which become the basis for many concepts of the atypical child. The theory of maturational lag, for example, is rooted in the analysis of child growth patterns.

Learning theorists have contributed to the analysis of school-subject content areas in behavioral terms, identifying tasks to be taught and behaviors to be expected. Reinforcement theory, operant conditioning, and behavior modification are among the contributions of learning theorists to learning disabilities research and teaching.

LANGUAGE STUDY

Workers in the fields of speech and language pathology, language development, linguistics, and psycholinguistics have recently recognized that many of their interests and concerns overlap those of the field of learning disabilities. Since speech teachers and language pathologists have traditionally allied themselves closely with the medical profession, their thinking and terminology readily follow the viewpoints and concepts developed by the medical field. Terms from the fields of speech and communication disorders found in the literature on learning disabilities include aphasia, dyslexia, anomia, and expressive and receptive language disorders.

The science of linguistics is the study of human language in all its forms. Psycholinguistics is a recently developed area that combines psychology and linguistics. These fields are making important contributions to our understanding of the relationship of language development to the learning process. A renewed interest in the puzzle of language acquisition, kindled by recent work in linguistics, shows promise of contributing to our understanding of the child with learning disabilites. Knowledge of how the normal child learns language will be invaluable in developing the ability to diagnose and treat language difficulties in children. Conversely, perhaps an understanding of the normal child's language acquisition will come through the study of the language disorders of exceptional children. Psycholinguistics and linguistics have contributed terms such as encoding, decoding, syntax, phonology, morphology, and semantics to the literature on learning disabilities.

EDUCATION

The field of education has a practical framework, for it must deal with the reality of teaching the child. Kirk (1972, p. 35) has noted that "education often begins where medicine stops." The training and experience of educators permit teachers, reading specialists, special educators, clinical teachers, psychoeducational diagnosticians, physical educators, and curriculum developers to focus on the learning behavior of the child. The educators' expertise includes knowledge about subject area sequences, an understanding of the relationship of curricular areas, an acquaintance with a variety of school organizational patterns, and knowledge of materials and methods. The very term *learning disabilities*, with its emphasis on the learning situation instead of the etiology of the disorder, is evidence of the impact of the educator in this field.

OTHER PROFESSIONS

Many other specialists play important roles in the research and literature on learning disabilities. Optometrists, who are concerned with the visual function, have made key contributions. Many of the child's percepts and concepts come to him through the visual field. Visual acuity, visual perception, visual memory, and visual motor learning are discussed by optometrists.

Audiologists, who work in the field of hearing, have contributed important concepts concerning auditory perception and auditory training. Social workers, occupational therapists, and guidance counselors have also made vital contributions to the growth of the field. In addition, research findings from fields such as genetics and biochemistry may provide additional important information.

LEARNING DISABILITIES SPECIALIST: THE COORDINATING AGENT

The learning disabilities specialist is the agent who is responsible for coordinating the efforts of the contributing professions. Kirk (1969, p. 4) describes the role of this specialist:

> A position for a person with interdisciplinary training will evolve in our schools, perhaps entitled "Diagnostic-Remedial Specialist." This individual will serve as the responsible agent for the child — responsible for adequate diagnosis, evaluation or assessment, and for the remediation or the organization of remediation for a child with a learning disability. All personnel involved in the assessment of the child — doctors, psychologists, and social workers — will report their findings and interpretations to this diagnostic-remedial specialist. She or he will be responsible for the collation and interpretation of information, for remediation, or for the prescription for remedial education. The diagnostic-remedial specialist will function somewhat as the family physician does — as the responsible agent for obtaining information from other specialists and for prescribing treatment.

One crucial role of the learning disabilities specialist within such a framework would be to build a cooperative interdisciplinary team that works together, rather than to permit team members to pursue a splintered and isolated approach that sometimes works at cross-purposes with the proposals of others. Although the learning disabilities specialist is not an expert in all of these contributing fields, intensive interdisciplinary training should include the vocabularies and basic concepts of the other specialists and what they can do. The learning disabilities specialist should not operate as an expert in the spheres of neurology or ophthalmology or psychoanalytic theory, but should serve as a highly skilled coworker and coordinator.

THE DEFINITION OF LEARNING DISABILITIES

The field of learning disabilities is relatively new, but it is growing at a phenomenally rapid rate. Through the intermingling of many professions, a multidisciplinary breadth is evolving. However, because so many diverse professions are concerned, a confusion of terminology and seemingly conflicting ideas pervade current discussions in the literature.

In the various attempts to identify the population of children with learning disabilities, several dimensions of the problem have been considered. Discussions of these different approaches to the problem of definition follow.

1. *Neurological dysfunction or brain impairment*. Definitions that focus on this dimension of the problem attempt to identify organic etiology. For example Cruickshank (1967) believes that specific neurological conditions give rise to learning dysfunction and refers to these children as "brain injured." The concept of *learning disability*, put forth by Johnson and Myklebust (1967, p. 8), implies a neurological dysfunction:

> . . . we refer to children as having a psychoneurological learning disability, meaning that behavior has been disturbed as a result of a dysfunction of the brain and that the problem is one of altered processes, not of a generalized incapacity to learn.

2. *Uneven growth pattern.* Another emphasis in the identification of the learning disability population is on the irregular development of mental abilities. An examination of profiles of subskills reveals that growth in the various areas is uneven and inconsistent. Myers and Hammill (1969) refer to this pattern as the "principle of disparity." Gallagher (1966, p. 28) focuses on such developmental imbalances in identifying the population:

> Children with developmental imbalances are those who reveal a developmental disparity in psychological processes related to education of such a degree (often four years or more) as to require the instructional programing of developmental tasks appropriate to the nature and level of the deviant developmental process.

3. *Difficulty in academic and learning tasks*. Another aspect of identifying the population of children with learning disabilities is that of considering the learning problems that such children encounter. Kirk's definition (1962, p. 263) emphasizes this problem:

A learning disability refers to a retardation, disorder, or delayed development in one or more of the processes of speech, language, reading, spelling, writing, or arithmetic resulting from a possible cerebral dysfunction and/or emotional or behavioral disturbance and not from mental retardation, sensory deprivation, or cultural or instructional factors.

4. *Discrepancy between achievement and potentiality*. Yet another focus in defining the population of learning-disabled children is the criterion of a significant discrepancy between what the child is potentially capable of learning and what in fact has been learned. Bateman (1965, p. 220), for example, defines children with specific learning disabilities as those who

> manifest an educationally significant discrepancy between their estimated intellectual potential and actual level of performance related to basic disorders in the learning processes, which may or may not be accompanied by demonstrable central nervous system dysfunction, and which are not secondary to generalized mental retardation, educational or cultural deprivation, severe emotional disturbance, or sensory loss.

5. *Definition by exclusion*. Another dimension of many of the definitions is that the children under consideration do not primarily fit into any other area of exceptionality; that is, children with learning disabilities are not primarily mentally retarded, emotionally disturbed, culturally deprived, sensorily handicapped. This dimension, among several others, is included in the definition by Johnson and Myklebust (1967, p. 9):

> In those having a psychoneurological learning disability, it is the fact of adequate motor ability, average to high intelligence, adequate hearing and vision, and adequate emotional adjustment together with a deficiency in learning that constitutes the basis for homogeneity.

Several committees, formed to channel these diverse perspectives, attempted to draw up a definition that was meaningful and acceptable to all concerned professional groups (Kass and Myklebust, 1969). Finally a definition was formulated by the National Advisory Committee on Handicapped Children in their annual report to Congress in 1968 (p. 4):

> Children with special learning disabilities exhibit a disorder in one or more of the basic psychological processes involved in understanding or using spoken or written languages. These may be manifested in disorders of listening, thinking, talking, reading, writing, spelling or arithmetic. They include conditions which have been referred to as perceptual handicaps, brain injury, minimal brain dysfunction, dyslexia, developmental aphasia, etc. They do not include learning problems which are due primarily to visual, hearing, or motor handicaps, to mental retardation, emotional disturbance, or to environmental disadvantage.

Congressional legislation concerning the child with learning disabilities incorporates this definition in the Children with Specific Learning Disabilities Act of 1969, PL 91-230, the Elementary and Secondary Amendments of 1969. This legislation was extended in 1974 as part of PL 93-380.

The definition resulted from the work of individuals representing many disciplines concerned with learning disorders. However, objections to this somewhat ambiguous and confining definition of the learning-disabled child were soon voiced (Hammill 1974). The objections centered on the exclusion dimension of the definition — the exclusion of disadvantaged children, of emotionally disturbed children, and of mentally retarded children. The critics correctly pointed out that many of these excluded youngsters also exhibit symptoms of learning disabilities and it is often impossible to discern which handicap is primary. While the desire for a broader definition has merit, it is important to understand the reason for the development of the present definition and to see it from a historical perspective.

Kirk (1974) explains that legislation passed by Congress in 1963 provided for the training of professional personnel and research for handicapped children. Handicapped children were defined specifically as mentally retarded, seriously emotionally disturbed, speech defective, auditorily handicapped, visually handicapped, crippled, and afflicted with other health impairments that require special education. No reference was made to learning disabilities, since the term was not used at that time. Parents from the Association for Children with Learning Disabilities (ACLD) and professionals from the field began to agitate for specific legislation for the problem of learning disabilities. Individuals appeared before Congressional committees during the years 1965–1967 to ask for special legislation and special funding — funding that would not have to be shared or come from other areas of exceptionality. The definition, establishment, and recognition of learning disabilities as a separate and discrete category were therefore essential to provide sufficient funds and appropriate legislation. An ACLD committee recently recommended amending this definition to include children with specific learning disabilities who also have sensory, motor, intellectual, or emotional problems, or are environmentally disadvantaged (Kirk 1974) [The risk involved in broadening this definition is over-identifying children who have problems in learning; this would result in a sharp increase in the prevalence of learning disabilities.]

In practice, the concepts of diagnosing and treating learning-disabled youngsters provide a practical framework for all categories of mildly handicapped youngsters. Many mildly retarded, hearing impaired, emotionally disturbed, and culturally different young people exhibit characteristics and symptoms that fit the learning disabilities concepts and respond to materials and methods designed for the learning disabled. Moreover, much of what is known of learning disabilities is derived from research in other categories of exceptionality, particularly in mental retardation (Hallahan and Cruickshank 1973). At present, however, the Congressional definition, as recommended in 1968 by the National Advisory Committee on Handicapped Children, still stands as the basis for many important decisions.

PREVALENCE OF LEARNING DISABILITIES

A variety of estimates of the prevalence of children who suffer from learning disabilities has been made, ranging from 1 percent to 30 percent of the school population, depending on the criteria used to determine the disability. One estimate, for example, was the result of a recent screening of almost 2,800 children in the third and fourth grades in a public school population; this screening was conducted as part of a research project at Northwestern University (Myklebust and Boshes 1969). The identification criterion used in this study was based on an educational-discrepancy definition of learning disabilities: the entire public school population was initially screened by administering a battery of psychoeducational tests and deriving a ratio between achievement and expectancy for each child tested. The criterion of underachievement was a ratio or learning quotient of less than 90; by this standard, 15 percent of the research population were identified as underachievers. However, further study and more stringent criteria for identification revealed that approximately one-half of those initially identified fell into the category of learning disabled. In this study, then, the prevalence of children with learning disabilities in the public school population examined was determined to be 7 to 8 percent.

A more conservative estimate has been made by the National Advisory Committee on Handicapped Children (1968) in their report to Congress. They recommended that 1 to 3 percent of the school population be considered as a prevalence estimate, at least until research provides objective criteria for identifying these children more clearly. Kirk (1974) explains that when the passage of learning disabilities legislation was being argued before Congress, senators and representatives were surprised to hear that 20 to 30 percent of public school children are learning disabled. If this prevalence is so high, they asked, can this truly be considered an area of special education? One senator questioned the 30 percent figure, noting that if an additional 15 percent have other handicapping conditions, then 45 percent of school children require special education.

To solve this confusion and provide some perspective, the National Advisory Committee for the Handicapped has estimated that the hard-core cases of learning disabilities constitute approximately 1 to 3 percent of the school population.

Nevertheless, it is clear that we are talking about a tremendous number of children. It is interesting to compare these prevalence estimates with those of other areas of exceptionality, as shown in Table 1.1. The number of children with learning disabilities, as estimated by studies such as the Northwestern project (Myklebust and Boshes 1969), is much larger than the number of children with any other kind of handicap listed in the table.

Table 1.1 Estimated prevalence of handicapped children in the school-age population

Type of Exceptionality	Estimated Percentage
Mentally retarded	2.3 percent
Deaf and hard-of-hearing (deaf: 0.1 percent) (hearing impaired: 0.5 percent)	0.6
Visually handicapped (partially seeing: 0.07 percent) (blind: 0.03 percent)	0.1
Crippled	0.8
Special health problems	0.8
Speech handicapped	3.5
Emotionally disturbed and socially maladjusted	2.0
Gifted	2.0
Total	12.1

Adapted from Romaine P. Mackie, *Special Education in the United States: Statistics 1946–1949*. New York: Teachers College Press, 1969, p. 61.

Whatever the prevalence is finally determined to be, there are likely to be at least several children in every classroom who can be identified as children with learning disabilities. The problem appears in boys four to six times more often than in girls.

SUMMARY

This chapter has presented an introduction to the enigmatic field of learning disabilities and the specialty fields within it, including medicine, psychology, language study, education, and other professions. We have examined the role of the learning disabilities specialist in coordinating these contributing disciplines. We have reviewed the history leading to the definition of learning disabilities, the legal definition used by Congress, and the current dissatisfaction with that definition. Finally, we have seen that the prevalence of learning disabilities in the general population underscores the importance of these issues.

REFERENCES

Bassler, John J. "Interdisciplinary Needs in Reading." *Illinois Journal of Education* 58 (December 1967): 3–4.

Bateman, Barbara. "An Educator's View of a Diagnostic Approach to Learning Disorders," pp. 219–236 in Jerome Hellmuth (ed.), *Learning Disorders,* Vol. 1. Seattle: Special Child Publications, 1965.

Cruickshank, William. *The Brain-Injured Child in Home, School and Community.* Syracuse, N.Y.: Syracuse University Press, 1967.

Gallagher, James. "Children with Developmental Imbalances: A Psychoeducational Definition," pp. 21–34 in W. Cruickshank (ed.), *The Teacher of Brain-Injured Children: A Discussion of the Bases of Competency.* Syracuse, N.Y.: Syracuse University Press, 1966.

Hallahan, D., and W. Cruickshank. *Psychoeducational Foundations of Learning Disabilities.* Englewood Cliffs, N.J.: Prentice-Hall, 1973.

Hammill, Donald. "Learning Disabilities: A Problem in Definition." *Division for Children with Learning Disabilities Newsletter* 4 (Spring 1974): 28–31.

Johnson, Doris, and Helmer Myklebust. *Learning Disabilities: Educational Principles and Practices.* New York: Grune & Stratton, 1967.

Kass, Corrine, and H. Myklebust. "Learning Disabilities: An Educational Definition." *Journal of Learning Disabilities* 2 (July 1969): 377–379.

Kirk, Samuel. *Educating Exceptional Children.* Boston: Houghton Mifflin, 1972.

———. Introduction to *State of the Art: Where Are We in Learning Disabilities?* Los Angeles: Association for Children with Learning Disabilities and California Association for Neurologically Handicapped Children Publications, 1974.

———. "Learning Disabilities: The View From Here," pp. 21–27 in *Progress in Parent Information, Professional Growth and Public Policy.* Selected papers, Association for Children with Learning Disabilities. San Rafael, Calif.: Academic Therapy Publications, 1969.

Mackie, Romaine P. *Special Education in the United States: Statistics 1946–1966.* New York: Teachers College Press, 1969.

Myers, P., and D. Hammill. *Methods for Learning Disorders.* New York: Wiley, 1969.

Myklebust, Helmer, and Benjamin Boshes. *Minimal Brain Damage in Children.* Final report, U.S. Public Health Service Contract 108–65–142. U.S. Department of Health, Education, and Welfare. Evanston, Ill.: Northwestern University Publication, June 1969.

National Advisory Committee on Handicapped Children. *Special Education for Handicapped Children.* First Annual Report. Washington, D.C.: U.S. Department of Health, Education, and Welfare, January 31, 1968.

Patten, Bernard M. "Visually Mediated Thinking: A Report of the Case of Albert Einstein." *Journal of Learning Disabilities* 6 (August/September 1973): 415–420.

Thompson, Lloyd J. "Language Disabilities in Men of Eminence." *Journal of Learning Disabilities* 4 (January 1971): 34–45.

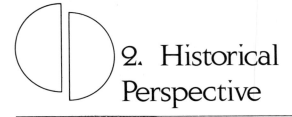

2. Historical Perspective

DEVELOPMENT OF A NEW FIELD

This chapter presents a brief history of the field of learning disabilities, which Wiederholt (1974) divides into three distinct periods of development: a foundation phase, a transition phase, and an integration phase. During the *foundation phase* (about 1800–1930), medical theories of brain function and dysfunction were formulated by studying behavioral characteristics of adults who acquired brain damage and consequently lost certain skills. During the *transition phase* (about 1930–1960), pioneering psychologists and educators attempted to translate the theoretical formulations of the first phase into remedial practices for children. The *integration phase* (about 1963 to the present) is characterized by the rapid growth of school programs for learning-disabled children and by eclectic use of a large variety of theories, assessment methods, and teaching strategies.

The enigma of the child who is unable to learn has been the concern of researchers for many years. In the late 1800s, Morgan (1896), an English ophthalmologist, reported on a condition he called "word blindness," which involved an inability to read. The concept of remedial reading began in the United States in the 1920s (Smith 1961). In the 1930s, Orton (1937), a neuropathologist, studied the relationship between cerebral dominance and developmental language disorders. Also during this period, McGinnis (1963), a speech pathologist, investigated and treated the problem of language disorders and aphasia. Learning disabilities as a comprehensive field of study, however, is generally considered to have begun in 1947, with the appearance of *Psychopathology and Education of the Brain-Injured Child,* by Alfred A. Strauss and Laura E. Lehtinen.

Since that time many have dedicated themselves to an intensive study of this problem. As new knowledge has accrued, the existing theories have often proved to be inadequate, and so have been treated as working hypotheses to be refined, modified, revised, and enlarged. The historic growth of any science is dependent on such a continuum of inquiry. Indeed, this is the essence of the scientific method. According to John Dewey (1938, p. 236):

> That earlier conclusions have the function of preparing the way for later inquiries and judgments, and that the latter are dependent upon facts and conceptions instituted in earlier ones are commonplaces in the intellectual development of individuals and the historic growth of any science.

In the field of learning disabilities, one consequence of the modifications and refinements of the working hypotheses since 1947 has been an accompanying change in terminology. The early work of Strauss focused on a new category of exceptional child conceptualized as *brain injured,* but this view was soon questioned in the light of new knowledge and insights. Many new concepts and terms were introduced, such as brain damage, the Strauss syndrome, perceptual handicap, neurophrenia, "the other child," minimal brain dysfunction, and learning disabilities. The historical development of the field of learning disabilities has been a process of building toward systematic knowledge.

THE BRAIN-INJURED CHILD

Educators and teachers have long been aware of children who have difficulty with school subjects or whose school achievement is far below their capability. However, the pioneering work in the field now called learning disabilities can be traced to the initial investigations in the late 1930s and early 1940s of Heinz Werner, a psychologist, and his associate, Alfred A. Strauss, a neuropsychiatrist. Their views were presented in the first volume of the now-classic work of Strauss and Lehtinen (1947).

Strauss and Werner perceived a common pattern in a group of children who had been previously classified in various exceptional categories, such as mentally retarded, emotionally disturbed, autistic, behaviorally maladjusted, and aphasic. A new category of exceptional children — *brain injured* — was created.

Strauss, a physician who had received his medical training in Germany, had emigrated to the United States prior to 1937 and joined the staff of the Wayne County Training School in Michigan. Later in Wisconsin and Illinois, he established the Cove Schools for brain-injured children. The subjects of Strauss' studies, most of whom exhibited such severe behavioral disturbances that they were excluded from the public schools, frequently had medical histories indicating that brain injury had occurred at some time.

Seeking a medical cause for the behavioral characteristics he observed, Strauss surmised that the behavior and learning patterns of these children were manifestations of brain injury. This hypothesis was unique because the behavioral abnormalities of many such children had been explained by others as having emotional causes or as being psychogenic. Strauss further speculated that children who exhibited characteristics similar to those of the children in his study had also experienced an injury to the brain that produced the abnormal behavioral symptoms. Strauss concluded that the injury to the brain could have taken place in the prenatal stages, during the birth process, or at some point after birth. He defined the brain-injured child as follows (Strauss and Lehtinen 1947, p. 4):

> The brain-injured child is the child who before, during or after birth has received an injury to or suffered an infection of the brain. As a result of such organic impairment, defects of the neuromotor system may be present or absent; however, such a child may show disturbances in perception, thinking, and emotional behavior, either separately or in combination. This disturbance can be demonstrated by specific tests. These disturbances prevent or impede a normal learning process. Special educational methods have been devised to remedy these specific handicaps.

Strauss theorized that such brain injury was *exogenous* rather than *endogenous*, that is, the impairment was due not to an inherited pattern or the genetic structure of the brain, but to an injury that occurred outside of the genetic structure. An example of an exogenous cause of brain injury before birth is an infection such as German measles contracted by the mother early in pregnancy and affecting the fetus. An example of an exogenous cause of injury during the birth is any condition that would seriously reduce the infant's supply of oxygen during the birth process. An example of exogenous brain injury after birth is a fall on the head or an excessively high fever in infancy or early childhood. The following are among the characteristics Strauss noted in the children he categorized as brain injured.

BEHAVIORAL CRITERIA

1. *Perceptual disorders*. When looking at a picture, the child with perceptual disorders sees parts instead of wholes, or sees figure-ground distortions that may confuse the background with the foreground. An example of seeing an object as a whole rather than as unrelated parts is the identification of a letter. When asked to identify the capital letter "A," the child with

perceptual disorders may perceive three unrelated lines rather than a meaningful whole.

Figure-ground distortion refers to an inability to focus on an object without having its setting interfere with the perception. Looking at the picture in Figure 2.1, one child saw a room rather than the door and, consequently answered that the initial consonant of the object in the picture was "r" instead of "d."

The classic illustration shown in Figure 2.2 illustrates the feelings of ambiguity that perceptual disorders present. This illustration contains a reversible figure-ground pattern, and a confusion or a shifting of background and foreground is expected. The ambiguity in perception that the normal observer senses in this ilustration can help one understand the unstable world of the child with a perceptual disorder. One teacher noted that

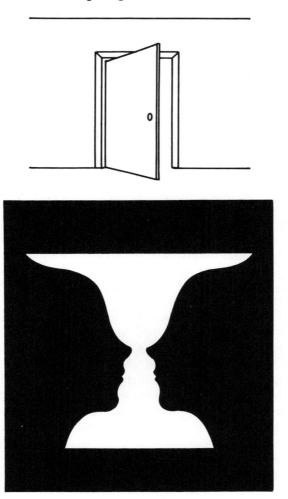

Figure 2.1

Figure 2.2

whenever she wore a particular dress with polka dots, children with perceptual disorders seemed compelled to touch in order to verify what they thought they perceived.

2. _Perseveration._ A child with perseverative behavior continues an activity once it has started and has difficulty in changing to another. For example, a child may not be able to stop after writing the letter "a" the three times required in a writing lesson, but, instead, continues this activity until the entire page is filled with a's. One such child continued the activity onto the desk and up the wall.

3. _Conceptual disorders._ A child with conceptual disorders is unable to organize materials and thoughts in a normal manner. This is a disturbance in the cognitive abilities, and it affects comprehension skills in reading and listening. One 10-year-old girl was unable to differentiate the concepts of "sugar" and "salt" and usually confused the words symbolizing the concepts.

4. _Behavioral disorders._ Children with behavioral disorders may be hyperactive, explosive, erratic, or otherwise uninhibited in behavior. The child who is continually in motion, blows up easily, and is readily distracted from the task at hand is exhibiting behavioral disorders.

BIOLOGICAL CRITERIA

1. _Slight neurological signs._ This term refers to subtle, rather than obvious or severe, evidence of neurological abnormalities. An awkwardness in gait, for example, is considered a slight neurological sign. The inability to perform fine motor skills efficiently is also included in this category.

2. _A history of neurological impairment._ This refers to evidence in the medical history of brain injury that occurred before, during, or after birth.

3. _No history of mental retardation in the family._ Strauss felt that it was important to rule out endogenous or genetic abnormalities of the brain, such as familial mental retardation. His concern was with exogenous brain damage to a potentially normal brain. He did not include within his category of the brain-injured child endogenous abnormalities caused by inherited factors.

In Strauss' thinking, a child could be diagnosed as brain injured without hard evidence of any of the three biological signs. Strauss' original subjects were known to have had an injury to the brain. These groupings of brain-injured children included youngsters who fell within the normal and above-normal intelligence ranges, as well as those who were classified as mentally retarded. Because these children known to be brain injured exhibited the appropriate behavioral characteristics, Strauss concluded that children who exhibited the same characteristic behavioral patterns could be presumed to have suffered a brain injury at some time.

One consequence of Strauss' initial work was that physicians were alerted to events that could be related to injury to the brain. An alarmingly large number of possibilities have been suggested as potential causes of exogenous brain injury. For instance, the mother's condition during pregnancy might be a possible cause of brain injury. Examples of such conditions include the RH factor, diseases during pregnancy such as rubella, and medication taken by the mother during pregnancy. Brain injury may be caused by factors in the birth process itself, including insufficient oxygen; prematurity; a long, hard labor; difficult delivery; or a purposely delayed birth. Examples of severe childhood diseases and accidents that have been related to brain injury include encephalitis, meningitis, dehydration, extremely high fevers, and head injuries.

It must be remembered that these events are merely potential causes of injury to the brain. Many children with case histories of such events apparently escape injury to the brain, while other children who evidence clear symptoms of brain injury have no such events in their case histories. Even in cerebral palsy clinics, which deal with grossly damaged brains, the causes of about one-third of the cases are obscure (Paine 1965).

In addition to the development of a theory of the brain-injured child, Strauss and Lehtinen presented a plan for teaching brain-injured children. Their suggested methods, materials, and settings were dramatically different from those of a regular classroom. For example, the learning environment was designed to reduce distraction and hyperactivity. All stimulating visual materials such as bulletin boards or pictures were to be removed and the windows were to be painted to conceal overstimulating outside views. Moreover, the teacher was to avoid jewelry and to dress in a manner that would reduce distractions still further. The children's desks were to be placed against a wall, behind a screen, or in a partitioned cubicle. Special materials were constructed to aid a child in perception of visual forms and in organization of space and form. The authors advised that many of the commercially prepared teaching materials designed for normal children were unsuitable for the brain-injured child.

Although the volume by Strauss and Lehtinen is still one of the best basic sources in the field, questions about the assumptions and implications of its framework arose soon after its publication. It should be remembered, however, that Strauss and his coworkers laid the foundation for the field of learning disabilities by (1) perceiving a homogeneity in a diverse group of children who had been misdiagnosed by specialists, misunderstood by parents, and often discarded by society; (2) devising diagnostic tests to specify and evaluate the characteristics of these children; (3) planning and implementing educational settings and procedures to teach such children successfully; and (4) alerting many professions to the existence of a new category of exceptional children.

Strauss has been called one of the founders of the learning disabilities movement. His search to understand and educate these children was a vital factor in recognizing that their complex problems require highly specialized educational methodology (Cruickshank and Hallahan 1973). Strauss' work filled a great void. There was finally another possible diagnosis for children who previously had been given many other labels, such as badly behaved, emotionally disturbed, lazy, careless, or stupid. For parents who had been blamed for causing psychological situations that created learning disorders in their children, for parents who had been told that their children did not fit into a public school setting, and for parents who had been vainly seeking a diagnosis, this framework was most welcome. It provided a meaningful, logical, and hopeful analytic view of their problem children.

An adaptation and refinement of the educational methods proposed by Strauss and Lehtinen were performed in a demonstration-pilot study by Cruickshank et al. (1961). The general educational plan for teaching these children, referred to as brain injured and hyperactive, called for the following conditions in the teaching environment:

1. reducing unessential visual and auditory environmental stimuli
2. reducing to a minimum the space in which the child works
3. providing a highly structured, daily school schedule
4. increasing the stimulus value of the teaching materials

Cruickshank et al. (1961) provide a detailed description of the program, as well as a report of its effectiveness.

THE STRAUSS SYNDROME

The terminology put forth by Strauss and his associates proved to be confusing. The terms *exogenous* and *brain injury* began to be consistently linked by some authors. Anomalies that were considered exogenous brain injuries by certain writers were viewed as endogenous by others (Doll 1951). For example, one condition that is difficult to place within either classification is the condition called phenylketonuria (PKU), a congenital defect that results in the lack of an enzyme needed to digest an amino acid in proteins. This lack leads, in turn, to deterioration of brain tissue. It is difficult to classify this biochemical disorder, which results in brain injury, as exogenous or as an inherited endogenous condition.

Further, it was observed that some children with brain injuries, for example, many with cerebral palsy, have no learning disorders. Some have even gone on to earn Ph.D. and M.D. degrees, while other brain-injured children have severe mental defects. Kirk (1963) has stated that applying the term *brain injury* does not constitute a diagnosis that leads to methods of treatment or teaching.

The term *brain injured,* then, was seen to have questionable value as a means of describing, categorizing, and teaching children. This objection was stated by Wortis (1956, p. 206):

> There is no "brain-injured child," but only a variety of brain-injured children whose problems are quite varied and whose condition calls for far more refined analysis than some of the current generalizations of the brain-injured child provide.

Educators and psychologists found the label *brain-injured child* a difficult one to use in communicating with parents, administrators, physicians, and others. If the diagnosis was based on behavior, there was frequently no medical evidence of brain injury. Since it was essentially a medical term, nonmedical personnel were reluctant to use it. Moreover, educators and others found the diagnosis a difficult concept to communicate, and it appeared excessively condemning on the child's school record. Parents understandably reacted in a negative, traumatic, or guilt-ridden manner when told their child had a brain injury.

Four objections to the term *brain-injured child* were presented by Stevens and Birch (1957):

1. The term *brain-injured child* is a cause-oriented or etiological concept. It does not relate to the symptoms or behavioral aspects of the condition. However, the condition of brain injury is described in terms of symptoms rather than of causation.
2. The term can be associated with other conditions, such as cerebral palsy or epilepsy, and these conditions have no relation to the kind of child under consideration.
3. The term *brain-injured child* does not help in the development of a sound teaching approach.
4. The term is not suited for use as a descriptive concept because it is too broad in meaning and easily leads to oversimplification.

Stevens and Birch (1957) recommended, therefore, that the name "Strauss syndrome" be used instead of *brain injured child* to describe the child who could not learn and did not easily fit into other classification schemes. The new label would focus on the collection of behavioral characteristics noted in these children, while having the additional virtue of paying tribute to an early pioneer and great worker in the field. The term "Strauss syndrome" thus was introduced to describe the child who exhibited several of the following behavior characteristics (Stevens and Birch 1957, p. 348):

1. erratic and inappropriate behavior on mild provocation
2. increased motor activity disproportionate to the stimulus
3. poor organization of behavior
4. distractibility of more than ordinary degree under ordinary conditions
5. persistent faulty perceptions
6. persistent hyperactivity
7. awkwardness and consistently poor motor performance

DEVELOPMENT OF OTHER NOMENCLATURE

Other authors or groups utilized different terminology to overcome the shortcomings of the term *brain-injured child*. Doll (1951) suggested *neurophrenia*, and Lewis (1960) used *the other child*. Others described this child as *perceptually handicapped,* which was actually one of the behavioral characteristics identified by Strauss.

Some researchers and clinicians noted that children exhibiting the Strauss syndrome were but a portion of the children with learning problems. For example, some children who were unable to learn readily did not exhibit hyperactive behavior, but instead were hypoactive: quiet, without excessive movement, and even withdrawn. Further, while some children exhibited perceptual disturbances along with the learning problems, many others did not.

In a review of selected literature, Clement (1966) identified 38 different terms that were being used to refer to this child and he divided them into two categories: those that identified "organic aspects" (cause-related terms) and those that identified "consequences" (behavior-related terms). An example of an organic label is *neurological dysfunction;* an example of a consequence label is *hyperkinetic syndrome.*

MINIMAL BRAIN DYSFUNCTION

Clements (1966) and others preferred the description *minimal brain dysfunction* or *minimal neurological impairment* These authors placed children with various brain impairments along a scale that ranges from mild to severe. At the severe end of the scale are children with obvious brain damage, such as cerebral palsy or epilepsy. At the opposite end of such a

Table 2.1 Classification guide of brain dysfunction syndromes

Minimal (minor, mild)	*Major (severe)*
1. Impairment of fine movement or coordination	1. Cerebral palsies
2. Electroencephalographic abnormalities without actual seizures, or possibly subclinical seizures, which may be associated with fluctuations in behavior or intellectual function	2. Epilepsies
3. Deviations in attention, activity level, impulse control, and affect	3. Autism and other gross disorders of mentation and behavior
4. Specific and circumscribed perceptual, intellectual, and memory deficits	4. Mental subnormalities
5. Nonperipheral impairments of vision, hearing, haptics, and speech	5. Blindness, deafness, and severe aphasia

From Sam D. Clements, *Minimal Brain Dysfunction in Children.* Washington, D.C.: Department of Public Health Services, Publication #1415, 1966, p. 10.

scale are children with minimal impairments that affect behavior and learning in a more subtle way. In 1966, Clements concluded that the term *minimal brain dysfunction syndrome* was the best way to describe the child with near-average intelligence and with certain learning or behavioral disabilities associated with deviations or dysfunctions of the central nervous system. This term differentiated the minimally involved child from the child with major brain disorders. Table 2.1 illustrates this dichotomy.

Still other authorities have noted that the so-called major brain injuries on the conceptualized brain-dysfunction scale may or may not be accompanied by difficulties in learning. While some individuals with obvious brain injury, such as cerebral palsy, have no learning difficulties, others exhibit conditions such as mental subnormalities, infantile autism, and childhood schizophrenia (Kirk 1967). Some educators have found that minimal brain dysfunction does not properly describe the behavior or learning characteristics of the child. The question then arises of how much is minimal. Some writers in the current literature prefer to keep the Strauss terminology of the brain-injured child. According to Cruickshank (1966), the inability of the diagnostician to be specific and to obtain positive proof of a brain injury does not imply that no injury to tissue exists. Cruickshank speculates that if diagnostic procedures were available to permit accurate evaluation of children possessing certain characteristic behaviors, tissue damage or injury would be demonstrated and thus the child would be accurately called brain injured.

CENTRAL PROCESSING DYSFUNCTIONS

Chalfant and Scheffelin (1969) express an awareness of the need to formulate several definitions, each of which would have relevance and function for different users. Their Task Force III report focuses attention upon the deviant behaviors that arise from dysfunction of the central processing mechanisms. More specifically, the term *central processing dysfunctions* comprises disorders in the analysis, storage, synthesis, and symbolic use of information.

LEARNING DISABILITIES

In many cases, the dysfunction of the brain has been inferred through observation of the behavior of the child, through analysis of the child's reactions to learning situations, or through the sampling of behavior through psychological tests. Since it is impossible to look at the physical brain injury inside the child's skull or to know for certain that specific cerebral tissue has been injured, guesses necessarily have been made on the basis of behavioral symptoms.

Some authorities therefore suggested the use of terminology that accurately and meaningfully describes the child's behavioral symptoms. One of the first writers to suggest the term *learning disabilities* was Kirk (1963), who used it to describe a group of children who had disorders in the development of language, speech, reading, and associated communication skills needed for social interaction. Children who had sensory handicaps, such as blindness or deafness, and children who had generalized mental retardation were excluded from this group. Children whose learning failure was primarily caused by emotional disturbances or experience deprivation were also excluded from the learning disabilities group.

Johnson and Myklebust (1967) suggested a variation: *psychoneurological learning disabilities.* Implied in this term is the concept that the "psychology of learning" is disturbed because of an impairment of the central nervous system. Because of a neurological deficit, the learning process of these children is different. The term "psychoneurological learning disabilities" assumes the concern with learning and education as well as an acknowledgement of medical pathology or etiology.

At the present, then, the concept *learning disabilities* appears to be a satisfactory one. Rather than emphasizing a presumed cause, it focuses on the problem the child faces. It is still a blanket term in that it does not specify the areas in which the child has learning problems nor does it specify the learning process in which the child is deficient. Although *learning disabilities* covers a wide range and diverse types of learning disorders, the term avoids the medical difficulties, focuses on the educational problem, and seems to be acceptable to parents as well as teachers.

There is evidence that the term is gaining general acceptance. For example, a separate division recently created within the Council for Exceptional Children is called the Division for Children with Learning Disabilities (DCLD); a national parent and professional organization has chosen the name Association for Children with Learning Disabilities (ACLD); and many states now use the term in their educational statutes and certification legislation. Finally, a Congressional bill entitled the Children with Specific Learning Disabilities Act became law in 1970 as part of the Elementary and Secondary Educational Amendments of 1969 (PL 91-230). An extension of this law, the Education of the Handicapped Act, known as the Education Amendments of 1974, is part of the Elementary and Secondary Education Act (PL 93-380), passed by Congress in 1974. This legislation included special programs for children with specific learning disabilities and authorized provisions for research, training of educational personnel, and the development of model centers in the field of learning disabilities.

Congress has officially accepted the term *learning disabilities*, and it probably will continue to be the term used to describe the children about whom we are concerned.

LEARNING DISABILITIES ORGANIZATIONS

Parents who were convinced that Strauss' views perceptively described their children welcomed the theories of diagnosis and treatment he presented. However, they soon discovered that educators, physicians, and psychologists were generally unaware of the concepts that Strauss had evolved and of the educational treatment that he had suggested. Many parents, believing that public schools should provide the special education required for their children, organized parent groups for the purpose of convincing schools that these exceptional children were educable and that it was the obligation of the schools to provide appropriate education. As has been typical in the history of special education, the pressure and impetus came from parent groups rather than from educators.

In the period 1950 to 1960, many parent groups were formed to bring the findings of this field to the attention of educators, physicians, legislators, other parents, and the lay public. Among the first such groups were the Fund for Perceptually Handicapped Children (Evanston, Illinois) and the New York [State] Association for Brain-Injured Children, both organized in 1957. The California Association for Neurologically Handicapped Children was organized in 1960. The formulation and growth of many other such local organizations were rapid.

One outcome of the Conference on Exploration into the Problems of the Perceptually Handicapped Child (1963) was a decision to formulate a national association for children with learning disabilities. The general acceptance of the term *learning disabilities* probably can be traced to decisions made at this meeting. As a result, a national organization, the Association for Children with Learning Disabilities (ACLD), was formed to strengthen the thrust of the many local parent organizations. ACLD chapters were established in most states, and by 1974 there were 47 affiliated states. These structures, in turn, have been the impetus for the establishment of additional local chapters. An illustration of the growth of these groups is Illinois, which by 1974 had 25 local chapters affiliated with the state association. An organizational newsletter is distributed from ACLD headquarters at 5225 Grace Street, Pittsburgh, Pennsylvania 15236. Membership in local chapters, which includes national membership, is open to any interested parent, professional, or student.

In 1968 the Council for Exceptional Children established its Division for Children with Learning Disabilities (DCLD). Membership information can be obtained from its headquarters at 1920 Association Drive, Reston, Virginia 22091.

SUMMARY

This chapter has reviewed the short history of the field of learning disabilities, which can be thought of as having three phases: the foundation phase, the transition phase, and the integration phase. The field is generally considered to have pioneered with the work of Strauss on the brain-injured child which appeared in 1947. Objections to Strauss' terminology led to modifications and revisions of both terminology and concepts. Terms used to identify this child include Strauss syndrome, minimal brain dysfunction, central processing dysfunction, and, finally, learning disabilities. In recent years there has been rapid development of organizations concerned with the learning-disabled child.

REFERENCES

Chalfant, James C., and Margaret A. Scheffelin. *Central Processing Dysfunctions in Children: A Review of Research.* NINDS monograph no. 9. Bethesda, Md.: U.S. Department of Health, Education, and Welfare, 1969.

Clements, Sam D. *Minimal Brain Dysfunction in Children.* NINDS monograph no. 3, Public Health Service Bulletin no. 1415. Washington, D.C.: U.S. Department of Health, Education, and Welfare, 1966.

Conference on Exploration in the Problems of the Perceptually Handicapped Child. Evanston, Ill.: Fund for Perceptually Handicapped Children, 1963.

Cruickshank, William. "An Introductory Overview," in W. Cruickshank (ed.), *The Teacher of Brain-Injured Children: A Discussion of the Bases of Competency.* Syracuse, N.Y.: Syracuse University Press, 1966.

Cruickshank, W., and D. Hallahan. "Alfred A. Strauss: Pioneer in Learning Disabilities." *Exceptional Children* 39 (January 1973): 321–329.

Cruickshank, W., F. Bentzen, F. Ratzburg, and M. Tannhauser. *A Teaching Method for Brain-Injured and Hyperactive Children.* Syracuse, N.Y.: Syracuse University Press, 1961.

Dewey, John. *Logic: The Theory of Inquiry.* New York: Henry Holt, 1938.

Doll, Edgar A. "Neurophrenia." *American Journal of Psychiatry* 108 (1951): 50–53.

Hallahan, D., and W. Cruickshank. *Psychoeducational Foundations of Learning Disabilities.* Englewood Cliffs, N.J.: Prentice-Hall, 1973.

Johnson, Doris, and Helmer Myklebust. *Learning Disabilities: Educational Principles and Practices.* New York: Grune & Stratton, 1967.

Kirk, Samuel A. "Behavioral Diagnosis and Remediation of Learning Disabilities," pp. 1–7 in *Conference on Exploration into the Problems of the Perceptually Handicapped Child.* Evanston, Ill.: Fund for Perceptually Handicapped Children, 1963.

———. "From Labels to Action," pp. 36–44 in *Interdisciplinary Approach to Learning Disabilities of Children and Youth.* Tulsa, Okla.: Association for Children with Learning Disabilities, 1967.

Lewis, Richard S., A. Strauss, and Laura Lehtinen. *The Other Child — The Brain-Injured Child.* New York: Grune & Stratton, 1960.

McGinnis, Mildred. *Aphasic Children: Identification and Education by the Association Method.* Washington, D.C.: Volta Bureau, 1963.

Morgan, W. P. "A Case of Congenital Word-Blindness." *British Medical Journal* 2 (1896): 1378.

Orton, Samuel T. *Reading, Writing and Speech Problems in Children.* New York: Norton, 1937.

Paine, R. S. "Organic Neurological Factors Related to Learning Disorders," pp. 1–29 in J. Hellmuth (ed.), *Learning Disorders,* Vol. 1. Seattle: Special Child Publications, 1965.

Smith, Nila B. "What Have We Accomplished in Reading? — A Review of the Past Fifty Years." *Elementary English* 38 (March 1961): 141–150.

Stevens, Godfrey D., and Jack W. Birch. "A Proposal for Clarification of the

Terminology Used to Describe Brain-Injured Children." *Exceptional Children* 23 (May 1957): 346–349.

Strauss, Alfred, and Laura Lehtinen. *Psychopathology and Education of the Brain-Injured Child.* New York: Grune & Stratton, 1947.

Wiederholt, J. Lee. "Historical Perspectives in the Education of the Learning Disabled," pp. 103–152 in L. Mann and D. Sabatino (eds.), *The Second Review of Special Education.* Philadelphia: Journal of Special Education Press, 1974.

Wortis, Joseph. "A Note on the Concept of the 'Brain-Injured' Child." *American Journal of Mental Deficiency* 61 (July 1956): 204–206.

 3. Emerging Directions
in Learning Disabilities

This chapter continues to describe the development of the field of learning disabilities by examining its current status and some emerging trends. In a new and burgeoning field, one expects many changes in direction and many new concepts and ideas. Some occur as a natural extension of ongoing programs; others result from shortcomings experienced in earlier programs; and still others come about because of outside pressures. The emerging directions discussed in this chapter include: early identification, language disorders,· the cross-categorical movement, mainstreaming, the learning-disabled adolescent, and the impact of the law.

EARLY IDENTIFICATION OF CHILDREN WITH POTENTIAL LEARNING PROBLEMS

A recent concern in special education is the early-identification of preschool children who may encounter difficulty in academic learning and the immediate provision of appropriate preventive services for them. In the past, children with learning disabilities were identified primarily in the elementary school age period; but by identifying these children as preschoolers before they encounter difficulty, it may be possible to diagnose their disabilities and institute remedial education to prevent potential learning problems from occurring (Haring and Ridgway 1967; Keogh 1970; Butenica 1971; Denhoff, Hainsworth, and Hainsworth 1972; Keogh and Becker 1973).

The crucial influence of the early childhood years on later success is becoming increasingly evident. The research of cognitive psychologists and language specialists clearly shows that by the time the child fails in school, much is already lost — in fact, it may be too late. The sooner such high-risk children are recognized, the greater the chances of preventing failure.

The early identification of handicapped children has received both state and national support. On the federal level, the Bureau of Education for the Handicapped (BEH) of the Office of Education has given top priority to early childhood programs (Martin 1971). Recent legislation in many states is designed to assure that schools develop programs for identifying potential failures and providing preventive services. Many states have passed laws that require schools to provide appropriate educational services for handicapped children from ages 3 through 21 with some states providing services for children as young as 2 years old. Texas, the first state to pass comprehensive mandatory legislation in 1970 as part of its "Plan A" (described in Chapter 13), provides educational help for all handicapped persons from ages 3 to 21. Of the 40,000 to 50,000 three-, four-, and five-year-olds screened in the first year of the Texas project, 2,500 were identified as learning disabled, which can be translated into a prevalence rate of 5 to 6 percent of learning-disabled preschoolers in the general preschool-population (*ACLD Newsbriefs* 1974).

PROBLEMS RELATED TO EARLY IDENTIFICATION

A number of important issues are inherent in providing screening, diagnostic, and treatment services for preschoolers. Some authorities are concerned with the potential dangers of early identification. By identifying and labeling a child at three or four years of age, educators actually may be creating certain problems. Since children do not mature at the same rate, readiness for school often is a matter of timing. Some children have developmental lags that may disappear by the time they are ready for formal schooling. The term *self-fulfilling prophecy* has been used by Rosenthal and Jacobson (1968) to describe effects of teacher expectancy on pupil performance. It is possible that early identification might serve to impose limits on teacher expectancies and to develop an atmosphere that reinforces the child's learning problems.

Another issue that arises is the paradox that at the time the child is identified, the learning disability has not yet occurred. If not treated the child may or may not develop a problem. Even if a treated child is successful in a later learning situation, one can never be certain if that success was due to the early identification and treatment. Predictive validity is therefore low (Keogh and Becker 1973). Another problem in early identification is the difficulty of determining a three-year-old's category of exceptionality. Diagnostic instruments are imprecise and an inappropriate label may stigmatize the child. Since the nature of the handicapping condition is not easily discernible at this age, early childhood programs generally include children with a variety of handicaps: learning disabilities, mental retardation, emotional disturbances, and language disorders. Most program developers feel that it is not as important to make a differential diagnosis to determine the precise category of the preschooler's problem as it is to find and help the child. Most preschool programs are therefore cross-categorical, seeking terms that will include all of these handicaps. Cross-categorical terms, such as *developmental disabilities* or simply *early childhood services,* are often used.

Keogh and Becker (1973) summarize concerns about early detection by asking three serious questions: (1) How valid are the identifying or predictive measures? (2) What are the implications of diagnostic data for remediation or early intervention? (3) Do benefits of early identification outweigh possible damaging or negative effects of such recognition? In spite of the implications of these questions, most special educators believe that effective early identification is critical and that it may accomplish much in preventing or reducing learning disorders.

PROGRAMS FOR EARLY IDENTIFICATION

Few established guidelines are available to aid in the development of early identification programs. Most are still in the developmental or experimental stages. Typically, the programs provide for the following phases: (1) screening to identify high-risk children; (2) intensive diagnosis of selected children to determine the nature of the problem and make further referrals if necessary; (3) placement of some children in a developmental disabilities class for further observation and teaching; and (4) making decisions for further educational placement, i.e., regular kindergarten, a transitional kindergarten or a special class. To avoid stigmatization, the school district might encourage *all* three- to five-year-olds to be brought in for initial screening. Problems encountered in this approach include finding the preschool children in the surrounding geographical area, notifying *all* parents that such services are available, encouraging them to bring in *all* children for initial screening, and, finally, informing parents of the results of the screening procedures.

Curriculum models of developmental disabilities classes are also in the process of evolving. One model for early childhood programs for children with potential learning disabilities described by Spicker (1973) includes a curriculum in three areas: cognitive development, perceptual-motor development, and preacademic skills development. The *cognitive development* program attempts to improve concept formation, general information and comprehension, problem-solving ability, memory, and discrimination learning. The *perceptual-motor* program stresses visual discrimination, visual-motor integration, gross and fine motor skills, and perceptual skills. The *preacademic skills* curriculum provides systematic instruction in certain readiness skills needed for reading and arithmetic. A fourth curricular area should be added — *language development*. This would help the child with oral language development, listening skills, vocabulary, and sentence development.

A Preschool Screening Model: DIAL

To help school districts in Illinois plan for the screening phase of early identification programs, the state sponsored a *Learning Disabilities/Early Childhood Research Project* known as *Developmental Indicators for the Assessment of Learning* (DIAL), which was conducted by Mardell and Goldenberg (1972, 1975). The DIAL preschool screening test was used to develop a system for observing and recording behavior of children between the ages of 2½ and 5½. It was designed to be administered by well-trained professionals or paraprofessionals, to assess many areas of behavior, to take less than 30 minutes, and to be of minimal cost per child for the school district.

The model for the DIAL project planned for the assessment of the following areas: (1) sensory, (2) motor, (3) affective, (4) social, (5) conceptual, and (6) language (communication). Children were screened in stations set up in a large room for each area of testing by trained operators. The child entered the testing room and was greeted by an operator. Certain basic information about the child was obtained from the parent, and a name identification card was prepared. The child was then introduced to a play area to relax, wait to be tested, and interact with other children. In the next step the child's picture was taken with a Polaroid camera. As the child progressed to the various testing stations, the operator noted performance on a single score sheet. The entire procedure required 25 to 30 minutes per child. Each of the assessment areas is briefly described in the following section.

1. *Sensory.* Children were screened for visual acuity and auditory acuity. If visual or auditory defects were suspected from the screening tests, the child was referred for a professional visual or hearing examination.

2. *Motor.* Children were screened for both gross motor and fine motor development. *Gross motor* tests included walking a balance beam; throwing and catching a beanbag (noting handedness); jumping, hopping, skipping, standing still for a 30-second time period; and identifying the parts of the body (nose, ear, neck, hip, knee, elbow, ankle, chin, wrist, shoulder). *Fine motor* tests included matching ten designs; building three-block designs from a model; cutting out two patterns with a scissors; copying four geometric designs (circle, cross, square, and triangle); copying four letters (D, N, E, and S); demonstrating finger agility (copying the operator's demonstration by consecutively touching each finger on one hand to the thumb of

the same hand, and then repeating the task on the other hand); and repeating a hand-clapping pattern.

3. *Affective.* The child's affective level — anxiety, emotional stability, attention, focus, and task persistence — was assessed on an observational rating check list that the operators filled out. In addition, the child's behavior was observed throughout the screening session.

4. *Social.* The developers of DIAL note that at present there are limited procedures for social skill assessment. However, the DIAL project used the same check list for social behaviors that was used for affective behaviors.

5. *Conceptual.* Tests included duplicating a learning task of sorting; identifying six colors; rote counting to 10; showing one-to-one correspondence of 1, 3, and 5; demonstrating five prepositions (on, beside, front, back, and under); following three verbal directions; and identifying fourteen given concepts (big, fast, hot, tall, empty, day, more, little, slow, cold, short, full, high, and less) on pictures.

6. *Language (communication).* In the communication component, children were tested in the skills of receiving and expressing language, including articulating sixteen words; repeating a series of numbers given verbally by the operator; describing ten pictorial figures for noun descriptions; describing six pictorial figures for verb description; answering four problem-solving questions about hunger, sleep, cold, and toys; self-identification of a Polaroid picture; self-identification of sex; naming foods; and describing a picture. In assessing the child's verbal description of the pictures, the operator recorded total output, sentence length, quality of story, and the parts of speech.

The DIAL screening tests were field tested in Illinois with 4,423 preschool children in eight regional sites. The instrument proved to aid in the identification of high-risk preschoolers.

Tests for Identification of High-Risk Preschool Children

Besides DIAL a few other tests for early identification screening of preschool-age children have been developed, including the *Meeting Street School Screening Test, Early Detection Inventory, Boehm Test of Basic Concepts, Evanston Early Identification Scale, Peabody Picture Vocabulary Test,* and *Comprehensive Assessment in Nursery School and Kindergarten* (CIRCUS). These tests are described in Appendix C.

In summary, children have suffered the consequences of school failure because their learning deficiencies were not detected at preschool ages; or, if these deficits were noted, appropriate teaching programs were not available. Hopefully, early identification of high-risk children and early compensatory training programs will be a means of preventing later problems. Most preschool identification programs are still in the process of development or have been in operation for only a short period of time. While it is difficult at this time to assess their effectiveness, the early identification movement is clearly a major development in the field of learning disabilities.

STUDY OF LANGUAGE DISORDERS

While language disorders will be discussed in Chapter 10, growing interest in the problems of language acquisition warrants inclusion of this subject as an emerging trend. As noted earlier in this chapter, language development is one of the areas that is tested to detect high-risk preschoolers; the child who has a language disorder is identified as a child with a potential learning disability.

The concern for children with language disorders is shared by two specialties: learning disabilities specialists (especially those interested in early childhood) and speech and language pathologists (especially those interested in language disorders). Lee (1974) notes that until very recently speech therapists were trained to work solely with *disorders of speech production,* such as voice, articulation, and fluency. Their case load included children who lisped, those who could not articulate certain sounds, and those who stuttered. Only recently have speech pathologists begun to view *language disorders,* such as delayed speech, as difficulties apart from speech disorders. Similarly, it is only recently that learning disabilities specialists have begun to see the critical importance of normal language development to later learning, including reading and writing.

It is strange that, until recently, the importance of language development to later learning was neglected by many groups, including reading specialists, linguists, and speech pathologists. Reading specialists were unfamiliar with the complexities and manifestations of language. In a discussion of factors related to success in beginning reading, Durrell (1956, p. 45) asserted, "Lack of oral language background is almost never found as a cause of reading disability." The linguists assumed that *all* children acquire a sophisticated level of language usage and understanding by the time they enter first grade and that *all* six-year-old children are sophisticated users of the language (Fries 1962). The speech pathologists limited their field to disorders of speech production (Lee 1974).

As new linguistic techniques for measuring and describing the child's acquisition of language became available, we began to discover that not all children are sophisticated users of their native language (Ruddell 1970). Moreover, children with various kinds of language disturbances as preschoolers seem to be handicapped in later years with a variety of language disorders in reading and writing. Studies show that youngsters with severe reading disabilities differ from normal children in their basic language skills (Vogel 1974). By viewing reading as a language process, reading disability could be interpreted as a language disorder (Lerner 1972). Thus, a first step in a comprehensive study of the reading process is an analysis of the language models that underlie reading (Athey 1971). The interests of the speech pathologist have broadened to take into account language disorders, including a consideration of vocabulary, word meanings, concept formation, and the learning of grammatical rules (Lee 1974, Lee et al. 1975).

Several types of language problems become the concern of the learning disabilities specialist. Language pathologists use the term *language disorder* to refer to children with a *language delay* or a *language deficit*. The language-delayed child may not be talking at all or may be using very little language at an age when language normally develops. The child with a language deficit may be talking, but using strange syntactical patterns, confused word order, or inappropriate words. Thus, the child who is not speaking at age four is language delayed; the child with a language deficit may be saying at age five, "Why not don't he eats?" Such disorders occur in spite of the fact that these children have encountered a rich language environment and ample opportunity to hear and participate in standard English. Problems of language disorders are sometimes referred to as childhood aphasia or developmental aphasia. *Acquired aphasia* is a medical term used to identify adults who lose the ability to speak because of brain damage due to a stroke, disease, or accident. *Childhood* or *developmental aphasia* refers to children who have not yet learned to speak; a neurological dysfunction is suspected.

Language difference (in contrast to a *language disorder*) is another language problem that may affect learning. Children with a language difference come from cultures where a language or dialect other than standard English is spoken. For example, the child's native language may be a dialect of standard English, such as black English. The child's language is appropriate for the surroundings, is similar to that of others in the immediate environment, and causes no difficulty in communicating with others within this environment. Although such children do not have a language deficit, their language or dialect difference apparently interferes with the learning of many of the language skills in standard English, and they often have difficulty learning to read (Shuy 1972). Similar observations concerning the relationship between language differences and later language learning can be made about youngsters with bilingual problems. For the child whose native language is foreign, learning language skills in English may be a difficult chore.

It should be emphasized that a language difference is neither a language deficit nor a language disorder. However, many teachers who work with black children in inner-city areas or with bilingual children suspect that some of the youngsters have a language disorder in addition to a language difference.

Ways of diagnosing and analyzing language disorders, as well as ways to teach language, are becoming available for the learning disabilities specialist. Learning language certainly should be considered an area of responsibility, and the learning disabilities specialist should learn methods for diagnosing language disorders and providing language therapy. These methods are discussed in Chapter 10.

CROSS-CATEGORICAL MOVEMENT

The cross-categorical movement, which is sometimes referred to as the noncategorical movement, provides a new view of special education, and the field of learning disabilities plays a pivotal role within this new view. Briefly, the cross-categorical approach means that rather than perceiving each category of special education as clearly differentiated from the others, we should emphasize the common characteristics among the categories. The implications of the cross-categorical issue were discussed at a conference sponsored by the Bureau of Education for the Handicapped (Meyen 1971).

The field of learning disabilities evolved as one of the categories in special education. A *category* is a term used to identify a specific type of handicapped child, such as visually impaired, hearing impaired, or crippled. The field of special education includes a collection of categories of atypical children. Each category, which is based largely on physical or medical characteristics of handicapped children, was separately established when there was enough support and sufficient interest in that type of exceptionality. Thus, the field of special education was structured within what are referred to as the traditional categories — hearing impaired, visually handicapped, mentally retarded, physically handicapped, etc. The last category of exceptionality to be recognized within this structure was the category of learning disabilities, which was created because the learning-disabled child does not fit into the other existing categories of special education; many children who are physically unimpaired and intellectually normal still cannot adequately talk, write, spell, calculate, think, or read.

The entire field of special education is currently undergoing change. The utility of the traditional classification system of categories is under serious question by leaders in the field (Dunn 1968, Quay 1968, Lilly 1970, Bateman 1971). Gallagher (1971) sees the special education scene as undergoing a major changeover from one pattern of dealing with the educational problems of handicapped children to another.

There are many reasons for dissatisfaction with the categorical approach to special education. First, the categories of exceptionality are not discrete and separate entities but have much in common with each other. Thus, children with mild problems — including those traditionally labeled as mentally retarded, emotionally disturbed, behaviorally disordered, educationally handicapped, or learning disabled — often are not easily differentiated through diagnostic methods. Moreover, treatment procedures are often overlapping, suggesting that diagnostic and intervention methods cut across the existing categories. In early childhood special education programs it often makes little sense to try to determine if a three-year-old is learning disabled, emotionally disturbed, language disordered, or a combination of all. What is important is the identification of what the child can and cannot do and the development of a program that will help those problems.

A second element in the growth of the cross-categorical movement is a cluster of court decisions supporting claims of discrimination by placement of children in special education categorical programs. Minority groups have charged through legal action that special education classes are discriminatory, often causing social or psychological harm. The term *six-hour retarded child* is used to describe children who are retarded only during the time they are in school.

A third factor in the cross-categorical movement is research that questions the benefits of a self-contained special education class designed for a specific category. This is particularly evident in the case of mental retardation (Goldstein, Moss, Jordon 1965). Children with similar handicaps who remained in the regular class made as much or more progress as the special education group.

The field of learning disabilities has a unique position in the cross-categorical movement, for it deals with the various areas of learning that are important to school success. It can act as a core since most categories of special education involve children who face learning problems; it provides a viable educational model that will serve as a better base for decision making; and it offers the kind of diagnostic and clinical training required by professionals who deal with the cross-categorical handicapped child. Other implications of the cross-categorical movement for learning disabilities are discussed in Chapter 7.

MAINSTREAMING

Along with the cross-categorical movement in special education, a new approach for providing educational services for exceptional children has emerged. This approach is called *mainstreaming*, an alternative to the traditional self-contained classroom of special education. Mainstreaming is a delivery system that integrates handicapped children into regular classrooms.

> Central to the mainstreaming movement is the theme that given the desire, facilities, and reasonable professional preparation, the average teacher can learn to educate exceptional youngsters in the regular classroom with the support and consultative services of special education personnel. (Birch 1974, p. 1)

Although many professionals agree with the major concepts and goals of mainstreaming, important questions have arisen from the actual implementation of mainstreaming programs. In a review of 30 such programs, Chaffin (1974) emphasizes that there are a number of ways to organize a mainstreaming delivery system, and Birch (1974) calls attention to key points for doing so:

1. The concerns of both regular classroom teachers and special education teachers should be considered.
2. Regular classroom teachers should have opportunities to talk and learn about mainstreaming prior to implementation.

3. The success of a mainstreaming program is strongly influenced by teacher attitudes.
4. In-service education is an essential preparation for mainstreaming programs.
5. Pupil placement calls for sensitive administration; this system is not appropriate for all handicapped youngsters.
6. Identified pupils should be kept in regular grades.
7. Educational assessment and diagnostic teaching should be emphasized.
8. The program should be flexible and modified by the local school educators to meet local needs.
9. The program must have strong administrative support.
10. Parents should be informed about the program.

Mainstreaming programs are still in developmental stages, and evaluation of ongoing projects is needed. Although mainstreaming is a controversial topic, the trend is gaining momentum and support. (See Chapters 7, 13, and 14 for more detailed discussion.)

PROGRAMS FOR THE LEARNING-DISABLED ADOLESCENT

New programs for the secondary school level have developed along with the early identification programs. In addition to junior high and senior high school systems, some colleges also have special accommodations. However, compared to the rapid growth of the learning disabilities movement for the preschool child, the secondary school has experienced a much slower development.

SPECIAL PROBLEMS AT THE SECONDARY SCHOOL LEVEL

While initial efforts historically have been directed toward the middle-age range of children with learning disabilities, many of these pupils still had their learning problems when they reached high school, aggravating the normative turmoil of adolescence. By this time in their school lives, learning-disabled adolescents frequently have low opinions of themselves, negative attitudes about learning and school, and emotional and behavioral problems. In fact, by this stage the emotional and behavioral problems may appear to be primary factors (Schloss 1971).

There are a number of other complications at the high school level. Many secondary school teachers are not oriented to working with the learning-disabled student. High school teachers are likely to be more "content" oriented than "child" oriented, and they may not see the need to adjust curricula for students with specific learning deficits.

Another problem relates to the background and training of the learning disabilities specialist for the high school. This person must not only be thoroughly acquainted with the field of learning disabilities, but also must be familiar with problems of the adolescent and the curriculum of the high school. Two possibilities for recruitment are (1) teachers trained in learning disabilities who do additional work in areas such as adolescent psychology, vocational guidance, and the secondary curriculum, or (2) high school teachers who acquire additional training in the fields of special education and learning disabilities.

The paucity of materials for this age group presents a major problem. Most are directed at learning disabilities in the preschool, primary, or elementary age groups. Some materials designed for the teenage retarded reader are excellent, and others designed for the educable mentally handicapped adolescent can be adapted. In general, however, creativity and ingenuity are required to gather and design appropriate materials. Examples of those currently used in secondary level programs are listed in Appendix B.

Diagnosing the adolescent's problem is also difficult because of the lack of appropriate tests. Moreover, deficit areas that interfered with learning at an earlier age may no longer be evident. While a severe auditory deficit may have been a key factor in keeping Joe from learning to read in the primary grades, that auditory problem may not be easily detected at age 16, even though he still cannot read. Just as specific tests are being designed for the preschool child, so, too, it is necessary to develop good testing and assessment instruments for the student at the secondary level.

DELIVERING SERVICES TO THE SECONDARY SCHOOL STUDENT

The secondary school needs several options for delivering educational services. The self-contained classroom may be beneficial for a few students; for most, however, a special resource room may provide a better system for enabling them to receive help for the specific difficulty that arises in class work. Within a resource room setting the learning disabilities specialist can act as a liaison between teacher and counselor, student and parent, etc.

In some secondary school programs, the high school offers an additional section of a course especially designed to offer the individualization required for students with various learning problems. For example, a student with a specific mathematics disability might enroll in all regular courses but enter a specially designed section for algebra; or a student with a severe writing problem might only need a special section of the English course. Such classes would be small enough to assure flexibility and individualization, and they would require an instructor who knows both the content area and the field of learning disabilities.

Resource teachers in high school learning disabilities programs must be familiar with the entire curriculum of the school. Their responsibilities may range from helping students with algebra problems, to aiding a student with a creative writing assignment in English, to helping a student with a mechanical drawing lesson, to explaining a science experiment. The immediacy and relevancy of the problem is of vital concern to the student, who will not be satisfied unless the help is directly related to that problem. For this reason, remediation must be closely tied to what is happening in the classroom.

A major task of the high school specialist is to help the content teachers understand the nature of a specific student's problem and the steps to be taken to help the student. For example, if the student has a severe reading disability, perhaps it may be possible to tape lessons. Certain books have been recorded for the blind and could be made accessible to nonreaders through local libraries (Talking Book Service 1974). In an examination situation, the student with a severe writing problem might be allowed to give answers orally, to tape answers, or to dictate answers to someone else. The student who works at a very slow rate, might be allowed additional time. Selling the learning disabilities concept so that high school teachers are willing to make such modifications requires skill in interpersonal relationships.

Russell (1974) suggests several conditions for developing a successful learning disabilities program in the secondary school:

1. The program should not isolate learning-disabled students from their peers.
2. The program should be made as invisible as possible among other course offerings.
3. The school should be flexible enough to make modifications in curriculum, teaching procedures, and testing methods to meet the needs of learning-disabled students.
4. The program should have high expectancy for normal achievement.
5. The program must be realistic and relevant to the youngster's immediate needs.

Another task of the learning disabilities teacher at the secondary level is to work closely with guidance counselors in helping the student prepare for the future. Some learning-disabled students have the desire and ability to prepare for college, but they must receive careful guidance. Others want specific preparation for vocational careers and the high school must offer guidance to them as well.

Finding an appropriate college placement for the student may be a difficult task. Moss (1971, 1975) has compiled a directory of colleges for learning-disabled youth for the Association for Children with Learning Disabilities. Through a questionnaire administered by Wells (1973), 20 colleges indicated that they had personnel specially trained in learning disabilities (see Appendix D). Webb (1974) describes one specific program at the college level.

IMPACT OF LAW

Recent litigation brought by parents against schools and legislation passed in several states are having a strong influence on the direction of special education and learning disabilities (Weintraub 1972; Abeson 1974; Kirp 1974; Gilhool 1973; Ross, DeYoung, and Cohen 1971). Parents are going to the courts and the legislatures to obtain decisions and actions that will insure adequate education for learning-disabled children. As noted earlier, legal action has been a major impetus in the development of the noncategorical movement.

Gilhool (1973) classifies litigation cases into three types. One type of lawsuit is classified as "right to treatment" cases. For example, he cites the San Francisco case of a dyslexic 18-year-old high school graduate who sued the school district for damages incurred through its failure to teach. Such claims are based on the premise that the handicapped are entitled to appropriate treatment, therapy, and education.

A second type of case deals with standards applied in assigning children to special education services. The charge here is that placement is often discriminatory. For example, minority children are more often placed in classes for the educationally retarded than other children. In some states such litigation has resulted in requirements that selection tests be standardized for the cultural and language subgroups of the children involved. For example, in some municipalities intelligence tests have been judged to be culturally biased and their use prohibited. Some localities require that the child whose native language is Spanish be given tests in Spanish by Spanish-speaking psychologists. Another outcome of this kind of legislation is the requirement that no child be assigned to a special education program without the consent of the parent.

A third class of cases involves the right to education for all children and is sometimes referred to as the "zero reject model." This means that the educational system must provide educational services for *all* handicapped children, and the school cannot reject certain children from school because they do not fit into the ongoing system. In the past many children have been denied access to public schooling because there was no program for that type of child. As noted in Chapter 2, many of the children whom Strauss identified as "brain injured" had previously been rejected from the public school setting.

There is much new legislation, both completed and pending, that will have significant effects on the field of learning disabilities. Many states have passed laws requiring that school districts provide education for all handicapped individuals from ages 3 to 21. Some recent legislation specifies that final decisions on placement must be approved by parents, who also have the right to see all records, data, test scores, etc., pertaining to their children. Finally, important legislation provides for certification and financial support of special education programs.

There is little doubt that we are entering a new era reflecting the law's influence on the handicapped and the learning disabled. Gilhool (1973, p. 609) writes that there is

> a new conception of the handicapped citizen, a new conception of that citizen's place in our society, a new conception of those obli-

gations owed to him by those who act in place of that society, a conception that suggests that handicapped citizens no longer have what they may have by the grace or by the good will of any other person but that they have what they must have by right. It is now a question of justice.

SUMMARY

This chapter has discussed several of the new issues and directions evolving in the field of learning disabilities. One major concern is the early identification of preschool children who are likely to have difficulty with academic learning and the provision of prevention programs for such children. Another trend is the interest in language disorders, apart from speech disorders, and in the relationship of such problems to all areas of learning. A third trend is the cross-categorical or noncategorical movement and the pivotal role that the field of learning disabilities plays in this movement. Mainstreaming provides an alternative to the traditional self-contained classroom by integrating exceptional children into the regular classroom.

The problems of the learning-disabled adolescent and the development of programs at the secondary school level constitute another direction in learning disabilities.

Finally, significant legal developments, including litigation instituted by parents and new legislation in many states, are having a substantial impact on the field of learning disabilities.

These topics certainly do not exhaust the many trends in this burgeoning field. Some of the directions and issues are incorporated in other sections of this book. The concepts of the resource room, of working with parents, and of the changing role of the learning disabilities specialist are discussed in Chapter 14. The behavioral movement, including behavior modification and precision teaching, is discussed in Chapter 12.

In a field as new, as vibrant, as interdisciplinary, and as expanding as learning disabilities, we must be continually alert to new ideas, new concepts, and changing directions.

REFERENCES

Abeson, Alan. "Movement and Momentum: Government and the Education of Handicapped Children II." *Exceptional Children* 41 (October 1974): 109–116.

ALCD Newsbriefs, no. 90, May 1974, p. 3.

Athey, Irene J. "Language Models and Reading." *Reading Research Quarterly* 7 (Fall 1971): 17–109.

Bateman, Barbara. "Implications of a Learning Disabilities Approach for Teaching Educable Retardates," pp. 297–304 in D. Hammill and N. Bartel (eds.), *Educational Perspectives in Learning Disabilities*. New York: Wiley, 1971.

Birch, Jack W. *Mainstreaming: Educable Mentally Retarded Classes.* Reston, Va.: Council for Exceptional Children, 1974.

Buktenica, Norman. "Identification of Potential Learning Disorders." *Journal of Learning Disabilities* 4, 7 (September 1971): 379–383.

Chaffin, Jerry D. "Will the Real 'Mainstreaming' Program Please Stand Up! (or . . . Should Dunn Have Done It?)" *Focus on Exceptional Children* 6 (October 1974): 1–18.

Denhoff, E., P. Hainsworth, and M. Hainsworth. "Learning Disabilities and Early Childhood Education: An Information-Processing Approach," pp. 111–150 in H. Myklebust (ed.), *Progress in Learning Disabilities,* vol II. New York: Grune & Stratton, 1971.

Dunn, Lloyd M. "Special Education for the Mildly Retarded — Is Much of It Justifiable?" *Exceptional Children* 35 (September 1968): 5–22.

Durrell, Donald. *Improving Reading Instruction.* New York: Harcourt, Brace & World, 1956.

Fries, Charles. *Linguistics and Reading.* New York: Holt, Rinehart and Winston, 1962.

Gallagher, J. J. "The Future Special Education System," pp. 1–13 in E. Meyen (ed.), *Proceedings — The Missouri Conference on the Categorical/ Non-Categorical Issue in Special Education.* Columbia, Mo.: University of Missouri Press, 1971.

Gilhool, Thomas H. "Education: An Inalienable Right." *Exceptional Children,* 38, 8 (May 1973): 597–610.

Goldstein, H., J. Moss, and L. Jordon. "The Efficacy of Special Class Training on the Development of Mentally Retarded Children." Urbana: University of Illinois Press, 1965.

Haring, N., and R. Ridgway. "Early Identifying of Children with Learning Disabilities." *Exceptional Children* 33 (1967): 387–395.

Keogh, Barbara, ed., "Early Identification of Children with Potential Learning Problems." *Journal of Special Education* 4, 3 (Fall 1970): 309–363.

Keogh, Barbara, and Laurence D. Becker. "Early Detection of Learning Problems: Questions, Cautions, and Guidelines." *Exceptional Children* 40 (September 1973): 5–13.

Kirp, D. L. "Student Classification, Public Policy, and the Courts." *Harvard Educational Review* 44 (1974): 7–52.

Lee, Laura L. *Developmental Sentence Analysis.* Evanston, Ill.: Northwestern University Press, 1974.

———. *Northwestern Syntax Screening Test.* Evanston, Ill.: Northwestern University Press, 1971.

Lee, Laura, Roy A. Koenigsknect, and Susan T. Mulhern. *Interactive Language Development Teaching.* Evanston, Ill.: Northwestern University Press, 1975.

Lerner, Janet W. "Reading Disability as a Language Disorder." *Acta Symbolica* 3, 1 (Spring 1972): 39–46.

Lilly, M. S. "Special Education: A Teapot in a Tempest." *Exceptional Children* 37 (September 1970): 43-49.

Mardell, Carol, and Dorothea Goldenberg. *Learning Disabilities/Early Childhood Research Project.* Springfield, Ill.: Office of the Superintendent of Public Instruction, 1972.

———. "For Pre-Kindergarten Screening: DIAL." *Journal of Learning Disabilities* 8 (March 1975): 140–147.

Martin, Edwin W. "Bureau of Education for the Handicapped Commitment and Program in Early Childhood Education." *Exceptional Children* 37 (May 1972): 661–665.

Meyen, E., ed. *Proceedings — The Missouri Conference on the Categorical/ Non-Categorical Issue in Special Education.* Columbia, Mo.: University of Missouri Press, 1971.

Moss, John R., ch. *A National Directory of Four Year Colleges, Two Year Colleges and Post High School Training Programs for Young People with Learning Disabilities.* Compiled for the Membership Committee of the Association for Children with Learning Disabilities. Commerce, Texas: East Texas State University, 1971, 1975.

Quay, H. C. "The Facets of Educational Exceptionality: A Conceptual Framework for Assessment Grouping and Instruction." *Exceptional Children,* 35 (September 1968): 25–32.

Rosenthal, R., and L. Jacobson, *Pygmalion in the Classroom.* New York: Holt, Rinehart and Winston, 1968.

Ross, Sterling, Jr., H. DeYoung, and J. Cohen, "Confrontation: Special Education Placement and the Law." *Exceptional Children* 38 (September 1971): 5–12.

Ruddell, Robert B. "Psycholinguistic Implications of a System of Communication Model," pp 239-258 in Harry Singer and Robert B. Ruddell (eds.), *Theoretical Models and Processes of Reading.* Newark, Del.: International Reading Association, 1970.

Russell, Robert. "The Dilemma of the Handicapped Adolescent," pp. 155–172 in R. Weber (ed.), *Handbook on Learning Disabilities.* Englewood Cliffs, N.J.: Prentice-Hall, 1974.

Schloss, Ellen. *The Educator's Enigma: The Adolescent with Learning Disabilities.* San Rafael, Calif.; Academic Therapy Publications, 1971.

Shuy, Roger W. "Speech Differences in Teaching Strategies: How Different is Enough?" pp. 55–72 in R. Hodges and E. Rudorf (eds.), *Language and Learning to Read.* Boston: Houghton Mifflin, 1972.

Siegel, Ernest. *The Exceptional Child Grows Up.* New York: Dutton, 1974.

Spicker, Harold H. "Intellectual Development Through Early Childhood Education." *Exceptional Children* 37 (May 1971): 629–642.

Talking Book Services, Commission for the Blind. Washington, D.C.: Library of Congress, 1974.

Vogel, Susan A. "Syntactic Abilities in Normal and Dyslexic Children." *Journal of Learning Disabilities* 7, 2 (February 1974): 103–109.

Webb, Gertrude. "The Neurologically Impaired Youth Goes to College," pp. 243–257 in R. Weber (ed.), *Handbook on Learning Disabilities.* Englewood Cliffs, N.J.: Prentice-Hall, 1974.

Weintraub, F. J. "Recent Influences of Law Regarding the Identification and Education Placement of Children." *Focus on Exceptional Children* 4, 2 (April 1972): 1-11.

Wells, Lorraine R. *Writing Disorders and the Learning Disability Student in the College English Classroom.* Unpublished Ph.D dissertation, Northwestern University, 1973.

4. Medicine and Learning Disabilities

The medical profession plays a crucial role in the field of learning disabilities. An underlying assumption of many theories of learning disability is that the condition is an organically based problem. As educators, psychologists, and guidance counselors become aware that a learning problem may have pathological implications, children are being referred to pediatricians, neurologists, ophthalmologists, otologists, and psychiatrists for further diagnosis. Medical specialists are becoming key members of multidisciplinary teams treating learning disabilities.

This chapter looks at the way in which the various medical specialties view the child with learning disabilities and at the contributions these specialties are making to diagnosis, prognosis, and treatment. In addition, certain physiological functions related to learning are discussed.

PEDIATRICS

The parent who becomes concerned about a child's behavior at home or poor performance in school often turns to the pediatrician for help. The parent might report that the child overreacts to everything, is constantly in motion, is silly at inappropriate times, does not see the consequences of actions, cannot control behavior, is overly affectionate, indiscriminate, and gullible. The child may have poor relations with peers, a low tolerance of frustration, and frequent temper tantrums. In school he or she may have a short attention span, be easily distracted, be disorganized in working, vary in mood from day to day, or even hour to hour. The child may have problems in reading and may not seem to understand numbers and arithmetic concepts.

Frequently, however, pediatricians have not been trained to detect those medical symptoms that indicate the likelihood of learning disabilities. If the symptoms are reported as school failures or emotional disturbances, pediatricians may feel these areas are out of the realm of their specialty.

On the other hand, many pediatricians see their role as a central one in the total management of the child in matters of both physical and mental health. They consider themselves to be concerned with such areas as language development, school adjustment, and academic learning of the child. Many pediatricians have commented on the change in the types of problems faced by their profession. For example, while there has been a decline in serious infectious diseases in children, there has been an increase in emphasis on biochemical abnormalities. At the present time, pediatricians are increasingly being alerted to learning disabilities. They are frequently panel members at educational conferences dealing with such problems as dyslexia; they are often part of diagnostic teams in various clinical settings in which learning disabilities are encountered; and they are beginning to make referrals when a cluster of symptoms suggestive of learning disabilities is noted.

Richmond and Walzer (1973) see pediatricians as responsible for enhancing the functional capacity of children in their psychosocial as well as biological development. Because there is no clear-cut taxonomy of learning disorders for the pediatrician to use, the complex task involves many responsibilities, including:

1. diagnosing and treating any physical and physiological handicaps that might impair learning, such as visual or auditory handicaps, undernutrition, or endocrinological and metabolic disorders
2. interpreting the nature of medical findings and their significance for

learning to parents, teachers, and other professionals working with the child

3. supporting and encouraging the family to procure special evaluative and educational procedures when indicated
4. specifying medical therapy for any defects or emotional problems
5. providing continuity of care for the family and the child in order to assess progress
6. utilizing the programs available for preventive intervention, including programs for the disadvantaged, early childhood screening, and intervention programs

Bateman and Frankel (1972) suggest three specific steps that pediatricians might take to effectively use and assist special education:

1. Pediatricians should know the special education personnel and services in their locality.
2. Pediatricians should adapt a "problem area" philosophy and an approach that insures their primary responsibility for delivery of medical services while also enabling them to function supportively and cooperatively as members of teams concerned with the delivery of educational services.
3. Pediatricians should recognize that the particular status accorded physicians in our society places on them the responsibility of recognizing the importance of educational services and supporting special education programs.

Pediatricians who are concerned with the mental and emotional facets of child development and health can be extremely helpful to parents. They can coordinate diagnosis and treatment and can become consultants and advisers in various treatment programs.

NEUROLOGY

The teacher who deals with learning disabilities should have some knowledge of the physiology and function of the brain and nervous system in order to evaluate new views and theories, to have a basis for meaningful diagnoses, and to help plan sound therapeutic strategies. Although it is often difficult to verify medical evidence of brain dysfunction, it is nevertheless important for the educator to have some familiarity with the current state of knowledge of the function of the brain and nervous system as it concerns learning and the language process.

THE BRAIN

All human behavior is mediated by the nervous system and the brain. Thus, the behavior of learning, one of the most important activities of the brain, has a physiological basis within the nervous system and brain. Gaddes (1969, p. 89) describes the brain activity during the learning process:

All of this mental activity is subserved by a rich and elaborated physiological excitation in the brain and the brain-stem of millions of tiny neurons or nerve cells firing many times a second and causing minute electrochemical changes. The human cortex alone is believed to contain about nine billion nerve cells, and these are interconnected by millions of neural pathways or fibers. The possibility of activity between various parts of the brain staggers the imagination. However, it is known that relatively large areas of the human cortex are involved with certain sensory and motor activities, and new information is gradually emerging regarding the correlative action of these areas and mental imaginative functions.

Modern medical techniques, such as refined neurosurgical procedures, electrical stimulation of the living brain tissues, and procedures in electroencephalography and neurophysiology, are providing new data about the structure and function of the brain. This material appears to have much relevance for understanding learning disabilities.

Much of our knowledge of how the human brain deals with language-related skills and the learning process has been derived from studies of the adult brain, usually an adult brain that has incurred some tissue damage from disease or injury. Science, however, has at last begun to develop new tools to enable the scientist to observe the functioning brain. One consequence of improved techniques of observation is that we are beginning to realize how little is really known about the very complex brain mechanism for learning.

The Cerebral Hemispheres

The human brain is composed of two halves, the right hemisphere and the left hemisphere, which appear to be almost identical in construction and metabolism. Each hemisphere contains a frontal lobe, a temporal lobe, an occipital lobe, a parietal lobe, and a motor strip area. The motor area of each hemisphere controls the muscular activities of the opposite side of the body. Thus, the right–hand and foot movements originate in the motor strip of the left hemisphere. Both of the eyes and ears are represented in both hemispheres (Bryan and Bryan, 1975).

Language function is thought to be located in one hemisphere of the brain. Research indicates that in more than 90 percent of adults, language function originates in the left hemisphere, regardless of whether the individual is left-handed, right-handed, or mixed. According to Geschwind (1968), the speech area is located in the left hemisphere in the majority of right-handed people; for left-handed people, the location for speech appears to occur with nearly equal frequency in each hemisphere. Similarly, Rossi and Rosadini (1967) found that about 98 percent of right-handed and 71 percent of left-handed patients had speech dominance in the left hemisphere.

Although the two halves of the brain appear to be almost identical in structure, they are quite different in function. Current research suggests that while the left hemisphere appears to react to and utilize language-related activities, the right hemisphere deals with nonverbal stimuli, including spatial perception, directional orientation, time sequences, and body awareness (Ketchum 1967, Teuber 1967). Thus, even though visual and auditory nerve impulses are carried to both cerebral hemispheres simultaneously, it is the left hemisphere that reacts to linguistic stimuli, such as words, symbols, and thought. Consequently, adult stroke patients with brain injury in the left hemisphere often suffer language loss along with an impairment in the motor function of the right half of the body.

However, the two hemispheres of the brain do not function altogether independently; there are many interrelating elements and functions. Faulty efficiency in either hemisphere reduces the total effectiveness of the individual and also results in reduced ability to deal with language and environment (Teuber 1967, Mountcastle 1962).

Cerebral Dominance Controversy

Orton (1937), one of the early investigators of reading difficulties, concluded that reversal of letters and words (which he called *strephosymbolia*, or twisted symbols) was symptomatic of a failure to establish cerebral dominance in the left hemisphere, the location of the speech area. According to this view, the interference of the right hemisphere during language activities was the cause of language confusion. Orton's therapeutic reasoning was therefore as follows: language function originates in the left cerebral hemisphere, and the left cerebral hemisphere is also the center for motor movement on the right side of the body; therefore, the language center in the left hemisphere could be strengthened and made dominant by strongly establishing the right-sided motor responses of the body. Right-handed and right-sided activities should be strongly encouraged and practiced, while left-sided activities should be discouraged or eliminated. This procedure, according to the Orton theory, would reduce the interference of the right cerebral hemisphere, which causes the language problems.

Most researchers today find the concept of cerebral dominance as put forth by Orton untenable (Ketchum 1967). Current findings suggest that, although the left hemisphere usually does specialize largely in language functions while the right hemisphere services nonverbal areas, both hemispheres contribute to the learning process. Faulty efficiency in either hemisphere reduces the total effectiveness of the individual and the handling of language. Concepts of cerebral dominance, mixed dominance, or nondominance have not proved to be useful in teaching language skills. The nondominant hemisphere does not retire to nonfunctional silence. According to Money (1966, p. 91), "A great deal of material about mixed dominance adds up to make sheer anatomical nonsense."

The laterality issue is a related controversial subject. The theory involved is that an individual's tendency to use either the right or left side of the body, or a preference in using one hand, foot, eye, or ear has a relationship to learning disorders. The term *established laterality* refers to the tendency to perform all functions with one side of the body, while *mixed laterality* refers to the tendency to mix the right and left preference in the use of hand, feet, eyes, and ears. In a test of lateral preference designed by Harris (1958), the child is asked to perform such tasks as throwing a ball, kicking a stick, sighting with a tube, and listening to a watch. In each case the child's lateral preference is noted.

Recent research suggest that there is no difference in reading ability between established and nonestablished laterality groups of public school children, and many research studies in reading conclude that the determination of laterality has dubious practical value as part of a reading diagnosis (Capobianco 1967, Belmont and Birch 1965). Spache (1968, p. 284) has come to a similar conclusion: "The tangential studies of the inter-relatedness of reading, [eye-preference] cerebral dominance, and the like are gradually disappearing under the weight of accumlated research which indicates that these areas do not yield significant findings for reading instruction."

Split-Brain Research

Studies of the separate reactions of each of the two hemispheres of the brain when they have been surgically separated give additional insight into the functions of the cerebral hemispheres (Sperry 1968). As noted earlier, the two hemispheres of the brain are contralaterally organized: the right hemisphere receives information from the left visual field and the left side of the body, while the left hemisphere gets input from the right visual field and the right side of the body. The sensory inputs are integrated through the *corpus callosum*, a bundle of nerve fibers connecting the two hemispheres.

Surgery severing the *corpus callosum* is performed to free patients from severe epileptic seizures that could be fatal but could not be cured with medication. Despite the benefits, however, splitting the two hemispheres of the cerebrum, creates the situation of two brains operating within a single body, each half acting independently of the other and each seeming to have its own sensations, perceptions, and memories, as well as cognitive and emotional experiences.

A number of investigations of split-brain patients have been carried out, using an apparatus that allows for the lateralized testing of the visual field separately or together. That is, the left eye and the right eye could be tested separately, or the right or left hand and leg could be tested separately with the vision excluded. Such tests show that these patients no longer have one visual inner world but two separate inner visual worlds — one serving the right half of the field of vision and the other serving the left half, each of course in its own respective hemisphere. For example, a picture of an object may be shown in the left visual field (right hemisphere), but the subject has no recollection of seeing it when it is shown to the right visual field (left hemisphere). Each half only remembers experiences from its own visual field.

The separate existence of the two brain hemispheres is further revealed by experiences in speech and writing, which are centered in the dominant hemisphere (left for most people). Visual material projected to the right visual field (left hemisphere) can be described in speech and writing. However, when the material is projected to the left visual field (right hemisphere), the subject does not see anything — only a flash of light. It is intriguing that emotional affects appear to get across to the language hemisphere, while the cognitive component cannot be articulated through the brain stem. In one experiment, when a nude pin-up was unexpectedly flashed to the left visual field of a split-brain patient, he said that he saw nothing but a flash of light. He then began to grin, blush, and giggle, but he could not say what had turned him on.

In another experiment, the split-brain patient was asked to identify objects put in his hand. When the object was placed in his right hand he could name the objects in speech or writing, but when the same objects were placed in his left hand, he made wild guesses in attempting to identify the object. Also, when a picture of the object was exposed to his left visual field, he had no trouble identifying the same object by touch with his left hand (both reached the same cerebral hemisphere — the right side). However, when a picture was seen with the left visual field, the patient could not match the object by touch with his right hand.

While split-brain research is still in basic research stages, it does provide insight into the differences in brain function between the two cerebral hemispheres and their relationship to learning. Since the field of learning disabilities is vitally concerned with the connection between brain dysfunction and learning anomalies, professionals should be aware of such current brain research.

NEUROLOGICAL EXAMINATION

If neurological impairment is suspected, the child may be referred to the neurologist, the medical specialist who evaluates the development and functioning of the central nervous system. Overt disturbances of motor function (such as cerebral palsy, epilepsies, and cortical blindness or deafness) and overt neurological abnormalities (such as the absence of certain reflexes or asymmetry of reflex responses) can be readily detected by the neurologist. However, children with learning disabilities rarely have such obvious impairments. They are more likely to manifest minimal, subtle, refined deviations called *soft signs.*

The conventional neurological examination would not reveal many soft signs. Medical specialists carrying on research in the field of learning disabilities have noted that the conventional neurological examination often fails to find any abnormalities in patients whose primary complaint is the inability to learn (Vuckovich 1968). Many children receive negative neurological reports because the neurologist may not be looking for subtle symptoms. Neurologists also face a number of further difficulties in interpreting neurological findings:

1. A wide range of soft signs of minimal neurological dysfunction occur among children who *are* learning satisfactorily.
2. Because the child's neurological system is not yet mature and is continually changing, it is often very difficult to differentiate between a lag in maturation and a dysfunction of the central nervous system.
3. Many of the tests for soft signs are psychological or behavioral rather than neurological tests.

For these reasons the value of the soft signs is open to question by some neurologists. Perhaps the best answer to these critical reservations has been suggested by Vuckovich (1968): the supreme test of healthy neurological function is efficient learning. The key difference between human beings and lower animals is our unique ability to learn, which is attributable to the highly complex organization of our brain and nervous system. The well-functioning nervous system will facilitate learning.

The neurological examination has been described for educators by medical specialists and pediatric neurologists (Vuckovich 1968, Grossman 1966a). In the conventional neurological examination, the neurologist first obtains a careful, detailed *medical history* to provide specific information and to obtain clues to the causes of the problem. The information collected includes a family history (for clues of a genetic nature), the details of the mother's pregnancy, the birth process, and the neonatal development. The neurologist records information about all illnesses, injuries, and infections that the child has had. The developmental history of the child's motor behavior (the age at which the child crawled, stood, walked) and language skills is also important. The neurologist collects further data on the child's hearing, vision, feeding, sleeping, toilet-training, and social and school experiences.

An *examination of the cranial nerves* gives information relating to vision, hearing, taste, facial expression, chewing, swallowing, vestibular function (equilibrium), and the ability to speak. Evaluation of the function of the various cranial nerves is derived by noting responses to certain stimuli, the condition of various organs, and the ability of the child to perform certain tasks.

Another area of the conventional neurological examination is the *assessment of all the components that control motor function*. A number of reflexes are tested in the neurological examination. Other aspects of the examination include an assessment of the sensory nerves through tests of perception, or tactile stimulation.

Electroencephalography, commonly called EEG, is a technical process of measuring the electrical activity of the brain. In this examination, electrodes are attached with a special paste to several locations on the head of the person being examined. The brain activity emanating from the various locations of the electrodes is represented on a chart by a graph-type pattern. The electroencephalographer reads the pattern that has been produced to determine if abnormalities in brain activity exist.

Although abnormal or borderline EEG patterns are found in many children with learning disabilities, many investigators believe that at the present time a diagnosis with this instrument is rather unreliable. Freeman (1971) asserts that the EEG is regarded with more awe than it deserves and that there are many technical problems in its use with children. For example, research findings indicate that many children who are not learning efficiently have normal EEG patterns, while some children with no apparent learning problems seem to have abnormal EEG patterns. In one study, when the EEG examinations of normal children were compared with those of children with learning disabilities, 35 percent of those with severe learning disabilities and 26 percent of the control, or normal, population were found to have abnormal EEG readings, a difference that was not reported to be significant. This study also reported that among 101 children with a moderate degree of learning disabilities, 48 percent had abnormal EEG readings; while among a control population of 101 children with no learning problems, 32 percent had abnormal EEG readings. The difference between these two groups was significant at the 5 percent level (Mylkebust and Boshes 1969).

Moreover, at present, researchers are unable to correlate the location of electroencephalographic abnormalities with the nature of the child's difficulty in learning. One example of the uncertainty of the interpretation of EEG patterns is the disagreement about the significance of the EEG pattern called "14- and 6-per-second positive spike discharges." This pattern is found quite frequently, yet there is difference of opinion among electroencephalographers as to whether or not such a pattern indicates an abnormality of the neurological system. In the research reported by Myklebust and Boshes (1969, p. 178), the type of EEG abnormality found most frequently was positive spikes; however, the percent of children found to have such an EEG reading was reported to be essentially identical in the experimental learning disabilities group and in the control group of children without learning problems. Freeman (1971) reports that 14- and 6-per-second positive spike patterns are quite common in young children and must be used as an indication of pathology only with extreme caution.

One interesting recent research finding suggests that a common clinical EEG abnormality in children with minimal brain dysfunction is an excessive amount of slow-wave activity and a slower than normal response to stimuli, as indicated on the brain-wave pattern (Satterfield et al., 1973, Shields 1973). In these studies children were exposed to a stimulus, such as a light flash, while taking an EEG examination. Analysis of the brain-wave patterns showed that children designated as learning disabled had a slower response than normal children.

Although many authorities feel that, in light of our present knowledge, the EEG has been overused and overemphasized in diagnosing learning disabilities (Grossman 1966a, Freeman 1971), other researchers predict that in the near future a relationship between EEG patterns and deficiencies in learning will be established and be of importance in diagnosis and management (Hughes 1968, Satterfield et al. 1973).

Other special medical procedures that might be requested by the neurologist include X rays of the skull and the blood vessels of the brain, biochemical studies, endocrinological studies, and genetic examinations.

Soft neurological signs can be detected with a neurological examination that is more complete than the conventional one. As previously noted, the neurological abnormalities most often seen in the child with learning disabilities are not the gross deviations but, rather, the fine, subtle, and minor symptoms. Many of the tests used to detect these symptoms have been borrowed or adapted from psychological assessment procedures. The soft signs include mild coordination difficulties, minimal tremors, motor awkwardness, visual-motor disturbances, deficiencies or abnormal delay in speech development, and difficulties in reading and arithmetic skills.

Vuckovich (1968) discusses a number of tests used by neurologists to detect soft signs of central nervous system dysfunction.

Visual-Motor Tests

Bender Visual-Motor Gestalt Test (Bender 1938). This test and others like it evaluate the visual-motor functioning of children by requiring them to copy various geometric forms. Following are some of the geometric forms used and the normal age at which the task can be performed (Ilg and Ames 1964):

Figure	Age
circle	3
cross	4
square	5
triangle	6–7
diamond	7

Draw-a-Man Test (Harris 1963). In this test the child is asked to draw a picture of a human figure. The scoring is dependent upon the body represented. This test is used by some diagnosticians to evaluate awareness of one's own body parts, as a measure of intelligence, or as a projective psychological test.

Gross-Motor Tests

Following are tests used to indicate postural skills, movement and balance, and the normal age at which the task can be performed (Vuckovich 1968):

Task	Age
Hopping on either foot	5
Standing on one foot	6
Tandem walking (heel-to-toe)	9
The child's walking gait is also observed.	

Tests of crossing the midline in execution of movements:

Touching nose and left ear and then nose and right ear. Observers note the rapidity with which the automatic level of takeover of motor movements is introduced.

Finger-nose test. The child is asked to touch his finger to his nose and to the examiner's finger repeatedly. Facility in alternating movement is observed.

Fine Sensory-Motor Tests

Finger-agnosia test. This test assesses the child's ability to recognize through a tactile sensation, often with eyes closed, which finger is being touched by the examiner. Following are the tasks and the normal age at which each task can be performed (Vuckovich 1968):

Task	Age
Recognition of thumb	4
Recognition of index finger	5–6

Other tests of tactile perception are recognition of objects by touch, recognition of two simultaneous contacts as the examiner touches two parts of the child's body (such as face and hand), recognition of letters or numbers by touch, recognition of letters or numbers drawn in the palm of the hand, and facility in moving the tongue (vertically and horizontally).

Hyperkinesis

The condition of hyperkinesis, a behavioral symptom related to extreme hperactivity, is considered to be one of the soft neurological signs of brain dysfunction. Hyperkinetic children can only sit for a few minutes at a time and even then often fidget and wiggle excessively. They have an extremely short attention span, are likely to talk too much in class, and constantly fight with friends, siblings, and classmates. Their actions have been described as impulsive or driven. Hyperkinetic children are easily distracted, racing from one idea and interest to another, unable to focus attention. The existence of hyperkinesis is interpreted as a soft sign of neurological dysfunction.

As noted earlier, many tests for soft signs of neurological dysfunction tend to overlap with the evaluation techniques used by psychologists.

According to Vuckovich (1968), there is no domain in neurology more controversial than the area of learning disabilities. Although it seems reasonable to presume that neurological disturbances have a detrimental effect on the learning processes, the precise nature of the relationship between neurological abnormalities and learning disabilities is still not clear. In the learning disabilities study reported by Myklebust and Boshes (1969, p. 214) neurological examinations were given to children in the experimental groups (203 children with varying degrees of learning disabilities) and to a control population (203 children who did not evidence learning problems). In the experimental groups, 50 to 53 percent were classified as normal in the neurological examination, while in the control groups 63 percent were classified as normal. The difference between these two groups was not statistically significant. As more knowledge is gained in the fields of neurology and pediatric neurology, and as the parameters of normal neurological development in children become more precise, the relationship between the neurological system and learning will become clearer. Vuckovich asserts:

> Knowledge of neurology as it relates to learning disabilities is still fragmentary. Parameters must be more clearly established so that the soft neurological signs can be more meaningful, not merely indications of a variation from the normal (Vuckovich 1968, p. 37).

OPHTHALMOLOGY

Whereas the pediatrician is usually the first to be consulted by the parent when the child has problems at home, the eye specialist is often consulted when the child has difficulty in school, particularly when the problem is poor reading. In fact, one of the first published papers on reading problems (Morgan 1896) was written by an ophthalmologist. It seems axiomatic that ocular comfort and visual efficiency are desirable attributes for reading success. Because reading is so obviously related to vision, it is not surprising that the eye specialist is involved when the child fails to learn to read.

The ophthalmologist is the specialist in the medical field who is responsible for the health of the eye, while the optometrist is the nonmedical specialist concerned with vision and its measurement and correction. The ophthalmologist considers the physiology of the eye, its organic aspects, diseases, and structure. The optometrist is more likely to stress the uses of the eye. There are differences in diagnosis and treatment procedures among eye specialists. While some treat deviations they consider significant by patching, lenses, and surgery, other specialists emphasize functional vision and the fact that visual skills are learned. Others treat weak or impaired visual skills by direct training procedures, as well as by lenses and other methods (Spache 1966).

Another way of presenting the contrast between these two views is to differentiate between an "eye problem" and a "visual problem." This point has been articulated well by Ilg and Ames (1955, p. 271) of the Gesell Institute of Child Development:

> One reason for overlooking the child's vision problem has been a lack of understanding by some educators and even by some eye specialists as to what constitutes a *visual* problem, and how it may differ from an eye problem. Many children have a visual problem, but not an eye problem. That is to say, the interior and exterior parts of their eyes are healthy, they have the ability to see small letters clearly at twenty feet (20/20 vision), and there are no obvious errors in the optical systems of either eye. Therefore, the diagnosis is healthy eyes and no visual problem.

In a proper visual examination, more than that is involved. In a visual examination, we should be concerned with the child's visual *abilities....*

The visual abilities to be examined are the following: (1) whether or not a child can focus and point the eyes together as a team (fusional ability), (2) whether or not a child can look from one object to another quickly and accurately (fixation ability), (3) whether or not a child can focus on an object moving closer (convergence ability), and (4) whether or not a child can maintain a clear focus at reading distance (accommodation ability).

> When a child lacks some of these essential visual skills, he may find himself classed as a reading problem, a behavioral problem, or more often just as a lazy child who could do the work if he would only try. When we speak of vision, we must be concerned with the child's ability to get meaning and understanding from what he sees by the skillful and efficient use of both eyes (Ilg and Ames 1955, p. 271).

VISUAL FINDINGS AS FACTORS IN READING PROBLEMS

Since visual deficiency may be a factor in certain cases of reading disability, children with reading problems should have an eye examination as part of their diagnosis. Teachers should be alert to such symptoms as facial contortions, head thrust forward or tilted, tension during close work or when looking at a distant object, poor sitting posture, frequent rubbing of eyes, excessive head movements, avoidance of close work, and frequent losing of place during reading.

In the eye examination, the eye specialist checks for visual acuity, refractive errors, and binocular difficulties. _Visual acuity_ refers to the ability to see forms or letters clearly from a certain distance. The Snellen chart, a visual screening test used in many schools, tests visual acuity at 20 feet from the chart, that is, *far-point visual acuity*. A score of 20/20 means that the subject sees at 20 feet what the normal eye sees at 20 feet. A score of 20/40 indicates that the subject sees at 20 feet what the normal eye sees at 40 feet. Other instruments are needed to assess *near-point visual acuity* at 16 inches, the distance used in reading. Persons who pass a far-point visual acuity test may fail the near-point test.

Refractive errors are due to a defect of the lens and are of three types: (1) *myopia* (nearsightedness), (2) *hyperopia* (farsightedness), and (3) *astigmatism* (the blurring of vision due to an uneven curvature of the front of the eye). Research studies have revealed that myopia has little or no correlation with poor reading and, in fact, is found as often or more often in good readers than in poor readers (Bond and Tinker 1967). The visual screening devices that detect only the condition of myopia may not detect those children with visual defects that appear to be significantly related to reading difficulties. Reading requires visual acuity at "near point," a distance of 14 to 16 inches, rather than at 20 feet. Astigmatism does not appear to be closely related to reading disability either. In fact, Robinson found that in some cases it is associated with better-than-average reading (Bond and Tinker 1967). Poor readers, however, do seem to have a slightly higher occurrence of hyperopia (Bond and Tinker 1967).

Binocular difficulties occur because the two eyes are not functioning together. Three binocular conditions are (1) *strabismus* (lack of binocular coordination), (2) *inadequate fusion* (poor accommodation of focus of the eye lens to fuse the two images), and (3) *aniseikonia* (ocular images of an object fixated are unequal in size or shape in the two eyes). Some research studies have indicated that problems of binocular vision have more implications for reading than refractive errors do.

In summing up the research studies of visual adequacy and reading, Park (1968, p. 328) reached the following conclusions:

1. Many visual deficiencies occurring in cases of reading retardation can be considered nothing more than coincidental.
2. Although visual acuity or the occurrence of refractive errors probably is not related directly to reading ability, lack of adequate coordination in the functioning of the two eyes probably contributes to reading disorders.
3. Although reading ability and visual functioning are not related directly, the detection and correction of visual difficulties may improve comfort and efficiency in reading.

Other ophthamologists concur. According to Lawson (1968), the role of ocular factors as *the cause* of reading retardation has been refuted, but there is general agreement that eye defects can aggravate a learning disorder. Goldberg (1959) concluded that defective vision and eye muscle imbalance are not significant factors in problems of spatial confusion or poor visual memory. Further, he believes that poor ocular motility is not a causal factor in poor reading comprehension (Goldberg 1970). Finally, the research in reading has not revealed much difference between the visual characteristics of good readers and those of poor ones (Bond and Tinker 1967).

Probably of greater importance to learning and reading than visual acuity or refractive errors is the process of visual discrimination and visual perception — the interpretation of visual sensory stimulation. Disturbances in visual perception, however, are not due to organic ocular abnormalities but rather to psychological or central processing dysfunctions.

Visual discrimination is the process of detecting differences in objects, forms, letters, or words. *Visual perception* is the cognition and interpretation of a visual sensation and the mental association of the present visual stimuli with memories of past experiences. The mechanisms of visual discrimination and visual perception are not strictly within the realm of the medical aspects of vision. They are, therefore, discussed more fully in a later chapter (Chapter 9) dealing with perceptual skills.

EYE MOVEMENTS DURING THE READING PROCESS

The eye movements of readers have been photographed and plotted with an instrument, made especially for this purpose, called an *ophthalmograph*. In visual terms, Spache (1966) describes the events that occur during the reading act: As the individual reads, the eyes do not make a continuous sweep across the page; instead they make a series of jumps and pauses from left to right, across the line of print, and then make a return sweep to the beginning of the next line. Observers of the eyes of readers through a peephole in a page have likened the movement of the eyes to that of a typewriter. Each pause is called a *fixation*. The reader reads only when the eyes are at rest during a fixation. During the *interfixation movement*, from one fixation to the next, vision is blurred and the reader sees nothing clearly. The fixations are the heart of the visual reading act, accounting for about 90 percent of the reading time, while interfixation movements and return sweeps account for the balance. During the entire process the two eyes must focus, relax, and move together. A backward movement and fixation called a *regression* is made when the reader fails to recognize or understand the material seen during the fixation.

The good reader has fewer, shorter, and more regular fixations than the poor reader, as well as fewer regressions. Inefficient eye movements, however, are symptoms rather than causes of poor reading. A recent research study with the eye camera (Taylor 1966) revealed that the average first-grade reader makes 240 fixations per 100 words. The average college student, reading at 340 words per minute, has 75 fixations per 100 words. The first grader makes over two stops per word, the sixth grader sees less than one word per fixation, and the college student sees about 1.3 words per fixation. The implication of these findings makes questionable the methods, materials, and machines that are designed to increase the span of recognition, the amount of material the eye takes in during a fixation. Accumulating research on eye movements during reading supports the following statement by Lawson (1968, p. 155):

> The average child cannot be expected to see several words in a single fixation. The individual has little voluntary control of his visual apparatus in reading. He cannot increase the rapidity of his eye movements automatically and expect his comprehension to remain the same or to increase. The brain controls the way the eyes work when various types of material are read; it must do the organizing and comprehending after perception takes place.
>
> The average reader cannot be trained to read at high speed. Those who obtain excessive speeds generally are superior readers before they take special training and usually have better than average vocabulary.

As we saw earlier, the relationship of eye dominance and eye laterality to reading has been controversial and findings are still not precise. However, it appears that there is not a significant relationship between eye preference and reading achievement (Belmont and Birch 1965, Balow and Balow 1964). Neither eye dominance nor the preference for one eye with the opposite hand seems to be a significant factor in differentiating good from poor readers (Tinker 1965).

DIFFERENCES OF OPINION CONCERNING VISION AND LEARNING

Professional differences of opinion concerning the eye and learning disabilities are reflected by the two professional specialties that deal with eye care, the opthalmologists and the optometrists. Benton (1973) observes that many optometrists are interested in developmental vision, visual perception, and visual training, as well as refractive errors. In contrast, Benton states that most ophthalmologists are concerned with the organic health of the eye, as well as refractive errors. Consequently, while the optometrist may see a need for eye training for a particular child, the ophthalmologist may find nothing wrong with the child's eyes.

The American Association of Ophthalmology, in conjunction with other medical associations, issued a position paper entitled "The Eye and Learning Disabilities" (Flax 1973), which presented the profession's opposition to visual training approaches to reading problems. Optometrists have attacked this position statement, charging that gross distortions and inaccuracies were used in reaching these conclusions (Flax 1973). One educator who reviewed the visual training research (Keogh 1974) concluded that while the research does indicate a relationship between visual perception and reading ability, there is insufficient evidence to support a direct causal interpretation. One problem is that the developmental training programs reported in the research used a variety of techniques, including an emphasis on language, so that it was difficult to consider visual perception independently of other program effects. It appears that additional study is needed to find definitive answers to this controversial question.

OTOLOGY

The ability to hear the sounds and language in the environment is a crucial factor in a child's learning. Language, for example, is learned largely through the sense of hearing. The medical specialist responsible for the diagnosis and treatment of auditory disorders is the otologist, and the branch of medicine dealing with the ear is called otology. A slightly broader area of medical specialization, otolaryngology, deals with the ear, nose, and throat.

The nonmedical specialist who is concerned with normal and abnormal aspects of hearing is called an audiologist. Audiology spans a number of functions, including the testing and measurement of hearing, the diagnosis and rehabilitation of the deaf and hard-of-hearing, the scentific study of the physical process of hearing, and the broadening of knowledge and understanding of the hearing process.

Hearing is most frequently measured with an electronic device called a pure-tone audiometer. Pure tones are produced near the outer ear, and the subject states whether or not a sound is heard. A second method of assessing hearing is through a bone conduction test. This method measures hearing in certain types of hearing loss by conducting sound waves directly to the inner ear by way of the bones of the ear. In testing for auditory disorders, two dimensions of hearing are considered — intensity and frequency.

Intensity refers to the relative loudness of the sound and is measured in decibels (db). The louder the sound, the higher the decibel measure. Ordinary conversation measures at 56 to 60 decibels. Silverman (1960) estimates a hearing threshold of 30 decibels as the minimum level at which children begin to encounter problems in school. *Frequency* refers to the pitch or vibrations of a given sound wave and is measured in cycles per second (cps). A person may have a hearing loss at one frequency but be able to hear well at another. In speech, consonant sounds such as *s, sh, z,* are high-frequency sounds; vowels, such as *o* and *u,* are low-frequency sounds.

Hearing level is the intensity level in decibels at which a person begins to detect sounds in various frequency levels. When screening children for hearing loss, the audiometer may be set at an intensity of 15 to 20 decibels. In a comprehensive sweep check test, the child is tested at frequencies of 250, 500, 1,000, 2,000, and 8,000 cycles per second.

Wooden (1963) suggests that a prevalence estimate of slightly more than one-half percent (0.6 percent) is probably a fair approximation of children in the school population with hearing loss. In addition, many children suffer temporary hearing losses due to infected adenoids or tonsils, wax in the ears, or other abnormalities that can be corrected. When such a temporary impairment occurs during certain developmental stages in early childhood, it may have a detrimental effect on learning, particularly language learning.

A sensory hearing impairment, then, is an important consideration in diagnosing and treating a child with learning disabilities. Occurring with greater frequency than impairments in auditory acuity, however, are deficits in auditory perception and auditory discrimination. A disability in auditory perception is not related to organic abnormalities of the ear. The subject of auditory perception is discussed in greater detail in Chapter 9.

PSYCHIATRY

Many children with learning disabilities are referred to child psychiatrists, who can play an important role in the field of learning disabilities. A study in Vancouver, Canada, revealed that 22 percent of individuals under age 18 who were referred to psychiatric facilities were referred because of academic difficulties (Nichol 1974). As we have come to recognize the emotional factors in learning disabilities, these medical specialists often assume important roles as members of diagnostic and treatment teams. Giffin (1968) believes that a psychiatric approach to learning disabilities should take into account the complex relationship between organic factors and psychotherapeutic elements. Psychatrists often work with parents and other family members, as well as the child. In addition, they must communicate and coordinate their efforts with the school or clinic and with the educational efforts that are being made. The child psychiatrist certainly is a very visible medical professional at conferences, in the literature, in research, and as an important member of the learning disabilities team.

PHARMACOLOGY

DRUGS AS MEDICATION

Many children with learning disabilities are given drugs intended to control behavior. It is hoped that an improvement in behavior will enhance the child's ability to learn. Although drug therapy is a medical problem, the teacher plays an important role in improving its effectiveness. To accomplish this, the teacher should be aware of the specific drug program a child is under in order to provide feedback to the doctors and parents concerning the effect of the drug on the child in school. With such feedback, the physician can gauge the effectiveness of the drug and make appropriate modifications.

Children with volatile behavior symptoms are most likely to receive drugs to aid in the management of behavior both at home and at school. The drug may decrease the child's hyperactivity and increase the length of attention span so that learning can take place.

The child with learning disabilities has been noted to have an unpredictable reaction to a particular drug or combination of drugs. Certain stimulants, used by adults as antidepressants and energizers, seem to have the effect of calming the behavior of children who are hyperactive, impulsive, and distractible (Grossman 1966b). On the other hand, sedatives such as phenobarbital have been reported to increase activity in the lethargic and hypoactive child. There are many exceptions to these generalizations, and no specific treatment is available for pediatric patients who have been diagnosed as having learning disabilities or minimal brain dysfunction because the causes and manifestations are so diverse.

Since these children often have an abnormal reaction to certain drugs, some physicians have suggested that trial of a drug can be a useful diagnostic tool to indicate the presence of a neurological abnormality. An atypical reaction to a drug such as Dexedrine or Ritalin could serve as part of the data in making a diagnosis. Normal use of such drugs is as an energizer, so a calming-down reaction to the drug could be a diagnostic indication of dysfunction in the central nervous system.

Some physicians have questioned the effectiveness of drugs as a means of improving learning or even of affecting behavior. Parents often report that their child's behavior and learning have improved after being given a placebo. Thus, a harmless substance given to a patient may have a beneficial psychological effect, but this result raises doubts concerning the effectiveness of genuine drugs. Many experimental studies on the effectiveness of drugs have been criticized because they have been poorly designed and inadequately controlled. For example, there is frequently little assurance that subjects actually follow the precise directions of the research design. In one two-year study designed partly to test the effect of a particular drug, the authors reported that this portion of the research had to be abandoned because it proved impossible to control administration of the drug to the subjects (Abrams and Belmont 1969).

The ideal drug for the treatment of children with minimal brain dysfunction should control hyperactivity, increase attention span, reduce impulsive and aggressive behavior without inducing insomnia, anorexia (loss of appetite), drowsiness, or other serious toxic effects (Millichap 1973). Because hyperactive behavior is substantially reduced at the onset of puberty, medication is typically stopped at age 12. The following groups of drugs are prescribed: *central nervous system* drugs (Ritalin, Dexedrine, Deaner); *tranquilizers* (Librium, Mellaril, Thorazine, Serpasil); *antidepressant* and *anticonvulsant* drugs (Dilantin, phenobarbital). Millichap (1972, p. 77) reports the following commonly used drugs according to their probable control:

Name of Drug	Expected Incidence of Control
Ritalin	84
Dexedrine	69
Librium	60
Mellaril	57
Thorazine	55
Deaner	47
Serpasil	34

In addition, a relatively new central nervous system drug, Cylert, is reported to be effective in reducing hyperactive behavior (Page et al. 1974).

The Child Development Laboratory at Harvard University has been researching the effectiveness of drug treatment with learning-disabled children for the past 10 years. This experience has led Conners (1973) to the following conclusions:

1. There is no simple available diagnostic category backed up by clear-cut procedures of assessment and validated methods that unequivocally lead to a prescription for drug treatment.

2. The effect of stimulant drugs, such as amphetamines, is more complex than a simple reduction of activity level. The drugs alter the quality of the child's activity and goal directedness. They can also have a significant effect on mood, personality, concentration, perception, and motor coordination. Since the effects are least apparent to the physician treating the child in an office, close liaison of the medical personnel with the school and the family is needed.

3. Drug treatment by itself is seldom a sufficient remedy for the child's total set of symptoms of maladaptive behavior. Educational and psychological treatment is also needed.

4. Careful follow-up of the course of treatment is essential to regulate dosage and to evaluate the side effects and behavioral effects of treatment. The drugs by themselves do not teach anything. The child still needs continued attention to educational inputs.

5. Despite these cautions, drugs have been shown to produce substantial academic and behavioral improvement. When indicated, they should be used. There is no support to the fear that drugs produce a susceptibility to addiction or drug abuse in later life.

All in all, drugs appear to be of considerable value in certain instances, but are of little or dubious help in other cases. Drug therapy is only part of the management picture and should be considered an adjunct to the educational procedure.

CONFERENCE REPORT ON USE OF STIMULANT DRUGS

The use of drugs is understandably regarded with some apprehension. Concern has been raised by the public and news media in regard to hazards and abuses; the use of amphetamines as a treatment for hyperactivity has particularly alarmed the public. Are drugs misused in lieu of other treatment methods? Does their use tend to oversimplify a complex problem? Could these drugs induce toxicity? Could their use create dependence on drugs in later years?

The Office of Child Development and the Office of the Assistant Secretary for Health and Scientific Affairs (1971) held a conference of experts to discuss the use of drugs in children with hyperkinetic disorders. Hyperkinetic children, estimated as 3 out of 10 elementary school children, were described as youngsters with an increase of purposeless physical activity and a significantly impaired span of attention. The report advised that excessive activity and attentional disturbances become less apparent after puberty.

While the report emphasized that medicine does not "cure" the condition, it stated that the child may become more accessible to educational and counseling efforts. Over a short period and at a critical age, the medication can provide the help needed for the child's development. Although stimulant medications are beneficial in only about one-half to two-thirds of the cases in which trials of the drugs are warranted, the report considered the stimulant drugs to be the first and least complicated of the medicine to be tried. The other medications, including the tranquilizers and antidepressants, were reserved for a small group of patients.

In treating a child, the physician cannot predict a response to the stimulant medicine. However, the doctor can quickly determine if the medication is successful, for when stimulants are given in adequate doses the child improves quickly. If doubtful benefits occur, or none at all, after a test of a few days or weeks, the treatment can be promptly terminated.

If it works, the drug appears to mobilize and increase the child's abilities to focus on meaningful stimuli and to organize bodily movements more purposefully.

A number of questions that had been raised by the news media were answered:

1. *Does the medication produce toxicity?* In the low dosage used for children, the questions of acute or chronic toxicity noted in the stimulant abuser is not a critical issue.

2. *Is there a risk of drug dependency in later years?* Clinical experience and several scientific studies show no association between medical use of stimulants in the preadolescent child and later drug abuse. Children do not have the pleasurable, subjective effects that would encourage misuse. They are often happy to stop the therapy, which they view as "medicine." The report concluded that use of drugs with young children does not appear to induce misuse. Several studies have failed to reveal an association between the medical use of stimulants in the preadolescent child and later drug abuse. In fact, the medical supervision seems to teach the child appropriate use of medicine; hazard of later drug abuse is minimal.

3. *Are there safeguards against misuse?* Sensible steps should be taken to guard against misuse. The child should not be given sole responsibility for taking the medication. If possible the drug should not be brought to school.

4. *Do stimulants for children create risk for others?* The panel stated that the prescribed dosage for an individual child constitutes an insufficient quantity to supply the confirmed abuser of stimulant. There is no present evidence that the prescriptions for the children who benefit from stimulants will require the manufacture of excessive and dangerously divertable supplies.

5. *Does medication handicap the child emotionally?* The report denies that treated children are unable to learn normal responses and master adjustments to the stresses of everyday life. The medication helps the child acquire the capacity to tolerate and master stress; in this way, drugs are an aid for satisfactory psychological development, although drug therapy should not allow children to avoid or escape the ordinary stresses of life.

6. *What are the rights of the parents?* Under no circumstances should any attempt be made to coerce parents to accept any particular treatment. The consent of both the patient and the parents should be obtained for treatment. School personnel can inform parents of a child's behavior problems, but they should not directly diagnose the hyperkinetic disturbance or prescribe treatment.

BIOCHEMICAL APPROACHES

In recent years there has been an interest in a number of biochemical and biomedical areas that may have an impact on the child's ability to learn. Several of these areas are discussed in this section.

One area under investigation is the connection between _nutrient deficiency_ and _learning impairment_. Much of the research has considered nutrient deficiency in relation to mentally retarded youngsters, but Hallahan and Cruickshank (1973) suggest that malnutrition may also be related to perception, attention, and other learning-related phenomena. Early malnutrition impairs growth, both of the body in general and the central nervous system in particular. The severity of the deficit is related to the age at which malnutrition occurs, the degree, and the duration. The first six months of life are a critical nutrient period because it is at this time that maximal postnatal brain cell division occurs in the human infant. Damage incurred during this period is probably permanent. Research indicating a causal link between early nutrient deprivation and later impaired learning function is reported by Birch and Gussow (1970) and Cravioto (1972).

Another recent area of interest is the use of _megavitamins_ as a treatment procedure. Cott (1972) discusses the results achieved with approximately 500 children who were treated by orally administering pills, capsules, or liquids containing massive doses of vitamins. While Cott reports that this treatment is effective for children with learning disabilities, many physicians feel the need for further research evidence before such treatment can be generally prescribed.

There are several diet-related theories concerning the cause or treatment of hyperactivity and learning disorders. One position suggests that _food additives_ in the child's diet cause hyperactivity and learning disorders. Feingold (1975) notes that artificial flavors, artificial preservatives, and artificial colors have been on the increase in the American diet and that today's youngsters consume a large variety of food additives. Therapy consists of the control of the child's diet and the removal of food additives.

Another diet-related theory of the cause of learning disorders suggests that many learning-disabled children have _hypoglycemia,_ a condition due to a deficiency in the level of blood sugar (Dunn 1973). Therapy consists of the control of the child's eating pattern so that the condition can be improved. Without diet control, according to the theory, there is a decrease in the blood-sugar level about an hour after eating, and the child's energy for learning is drained.

The belief that many children develop _allergies_ that adversely effect learning is both a diet-related and environment-related theory (Harvard 1973). Removal of the element causing the allergy is the treatment in this approach. Another theory is that coffee can be used as an alternative treatment for drugs in decreasing hyperactivity (_Perception_ 1975).

In general, however, these biochemical approaches are still in theory stages and require additional research before general acceptance (Brown 1974, Silver 1975).

Finally, research in biochemistry may result in discoveries that will enable us to alter the intellectual capacity of children. Biochemical experimentation has shown that rats given a memory drug containing RNA (ribonucleic acid) improved their learning capacity up to 500 percent (Smith 1968).

Will we someday be able to substitute administration of a memory pill for long and difficult sessions of remedial therapy?

OTHER MEDICAL SPECIALTIES

The discussion in this chapter does not exhaust the medical specialties concerned with or contributing to the field of learning disabilities. Practitioners and researchers in the fields of endocrinology, biochemistry, and genetics are very much involved with the problems of the child who cannot learn in a normal fashion. They are treating such children, are members of diagnostic teams, and are contributing important findings to the literature. The future may hold important breakthroughs from these disciplines.

IMPLICATIONS OF MEDICAL INFORMATION FOR EDUCATORS

Because of the nature of the medical profession, medical specialists involved in learning disabilities are largely engaged in seeking the cause of the problem. Medical members of the learning disabilities team often perform an important function in aiding in the identification of children with learning disabilities. The task of treatment, however, falls primarily to educators. Medical information, such as an analysis of a child's EEG brain pattern or the physician's conjecture of the location of the dysfunction in the brain, does not guide the educator in selecting the appropriate method for teaching or improving academic performance. For this reason, Bateman (1974) sees little educational relevance of a diagnosis of MBD (minimal brain dysfunction) while (Cohen 1973, p. 251) suggests that neither medical labels nor the diagnosis of the medical cause of the child's problem helps the teacher in "practical matters such as teaching kids to read."

At present, then, there is no precise and immediate translation of medical findings to specific teaching procedures. Nevertheless, it seems essential for professionals in learning disabilities to be familiar with medical findings and with the perspectives of the various medical specialties. They should be in a position to communicate with other specialists and parents; they should be concerned with a broad base of child learning problems — not only those elements that have immediate applicability; and they should seek to maintain the interests of medical professionals in the learning-disabled child.

SUMMARY

This chapter has presented an overview of the contributions of various medical specialties to the field of learning disabilities. In addition, certain physiological functions related to learning and medical issues were discussed.

Pediatricians are probably the central medical specialists in many cases.

Their changing responsibilities include the psychosocial development as well as the biological health of the child.

The neurologist, as the medical specialist who evaluates the development and functioning of the brain and the central nervous system, is in a key position to diagnose children with learning disabilities. Some pediatric neurologists specialize in working with this type of child.

Because so many children with learning disabilities have difficulty learning to read, they often are referred to an ophthalmologist, who is the medical eye specialist. In addition, the optometrist, the nonmedical eye specialist, can contribute expertise in visual function.

The otologist is the medical hearing specialist, while the audiologist is the nonmedical hearing specialist. Both are concerned with auditory impairment, an important consideration in learning disabilities.

Psychiatrists are medical specialists concerned with the emotional factors that are often involved in learning disabilities. The psychologist is the nonmedical professional who works with the emotional aspect.

Finally, this chapter reviewed the use of drugs as medication for controlling the behavior of the learning-disabled child.

REFERENCES

Abrams, Jules C., and Herman S. Belmont. "Different Approaches to the Remediation of Severe Reading Disabilities in Children." *Journal of Learning Disabilities* 2 (March 1969): 136–145.

Balow, I. H., and B. Balow. "Lateral Dominance and Reading Achievement in the Second Grade." *American Educational Research Journal* 1 (1964): 139–143.

Bateman, Barbara. "Educational Implications of Minimal Brain Dysfunction." *Reading Teacher* 27 (April 1974): 662–668.

Bateman, Barbara, and Herman Frankel, "Special Education and the Pediatrician." *Journal of Learning Disabilities* 5 (April 1972): 178–186.

Belmont, Lillian, and H. C. Birch. "Lateral Dominance, Lateral Awareness, and Reading Disability." *Child Development* 34 (March 1965): 57–71.

Bender, Loretta. *A Visual-Motor Gestalt Test and its Clincal Uses.* Research monograph no. 3. New York: American Orthopsychiatric Association, 1938.

Benton, Curtis D. Jr. "Comment: The Eye and Learning Disabilities." *Journal of Learning Disabilities* 6 (May 1973): 334–336.

Birch, H., and J. Gussow. *Disadvantaged Children: Health, Nutrition, and School Failure.* New York: Grune & Stratton, 1970.

Bond, Guy L., and Miles A. Tinker. *Reading Difficulties: Their Diagnosis and Correction,* 2nd ed. New York: Appleton-Century-Crofts, 1967.

Brown, G. W. "Food Additives and Hyperactivity." *Journal of Learning Disabilities* 7 (December 1974): 62–63.

Bryan, T. H. and J. H. Bryan. *Understanding Learning Disabilities.* Pt. Washington, N.Y.: Alfred Publishing Co., 1975.

Capobianco, R. J. "Ocular-Manual Laterality and Reading Achievement with Special Learning Disabilities." *American Educational Research Journal* (March 1967): 133–183.

Cohen, S. Alan. "Minimal Brain Dysfunction and Practical Matters such as

Teaching Kids to Read," pp. 251–261 in F. De La Cruz, B. Fox, and R. Roberts (eds.), *Minimal Brain Dysfunction*. Annals of New York Academy of Sciences 205 (February 1973).

Conners, C. Keith. "What Parents Need to Know About Stimulant Drugs and Special Education." *Journal of Learning Disabilities* 6 (June/July 1973): 349–351.

Cott, A. "Megavitamins: The Orthomolecular Approach to Behavioral Disorders and Learning Disabilities." *Academic Therapy* 7 (Spring 1972): 245–259.

Cravioto, J. "Nutrition and Learning in Children," pp. 25–44 in N. S. Springer (ed.), *Nutrition and Mental Retardation*. Ann Arbor, Mich.: Institute for the Study of Mental Retardation and Related Disabilities, 1972.

Dunn, P. "Neurological Disorders and Learning Disabilities Called a Major Problem." *Pediatric Herald* (June 1973).

Feingold, Ben F. *Why Your Child is Hyperactive*. New York: Random House, 1975.

Flax, Nathan. "The Eye and Learning Disabilities." *Journal of Learning Disabilities* 6 (May 1973): 328–333.

Freeman, Roger D. "Special Education and the Electroencephalogram: Marriage of Convenience," pp. 41–58 in D. Hammill and H. Bartel (eds.), *Educational Perspectives in Learning Disabilities*. New York: Wiley, 1971.

Gaddes, William H. "A Neurological Approach to Learning Disorders," pp. 88–102 in *Successful Programming: Many Points of View*. San Rafael, Calif.: Academic Therapy Publications, 1969.

Geschwind, Norman. "Neurological Foundations of Language," pp. 182–199 in H. Myklebust (ed.), *Progress in Learning Disabilities*, Vol. 1. New York: Grune & Stratton, 1968.

Giffin, Mary. "The Role of Child Psychiatry in Learning Disabilities," pp. 75–99 in H. Myklebust (ed.), *Progress in Learning Disabilities*, Vol. 1. New York: Grune & Stratton (1968).

Goldberg, Herman. "The Ophthalmologist Looks at the Reading Problem." *American Journal of Ophthalmology* 47 (1959): 67–74.

Grossman, Herbert J. "The Child, the Teacher, and the Physician," pp. 57–68 in W. Cruickshank (ed.), *The Teacher of Brain-Injured Children*. Syracuse, N.Y.: Syracuse University Press, 1966.

————. "Psychopharmocology," pp. 245–254 in W. Cruickshank (ed.), *The Teacher of Brain-Injured Children*. Syracuse, N.Y.: Syracuse University Press, 1966.

Hallahan, Daniel P., and William M. Cruickshank. *Psychoeducational Foundations of Learning Disabilities*. Englewood Cliffs, N.J.: Prentice-Hall, 1973.

Harris, Albert. *Harris Test of Lateral Dominance*, rev. 3rd ed. New York: Psychological Corporation, 1958.

Harris, Dale. *Children's Drawings as Measures of Intellectual Maturity*. New York: Harcourt, Brace & World, 1963.

Harvard, Janice. "School Problems and Allergies." *Journal of Learning Disabilities* 6 (October 1973): 492–494.

Hughes, John R. "Electroencelphalography and Learning," pp. 113–146 in H. Myklebust (ed.), *Progress in Learning Disabilities*, Vol. 1. New York: Grune & Stratton, 1968.

Ilg, Frances, and Louis B. Ames. *Child Behavior*. New York: Harper and Row, 1955.

Keogh, Barbara K. "Optometric Vision Training Program for Children with Learning Disabilities: Review of Issues and Research." *Journal of Learning Disabilities* 7 (April 1974): 219–231.

Ketchum, E. Gillet. "Neurological and/or Emotional Factors in Reading Disabilities," pp. 521–525 in J. Figurel (ed.), *Vistas in Reading*. Newark, Del.: International Reading Association, 1967.

Lawson, Lawrence J. "Ophthalmological Factors in Learning Disabilities," pp. 147–181 in H. Myklebust (ed.), *Progress in Learning Disabilities*, Vol. 1. New York: Grune & Stratton, 1968.

Millichap, J. Gordon. "Drugs in Management of Minimal Brain Dysfunction," pp. 321–335 in F. De La Cruz, B. Fox, and R. Roberts (eds.), *Minimal Brain Dysfunction*. Annals of the New York Academy of Sciences 205 (February 1973).

———. "Drugs in the Management of Minimal Brain Dysfunction." *International Journal of Child Psychotherapy* 1 (1972): 65–81.

Money, John. "The Laws of Constancy and Learning to Read," pp. 80–99 in *International Approach to Learning Disabilities of Children and Youth*. Tulsa, Okla.: Association for Children with Learning Disabilities, 1966.

Morgan, W. P. "A Case of Congenital Word Blindness." *British Medical Journal* 2 (November 1896): 1375–1379.

Mountcastle, V. B., ed. *Interhemispheric Relationships and Cerebral Dominance*. Baltimore: Johns Hopkins Press, 1962.

Myklebust, Helmer R., and Benjamin Boshes. *Minimal Brain Damage in Children*. Final report. U.S. Public Health Service Contract 108-65-142. U.S. Public Health Service, Neurological and Sensory Disease Control Program, U. S. Department of Health, Education, and Welfare. Evanston, Ill.: Northwestern University Publications, June 1969.

Nichol, Hamish. "Children with Learning Disabilities Referred to Psychiatrists: A Follow-up Study." *Journal of Learning Disabilities* 7 (February 1974): 118–122.

Office of Child Development and the Office of the Assistant Secretary for Health and Scientific Affairs. *Report of the Conference on the Use of Stimulant Drugs in the Treatment of Behaviorally Disturbed Young School Children*. Washington, D.C.: Department of Health, Education, and Welfare, January 1971.

Orton, Samuel T. *Reading, Writing, and Speech Problems in Children*. New York: W. W. Norton, 1973.

Page, John G., Robert S. Janicki, Joel E. Bernstein, Charles F. Curran, and Frank A. Michelli. "Pemoline (Cylert) in the Treatment of Childhood Hyperkinesis." *Journal of Learning Disabilities* 7 (October 1974): 498–503.

Park, George E. "The Etiology of Reading Disabilities: An Historical Perspective." *The Journal of Learning Disabilities* 1 (May 1968): 318–330.

Perception (January 1975): 4.

Richmond, J., and S. Walzer. "The Central Task of Childhood — Learning. The Pediatrician's Role," pp. 390–394 in F. De La Cruz, B. Fox, and R. Roberts (eds.), *Minimal Brain Dysfunction*. Annals of the New York Academy of Sciences 205 (February 1973).

Rossi, Gian F., and G. Rosadini. "Experimental Analysis of Cerebral Dominance in Man," pp. 167–175 in C. Millikan (ch.) and F. L. Darley (ed.), *Brain Mechanisms Underlying Speech and Language*. New York: Grune & Stratton, 1967.

Satterfield, James, L. Lesser, R. Saul, and D. Cantwell. "EEG Aspects in the Diagnosis and Treatment of Minimal Brain Dysfunction," pp. 274–282 in F. De La Cruz, B. Fox, and R. Roberts (eds.), *Minimal Brain Dysfunction*. Annals of the New York Academy of Sciences 205 (February 1973).

Shields, Dianne T. "Brain Responses to Stimuli in Disorders of Information Processing." *Journal of Learning Disabilities* 6 (October 1973): 501–505.

Silver, Larry B. "Acceptable and Controversial Approaches to Treating Learning Disabilities," *Pediatrics* (March 1975): 406–415.

Silverman, S. R. "Hard of Hearing Children," pp. 452–458 in Davis, Hallowell, and S. R. Silverman (eds.), *Hearing and Deafness,* 2nd ed. New York: Holt, Rinehart and Winston, 1960.

Smith, Nila B. "Perspectives in Reading Instruction: Past Perfect? Future Tense?" *Elementary English* (April 1968): 440–445.

Spache, George. "Contributions of Allied Fields to the Teaching of Reading," pp. 237–290 in Helen Robinson (ed), *Innovation and Change in Reading Instruction.* National Society for the Study of Education Yearbook, Part II. Chicago: University of Chicago Press, 1968.

————. "What Teachers Should Know About Vision and Reading." *The Optometric Weekly,* October 20, 1966.

Sperry, R. W. "Hemisphere Deconnection and Unity in Conscious Awareness," *American Psychologist* 23 (October 1968): 723–733.

Taylor, E. *The Fundamental Reading Skill as Related to Eye-Movement Photography and Visual Anomalies.* Springfield, Ill.: Charles C. Thomas, 1966.

Teuber, Hans-Lukas. "Lacunae and Research Approaches to Them, I," pp. 204–216 in C. Millikan (ch.) and F. Darley (ed.), *Brain Mechanisms Underlying Speech and Language.* New York: Grune & Stratton, 1967.

Tinker, Karen J. "The Role of Laterality in Reading Disability," pp. 300–303 in *Reading and Inquiry.* Newark, Del.: International Reading Association, 1965.

Vuckovich, D. Michael. "Pediatric Neurology and Learning Disabilities," pp. 16–38 in H. Myklebust (ed.), *Progress in Learning Disabilities,* Vol. 1. New York: Grune & Stratton, 1968.

Wooden, Harley Z. "Deaf and Hard-of-Hearing Children," pp. 339–412 in Lloyd M. Dunn (ed.), *Exceptional Children in the Schools.* New York: Holt, Rinehart and Winston, 1963.

TWO

The Diagnosis/ Teaching Process

5. Diagnosis

PURPOSE OF DIAGNOSIS

DIAGNOSTIC PROCESS

OBTAINING DATA FOR DIAGNOSIS
Case History
Clinical Observation
Informal Tests
Formal Standardized Tests

INTERPRETING TEST SCORES
Wechsler Intelligence Scale for Children
Illinois Test of Psycholinguistic Abilities

QUANTIFYING THE LEARNING DISABILITY

SUMMARY

In examining the first part of the diagnosis/teaching process — the diagnosis of learning disabilities — this chapter discusses (1) the purpose of diagnosis, (2) the diagnostic process, (3) ways of gathering diagnostic data via the case history or interview, clinical observation, informal tests, and standardized tests, and (4) ways of interpreting the scores of certain tests. The second part of the diagnosis/teaching process, is examined in chapter 6. Both diagnosis and teaching are shaped, in large part, by the perspective and theoretical framework of the diagnostician and teacher. The various theories of learning disabilities that might affect this perspective are discussed in Part Three.

PURPOSE OF DIAGNOSIS

The reason for conducting a diagnosis is to gather pertinent information concerning a specific child and to analyze and synthesize the information in making the crucial decisions about teaching. The child can be referred for an educational diagnosis by several sources: the school, a physician, the parents, or some other professional person who has contact with the child.

The phases of the total evaluation within the school are [(1) an identification process to detect pupils who *may* be learning disabled, (2) the actual diagnosis of children who have been identified in the screening process, and (3) the decisions about appropriate services and instructional methods (McGrady, 1974).

In the first phase of the school evaluation, several methods can be employed to identify children who may have learning disabilities. Classroom teachers may be asked to make referrals of suspected children, or the school may use some test for mass screening of all pupils, or teachers may be asked to complete a behavior rating scale to rate characteristics of all students in their classes. Once suspected pupils are identified, the actual selection of pupils for the program is made with a more intensive diagnosis (phase two). Phase three includes administrative decisions about placement and instructional decisions about teaching (Senf 1974).

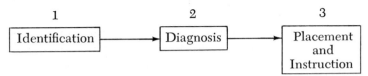

Figure 5.1 Phases of school evaluation

Diagnosis and teaching should be interrelated parts of a continuous process of trying to understand a child and to help the child learn. The instructional program that consists merely of the routine teaching of skills or the blind use of methods and materials without regard to diagnostic information about the unique problem of the child may not only waste time and effort but may also prove detrimental to the child. A diagnosis that culminates in merely attaching a label, such as dyslexia, or that names the presumed cause of the learning problem, such as a lesion in the angular gyrus or perhaps an overindulgent mother, is not operational because it provides insufficient guidelines for devising strategies to help the child learn. Terminology that has recently appeared in the literature emphasizes the interrelatedness of diagnosis and teaching as a total process: for example, *diagnostic teaching, remedial diagnosis,* and *psychoeducational remedial diagnostician.*

DIAGNOSTIC PROCESS

Children with learning disabilities are a heterogeneous group. The wide range of both degree and type of learning disorders requires a diversity of approaches and of diagnostic techniques. While a child with a severe and complex disorder may need a complete, intensive diagnosis provided by an entire interdisciplinary team of specialists, a child with milder problems may be helped with a less thorough examination given by a psychoeducational or learning disabilities specialist. Sometimes the learning disabilities specialist receives a case after the child has had a diagnostic evaluation by specialists in other disciplines. In that case some diagnostic data accompany the referral. If the learning disabilities specialist is the first professional to see the child, the specialist may need diagnostic information from other disciplines and will then take the initiative in making referrals.

The purpose of the diagnosis is to collect and analyze information that will help in planning an educational program to improve the child's learning. The steps in the process of diagnostic evaluation have been described by Kirk (1972), Bateman (1965), and others. Depending upon many variables, a specialist in each of the contributing disciplines could provide data and information at any of these stages; the learning disabilities specialist has the responsibility of bringing the information together. Most authorities agree that the following steps are essential in making the diagnosis:

1. *Determine whether the child has a learning disability.* Implicit in most definitions of learning disability is a discrepancy between what a child is actually learning and what the child ought to be learning. Actual learning is determined by measurement of the child's present achievement, while what the child ought to be learning is estimated through measures of capacity to learn. A number of ways of measuring this discrepancy are discussed later in this chapter under "Quantifying the Learning Disability."

Another kind of discrepancy that may indicate a learning disability can be detected by an analysis of the relationship of various subskills of the child's mental functioning. An uneven pattern (sometimes referred to as *developmental imbalances*) suggests that a weakness in specific areas of mental functioning is preventing the child from reaching full learning potential. A profile of subtest scores on certain tests is useful in determining whether the child does have an uneven pattern of mental functioning.[1]

2. *Measure the child's present achievement* to detect the specific areas of failure and the levels that appear to be blocked. For example, to determine the present achievement level in reading, a reading test is given. Another approach to this diagnostic step is to determine the developmental level of the learning problem — whether it is a motor problem, a perceptual problem, a memory problem, a language problem, or a cognitive problem. Evaluations of performance in these areas of learning should be made. Clinical observations, informal tests, and standardized instruments can all provide useful data and information.

3. *Analyze how the child learns.* What are the child's approaches to processing information? The framework of theory within which the diagnostician views the child will have an important impact on the analysis of how the child learns.[2] Questions that might be asked at this stage include: Is

---

[1] The concept of developmental imbalances is also discussed in Chapter 11.
[2] The various theories of learning disabilities with which the diagnostician may approach the child's problem are discussed in Part Three.

the child's problem one of receiving information, expressing information, or processing and associating information? What are the child's strengths and weaknesses in learning visually, auditorily, and in intersensory tasks? What behavior characteristics does the child display? How does the child attack a learning problem, such as new words in reading, and what kinds of errors are made? Data for such analysis can be obtained through both informal observations and standardized tests.

4. *Explore why the child is not learning.* It is difficult to establish clear cause-effect correlates, and these may not always be directly relevant to therapeutic planning. Nevertheless, it is useful to note all the possible causes of the learning problem, as well as contributing factors. Emotional, environmental, and psychological factors should be considered. Data from various sources, the case history, informal tests and observations, and standardized formal tests can help identify these factors.

Clusters of factors and characteristics revealed in the diagnosis sometimes constitute a syndrome that leads to a useful analysis and a practical teaching plan. For example, one such cluster of organic factors might include soft signs of neurological dysfunction, motor awkwardness, poor performance in motor tests, and low scores on subtests related to spatial orientation. Another set of correlates might point to a deficiency in auditory processing. This set might include slow language development, articulation substitutions, poor performance in auditory discrimination and sound-blending tests, poor auditory memory, poor reading, and an inability to learn phonics.

5. *Collate and interpret data and formulate a diagnostic hypothesis.* This hypothesis sums up all that has gone before and points the way for educational planning. Technical terminology should be avoided where possible. An opinion about any specific area of disability should be substantiated by several objective measures plus clinical observations. A single random shortcoming revealed by one subtest score is insufficient evidence for a diagnostic decision. Further, any single isolated area of disability should be examined for possible relatedness to a larger syndrome of characteristics. The formulation of the hypothesis will obviously be affected by the theoretical outlook of the diagnostician.

6. *Develop a plan for teaching* in the light of the hypothesis that has been formulated. This plan should specify areas of the child's strengths and weaknesses and should suggest approaches that take these into account. Most authorities feel that strategies for teaching should include plans to teach through areas of strength while helping to develop and build deficient areas. The plan must also take into account the child's developmental levels, that is, the specific skills already learned as well as those not yet assimilated. In addition, the pupil's interests, age, and attitudes should be considered. Planning such strategies requires that the diagnostician have a broad knowledge of methods, materials, approaches, curriculum areas, child development, and, most important, children themselves. Since the

earlier steps of the diagnostic process were shaped in part by a framework of theory, teaching plans similarly will be affected by such views.

The diagnosis is continuous and must be revised and modified as more knowledge of the child is acquired through teaching, and as the students themselves change through learning. It involves continuous reappraisal. In order to accomplish each step of the diagnostic process just outlined, data must be obtained to provide the basis for decisions. The next section discusses methods and techniques of data collection.

OBTAINING DATA FOR DIAGNOSIS

Data for diagnosis can be obtained in four major ways: (1) a case history or interview, (2) clinical observation, (3) informal testing, and (4) formal standardized testing. In practice, these four methods are not separated, but are often accomplished simultaneously. One procedure may suggest the others. As a result of astute clinical observation, specific formal tests may be selected. For example, speech misarticulation, along with frequent misunderstanding of the examiner's conversation, could suggest an auditory difficulty and lead to a decision to administer formal tests of auditory acuity and discrimination. For purposes of discussion, however, it is useful to separate these four areas of data gathering.

In an interdisciplinary approach, any of the various specialists could contribute to the diagnostic information obtained through any of these techniques. For example, the physician could obtain a medical history, observe the child during the medical examination, and give standardized medical tests.

CASE HISTORY

The case history provides information, insights, and clues about the child's background and development. The following kinds of information are obtained, usually from the parents: learning problems of other members of the family (indicating possible genetic traits); the child's prenatal history, birth conditions, and neonatal development; the child's age when developmental milestones such as sitting, walking, toilet training, and talking were attained; and the child's health history, including illnesses (particularly those with high fevers) and accidents. Additional information, such as the school history, can be obtained from parents, from files, and from school personnel, including teachers, nurses, and guidance counselors.

It requires a skillful interviewer to obtain a maximum amount of useful data. The interviewer must try to establish a feeling of mutual trust with the persons being interviewed being careful not to ask questions that might alarm parents or make them defensive by indicating disapproval of their actions. The interviewer's attitude should convey a spirit of cooperation, acceptance, and empathy while maintaining a degree of professional objectivity to guard against excessive emotional involvement and consequent ineffectiveness.

If the history taking is to be useful in making a diagnosis, it must go beyond routine questions and gather more information and impressions than the questions themselves ask. The skillful interviewer is able to gather information in a smooth, conversational manner while fulfilling all the other requirements of case-study technique. The data and impressions thus gained are integrated with information obtained through clinical observation and formal testing procedures.

Many school systems have designed screening interviews or questionnaires that are used with the parents of all incoming kindergarten children. Questions are designed to detect those children who are likely to have learning difficulty. The hope is that early detection of high-risk cases will permit plans to be made to help prevent the development of learning disabilities. Below are some questions that might be used in such a screening interview:

Questions concerning general background and health:
How old is the child in years and months?
Was there anything unusual in the birth history?
How is the child's general health?
Has the child had any periods of illness or hospitalization?
Have you ever suspected that the child has poor eyesight?
What were the results of any visual examination?
Have you ever suspected that the child has poor hearing?
If an examination was given, what were the results?

Questions concerning development:
At what age did the child sit up, crawl, walk?
At what age was the first word spoken?
At what age did the child begin to use sentences?

Questions concerning present activities:
Can the child use pencils, crayons, scissors?
Can the child ride a bicycle?
Can the child write his or her name?
Does the child have any nervous tendencies such as bed-wetting, unusual fears, extreme moods of depression, anxiety, temper tantrums?
Is the child overly active or restless?
Can the child use language for intelligent expression?
Does the child like to listen to stories?
What responsibilities or independent activities does the child accept and perform with some regularity?
How does the child spend time at home?

A variety of forms designed to obtain information about the case history by means of an interview have been developed. Some are quite lengthy and complete, procuring information in many categories. Working somewhat like a detective, the diagnostician must gather enough information to analyze the child's learning failure and to design an appropriate treatment procedure. Not all cases require all the information found on some forms. Case history forms generally contain questions in the following categories:

Identifying information
   Child: name, address, telephone, date of birth, school, grade
   Parents: father's name and occupation; mother's name and occupation
   Family: siblings' names and ages; others in the home
   Clinic: date of interview, referral agency; name of examiner

Birth History
   Pregnancy: length, condition of mother, unusual factors
   Birth conditions: mature or premature, duration of labor, weight, unusual circumstances
   Conditions following birth

Physical and Developmental Data
   Health history: accidents, high fevers, other illnesses
   Present health: habits of eating and sleeping, energy and activity level
   Developmental history: age of sitting, walking, first words, first sentences, language difficulties, motor difficulties

Social and Personal Factors
   Friends
   Sibling relationships
   Hobbies, interests, recreational activities
   Home and parent attitudes
   Acceptance of responsibilities
   Attitude toward learning problem

Educational Factors
   School experiences: skipped or repeated grades, moving, change of teachers
   Preschool education: kindergarten, nursery school
   Special help previously received
   Teachers' reports
   Child's attitude toward school

No one case history form will be entirely suitable without revision and modification from one clinical setting to another. Each diagnostic center must develop a form that meets its own needs and provides the information it desires.

CLINICAL OBSERVATION

Many attributes of the child are inadequately identified through either standardized test instruments or through interview. The skillful diagnostician, however, is able to detect many of these characteristics through astute observation of the child's behavior and through the proficient use of informal tests. Further, informal tests and observation of behavior provide an opportunity to corroborate findings of the other two areas of assessment. For example, the skillful observer can determine whether the behavior of a child who appears to be deaf is characteristic of children with actual deafness or of children with other types of problems such as aphasia, emotional disturbance, or mental retardation.

Norman, who was being diagnosed because of poor reading, was overheard by the diagnostician warning another child that for his bad behavior he would no doubt get "H-A-L-L." The diagnostician perceptively inferred that Norman's incorrect spelling might be related to a deficit in auditory processing. A formal test of auditory discrimination was subsequently given, and Norman's poor performance substantiated that hypothesis.

An assessment of the child's general _personal adjustment_ can be made through observation techniques. For example, in the testing situation the examiner observed that when the work became difficult, Ricky gave up completely and simply filled in the blank spaces with any answer; Pat tensed up and refused to continue the work; and Jane, refusing to guess and afraid to make a mistake, struggled with a single item for as long as she was permitted. Through such observations, questions such as the following should be probed: How does the child react to new situations and people? What is the child's attitude toward the learning problem? Has the school problem interfered with other aspects of the child's life? Has it drained the child's energy? Is the child's attitude one of interest or of indifference?

Motor coordination and development can be at least partially assessed by observing the child's movements and gait. How does the child attack a writing task? Does he contort his entire body while writing? What is the general appearance of the child's handwriting? How does the child hold a pencil? Does the child move continuously during the session or constantly touch things in the room?

One can also informally assess the child's _use of language_. Is there evidence of infantile speech articulation? Does the child have difficulty finding words? Does the child have an adequate vocabulary? Does the child speak easily or haltingly or perhaps excessively? Does the child use complete sentences or single words and short partial phrases? Is the sequence of sounds correct in words? Does the child commit major errors of grammar and syntax?

Games, toys, and informal activities are useful to the diagnostician both as a means of building rapport with the child and as an aid in making informal clinical observations. For example, the child's ability to zip a zipper, tie a shoelace, button clothing, or lock a padlock gives clues to _fine motor coordination and eye-hand relationships._ Games such as phonic rummy or phonic bingo gives clues to the child's _auditory skills_.

Many of the clues that can be used in planning the instructional programs are best detected by observing the pupil's everyday classroom behavior (Wallace and Kauffman 1973). For example, while the student is reading, the teacher can observe how he or she responds to an unknown word. Does the reader look at the initial consonant and then take a wild guess, attempt to break the word into syllables, or try to infer the word from context. Such information, gathered through observation in the class-room, can prove to be valuable data in the diagnosis.

Rating Scales of Student Characteristics

Teachers' observations of children can also be recorded in a behavior-rating scale. These scales record the teacher's judgment or impression of the child in a measurable fashion. For example, the teacher is asked to judge the child's ability to follow directions on a 5-point scale. A rating at level 1 indicates that the teacher judges the child as being unable to follow direc-tions while a rating at level 5 indicates that the child is skillful at following directions.

Teachers involved in one study were asked to judge 24 behavioral char-acteristics of children by rating them on a 5-point scale (Myklebust and Boshes 1969). A score of 1 represented the lowest rating of function, a score of 5 represented the highest, and a score of 3 was considered average. The behavioral categories rated were:

Auditory Comprehension
1. Ability to follow oral directions
2. Comprehension of class discussion
3. Ability to retain auditory information
4. Comprehension of word meaning

Spoken Language
5. Complete and accurate expression
6. Vocabulary ability
7. Ability to recall words
8. Ability to relate experience
9. Ability to formulate ideas

Orientation
10. Promptness
11. Spatial orientation
12. Judgment of relationships
13. Learning directions

Behavior
14. Cooperation
15. Attention
16. Ability to organize
17. Ability to cope with new situations
18. Social acceptance
19. Acceptance of responsibility
20. Completion of assignments
21. Tactfulness

Motor
22. General coordination
23. Balance
24. Ability to manipulate equipment

Since 5 was the highest possible rating on any one factor, the highest total possible score was 120. The mean score of children identified as normal was 81, while the mean score of the learning disabilities group was 61.

Teacher judgment of behavioral characteristics of children has proved to be a reliable technique for identifying children with learning disabilities, and rating scales have been found to be useful instruments (Bryan and McGrady 1972). A behavior-rating scale used by teachers in Aurora, Colorado, is presented in Gearhart (1973, pp. 14–20). Two scales, the *Pupil Rating Scale* and the *Devereaux Behavior Scales*, are listed in Appendix C.

Behavioral Approach to Observation

Within the behavioral approach to teaching children with learning problems, the concept of observation takes on a very specific meaning since quantified observational data are required (Lovitt 1967, Haring and Phillips 1972). Direct and structured observational techniques are used in this approach to provide data for measuring the child's behavior over a period of time, to determine a base line of initial behavior, and to determine and measure those events that appear to modify behavior. The data obtained through these detailed quantitative observations provide the basis for planning ways to teach and meet explicit behavioral goals in reading, speaking, and computation.

It should be noted, however, that traditional methods of data collection, such as information obtained from a case history report, are thought to be unimportant by those educators who approach assessment from a behavioral approach. Evaluation from this perspective is not based on reported events from the case history or the past but, rather, on the child's present performance and symptoms of learning failure.

For the behavior-modification approach, therefore, certain methods of assessment are needed, as specified in greater detail in Chapter 12.

INFORMAL TESTS

A number of informal nonstandardized tests are extremely useful in diagnosis:

Informal Reading Inventory

The *Informal Reading Inventory* can be quickly and easily administered, yet it provides a wealth of information concerning reading skills, reading levels (independent, instructional, and frustration), types of errors, the child's techniques of attacking unknown words, and related behavioral characteristics (Johnson and Kress 1965).

Briefly, the technique of the informal reading inventory is as follows: the examiner chooses selections approximately one hundred words in length from various graded reading levels. To assure that the selections represent the difficulty level desired, their readability may be checked using such procedures as the Spache (1953), Dale and Chall (1948), or "cloze" readability methods (Bormuth 1968). The child is asked to read aloud from several graded levels and errors are recorded in a systematic manner. If more than five errors per hundred words are made, the child is given progressively easier selections until a level is found at which there are no more than two errors per hundred words. The child is asked approximately four questions about each selection to check comprehension. Using the following criteria, three reading levels can be determined through the use of an informal reading inventory:

1. *Independent reading level*. Criteria: The child is able to recognize about 98 percent of the words and is able to answer all of the comprehension questions correctly. This is the level at which the child is able to read independently in library books or do self-work.

2. *Instructional reading level*. Criteria: The child is able to recognize about 95 percent of the words in the selection with a comprehension score of about 75 percent. This is the reading level at which the child will profit from directed reading instruction.

3. *Frustration reading level*. Criteria: The child is able to recognize less than 90 percent of the words with a comprehension score of 50 percent or less. This reading level is too difficult for the child, who does not understand the material. It should not be used for instruction.

Informal Graded Word-Recognition Test

This sort of test can be used as a quick method to determine the child's approximate reading level. Such a test is also useful in detecting the child's errors in word analysis. An informal graded word-recognition test can be constructed by selecting words at random from graded basal reader glossaries. The list below illustrates the informal graded word-recognition test. Words from the preprimer through third-grade levels were selected from several basal reader series. Words from grades four through six were from the Durrell-Sullivan reading vocabularies for grades four, five, and six (Durrell 1956).

The informal graded word list can be given as follows: (1) type the list of words selected for each grade on separate cards; (2) duplicate the entire test on a single sheet; (3) have the child read the words from the cards while the examiner marks the errors on the sheet, noting the child's method of analyzing and pronouncing difficult words; and (4) have the child read from increasingly difficult lists until three words are missed. The level at which there are two missed words suggests the instructional level at which the child is able to read with help. The level at which one word is missed suggests the child's independent reading level — that at which the child can read alone. The level at which three words are missed suggests a frustration level, and the material is probably too difficult.

Trial Lessons

Trial lessons provide a means of informally assessing the way a child responds and learns through several teaching methods. In contrast to standardized testing requirements, the informal situation can engender a free and spontaneous atmosphere permitting the clinician to enlist the student's participation in the search for ways to overcome the learning problem. Roswell and Natchez (1971) describe the technique of trial lessons used

Informal Graded Word Reading List

Preprimer	Primer	Grade 1	Grade 2
see	day	about	hungry
run	from	sang	loud
me	all	guess	stones
dog	under	catch	trick
at	little	across	chair
come	house	live	hopped
down	ready	boats	himself
you	came	hard	color
said	your	longer	straight
boy	blue	hold	leading

Grade 3	Grade 4	Grade 5	Grade 6
arrow	brilliant	career	buoyant
wrist	credit	cultivate	determination
bottom	examine	essential	gauntlet
castle	grammar	grieve	incubator
learned	jingle	jostle	ludicrous
washed	ruby	obscure	offensive
safety	terrify	procession	prophesy
yesterday	wrench	sociable	sanctuary
delight	mayor	triangular	tapestry
happiness	agent	volcano	vague

as informal tests. This technique consists of giving small sample lessons using various approaches to help both teacher and pupil find the student's best style of learning. These authors have described trial lesson techniques for reading levels ranging from grade 1 to grade 12. In addition, the *Learning Methods Test* by Mills (1956) is designed for this purpose.

The procedures suggested by Roswell and Natchez for trial lessons for reading levels 1 to 3 are described below. For the nonreader or the reader who has a minimum of word-analysis techniques, the following major word-recognition approaches are tried: (1) visual, (2) phonic, (3) visual motor, and, if all of these are unsuccessful, (4) kinesthetic. At the conclusion of the trial lessons, the teacher and pupil should both have a clear picture of the methods that can be used most successfully.

In the *visual* method, the teacher selects about five words not known by the child, such as *pencil, lady, sock,* and prints each of them on a separate card. (The examiner first administers tests to make sure the child does not already know the words.) The examiner then writes each word on another card, along with the picture of the object denoted. The examiner points to the word on the picture card, pronounces it, and then asks the child to look at the word and say it several times. After a lapse of time, the child is tested on the nonillustrated cards.

The *phonics* trial lesson consists of several parts. First, the teacher asks the child to make new words by substituting beginning consonants: change *run* to *sun, fun, bun,* and so on. Then the teacher pronounces single phonemes in one-syllable words slowly and distinctly and asks the child to combine the sounds to make a word: *k-a-t* blends to *cat.* The teacher next asks the child to substitute final consonants in short-vowel words using sounds taught in the first part: *fat* to *fan, cat* to *can, run* to *rub.* Finally, the teacher asks the child to read in mixed order the words learned through the phonic approach: *run, cat, rub, man.*

In the *visual-motor* trial lesson, the teacher chooses three unknown words five to seven letters in length (for example, *fight, missile, horse*) and presents each word separately on a card, asking the pupil to look carefully, to shut his eyes and try to visualize the word, to open his eyes and check his visual image by looking at the word, and finally to say the word. Then the card is removed and the child writes the word from memory.

The *kinesthetic* trial lesson is attempted if all the other methods have failed. The teacher writes or prints an unfamiliar word on unlined paper, each letter approximately two inches high. The child is told that she will learn a new way to read through her fingers. She looks at the word and traces it with her index finger while simultaneously pronouncing it very slowly. This trace-and-say process is repeated several times, and the child is then asked to write the word without reference to the model.

Other trial lesson techniques are suggested by Roswell and Natchez for older students reading at higher grade levels. Again, at the conclusion of the trial lesson session both teacher and student have a better idea of how to begin and where to go. Roswell and Natchez (1964, pp. 46–47) state:

> In this way, trial lessons at all levels are extremely helpful in preparing the pupil for remedial instruction. Instead of leaving the examination with a vague feeling of "something is wrong with my reading," he knows what is wrong. He has been shown in which areas he needs help. . . . As the pupil recognizes his problem and understands what he can do about it, he becomes more hopeful. His anxiety is lessened and the foundation is laid for effective remedial treatment.

Analysis of Spelling Errors

Another informal test to determine what processes the child is using in learning situations is the analysis of the kinds of *spelling errors* the child makes (Boder 1968). Such an analysis might give clues about whether the child is relying on auditory or visual processes to spell the words. The child who is strong in auditory perception and in the ability to remember the sounds of words but poor in visual memory and visual learning may misspell the words, but the errors follow some kind of phonic generalization. The child may spell *attention* as *atenchen,* or *peace* as *pese,* or *almost* as *olmoste.* In contrast, the child who is strong in visual learning and visual memory but low in auditory perception and learning makes spelling errors that do not follow any phonic generalization. That child may remember the correct letters, but they may be in the wrong order. *Mark* may be spelled as *mrak, eat* as *aet, orange* as *ronaeg.* As in the trial lesson technique, spelling pattern errors are analyzed to discover how the child is learning.

Informal Arithmetic Test

An informal arithmetic test can be easily devised to point up weaknesses in the basic computational skills. Otto, McMenemy, and Smith (1973) suggest the following informal survey test for sixth grade. The difficulty level of the test could be increased or decreased, depending on the grade level being tested.

Informal Survey Test: Sixth-Grade Level

Addition	300	37			
	60	24		234	123
	407	6	271	574	324
	2	19	389	261	451
Subtraction	765	751	7054	8004	90327
	-342	-608	-3595	-5637	-42827
Multiplication	36	44	721	483	802
	$\times 10$	$\times 83$	$\times 346$	$\times 208$	$\times 357$
Division	$2\overline{)36}$	$12\overline{)36}$	$6\overline{)966}$	$16\overline{)1081}$	$13\overline{)8726}$

From W. Otto, R. McMenemy, and R. Smith. *Corrective and Remedial Teaching.* Boston: Houghton Mifflin, 1973, p. 284.

The informal arithmetic test should include several items of each kind so that a simple error will not be mistaken for a more fundamental difficulty. Otto, McMenemy, and Smith suggest that errors can be charted:

Addition	Subtraction
errors in combinations	combinations
counting	counting
carrying	regrouping
faulty procedures	faulty procedures

Multiplication	Division
combinations	combinations
counting	counting
remainder difficulties	carrying
faulty procedures	faulty procedures

FORMAL STANDARDIZED TESTS

Formal standardized tests are used in the diagnosis to sample performance in particular aspects of learning. Norms for these tests should be standardized on a large population, and statistics concerning the reliability and validity of the tests should be available from the publishers. Different kinds of standardized tests are given by psychologists, medical specialties, and by classroom teachers. The learning disabilities specialist might serve in a role that incorporates the diagnostic responsibilities of several of these professional people.

Limitations of Formal Tests

The examiner should have a sound foundation in the techniques of using and interpreting tests in general, and should be thoroughly familiar with the specific test being used. Frequently the value of a test may not be so much in the final test score as in the measurement of a particular subtest performance, the profile of all the subtest scores, or the clinical observations of the child during the test. The diagnostician who has had extensive experience with a test may find that some parts used alone yield the necessary information.

Caution must be exercised in the interpretation of test scores. The score indicates only a small sample of the child's performance at one moment in time. All tests, by their very nature, give only a limited measure of a child's abilities. Moreover, the statistical validity and reliability of a number of widely used learning disabilities tests have been seriously questioned in recent investigations. Some studies challenge the diagnostic value of mental and perceptual processing tests, such as the *Illinois Test of Psycholinguistic Abilities* (Newcomer et al. 1974), the *Frostig Visual Perceptual Test* (Hammill and Wiederholt 1973), and the *Detroit Tests of Learning Aptitude* (Buros 1939). Serious statistical limitations in making a diagnostic interpretation from the individual subtest scores of the *Wechsler Intelligence Scale for Children* (WISC) are explained by Anastasi (1968) and Simensen and Sutherland (1974). The fallibility of the scores of diagnostic reading tests in terms of statistical reliability is illustrated by Thorndike (1973), who concludes that in their use in diagnostic studies, the confidence level of the diagnostic reading tests is often distressingly low. In an analytical study of reading tests, Farr (1969) cautions that a serious deficiency in using standardized tests to diagnose reading achievement is the lack of discriminant validity for the various subtests of reading.

The child with a learning disability, however, cannot wait until we have diagnostic tools that are without fault. Moreover, data from informal tests and observations are subject to similar fallibility. In spite of the doubts raised by such critical reports, formal tests can be useful in obtaining information that helps formulate a diagnosis when the tests are wisely used. It is important for the diagnostician to know the limitations of the test and to use the information in proper perspective. Any single score, of course, gives only a small part of the information and it should always be interpreted with extreme caution.

Formal tests can be viewed as a means of providing two levels of information about the child: (1) *General tests* sample general or global areas of functioning. Such tests determine whether a child is performing at, above, or below age level in a given area. (2) *Diagnostic tests* provide a microscopic view of the component elements of some area of performance. Such tests enable the diagnostician to analyze the child's functioning within specific subskill areas and supply direction for remediation. Some commonly used formal tests of both types are discussed below. A listing of these tests and their publishers is presented in Appendix C; many are discussed in greater detail in Part Three.

Tests of Mental Abilities and Mental Processes

The purpose of the general intelligence tests is to assess the global aspects of intelligence, usually for classification or categorization. The most commonly used individual general intelligence tests are: the *Wechsler Intelligence Scale for Children* (WISC) and the revised version WISC-R, and the *Stanford-Binet Intelligence Scale.* While the *Stanford-Binet* yields a single score of general intelligence, the WISC and the WISC-R provide a verbal IQ and a performance IQ in addition to the full-scale score.[1] The *Slosson Intelligence Test for Children and Adults* and the *Peabody Picture Vocabulary Test* are also frequently used as tests of intelligence. Such tests provide initial data for classifying a child as high, average, or low in general mental abilities. However, the universal nature of such tests may limit their usefulness in analyzing the characteristics of a child's learning problem and in designing suitable treatment procedures.

While intelligence tests provide an overall estimate of general intelligence, other tests are required to examine specific mental abilities. A second stage in diagnosis, then, is the use of tests to analyze mental processing and specific intellectual, perceptual, and/or cognitive factors (Kirk and Kirk 1971). One test designed expressly for analysis of the subskills of intellectual

---

[1] Interpretation of the WISC subscore tests is discussed in a later section of this chapter.

function is the *Illinois Test of Psycholinguistic Abilities* (ITPA). The stated purpose of the ITPA is to provide an instrument that will aid in diagnosis by identifying specific areas of learning difficulty. ITPA subtests attempt to measure certain perceptual and cognitive abilities that seem to bear a relationship to intellectual development and academic learning. The ITPA yields a global psycholinguistic age, a psycholinguistic quotient, as well as scores indicating at what level the child is functioning in 12 specific areas of mental processing. The ITPA yields an age score and a scaled score for each of the 12 areas tested so that the diagnostician has a profile of the child's abilities and disabilities. Interpretation of the ITPA is discussed in greater detail in a later section of this chapter.

Another diagnostic test battery that assesses several subareas of mental abilities is the *Detroit Tests of Learning Aptitude*. These tests yield an overall age score as well as specific age scores in 19 areas of mental functioning. There are also a number of other diagnostic tests that sample only one or a few of the subareas of mental processing. Tests of visual-motor perception include: the *Bender Visual-Motor Gestalt Test for Children*, the *Developmental Test of Visual-Motor Integration*, the *Marianne Frostig Developmental Test of Visual Perception*, and the *Monroe Reading Aptitude Tests*. A test that estimates visual perception development and intelligence is the *Goodenough-Harris Drawing Test*. Auditory perception tests include the *Wepman Test of Auditory Discrimination* and the *Roswell-Chall Auditory Blending Test*.

Reading Tests

There are many global or general survey-type tests of reading. Among them are the *Gates-MacGinitie Reading Tests;* the *Stanford Achievement Test: Reading; California Reading Test; Metropolitan Achievement Tests: Reading; SRA Achievement Series: Reading*. These tests yield a general score of silent reading, and they give an indication of the level at which a child reads.

A diagnostic reading test differs from a general reading test in that it analyzes the processes by which the child attempts to read — it gives information on *how* the child reads rather than only indicating reading level. Analysis of specific errors, for example, might indicate poor word-attack skills, a lack of familiarity with certain phonic elements (vowels, consonant blends, diphthongs), inadequate sight vocabulary, or a slow reading rate. Some of the useful diagnostic reading tests include: *Gates-McKillop Reading Diagnostic Tests*, the *Durrell Analysis of Reading Difficulty, Roswell-Chall Diagnostic Reading Test of Word-Analysis Skills, Gray Oral Reading Tests, Spache Diagnostic Reading Scales*, and *Woodcock Reading Mastery Scales*.

Tests of Other Academic Skills

Some of the general tests that measure performance in academic subjects such as reading, arithmetic, spelling, and grammar are: the *Iowa Every-*

Pupil Tests of Basic Skills, the *California Achievement Test*, the *Metropolitan Achievement Tests*, *SRA Achievement Test*, the *Stanford Achievement Test*, and the *Wide-Range Achievement Test* (WRAT).

Fewer tests of a diagnostic nature are available for academic areas other than reading. Some of them are: *Diagnostic Tests and Self-Helps in Arithmetic*, the *Gates-Russell Spelling Diagnostic Tests*, the *Stanford Diagnostic Arithmetic Test*, the *Peabody Individual Achievement Test* (PIAT) and the *Key Math Diagnostic Arithmetic Test*.

Motor Tests

A general assessment of motor skill can be made with the *Heath Railwalking Test*. Examples of diagnostic tests that examine the component parts of motor performance are the *Lincoln-Oseretsky Motor Development Scale, Purdue Perceptual Motor Survey,* and the *Southern California Perceptual-Motor Tests*.

Language Tests

In the area of language tests it is important to differentiate between speech assessment and language assessment. A speech test evaluates the child's skills in articulation and voice quality. A language test evaluates linguistic abilities. Many of the tests previously mentioned in this section (such as the ITPA) have subtests of language ability.

Speech screening tests of articulation are the *Templin-Darley Screening and Diagnostic Tests of Articulation* and the *Goldman-Fristoe Test of Articulation*. Two tests of the ability to understand words are the *Peabody Picture Vocabulary Test* and the *Ammons Full-Range Picture Vocabulary Test*. The *Northwestern Syntax Screening Test* and the *Test of Auditory Comprehension of Language* (Carrow) measure syntax development. Other language measures are the *Houston Test for Language Development* and the *Mecham Verbal Language Development Scale*. A test of written language is made by the *Picture Story Language Test*, in which the child writes a story.

Social Maturity Assessment

The *Vineland Social Maturity Scale* is an instrument that uses the technique of interviewing an informant (usually the mother) to assess several areas of the child's maturity. Six categories of maturity are measured on this scale: (1) self-help, (2) locomotion, (3) occupation, (4) communication, (5) self-direction, and (6) socialization. The scale yields a "social age score" and a social quotient, with an average social quotient score of 100.

Screening Tests for Visual and Auditory Acuity

Since defects in vision or hearing may adversely affect the learning processes, it is important for children with learning disabilities to be checked for such sensory deficits. Vision- and hearing-screening tests may be given by the learning disabilities specialist who has been trained in the administration of these tests, or sensory screening may be conducted by the school nurse or some other member of the interdisciplinary team. Those children who fail the screening tests are referred to an eye or ear specialist for a thorough and intensive professional examination.

There are several vision-screening instruments that are useful in detecting children who require further testing. Among them are the telebinocular of the *Keystone Vision Screening for Schools* and the *Ortho-Rater*. These instruments use stereoscopic slides to screen for near-vision and far-vision acuity, eye-muscle balance, and fusion.

The *audiometer* is an auditory screening instrument for detecting children who should be referred for a more thorough and intensive examination. Two attributes of the child's ability to hear sound are measured: *frequency* and *intensity*. The frequency of a sound is measured by the number of vibrations that occur per second; as the frequency of sound increases, the pitch of the sound becomes higher. The intensity of a sound wave refers to the strength (or loudness) measured in decibels. The child who, in a threshold audiometric examination, exhibits hearing levels of 20 decibels or greater at any two frequencies in either ear should be referred for an otological examination (Newby 1964, p. 233). Considerable training is required before a diagnostician is able to use an audiometer and interpret the findings of an audiometric test.

INTERPRETING TEST SCORES

In using test scores, the examiner should be aware of the test's reliability and validity. Moreover, a child's performance on any one day is subject to many factors such as fatigue, interest, and motivation. Tests have limitations and any single test score must be viewed with caution.

WECHSLER INTELLIGENCE SCALE FOR CHILDREN

One of the most widely used tests for general intelligence for children aged 5 to 15 is the Wechsler Intelligence Scale for Children (WISC, 1949). A 1974 revision, called the WISC-R, was standardized on the 1970 census. The revision, which spans the age range of 6–0 to 16–11, added new items and dropped items considered unfair, obsolete, or ambiguous (*Manual for the Wechsler Intelligence Scale for Children — Revised*, 1974). The complete test, which is administered by a trained psychological examiner, consists of five verbal and five performance subtests, plus two optional tests. The test yields a full-scale IQ, a verbal IQ, and a performance IQ. Although it was designed as a measure of general intelligence, some clinicians use it as a diagnostic instrument by analyzing the subtest patterns. Other investigators caution that there is little empirical evidence to support such diagnostic use of the WISC (the 1949 version) subtest patterns (Anastasi 1968, Glasser and Zimmerman 1967).

The WISC is designed so that a scaled or standard score of 10 indicates average ability for age in the particular subtest. A general idea of the kinds of abilities sampled in each of the subtests is given below:

Verbal Tests. These tests use oral language for administration and responses of the subject.

Information — a test of how much general knowledge the child has acquired through living in the surrounding environment.

Comprehension — an assessment of a child's ability to make judgments about social situations.

Arithmetic — a test of ability to do arithmetic reasoning problems within a time limit.

Similarities — a test of a child's skill at detecting analogies, or similar elements in different objects.

Vocabulary — a test of the child's ability to describe selected spoken words.

Digit span — an optional test measuring the child's ability to remember and repeat a series of digits after the examiner says them.

Performance Tests. These tests are presented in a visual manner and the subject responds by performing some task.

Picture completion — requires the child to detect missing elements in pictures.

Picture arrangement — the child must rearrange a set of pictures so that they relate a sequential story.

Block design — the subject must arrange small colored blocks to copy a geometric design.

Object assembly — the child must assemble the parts of a puzzle that represent an object.

Coding — the child must remember associations between numbers and geometric symbols and quickly record these associations.

Mazes — an optional paper and pencil test measuring the child's ability to find the way out of a maze.

Clements (1964) has isolated three WISC patterns that occur in the subtest peformance of children with learning disabilities:

Pattern 1. A scatter is evidenced in both the verbal and performance scores, with a wide range between high and low scores of 7 to 12 points. Such a pattern suggests specific deficits in certain mental processes.

Pattern 2. The verbal score is 15 to 40 or more points higher than the performance score. Children displaying this pattern have difficulty in perceptual-motor areas, but they are strong in language areas.

Pattern 3. The performance score is 10 to 30 points higher than the verbal score. Children with this pattern are likely to have difficulty in expressing (Ackerman, Peters, and Dykman 1971) found no characteristic WISC themselves verbally.

One study of the WISC profiles of children with learning disabilities profile that would single out children with learning disabilities. Probably the diversity of problems encountered by children with learning disabilities accounted for this.

Bannatyne (1968) suggested another technique for analyzing the WISC subscore patterns by grouping them:

Spatial score = sum of scaled scores of *Picture Completion + Block Design + Object Assembly*. This category requires the ability to manipulate objects directly or symbolically in multidimensional space.

Conceptualization score = sum of scaled scores of *Comprehension + Similarities + Vocabulary*. This category requires abilities more closely related to language functioning.

Sequencing score = sum of scaled scores of *Digit Span + Picture Arrangement + Coding*. This category requires the ability to retain sequences of auditory and visual stimuli in short-term memory storage.

Since the average scaled score on the WISC is 10, the composite scaled score for each of these three groups of subtests should average 30. By comparing a child's spatial score, conceptualization score, and sequencing score, Bannatyne suggested that the diagnostician can obtain information about the child's strengths and weaknesses.

Rugel (1974) reviewed 25 studies that reported WISC scores of disabled readers and concluded that the Bannatyne recategorization of the WISC subtests scores into spatial, conceptual, and sequential groups is a useful method. In a recent article, Bannatyne (1974) suggested a revised method of regrouping the WISC subtests into four categories: *spatial ability* (picture completion, block design, object assembly); *verbal conceptualization ability* (comprehension, similarities, vocabulary); *sequencing ability* (digit span, arithmetic, coding); and *acquired knowledge* (information, arithmetic, vocabulary). The average scaled score for each category totals 30 points.

ILLINOIS TEST OF PSYCHOLINGUISTIC ABILITIES

The ITPA (Kirk, McCarthy, and Kirk 1968) was designed to diagnose problems of learning by assessing specific and discrete underlying psychological functions of young children. In designing the test, the authors attempted to consider mental functioning in three ways (Paraskevopoulos and Kirk 1969): (1) They wanted to consider *levels of organization*, or the degree to which habits of communication have developed within the child. The representational level requires the mediating process of utilizing symbols that carry the meaning of an object; while the automatic level reflects the more habitual, less voluntary, but highly organized and integrated functions. (2) Another consideration was *channels of communication*, or the input and output routes through which communication flows: auditory-vocal, auditory-motor, visual-motor, visual-vocal. (3) *Psycholinguistic processes* were the third consideration involving the acquisition and use of language — the receptive process, the expressive process, the associative process.

There are 12 subtests in the ITPA designed to sample various components of mental functioning. They are:

Representational Level

The Receptive Process

AUDITORY RECEPTION TEST. This test samples the child's ability to understand what is said. The child responds by answering *yes* or *no*. For example, "Do birds fly?"

VISUAL RECEPTION TEST. This test assesses the child's ability to derive meaning from pictures and respond by pointing.

The Associative Process

AUDITORY ASSOCIATION. This test assesses the child's ability to relate concepts that are presented orally. The child supplies the missing word in verbal analogies. For example "I cut with a saw; I pound with a _____."

VISUAL ASSOCIATION. In this test the child must associate concepts that are presented visually through pictures. The child responds to the question "What goes with this?" by pointing to the appropriate picture from four options.

The Expressive Process

VERBAL EXPRESSION. This test examines the child's ability for vocal expression about objects seen and touched. The child is asked to tell about familiar objects that are shown — for example, a ball — with the injunction "Tell me all about this."

MANUAL EXPRESSION. In this test the child must express ideas by gesture and is asked to show what we do with various objects — for example, a telephone.

Automatic Level

Closure

GRAMMATIC CLOSURE. This test measures how well the child has learned automatic habits for handling linguistic constructs of grammar and syntax of the English language. The child is asked to supply the missing grammatical elements in incomplete sentences. For example, "Here is a dog; here are two _____."

AUDITORY CLOSURE. This test measures the child's ability to complete a word by filling in missing parts that are deleted when the word, with certain sounds omitted, is spoken by the examiner. For example, the examiner might say "tele/one" and the child is to respond "telephone."

SOUND BLENDING. This test taps the child's ability to blend or synthesize the isolated phoneme sounds of a word. Thus, the examiner says "c—a—t." The child is to respond: "cat."

VISUAL CLOSURE. This test measures the ability of the child to identify common objects in pictures from an incomplete visual presentation. Objects are partially hidden in pictures shown to the child.

Sequential Memory

AUDITORY SEQUENTIAL MEMORY. This test measures the child's ability to remember and reproduce sequences of numbers or digits that are spoken. For example, the child might be asked to repeat the sequence "4—7—2."
VISUAL SEQUENTIAL MEMORY. This test measures the child's ability to remember sequences of nonmeaningful figures.

The ITPA is designed to permit a comparison of an individual child's specific and discrete areas of development. Thus, while the normal child exhibits a relatively flat profile of performance on the 12 subtests, with little deviation between a single area of development and the average of all the child's scores, the learning-disabled child is likely to show discrepant growth patterns, with large deviations of individual subtest scores from the average of all subtest scores. Data on the deviation patterns of normal children on whom the ITPA was standardized is provided by Paraskevopoulos and Kirk (1969). In addition, these authors describe a technique to evaluate the likelihood that the difference between two ITPA subtest scores is a statistically significant difference (Paraskevopoulos and Kirk 1969, pp. 113–120). An analysis of construct validity conducted by Newcomer et al. (1974, 1975) indicated that the ITPA appears to measure discrete, independent abilities, with a few exceptions; and support was found for the ITPA constructs of level and process. The channel concept had the least empirical substantiation in this study.

The 12 subtests each yield both age scores and scaled scores. Figure 5.2 illustrates the profile of a child's scaled scores on the ITPA. The mean scaled score was 33. Since one standard deviation is 6, one standard deviation above the mean is 39, while one standard deviation below the mean is 27. In this way it is easy to note individual high scores and low scores at a glance (Kirk and Kirk 1971).

Further analysis may be made by combining the subscores to discover various factors of mental functioning. To determine the existence of significant discrepancies in areas of mental functioning, the subscores can be combined to evaluate the child in each of the three dimensions of the ITPA: levels of organization, channels of communication, and psycholinguistic processes (Kirk and Kirk 1971).

Levels of organization. The mean score of the tests at the representational level can be compared to the mean score of the tests at the automatic level. Such an examination would compare the child's abilities in habitual but highly organized and integrated responses (automatic level) with responses requiring the more complex mediating processes that utilize symbols carrying the meaning of an object (representational level).

Channels of communication. Scores on tests in the auditory-vocal channel may be compared to scores in the visual-motor channel. The child's per-

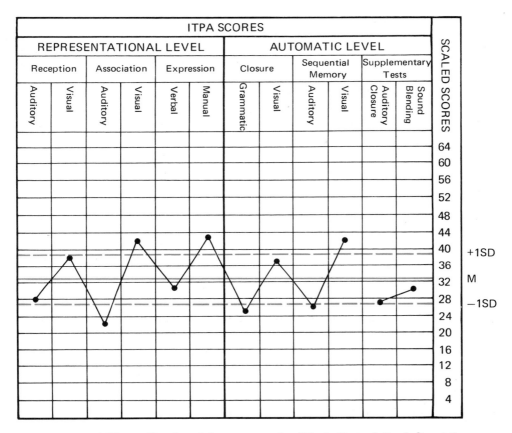

Figure 5.2 A child's profile of scaled scores on the Illinois Test of Psycholinguistic Abilities

From Samuel A. Kirk and Winifred D. Kirk. *Psycholinguistic Learning Disabilities: Diagnosis and Remediation*. Urbana, Ill.: University of Illinois Press, 1971.

formance in tasks that require listening to language and speaking (auditory-vocal) is compared to tasks that require looking and performing motor action (visual-motor).

Psycholinguistic processes. Scores on the three processes of receiving information, associating it, and expressing it can be compared. Thus the child's ability to recognize and/or understand what is seen or heard (receptive process); to relate and organize what is seen or heard (association process); and in expressing ideas verbally or by gesture (expressive process) are compared.

Analysis of the three dimensions of the ITPA for the scores of the child in Figure 5.2 is shown on p. 96 in Table 5.1 (Kirk and Kirk 1971). The table shows the child's age scores as well as the scaled scores pictured in the profile in Figure 5.2.

Table 5.1 Analysis of child's scores in Figure 5.2

	Age Scores	Scaled Scores
Levels of Organization		
Representational	6–4	34
Automatic	5–11	33
Channels of Communication		
Auditory-vocal	4–9	26
Visual-motor	7–5	40
Psycholinguistic Processes		
Reception	5–9	33
Association	6–2	32
Expression	6–11	37

From Samuel A. Kirk and Winifred D. Kirk. *Psycholinguistic Learning Disabilities: Diagnosis and Remediation.* Urbana, Ill.: University of Illinois Press, 1971.

Analysis of scores classified this way indicates that (a) there are no significant differences between the representational and automatic levels of organization, (b) there are no significant differences among the psycholinguistic processes, but (c) there is a significant difference between the visual-motor and auditory-vocal channels. Further analysis and testing did substantiate the diagnostic hypothesis that for this child the auditory-vocal channel was the weak area of functioning. A treatment plan based on this diagnosis was thereby designed (Kirk and Kirk 1971).

QUANTIFYING THE LEARNING DISABILITY

Most definitions of learning disability state that a significant discrepancy exists between what the child has actually learned and what the child is potentially capable of learning. Three difficult questions are implied in this statement: (1) What has the child actually learned and what is the child's present achievement level? (2) What is the child potentially capable of learning and how can this potential be measured? (3) What amount of discrepancy between achievement and potential should be considered significant?

The first question involves the difficulty of determining the child's present achievement level. Because of the problem of measurement error, it is never certain that a test score actually represents the child's present ability. The second question, concerning assessment of the child's potential capacity, is difficult because of the problems inherent in judging intelligence. Group tests, individual tests, verbal and nonverbal tests — all give vastly different measures of intelligence; and the relationship between various factors of intelligence and learning capacity is still not clear. Further, the entire concept of IQ and mental age as an accurate means of judging intelligence is under severe attack on a number of grounds. The third question deals with the amount of discrepancy between potential and achievement that is to be considered significant. This amount differs from grade to grade and age to age. A child with a six-month discrepancy in reading in the first grade has a much greater learning problem than an eleventh grader with a six-month discrepancy.

In spite of the difficulties raised by these questions, it is necessary for the practitioner to make decisions using the quantitative data that is available. Several methods of measuring the learning disability have been suggested; three of these are discussed here: the mental grade method, the years-in-school method, and the learning quotient method. Still other recommended procedures are the computation of differential indices (Woodbury 1963) and the Z-score discrepancy method (Erickson 1975).

MENTAL GRADE METHOD (Harris 1961). This is the simplest method. It uses the child's mental age to assess reading expectancy. To determine reading expectancy grade, the examiner subtracts five years from the child's mental age.

$$RE \text{ (reading expectancy grade)} = MA \text{ (mental age)} - 5$$

Thus a child with a mental age of thirteen is expected to read as well as the average thirteen-year-old or average eighth-grade student. An MA of seven suggests a reading expectancy of the average seven-year-old or second-grade child.

A comparison is made between the expected reading level and the child's present reading level to determine whether a discrepancy exists. For example, Tony is 10 years 0 months old and has an IQ of 120. Using the mental grade method, his reading expectancy grade is 7.0. If he reads at 4.0 grade level, he has a 3-year discrepancy in reading.

$$7.0 \text{ (RE)} = 12(MA) - 5$$

YEARS-IN-SCHOOL METHOD. Bond and Tinker (1967, pp. 198–203) suggest that the mental grade method does not take into account the years of teaching exposure and therefore gives an inaccurate expectancy in some cases, especially when the IQ is particularly high or particularly low. In the first case it overestimates expectancy, while in the second it underestimates it. These authors suggest calculating expectancy grade with the formula

$$RE \text{ (reading expectancy grade)} = \frac{\text{years in school} \times IQ}{100} + 1.0$$

Ten-year-old Tony is in the middle of the fifth grade and therefore has been in school for 4.5 years. Using this formula with his IQ of 120, his reading expectancy is grade 6.4.

$$RE = \frac{4.5 \times 120}{100} + 1.0 = 6.4$$

If he reads at 4.0 grade level, the discrepancy between his expectancy and achievement levels is 2.4 years.

LEARNING QUOTIENT METHOD. Another method that has been suggested to quantify a learning disability first takes three factors into consideration: mental age (MA), chronological age (CA), and grade age (GA) (Myklebust 1968). Since each factor contains certain errors, an average of the three — called expectancy age (EA) — tends to minimize error. In this method the MA is considered separately as a verbal MA and as a performance MA, as measured by the *Wechsler Intelligence Scale for Children*.

$$\text{EA (expectancy age)} = \frac{MA + CA + GA}{3}$$

The learning quotient is then the ratio between present achievement level (achievement age, or AA) and the expectancy age (EA).

$$\text{LQ (learning quotient)} = \frac{AA \text{ (achievement age)}}{EA \text{ (expectancy age)}}$$

A learning quotient (LQ) of 89 or below is one basis for classifying a child as having a learning disability.

An estimate of verbal mental age (MA) is obtained by multiplying verbal IQ by chronological age and dividing by 100:

$$\frac{\text{Verbal IQ} \times CA}{100}$$

Similarly with performance MA:

$$\frac{\text{Performance IQ} \times CA}{100}$$

An estimate of grade age (GA) is made by adding 5.2 to present grade placement (Grade + 5.2).

We can look at Tony using this method. He is 10.0 years old, is in grade 5.5, and has a WISC IQ of 120. His verbal IQ is 110 and his performance IQ is 130. His reading achievement score was 4.0, which gives him a reading achievement age of approximately 9.2.

$$\textit{Verbal MA} \quad \frac{11(MA) + 10\ (CA) + 10.7\ (GA)}{3} = 10.6\ (EA)$$

$$\frac{9.2\ (AA)}{10.6\ (EA)} = .87\ (LQ)$$

$$\textit{Performance MA} \quad \frac{13(MA) + 10(CA) + 10.7\ (GA)}{3} = 11.2\ (EA)$$

$$\frac{9.2\ (AA)}{11.2\ (EA)} = .82\ (LQ)$$

By using the learning quotient method, Tony would be designated as having a learning disability because on the basis of his verbal mental age he has a learning quotient of 87 and in his performance mental age he has a learning quotient of 82. These quotients suggest that he has learned 87 percent of what he is capable of in one case and 82 percent of what he is capable of in the other. Both are below the cutoff point of 89.

Another technique of estimating expectancy age is suggested by Harris (1970). This method, which gives priority to intelligence but also gives weight to experience, involves giving mental age twice the weight of chronological age. Thus:

$$\text{EA (expectancy age)} = \frac{2 \text{ MA} + \text{CA}}{3}$$

This calculation can be substituted for step one of the learning quotient method. However, Harris suggests subsequent calculations for estimating a reading expectancy quotient and a reading quotient (Harris 1970, pp. 212–214).

A similar method of measuring reading proficiency has been suggested by Monroe (1932), using a reading index in which an expected reading age is obtained by averaging chronological age, mental age, and arithmetic computation age. The reading index is then obtained by dividing the reading achievement age by the expected reading age.

These methods of quantifying a learning disability may be useful in deciding whether a child is learning disabled and in making decisions concerning school programs. However, it must be noted that a number of flaws are inherent in these techniques (Spache 1969). The use of MA as a measure of expectancy has been questioned. Can a 9-year-old with an MA of 13 be expected to perform like a 13-year-old? Further, the techniques are not useful for the preschool youngster or the first-grade child who has not yet learned to read, since an achievement score is required by the formula. Such techniques have also been criticized because they neglect many important variables such as background, environment, language, motivation, and psychodynamics. Nevertheless, there are many times when such methods are helpful in making decisions.

SUMMARY

This chapter has looked at the first of the two parts of the diagnosis teaching process — the diagnosis of learning disabilities.

The purpose of a diagnosis is to gather information and to analyze and synthesize this data so that the teacher can help the child learn.

The process of diagnosing a child can be separated into six stages: (1) determining whether the child has a learning disability, (2) measuring the child's present achievement, (3) analyzing how the child learns, (4) exploring why the child is not learning, (5) collating and interpreting data to formulate a hypothesis, and (6) developing a plan for teaching.

Ways of collecting data for the diagnosis were discussed and included: (1) case history or interview, (2) clinical observation, (3) informal testing, and (4) formal standardized testing.

Finally, ways of interpreting test scores in widely used tests were presented, and methods of quantifying the disability were discussed.

The next chapter deals with the second part of the diagnosis/teaching process — clinical teaching.

REFERENCES

Ackerman, Peggy T., John E. Peters, and Roscoe A. Dykman. "Children with Specific Learning Disabilities: WISC Profiles." *Journal of Learning Disabilities* 4 (March 1971): 150–166.

Anastasi, Anne. *Psychological Testing*, 3rd ed. New York: Macmillan, 1968.

Bannatyne, Alex. "Diagnosing Learning Disabilities and Writing Remedial Prescriptions." *Journal of Learning Disabilities* 1 (April 1968): 28–34.

————. "Diagnosis: A Note on Recategorization of the WISC Scaled Scores." *Journal of Learning Disabilities* 7 (May 1974): 272–274.

Bateman, Barbara. "An Educator's View of a Diagnostic Approach to Learning Disorders," pp. 219–237 in J. Hellmuth (ed.), *Learning Disorders*, Vol. I. Seattle: Special Child Publications, 1965.

Boder, Elena. "Developmental Dyslexia: Diagnostic Screening Patterns Based on Three Characteristic Patterns of Reading and Spelling." *Claremont Reading Conference*, 1968.

Bond, Guy, and Miles Tinker. *Reading Difficulties: Their Diagnosis and Correction*, 2nd ed. New York: Appleton-Century-Crofts, 1967.

Bormuth, John R. "The Cloze Readability Procedure." *Elementary English* 45 (April 1968): 429–436.

Bryan, Tanis, and Harold McGrady. "Use of a Teacher Rating Scale." *Journal of Learning Disabilities* 5 (April 1972): 199–208.

Buros, Oscar K. *The 1938 Mental Measurements Yearbook*, Entry 1058. New Brunswick, N.J.: 1938.

Clements, Sam D., Laura E. Lehtinen, and Jean Lukens. *Children with Minimal Brain Injury*. Chicago: National Society for Crippled Children and Adults, 1964.

Dale, Edgar, and Jeanne S. Chall. *A Formula for Predicting Readability*. Columbus: Ohio State University, Bureau of Educational Research, 1948.

Durrell, Donald D. *Improving Reading Instruction*. New York: Harcourt, Brace & World, 1956.

Erickson, Marilyn T. "The Z-Score Discrepancy Method for Identifying Reading-Disabled Children." *Journal of Learning Disabilities* 8 (May 1975): 308–312.

Farr, Roger. *Reading: What Can Be Measured?* ERIC/CRIER, Reading Review Series. Newark, Del.: International Reading Association, 1969.

Gearhart, B. R. *Learning Disabilities: Educational Strategies*. St. Louis: Mosby, 1973.

Glasser, A. J., and I. L. Zimmerman. *Clinical Interpretation of the Wechsler Intelligence Scale for Children*. New York: Grune & Stratton, 1967.

Hammill, D. D., and J. L. Wiederholt. "Review of the Frostig Visual Perception Test and the Related Training Program," pp. 33–48 in L. Mann and D. Sabatino (eds.), *The First Review of Special Education*. Philadelphia: Journal of Special Education Press, 1973.

Haring, N. C., and E. L. Phillips. *Analysis and Modification of Classroom Behavior*. Englewood Cliffs, N.J.: Prentice-Hall, 1972.

Harris, Albert. *How to Increase Reading Ability*, 4th ed. New York: David McKay, 1961; 5th ed., 1970.

Johnson, Margorie, and Roy Kress. *Informal Reading Inventories*. Newark, Del.: International Reading Association, 1965.

Kirk, Samuel A. *Educating Exceptional Children*. Boston: Houghton Mifflin, 1972.

Kirk, Samuel A., and Winifred D. Kirk. *Psycholinguistic Learning Disabilities: Diagnosis and Remediation*. Urbana, Ill.: University of Illinois Press, 1971.

Kirk, Samuel A., James P. McCarthy, and Winifred D. Kirk. *The Illinois Test of Psycholinguistic Abilities*, rev. ed. Urbana, Ill.: University of Illinois Press, 1968.

Lovitt, Thomas C. "Assessment of Children with Learning Disabilities." *Exceptional Children* 34 (December 1967): 233–240.

McGrady, Harold J. Lecture at the University of Denver. Denver, Colo., July 15, 1974.

Mills, Robert E. *Learning Methods Test*. Fort Lauderdale, Fla.: 1612 E. Broward Boulevard, 1956.

Monroe, Marion. *Children Who Cannot Read*. Chicago: University of Chicago Press, 1932.

Myklebust, Helmer. "Learning Disabilities: Definition and Overview," in *Progress in Learning Disabilities*, Vol. I. New York: Grune & Stratton, 1968.

Myklebust, H., and B. Boshes. *Minimal Brain Damage in Children: Final Report*. U.S. Public Health Service Contract 108–65–142. Department of Health, Education and Welfare. Evanston, Ill.: Northwestern University Publication, June 1969, pp. 293–301.

Newby, Hayes A. *Audiology*. New York: Appleton-Century-Crofts, 1964.

Newcomer, Phyllis, B. Hare, D. Hammill, and J. McGettigan. "Construct Validity of the ITPA." *Exceptional Children* 40 (April 1974): 509–510.

———. "Construct Validity of the Illinois Test of Psycholinguistic Abilities." *Journal of Learning Disabilities* 8 (April 1975): 220–231.

Otto, W., R. McMenemy, and R. Smith. *Corrective and Remedial Teaching*. Boston: Houghton Mifflin, 1973.

Paraskevopoulos, John N., and Samuel A. Kirk. *The Development and Psychometric Characteristics of the Revised Illinois Test of Psycholinguistic Abilities*. Urbana, Ill.: University of Illinois Press, 1969.

Roswell, Florence, and Gladys Natchez. *Reading Disability: Diagnosis and Treatment*. New York: Basic Books, 1964. Revised 1971.

Rugel, Robert P. "WISC Subtest Scores of Disabled Readers: A Review with Respect to Bannatyne's Recategorization." *Journal of Learning Disabilities* 7 (January 1974): 57–64.

Senf, Gerald. *Model Centers Program for Learning-Disabled Children: Historical Perspective*. Preview Series. Tucson: Leadership Training Institute for Learning Disabilities, University of Arizona, 1974.

Simensen, R. J., and J. Sutherland. "Psychological Assessment of Brain Damage: The Wechsler Scales." *Academic Therapy* 10 (Fall 1974): 69–81.

Spache, George. "A New Readability Formula for Primary-Grade Materials." *Elementary School Journal* 53 (March 1953): 410–413.

———. "Review of Progress in Learning Disabilities." *Journal of Reading Behavior* 1 (Summer 1969): 93–97.

Thorndike, Robert L. "Dilemmas in Diagnosis," pp. 57–67 in *Assessment Problems in Reading*, Newark, Del.: International Reading Association, 1973.

Wallace, G., and J. Kauffman. *Teaching Children with Learning Problems*. Columbus: Merrill, 1973.

Wechsler Intelligence Scale for Children. New York: Psychological Corporation, 1949. Revised as WISC-R, 1974.

Woodbury, Charles A. "The Identification of Underachieving Readers." *Reading Teacher* 16 (January 1963): 218–223.

6. Clinical Teaching

In successful clinical teaching the diagnosis provides only a starting point. This chapter reviews the teaching portion of the diagnosis/teaching process. A special kind of teaching is required to help children who are handicapped by learning problems; to differentiate it from regular classroom teaching and other kinds of special help, it is called *clinical teaching*.

The goal of clinical teaching is to tailor learning experiences to the unique needs of a particular child. Using all the information gained in the diagnosis and through the hypothesis of the child's learning disabilities, a specific teaching program is designed. In clinical teaching, diagnosis does not stop when treatment procedures begin, and, in fact, continuous diagnosis and treatment become the essence of clinical teaching. This means that the teacher modifies teaching procedures and plans as new needs become apparent.

A clinical teacher is a child-watcher. Instead of concentrating only on what the child *cannot* do, such a teacher observes in detail what the child *does* do. Knowing what kinds of errors are made is as important as knowing about the child's successes. Errors provide clues about the child's mental functions and present level of development.

Clinical teaching can be viewed as an alternating teach-test-teach-test process, with the teacher alternating roles between teacher and tester. First the child is tested; a unit of work based on the resulting information is then taught to the child. Then the child is again tested to determine what has in fact been learned. If the child passes the test, the clinical teacher is informed that the teaching has been successful and plans the next stage of learning. If the child fails the test, analysis of the errors is valuable for determining the cause of failure and for planning subsequent teaching.

For example, a clinical teacher might make use of oral reading errors. Kenneth Goodman's studies (1969) of the analysis of errors (or miscues) in oral reading show that such errors provide excellent clues to the child's mental processes underlying reading. According to Yetta Goodman (1970), oral reading miscues should not be viewed as mistakes which must be eradicated, but as overt behavior which may reveal aspects of intellectual processing.

One child, Ann, read "I saw a large white house," as "I saw a large white horse." The teacher might respond by concluding that Ann is wrong and her error must be corrected. The clinical teacher would respond by thinking, "That's an interesting error. I wonder what caused that behavior? What is involved in Ann's mental functioning that caused her to do that?" The teaching that followed, then, would depend on analysis of this error — whether it is related to a deficiency in visual perception, in visual-motor processes, a poor sight vocabulary, inadequate visual memory, or lack of word attack skills. Subsequent teaching and testing would evaluate the analysis.

John read "Now he had been caught" as "Now he had been catched." Again, teaching will depend on whether the clinical teacher analyzes such an error as lack of phonics skills, not paying attention to word endings, or as an underlying linguistic difference between the reader and the text.

In another area of academic performance, Debby failed the arithmetic story problems in the testing situation. Observation revealed that though she could read the words of the story and perform the arithmetic calculations required, she could not visualize the story's setting. She could not picture in her mind's eye the items to be calculated. The clinical teacher speculated that Debby's arithmetic failures were related to her problems in spatial orientation and visualization. This hunch was supported by the observation that Debby could not remember how to get to school, the store, or a friend's house from her home and that she constantly lost her way in the hall outside the clinic. The teaching in this case was directed toward strengthening Debby's formulation of space and improving her skills of visualization.

Clinical teaching, then, implies a concept about teaching. It requires flexibility and continuous probing by the teacher, but it does not require any one particular system of educational services, setting, form, or style of teaching. The concept of clinical teaching can be applied to teaching an individual child in many settings: for instance, in an individual tutorial arrangement, a small group, or even in a whole classroom. Moreover, clinical teaching can be used in a variety of delivery systems such as the resource room plan, the itinerant plan, or the self-contained classroom.[1] In many ways, clinical teaching is similar to what has been called individualized teaching, but there is a difference in the way the child's disability is analyzed.

CLINICAL TEACHING CYCLE

Clinical teaching requires continual decision making by the person doing the planning and teaching. The complete clinical teaching process can be viewed as a cycle, with each stage of the process as a point along a circle, as diagrammed in Figure 6.1. The phases of the clinical teaching process are (1) diagnosis, (2) planning, (3) implementation, and (4) evaluation, leading to (5) a modification of the diagnosis, and then to new planning, new forms of implementation, and a continuing cycle of clinical teaching (Lerner 1967).

Clinical teaching differs from regular teaching in several ways. First, while in clinical teaching continual decision making is required, in the regular classroom the routine often appears to be designed to minimize decision-making points. For example, in the regular classroom, curriculum procedures are often determined not by the teacher but by the materials being used. The search for the "perfect package" to teach academic skills and "foolproof" programed materials can be viewed as an attempt to minimize the teacher's need to make decisions. One example of classroom methods that tend to reduce decision making is the widespread use of a highly planned basal reader, the predominant instrumental tool in reading in 90 to 95 percent of the classrooms across the country. Once the choice of which basal reader should be adopted has been made, the implementation of the decision is largely formed by the nature of the basal reader itself. The initial decision can stand for five years or more. The rapid implementation of modern math programs is partly due to the minimizing of decision making made

---

[1] These systems for delivering educational services are in Chapter 13.

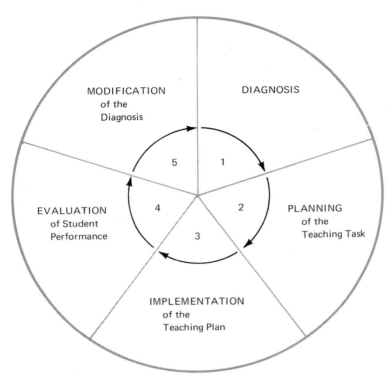

Figure 6.1 Diagram of the clinical teaching cycle

possible by the materials. Step-by-step and day-by-day directions are laid down in the mathematics series. Even if grade-level materials are merely given to each classroom teacher without further explanation, the workbook, textbook, and teacher's manual become the decision makers.

Another difference between clinical teaching and regular teaching is that while clinical teaching is designed for a unique child, lessons and materials in the regular class are designed for the "average" child of a given grade level or classroom. Educational research is frequently designed for the average child when its goal is to find the *best* method to teach a subject area. Such research is intended to measure the average or mean achievement level that results from the use of various methods or materials, rather than to study appropriate methods for teaching a unique child with a highly individualized learning style.

To summarize, clinical teaching differs from regular teaching because it is planned for an individual child rather than for an entire class; for an atypical child rather than for the mythical "average" child. The child may be taught within a group setting, but, even so, clinical teaching implies that the teacher is fully aware of the individual student's learning style, interests, shortcomings and areas of strength, levels of development and tolerance in many areas, feelings, and adjustment to the world. With such knowledge, a clinical teaching plan that meets the needs of a particular child can be designed and implemented. An important aspect of clinical teaching is the skill of interpreting feedback information and the need for continuous decision making.

MANIPULATING VARIABLES IN CLINICAL TEACHING

The teacher and the school are able to do relatively little about many factors related to learning disabilities. The home situation or the genetic or biological makeup of the child may be key elements producing the learning problem, but frequently such variables are not open to modification by the teacher. Some variables, however, can be changed or manipulated by the school, and these should be carefully analyzed for optimum effect.

Barsch (1965) has suggested six factors in learning that can be readjusted by the clinical teacher: space, time, multiplicity, difficulty level, language, and interpersonal relationships.

1. *Space* refers to the physical setting, which should be conducive to learning. Among the ways to modify space are the use of partitions, cubicles, screens, special rooms, and quiet corners, and the removal of distracting stimuli. Other areas to be considered in space are the actual work area, the size of the paper, and the desk surface. Strauss and Lehtinen (1947) and Cruickshank (1961) suggest that a nondistracting school environment be provided. Translucent rather than transparent windows are advised to reduce the visible space and minimize distractions. Another recommendation is that the teacher's clothing be plain and free from distracting ornaments.

The goal of space control is to slowly increase the amount of space with which the child must contend. Gradually children must internalize their own controls so that they can get along in an unmodified space environment.

2. There are a number of ways to control *time* in the clinical teaching setting. For the child with a very short attention span, lessons can be designed to be completed in a shorter time. For example, one row of mathematics problems can be assigned instead of an entire page. The work page can be cut into squares or strips to shorten the time required to complete one section. In timed exercises, the time can be increased. Time can be broken into shorter units by varying the types of activity so that quiet ones are followed by more active ones. Planned interruptions of long lessons, such as having the child come to the teacher's desk or walk to a shelf to get supplies, can be useful.

3. The *multiplicity* variable refers to the number of factors the child

must deal with in a task. The teacher can control the factors the child must contend with and avoid overloading the child by limiting (1) the number of pieces of work to be dealt with, (2) the environment, or extraneous stimuli, and (3) the modality channels of various teaching methods.

The number of pieces of work can be reduced by giving the child fewer pages to complete or fewer spelling words to learn. The teacher can limit the number of pictures on walls and bulletin boards, can control the lighting and the color of the room or furnishings, and can reduce his or her own verbalization. Cruickshank (1961) urged that the elimination of unnecessary visual and auditory environmental stimuli is essential when creating a good teaching environment for brain-injured and hyperactive children.

For some children the modalities stimulated during learning should be limited. The multisensory approach may, in fact, actually disturb their learning. That is, stimulation of the auditory, visual, tactile, and kinesthetic sensory modalities all at the same time may prevent rather than enhance learning.

4. The *difficulty level* of material used can be modified to the tolerance level of the child. The concept of readiness applies here. Many children are failing tasks simply because the tasks are too difficult and the level of performance required is far beyond their present ability. Expecting a child to perform a task far beyond tolerance level can result in a complete breakdown in learning. Strauss recognized such a reaction, calling it a "catastrophic response."

Another factor to be considered is the developmental hierarchy of the subject area. Certain tasks normally precede others. The child who has not learned to handle the oral language will probably do poorly in written language tasks of reading and writing. The child with poor word recognition skills cannot be expected to succeed in reading-comprehension exercises.

Some skills or responses must be overlearned so that they become automatic. If skills are to be utilized or transferred to new situations, they must be internalized. This internalization permits a shift from the representational level (the conscious, cognitive level) to the automatic response level (the subconscious, habitual level). For example, in reading, the child may initially use phonic skills in a conscious, deliberate way to decode words, but later the process should become automatic (at a subconscious level) for effective reading. The conscious sounding out of words may actually interfere with reading. Syntax and grammar must become automatic if the child is to understand and use language effectively.

5. *Language* can also be modified to enhance the child's learning. To assure that language clarifies rather than disturbs, clinical teachers should examine the wording of directions. They should plan communication so that the language used does not exceed the child's level of understanding. For some children, particularly those with auditory language disorders, language quantity must be reduced to the simplest statements. Barsch

(1965) has suggested the following techniques to simplify language: reduce directions to "telegraphic speech," using only essential words; maintain visual contact with the learner; avoid ambiguous words and emphasize meaning with gesture; speak in a slow tempo; touch the child before talking; and avoid complex sentence structure, particularly negative constructions. In summary, do not overload a child's capacity to handle language.

6. The _interpersonal relationship factor_, the rapport between the pupil and teacher, is of paramount importance. Without it, learning is not likely to take place, while with it, learning frequently occurs in spite of inappropriate techniques, materials, or other shortcomings. Both the pupil's self-concept and concept of the teacher must be considered. The importance of the pupil-teacher relationship is discussed in greater detail in this chapter under "Establishing Therapeutic Relations in Clinical Teaching."

TASK ANALYSIS

The first two sections of this chapter considered clinical teaching in terms of analysis of the student and the surrounding environment. This section considers ways to analyze the task itself.

In general, task analysis is a method that is used to provide further diagnostic information; it is an approach to evaluation designed to lead directly to appropriate teaching. Two ways to think about task analysis are presented: (1) the _modality-processing approach_, to evaluate and analyze the processing abilities that underlie the learning task; and (2) the _skills-sequence approach_, to analyze and evaluate what is to be learned — the task itself. The first analyzes the child, while the second analyzes the content to be learned.

MODALITY-PROCESSING APPROACH

The modality-processing approach to task analysis attempts to identify and analyze the underlying processing abilities and disabilities of the child as revealed through performance of the task. The key questions being asked are: "How does this child process information?" or "What are the child's central processing dysfunctions?" (Chalfant and Scheffelin 1969). The primary concern is the identification of cognitive processes presumed to cause inadequate learning in order to prescribe differential remediation of the processing abilities themselves (Ysseldyke and Salvia 1974).

A presentation of the modality-processing approach to task analysis is given by Johnson (1967). Two aspects of the task the child is expected to accomplish are analyzed: the manner of the _presentation_ of the task and the expected mode of _response_. These two aspects are then considered in relationship to the child's success or failure in performing the task.

The task can be analyzed in a number of ways: (1) What _perceptual_ *channels* are required in order to receive the presentation and perform the task? These channels could be auditory, visual, kinesthetic, or tactile in nature. (2) Is a *single sensory-perceptual* system needed, or is a *cross-modal* shifting from one sensory system to another required? (3) Is the task primarily *verbal* or *nonverbal* in nature? (4) Does the task require *social* or *nonsocial* judgments? (5) What *skills and levels of involvement* (perception, memory, symbolization, conceptualization) are required?

If a child fails a task, then the teacher analyzes whether failure is due to the manner of presentation or to the mode of response expected, and the teacher probes for the factor that accounts for the failure.

For example, two spelling tasks might differ significantly in presentation and mode of response: one spelling test might require the pupil to underline the correct spelling from among four choices, and another might require the child to spell orally a spoken word. The visual-memory, language, and motor requirements of these two spelling tasks are quite different.

As another example, two pictures in a workbook exercise represent a *ball* and a *rake*. The teacher orally asks the child to circle the one that rhymes with *bake*. If the child fails, one can analyze the task to discover why. The manner of presentation was verbal and auditory (from the teacher) and visual (from the page). The child had to understand language, including the meaning of *rhyme* and *circle*, follow directions, and have good visual perception of the two-dimensional graphic representation of objects on the page. The mode of response was motor. Prerequisites for performing the task included previous knowledge of and experience with the items represented by the pictures, and adequate auditory memory of the sounds of the words represented by the pictures and the words spoken by the teacher, the skill to compare words and identify rhymes, and the motor ability to draw a circle. Failure to complete the task could have been due to a lack of any of these requirements.

In another task, the child is required to match a printed geometrical form with one of three choices by circling the matching form. This task, a common one in readiness tests and exercises, can be analyzed as being on the perceptual level, nonverbal and nonsocial. The presentation is visual, and the response is motor.

The use of such task analysis in examining workbooks and test materials often reveals that the name of the exercise has little to do with the abilities required to understand and perform the task. Clinical teaching requires the ability to understand the processing requirements of the task and to compare these with the abilities of the child.

SKILLS-SEQUENCE APPROACH

The second approach to task analysis is oriented toward an analysis of the task itself so that learning experiences can be designed to direct a child to reach specific objectives. Ysseldyke and Salvia (1974) maintain that the skills approach advocates assessment of academic skills development and differential instruction tailored to move the child to the desired level of skill achievement. The emphasis is on component skills and their integration into complex terminal behaviors. The skill of buttoning, for example, entails a sequence of component sequential subskills: grasping the button, aligning the button with the buttonhole, etc.

Bateman (1967, 1974) describes this approach as one that places relatively little emphasis on discovering abilities or disabilities within the child, while it places major emphasis on the specific educational tasks to be taught. The important questions behind curriculum planning using this approach are: (1) What specific educational tasks are important for the child to learn? (2) What are the sequential steps in learning this task? and (3) What specific behaviors does the child need to perform this task?

In other words, an educational objective is operationally determined. For example, reading may be the objective that is operationally defined as pronouncing certain words. The desired educational task is broken up into small component parts or sequential steps, i.e., learning certain initial consonants, short vowels, blending certain sounds into words. Finally, specific desired behaviors of the child are determined for each step.

Frank (1973) specifies four steps in the sequence approach to task analysis. Step one: clearly state the learning task (behavioral objective); step two: list all of the components or subskills necessary to meet these objectives and to place these subskills in a logical teaching sequence; step three: test informally to determine what subskills the child can already perform; and step four: begin teaching in sequential order the next skill on the task-analysis hierarchy.

Several curriculum plans are purported to be built on a skills approach, for example, the *Distar* programs for reading, arithmetic, and language (Engelmann et al. 1969). The criterion-referenced reading programs (such as the *Wisconsin Design for Reading Skill Development*) identify operationally defined tasks in a sequential-skills hierarchy of reading and testing to determine which skills the child knows and does not know.

The basic philosophy of the skills-sequence approach to task analysis is summed up in a set of principles formulated by Engelmann (1969, p. 37):

1. Educational objectives must be stated as a series of specific tasks.
2. Everything that follows — the analysis, the development of specific teaching presentations, and the teacher's behavior — must derive from the objective tasks.
3. The analysis must be made by noting every concept needed for successful performance of the tasks.
4. Tasks that teach these concepts must be specified.
5. Each presentation designed to teach a given concept must admit of one and only one interpretation.
6. For clarity and maximum feedback of information from per-

formance, the program should be designed so that the child learns one new concept at a time.

7. Teachers must infer from the children's performance whether they have mastered a concept. They must provide appropriate remedies for children who have developed misconceptions or inadequate formulations of a given concept. They must recognize that teachers deal only in concepts and that the child's responses must be interpreted in terms of concepts.

8. The program must be evaluated in terms of whether the children meet the various criteria of performance specified by the objectives.

COMBINING MODALITY-PROCESSING AND SKILLS-SEQUENCE APPROACHES

The two approaches to task analysis, the modality-processing and the skills-sequence approaches, are often debated and contrasted in an effort to determine the better method for clinical teaching (Ysseldyke and Salvia 1974). Yet they need not be considered dichotomous; rather, clinical teachers should be proficient in both types of task analysis. They must know the sequence of skills in academic subjects and be able to analyze the tasks in the sequence of skills. At the same time, they must also be able to perform a modality-processing analysis that shifts the orientation from the subject matter to the processing abilities of the child.

Some writers recommend that the two approaches be combined. Siegel (1972) suggests that the clinical teacher should (1) select a relevant and appropriate task, (2) know or create a specific sequence of steps based on the hierarchy of competencies needed to perform the task, and (3) make the necessary modifications based on the individual child's profile of strengths and weaknesses. Junkala (1947) writes that the clinical teacher must be able to identify the demands that a task will make on a child in order to prepare the child to meet each demand. Miller et al. (1974) compiled a guide that presents hierarchical sequences of skills in various curriculum areas; each skill is accompanied by an analysis of the task from a behavioral- and modality-processing standpoint.

Competencies in both approaches to task analysis, then, should be part of the professional repertory of the clinical teacher (McCarthy 1970):

1. *Task analysis of the learner* involves specifying how a particular child functions — the things the child can and cannot do, modality-processing areas of strengths and weaknesses, and attitudes and emotions as they affect learning.

2. *Task analysis of the curriculum* involves knowing the content of developmental skills and the hierarchy of components needed to perform such skills.

3. *Relating the curriculum task to the learner* involves the ability to

coordinate data gathered from the analysis of the learner with the analysis of curriculum skills to be learned.

4. *Making appropriate clinical decisions* involves the ability to decide on ways of using this information to bring about improvement in the child.

ESTABLISHING THERAPEUTIC RELATIONSHIPS IN CLINICAL TEACHING

Clinical teaching does not imply a mechanistic or unsympathetic view of the child. Clinical teaching does demand objectivity to analyze the way a child learns and the skills to be taught and to implement specific teaching plans, but it also requires a subjective understanding of the pupil as a child — as a whole child with feelings, emotions, and attitudes. Abrams (1970) refers to this emotional dimension of the child with learning disabilities as "ego status," while Strang (1968) puts it within the framework of the child's self-concept.

Within such a framework, Roswell and Natchez (1971) present a sensitive and empathetic description of the feelings of the child with learning disabilities. They point out that this student is a lost and frightened person who has often suffered years of despair, discouragement, and frustration. Feelings of rejection, failure, and hopelessness about the future are always present, affecting every subject in school and every aspect of the child's life.

> For twelve long years of school and after, he contends with a situation for which he can find no satisfactory solution. When schoolwork becomes insurmountable, the child has few alternative resources. An adult dissatisfied with his job may seek a position elsewhere or find solace outside of his work; he may even endure these difficulties because of a high salary or other compensations. For a child who fails, however, there is no escape. He is subjected to anything from degradation to tolerance. Optimum conditions may lessen the child's misery, but proof of his inadequacies appears daily in the classroom. In the end, he is held in low esteem, not only by his classmates, but also by his family (Roswell and Natchez 1971, p. 2).

The clinical teacher should realize that a learning disability may influence every aspect of the child's world. Deploring such statements as "There's no point in trying to teach until the child's emotional problems are cured," Roswell and Natchez note that clinical teaching can provide therapeutic results. Experience has shown that success in learning has a beneficial effect on personality, enhances feelings of self-worth, and rekindles an interest in learning. In fact, these authors refer to teaching that results in such changes as "psychotherapeutic." In addition to knowledge and skill in the use of clinical teaching techniques, the clinical teacher must understand the emotional impact of failure on the child.

Not only are his parents and teachers displeased with him, but their anxiety often becomes uncontrollable. The parents wonder whether their child is retarded or just plain lazy. If they are assured that his intelligence is normal, even the most loving parents can become so alarmed at their child's inability to learn that they tend to punish, scold and threaten, or even reward with the hope of producing the desired results. Teachers also feel frustrated by their inability to reach the child.

It is under such adverse conditions that the child tries his best to function. When he continues to fail, he can become overwhelmed and devastated. These feelings linger with him after school and on weekends. The notion that he does not measure up hangs over him relentlessly (Roswell and Natchez 1971, p. 68).

An important goal of clinical teaching, therefore, is to motivate children who have been failing, to build their self-concept, and to interest them in learning. To accomplish such ends, Roswell and Natchez suggest consideration of the following "psychotherapeutic principles" of teaching.

Rapport. A good relationship between the teacher and student is an essential first step in educational therapy. In fact, it has been said that much of the success in clinical teaching depends on the establishment of rapport. There must be total acceptance of the child as a human being worthy of respect in spite of failure to learn. A good relationship implies compassion without overinvolvement, understanding without indulgence, and a genuine concern for the child's development. Since the child lives in a continuing atmosphere of rejection and failure, the relationship with the clinical teacher should provide a new atmosphere of confidence and acceptance. It is extremely difficult for a parent to retain an accepting yet objective attitude, and the child becomes very sensitive to the parents' disappointment. Parents are often unaware of the child's reaction to their efforts. For example, one well-intentioned father, who was observed in a public library helping his son pick out a book and listening to him read, was overheard to say, "I'll tell you that word one more time, and then I don't want you to forget it for the rest of your life." This hardly reflects an attitude conducive to learning.

Collaboration. Involvement of both the pupil and the teacher in their joint task provides another step toward psychotherapeutic treatment. Pupils should be involved in both analysis of their problems and evaluation of their performance. In the same collaborative spirit, the child should take an active role in designing lessons and choosing materials.

Structure. Both structure and limits are important elements in teaching children with learning disorders because they introduce order into the children's chaotic lives. Many of these children need such order and welcome it. Structure can be provided in many aspects of clinical teaching — in the physical environment, in the routine sequence of activities, and in the manner in which lessons are taught. Cruickshank (1967) provides numerous examples of program and environment structure.

Sincerity. Children are skillful in detecting insincerity. Honest appraisal is necessary. Children soon detect dishonesty if told that they are doing well when they know they are not. Instead, the teacher might try to minimize anxiety about errors by saying that many children have similar difficulties and by conveying a confidence that together they will find ways to overcome them.

Success. Achieving goals in learning and acquiring a feeling of success are of prime importance for the child with learning disabilities. This means that the materials selected must be at a difficulty level that will permit success.

The popularity of reading material printed on cardboard and packaged in boxes (instead of on pages bound into books), such as the *SRA Reading Laboratory,* is partly due to the fact that such programs are designed to assure success. Learning-disabled children are reluctant to read books at the appropriate difficulty level for them if the books are obviously labeled for a grade level lower than their own. Rather than identifying difficulty level by a grade level, the publishers of some new materials have identified difficulty levels by color cuing the reading selections. Fourth graders who would refuse to read a second-grade book can now meet success because they do not hesitate to read material at the purple level.

In addition to carefully selecting the level of difficulty of teaching materials the teacher can also make children conscious of success and progress by praising good work, by using extrinsic rewards as reinforcement, and by developing visual records of progress through charts and graphs.

Interest. The chance of successful achievement is greatly increased when materials based on the child's special interests are provided. Such interests can be determined through conversations with the pupil or by administering interest inventories. If reading material can be found in the child's area of interest, this may prove to be a strong motivation for learning. However, it is frequently difficult to find material in the child's area of interest that is also written at the appropriate difficulty level, particularly if knowledge of the subject is quite advanced. In that situation, books written on the child's difficulty level are too simple in content and therefore not interesting.

Middle-grade boys with an interest in Greek and Roman mythology have been observed to improve their reading skills greatly by devouring all the myths. The first real interest in reading shown by some high school students is stimulated by the necessity of passing a written test in order to get a driver's license. Utilizing this interest, some teachers have successfully used the driver's manual to teach reading. Series books have been the impetus for other youngsters to become readers. An interest in a series such as the Freddy books, Landmark books, or Nancy Drew mysteries or an interest in an author, television series, or movie based on a book can spark reading if the clinical teacher can capture this interest. Once a real interest is tapped, great progress can be made. One eighth-grade boy found the first book he ever read from cover to cover, *The Incredible Journey,* so fascinating that he was completely oblivious to class changes, ringing bells, and classroom incidents from the time he started the book until it was completed.

One teacher reported as follows about a boy with a reading disability who became interested in the simplified Dolch version of *Robinson Crusoe:*

> He became so immersed in the story that he would grab the book as soon as he entered the room for our daily session. At first he couldn't allow me to read any part of the story, even trying phonetically to read new words. But as the story became more exciting, he'd ask me to tell him the words because he did not want to lose the thread of the plot while seeking the correct word.

Once in a while dramatic changes occur in the attitude and outlook of a child because of clinical teaching. When such changes occur because of a book the child has read, it is sometimes called *bibliotherapy*. Learning about the experiences of others fosters release and insight, as well as hope and encouragement. Fairy tales, for example, have great appeal for many children, and primary teachers are aware of the sheer delight and excitement of children when they read a simple version of the classic themes in their reading books. Children with personal problems (for example, children who are short, fat, unpopular, or physically or academically handicapped) identify with characters in books suffering similar problems and are helped by the characters' resolution of them.

One boy in a learning disabilities group in seventh grade who was without goals, direction, or adult identification, was able to identify with Houdini, the great escape artist. He read all the books he could find on Houdini in the school library and in the public library. At the same time, personality and attitude changes as well as tremendous improvement in reading were observed by his teachers. The boy who found an interest in *Robinson Crusoe* identified with the chief character and his predicaments. His teacher reported:

> Many times he would tell what he thought he would do if he were in a particular situation that Crusoe was in, and then he would be so delighted that the main character had done similarly. If Crusoe had taken another course of action, we would have to decide whose plan was better.

The right book can be a powerful tool to build interest, provide motivation, and improve reading.

A CLASSIFICATION SYSTEM OF REMEDIAL APPROACHES

Remediation, a term frequently used instead of clinical teaching, has many meanings to scholars and practitioners in learning disabilities, special education, and general education. While many of these interpretations are discussed elsewhere in this book, this section presents an organized system, or taxonomy, to provide an overall perspective.

The model used for organizing remedial approaches, shown in Figure 6.2, is but one possible system of classification. Other taxonomies of remediation may also serve to organize remediation approaches. In this model remediation is divided into three kinds of analysis: analysis of the *child,* of the *content* to be learned, and of the *environmental conditions* under which the child learns. Each analytic approach is further subdivided into three specific categories of remediation, making a total of nine. While each of the nine categories of remediation has merit, each also has certain limitations

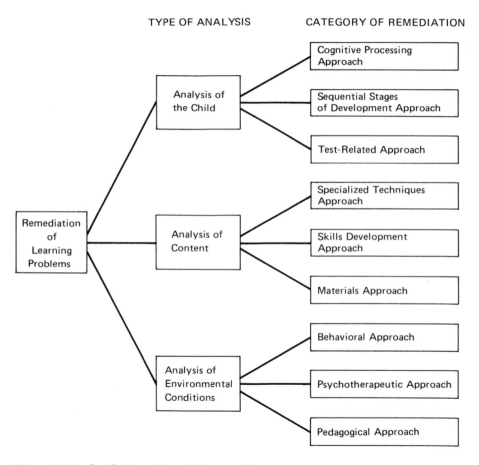

Figure 6.2 A classification of remedial approaches

and shortcomings. The remedial method and the nature of the criticism of each of the nine approaches are briefly described in this section.

The purpose of this classification scheme is simply to sort out the many categories or approaches to remediation. Another conceptual framework might well be devised wherein the categories of remediation would be ordered in a different manner. The importance of this classification model is that it offers *one* working system to organize the confusion of remedial and teaching methods.

ANALYSIS OF THE CHILD

The first three categories of remediation concentrate on an analysis of the child and how this learner functions.

Cognitive Processing Approach

The approach to remediation most readily associated with learning disabilities is probably that of cognitive processing. "Cognitive processing" refers to the child's abilities in processing. information, perceptual modalities (Chapter 9), or pathways of learning. By assessing a child's processing abilities (visual, auditory, memory, haptic abilities, etc.) and comparing and contrasting the areas of processing strengths and weaknesses, the clinician gathers information to plan remediation. Several approaches are suggested by various authorities: one is to remediate the child's processing deficits; another is to teach the child through modalities that are intact; and a third is to do both simultaneously,

The value of this approach has been recently questioned by a number of investigators (Mann and Phillips 1971, Hammill, Goodman, and Wiederholt 1974, Cohen 1969, Hammill and Larsen 1974, 1974a). They challenge the premise that instruction in cognitive processing leads to improvement in academic learning.

Nonetheless, the concept of cognitive processing remains a cornerstone of the field of learning disabilities. It provides a way of thinking about how a child learns and offers a framework for teaching.

Sequential Stages of Development Approach

In the "sequential stages of development" approach to remediation, the child is analyzed in terms of a specific hierarchy of stages of normal child development. Examples of such hierarchies are Getman's Visuomotor model (Chapter 8) and Piaget's developmental stages (Chapter 12). In this approach, the child begins remediation at the lowest unaccomplished stage in the hierarchy, proceeding to the next stage when ready. For example, according to one hierarchy model, if the child has inadequate gross motor skills, remediation would be geared to helping the child attain proficiency at that level. Once skills at this stage are learned, remediation moves on to the next sequential stage, e.g., fine motor development.

Specific models and programs of the sequential approaches to remediation have been critiqued by Goodman and Hammill (1973) and others. They question the need to develop proficiency at each stage of the hierarchy as well as the transferability of skills learned in the hierarchy to areas of academic learning.

A number of remedial programs are based on the sequential stages of development theory, a framework that rests on a child development perspective. Many of the motor development programs, for example, are based on such a model.

Test-related Approaches

The "test related" approaches to remediation analyze the child through a particular diagnostic instrument, which provides a system for pinpointing areas that need remediation. The model underlying the test is accepted as the model of learning disabilities. For example, if the examiner administers the *Illinois Test of Psycholinguistic Abilities* (ITPA), this model provides the framework for remediation. Certain materials have been specifically designed for test-related approaches. Bush and Giles (1969), the *WMW Program* (Minskoff, Wiseman, and Minskoff 1973), and the *Goal Program Language Development Game* (Karnes 1972) provide exercises and materials designed for remediating deficit areas as indicated by the ITPA test.

The test-related approach to remediation has also been questioned by several writers (Mann and Phillips 1971, Newcomer et al. 1974, Hammill and Wiederholt 1972, Hammill and Larsen 1974, Newcomer and Hammill 1975). While the child often improves in the specific skill areas being tested and taught, the carry-over to broader kinds of learning is uncertain. Moreover, critics ask test makers why the areas chosen for assessment are more important than others that might have been chosen. They also question the construct validity of the tests themselves.

Remediation in test-related approaches is dependent on the test being used and the quality of the theory underlying the test. The child's performance in the test directs the remedial procedure.

ANALYSIS OF CONTENT TO BE LEARNED

The next three approaches to remedial instruction emphasize the content to be learned rather than analysis of the child who is to learn it.

Specialized Techniques Approach

Unlike the usual developmental methods that are used in the regular classroom, "specialized techniques" are purported to be highly differentiated

ways of attacking specific learning problems. A specific method is sometimes named after the originator or the person who popularized the approach, i.e., the Gillingham method or the Fernald method. These approaches often require the teacher to follow certain steps in a prescribed
order and fashion and for a specified period of time. The same method is
used for all children, regardless of each child's specific abilities.

Since most research compares methods as they affect large groups, it is
difficult to know if any one particular method has been *the* best for an
individual child. Few research studies have been conducted to measure the
superiority of one specialized technique. In fact, on close inspection the
highly specialized techniques often turn out to be similar to remedial and
developmental approaches that have been used over the years.

Skills-Development Approach

Another category of remediation that analyzes the content to be learned is
the "skills-development approach." A hierarchy of skills in a subject area
(reading, arithmetic, spelling, etc.) is postulated. The remedial specialist
attempts to determine how far the child has gone along the skills hierarchy
in a specific subject area, what the child does not know within the skills
hierarchy, and where in the hierarchy teaching should begin. The ability
to read, for example, is assumed to be composed of many skills and subskills; by mastering the component subskills, it is presumed that the child
will thereby master the skill of reading. The remedial specialist must have a
thorough understanding of normal developmental skills in each subject area.
Criterion-referenced systems of teaching (discussed in Chapter 12) embody
the skills-development approach to remediation.

Critics have questioned the premise that a specific empirically derived
hierarchy of skills exists. In the field of reading, for example, Thompson
and Dzuiban (1973) state that there is lack of evidence to support this
contention. Some children may be better able to learn by using a different
set or ordering of skills.

The skills-development approach focuses on the analysis of the task to
be learned rather than on the child who is to learn it. Because growth is
assumed to proceed through a sequence of skills, each phase of developmental growth is likened to climbing the rungs on a ladder. The premise of
this approach is that each rung must be touched in climbing to the top;
the learner who misses some rungs may fall off altogether.

Materials Approach

Publishers' materials become the basis of yet another category of remediation, guiding and directing the procedure of remediation. The basic decision within this approach is thus the choice of materials. Once this decision
is made, the materials themselves become the decision makers, guiding the
skills sequence, providing practice activities, suggesting questions to be

used, and giving step-by-step instructional procedures. The use of *Distar* is an example of this category of remediation.

The materials method thus minimizes decision making, for the materials themselves become the remedial procedure. However, as noted earlier in this chapter, clinical teaching should require constant decision making. Durkin (1974), after observing teachers of reading who followed the materials approach, noted that some of them had become educational clerks, allowing materials to dictate what was to be taught and how. In effect, the materials can become the master rather than the servant of the teacher.

Nevertheless, publishers' materials can prove to be a valuable tool in remediation if they are not misused. Certainly, the clinical teacher should be familiar with a wide variety of materials.

ANALYSIS OF ENVIRONMENTAL CONDITIONS SURROUNDING LEARNING

Behavioral Approaches

A growing movement in remediation is the behavior-modification approach. Unlike the categories discussed earlier — which analyze the child, the content to be learned, or the materials to be used — this approach concentrates on the environmental conditions surrounding learning. Based on principles of operant conditioning, the behavioral approach is used to remediate children in two ways: to eliminate undesired behaviors and to establish specific desired behaviors.

Behavior modification is the application to human beings of the knowledge about animal behavior obtained through experimental psychology. As presented in Chapter 12, the theory states that if a response is rewarded (reinforced) when it occurs, it will tend to be repeated. Advocates of behavior modification are not concerned about the cause of a child's learning problem, or how the child processes information, or with a hierarchy of stages; rather, they focus on how the environment can be manipulated to bring about desired behavior. They do not search for underlying causes or explanations, but for ways of changing specific behavior (Poteet 1973).

Cases in which behavior-modification approaches to teaching were used indicate that manipulation of consequent events (reinforcement) improved the child's performance. Evidence of the success of the behavioral method is demonstrated by a series of graphs (see page 341) showing the change in learning behavior. Despite such apparent evidence, however, many educators find this approach to teaching to be narrow, confining, and contrary to the concepts of freedom and learning. Goodman (1974, p. 823), for example, says:

> We've got to tell the operant conditioners and the contingency reinforcers that kids can learn like pigeons but pigeons can't learn like kids and that learning theories that try to reduce learning to

read to bite-size pellets that pigeons can swallow are inappropriate and ultimately harmful to at least some kids. . . .

Using the behavioral approach, the objectives of remediation must be precise, observable, and measurable. The approach does not ask why — just what reinforcement will change the behavior.

Psychotherapeutic Approach

This category of remediation concentrates on the <u>feelings of the child and on the relationship with the teacher</u>. The psychodynamics of remediation are too often lost in the labyrinth of materials, techniques, methods, modalities and base-line data. These failing children are unhappy in the learning situation. Their frustrations, poor ego development, and feelings of inadequacy, all lead to continued failure in learning. What is needed, this approach suggests, is to reverse this cycle by building feelings of success and establishing a healthy psychodynamic relationship between teacher and student.

Even if a child is well adjusted when entering school, continued failure in school learning is likely to have unfavorable effects. As the pupil gets older, these feelings of failure, frustration, and oversensitivity tend to increase. Thus, in the learning-disabled adolescent, emotional problems are almost always in evidence. Many children with learning problems are, in fact, referred to psychological or psychiatric therapy. A study of persons under age 18 referred to psychiatric facilities revealed that 22 percent were referred because of academic difficulty (Nichol 1974). Harris (1970) found that close to 100 percent of reading disability cases at Queens College Clinic showed some maladjustment problems. Remediation thus involves the task of <u>rebuilding the child's ego</u>, fostering <u>confidence and assurance</u>, and letting the child know that the teacher understands the problem and has confidence in the child's ability to learn and succeed. There are many reported cases of children who improved dramatically in academic learning after working with a tutor who was untrained in the sophisticated skills and knowledge of the learning disabilities profession; yet the tutor was able to establish a point of meaningful contact between the teacher and the child. Specific techniques are presented in an earlier section of this chapter, "Establishing Therapeutic Relationships in Clinical Teaching," and in Chapter 12.

The psychotherapeutic approach to remediation also has its critics. Despite the need for considering psychodynamic factors, many authorities question the overdependence of this approach alone. They point out that exclusive use of psychotherapeutic therapy may result in the creation of "happy failures," children who have learned to be content with their disabilities. McCarthy (1971, pp. 12–13) comments on the limits of psychotherapeutic treatment:

After several decades of often fruitless efforts at manipulating the child's attitude toward learning, it became apparent . . . that tender loving care, or a deeper understanding of his own motivation, could at best produce a child who was comfortable, albeit euphoric, with his nonlearning.

The emphasis in this approach to remediation, then, is on providing appropriate environmental conditions to improve the child's self-confidence and establish a healthy relationship with the teacher.

Pedagogical Approach

The last category of remediation has the old-fashioned title "pedagogy." According to Cohen (1971), the major cause of reading failure is *dyspedagogia,* a term coined to indicate a lack of good teaching. It follows, therefore, that good teaching is itself a method of remediation. A number of research studies have concluded that the teacher is the most important variable in a child's learning (Bond and Dykstra 1967, Chall and Feldmann 1966, Harris et al. 1968). These studies have shown that children in certain classes in school do better than children in other classes, regardless of the methods or materials used, even when the data is controlled for intelligence and socioeconomic level. The most important component in these situations was not the materials nor the methods but the teacher. Bateman (1974) suggests that the term *learning disabilities* be replaced by the term *teaching disabilities* to emphasize the shift in focus from something deviant or pathological within the child to inadequacies in the child's teacher and the teaching environment.

Despite this frequent observation that the teacher is the key ingredient for successful remediation, the research has not yet revealed precisely what qualities the successful teacher possesses. Is it empathy, kindness, ability to structure the class, enthusiasm, creativity, punctuality, ability to individualize instruction, consistency, knowledge of the field, love of children, diagnostic skills, familiarity with materials, competency in specific skills, clinical intuition, or something else? Without a clear answer to what qualities make the good teacher, the plea for "good teaching" is nebulous.

A classification system of remediation, consisting of three kinds of analysis and nine categories, has been presented. Of course, in practice these categories are not mutually exclusive, and teachers may use several concurrently. Each of the categories has strong arguments to support it; yet each is also vulnerable to criticism. Learning disabilities specialists must have a certain degree of knowledge, skill, and expertise in each of the categories while also recognizing the shortcomings and limitations of each. Each category of remediation has a contribution to make to the total system of clinical teaching.

Overdependence on one approach to remediation should be avoided.

Such an error is exemplified in this fable (*Reading Today International,* 1974):

Once upon a time the animals decided they must do something educational to help their young meet the problems of the world. A school was organized where they adopted a curriculum consisting of running, climbing, and swimming. To make it easier to administer, all of the animals took all the subjects. Of course, the duck was excellent in swimming — in fact he was better than the instructor; running, however, was a weak area for him. Therefore, he had to stay after school and drop swimming in order to practice running. Now, this was kept up until his webbed feet were badly worn and soon he became only average in swimming. However, average was an acceptable criterion in this school so no one was concerned about it — except, of course, the duck. While the rabbit was good in running, he was not up to par in swimming and suffered a nervous breakdown because of the makeup work required to improve his swimming. By the end of the year, an abnormal eel that could swim exceedingly well and also run and climb had the overall highest average and was consequently named valedictorian of the class.

The point of the fable is that no one method of remediation can be relied on as *the* way to provide remediation in every case. After a five-year follow-up study of children with learning disabilities who were enrolled in special education classes, Koppitz (1973, p. 137) concluded:

> . . . learning disabilities cannot be corrected or "cured" by a specific teaching method or training technique. It is imperative that teachers have a wide range of instructional materials and techniques at their disposal and that they are imaginative and flexible enough to adapt these to the specific needs of their pupils.

The teaching competencies of learning disabilities specialists, then, should include knowledge and skill in each of the categories of remediation. They should also be aware of the limitations of each of the categories of remediation.

SUMMARY

This chapter has reviewed the clinical-teaching portion of the diagnosis/teaching process. The concept of clinical teaching as a way of tailoring learning experiences to the unique needs of a particular child was discussed. The clinical-teaching process was examined in terms of a five-stage cycle of decision making. Ways that the teacher can manipulate variables in the school setting were presented. The subject of task analysis was discussed from several perspectives. Several ways that the teacher can establish a therapeutic relationship in clinical teaching were presented. Finally, a system of classifying remedial approaches was suggested.

At many stages within the diagnostic/teaching process decisions must be made. These will be colored, in large measure, by the theoretical framework of those making the decisions. Part Three reviews theories of learning disabilities, along with teaching strategies evolving from these theories.

REFERENCES

Abrams, Jules C. "Learning Disabilities. A Complex Phenomenon." *Reading Teacher* 23 (January 1970): 299–303.

Barsch, Ray. "Six Factors in Learning," pp. 329–343 in J. Hellmuth (ed.), *Learning Disorders*, Vol. 1. Seattle: Special Child Publications, 1965.

Bateman, Barbara. "Educational Implications of Minimal Brain Dysfunction." *Reading Teacher* 27 (April 1974): 662–668.

———. "Three Approaches to Diagnosis and Educational Planning for Children with Learning Disabilities." *Academic Therapy Quarterly* 2 (1967): 215–222.

Bond, L., and R. Dykstra. "The Cooperative Research Program in First Grade Reading Instruction." *Reading Research Quarterly* 2 (Summer 1967).

Bush, Wilma Jo, and Marion T. Giles. *Aids to Psycholinguistic Teaching.* Columbus: Merrill, 1969.

Chalfant, J., and M. Scheffelin. *Central Processing Dysfunctions in Children.* NINDS monograph no. 9. Bethesda, Md.: U.S. Department of Health, Education and Welfare, 1969.

Chall, Jeanne, and Shirley Feldmann. "First Grade Reading: An Analysis of the Interactions of Professed Methods, Teaching, Implementation, and Child Background." *Reading Teacher* 19 (May 1966): 569–575.

Cohen, S. Alan. "Studies in Visual Perception and Reading in Disadvantaged Children." *Journal of Learning Disabilities* 2 (October 1967): 8–13.

———. "Dyspedagogia as a Cause of Reading Retardation in Learning Disorders," pp. 269–293 in B. Bateman (ed.), *Learning Disorders—Reading*, Vol. 4. Seattle: Special Child Publications, 1971.

Cruickshank, W. A. *The Brain-Injured Child in Home, School, and Community.* Syracuse, N.Y.: Syracuse University Press, 1967.

Cruickshank, W. A., B. Bentzen, F. Ratzeburg, and M. Tannhauser. *A Teaching Method for Brain-Injured and Hyperactive Children.* Syracuse, N.Y.: Syracuse University Press, 1961.

Durkin, Dolores. "Some Questions About Questionable Instructional Material." *Reading Teacher* 28 (October 1974): 13–17.

Engelmann, Siegfried. *Preventing Failure in the Primary Grades.* Chicago: Science Research Associates, 1969.

Engelmann, Siegfried, et al. *Distar Reading, Distar Arithmetic, Distar Language.* Chicago: Science Research Associates, 1969.

Flavel, John H. *The Developmental Psychology of Jean Piaget.* Princeton, N.J.: Van Nostrand, 1963.

Frank, Alan R. "Breaking Down Learning Tasks: A Sequence Approach." *Teaching Exceptional Children* 6 (Fall 1973): 16–29.

Getman, Gerald M. "The Visuomotor Complex in the Acquisition of Learning Skills," pp. 49–76 in J. Hellmuth (ed.), *Learning Disorders*, Vol. 1. Seattle: Special Child Publications, 1965.

Goodman, Kenneth S. "Effective Teachers of Reading Know Language and Children." *Elementary English* 5 (September 1974): 823–828.

———. "Analysis of Oral Reading Miscues: Applied Psycholinguistics." *Reading Research Quarterly* 5 (Fall 1969): 9–30.

Goodman, Libby, and Donald D. Hammill. "The Effectiveness of Kephart-Getman Activities in Developing Perceptual Motor and Cognitive Skills." *Focus on Exceptional Children* 4 (February 1973): 1–9.

Goodman, Yetta M. "Using Children's Reading Miscues for New Teaching Strategies." *Reading Teacher* 23 (February 1970): 455–459.

Hammill, Donald D., Libby Goodman, and J. Lee Wiederholt. "Visual-Motor Processes — Can We Train Them?" *Reading Teacher* 27 (February 1974): 469–480.

Hammill, Donald D., and Stephen C. Larsen. "The Effectiveness of Psycholinguistic Training," *Exceptional Children* 41 (September 1974): 3–15.

————. "The Relationship of Selection Auditory Perceptual Skills and Reading Ability." *Journal of Learning Disabilities* 7 (August/September 1974): 429–436. (a)

Hammill, Donald D., and J. L. Wiederholt. "Review of the Frostig Visual Perceptions Test and the Related Training Program," pp. 33–48 in L. Mann and D. Sabatino (eds.), *The First Review of Special Education.* Philadelphia: Journal of Special Education Press, 1972.

Harris, A. *How to Increase Reading Ability,* 5th ed. New York: David McKay, 1970.

Harris, Albert, et al. *A Continuation of the CRAFT Project: Comparing Approaches with Disadvantaged Urban Negro Children in Primary Grades.* USOE no. 5–0570–2–12–1. New York: Selected Academic Readings, 1968.

Hewett, Frank M. "Hierarchy of Educational Tasks for Children with Learning Disorders." *Exceptional Children* 31 (December 1964): 207–214.

Johnson, Doris. "Educational Principles for Children with Learning Disabilities." *Rehabilitation Literature* 28 (October 1967): 317–322.

Junkala, John. "Task Analysis and Instructional Alternatives," pp. 483–489 in S. Kirk and F. Lord (eds.), *Exceptional Children: Educational Resources and Perspectives.* Boston: Houghton Mifflin, 1974.

Karnes, Merle. *Goal Program Language Development Game.* Springfield, Mass.: Milton Bradley, 1972.

Kirk, S., James McCarthy, and Winifred Kirk. *Illinois Test of Psycholinguistic Abilities,* rev. ed. Urbana, Ill.: University of Illinois Press, 1968.

Koppitz, Elizabeth. "Special Class Pupils with Learning Disabilities: A Five-Year Follow-up Study." *Academic Therapy* 13 (Winter 1972–1973): 133–140.

Lerner, Janet W. "A New Focus for Reading Research — The Decision-Making Process." *Elementary English* 44 (March 1967): 236–242.

Mann, Lester and William A. Phillips. "Fractional Practices in Special Education," pp. 314–325 in D. Hammill and N. Bartel (eds.), *Educational Perspectives in Learning Disabilities.* New York: Wiley, 1971.

McCarthy, Jeanne M. "Learning Disabilities: Where Have We Been? Where Are We Going?" pp. 10–19 in D. Hammill and N. Bartel (eds.), *Educational Perspectives in Learning Disabilities.* New York: Wiley, 1971.

McCarthy, Jeanne M., ch. "Group Report," pp. 48–60 in *Final Report: USOE Contract No. OEG–0–9–121013–3021(031). Advanced Institute for Leadership Personnel in Learning Disabilities.* Tucson: University of Arizona, Bureau of Education for the Handicapped, U.S. Office of Education, 1970.

Miller, Roselle J., John Junkala, Ronald E. Netter, and Lynn F. Ellis. *Teachers' Guide for Exceptional Children and Youth.* USDESEA Pam 352–623, Directorate, United States Department of Dependent Schools, European Area, PAO New York 09164, 1973.

Minskoff, E. H., D. E. Wiseman, and J. C. Minskoff. *The MWM Program of Developing Language Abilities.* Ridgefield, N.J.: Educational Performance Associates, 1973.

Newcomer, Phyllis B., and Donald D. Hammill. "ITPA and Academic Achievement: A Survey." *Reading Teacher* 28 (May 1975): 731–741.

Newcomer, Phyllis, B. Hare, D. Hammill, and J. McGettigan. "Construct Validity of the ITPA." *Exceptional Children* 40 (April 1974): 509–510.

Nichol, Hamish. "Children with Learning Disabilities Referred to Psychiatrists: A Follow-up Study." *Journal of Learning Disabilities* 7 (February 1974): 118–122.

Poteet, James A. *Behavior Modification: A Practical Guide for Teachers.* Minneapolis: Burgess Publishing, 1973.

Reading Today International, "A Fable for Teachers," Vol. III, No. 2 (May 1974): 1.

Roswell, Florence, and Gladys Natchez. *Reading Disability: Diagnosis and Treatment.* New York: Basic Books, 1971.

Siegel, Ernest. "Task Analysis and Effective Teaching." *Journal of Learning Disabilities* 5 (November 1972): 519–532.

Skinner, B. F. "Operant Behavior." *American Psychologist* 18 (1963): 505–515.

Strang, Ruth. *Reading Diagnosis and Remediation.* Newark, Del.: International Reading Association, ERIC-CRIER, 1968.

Strauss, Alfred A., and Laura Lehtinen. *Psychopathology and Education of the Brain-Injured Child,* Vol. 1. New York: Grune & Stratton, 1947.

Thompson, Richard A., and Charles D. Dzuiban. "Criterion-Referenced Reading Tests in Perspective." *Reading Teacher* 37 (December 1973): 292–294.

Ysseldyke, James E., and John Salvia. "A Critical Analysis of the Assumptions Underlying Diagnostic-Prescriptive Teaching." *Exceptional Children* 41 (November 1974): 181–187.

THREE

Learning Disabilities: Theories and Teaching Strategies

7. The Role of Theory

"If you don't know where you are going, any road will take you there." This counsel is as applicable to learning disabilities as other facets of life. Theory is needed to understand the learning problem encountered by the child and to provide a basis for the methodology that will be used. Teaching without theory may follow the road that leads nowhere.

In a visit to a hypothetical classroom, we might see all the children in a room, or in a school district, or even in an entire city, using the latest in educational technology — "Mother Hubbard's Cure-all," enticingly packaged material composed of colorful boxes, machines, and supplementary items. This program, which the publisher assures the user is based on extensive research and the most recent scientific evidence, is purported to cure children with learning disabilities and to improve children without learning disabilities. The program contains all teaching media: films, tapes, ditto sheets, workbooks, computers, muscle exercises, and even books. It also has a teacher's manual that describes the foolproof step-by-step directions on *how* to use the equipment. Everything is carefully described, except *why* a particular activity is to be used. The theoretical basis for the method has been eclipsed by the latest educational technology. The answer to the question of *why* a particular activity is being performed may be that the teacher's manual specified that this activity is to be completed two times a day for a period of three weeks before Book Three can be used with the audio-visual-motor-computer machine.

The point of this somewhat cynical view of children engulfed in orderly technology without a theoretical basis is that such activity may be wasteful. In their enthusiasm to "do something," education students often question the need to study theory. What is needed, they imply, are "practical" methods and techniques to help children. Knowledge of methods and techniques is indispensable, but one must inquire *what* techniques do and *why*. In many classrooms and clinics across the country, teachers are busily engaged in neat, orderly techniques, completing page after page or step after step in sequential fashion without knowing why. As a result, much of the work is probably wasteful of all resources — time, effort, money — and, most important, children. There has been too great an emphasis in some classes on practical arts and practical academics, with a neglect of the theory underlying the methodology.

THEORY AND LEARNING DISABILITIES

An understanding of the theories and concepts contributing to the field of learning disabilities is a basic requirement for people in the profession. Theory provides perspective for viewing the various branches of the field. It also helps to sort and evaluate the bewildering deluge of new materials, techniques, machines and gadgets, methods and mediums confronting the educator (Lerner 1968).

Theories in this context are meant to be working statements. As John Dewey (1946) expressed it, "They are not meant to be ideas frozen into absolute standards masquerading as eternal truth or programs rigidly adhered to; rather, theory is to serve as a guide in systematizing knowledge and as a working concept to be modified in the light of new knowledge." This process of theory building can be useful in separating what we know from what we believe or infer. Dewey contended that theory is the most practical of all things.

The purpose of theory is to bring form, coherence, and meaning to what we observe in the real world. Theory is practical in that it provides a guide for action, creates a catalyst for further research and theory building, and clarifies and structures the processes of thought. Without a theoretical basis for diagnosis and treatment, decisions are based on faith in what the experts say, intuitive homilies and principles, or the bandwagon approach to decisions in education — the use of materials or techniques that appear to be popular at the moment.

What is needed in both learning disabilities and special education — if they are to continue as dynamic and growing fields of study — is the development of conceptual models on which to build treatment. Progress in special education has been hampered by practices whereby children have been diagnosed only for the purpose of classifying them within a certain educational category and finally removing such children from the mainstream of general education to isolated special education classes and schools. Diagnosis in the past has been a search for an appropriate label, such as "mentally retarded," "perceptually impaired," "emotionally disturbed," "minimally brain injured," or some other such term that would permit the child to be enrolled in some special group. Once the goal of placement was achieved, the diagnostic process was thought to be completed. Research studies have indicated that such isolation has not, in fact, been the best kind of treatment for these children.

The practice of special classification and educational placement has been acceptable to those in general education, since it does succeed in removing pressures on regular teachers and pupils, although often at the expense of the handicapped child. Kirk (1964) and others state that special education research strongly indicates that such procedures have not been successful. Indeed, in the case of mentally retarded pupils, children who stayed in the regular grades made as much or more progress as those who were placed in special education classes. Special education as it has operated in the past is obsolete (Dunn 1968).

Instead of emphasizing procedures of identification, classification, and special education placement, we should concentrate on the specific areas of learning difficulties found in children who are not progressing in school as expected. Those responsible for special education should stop trying to squeeze children who have learning problems into the existing categories of special education programs by fitting them with labels that make them eligible for special classes. To help children with school learning disorders, we must recognize, diagnose, and treat specific areas of learning difficulty. Conceptual models and frameworks are needed to analyze each of these areas of learning difficulty and to develop teaching strategies that will help children improve in each of these areas (Dunn 1968).

The role of theory in the field of learning disabilities, then, is to develop conceptual frameworks for approaching each of the broad areas in which children have difficulty learning. The conceptual models discussed as theories of learning disabilities in Part Three are organized within the following broad areas: motor development, perception and memory, language skills, cognitive skills, and personality and behavioral development. For each of these broad areas, several theories or conceptual models are presented.

LEARNING DISABILITIES AND
SPECIAL EDUCATION

The cross-categorical movement in special education, as discussed in Chapter 3, assigns a pivotal role to the field of learning disabilities. The field of special education evolved, historically, as a collection of categories of atypical children, i.e., children who were visually impaired, hearing impaired, mentally retarded, physically handicapped, speech impaired, emotionally disturbed, and so on. Each category of special education was established when there was sufficient interest in that type of exceptionality, and learning disabilities is the most recent category to join the classification system. The categorical classification system paved the way for many kinds of decisions: labeling a child, organizing special education programs, budgeting, teaching education, and curriculum planning.

The utility of the traditional or historical classification system is currently under serious question (Dunn 1968, Quay 1968, Schwartz 1971, Reynolds and Balow 1972). The various categories are not, in fact, discrete and separate entities, but they have much in common with each other. Because this system of classification may not provide the optimal way to cope with many of the problems in special education, an alternative classification system has been suggested — one that will cut across the commonalities of the categories. What is suggested is a functional system that will focus on teaching and on the learning disorders common to all the categories. Functional categories could be divided by areas of learning problems rather than by types of exceptionality.

Figure 7.1 shows a matrix relating the *historical categories* of special education to the *functional categories* of learning. The functional classification provides a new perspective of special education. Rather than making decisions regarding budgeting, curriculum planning, and placement on the basis of historical categories, they could be made on the basis of functional activities, using a systems-analysis approach (Lerner 1974, Lerner and James 1975).

The field of learning disabilities could be broadly viewed as the study of

HISTORICAL CATEGORIES	FUNCTIONAL CATEGORIES					
	Motor Development	Perception	Language	Cognitive Development	Social Development	Others...
Mentally Retarded						
Visually Impaired						
Hearing Impaired						
Crippled						
Speech Impaired						
Emotionally Disturbed						
Others...						

Figure 7.1 Matrix of historical categories and functional categories

From J. W. Lerner. "Systems Analysis and Special Education." *Journal of Special Education* 7 (Spring 1973):19.

learning disturbances, which provides a key to the problems of special education. Since most children in special education have learning problems, knowledge of the field of learning disabilities should enhance the effectiveness of all persons involved in the field.

LEARNING DISABILITIES AND GENERAL EDUCATION

The field of learning disabilities also provides a way of bridging the gap between special education and general education, which currently seem to be moving closer together. As stated earlier, special educators realize that problems in special education will not be solved by isolating exceptional children and that there are many benefits to be obtained from placement in a regular classroom. At the same time, changes are occurring in general education. The present philosophy of general education makes it more adaptable to the problems of the atypical child; and schools today are more concerned with individual differences. Moreover, schools have developed more flexible organizational patterns, there are better trained teachers and more ancillary school personnel available, the curriculum is more flexible, and a greater variety of teaching materials and media are to be found in the regular schools and classrooms.

One administrative pattern designed to bridge the gap between regular education and special education offers educational services for handicapped children through a system called *mainstreaming*, which keeps the handicapped child in the regular classroom.

The rapid growth of special education in the past 25 years has been, until very recently, in the direction of removing atypical children from the mainstream of regular education and placing them into special programs. General education supported this movement, which had the effect of transferring the responsibilities of educating children with a variety of learning problems to the domain of special education. Mainstreaming, a placement practice that reverses this trend, has occurred for several reasons. First, as noted earlier, scholars have begun to question classification and isolation, citing research to suggest that self-contained special education classrooms have been disappointing in terms of academic achievement (Goldstein et al. 1965, Kirk 1964). Secondly, parent groups have complained that self-contained special education classrooms discriminated against their children, and they have instigated legislation to prevent such discriminatory practices. Finally, some educators have stated that segregated classes have detrimental effects on the feelings of exceptional children. For these reasons many schools are beginning to integrate special education youngsters into the regular classroom (Grosnick 1971; Yates 1973; Christopolos 1973; Beery 1972, 1974; Birch 1974; Chaffin 1974). (Mainstreaming programs are described in Chapters 3, 13 and 14.)

When the handicapped child is placed in a regular classroom, it is essential that additional guidance be available to help both the child and the classroom teacher. Specialists in learning disabilities should be prepared to serve in this capacity. Regular classroom teachers should also be familiar with the field of learning disabilities as well as special education in general, so that they can identify and help the atypical pupil.

THEORY AND TEACHING STRATEGIES

Emerging from the theories within each of the broad areas of learning disabilities are the teaching methods that are presumed to be appropriate for that area of disability. Strang (1968) and others acknowledge that compared to diagnosis and testing, remediation and treatment have received relatively little attention. There has been more work on theory and diagnosis than on remedial procedures.

The gap between theory and practice is very wide in this field. There is still little evidence of a clear-cut relationship between theoretical discussions of problem areas and remedial methods or therapeutic treatment to resolve these learning difficulties. Teachers, however, cannot wait for researchers to close the gap and to verify teaching methods. Teachers must face children with problems every day and must take some action to help them. Therefore, despite the lack of definitive evidence relating theory to methods, teaching strategies are presented here.

Part Three presents the major theories, developed at a number of different research centers, about each of the areas in which learning disorders occur: motor skills; perception and memory; language; cognitive skills; and maturational, psychological, and social factors. The second part of each of the chapters deals with teaching strategies that have been developed to improve skills in that area. These activities are gathered from many sources, and they are designed to serve as springboards for teaching ideas and plans. They are not meant to be a specific or structured way to teach any particular skill.

Dunn (1968) suggests that a first step in establishing specialized programs of study for children with learning disorders is to evolve conceptual models on which to build treatment. The organization of this section builds upon Dunn's taxonomy of broad areas to be considered. The broad areas, roughly following the hierarchy of developmental stages of human growth and learning discussed in the balance of Part Three include: sensory-motor/perceptual-motor development, perception, memory, language, cognition, social and emotional development. Such a hierarchy of development has a long tradition in scholarly studies. For example, Aristotle in his treatise on the Soul (the ancient Greek equivalent of psychology) uses a very similar hierarchy in his analysis and discussion of the development of the human mind and man's state of knowing (McKeon 1944).

SUMMARY

The role of theory and its relationship to teaching strategies, discussed in this chapter, provides an important framework for the professional person.

This chapter has examined the way in which theory continually changes our perspective on learning disabilities. The impact of the study of learning disabilities on theoretical development in special education was discussed. The relationship between learning disabilities and regular education was analyzed. Finally, the linkage between theory and teaching strategies was reviewed.

FORMAT OF PART THREE

Chapter 8 presents models of *sensory-motor/perceptual-motor* development, and teaching strategies for sensory-motor/perceptual motor development are suggested. In Chapter 9 theories of *perception* and *memory* are discussed, with related teaching strategies. In Chapter 10 various theories of *language* that have an impact on learning disabilities are discussed, followed by suggestions for teaching strategies in five language categories: *listening, speaking, reading, writing,* and *spelling.* Chapter 11 is a discussion of *cognitive development,* with teaching strategies for developing these skills in arithmetic and reading comprehension. Theories of *maturational, psychological,* and *social* factors are discussed in Chapter 12, with teaching strategies for *self-concept development, social perception,* and *behavior modification.*

Although these somewhat arbitrary categories are useful for an organized presentation, the theories formulated by various writers do not always fit the abstraction. Concepts often relate to several of the categories, and the boundaries merge and overlap. However, for the purpose of presentation and discussion, these groupings appear to be useful.

REFERENCES

Beery, Keith. "Mainstreaming: A Problem and an Opportunity for General Education." *Focus on Exceptional Children* 6 (November 1974): 1–7.

————. *Models of Mainstreaming.* San Rafael, Calif.: Dimensions Publishing, 1972.

Birch, Jack W. *Mainstreaming: Educable Mentally Retarded Children in Regular Classes.* Reston, Va.: Council for Exceptional Children, 1974.

Chaffin, Jerry D. "Will the Real 'Mainstreaming' Program Please Stand Up! (Or . . . Should Dunn Have Done It?)" *Focus on Exceptional Children* 6 (October 1974): 1–18.

Christopolos, Florence. "Keeping Exceptional Children in Regular Classes." *Exceptional Children* 39 (April 1973): 569–572.

Dewey, John. *The Public and Its Problems.* Chicago: Gateway Books, 1946.

Dunn, Lloyd M. "Special Education for the Mildly Retarded — Is Much of It Justifiable?" *Exceptional Children* 35 (September 1968): 5–22.

Goldstein, H., H. Moss, and L. Dordon. *The Efficacy of Special Class Training on the Development of Mentally Retarded Children.* U.S. Office of Education, Cooperative Research Project no. 619. Urbana, Ill.: University of Illinois Press, 1965.

Grosnick, Judith K. "Integration of Exceptional Children in Regular Classes: Research and Procedure." *Focus on Exceptional Children* 3 (October 1971): 1–11.

Kirk, S. A. "Research in Education," pp. 57–99 in H. A. Stevens and R. Heber (eds.), *Mental Retardation*. Chicago: University of Chicago Press, 1964.

Lerner, Janet W. "A Global Theory of Reading — and Linguistics." *Reading Teacher* 21 (February 1968): 416–421.

———. "Systems Analysis and Special Education." *Journal of Special Education* 7 (Spring 1973): 15–26.

Lerner, Janet W., and Kenneth W. James. "Systems and Systems Applications in Special Education," pp. 273–307 in L. Mann and D. Sabatino (eds.), *The Second Review of Special Education*. Philadelphia: Journal of Special Education Press, 1974.

McKeon, Richard, ed. *The Basic Works of Aristotle*. New York: Random House, 1941.

Quay, H. "The Facets of Educational Exceptionality: A Conceptual Model for Assessment, Grouping, and Instruction." *Exceptional Children* 35 (January 1968): 25–32.

Reynolds, Maynard C., and Bruce Balow. "Categories and Variables in Special Education." *Exceptional Children* 38 (January 1972): 357–366.

Schwartz, Louis. "A Clinical Teacher Model for Interrelated Areas of Special Education." *Exceptional Children* 37 (April 1971): 565–572.

Strang, Ruth. *Reading Diagnosis and Remediation*. Newark, Del.: International Reading Association, ERIC-CRIER, 1968.

Yates, James R. "Model for Preparing Regular Classroom Teachers for 'Mainstreaming.'" *Exceptional Children* 39 (March 1973): 471–472.

8. Sensory-Motor/ Perceptual-Motor Development

THEORY

Since the beginning of Western civilization philosophers and educators have recognized the important relationship that exists between motor development and learning. Plato places gymnastics at the first level of education in the training of the philosopher-king. Aristotle writes that a person's soul is characterized by two faculties: sense and mind. Spinoza advises, "Teach the body to do many things; this will help you to perfect the mind and to come to the intellectual level of thought." Piaget (1936) emphasizes the importance of early sensory-motor learnings as fundamental building blocks for later, more complex perceptual and cognitive development. From the neuropsychological focus, Hebb (1949) stresses the importance of early motor learnings as an integral part of the buildup of cortical cell assemblies. Interest in the relationship between motor learning and language and cognitive development is evident in the work of Russian scholars such as Luria (1966). It is not surprising, therefore, to find a number of approaches to learning disabilities that focus on the sensory-motor or perceptual-motor development of the child.

Sensory-motor refers to a combination of the input of sensations and output of motor activity. It reflects what is happening in the child's central nervous system. The human being has six sensitivity systems serving as intake channels for obtaining raw data about the world: the visual (sight), auditory (sound), tactual (touch), kinesthetic (muscle feeling), olfactory (smell), and gustatory (taste).

Some writers prefer the term *perceptual-motor* development. The process of organizing the raw data obtained through the senses and interpreting its meaning is called *perception.* Perceptual information, then, is a refinement of sensory information; perceptual-motor refers to the interaction of the various channels of perception with motor activity.

In the motor learning process, several input channels of sensation or perception are integrated with each other and correlated with motor activity, which in turn provide feedback information to correct the perceptions. Thus, in performing a motor activity such as a somersault the child *feels* the surface of the floor; has a body *awareness* of space, changing body position, and balance; *sees* the floor and other objects in relation to changing positions; *hears* the body thump on the floor; and *moves* in a certain fashion. In education, emphasis is usually placed on the visual, auditory, kinesthetic, and tactile systems as the most practical approaches to sensory-motor and perceptual-motor development.

Medical terms are frequently used in discussions of sensory or motor disturbances. The inability to obtain information through one of the input channels or senses when the sense organ is not significantly defective is called *agnosia* (lack of knowledge). To illustrate, auditory agnosia is the inability to recognize or interpret sound even though it is heard; thus an individual might hear but not recognize the ring of a telephone. Difficulty in motor output in performing purposeful movements is called *apraxia.* For example, persons who cannot produce the motor movements required to speak, in spite of the fact that they know the word and do not have paralysis, are subject to apraxia. *Dysgraphia*, a condition in which the person has difficulty performing the motor act of writing, is another type of apraxia.

Professionals from various disciplines, when working with learning-disabled children, investigate motor skills as they are related to their specialties. The physician, the psychologist, the language pathologist, and the educator — all realize the importance of obtaining information on motor functioning as an indicator of learning disability, since sensory-motor and perceptual-motor skills reflect the condition of the child's nervous system, past motor-learning experiences, and the present stage of motor development.

Our present concern for sensory-motor and perceptual-motor development is derived from a rich background of educational and experimental literature, including contributions from Itard (1801), Sequin (1894), Montessori (1912), Piaget (1936), and Gesell and Ilg (1943). The concern for motor development is a recurring theme throughout the history of special education. This section presents several schools of theory representative of current sensory-motor and perceptual-motor approaches to learning disabilities: the *visuomotor theory* of Getman, the *perceptual-motor theory* of Kephart, the *movigenic theory* of Barsch, the *patterning theory of neurological organization* of Doman and Delacato, the *physical education approach* of Cratty, and the *sensory-integration approach* of Ayres. These are not the only motor theories of learning disabilities, but they serve as a vehicle for discussion of the key concepts of motor development and its relationship to learning disabilities.

VISUOMOTOR THEORY: GETMAN

A model of the development of the motor system and its interaction with learning has been devised by Getman (1965). Because Getman is an optometrist, the approach reflects his primary interest in the development of vision, which is equated with perception in this model. Vision is defined as the learned ability to understand things that cannot be touched, tasted, smelled, or heard; it is the process whereby space is perceived as a whole. Vision is differentiated from both sight and acuity: sight is simply response to light, while acuity refers to the clarity of the light pattern striking the retina. Vision, within this framework, is learned and refers to the child's ability to interpret the world and one's own relationship to the world.

VISUOMOTOR MODEL

The visuomotor model of Getman (Figure 8.1) attempts to illustrate the developmental sequences of a child's performance in acquiring motor and perceptual skills. The model is designed to illustrate the dependence of each successive stage of development upon an earlier level. Each level or row is composed of a number of separate activities.

The innate response system: row A. The infant is born with the innate response system, represented by row A, which is the beginning of all learning. The motor responses within this system are unlearned and must be reasonably intact and operable at birth. They include: the *tonic neck reflex*, which is the basic position or starting point from which the child moves; the *startle reflex*, which is a bodily reaction to a sudden loud noise and sudden flash of light; the *light reflex*, at first as a tightening of the eyelids and later as a reduction in the size of the pupil during exposure to bright light; the *grasp reflex*, which is a grasping of objects and is related to atten-

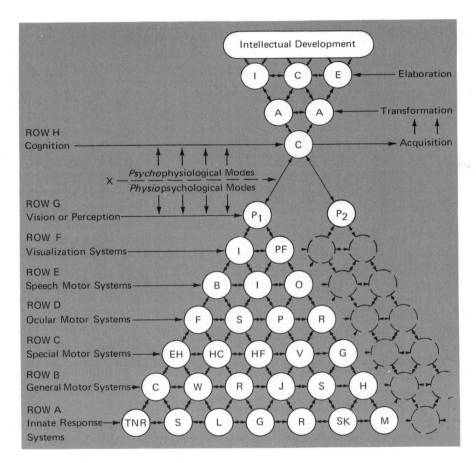

Figure 8.1 The visuomotor complex

From G. N. Getman. "The Visuomotor Complex in the Acquisition of Learning Skills," in J. Hellmuth (ed.), *Learning Disorders, Vol. I.* Seattle, Wash.: Special Child Publications, 1965, p. 60.

tion span; the *reciprocal reflex,* which refers to the facility of thrust and counterthrust of bodily movements; the *stato-kinetic reflex,* the state of relaxed attentiveness or a readiness to act; and the *myotatic reflex,* a stretch reflex system that provides the body with information concerning its own status. The innate response system becomes the basis, then, for all further learning.

The general motor system: row B. The next level of learning, according to Getman, is the general motor system. Row B of the model represents the general motor system of locomotion or mobility skills: *creeping, walking, running, jumping, skipping, hopping.* Through such activities the child is able to build on information obtained in the innate response system, thus acquiring skills of mobility, reciprocity, and coordination. The child who does not master the skills of row B may be awkward and lacking in coordination. Moreover, the child who does not perfect the general motor skills at this level will not be able to build the solid base needed to continue building the pyramid of learning. For this reason, children need the physical activities that will permit the development of general or gross motor skills.

Special motor system: row C. Row C represents special motor systems and builds on the first two levels to more selective and elaborate combinations of motor skills: *eye-hand* relationships, *combinations of two hands* working together, *hand-foot* relationships, *voice* and *gesture* relationships. Children are too often required to perform these fine motor tasks before they have facility with earlier and more basic skills. Getman observes that the child who cannot color a square or cut corners may not have learned to manipulate or move around corners using the entire motor system.

Ocular motor system: row D. Row D represents the ocular motor system. The movement of the eyes must be developed and controlled in a special manner for success in classroom tasks. The ocular system has two information-receiving, processing, and effector circuits — one for each eye — that have to be constantly matched and balanced. Getman contends that skills of eye movement are often taken for granted. Children may test out with perfect 20/20 eyesight, yet have an inadequacy in the bilateral relationships, creating stress or even double vision when doing close academic work. The child must learn to control and team the eyes across the lines of print. The ocular skills include: *fixation,* the ability to visually locate a target; *saccadics,* the visual movement from one target to another; *pursuits,* the ability to have both eyes follow a moving target; and *rotation,* free movement of both eyes in any and all directions.

The speech-motor system: row E. Row 1 of this model refers to the speech-motor and the auditory integration system, which includes the skills of *babbling, imitative speech,* and *original speech.* Getman sees an interplay at this level between vision and language processes. As an optometrist, he believes that skill in the speech-motor system is dependent on efficient and intact visual and ocular systems.

The visualization system. row F. The term *visualization* refers to the ability to recall or remember not only what has previously been seen by the eye, but also what has been heard, touched, or felt. Row F refers to the ability to visualize, recall, or picture a response in one's mind when the original sensory stimulus is not present. All senses (tactile, auditory, sight, kinesthetic, etc.) contribute to this ability. This level of learning is sometimes called imagery.

Two kinds of visualization are considered: *immediate*, whereby one can "see" a coin felt in one's pocket; and *past-future*, whereby one can review an event that happened yesterday or preview an event that will occur tomorrow.

Vision or perception: row G. Row G represents vision or the perceptual event, used in this model as synonymous terms. All the experiences, skills, and systems represented by the underlying levels or rows contribute to vision or the perceptual event. In this model, then, vision or perception is both the result of intact and complete learning in the supporting development levels. Vision or perception is learned through the development of earlier motor skills.

P_2. All of these experiences lead to P_1, a single perceptual event. P_2 signifies another perceptual event reached through a comparable pyramid of experiences. The letter C on the model represents cognition, which is reached through the process of integrating many perceptions. The three levels above cognition represent the higher symbolic and more abstract mental processes leading to intellectual development.

Cognition: row H. Row H represents cognition, and the portion of the model above this point refers to abstractions and elaborations of intellectual development. Cognition and concepts are derived from many interrelating perceptions. The development of cognition and intellectual thought, as presented in this model, is the result of a solid base of the various levels of motor learning.

IMPLICATIONS OF VISUOMOTOR MODEL

The Getman model of learning is one of visual development and learning. The pyramid shape indicates that a solid base of learning is required at each level before moving to the next level with security. Each level of motor learning is more precise and exacting than the preceding system. Getman believes that many learning programs utilized today approach children as if they had successfully achieved the motor and perceptual levels and were moving toward the cognitive levels. Such programs may not succeed if the foundation is not solidly built because cognitive learning will then be insecure and shaky. The implication is that many children need more experience in the base levels of motor development.

What is the implication of this framework in the case of Tony? Tony is unable to read; but he also never learned to skip, is awkward in running, and cannot keep his balance while hopping on one foot. In the light of this model, Tony's problem in reading can be traced to an inadequate development of the general motor system. The view suggests that Tony needs more practice and experience in perfecting motor skills.

Several teaching programs based on this model have been designed. One, *Developing Learning Readiness: A Visual-Motor Tactile Skills Program* (Getman et al. 1968), has activities for six areas of development: general coordination, practice in balance, practice in eye-hand coordination, practice in eye movement, practice in form recognition, and practice in visual memory.

The visuomotor model has been criticized for presenting an overly simplified picture of the development of learning, for overextending the role of vision, and for overemphasizing the role of visual perception (Myers and Hammill 1969). The fact that Getman is an optometrist is reflected in the key role that vision plays, while the role of language and speech in the learning process is relatively neglected. An inference can be drawn from this model that the blind or crippled child who could not experience the hierarchy would be unable to achieve skills of cognition or abstraction. Such children, of course, are not necessarily severely limited in mental growth. Further, the model does not clarify how the child moves from motor and physical development to the cognition stages of learning. The complex role of feedback in providing information and another mode of learning is omitted from the model. Finally empirical evidence to support the theoretical framework is lacking. Discussion of research of the Getman program is included in the section, "Discussion of Motor Theories," later in this chapter.

PERCEPTUAL-MOTOR THEORY: KEPHART

The perceptual-motor theory of learning disabilities put forth by Kephart (1963, 1967, 1971) postulates that normal perceptual-motor development helps a child establish a solid and reliable concept of the world. In Kephart's terms, the child establishes a stable *perceptual-motor world*. This approach examines the normal sequential development of motor patterns and motor generalizations and compares the motor development of children with learning problems to that of normal children.

Normal children are able to develop a rather stable perceptual-motor world by the time they encounter academic work at the age of six. For many children with learning disabilities, however, their perceptual-motor world is unstable and unreliable. These children encounter problems when confronted with symbolic materials because they have an inadequate orientation to what Kephart calls the basic realities of the universe that surrounds them — specifically the dimensions of space and time. To deal with symbolic materials the child must learn to make some rather precise observations about space and time and relate them to objects and events.

Most educational approaches assume that these relationships have already been established and therefore build upon presumed competencies in programs designed to develop conceptual and cognitive abilities. The perceptual-motor theory suggests that for many children such assumptions cannot be made, for these children have not had the necessary experiences to internalize a comprehensive and consistent scheme of the world. These children have been unable to adequately organize their information-processing systems to the degree necessary to benefit from such a curriculum. As a consequence, they are disorganized motorically, perceptually, and cognitively.

DEVELOPMENT OF MOTOR PATTERNS

An individual's first learnings are motor learnings — muscular and motor responses. Through motor behavior the child interacts with and learns about the world. According to Kephart, learning difficulty may begin at this stage because the child's motor responses do not evolve into motor patterns. The differentiation between a *motor skill* and a *motor pattern* is an important element of this framework.

A *motor skill* is a motor act that may have a high degree of precision, but it has a purpose of performing a specific act or the accomplishment of a certain end. The *motor pattern* may have less precision, but it has more variability. The purpose of the motor pattern is broader, beyond mere performance; it provides feedback and more information to the individual. For example, throwing a ball at a target may be a motor skill, but the ability to utilize this skill as part of a baseball game may be called a motor pattern. Another illustration is Kephart's use of the trampoline. He is not trying to develop expertise in trampoline but, rather, using the activity to develop certain motor patterns.

When outside pressure is exerted on the child to perform a certain motor act not within the child's current sequential development, such a skill may be acquired; but it becomes a *splinter skill.* Splinter skills are not an integral part of the orderly sequential development. Kephart illustrates a splinter skill with the example of a child who was required to learn to write even though he had not developed the physiological readiness to perform this act. The child acquired a splinter skill permitting him to write his name by memorizing a series of fine finger movements that were unrelated to the wrist or other parts of the arm or of the body (Kephart 1963). Some people dance as though it were a splinter skill, and the movement of their legs seems unrelated to the rest of their bodies. Barsch (1966) takes a similar approach in his discussion of movement training: "Movement training is not for the arms and legs; it is for alignment and balance. Movement training is not for muscle development but rather for kinesthetic awareness."

MOTOR GENERALIZATIONS

Extensions and combinations of motor patterns lead to motor generalizations. *Motor generalizations* are the integration and incorporation of motor patterns into broader motor tasks. In the realm of intellectual development, generalizations are formed by combining concepts into higher abstractions of thought. Similarly, in motor learning, motor generalizations are the result of combining and integrating many motor patterns.

Four motor generalizations are discussed by Kephart as important to success in school: balance and maintenance of posture, contact, locomotion, and receipt and propulsion. The relationship of each of these generalizations to learning is discussed in the following paragraphs.

Balance and maintenance of posture. This motor generalization involves those activities by which the child becomes aware of and maintains a relationship to the force of gravity. Gravity is a basic force and the point of origin for all learning, so it is very important that the child learn to be aware of the pull of gravity and learn to manipulate her body accordingly. The child gropes with gravitational forces in almost all situations — for example, when she first lifts her head against the gravitational pull; stands in an erect position; or keeps her balance in walking, going across a balance beam, or tandem (heel-to-toe) walking.

Contact. Through the motor generalization of contact, the child obtains information about things in the world by manipulating objects. The activities of reaching for, grasping, and releasing objects enable the child to investigate the objects via many sensory avenues, including looking, tasting, mouthing, listening, feeling, and even smelling. Through such extensive sensory-motor activities, the child observes the attributes and characteristics of objects and eventually develops skill in form perception, figure-ground relationships, and others.

Locomotion. A third kind of motor generalization is locomotion, which enables the child to observe relationships between one object and another in space. The motor patterns of crawling, walking, running, jumping, and hopping permit the child to move through space to investigate the properties of surrounding space and the relationship between objects. She now moves her body to explore "out there."

Receipt and propulsion. The first three generalizations were static; objects remained in a place in space. *Receipt and propulsion* are dynamic; now the child learns about the movement of objects in space through motor activities such as catching, pushing, pulling, throwing, and batting. According to Kephart, the child is at first egocentric, seeing his own body as the center of the universe and the point of origin. All directions are interpreted in terms of movements away, from, or toward himself: a ball rolling past him at first appears to be approaching him; but as it crosses the midline or center of his body, it appears to be going away from him. The concept of the midline plays an important part in Kephart's framework of laterality and directionality. He suggests the child must learn to deal with three midline planes within his body: (1) the lateral, or side-to-side midline; (2) the forward and backward midline; and (3) the vertical, or upper-to-lower midline. *Receipt* refers to those activities in which the child makes observations of objects coming toward him; *propulsion* refers to activities and observations concerning objects pushed away from his body. By combining these movements and observations, he also investigates movements lateral to himself, up and down, back and forth, and left and right.

It is through the four motor generalizations that children gain information about the space structure of their world.

PERCEPTUAL-MOTOR MATCH

As children gain information through motor generalizations, they also begin to note perceptual information. Since they cannot investigate all objects in motor fashion, they begin to learn to investigate them perceptually. Perceptual data only becomes meaningful when it is correlated with previously learned motor information; thus, perceptual information must be matched or aligned with the built-up body of motor information. Kephart terms the process of comparing and collating the two kinds of input data perceptual-motor match.

We know that the perceptual world is one of many seeming distortions. For example, when a circle is seen from an angle, it looks like an ellipse, or from certain angles the circle may appear to be a straight line. A rectangle from an angle may look like a trapezoid. This distortion of perception is utilized by the artist in creating perspective. In the process of perceptual-motor match, the distorted perceptions are equated to the stored information developed through motor generalizations and the distorted perceptions are thereby adjusted.

If the perceptual-motor match is not properly made, the child lives in two conflicting worlds — a perceptual world and a motor world. The child cannot trust the information being received because the two kinds do not match and cannot be collated. The world for such a child is indeed an uncomfortable, inconsistent, and unreliable place, and, unsure of what reality is, the child's behavior frequently becomes bizarre. Children who constantly touch objects may do so because they are not sure what they are seeing. One teacher of children with learning disabilities reported that whenever she wore a certain polka-dot dress, the children wanted to touch the dots because they did not understand what they saw. Figure 8.2 illustrates the match that must be made between the motor information of what a tabletop looks like and the perceptual information of what one actually views. The perceptual view of the table is distorted and must be matched to the motor information.

Another illustration of a motor-perceptual match that must be made is the apparent equal height of two unequal structures. From a certain perspective, the 555-foot Washington Monument in Washington, D.C., appears to be equal to the height of a 74-foot national Christmas tree. The child who has not developed perception of shapes, such as squares and rectangles, will have many difficulties in school subjects that assume such perceptual ability.

According to this view, vision is the sensory avenue that gives the greatest amount of information, since the child learns to explore objects by eye that

Motor Information   Perceptual Information

Figure 8.2 Two views of a tabletop

previously had to be explored by hand. Ocular control, therefore, is important in the establishment of perceptual-motor match.

DEVELOPMENT OF TIME STRUCTURE

The preceding discussion of the Kephart framework was largely in terms of a space structure; but the development of a time structure also begins with motor responses, continues with perceptual information, and then develops into conceptual information. Kephart identifies three aspects of time important to learning: _synchrony_, or the concept of simultaneity — things happening at the same time; _rhythm_, or equal time intervals; and _sequence_, or the ordering of events on the temporal scale.

As with the dimension of space, many children with learning disabilities have an unstable world of time. One example of timing _synchrony_ in motor movement is the changing of direction in running. All parts of the body involved in running must be ready for the change at a simultaneous moment in time or running movement will be awkward and clumsy. Another example of synchrony of timing is an activity that requires two parts of the body to perform a movement at the same time; for example, in cutting food two simultaneous hand movements are required.

Through _rhythm_ the development of a temporal scale of the world is acquired. Motor activities such as walking, running, skipping, and talking require a sense of rhythm. Another function related to the temporal scale is awareness of time units. Some children cannot estimate time and cannot differentiate between a minute and an hour. Other children with a rhythm disorder cannot imitate tapped-out rhythm patterns.

Sequence is the third aspect of time. The child learns that events have an order in time. To perform activities, certain body movements must follow others. For example, in playing jacks the girl who tries to pick up the jacks before throwing the ball has a sequence problem. The child who confuses the order of sounds in talking and says *pusghetti* instead of *spaghetti*, or *cimmanon* instead of *cinnamon*, or *flutterby* for *butterfly* may have a time-sequencing problem.

A concept of time, then, in addition to space, is established through perceptual-motor learning. The rhythm of speech, the timing of movement, the temporal sequence of steps in an activity are dimensions of time in perceptual-motor learning.

IMPLICATIONS OF PERCEPTUAL-MOTOR FRAMEWORK

In analyzing the case of Tony, a child with learning disabilities, the perceptual-motor approach suggests that the basis of Tony's academic difficulties may be a more fundamental disturbance than an inability to deal with abstract symbols. The theory implies that children like Tony have a disturbed orientation to the physical universe that surrounds them. By helping such children establish a more secure orientation to the physical universe, many of their academic problems can be alleviated.

One test built on this framework is the *Purdue Perceptual-Motor Survey* (Roach and Kephart 1966). Kephart (1971) describes a teaching program developed from this theory includes the following skills: walking a board or balance beam, jumping and hopping, identification of body parts, imitation of movement, ability to move through an obstacle course, movement of arms and legs (angels in the snow), steppingstones, chalkboard drawing, ocular pursuits, and visual achievement forms (copying geometric shapes).

The perceptual-motor theory of learning disabilities concentrates on perceptual and motor development with relatively little emphasis on the transition from this development to academic and cognitive development, and, consequently, the framework neglects to formulate guidelines for helping the child bridge this gap. The role of speech and language in the learning process is not clearly incorporated within the theory. As noted in the section "Discussion of Motor Theories" later in this chapter, there is limited research evidence to indicate that practice in the Kephart motor training directly results in increased academic achievement.

MOVIGENIC THEORY: BARSCH

The moviegenic theory of learning difficulties, developed by Barsch (1965, 1967, 1968), proposes that difficulties in learning are related to the learner's inefficient interaction with space.

THEORY OF MOVIGENICS

Movigenics is defined as a theory of movement as it relates to learning. It is the study of the origin and development of patterns of movement in human beings and the relationship of these movements to learning efficiency. The concept of movigenics is based upon Barsch's premise that human learning is highly related to motor efficiency — to the individual's performance of basic movement patterns.

> Perception is movement and movement is perception. According to this view, any effort to enrich perception and cognition must be initiated as a frank approach to attaining the highest possible state of efficiency in the fundamental patterns of physical movement (Barsch 1968, p. 299).

Movement and learning are seen as reciprocal elements throughout the life of the individual. Barsch (1967) has formulated 10 theses that provide the foundation of the movigenic theory:

1. *Man is designed for movement.* Movement is the key to life. The human being is designed to move and is in constant motion in all activities.

2. *The objective of movement is survival.* Just as the history of humanity has been a story of survival, so each individual must learn to survive in the world. Survival is dependent on the individual's ability to move efficiently. There are many kinds of survival: physiological, psychological, and environmental.

3. *Movement occurs in an energy surround.* The human being is a constant and active seeker of information whose survival depends on skill in attaining it.

4. *Man acquires information through his percepto-cognitive system.* The human being is capable of converting energy forms into information. The six systems of sensitivity for obtaining information are taste, touch, muscle feeling, smell, sight, and hearing.

5. *The terrain of movement is space.* Movement occurs within space; therefore, in learning to move efficiently, human beings must learn to cope with space.

6. *Developmental momentum thrusts the learner toward maturity.* Developmental momentum is a continuous and compelling force that moves an individual toward a peak of growth.

7. *Movement occurs in a climate of stress.* Man lives in a climate of stress. A certain level of stress is essential for learning and is part of life. However, each individual has a stress threshold beyond which he can no longer function.

8. *Feedback is essential for efficiency.* The human organism can be viewed as a homeostatic system seeking a steady state of equilibrium. An individual's "feedback system" provides the organism with information that enables one to make corrections in movement to maintain a steady state.

9. *Development occurs in segments of sequential expansion.* Each segment of development in a human being develops in a sequential, orderly fashion from the simple to the highly complex. However, since all types of behavior may not develop at the same rate, there may be an imbalance in the development of various segments of behavior.

10. *Communication of efficiency is derived from the visual spatial phenomenon called language.* An individual's language or symbol system is a reflection of background and experience. Movement efficiency is thus a crucial variable in the development of language efficiency.

TEACHING MOVIGENICS

In addition to describing the movigenic theory, Barsch deals with two essential components of the movigenic program: the necessary attributes of the teacher of movigenics and the nature of the curriculum in a movigenic program.

The teacher of this program must have certain essential attitudes, according to Barsch, including a firm belief in the importance of movement to learning, the ability to flexibly arrange the furniture of the classroom to create an environment that will encourage the learning of movement within space, and an awareness of developmental growth.

The curriculum designed to improve motor efficiency should have several goals, including developing body awareness, developing flexibility in movement, learning to readily shift from one motor movement to another, and changing both the rate and pattern of movement.

IMPLICATIONS OF MOVIGENIC FRAMEWORK

The movigenic perspective would suggest that Tony, who cannot perform academic tasks, has not had the opportunity to learn efficient movement under a teacher and curriculum geared to the goal of movement efficiency. The movigenic approach presumes that when basic motor patterns have been established and the individual achieves movement efficiency, the academic content will be easily accomplished.

Barsch separates the two fields, learning disabilities and motor training, stating that it is by chance that their development coincided. He contends that although children with learning disabilities need motor training, such training is also required by a much larger population than those identified as children with learning disabilities (Barsch 1968).

As with the previous motor models of learning presented in this chapter, the roles that language development and auditory skills play in learning are relatively neglected. Moreover, guidelines to help the teacher bridge the gap from motor skill devlopment to academic skills are not clearly specified.

PATTERNING THEORY OF NEUROLOGICAL ORGANIZATION: DOMAN AND DELACATO

The "patterning" theory of neurological organization — developed by a physical therapist, Glenn Doman, and an educator, Carl Delacato, in their work at the Institute of the Achievement of Human Potential in Philadelphia (Delacato 1966) — has been among the most controversial of the motor approaches to learning problems. The goal of this framework, according to its authors, is to establish in brain-injured, mentally retarded, and reading-disabled children the neurological developmental stages observed in normal children. The authors also suggest that the procedures are beneficial with normal children as well.

PATTERNING CONCEPTS

The concept providing the basis for the methods advocated is that the well-functioning child develops what the authors call "full neurological organization." The theory assumes that "the ontogeny recapitulates the phylogeny," or that the process that an individual member of the human species goes through in maturing follows the same developmental stages of the entire species in the long process of evolution. Thus, in the progression toward full neurological organization, the human being proceeds in an orderly way anatomically in the central nervous system, progressing sequentially through higher levels of the nervous system: (1) spinal cord medula, (2) the pons, (3) the midbrain, (4) the cortex, and finally (5) full neurological organization or the establishment of cortical hemispherical dominance.

Doman and Delacato maintain that there are six functional attainments of the human being: motor skills (mobility in walking upright and in cross-pattern fashion), speech, writing, reading (visual skills), understanding speech (auditory), and stereognosis (tactile). The attainment of these six skills is related to and dependent on the individual's anatomical progress toward neurological organization.

The failure to pass through a certain sequence of development at any stage indicates poor neurological organization and will result in problems in mobility or communication. Proponents of the theory maintain that by measuring the level of neurological organization, it becomes theoretically possible to prescribe activities that will improve neurological development and thereby eliminate or prevent learning disorders. Following are the kinds of behavior that are evaluated to determine the child's level of neurological development (Delacato 1963):

Spinal cord medulla level. Normal reflex movements of the infant indicate good neurological organization at this level.

Pons level. Good neurological development at the pons level is evaluated through the child's sleeping position; it should be appropriate to the child's laterality.

Midbrain level. Good neurological organization at this level is indicated by the child's creeping pattern; it should be smooth, rhythmical cross-pattern creeping.

Early cortex level. Good neurological organization at this level is indicated by walking that is cross-patterned, balanced, smooth, and rhythmical.

Cortical hemispheric dominance. The highest level of neurological organization is achieved with cortical hemispheric dominance. This is indicated with a clear dominance of one side of the body; the dominant hand, eye, and foot are all on the same side of the body and consistent with the dominant hemisphere of the brain.

Those neurological stages that are found to be underdeveloped are overcome by engaging the child in activities designed to develop those levels of neurological growth. For children who are physically unable to perform the prescribed motor activities, the activities are passively imposed on their nervous systems by moving their limbs. According to the theory, when the neurological organization is completed, the problem in learning is overcome. The sequence of stages toward the attainment of mobility are (Doman, et al. 1967): (1) rolling over, (2) crawling in a circle or backwards, (3) crawling without a pattern, (4) crawling homologous, (5) crawling homolaterally, (6) crawling cross-pattern, (7) creeping without pattern, (8) creeping homologous, (9) creeping homolaterally, (10) creeping cross-pattern, (11) cruising (walking holding), (12) walking without pattern, (13) walking cross-pattern.

The treatment requires children to pass through the above sequential stages to develop neurological organization. In severe cases of brain damage, the patterning is imposed by adults who manipulate the limbs and head of the child in prescribed positions determined by the authors. This "patterning" is to be carried out in strict observance to the plan for five minutes at least four times each day, seven days each week (Doman 1967). Other techniques include sensory stimulation; breathing exercises; restriction of fluids, salt, and sugar; early teaching of reading; sleeping in prescribed body positions; elimination of exposure to music; and training of eye and hand use. The goal of all of these activities is the establishment of hemispheric dominance and thereby full neurological organization.

IMPLICATIONS OF PATTERNING THEORY

The approach and techniques suggested in this program have been used in many types of cases including individual therapy with severely retarded and brain-injured children as well as group classroom instruction with normal children. Through the patterning approach, Tony must relearn and perform each stage of motor learning identified by the developers of the theory to overcome his problem. He must relearn to properly creep, crawl, walk, etc., since these motor activities are presumed to have an effect on reorganizing the structure of his brain.

A number of reports of the success of the method have been presented in the literature (Delacato 1966). However, other writers, including educators (Robbins 1966), researchers (Glass and Robbins 1967), and medical and health specialists (Freeman 1967), have found the theory, approach, treatment, and research to be lacking.

Ten medical, health, and educational organizations have jointly expressed concern about the Doman-Delacato treatment of neurologically handicapped children in an official statement (Cruickshank 1968), giving the following reasons:

1. Promotional methods appear to put parents in a position where they cannot refuse such treatment without calling into question their adequacy and motivation as parents;
2. The regimens prescribed are so demanding and inflexible that they may lead to neglect of other family members' needs;
3. It is asserted that if therapy is not carried out as rigidly prescribed, the child's potential will be damaged and that anything less than 100 percent effort is useless.
4. Restrictions are often placed upon age-appropriate activities of which the child is capable, such as walking or listening to music, though unwarranted by any supportive data and knowledge of long-term results published to date;
5. Claims are made for rapid and conclusive diagnosis according to a "Developmental Profile" of no known validity. No data on which construction of the Profile has been based has ever been published, nor do we know of any attempt to cross-validate it against any accepted methods;
6. Undocumented claims are made for cures in a substantial number of cases, extending even beyond disease states to making normal children superior, easing world tensions, and possibly "hastening the evolutionary process";
7. Without supporting data, Doman and Delacato have indicated many typical child-rearing practices as limiting a child's potential, increasing thereby the anxiety of already burdened and confused parents.

In spite of strong opposition from doctors and educators to the patterning method, many parents have become ardent advocates of the theory and techniques. In severe cases where all other professionals had counseled parents that there was no hope, patterning was the one avenue of action open. Many of these parents claim the method was successful and are enthusiastic supporters of the technique. The question is whether improvement is due to the techniques or to other factors.

MOTOR LEARNING AS PHYSICAL EDUCATION: CRATTY

Cratty (1969, 1971, 1973), a physical educator, emphasizes the importance of movement games as a way of helping the child with learning problems. Although Cratty is cautious about the academic benefits of motor training, he believes that there are indications that gross movement activities can provide a sensory experience that will enhance general classroom learning.

Cratty provides numerous examples of how physical education can be related to classroom learning. For example, the child's attention span can be lengthened through games and physical activities; the increased ability to pay attention can hopefully be transferred to academic learning. Cratty presents the learning of letters as a physical activity by placing large letters on a playground and devising games in which the child runs or walks over the shape of letters. Activities that involve the total body may also serve to focus the attention of the hyperactive child.

Cratty notes that a child's ability to play games can serve to enhance self-concept, social acceptance by peers, and academic performance. Motor activities — such as riding bicycles, playing games, and dancing — signal the emergence of various developmental levels. Inability to accomplish these activities with reasonable proficiency may precipitate a chain of failure.

Cratty (1971) has developed a motor program designed to use games for enhancing academic learning.

SENSORY-INTEGRATION APPROACH: AYRES

Ayres (1965, 1968, 1972, 1973) presents a theoretical construct of motor learning from the perspective of occupational therapy. She believes that treatment should be directed toward influencing basic neurophysiological integration through control of sensorimotor behavior. Human learning is seen as a highly complex function of the central nervous system. The human brain, which has evolved over millions of years of evolutionary development, is adaptable and has developed in response to the complex cognitive needs of the human being. The brain's ability to function effectively, however, is dependent on lower neural structure. Since the child's brain still has the quality of plasticity or adaptability, the assumption is that the brain of a child with motor defects can be reorganized through activities designed to enhance sensory integration and thereby normalize behavior.

Ayres (1969) has developed a battery of motor tests that includes tests in motor accuracy, perceptual-motor skills, figure-ground visual perception, kinesthesia and tactile perception, and space perception.

DISCUSSION OF MOTOR THEORIES

Sensory-motor and perceptual-motor approaches to learning disabilities emphasize the motor development of the child and assume that there is a sequence of developmental stages to be successfully learned by the child before the next stage can be added. Once the child's present developmental stage is determined, remediation consists of helping the child learn skills at the most basic level. After those skills have been successfully attained, the child moves on to learning the skills at the next sequential level. Theorists who stress the importance of motor learning conclude that when the various sensory-motor and perceptual-motor systems have been fully developed and integrated, the child is ready for the next stages of development — perception and concept formation. Concept formation depends on intact perception, which in turn depends on sound motor development. The authors of the motor theories of learning disabilities caution that a preoccupation with conceptual and cognitive learning may lead to a neglect of the basic foundation of motor learning. As a consequence, there may be gaps in the developmental sequence that will affect all future learning by either limiting or distorting it. In this view the study of human movement is inseparable from the study of learning because as human beings move, they learn. An understanding of the dynamics of learning thereby necessarily involves the understanding of movement.

RESERVATIONS

Research with exercises to develop motor skills and thereby improve academic learning is currently in progress, but thus far there is little conclusive evidence to indicate that motor programs result in significant academic gains. As a group, children who have difficulty learning appear also to have difficulty with motor performance. One hypothesis for this high correlation is that the motor problem is not the direct cause of the learning problem, but, rather, a concomitant difficulty that children are likely to have. According to this view, training in motor skills leads to improvement in motor learning, but it does not necessarily lead to improvement in academic ability and learning. A further consideration is that the role of language development in learning is relatively neglected in most motor theories. Finally, the correspondence between motor growth and learning can be questioned by the observation that some children with superior motor skills are unable to learn to read or to succeed in other academic areas, while some children with excellent academic skills are inferior in motor performance and physical activities.

One study that reviewed research of motor programs in order to determine the efficacy of motor training was reported by Goodman and Hammill (1973) and Hammill, Goodman, and Wiederholt (1974). Of the 42 research studies reviewed, only 16 satisfied their criteria for an adequate study: (1) involving at least 20 experimental subjects; (2) providing at least 12 weeks, or 60 sessions, of training; and (3) utilizing an experimental-control group design. The projects mainly used Getman- and Kephart-type activities. Analysis of the research indicated that of the 16 "better" designed reports, 11 were concerned with the effects of visual-motor training on visual-motor performance. The results of these training programs were termed insignificant in this review. Eight studies measured the effects of visual-motor training on school readiness. Only three of the nine post-test scores of readiness used in these studies favored the trained subjects. Ten studies measured the effects of visual-motor training on intelligence, school achievement, and language functions. Experimental subjects performed significantly better in only 6 of 15 post-tests. Overall, the authors concluded that motor training procedures did not demonstrate that the techniques significantly improved readiness skills, intelligence, academic achievement, or perceptual-motor performance.

Other studies that have failed to find a significant relationship between motor training and reading achievement are Spache (1968), Harris (1968), and Grattan and Matin (1965).

PERSPECTIVES

While studies such as those described above seriously question the efficacy of motor training, we cannot conclude that motor development is unimportant or that this aspect of learning should be discarded. Rather, these studies suggest that plans are needed for building the bridge between motor training and academic learning. Efficient motor movement may be a prerequisite but alone it is insufficient. We still must teach academic skills. As an analogy, a child who cannot read because he needs corrective lenses may still be unable to read after he obtains the spectacles. While the glasses are needed to see, successful reading instruction is also required. In discussing motor training, Early and Sharpe (1970, p. 241) advise,

> When abilities basic to academic learning are improved, further training must be instituted in order to assure the successful transfer of skills to academic achievement. We cannot assume that this transfer will be realized automatically when we consider the persistence of old attitudes and habits.

Another factor to be considered is that assessment devices are very gross and insensitive measures. The growth of a child who is happier, more confident, more available for learning and has begun to make progress in school cannot be measured by the typical achievement test. Moreover, some clinicians have observed that work in motor development may bring about unanticipated and probably unmeasurable improvement. For example, when the motor training requires the child to go *through, under, over, between,* and *around* obstacles, the child is also learning important language concepts. Finally, perhaps a more viable model of learning is needed to see the relationships among the various components of learning. A systems-analysis model of learning, rather than a cause-effect model, may be closer to the way the child's learning system operates. Thus, the improvement of a single component within such a complex system will not by itself change the total system to any measurable extent (Lerner 1973, Lerner and James 1974). Perhaps changes in several components are needed to trigger a measurable improvement.

The conviction that movement and motor learning provide essential learning experiences for the child has a long and respectable tradition in the history of educational thought. Undoubtedly, motor learning is important in the total development of the child. Its precise contribution to academic learning, however, is being questioned and this questioning requires additional investigation.

TESTS OF MOTOR DEVELOPMENT

Among the available tests to measure motor development and to screen for motor deficits are: *Purdue Perceptual Motor Survey, Heath Railwalking*

Test, Lincoln-Oseretsky Motor Development Scale, and the _Southern California Test Battery for Assessment of Dysfunction_ (which includes the _Southern California Kinesthesia and Tactile Perception Tests_, the _Southern California Figure-Ground Visual Perception Test_, the _Southern California Motor Accuracy Test_, the _Southern California Perceptual-Motor Tests_, and the _Ayres Space Test_). Descriptive data concerning these tests appear in Appendix C.

TEACHING STRATEGIES

Jim is an example of children with academic learning problems who also show indications of immature motor development, laterality confusion, and poor awareness of their own bodies. Jim was brought to a learning disabilities clinic at age 12 for a diagnosis because he was doing badly in school, particularly in reading and arithmetic. An individual intelligence test indicated that his intelligence was normal, and a screening test for auditory and visual acuity showed no abnormalities. His oral language skills seemed good for his age. At first Jim's posture gave the impression of being unusually straight, almost military in bearing. During the motor testing, however, it was evident that this seemingly straight posture was actually rigidity. When a change in balance occurred because of a required movement, he was unable to make the correction within his body position and his relationship to gravity. He fell off the balance beam after the first few steps. When a ball was thrown to him, he was unable to catch it, losing his balance. Jim's trials at catching the ball were similar to those of a child of four or five. He was noted to work at times with his left hand, at other times with his right hand; he had not yet established hand preference. Although he had been given swimming lessons several times, he still was unable to swim. All the children in his neighborhood played baseball after school and on weekends but Jim could not participate in this sport with children his own age. Consequently he had no friends, and his teacher identified him as a loner. Evidence of poor motor skills appeared in many academic activities. For example, his handwriting was almost illegible, reflecting his perceptual-motor dysfunction. Jim's father, who had excelled in athletics and had won several sports championships in high school and college, had little patience for working or playing with a child who did not catch on quickly. In fact, because of Jim's abysmal failure in sports, his father was convinced his son was mentally retarded and not "a real boy." Looking at Jim as a totality, reading was but one part of the difficulty he had in relating to the world; a diagnosis should take into account his poorly developed motor skills, and a treatment plan should help him establish himself motorically within the world.

Many children with learning disabilities show motor behavior that is typical of a much younger child. Examples are overflow movements (when the child wishes to perform a movement with the right arm, the left arm involuntarily performs a shadow movement), poor coordination in motor activities, difficulty in fine-motor coordination, poor body image, lack of directionality, and confused laterality. These children are easily spotted in gym class, since they are poor in the physical education activities for their age level. Such children frequently disturb others in the classroom by bumping into objects, falling off chairs, dropping pencils and books, and appearing generally clumsy.

Deficiencies and lags in basic motor development may lead to subsequent difficulties in other areas of learning. However, not all children with learning disabilities have a deficiency in motor development, and a routine recommendation of motor training for all children with learning disabilities should be avoided. For many children, the break in learning developed at some other point in the developmental process.

Moreover, if a deficit in sensory-motor function is diagnosed, this does not mean that the teaching of academic material is necessarily to be delayed (Frostig 1968). As noted earlier, motor training alone will not teach a child to read, any more than eyeglasses alone will instantly transform a nonreader into a bookworm. Simultaneous work in motor development and academic skills can be designed to reinforce and enhance each other. For example, in one summer camping and academic program for children with learning disabilities, children were noted to have a breakthrough in reading and other academic work at the same time they learned to swim (Lerner et al. 1971). Further, as noted in the discussion of research on motor training, a period of motor training has not automatically resulted in academic improvement.

ACTIVITIES FOR MOTOR DEVELOPMENT

The balance of this chapter lists some representative activities for teaching sensory-motor and perceptual-motor functions. These activities are not organized to implement any particular motor theory, nor do they represent any particular curriculum program. They are simply a representative collection of motor activities designed to give the reader an idea of the kinds of activities used for motor development.

It is readily noted that many of these activities are similar to those in a physical education program. When learning disabilities specialists have been able to obtain the cooperation of physical educators in the school, these specialists become ardent team members, taking the responsibility for developing and implementing a motor development curriculum for children with learning disabilities. Utilization of such personnel has proved beneficial to both the academic and physical education programs.

Teaching strategies are subdivided into three areas: gross motor skills, body-awareness and body-image development, and fine motor skills.

GROSS MOTOR ACTIVITIES

Gross motor activities involve the total musculature of the body and the ability to move various parts of the body on command, controlling body movements in relationship to various outer and inner elements, such as gravity, laterality, and body midlines. The purpose of these activities is to develop smoother, more effective body movements and also to add to the child's sense of spatial orientation and body consciousness. Activities of gross motor movement are grouped as walking activities, floor activities, balance beam activities, and other gross motor activities.

Walking Activities

1. *Forward walk.* Have the child walk through a straight or curved path marked on the floor to a target goal. The path may be wide or narrow, but the more narrow the path, the more difficult the task. A single line requiring tandem walking (heel-to-toe) is more difficult than a widely spaced walk. A slow pace is more difficult than a running pace. Walking without shoes and socks is more difficult than walking with shoes.

2. *Backward walk.* Walk through the same course backwards.

3. *Sideways walk.* Walk a predetermined course sideways to the right one step at a time; then to the left one step at a time; finally, walk sideways with one foot crossing over the other.

4. *Variations.* Walk the above with arms in different positions, carrying objects, dropping objects along the way, such as balls into containers, or with eyes focused on various parts of the room.

5. *Animal walks.* Imitate the walks of various animals: elephant walk (bend forward at the waist, allowing arms to hang down, taking big steps while swaying from side to side); rabbit hop (placing hands on the floor, do deep knee bends, and move feet together between hands); crab walk (crawl forward and backward face up); duck walk (walk with hands on knees while doing a deep knee bend); worm walk (with hands and feet on the floor, take small steps first with feet, then with hands).

6. *Moon walk.* Imitate the leaping kangaroo-like steps of the astronauts on the moon.

7. *Cross-pattern walking.* Step off with one foot and the opposite hand pointed to the foot. Eyes and head follow the hand.

8. *Steppingstones.* Place objects on the floor for steppingstones identifying placement for right foot and left foot by color or the letters R and L. Child is to follow course by placing the correct foot on each steppingstone.

9. *Box game.* The child has two boxes (the size of shoe boxes), one behind and one in front. The child steps into the front box with both feet, moves rear box from behind to front and then steps into that. The child can use different hands to move boxes and use alternating feet. Move toward a finish line.

10. *Line walks.* Draw lines in colors on the floor. Lines can be curved, angular, or spiral. Also use a rope placed on the floor and have the child walk along the side of the rope.

11. *Ladder walk.* Place ladder flat on the ground. Have the child walk between rungs forward, backward, hopping.

Floor Activities

12. *Angels in the snow.* Have the child lie down with back on the floor and move limbs on command. Begin with bilateral commands: i.e., move feet apart as far as possible, move arms along ground until they meet above the head. Follow with unilateral commands: move left arm only, move

left leg only. Finally give cross-lateral commands: move left arm and right leg out.

13. *Crawling.* Since the child's first developmental motor activities are on the floor, some authorities feel it is important to have the child re-experience such movements. Creeping (creep with stomach touching the floor); unilateral crawl (moving arm and leg on one side of the body together); cross-lateral crawl (moving left arm with right leg and right arm with the left leg while crawling).

14. *Obstacle crawl.* Create an obstacle course with boxes, hoops, tables, barrels, chairs, etc., and have the child cover a predetermined course, going *through, under, over* and *around* various objects.

Balance Beam Activities

The balance beam can be a flat board, commercially purchased, or made from a two-by-four. It can be of various widths; the narrower the width, the more difficult the activities. Kephart (1971) suggests a section of two-by-four measuring 8 to 12 feet long. Each end of the board is fitted into a bracket that serves as a brace and prevents the board from tipping over. The board can be set flat with the wide surface up or set on its edge with the narrow surface up.

15. *Walking forward.* Have the child walk forward slowly across the board, walking with a normal stride or a tandem walk (heel-to-toe). The task is more difficult with bare feet than with shoes on.

16. *Walking backward.* Walk backward while keeping balance.

17. *Sideways walking.* Walk across board sideways starting with the left foot, then with the right. One foot could slide to the other or cross over the other.

18. *Variations.* Variations and more complex activities for the balance beam can be devised by adding activities such as turning, picking up objects on the board, kneeling, dropping objects such as balls or beanbags into containers while going across, following oral or recorded commands while on the board, walking while blindfolded or with eyes focused on an object.

Other Gross Motor Activities

19. *Skateboard.* The skateboard provides another technique for gross body-movement activities. This can be done lying on the stomach, kneeling, or standing; and the surface can be flat or on a downhill slope. The *balance board* is another variation. This is a square board placed on a block-shaped piece of wood. Unless the weight of the body is correctly distributed, the board will tilt to one side.

20. *Stand-up.* Have the children sit on the floor with their knees bent and feet on the floor. Ask them to get up and sit down again. Vary this exercise by having them do it with or without the use of their hands, with the eyes closed, and with the eyes open.

21. *Jumping jacks.* Jump, putting feet wide apart, while clapping hands above the head. Variations of this can be made by asking the child to make quarter turns, half turns, and full turns, or by asking the child to jump to the left, right, north, or south.

22. *Hopping.* Hop on one foot at a time. Alternate feet while hopping. Hop in rhythmical patterns: left, left, right, right; or left, left, right — right, right, left.

23. *Bouncing* activities and other variations can be accomplished on a trampoline, bedsprings, mattress, or on a large truck tire tube.

24. *Galloping steps.* These can be done to the accompaniment of rhythmic clapping or music. The speed can be regulated and changed from fast to slow.

25. *Skipping.* This is a difficult activity for children with poor motor coordination. It combines rhythm, balance, body movement, and coordination. Many children need help to learn to skip.

26. *Hopscotch games.* Hopscotch games can be made on the concrete outdoors, or put on plastic or oilcloth for indoor use.

27. *Hoop games.* Hoops of various sizes from the hula hoop down can be used to develop motor skills. Twist them around the arms, legs, waist; bounce balls in them; toss beanbags in them, step in and out of them.

28. *The "Stegel."* The stegel is a multi-use piece of equipment for outdoors. It is made up of a balance board, a ladder, a springboard, and sawhorses. This apparatus, adapted from Germany, has been found to be adaptable for a wide variety of motor activities. Some exercises to use with the stegel are to have children weave in and out of the ladder rungs, reverse the direction of an exercise, jump off the springboard, go forward and backward on the individual beams.

29. *Rope skills.* A length of rope can be used to perform a variety of exercises. Have the child put the rope around designated parts of the body (knees, ankles, hips) to teach body image. Have the child follow directions, put the rope around chairs, under a table, through a lampshade, jump back and forth or sideways over the rope, or make shapes, letters, or numbers with the rope.

BODY-IMAGE AND BODY-AWARENESS ACTIVITIES

The purpose of these activities is to help the child develop accurate images of the location of the parts of the body and the function of these body parts.

1. *Point to body parts.* Ask the child to point to the various parts of the body: i.e., nose, right elbow, left ankle, etc. This activity is more difficult with the eyes closed. Children can also lie down on the floor and be asked to touch various parts of their bodies. This activity is more difficult if done in a rhythmic pattern — use a metronome, for example.

2. *The robot man.* A man made from cardboard, held together at the joints with fasteners, can be moved into various positions. The children can

move the limbs of the robot on command and match the positions with their own body movements.

3. *Simon Says.* This game can be played with eyes open and with eyes closed.

4. *Puzzles.* Puzzles of people, animals, objects, etc., can be cut to show functional portions of the body.

5. *What is missing?* Use pictures with body parts missing. Have a child tell or draw what is missing.

6. *Life-sized drawing.* This can be made by having the child lie down on a large sheet of paper and tracing an outline around him. He fills in and colors the clothes and the details of the face and body.

7. *Awareness of the body parts through touch.* Touch various parts of the child's body while her eyes are closed and ask her which part was touched.

8. *Games.* Games such as Lobby Loo, Hokey-Pokey, and Did You Ever See a Lassie, help develop concepts of left, right, and body image.

9. *Pantomime.* The children pantomime actions that are characteristic of a particular occupation, such as bus driver driving a bus, a police officer directing traffic, a mail carrier delivering a letter, or a chef cooking.

10. *Following instructions.* Instruct child to put his left hand on his right ear, and right hand on his left shoulder. Other instructions might be to put his right hand in front of his left hand; turn right, walk two steps, and turn left.

11. *Twister.* Make rows of colored circles on the floor, or use on oilcloth or plastic sheet, or use the commercial game. Make instruction cards: put left foot on green circle and right foot on red circle.

12. *Estimating.* Have the child estimate the number of steps it will take her to get to a goal.

13. *Facial expression.* Have the child look at pictures of people and tell if a person is happy, sad, or surprised. Tell a story and ask the child to match the appropriate facial expression to the story. How does the person in the story feel?

14. *Water activities.* Gross motor movements done in a pool or lake allow the child some freedom from the force of gravity. Some activities are easier for the child to learn in the water, since it affords greater control and can be done at a slower pace. Swimming is also an excellent activity to strengthen general motor functioning.

FINE MOTOR ACTIVITIES

While some children may do well at gross motor activities, their performance may be poor when it comes to fine motor activities. Teaching strategies in this section are grouped as: [(a) throwing and catching activities, (b) eye-hand coordination activities, (c) chalkboard activities, and (d) eye movement.]

Throwing and Catching Activities

1. *Throwing.* Throwing objects at targets or to the teacher or other children can be performed with balloons, wet sponges, beanbags, yarn balls, and rubber balls of various sizes.

2. *Catching.* Catching is a more difficult skill than throwing, and the child can practice catching the above objects thrown by the teacher or other children.

3. *Ball games.* Many ball games help in the development of motor coordination. Balloon volleyball, rolling ball games, bouncing balls on the ground, and throwing balls against the wall are some examples.

4. *Tire-tube games.* Old tire tubes provide good objects for games of rolling and catching.

5. *Rag ball.* Many children find that throwing and catching a rubber ball is too difficult a task. Initially a rag ball can be used. It can be made by gathering rags or discarded nylon hosiery and covering them with cloth.

Eye-Hand Coordination Activities

6. *Tracing.* Trace lines, pictures, designs, letters, or numbers on tracing paper, plastic, or stencils. Use directional arrows, color cues, and numbers to help the child trace the figures.

7. *Water control.* Carrying and pouring water into measured buckets from pitchers to specified levels. Use smaller amounts and finer measurements to make the task more difficult. Use of colored water makes the activity more interesting.

8. *Cutting with scissors.* Have the child cut with scissors, choosing activities appropriate to her needs. Easiest are straight lines marked near the edges of the paper. Then cut along straight lines across the paper. Some children might need a cardboard attached to the paper to help guide the scissors. Cut out marked geometric shapes, such as squares, rectangles, and triangles. Draw a different color line to indicate change of direction in cutting. Cut out curving lines and circles. Cut out pictures. Cut out patterns made with dots and faint lines. Lazarus (1965) has additional specific suggestions for methods of using scissors.

9. *Stencils or templates.* Have the child draw outlines of patterns of geometric shapes. Templates can be made from cardboard, wood, plastic, old x-ray films or containers for packaged meat. Two styles can be made: a solid shape or frames with the shape cut out.

10. *Lacing.* A cardboard punched with holes or a pegboard can be used for this activity. A design or picture is made on the board and the child follows the pattern by weaving or sewing through the holes with a heavy shoelace, yarn, or similar cord.

11. *Rolling-pin game.* Place colored strips on a rolling pin. Hang a ball from a string at eye height and place a cardboard with stripes behind it. The ball is hit with a rolling pin at a place of a particular color and aimed

to hit a designated color stripe on the cardboard. For example, hit the ball with the red stripe of the rolling pin and have the ball hit the cardboard on the green stripe.

12. *Primary games.* Many primary and preschool games and toys, such as pounding pegs with a hammer, hammer and nail games, and dropping forms into slots, can be useful to practice fine motor control.

13. *Paper and pencil activities.* Coloring books, readiness books, dot-to-dot books, and kindergarten books frequently provide good paper and pencil activities for fine motor and eye-hand development. The materials published by Continental Press and Marianne Frostig (1964) are useful.

14. *Jacks.* The game of jacks provides opportunity for development of eye-hand coordination, rhythmical movements, and fine finger and hand movements.

15. *Clipping clothespins.* Clothespins can be clipped onto a line or a box. Children can be timed in this activity by counting the number of clothespins clipped in a specified time.

16. *Copying designs.* Children look at a geometric design and copy it onto a piece of paper.

17. *Paper folding or Japanese origami.* Simple paper-folding activities are useful for the development of eye-hand coordination, following directions, and fine motor control. The appendix in the *Perceptual Training Activities Handbook* by Van Witsen (1967) illustrates the steps to follow to make a number of objects.

Chalkboard Activities

Kephart (1971) suggests that chalkboard activities should be tackled before paper and pencil work. Chalkboard work encourages a freer use of large muscles of the shoulder and elbow rather than the tight, restricted "splinter" movement of the fingers that children often develop in paper and pencil tasks.

18. *Dot-to-dot.* The child connects two dots on the chalkboard with a line. Dots can be placed in various positions and in varying numbers, and the child must plan the lines of connection.

19. *Circles.* The child can practice making large circles on the board with one hand and with two hands, clockwise and counterclockwise.

20. *Geometric shapes.* Do similar activities to those described above with lines (horizontal, vertical, and diagonal), triangles, squares, rectangles, and diamonds. At first the child can use templates to make these shapes at the board; later the shapes can be copied from models.

21. *Letters and numbers.* The child can practice making letters and numbers on the chalkboard. Letters can be written in either manuscript or cursive style.

Eye-Movement Activities

One of the most controversial areas of motor training is that of eye-movement training. While some eye specialists discount it entirely, others believe it to be beneficial in certain cases. Kephart (1971) states that children must have a reasonably solid motor functioning and eye-movement pattern before training in ocular control can improve the child's ability to gain spatial and orientational information. Therefore, ocular pursuit training should be started only after the child has developed sufficient laterality and directionality to form the basis for adequate matching. Activities for eye-movement training are presented in detail by Kephart (1971) and Getman, Kane, and McKee (1968).

22. *Ocular-pursuit training.* In this activity the child is to follow a moving target with his eyes. The target could be the eraser end of a pencil, a penlight, or the examiner's finger. The target is moved in a horizontal arc, eighteen inches to the left and to the right; the target is moved in a vertical arc up and down; it is moved in a diagonal movement and in a rotating movement. Similar activities can be done with one eye covered.

23. *Finger and penlight.* The child can follow the light of a penlight or flashlight with her eyes and with her finger and eyes. She can also try to follow the teacher's light with her own.

24. *Moving ball.* Have the child follow the motions of a ball. The teacher can hold a large ball, then smaller balls, or a ball can be hung from a hook in the ceiling or wall.

25. *Quick focus.* Have the child look at a pencil about a foot in front of him, and then look to a target on the wall as quickly as possible, then back to the pencil, then to the target. Repeat a dozen times. Change targets, using other points of reference in the room.

26. *Visual tracking.* Have students trace pathways on paper using crayon, then the finger, finger above the paper, and follow the line with only the eye. These pathways can become increasingly complex as they cross and overlap each other and change directions.

PROGRAMS FOR MOTOR TRAINING

A number of programs for motor training have been developed. Below is a partial list of sources for motor development programs.

Barsch, Ray. *Perceptual Motor Curriculum,* Vol. 1. Seattle, Wash.: Special Child Publications, 1967.
————. *Enriching Perception and Cognition.* Vol. 2. Seattle, Wash.: Special Child Publications, 1968.
Braley, William T., G. Konicki, and C. Leedy. *Daily Sensorimotor Activities.* Freeport, N.Y.: Educational Activities, 1968.
Cratty, Bryant. *Active Learning: Games to Enhance Academic Abilities.* Englewood Cliffs, N.J.: Prentice-Hall, 1971.
Cratty, J. S. *Developmental Sequences of Perceptual Motor Tasks.* Freeport, N.Y.: Educational Activities, 1967.
Fairbanks, Jean S., and Janet Robinson. *Fairbanks, Robinson Program.* Boston: Teaching Resources, 1969.

Frostig, M. *Move-Grow-Learn.* Chicago: Follett, 1969.

Getman, G. N., E. R. Kane, M. R. Halgren, and G. W. McKee. *The Physiology of Readiness Programs.* Chicago: Lyons and Carnahan, 1966.

Getman, G. N., E. R. Kane, and G. W. McKee. *Developing Learning Readiness Program.* Manchester, Mo.: Webster Division, McGraw-Hill, 1968.

Hackett, Layne C., and Robert C. Jenson. *A Guide to Movement Exploration.* Palo Alto, Calif.: Peek Publications, 1967.

Hatton, Daniel, Frank J. Pizzat, and Jerome M. Pelkowski. *Erie Program Perceptual-Motor Exercises.* Boston: Teaching Resources, 1969.

Kephart, N. C. *The Slow Learner in the Classroom.* Columbus: Merrill, 1971.

Manual of Perceptual-Motor Activities. Johnstown, Pa.: Mafex Associates.

O'Donnell, Patrick. *Motor and Haptic Learning.* San Rafael, Calif.: Dimension Publishing, 1969.

Radler, D. H., and N. C. Kephart. *Success Through Play.* New York: Harper, 1960.

Raven, Betty. *Learning Through Movement.* New York: Teachers College, Columbia University Press, 1963.

Teaching Through Sensory-Motor Experiences. San Rafael, Calif.: Academic Therapy Publications, 1969.

Valett, Robert E. *The Remediation of Learning Disabilities.* Palo Alto, Calif.: Fearon Publishers, 1967.

Van Witsen, Betty. *Perceptual Training Activities Handbook.* New York: Teachers College, Columbia University Press, 1967.

SUMMARY

This chapter has reviewed sensory-motor and perceptual-motor theories of learning disabilities and has presented teaching strategies for developing a child's motor skills.

There are several theories of motor development. The visuomotor model of Getman is an example of an optometrist's view of motor learning, emphasizing the role of vision. Kephart's perceptual-motor theory has become the basis for much of the thinking about motor development in learning disabilities. It reflects the view that many youngsters with academic learning problems have not developed a stable and reliable perceptual-motor conception of the world. Barsch's movigenic theory is based on the premise that human learning is highly related to motor efficiency and the individual's performance of basic movement patterns. The presumption that provides the basis for Doman and Delacato's patterning theory of neurological organization is that the well-functioning child develops full neurological organization. This perspective counsels that when the child with problems performs a certain sequence of patterning and motor activities, the child's neurological organization will improve, thus promoting academic gains. Cratty discusses the importance of movement and games from the physical educator's perspective. The discipline of occupational therapy is represented by Ayres, who has developed a theory relating sensorimotor learning to basic neurophysiological integration.

The section "Discussion of Motor Theories" includes an overview of the motor development approaches, a discussion of reservations in light of critical research, and a response to the criticism.

The *Teaching Strategies* part of this chapter presented a collection of activities representing those used in motor programs. The activities were organized into the following categories: gross motor skills, body-awareness and body-image development, and fine motor skills.

REFERENCES

Ayres, A. Jean. "Improving Academic Scores Through Sensory Integration." *Journal of Learning Disabilities* 6 (June/July 1972): 338–343.

————. "Patterns of Perceptual-Motor Dysfunctions in Children: A Factor Analytic Study." *Perceptual and Motor Skills* 20 (1965): 335–368.

————. "Reading — A Product of Sensory Integrative Processes," pp. 77–82 in Helen K. Smith (ed.), *Perception and Reading*. Newark, Del.: International Reading Association, 1968.

————. *Sensory Integration and Learning Disorders*. Los Angeles: Western Psychological Services, 1973.

————. *Southern California Test Battery for Assessment of Dysfunction (Southern California Motor Accuracy Test; Southern California Perceptual Motor Tests; Southern California Figure-Ground Visual Perception Test; Southern California Kinesthesia and Tactile Perception Tests; Ayres Space Test)*. Los Angeles Western Psychological Services, 1969.

Barsch, Ray H. *Achieving Perceptual-Motor Efficiency*, Vol. 1. Seattle: Special Child Publications, 1967.

————. *Enriching Perception and Cognition*, Vol. 2. Seattle: Special Child Publications, 1968.

————. *A Movigenic Curriculum*. Bulletin no. 25. Madison, Wis.: Department of Public Instruction, Bureau for the Handicapped, 1965.

————. "Teacher Needs — Motor Training," pp. 183–195 in William Cruickshank (ed.), *The Teacher of Brain-Injured Children: A Discussion of the Bases of Competency*. Syracuse, N.Y.: Syracuse University Press, 1966.

Cratty, Bryant. *Active Learning: Games to Enhance Academic Abilities*. Englewood Cliffs, N.J.: Prentice-Hall, 1971.

————. *Intelligence in Action*. Englewood Cliffs, N.J.: Prentice-Hall, 1973.

————. *Perceptual-Motor Behavior and Educational Processes*. Springfield, Ill.: Charles C. Thomas, 1969.

Cruickshank, William M. "To the Editor." *Exceptional Children* 35 (September 1968): 93–94.

Delacato, Carl H. *The Diagnosis and Treatment of Speech and Reading Problems*. Springfield, Ill.: Charles C. Thomas, 1963.

————. *Neurological Organization and Reading*. Springfield, Ill.: Charles C. Thomas, 1966.

Doman, Robert J., et al. "Children with Severe Brain Injuries: Neurological Organization in Terms of Mobility," pp. 363–386 in Frierson and Barbe (eds.), *Educating Children with Learning Disabilities*. New York: Appleton-Century-Crofts, 1967.

Early, George H., and T. M. Sharpe. "Perceptual-Motor Training and Basic Abilities." *Academic Therapy* 5 (Spring 1970): 235–240.

Freeman, Roger D. "Controversy over 'Patterning' as a Treatment for Brain Damage in Children." *Journal of the American Medical Association* 202 (October 1967); 385–388.

Frostig, Marianne. "Education for Children with Learning Disabilities," pp. 234–266 in H. Myklebust (ed.), *Progress in Learning Disabilities*, Vol. 1. New York: Grune & Stratton, 1968.

Frostig, Marianne, and David Horne. *The Frostig Program for the Development of Visual Perception*. Chicago: Follet, 1964.

Gesell, A., and F. Ilg. *Infant and Child in the Culture of Today*. New York: Harper, 1943.

Getman, Gerald N. "The Visuomotor Complex in the Acquisition of Learning Skills," pp. 49–76 in J. Hellmuth (ed.), *Learning Disorders*, Vol. 1. Seattle: Special Child Publications, 1965.

Getman, Gerald N., E. R. Kane, and G. W. McKee. *Developing Learning Readiness: A Visual-Motor Tactile Skills Program*. Manchester, Mo.: Webster Division, McGraw-Hill, 1968.

Glass, Gene V., and Melvyn P. Robbins. "A Critique of Experiments on the Role of Neurological Organization in Reading Performance." *Reading Research Quarterly* 3 (Fall 1967): 5–52.

Goetzinger, C. "A Re-evaluation of the Heath Railwalking Test," *Journal of Educational Research* 54 (1961): 187–191.

Goodman, Libby, and Donald Hammill, "The Effectiveness of the Kephart-Getman Activities in Developing Perceptual-Motor and Cognitive Skills." *Focus on Exceptional Children* 4 (February 1973): 1–9.

Grattan, Paul E., and Milton B. Matin. "Neuro-muscular Coordination Versus Reading Ability." *American Journal of Optometry and Archives of the American Academy of Optometry* 42 (August 1965): 450–458.

Hammill, Donald, Libby Goodman, and J. Lee Wiederholt. "Visual-Motor Processes: Can We Train Them?" *Reading Teacher* 27 (February 1974): 469–480.

Harris, Albert J. "Diagnosis and Remedial Instruction in Reading," in Helen Robinson (ed.), *Innovation and Change in Reading Instruction*, Part 2. Chicago: University of Chicago Press, 1968.

Harris, Dale. *Children's Drawings as Measures of Intellectual Maturity*. New York: Harcourt, Brace & World, 1963.

Hebb, D. O. *The Organization of Behavior*. New York: Wiley, 1949.

Itard, J. M. G. *De l'education de l'homme sauvage*. Paris, 1801.

———. *The Wild Boy of Aveyron*. New York: Appleton-Century-Crofts, 1962.

Johnson, Doris, and H. Myklebust. *Learning Disabilities: Educational Principles and Practices*. New York: Grune & Stratton, 1967.

Kephart, Newell C. *The Brain-Injured Child in the Classroom*. Chicago: National Society for Crippled Children and Adults, 1963.

———. "Perceptual-Motor Aspects of Learning Disabilities," pp. 405–413 in Frierson and Barbe (eds.), *Educating Children with Learning Disabilities*. New York: Appleton-Century-Crofts, 1967.

———. *The Slow Learner in the Classroom*. 2nd ed. Columbus: Merrill, 1971.

Kraus, H. "Kraus-Weber Test for Minimum Muscular Fitness," pp. 125–126 in *Therapeutic Exercises*. Springfield, Ill.: Charles C. Thomas, 1963.

Lazarus, Phoebe, and Harriet Carlin. "Cutting: A Kinesthetic Tool for Learning." *Exceptional Children* 31 (1965): 361–364.

Lerner, Janet W. "Systems Analysis and Special Education." *Journal of Special Education* 7 (Spring 1973): 15–26.

Lerner, Janet, Dorothy Bernstein, Lillian Stevenson, and Anne Rubin. "Bridging the Gap in Teacher Education: A Camping-Academic Program for Children with School Learning Disorders." *Academic Therapy Quarterly,* (Summer, 1971): 367–374.

Lerner, Janet W., and Kenneth James. "Systems Applications in Special Education," pp. 273–306 in L. Mann and D. Sabatino (eds.), *Second Annual Review of Special Education.* Philadelphia: Journal of Special Education Press, 1974.

Lincoln-Oseretsky Developmental Scale. Los Angeles: Western Psychological Services, 1965.

Luria, A. R. *Higher Cortical Functions in Man.* New York: Basic Books, 1966.
————. *Human Brain and Psychological Processes.* New York: Harper & Row, 1966.

Montessori, M. *The Montessori Method,* A. E. George, trans. New York: Frederick Stokes, 1912.

Myers, Patricia, and Donald Hammill. *Methods for Learning Disorders.* New York: Wiley, 1969.

O'Donnell, Patrick. *Motor and Haptic Learning.* San Rafael, Calif.: Dimensions Publishing, 1968.

Piaget, J. *The Origins of Intelligence in Children,* M. Cook, trans. New York: International Universities Press, 1952 (originally published 1936).

Reading Readiness Series. Elizabethtown, Pa.: The Continental Press.

Roach, C., and N. Kephart. *The Purdue Perceptual-Motor Survey Test.* Columbus: Merrill, 1966.

Roach, Eugene C. "Evaluation of an Experimental Program of Perceptual Motor Training with Slow Readers," pp. 446–450 in *Vistas in Reading.* Newark, Del.: International Reading Association, 1967.

Robbins, Melvyn P. "A Study of the Validity of Delacato's Theory of Neurological Organization. *Exceptional Children* 32 (April 1966): 517–523.

Sequin, E. *Idiocy: And Its Treatment by the Physiological Method.* New York: Columbia University Press, 1907 (originally published in 1864).

Spache, George D. "Contributions of Allied Fields to the Teaching of Reading," pp. 237–290 in Helen Robinson (ed.), *Innovation and Change in Reading Instruction,* Part 2. Chicago: University of Chicago Press, 1968.

Van Witsen, B. *Perceptual Training Activities Handbook.* New York: Teachers College Press, Columbia University, 1967.

9. Perception and Memory

THEORY

This chapter examines (1) the relationship of various views of perception to learning disabilities and (2) the role of memory and imagery in learning disabilities. The "Teaching Strategies" section presents methods to teach perception and memory.

PERCEPTION

Perception is used to mean recognition of sensory information, or the mechanism by which the intellect recognizes and makes sense out of sensory stimulation. Several constructs of perception have implications for children with learning problems: the perceptual-modality concept, overloading of the perceptual systems, whole and part perception, visual perception, auditory perception, haptic perception, cross-modal perception, form and directional perception, and social perception. It is important for the teacher to know that perception is a learned skill and that the teaching process can have a direct impact on the child's perceptual facility. Appropriate teaching procedures can be selected to improve various subskills of perception or to modify the learning process in light of the child's perceptual abilities and disabilities.

PERCEPTUAL-MODALITY CONCEPT

Major differences exist in the way children learn. Some children learn best by listening; some learn best by looking; and some learn best by touching or performing an action. Each of these ways of learning and receiving information is called a *perceptual modality.* Many children with learning problems have a much greater facility in using one perceptual modality than in using another. Further, a particular perceptual modality may be so inefficient for some children that it is an unproductive pathway for learning (Wepman 1968).

Children appear to have one optimal perceptual modality for learning. While some children learn most efficiently through their ears or by listening (auditory modality), others learn best through their eyes (visual modality), and a few children seem to learn best by touch (tactile modality), or even by muscle feeling (kinesthetic modality).

Adults too have individual learning styles. Some learn best by listening to an explanation; others know that to learn something they must read about it or watch it being done; while still other individuals learn best by writing it down or going through the action themselves. As early as 1886, the clinical observation that individuals have a predilection for one perceptual input avenue over others was made by Charcot (1953), who categorized people as "audile," "visile," and "tactile" learners.

One example is eight-year-old Sandra, who failed many tasks that involved learning through the auditory modality. She could not learn nursery rhymes; she was unable to get messages straight over the telephone; she forgot spoken instructions; she could not discriminate between pairs of spoken words with minimal contrast or a single phoneme difference (cat-cap); she found phonics instruction baffling. Sandra was failing in reading; yet she had passed the reading readiness test with ease because it tested performance requiring skills within the visual modality. At first Sandra could not remember the arithmetic facts, but there was a sudden spurt in arithmetic achievement during the second half of first grade. She explained that she solved her arithmetic problems by putting the classroom clock in her head. By "looking" at the minute marks on the clock to perform arithmetic tasks, Sandra was using her superior visual modality to compensate for her deficit in auditory processing.

In contrast, John, at age eight, performed several years above his age level on tasks requiring auditory processing. He had easily learned to say the alphabet letters in sequence, he learned poems and nursery rhymes, he remembered series of digits and phone numbers, he remembered verbal instructions, and he quickly learned to detect phoneme differences in words. Visual tasks, however, were difficult for John. He had trouble putting puzzles together, seeing and remembering forms in designs, doing block arrangements, remembering the sequence and order of things he saw, and recalling what words looked like in print.

To choose the optimum method of teaching, the teacher should know a child's learning type — the child's best modality for learning. Before the appropriate approach to learning can be determined, the child's strengths and weaknesses in learning through visual, auditory, and tactile modes need to be evaluated. Once an evaluation of a child's modalities of strength and weakness is made, several alternative approaches are possible for teaching (Wepman 1964, 1968):

1. *Teach through the intact modality.* In this approach, once the modality of strength is determined, materials and methods that utilize the intact modality are selected. For example, if the child is high in auditory but low in visual perception, then an auditory teaching method would be selected.

2. *Strengthen the modality of deficit.* In this approach, the teaching procedure is designed to improve performance in the poor modality. The goal of this approach is to build the ineffective modality so that it can become a productive pathway for learning. The child who manifests a deficit in auditory perception would be taught with methods designed to improve auditory processing.

3. *Combination approach.* This is a two-pronged approach to teaching; the stronger modality is initially used, but, meanwhile, separate lessons are also used to build the deficit modality. Care must be taken so the child is not overtaxed in the tasks that require processing within the weak modality (Johnson and Myklebust 1967). For example, in the case of children who have a strong visual but weak auditory modality the clinical teacher might teach them to read using a visual method, while strengthening their auditory skills in separate lessons.

A similar view of perception is presented as the *semiautonomous systems model of brain function* (Johnson and Myklebust 1967). Briefly, this view conceptualizes the brain as made up of semi-independent modality systems such as the auditory system, a visual system, a tactile system, and a kinesthetic system. A given modality system can function in three ways: (1) semi-independently of the other modalities, (2) in a supplementary way with another system, or (3) with all systems contributing as a unit. The following terms are used to refer to these three types of brain system functions: (1) intraneurosensory, (2) interneurosensory, and (3) integrative.

The *intraneurosensory system* refers to learning that takes place predominantly through one sense modality; that is, learning that takes place through one input pathway that functions relatively independently. For example, during a hearing test the auditory modality functions relatively independently, and this represents an intraneurosensory task. An implication of this model is that a disability may be found in only one modality and this disability may not be disrupting to the other systems. Conceptually, then, there may be an impairment in the auditory system without involvement of the visual system.

The *interneurosensory system* refers to learning that results from the interrelated function of two or more systems in combination. The brain serves as a mechanism for converting one type of information to another, such as visual to auditory, or auditory to motor. The interneurosensory system includes the inner processes where one type of neurosensory information is converted into another within the brain. An illustration of an interneurosensory task is copying a circle. The child looks at the circle using the visual modality, and the visual information must then be converted to the kinesthetic modality, or motor movement. If the child cannot perform the act, the disturbance may lie in the interneurosensory system, the ability to convert information from one modality to another.

Integrative learning is the third system of the semiautonomous concept of brain function. In this type of learning all of the systems function simultaneously, working together as a unit. Many learning difficulties are in the area of integration. It is speculated that deficiencies in nonverbal learning, social perception, conceptualization, or comprehension may be due to an impairment in the integrative system.

Ketchum (1967) also sees integrative processing as a factor in learning disorders. He observes that there is a segment of the population whose reading disorders appear to be some form of dysfunction within or between hemispheres of the cerebral cortex.

Similarly, Eisenberg (1969, p. 179) has stated:

> The central nervous system is not to be regarded as a network of telephone circuits but, rather, as a complex of transient electrical fields whose reciprocal interrelations is the essence of normal function. . . . Any distortion in the felt-work of the cortex will alter the social adaptability of the organism.

Overloading Perceptual Systems

The concept of overloading the perceptual systems within the brain means that the reception information comes from another input modality. The child with learning disabilities may have a lower tolerance than the normal child for receiving and integrating information from several input systems at the same time. An analogy might be made to an overloaded fuse that blows out when it cannot handle any more electrical energy. Unable to accept and process an excess of data, the brain becomes overloaded and breaks down. Symptoms of such overloading include confusion, poor recall, retrogression, refusal of the task, poor attention, temper tantrums, or even seizures (Johnson and Myklebust 1967). Strauss called such reactions "catastrophic responses."

Many implications for teaching are implied in the concept of overloading. One recommendation stemming from such a view is that teachers be cautious in the use of multisensory techniques and that they evaluate the child before selecting methods that stimulate several perceptual modalities. Such recommendations differ substantially from teaching plans stemming from certain other theories. Some theoretical approaches use a simultaneous stimulation of all input modalities to reinforce learning (Fernald 1943, Gillingham and Stillman 1966). Such methods advocate that in learning to read a word, stimulating the eye, ear, touch, and motor avenues simultaneously will aid in the learning of the word. The child will hear the word, say the word, see the word, feel the word, write the word, and perhaps spell the world. In contrast, the concept of overloading implies that for certain children multisensory teaching procedures may cause a breakdown of learning by overstimulating the brain.

Wepman (1964) also advises against indiscriminate multisensory approaches to teaching. He suggests that two modalities should be trained quite independently since combining the two approaches before the child is capable of utilizing both often leads to confusion.

Children sometimes learn by themselves to adapt their behavior to avoid overloading perceptual modality input. One boy was observed to avoid looking at an individual's face whenever he was engaged in conversation. When asked about this behavior, the boy explained that he found he could not understand what was being said if he watched the speaker's face while listening. The visual stimuli, in effect, interfered with the ability to comprehend through the auditory modality.

Whole and Part Perception

In addition to differences in perceptual modalities of learning, another difference in perceptual styles has been observed — "whole perceivers" and "part perceivers" (Goins 1958). Some children apparently perceive an object in its entirety — its entire gestalt — while others tend to focus on minute details, missing the gestalt. This perceptual characteristic is similar to the background-foreground confusion Strauss and Lehtinen (1947) noted in some brain-injured children. Both the ability to see the whole and the ability to see parts are needed for effective learning. In a task such as reading, children must be able to move flexibly from whole to parts as their purpose dictates. At times they must see the word in its entirety, and at other times see a small detail that differentiates it from another word. For example, to differentiate between *house* and *horse* the child must be able to note details in words. The word *elephant*, however, is likely to be recognized as a whole or as a sight word. Children who rely on only one of these perceptual styles appear to have difficulty learning to read.

Children with learning disabilities often manifest this characteristic in their coloring of pictures. The sleeve may be colored red, while the body of the shirt is blue, and the other sleeve is yellow. One girl colored each side of the crease in the trousers a different color. She saw the parts but not the whole. Jerry, another child who was a "part perceiver," identified a tiny difference that the artist had made in two illustrations of an automobile that accompanied a story. Jerry was so concerned with the suspicion that it was a different automobile that he could no longer concentrate on the story. Children with such atypical styles of perception may be noted by teachers, but frequently such behavior is misinterpreted. One kindergarten teacher described a child who was subsequently found to have severe learning and perception problems as follows: "Paul has a good deal of ability; he shows originality; and he has a knack for describing in detail. He is unusually perceptive."

VISUAL PERCEPTION

Visual perception plays a significant role in school learning — particularly in reading. Some children have difficulty in tasks requiring the visual discrimination of geometric designs and pictures. Other children succeed at this task, but fail in the visual discrimination of letters and words.

Within the broad scope of visual perception, several component skills of visual perception can be identified. Chalfant and Scheffelin (1969) identify the following components:

Spatial relations refers to perception of the position of objects in space. This dimension of visual functioning implies the perception of the placement of an object or a symbol (pictures, letters, numbers) and the spatial relation of that entity to others surrounding it. In reading, words must be seen as separate entities surrounded by space.

Visual discrimination refers to the ability to differentiate one object from another. In a readiness test, for example, the child may be asked to find a rabbit that is different — to discover the rabbit with one ear in a row of rabbits with two ears. When asked to visually distinguish between the letters *m* and *n*, the child must perceive the number of humps in each letter. The skill of matching identical pictures, designs, shapes, letters, and words is another visual discrimination task. Objects may be discriminated by color, shape, pattern, size, position, or brightness. The ability to visually discriminate letters and words becomes essential in learning to read (Barrett 1965).

Figure-ground discrimination refers to the ability to distinguish an object from the background surrounding it. The child with a deficit in this area cannot focus on the item in question apart from the visual background. Consequently, the child is distracted by irrelevant stimuli.

Visual closure is a task in which the subject is asked to recognize or identify an object, despite the fact that the total stimulus is not presented. For example, in a picture of a man the leg may be missing, yet the picture can be identified. A competent reader can read a line of print when the top half of the print is covered. There are enough letter clues in the remaining bottom portion for the reader to provide visual closure to read the line.

Object recognition refers to the ability to recognize the nature of objects when viewing them. This includes recognition of geometric shapes, such as a square; of objects, such as a cat, a face, or a toy; of alphabetic letters and numbers; and of words. The kindergartener's ability to recognize geometric patterns, letters, and numbers has been found to be a good predictor of reading achievement (Barrett 1965).

Frostig (1964) has designed a test that samples the child's ability in visual perception. The five subskills evaluated in the *Frostig Development Test of Visual Perception* are:

1. *Visual-motor coordination* — the ability to coordinate vision with the movements of the body or parts of the body
2. *Figure-ground perception* — the ability to attend to one aspect of the visual field while perceiving it in relation to the rest of the field
3. *Perceptual constancy* — the ability to perceive objects possessing invariant properties such as shape, position, size, etc., in spite of the variability of the impression on the sensory surface
4. *Perception of position* — the perception in space of an object in relation to the observer
5. *Perception of spacial relationships* — the ability to perceive the positions of two or more objects in relation to each other

The ITPA has several stubtests that assess aspects of visual perception: *Visual Reception, Visual Association, Visual Closure,* and *Visual Sequential Memory* (Kirk, McCarthy, and Kirk 1968). Subtests of the *Detroit Tests of Learning Aptitude* that sample aspects of visual perception include: *Pictorial Opposites, Visual Attention Span for Objects, Memory for Designs, Visual Attention Span for Letters* (Baker and Leland 1935).

Other tests of visual perception are: the *Bender Visual-Motor Gestalt Test* (Koppitz 1964, Bender 1938); the *Developmental Test of Visual-Motor Integration* (Beery and Buktenica 1967); the *Motor-Free Test of Visual Perception* (Colarusso and Hammill 1972); *Southern California Figure-Ground Perception Test* (Ayres 1969); and *A Perceptual Testing and Training Handbook for First-Grade Teachers* (Sutphin 1964). Clues to the child's skills in visual perception tasks can be obtained from subtests of the *Wechsler Intelligence Scale for Children* (WISC): *Picture Arrangement,*

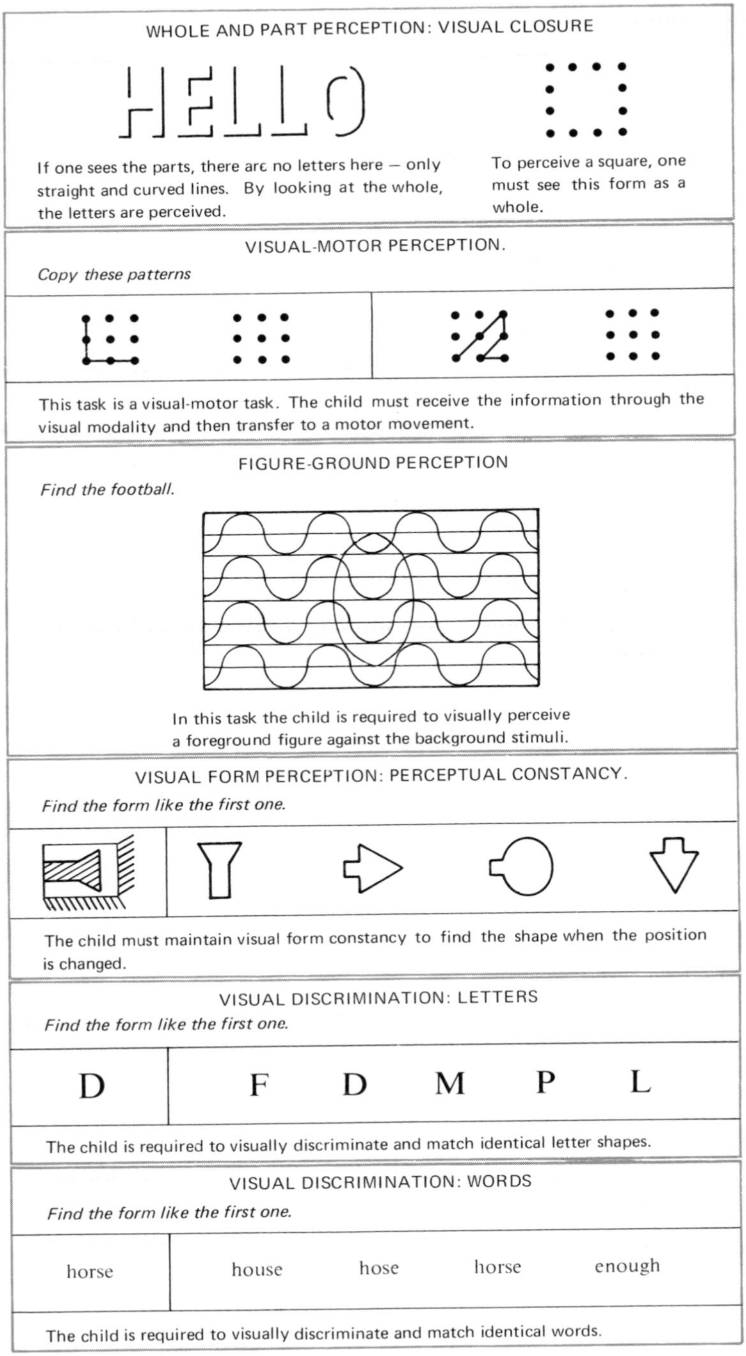
WHOLE AND PART PERCEPTION: VISUAL CLOSURE
If one sees the parts, there are no letters here — only straight and curved lines. By looking at the whole, the letters are perceived.
To perceive a square, one must see this form as a whole.
VISUAL-MOTOR PERCEPTION.
Copy these patterns
This task is a visual-motor task. The child must receive the information through the visual modality and then transfer to a motor movement.
FIGURE-GROUND PERCEPTION
Find the football.
In this task the child is required to visually perceive a foreground figure against the background stimuli.
VISUAL FORM PERCEPTION: PERCEPTUAL CONSTANCY.
Find the form like the first one.
The child must maintain visual form constancy to find the shape when the position is changed.
VISUAL DISCRIMINATION: LETTERS
Find the form like the first one.
D
F D M P L
The child is required to visually discriminate and match identical letter shapes.
VISUAL DISCRIMINATION: WORDS
Find the form like the first one.
horse
house hose horse enough
The child is required to visually discriminate and match identical words.

Figure 9.1 Examples of visual perception tasks

Block Design, Object Assembly, and *Coding* (Wechsler 1949, 1974). Descriptive data about these tests appear in Appendix C. Some informal tests of visual perception of letters and words are suggested by Durrell (1956).

Several illustrative items used in exercises to test or improve visual perception are shown in Figure 9.1.

AUDITORY PERCEPTION

Dysfunction of the auditory modality as a pathway for learning has been relatively neglected by researchers. At present more tests and teaching materials have been designed for evaluating or improving visual perception than for auditory perception. Many of the children who have difficulty learning phonics are found to have poor auditory processing skills. This is not a problem of hearing or auditory acuity, but a disability in auditory perception — the ability to recognize or interpret what is heard. The auditory mode of perception can be divided into the following subskills to differentiate more specific auditory functions: (1) auditory discrimination, (2) auditory memory, (3) auditory sequencing, and (4) auditory blending.

Auditory discrimination refers to the ability to recognize a difference between phoneme sounds and to identify words that are the same and words that are different. In the *Wepman Test of Auditory Discrimination* (1973), the child must decide whether a pair of words are the same or different. The different words have a minimal sound difference or contrast of a single phoneme sound. The child is faced away from the examiner — so there is no visual cue of watching the speaker's mouth — and is asked whether a pair of words is the same or different, i.e., "mit-mat" or "big-pig." Ability to discriminate between long and short vowels and between initial consonants and consonant blends is assessed in the STAP (Kimmel and Wahl 1969). The *Goldman-Fristoe-Woodcock Test of Auditory Discrimination* (1970) includes tests of auditory discrimination of phonemes against a quiet and noisy background.

Auditory memory is the ability to store and recall what one has heard. For example, the child could be asked to do three activities, such as: "Close the window, open the door, and place the book on the desk." Is the child able to store and retrieve through listening to such directions? Two subtests of the *Detroit Tests of Learning Aptitude — Oral Directions and Oral Commissions* (Baker and Leland 1935) — are designed to assess such functions. The STAP (Kimmell and Wahl 1969) has a section on the ability to remember and identify rhymes.

Auditory sequencing is the ability to remember the order of items given orally in a sequential list. For example, the sequences "A, B, C..." and "January, February, March..." are examples of the importance of sequence. Tests of auditory sequencing are found in the ITPA, *Auditory Sequential Memory* (Kirk, McCarthy, and Kirk 1968); WISC, *Digit Span* (Wechsler 1949, 1974); *Detroit Tests of Learning Aptitude, Auditory Attention Span for Unrelated Words* (Baker and Leland 1935); and tests of the ability to remember a rhythmic pattern, STAP (Kimmell and Wahl 1969).

Auditory blending is the ability to blend single phonic elements or phonemes into a complete word. Children with such disabilities are not able to blend the phonemes "m-a-n" to form the word *man*. Tests of this auditory skill include the ITPA subtests, *Sound Blending* and *Auditory Closure* (Kirk, McCarthy, and Kirk 1968); and the *Roswell-Chall Auditory Blending Test* (Roswell and Chall 1963).

All of the auditory subskills can be sampled through clinical observations during teaching sessions, through informal tests, or through formally designed standardized tests. Durrell (1956) has many suggestions for informal tests of auditory perception of sounds and words. The *Goldman-Fristoe-Woodcock Auditory Skills Test Battery* assesses several auditory perception skills.

Haptic Perception: Tactile and Kinesthetic Skills

Haptic perception refers to information received through two modalities — tactile and kinesthetic. The term *haptic* is used to refer to both systems.

Tactile perception is obtained through the sense of touch via the fingers and skin surfaces. The ability to recognize an object by touching it, to identify a numeral that is drawn on one's back or arm, to discriminate between smooth and rough surfaces, to identify which finger is being touched — all are examples of tactile perception.

Kinesthetic perception is obtained through body movements and muscle feeling. The awareness of positions taken by different parts of the body, bodily feelings of muscular contraction, tension, and relaxation are examples of kinesthetic perception. The discussion of body image and motor information in the previous chapter provides a broader view of the kinesthetic system.

It is sometimes difficult to conceptualize the difference between the two types of haptic perception. Perhaps the features distinguishing tactile perception from kinesthetic can be clarified by the illustration of shopping for mattresses. Both the tactile and kinesthetic modalities provide perceptual information about an innerspring mattress and a foam rubber mattress. By simply touching the covering on the two mattresses (tactile perception) it is difficult to tell the innerspring from the foam rubber. However, the body feeling received by sitting on each mattress differs considerably (kinesthetic perception). With such kinesthetic perceptual information, one can easily differentiate the innerspring mattress from the foam rubber one.

Both dimensions of the haptic system are important for obtaining information about object qualities, bodily movement, and their interrelationships. Most school tasks, as well as most acts in everyday life, require both touch and body movement. Chalfant and Scheffelin (1969) point out that in comparison to visual and auditory perception, little information is available concerning tactile and kinesthetic perception in the educational journals. Yet tactile and kinesthetic perception play important roles in learning. There is a need to know more about dysfunction in the haptic areas and their relationship to other areas of learning.

One test designed to assess haptic functions is the *Southern California Kinesthetic and Tactile Perception Test* (Ayres 1969). Several informal tests of tactile and kinesthetic perception are described by Chalfant and Scheffelin (1969, Chapter 4).

CROSS-MODAL PERCEPTION

There is growing evidence that a major difficulty in learning is the inability to integrate one modality of function with another modality (Chalfant and Scheffelin 1969). The neurological process of converting information within the brain from one modality to another has been referred to as cross-modality perception. This process is also termed "intersensory integration," "intermodal transfer," and "transducing" in the literature (Wallace and McLoughlin, 1975).

In many types of learning, information received through one sensory input system must be transferred or integrated with another perceptual system; and the learner must be able to shift or cross from one to the other, integrating the two systems. Some children appear quite adequate in both visual and auditory systems when they are assessed alone, but the deficit appears when a task requires the integration of the two systems.

An example of cross-modal perception is found in the reading process, where the reader must integrate visual symbols with their auditory equivalents. Johnson and Myklebust (1967) propose that some reading disorders are due to an inability to make such conversions within the neurosensory system. Thus the child who cannot convert from the visual modality to the auditory modality is able to learn what letters look like but cannot associate these visual images with their sound equivalents. Conversely, the child who cannot convert from the auditory modality to the visual learns what letters sound like but cannot associate it with the visual form of the letters.

Ayres (1968) believes that integration of other perceptual modalities is also required in reading. She proposes that intersensory integration of the modalities of visual, tactile, and kinesthetic perception is essential. Another illustration of a deficit in cross-modal perception is the child who has difficulty planning and executing motor movements. For example, to talk the child must convert an auditory memory of a word by implementing a motor plan in order to say the word (auditory system to motor system). The inability to plan and execute the proper motor action, to convert the auditory input into motor output, is sometimes called *apraxia*. Ayres notes that such children are characterized by poor tactile and kinesthetic perception.

Although there is as yet little information concerning the growth and development of the integration of perceptual systems, researchers believe that the appearance of higher and more complex learning is dependent on the gradual integration of the modality systems. Research studies of cross-modality integration that have been conducted thus far suggest that there are differences in intersensory integrative ability between normal children and neurologically impaired children. Further, there is evidence that some individuals who apparently function normally with a task requiring a single perceptual modality have difficulty when the task involves simultaneous or successive functioning of several modalities. The breakdown occurs in tasks requiring cross-modal perception and has been referred to as an integrative disorder (Chalfant and Scheffelin 1969).

Frostig (1965, 1968) advocates exercises in cross-modality associations for children found to have difficulty with the cross-modal process. Examples of such activities are: following spoken directions (auditory-verbal to motor); describing a picture (visual to auditory-verbal); finding certain objects in pictures (auditory-verbal to visual); feeling objects through a curtain and drawing their shapes on paper (tactile to visual-motor); determining whether two objects are the same or different when one is touched while the other is seen (tactile to visual); determining whether two patterns are the same or different when one is touched and the other heard — i.e., *dot-dot-dash* patterns (tactile to auditory). Activities designed to have the child perform cross-modal functions are suggested later in this chapter.

Probably many tests that purport to be testing a single perceptual modality actually require the integration of two or more perceptual modalities. That is, a visual perception test may actually require integration of the visual, motor, and auditory functions. While many tests require cross-modal functions in performance, at the present time few tests, if any, are available designed specifically to assess cross-modal perception. Certain researchers who are actively investigating this area of performance have developed tests of cross-modal processing designed to investigate their research problem. These include the studies of Birch and Belmont (1964), Birch and Lefford (1963), and Belmont, Birch, and Karp (1965).

FORM AND DIRECTIONAL PERCEPTION

An interesting analysis of perception has been made by Money (1966), in regard to the relationship of the perceptual world of objects and the perceptual world of letters and words. A perceptual generalization made by children in the prereading stage of development is the "law of object constancy." A child concludes that an object retains the same name or meaning regardless of the position it happens to be in, the direction it faces, or the modification of slight additions or subtractions. A chair, for example, is a chair regardless of whether it faces left or right, back or front, upside down or right side up, of whether it is upholstered or has additional cushions, or even if it has a leg missing. It is still called a chair. The child has made similar generalizations about dogs; no matter what its position, size, color, or quantity of hair, it is still called a dog.

When beginning to deal with letters and words, however, the child finds that this perceptual generalization no longer holds true. The placement of a circle on a stick from left to right, or top to bottom, changes the name of the letter from *b* to *d* to *p* to *q*, and the addition of a small line changes *c* to *e*. The direction the word is facing changes it from *was* to *saw*, or *no* to *on*, or *top* to *pot*. One incident of such confusion happened during a teachers' strike. A boy with directional perception difficulties looked at the picket signs and asked why they were picketing if the strike was called off. The sign, lettered *ON STRIKE*, was read by the youngster as *NO STRIKE*.

The implication, then, is that some children with reading disabilities fail to make the necessary amendments to an earlier perceptual generalization they have formulated. An instrument that Money found useful in assessing such space-form-direction perceptual difficulties in children is the *Road Map Test* (Money, Alexander, and Walker 1965). Another instrument to evaluate space and direction ability is the *Ayres Space Test* (Ayres 1969).

SOCIAL PERCEPTION

The preceding sections of this chapter considered disturbances in the perception of physical objects and events. Psychologists have recently turned their attention to another dimension of perception — that of social perception (Hochberg 1964). The skill of interpreting stimuli in the social environment and appropriately relating such interpretations to the social situation is called *social perception*. Compared to the quantity of research on the perception of physical phenomena, the area of social perception is relatively unexplored. Certain children appear to have difficulty perceiving social data, and they consequently have trouble learning how to make social judgments and how to adapt their behavior to the social situation (Johnson and Myklebust 1967, Bryan 1974).

Jimmy, nine and one-half years old, is an example of a child with a disability in social perception. On the *Stanford-Binet Intelligence Test*, Jimmy received an IQ score of 127, putting him in a high intelligence classification. He did particularly well on the sections that required verbal and language responses. Yet on the *Goodenough-Harris Drawing Test* (Harris 1963), his drawing ranked at the sixth percentile for his age (Figure 9.2).

Jimmy had many problems in the area of social perception. While he performed satisfactorily in many academic subjects, his teachers consistently reported that his social behavior in school was both strange and disturbing. The speech teacher dismissed him because of his abnormal delight and hilarity when others in the class made mistakes. Another teacher reported that he seemed unconscious of wrongdoing, that he made odd statements totally out of context, and that he was not well accepted by other children. Another report commented that Jimmy had not developed skills in social situations. Although he wanted to be accepted by others and have friends,

Figure 9.2 Drawing of a man made by a boy, age 9 years, 8 months, with a disability in social perception

he did not seem to know the appropriate manner of gaining friends, and instead tended to antagonize other children. As seems to be true of some other children with a disability in social perception, Jimmy also did poorly in perceptual-motor tasks and seemed to have a poor understanding of space relationships. The psychologist reported poor performance in perceptual-motor and coordination activities on the *Bender Visual-Motor Gestalt Test*.

Problems of social development and teaching strategies for social development are discussed further in Chapter 12.

MEMORY

The fact that some children who are unsuccessful learners have poor memories was observed long before learning disabilities was recognized as a field of study. Yet there is now a renewed interest in the role of memory in learning, in the kinds of memory operating within a learning task, and in ways to improve memory. The fields of psychology, biochemistry, and neurology have directed increased attention to the mechanism of human memory.

Sensation and perception take place when the stimulus is present; they are ongoing activities. Memory pertains to sensations and data *already* received and perceived. The ability to store and retrieve previously experienced sensations and perceptions when the stimulus that originally evoked them is no longer present is called memory, imagery, recall, or sometimes "the mind's eye."

Examples of sensations and perceptions that occur only in the mind are the musician "listening" to music played at an earlier time; the cook "tasting" the sourness of a lemon to be used; the carpenter "feeling" the roughness of sandpaper used yesterday in a job; the gardener "smelling" the sweetness of lilacs while looking at the buds on the tree. McCarthy (1968) describes how she helped her three-year-old understand the qualities of memory. She explained the word "mind" by asking the youngster to close her eyes and think about a peanut butter and jelly sandwich. Yes, the child could "see" the jelly dripping down the sides of the bread; she could "smell" the peanut butter; and she could even "taste" the first bite. Where was this sandwich that had become so vivid? It was, so went the explanation, in the same place her mind was.

MEMORY MECHANISMS

There are at least three stages of memory in which the child with learning disabilities could have difficulty: *reception*, *storage*, or *retrieval* (Howe 1970). First the child must *receive* the information, that is, be able to clearly understand what is to be remembered. A child may not remember something if it was not initially perceived clearly. Poor reception may also be related to inability to attend. Secondly, the information must be *stored* within the brain. There seem to be several stages and ways for the brain to store information. Thirdly, to remember something it must be *retrieved* from storage. Some children have difficulty getting the information back from storage. Most of us have had the experience of having a name or a word on the tip of our tongue but being unable to retrieve it.

Researchers in the field of human memory refer to three types of memory storage systems: (1) a sensory storage or register, (2) a short-term store, and (3) a long-term store (Kumar 1971). Information is first contained in the *storage register;* then it is identified and retained in the *short-term store;* finally, selected information is assimilated into what already is stored in the *long-term store*. Information that is not coded successfully for long-term storage fades away and is largely forgotten. Rehearsal is needed to maintain the information in short-term store.

There is ongoing biochemical research into the subject of memory, particularly the effects of the enzyme RNA (ribonucleic acid) on memory and learning in animals (McConnell 1962). However, the development of a "memory pill" to improve human memory is still considered speculative.

Effect of Memory on Other Mental Abilities

Memory is separable in concept from other facets of the intellect; it is not synonymous with intelligence. The individual may have a poor visual memory, yet excell in abstract reasoning. Conversely, a person with poor comprehension may possess an above average memory. Einstein's childhood, as noted in Chapter 1, suggests that he exhibited certain deficits in auditory memory while possessing qualities of a genius in quantitative thinking.

A fascinating account of a man who possessed an unusual ability to remember while he manifested poor abstract reasoning ability is reported by the Russian psychologist Luria (1968). The memory of this man, whom Luria referred to as "S," was so remarkable that he became a professional mnemonist, that is, a man who earns his living by demonstrating his remarkable capacity to remember. Luria had S memorize a table containing 50 numbers arranged in 4 columns and 13 rows. After 3 minutes of studying, S could reproduce the items perfectly in any pattern—column by column, diagonally, or in the form of one 50-digit number. Moreover, he was able to reproduce the table perfectly several months later. Even after 15 or 16 years, S was able to repeat a series of numbers Luria had given him, and he had complete recall of the setting 15 years earlier—Luria's clothing, the appearance of the room, etc.

Yet this remarkable mental subskill was not accompanied by superiority in other intellectual abilities, and this isolated ability brought its own frustrations. S's problem was that although he remembered almost everything he had experienced, he lacked an ability that most of us recognize only as a limitation—the ability to forget. Because S found it very difficult to eliminate images no longer useful, his vivid imagery blocked his understanding of the meaning of written descriptions and made abstract reasoning extremely difficult for him.

The saga of Luria's subject illustrates the concept that memory is an ability that is separable from other elements of the intellect.

Kinds of Memory

Children with learning disabilities frequently have difficulty recalling what things looked like or sounded like. Memory of past experiences must be retained and compared in order to organize and interpret experience. Otherwise each experience is unique, with no connection to previous experience and learning. Memory refers to the recall of nonverbal as well as verbal experiences — for example, the inability to recall the meanings of sounds made by dogs, horns, bells, and certain voice qualities, or to recall the meanings conveyed by facial expressions. The inability to remember words, directions, and explanations are examples of disabilities of remembering language. Memory problems can also be related to a specific perceptual modality, e.g., visual-memory, or auditory memory. There are other categories of memory that can be differentiated, such as rote memory, immediate or short-term memory, sequential or serial memory, and long-term memory.

Rote memory connotes repetition carried out mechanically without understanding. Thus, one child who through rote memory learned to repeat the alphabet without realizing the meaning of the letters asked what an "ele-menopee" is.

Short-term or *immediate memory* is required in tasks in which the subject is expected to hold information in the mind for a relatively short period of time before retrieval. Tasks such as repeating digits, repeating a string of words, following a short series of instructions, remembering and reproducing designs, or spelling a word for a test are examples of tasks requiring short-term memory. Research findings using the ITPA indicate that reading disability cases tend to perform poorly on auditory and visual short-term memory tests (Paraskevopoulos and Kirk 1969). Carroll (1967) found that people who had a poor aptitude for learning foreign language were also poor at the task of repeating nonsense syllables after a short delay, while people with high language aptitude had no trouble with this task.

Serial or *sequential memory* is another type of automatic response requiring a specified order to the items being recalled. For example, in saying the days of the week or in the act of counting, the order of the elements is of paramount importance. The order of the words in a sentence is crucial, particularly in the English language. The child who formulates a sentence in the order of object-verb-subject, "milk want baby," may be exhibiting a disturbance in sequential memory.

In *long-term memory* knowledge must be retained and stored for a long period of time before retrieval of the information is required. There is some physiological evidence to suggest that long-term and short-term memories are located within different structures of the brain (Magoun 1967). The phenomenon of memorizing material shortly before an examination and forgetting the bulk of it shortly thereafter is well known to most students. Long-term memory requires the ability to assimilate, store, and retrieve information when it is needed. It is dependent on the learner's skill in seeing the relevancy of the material and relating it to past knowledge.

Retrieval of odd bits of long-term memory traces sometimes are triggered by strange events. For example, at a recent national education conference a professor noted a vaguely familiar woman in the lobby. He observed her for several minutes, walked up to her, and blurted out, "Hilltop 5-4260." Indeed, that had been her telephone number some 25 years earlier; however, the professor could not remember the woman's name.

For efficient learning, an individual's memory in many areas of performance must become an automatic, habitual response to a stimulus. Examples of such automatic responses include remembering words when speaking, inserting the proper syntactic word form in a sentence, and remembering a word by sight when reading. Many factors have an effect on memory: the child's intensity of attention, meaningfulness of the material, interest in the subject, and the amount of drill and overlearning. Research indicates that appropriate environmental factors and teaching can help children improve in what they can remember (Vergason 1968; Wiseman 1965).

Tests of Memory

Some of the tests previously listed as useful in determining skills in perception also assess elements of memory. The *Benton Visual Retention Test* (Benton 1963); several subtests of the ITPA — *Grammatic Closure, Auditory Sequential Memory,* and *Visual Sequential Memory* (Kirk, McCarthy, and Kirk 1968); several subtests of the *Detroit Tests of Learning Aptitude* — *Memory for Designs* and *Oral Directions* (Baker and Leland 1935); and the *Memory-for-Designs Test* (Graham and Kendall 1960) are useful instruments for evaluating memory.

IMPLICATIONS OF THEORIES OF PERCEPTION AND MEMORY

This chapter thus far has reviewed various elements of perception and memory, which for some children are areas of disturbance that seem to interfere with learning. We have examined several constructions of perception and considered the impact of memory and memory disorders on learning. An important implication is that learning in these areas can be improved with appropriate teaching.

Teachers should be aware of criticism of perception and memory theories as they relate to learning disabilities. One type of critical judgment is expressed by Mann and Phillips (1971), who argue that perceptual approaches fractionate behaviors and that perceptual training programs tend to be a collection of activities that merely duplicate perceptual test items. They further argue that current research has not supported these approaches to teaching. Ysseldyke and Salvia (1974) question the assumptions underlying what they call the ability training model in terms of relevance to instruction, the assessment measures, and the effectiveness of differential instruction based on aptitude measures.

Studies that investigated the *perceptual modalities concept* were reported by Jones (1972), Robinson (1972), and Sabatino and Dorfman (1974). In these studies children were first given tests to determine their modal preference, and then were given differential instruction in reading in order to stress each child's modal preference — either the visual or the auditory modality. In general, these studies did not show a significant interaction between modal preference and method of reading instruction.

There are several explanations for the lack of significant interaction between modality preference and method of instruction (Jones 1972). First, the available tests of perception may not accurately measure perceptual modality preference. Secondly, perhaps both the visual and auditory modalities are so strongly involved in the reading process that learning to read words without the inclusion of both the auditory and visual perceptual modalities is not likely. According to Lilly and Kelleher (1973), a new approach to modality research is needed to avoid these pitfalls. Among the problems they noted in previous modality studies were: (1) a weakness in the instruments that measure modality, (2) treatment procedures differing along dimensions that were broader than the modality dimension, and (3) the design of the modality studies obscuring the interactions.

A review of *auditory perception* in terms of auditory development, tests, and teaching programs by Sabatino (1973) indicates that we still know relatively little about the diagnosis and remediation of auditory problems and that experts do not agree on what constitutes auditory perception. Sabatino notes that the correlational studies have established a positive relationship between auditory perception skills and reading. Hoping that we will soon have new information concerning the measurement of auditory perception abilities, training, and remediation, Sabatino advises that practitioners meanwhile continue using the available auditory perception tests, teaching strategies, and training programs.

A different interpretation of studies of auditory perception was reported by Hammill and Larsen (1974), who reviewed studies using correlational statistical procedures to examine the relationship between reading ability and measures of auditory discrimination, memory, blending, and auditory-visual integration. They concluded that auditory skills are not sufficiently related to reading to be useful in school practice. In contrast, the studies of Flynn and Byrne (1970) and Dykstra (1966) suggest a significant difference between the various measures of auditory perception of good and poor readers.

Studies of *visual perception* have been reviewed by Bortner (1974), Hammill and Wiederholt (1973), Hammill, Goodman, and Wiederholt (1974), and Cohen (1969). The visual perception program and test that have stimulated the most efficacy research is the *Frostig Program for the Development of Visual Perception* (Frostig and Horne 1964), which was revised in 1972 by Frostig, Miller, and Horne, and the *Developmental Test of Visual Perception* (Frostig et al. 1964). In general, the reviewers concluded from an analysis of the studies that the use of this visual perception training program alone did not have a significant effect on reading achievement.

There are several responses to the critiques of the visual perception programs, as well as the auditory perception approach. Frostig and Maslow (1969) stress that negative findings underscore the need for continued investigations of perceptual abilities and their relation to different learning tasks at various stages of development and performance. Bortner (1974) sees the need for a more encompassing theoretical framework of perception. In addition, the responses to criticisms of motor theories, as discussed in Chapter 8, are pertinent here. (1) A bridge is needed between perceptual training and academic achievement; adequate perception should be considered only as a prerequisite for learning such skills as reading. (2) Tests for assessing perceptual modalities are still imprecise and need improvement. (3) A systems-analysis approach to learning is needed to understand how the components of perception relate to the total learning process. Perhaps perception is but one important element that, along with others, must be improved before academic growth can be triggered.

Several reservations concerning remediation of *memory* are noted by Chalfant and Scheffelin (1969). Research on memory dysfunction is limited, and there is little research showing that memory can be improved through outside intervention. However, Chalfant and Scheffelin conclude that with our present knowledge educators should identify the specific memory problem of the child and intervene with specific techniques designed to improve learning.

In conclusion, it appears that the child's perceptual and memory abilities should be taken into account in diagnosing and remediating learning problems. While some current research suggests that a cautious attitude is wise, teachers cannot wait for definitive research but must use what is available to help the children they meet each day. One implication of theories of perception and memory is that it is fruitless to search for one *best* method to teach a subject such as reading to all children in the nation, the school, or even the classroom. A method that is good for one child in the class may not provide a satisfactory learning medium for another. Just as each child is unique in appearance, personality, intelligence, and motor development, so, too, each is different from others in learning characteristics.

TEACHING STRATEGIES

This second part of the chapter presents teaching strategies to help the child in two areas of learning: perception and memory. The ideas presented are merely representative of activities that can be used to improve each subskill. These activities, which represent many sources, are given as samples of activities used in learning disabilities programs.[1]

PERCEPTION

Many children with learning disabilities live in a warped perceptual world. Although they have no basic impairment in their sensory organs, they

---

[1] Other techniques are suggested in the following sources: *Perceptual Training Activities Handbook* by Van Witsen (1967); *The Remediation of Learning Disabilities* by Valett (1967); *Language and Learning Disorders of the Pre-Academic Child* by Bangs (1968); *Psychopathology and Education of the Brain-Injured Child* by Strauss and Lehtinen (1947); *Teaching Educationally Handicapped Children* by Arena (1967); *Learning Disabilities* by Johnson and Myklebust (1967); *Educational Therapy* by Ashlock and Stephen (1966); *Teaching Reading to Individuals with Learning Difficulties* by Ashlock (1969); *Auditory Learning* by Zigmond (1968); *Visual Learning* by Buktenica (1968); *Methods for Learning Disorders* by Myers and Hammill (1969); *Aids to Psycholinguistic Teaching* by Bush and Giles (1969); *Listening Aids* by Russell and Russell (1959); *Teaching Children with Learning Problems* by Wallace and Kauffman (1973); *Learning Problems in the Classroom* by Frostig and Maslow (1973); *Educational Therapy Materials* by Ashlock and Grant (1972), and *Handbook in Diagnostic Teaching* by Mann and Suiter (1974).

cannot interpret sensations in a normal manner. They do not hear, see, feel, or integrate sensory stimuli in their environmental surroundings the way other children do. The abnormality is not in the sensory organ itself, but in perception resulting from stimulation to the sensory organ. Auditory perception takes place in the brain — not in the ear; similarly, visual perception takes place in the brain — not in the eye. There is evidence that perceptual disturbances are important factors in the failure to learn, particularly at the early stages of academic instruction. The widely used term *perceptually handicapped child* stems from the abnormalities such children have with perception.

The perceptual activities suggested in this section are divided into the following categories: visual perception, auditory perception, haptic perception, and cross-modal perception. The teaching strategies are representative of activities that follow from conceptual models of perception and learning disabilities, and many additional teaching activities can be created. The classification of these activities is somewhat arbitrary, since many overlap with other processes and other areas of learning.

Visual Perception Activities

Numerous studies have established that visual perception is highly related to academic performance, particularly reading. Various authors and studies have found a number of visual perception subskills to be essential. Frostig (1968) identifies *five visual perception functions:* visual-motor coordination, figure-ground perception, perceptual constancy, perception of position in space, and perception of spatial relationships.

In a study of visual discrimination tasks as a predictor of first-grade reading achievement, Barrett (1965) concluded that *three visual discrimination tasks* make the strongest contribution to such a prediction: the ability to read letters and numbers, the ability to copy geometric patterns, and the ability to match printed words. DeHirsch's study (1966) similarly indicated that a number of visual perception tasks significantly contribute to a predictive reading index. They include the Bender *Visual Motor Gestalt Test*, word matching, letter matching, and word recognition. It is interesting to note that some of these highly predictive tasks are closer to the category of reading skills than to basic visual perception skills.

The implication of such studies is that direct teaching of visual perception leads to improvement in academic learning. Of course prediction of reading failure does not demonstrate cause and effect, and many of the factors found to be significant are not purely visual in nature. Nevertheless, direct teaching of visual perception skills appears to be a promising approach. Following is a collection of techniques designed to improve visual perception.

1. *Pegboard designs.* Reproduce colored visual geometric patterns to form the design on a pegboard using colored pegs.

2. *Parquetry blocks.* Have the child copy patterns using parquetry blocks.

3. *Block designs.* Using wood or plastic blocks that are all one color, or have faces of different colors, have the child match geometric shapes and build copies of models.

4. *Finding shapes in pictures.* Find all the round objects or designs in a picture. Find all the square objects, etc.

5. *Bead designs.* Copy or reproduce designs with beads on a string, or simply place shapes in varying patterns.

6. *Puzzles.* Have the child put together puzzles that are teacher made or commercially made. Subjects such as people, animals, forms, numbers, or letters can be cut in pieces to show functional parts.

7. *Classification.* Have the child group or classify geometric shapes of varying sizes and colors. The figures may be cut out of wood or cardboard or be placed on small cards.

8. *Rubber-band designs.* Have the child copy geometric configurations with colored rubber bands stretched between rows of nails on a board.

9. *Worksheets.* Ditto sheets can be purchased (or teacher made) that are designed to teach visual perception skills. Find the objects or shapes that are different, match the same objects, find objects in varying spatial positions, and separate the shapes and figures from the background. Some publishers put this material into workbooks. The use of an acetate cover is helpful if the workbook is to be reused.

10. *Matching geometric shapes.* Place shapes on cards and play games requiring the matching of these shapes. Collect different-sized jars with lids. Mix the lids and have the child match lids with jars.

11. *Dominoes.* Make a domino-type game by making sets of cards using sandpaper, felt, self-adhesive covering, or painted dots to be matched.

12. *Playing cards.* A deck of playing cards provides excellent teaching material to match suits, pictures, numbers, and sets.

13. *Letters and numbers.* Visual perception and discrimination of letters is an important reading readiness skill. Games that provide opportunities to match, sort, or name shapes can be adapted to letters and numbers.

14. *Letter bingo.* Bingo cards can be made with letters. As letters are called, the child recognizes and covers up the letters.

15. *Finding missing parts.* Use pictures from magazines and cut off functional parts of the pictures. The child finds and fills in the missing parts from a group of missing parts.

16. *Visual perception of words.* The ability to perceive words is, of course, highly related to reading. Games of matching, sorting, grouping, tracing, and drawing geometric shapes and letters could be applied to words.

17. *Rate of perception.* Use a tachistoscope or flash card to reduce the length of time that the child has to recognize pictures, figures, numbers, words.

18. *Far-point visual perception.* Use the overhead projector and a screen for far-point practice in visual perception. Shapes and letters can be cut out of colored transparencies. Overlays of background designs can be placed over shapes for background-foreground practice.

AUDITORY PERCEPTION ACTIVITIES

Although more emphasis has been given to visual perception in building readiness skills, we are beginning to fully realize the crucial role auditory perception plays in learning. In order to design teaching strategies for building perception skills, it is necessary to identify the subskills that make up auditory perception and to formulate a sequential hierarchy of these subskills. Messing (1968) has isolated eight categories of auditory perception skills. They are: auditory awareness, auditory focus, auditory figure-background, auditory discrimination, auditory memory, auditory scanning, auditory integration and synthesis, and auditory feedback. Flower (1968) identifies similar auditory processes: auditory sensitivity, auditory attending, auditory discrimination, auditory memory, auditory integration, auditory-visual integration. Flower suggests that such a hierarchy of auditory perception subskills presents certain inherent difficulties for designing both tests and teaching methods.

First, in both testing and teaching, each auditory subskill becomes contaminated with demands of other learning processes. A second difficulty has been that some children who are successful in academic performance fail certain auditory subtests. Third, the relationship between training in an auditory subskill and academic improvement has not yet been clearly established.

What has research shown about the relationship between deficits in auditory perception and academic achievement? DeHirsch's research (1966) showed that two auditory perception tasks made a significant contribution to the predictive reading index: the *Wepman Auditory Discrimination Test* and the *Imitation of Tapped-out Patterns Test*. It can be noted that these tests do not assess auditory perception solely, but also other learning processes, such as short-term memory. Dykstra (1966) found that five auditory discrimination measures made a significant contribution to a prediction of reading achievement: (1) discrimination between spoken words that do or do not begin with identical sounds, (2) detection of rhyming elements at the ends of words, (3) identification of the correct pronunciation of words, (4) using auditory clues with context clues to identify strange words, and (5) recognizing similarities and differences in final consonants and rhymes. Again, these tests require other processes besides pure auditory perception. Research with the *Illinois Test of Psycholinguistic Abilities* indicates that reading disability cases do poorly in the subtests of auditory short-term memory, and grammatic closure.

In spite of the lack of clear-cut evidence showing cause-effect relationships and the impreciseness of our knowledge of the subskills that make up auditory perception, most authorities do agree that auditory perception is an essential factor in learning and that children should be helped to acquire these skills. Following is a collection of teaching strategies designed to help children improve their auditory perception.

Auditory Sensitivity to Sounds

1. *Listening for sounds.* Have the children close their eyes and become auditorily sensitive to environmental sounds about them. Sounds like cars, airplanes, animals, outside sounds, sounds in the next room, etc., can be attended to and identified.

2. *Recorded sounds.* Sounds can be placed on tape or records, and children are asked to identify them. Planes, trains, animals, and typewriters are some of the sounds that may be recorded.

3. *Teacher-made sounds.* Have the children close their eyes and identify sounds the teacher makes. Examples of such sounds include dropping a pencil, tearing a piece of paper, using a stapler, bouncing a ball, sharpening a pencil, tapping on a glass, opening a window, snapping the lights, leafing through pages in a book, cutting with scissors, opening a drawer, jingling money, or writing on a blackboard.

4. *Food sounds.* Ask the children to listen for the kind of food that is being eaten, cut, or sliced: celery, apples, carrots.

5. *Shaking sounds.* Place small hard items such as stones, beans, chalk, salt, sand, or rice into small containers or jars with covers. Have the children identify the contents through shaking and listening.

Auditory Attending

6. *Attending for sound patterns.* Have the children close their eyes or sit facing away from the teacher. Clap hands, play a drum, bounce a ball, etc. Ask how many counts there were, or ask that the patterns made be repeated. Rhythmic patterns can be made for children to repeat. For example: slow, fast, fast.

7. *Sound patterns on two objects* provides a variation on the above suggestion; for example, use a cup and a book to tap out sound patterns.

Discrimination of Sounds

8. *Near or far.* With eyes closed, children are to judge what part of the room a sound is coming from, and whether it is near or far.

9. *Loud or soft.* Help the children to judge and discriminate between loud and soft sounds.

10. *High and low.* Children learn to judge and discriminate between high and low sounds.

11. *Find the sound.* One child hides a music box or ticking clock and the other children try to find it by locating the sound.

12. *Follow the sound.* The teacher or a child blows a whistle while

walking around the room. Other children should try to follow the route taken through listening.

13. *Blindman's bluff.* One child in the group says something, like an animal sound, sentence, question, or phrase. The blindfolded child tries to guess who it is.

14. *Auditory figure-background.* To help children attend to a foreground sound against simultaneous irrelevant environmental noises, have them listen for pertinent auditory stimuli against a background of music.

Awareness of Phonemes or Letter Sounds

For success at the beginning stages of reading the child must perceive the individual phoneme sounds of the language and must learn to discriminate each language sound that represents a letter shape from other sounds. Such abilities are essential for decoding written language.

15. *Initial consonants.* Have the child tell which word begins like *milk.* Say three words like "astronaut, mountain, bicycle." Ask the child to think of words that begin like *Tom.* Find pictures of words that begin like *Tom,* or find pictures of words in magazines that begin with the letter *T.* Find the word that is different at the beginning: *"paper, pear, table, past."*

16. *Consonant blends, digraphs, endings, vowels.* Similar activities can be devised to help the child learn to auditorily perceive and discriminate other phonic elements.

17. *Rhyming words.* Learning to hear rhyming words helps the child recognize phonograms. Games similar to those for initial consonants can be used with rhyming words. Experience with nursery rhymes and poems that contain rhymes is useful.

18. *Riddle rhymes.* Make up riddles that rhyme. Have the child guess the last rhyming word. For example: "It rhymes with book. You hang your clothes on a _____."

19. Additional activities for the development of auditory perception of letter sounds and words are presented in Chapter 10 under listening skills.

HAPTIC PERCEPTION ACTIVITIES: TACTILE AND KINESTHETIC SKILLS

For children who do not learn easily through the visual modality or the auditory modality, haptic perception provides an avenue for learning. The following activities are representative of activities designed to stimulate tactile and kinesthetic perception.

1. *Feeling various textures.* Have the child feel various textures such as smooth wood, metal, sandpaper, felt, flocking, sponge, wet surfaces, foods, etc.

2. *Touch boards.* These boards are made by attaching different materials to small pieces of wood. The child touches the boards without looking and learns to discriminate and match the various surfaces.

3. *Feeling shapes.* Various textures cut in geometric patterns or letters

can be placed on boards and felt, discriminated, matched, identified through the tactile perception. These shapes can also be made of plastic, wood, cardboard, clay, etc.

4. *Feeling temperatures.* Fill small jars with water to touch as a way of teaching warm, hot, and cold.

5. *Feeling weights.* Fill small cardboard spice containers with beans, rice, etc., to different levels. Have the child match weights through shaking and sensing the weights.

6. *Smelling.* Put materials of distinctive scents in bottles (cloves, cinnamon, vinegar, etc.). Have the child match the smells.

7. *Stereognosis.* Trace designs, numbers, or letters on the child's palm. Ask him to reproduce or to identify the shape he has felt.

8. *Identifying letters by feel.* Have the child learn to identify shapes, numbers, and letters by feeling them.

9. *Grab bag.* Put various objects in a bag or box. Have the child recognize the object through the sense of touch.

10. *Arranging sizes by feel.* Arrange geometric shapes of varying sizes according to size while blindfolded.

11. *Feel and match.* Match pairs of objects by feeling their shape and texture. Use a variety of textures pasted on pieces of wood, masonite, or plastic.

12. Additional activities for development of kinesthetic perception are included in Chapter 8 under body-image and body-awareness activities.

CROSS-MODAL PERCEPTION ACTIVITIES

For many children the difficulty in learning is due to an inability to transfer information from one perceptual modality to another or an inability to integrate two perceptual modalities. Most academic tasks require such intersensory or cross-modal perception. Below are some activities that require two or more perceptual modalities to function jointly.

1. *Visual to auditory.* Look at a pattern of dots and dashes and repeat it in a rhythmical form on a drum.

2. *Auditory to visual.* Have the child listen to a rhythmical beat and select the matching visual pattern of dots and dashes from several alternatives.

3. *Auditory to motor-visual.* Have the child listen to a rhythmical beat and transfer it to a visual form by writing out matching dots and dashes.

4. *Auditory-verbal to motor.* Play a game similar to Simon Says. The child listens to commands auditorily and transfers commands to movements of body parts.

5. *Tactile to visual motor.* Have the child feel shapes in a box or under a covering and draw the shapes that are felt on a piece of paper.

6. *Auditory to visual.* Record and play sounds of common objects, pets, household appliances, etc., and ask the child to match the sounds with the appropriate picture from several alternatives.

7. *Beat out names.* Beat the syllables in the rhythm and accent of names of the children in the group. For example: Marilyn McPhergeson.

Drumbeat: *Loud*-soft-soft   soft-*loud*-soft-soft
1   2   3   4   1   2   3

Have the children guess the name being played. Holidays or songs can also be used.

8. *Visual to auditory-verbal.* Have the child look at pictures. Ask: "Which begins with *F*? Which rhymes with *coat*? Which has a short *O* sound?"

9. *Auditory-verbal to visual.* Describe a picture to a child. Then have her choose the picture you were describing from several alternatives.

MEMORY

Memory plays a key role in almost all kinds of learning. Memory refers to the ability to store information that has been sensed, perceived, and learned; and memory also refers to the ability to retrieve that information from storage when it is needed. Memory is discussed under a variety of terminologies and subskills, i.e., imagery, retrieval, memory span, auditory memory, visual memory, sequential or serial memory, immediate or short-term memory, and long-term memory. Moreover, it is difficult to discuss, test, or teach memory alone without involving other learning processes.

Because memory plays such a vital role in every aspect of learning, a disability in this function impedes many areas of learning. While there is little research evidence to verify that memory can be improved by practice, Chalfant and Scheffelin (1969) do suggest that it seems possible to expedite the storage and retrieval of specific kinds of information through improving techniques of selective observation, organization of materials, and repetition. The following teaching strategies are representative of activities designed to provide practice in memory tasks. The activities quite obviously overlap those in many other areas of learning.

GENERAL MEMORY ACTIVITIES

1. *Importance of review.* Use *repetition* to make sure that the child learns the material well. The child forgets when the brain trace, which is a physical record of memory, fades away. Recitation and test questions can provide repeated exposure, and frequent *review sessions* will help the student remember the material.

2. *Organization of the material.* The organization of material has a great deal to do with how fast we can learn it and how well we can remember it. Already existing memory units are called chunks, and through *chunking* new material is reorganized into already existing memory units. The more children can relate what they are learning to what they already know, the better they will remember the material.

3. *Mnemonic strategies.* If new material is anchored to old knowledge, children are more likely to remember it. For example, one child remem-

bered the word "look" because it had two eyes in the middle. Some pupils can only alphabetize if they sing the "ABC" song. Some adults can remember people's names by using a mnemonic device that associates the name with a particular attribute of that individual, e.g., "tall Tony."

AUDITORY MEMORY ACTIVITIES

4. *Do this.* Place five or six objects in front of the child and give a series of directions to follow. For example: "Put the green block in Jean's lap; place the yellow flower under John's chair; and put the orange ball into Joe's desk." The list can be increased as the child improves in auditory memory.

5. *Following directions.* Give the child several simple tasks to perform. For example: "Draw a big red square on your paper, put a small green circle underneath the square, and draw a black line from the middle of the circle to the upper right-hand corner of the square." Such activities can be taped for use with earphones at a listening center.

6. Help the child hold in mind a list of numbers or single words. Start with two and ask for repetition. Gradually add to the list as the child performs the task. At first a visual reminder in the form of a picture clue may be helpful.

7. The learning of nursery rhymes, poems, finger plays, etc., may be useful in developing auditory memory.

8. Give a series of numbers and ask the child to answer questions about the series. For example, "Write the fourth one: 3, 8, 1, 9, 4." Other directions could include the largest, smallest, closest to five, last, the one nearest your age, etc.

9. Ask the child to watch a television program and remember certain things. For example: "Watch *The Wizard of Oz* tonight and tomorrow tell me all the different lands that Dorothy visited."

10. *Going to the moon.* Update the game of "Grandmother's Trunk" or "Going to New York." Say, "I took a trip to the moon and took my space suit." The next child repeats the statement but adds one item, for example, "helmet." Pictures may be used to help with auditory memory.

11. *Repetition of sentences.* Dictate sentences and have the student repeat them. Start with short simple sentences; then add compound sentences and complex clauses.

12. *Serial order of letters and numbers.* Say several letters in alphabetical order, omitting some. Ask the pupil to supply omitted numbers or letters: d, e, f (pause or tap) h; 3, 4 (pause or tap) 6, 7.

13. Read a selection that relates a short series of events. Have the students retell the story mentioning each event in order.

VISUAL MEMORY ACTIVITIES

14. Expose a collection of objects. Cover and remove one of the objects. Show the collection again, asking the child to identify the missing object.

15. Expose a geometrical design, letters, or numbers. Have the child select the appropriate one from several alternatives or reproduce the design on paper.

16. Expose a short series of shapes, designs, or objects. Have the child place another set of these designs in the identical order from memory. Playing cards, colored blocks, blocks with designs, or Mah-Jongg tiles are among the materials that might be used for such an activity.

17. Tachistoscopic exposure or flash cards can be used for recall of designs, digits, letters, or words that have been seen.

18. Place pictures of activities that tell a story on a flannel board. Remove the pictures and have the pupils tell the story depending on visual memory of the pictures.

19. Have the student look out the window, and then come into the room and tell how many things were seen.

20. Use an overhead projector to show numbers, pictures, or letters. Have the child look and then cover one. Ask which is missing.

21. Make a pattern of wooden beads or buttons. Have the child look for a few seconds; then ask for repetition of the pattern.

22. Arrange blocks to show a pattern or use drawings of blocks to show the pattern. Have the child reproduce the pattern from memory with actual blocks.

SUMMARY

This chapter has reviewed various elements of perception and memory and presented teaching strategies to help children build perceptual and memory skills.

Perception refers to the recognition of sensory information or the mechanism by which the intellect makes sense out of sensory stimulation. The perceptual-modality concept suggests that each child has a preferred perceptual modality for learning and that individual learning styles can be matched to appropriate teaching methods. Several constructs of perception that have implications for learning disabilities are: the perceptual-modality concept, overloading the perceptual modalities, whole and part perception, tactile perception, kinesthetic perception, cross-modal perception, form and directional perception, and social perception. Since perception is a learned skill, environmental influences, including teaching procedures, can modify and strengthen perceptual learning.

Memory pertains to sensations and data already received and perceived. Memory is the ability to store and retrieve previously experienced sensations and perceptions when the stimulus that originally evoked them is no longer present. Three stages of memory are *reception, storage,* and *retrieval.* Memory storage systems include sensory register, short-term store, and long-term store. The kinds of memory that are important for learning disabilities include rote memory, short-term memory, serial memory, and long-term memory.

The "Teaching Strategies" section of this chapter has presented methods for building the various perceptual skills and for improving the child's memory skills.

REFERENCES

Arena, John I., ed. *Teaching Educationally Handicapped Children*. San Rafael, Calif.: Academic Therapy Publications, 1967.

Ashlock, Patrick. *Teaching Reading to Individuals with Learning Difficulties*. Springfield, Ill.: Charles C. Thomas, 1969.

Ashlock, Patrick, and M. Grant. *Educational Therapy Materials*. Springfield, Ill.: Charles C. Thomas, 1972.

Ashlock, Patrick, and Alberta Stephen. *Educational Therapy in the Elementary School*. Springfield, Ill.: Charles C. Thomas, 1966.

Ayres, A. Jean. *Ayres Space Test; Southern California Figure-Ground Visual Perception Test; Southern California Kinesthetic and Tactile Perception Test*. Los Angeles: Western Psychological Services, 1969.

————. "Reading — A Product of Sensory Integrative Process," pp. 77–82 in Helen K. Smith (ed.), *Perception and Reading*. Newark, Del.: International Reading Association, 1968.

Baker, Harry J., and B. Leland. *Detroit Tests of Learning Aptitude*. Indianapolis: Bobbs, Merrill, 1935.

Bangs, Tina E. *Language and Learning Disorders of the Pre-Academic Child*. New York: Appleton-Century-Crofts, 1968.

Barrett, Thomas C. "Visual Discrimination Tasks as Predictors of First-Grade Reading Achievement." *Reading Teacher* 18 (January 1965): 276–282.

Beery, Keith E., and Norman Buktenica. *Developmental Test of Visual-Motor Integration*. Chicago: Follett, 1967.

Belmont, I., H. G. Birch, and E. Karp. "The Disordering of Intersensory and Intrasensory Integration by Brain Damage." *Journal of Nervous and Mental Diseases* 141 (1965): 410–418.

Bender, Lauretta. *Visual-Motor Gestalt Test and Its Clinical Use*. Research monograph no. 3. New York: American Orthopsychiatric Association, 1938.

Benton, A. L. *The Revised Benton Visual Retention Test*. New York: Psychological Corporation, 1963.

Birch, Herbert G., and Lillian Belmont. "Auditory-Visual Integration in Normal and Retarded Readers." *American Journal of Orthopsychiatry* 34 (1964): 851–861.

Birch, Herbert G., and A. Lefford. "Intersensory Development in Children." *Monograph of the Society for Research in Child Development* 28 (1963): whole no. 89.

Bortner, M. "Perceptual Skills and Early Reading Disability," pp. 79–103 in L. Mann and D. Sabatino (eds.), *Second Annual Review of Special Education*. Philadelphia: Journal of Special Education Press, 1974.

Bryan, Tanis. "Peer Popularity of Learning-Disabled Children." *Journal of Learning Disabilities* 7 (December 1974): 621–625.

Buktenica, Norman. *Visual Learning*. San Rafael, Calif.: Dimensions Publishing, 1968.

Bush, Wilma Jo, and Marion T. Giles. *Aids to Psycholinguistic Teaching*. Columbus: Merrill, 1969.

Carroll, John B. "Psycholinguistics in the Study of Mental Retardation," pp. 38–53 in Schiefelbusch, Copeland, and Smith (eds.), *Language and Mental Retardation*. New York: Holt, Rinehart, and Winston, 1967.

Chalfant, James C., and Margaret A. Scheffelin. *Central Processing Dysfunction in Children: A Review of Research.* NINDS monograph no. 9. Bethesda, Md.: U.S. Dept. of Health, Education, and Welfare, 1969.

Charcot, J. M. "New Lectures, 1886," in S. Freud (ed.), *On Aphasia.* New York: International Universities Press, 1953.

Cohen, S. Alan. "Studies in Visual Perception and Reading in Disadvantaged Children." *Journal of Learning Disabilities* 2 (October 1969): 498–507.

Colarusso, R., and D. Hammill. *The Motor Free Test of Visual Perception.* San Rafael, Calif.: Academic Therapy Publications, 1972.

Cruickshank, William A., et al. *A Teaching Method for Brain-Injured and Hyperactive Children.* Syracuse, N.Y.: Syracuse University Press, 1961.

DeHirsch, Katrina, et al. *Predicting Reading Failure.* New York: Harper & Row, 1966.

Durrell, Donald. *Improving Reading Instruction.* New York: Harcourt, Brace & World, 1956.

Dykstra, Robert. "Auditory Discrimination Abilities and Beginning Reading Achievement." *Reading Research Quarterly* Vol. 1, no. 1 (Spring 1966): 5–34.

Eisenberg, Leon. "Psychiatric Implications of Brain Damage in Children," pp. 171–187 in E. Frierson and W. Barbe (eds.), *Educating Children with Learning Disabilities.* New York: Appleton-Century-Crofts, 1967.

Fernald, Grace. *Remedial Techniques in Basic School Subjects.* New York: McGraw-Hill, 1943.

Flower, Richard M. "Auditory Disorders and Reading Disorders," in Flower, Gofman, and Lawson (eds.), *Reading Disorders.* Philadelphia: F. A. Davis, 1965.

———. "The Evaluation of Auditory Abilities in the Appraisal of Children with Reading Problems," pp. 21–24 in Helen K. Smith (ed.), *Perception and Reading.* Newark, Del.: International Reading Association, 1968.

Flynn, P. T., and M. C. Byrne. "Relationship between Reading and Selected Auditory Abilities of Third Grade Children." *Journal of Speech and Hearing Research* 13 (1970): 731–740.

Frostig, Marianne. "Corrective Reading in the Classroom." *Reading Teacher* 18 (April 1965): 573–580.

———. "Education for Children with Learning Disabilities," ch. 10 in H. Myklebust (ed.), *Progress in Learning Disabilities.* New York: Grune & Stratton, 1968.

Frostig, Marianne, et al. *The Marianne Frostig Developmental Test of Visual Perception.* Palo Alto, Calif.: Consulting Psychologists Press, 1964.

Frostig, Marianne, and D. Horne. *The Frostig Program for the Development of Visual Perception.* Chicago: Follett, 1964.

Frostig, Marianne, and Phyllis Maslow. *Learning Problems in the Classroom.* New York: Grune & Stratton, 1973.

Frostig, Marianne, and Phyllis Maslow. "Reading, Developmental Abilities, and the Problem of Match." *Journal of Learning Disabilities* 2 (November 1969): 571–578.

Frostig, Marianne, A. Miller, and D. Horne. *Pictures and Patterns,* rev. ed. Chicago: Follett, 1972.

Gillingham, A., and B. Stillman. *Remedial Training for Children with Specific Disability in Reading, Spelling, and Penmanship,* 7th ed. Cambridge, Mass.: Educators Publishing Service, 1966.

Goins, Jean T. *Visual Perceptual Abilities and Early Reading Programs.* Supplementary Educational Monographs no. 87. Chicago: University of Chicago Press, 1958.

Graham, F., and B. Kendall. *Memory-for-Designs Test*. Missoula, Mont.: Psychological Test Specialists, 1960.

Hammill, Donald D., Libby Goodman, and J. Lee Wiederholt. "Visual-Motor Processes: Can We Train Them?" *Reading Teacher* 27 (February 1974): 469–478.

Hammill, Donald D., and Stephen C. Larsen, "The Relationship of Selected Auditory Perceptual Skills and Reading." *Journal of Learning Disabilities* 7 (August/September 1974): 429–435.

Hammill, Donald D., and J. Lee Wiederholt. "Review of the Frostig Visual Perception Test and the Related Training Program," pp. 33–48 in L. Mann and D. Sabatino (eds.), *The First Review of Special Education*, Vol. 1. Journal of Special Education Press, 1973.

Hochberg, Julian. *Perception*. Englewood Cliffs, N.J.: Prentice-Hall, 1964.

Howe, Michael. *Introduction to Human Memory*. New York: Harper & Row, 1970.

Johnson, Doris, and H. Myklebust. *Learning Disabilities: Educational Principles and Practices*. New York: Grune & Stratton, 1967.

Jones, John Paul. *Intersensory Transfer, Perceptual Shifting, Modal Reference and Reading*. Newark, Del.: International Reading Association ERIC/CRIER-IRA, 1972.

Ketchum, E. G. "Neurological and/or Emotional Factors in Reading Disability," pp. 521–526 in J. Figurel (ed.), *Vistas in Reading*. Newark, Del.: International Reading Association, 1967.

Kimmell, Geraldine M., and Jack Wahl. *The STAP (Screening Test for Auditory Perception)*. San Rafael, Calif.: Academic Therapy Publications, 1969.

Kirk, Samuel, James McCarthy, and Winifred Kirk. *Illinois Test of Psycholinguistic Abilities*, rev. ed. Urbana, Ill.: University of Illinois Press, 1968.

Koppitz, Elizabeth. *Bender-Gestalt Test for Young Children*. New York: Grune & Stratton, 1964.

Kumar, V. K. "The Structure of Human Memory and Some Educational Implications." *Review of Educational Research* 41 (5): 379–417.

Lilly, M. Stephen, and John Kelleher. "Modality Strengths and Aptitude-Treatment Interaction." *Journal of Special Education* 7 (Spring 1973): 5–14.

Luria, A. R. *The Mind of a Mnemonist*. New York: Basic Books, 1968.

Magoun, H. W. "Commentary," pp. 199–201 in F. Darley and C. Millikan (eds.), *Brain Mechanisms Underlying Speech and Language*. New York: Grune & Stratton, 1967.

Mann, L., and W. Phillips. "Fractional Practices in Special Education: A Critique," pp. 314–325 in D. Hammill and N. Bartel (eds.), *Educational Perspectives in Learning Disabilities*. New York: Wiley, 1971.

Mann, Philip H., and Patricia Suiter. *Handbook in Diagnostic Teaching: A Learning Disabilities Approach*. Boston: Allyn and Bacon, 1974.

McCarthy, Jeanne M. Speech delivered for the Council on Understanding Learning Disabilities, April 1968, at Deerfield, Illinois.

McConnell, J. V. "Memory Transfer Through Cannibalism in Planaria." *Journal of Neuropsychiatry* 3 (45) (1962): 542–548.

Messing, Eleanor S. "Auditory Perception: What Is It?" pp. 439–452 in John I. Arena (ed.), *Successful Programming: Many Points of View*. Fifth Annual Conference Proceedings, Association of Children with Learning Disabilities. San Rafael, Calif.: Academic Therapy Publications, 1969.

Money, John. "The Laws of Constancy and Learning to Read," pp. 80–97 in *International Approach to Learning Disabilities of Children and Youth*, ACLD Conference. Tulsa, Okla.: Association of Children with Learning Disabilities, 1966.

Money, J., D. Alexander, and H. T. Walker, Jr. *A Standardized Road Map Test of Direction Sense*. Baltimore: Johns Hopkins Press, 1965.

Myers, Patricia, and Donald Hammill. *Methods for Learning Disorders*. New York: Wiley, 1969.

Myklebust, Helmer. "Learning Disorders: Psychoneurological Disturbances in Childhood." *Rehabilitation Literature* 25 (December 1964): 354–360.

Paraskevopoulos, John N., and Samuel A. Kirk. *The Development and Psychometric Characteristics of the Revised Illinois Test of Psycholinguistic Abilities*. Urbana, Ill.: University of Illinois Press, 1969.

Robinson, Helen M. "Visual and Auditory Modalities Related to Methods for Beginning Reading." *Reading Research Quarterly* 8 (Fall 1972): 7–41.

Roswell, Florence, and Jeanne Chall. *Roswell-Chall Auditory Blending Test*. New York: Essay Press, 1963.

Russell, David, and E. Russell. *Listening Aids Through the Grades*. New York: Bureau of Publications, Teachers College, Columbia University, 1959.

Sabatino, David A. "Auditory Perception: Development, Assessment, and Intervention," pp. 49–82 in L. Mann and D. Sabatino (eds.), *The First Review of Special Education*, Vol. I. New York: Grune & Stratton, 1973.

Sabatino, David A., and Nancy Dorfman. "Matching Learning Aptitude to Two Commercial Reading Programs." *Exceptional Children* 4 (October 1974): 85–90.

Strauss, Alfred, and Laura Lehtinen. *Psychopathology and Education of the Brain-Injured Child*. New York: Grune & Stratton, 1947.

Sutphin, Florence A. *A Perceptual Testing and Training Handbook for First-Grade Teachers*. Winter Haven, Fla.: Winter Haven Lyons Research Foundations, 1964.

Valett, Robert E. *The Remediation of Learning Disabilities*. Palo Alto, Calif.: Fearon, 1967.

Van Witsen, Betty. *Perceptual Training Activities Handbook*. New York: Teachers College Press, Columbia University, 1967.

Vergason, Glenn A. "Facilitation of Memory in the Retardate." *Exceptional Children* 34 (April 1968): 589–594.

Wallace, G., and J. Kauffman. *Teaching Children with Learning Problems*. Columbus: Merrill, 1973.

Wallace, Gerald, and James A. McLoughlin. *Learning Disabilities: Concepts and Characteristics*. Columbus: Merrill, 1975.

Wechsler, David. *Wechsler Intelligence Scale for Children*. New York: Psychological Corporation, 1949. Revised WISC-R 1974.

Wepman, Joseph. "The Modality Concept," pp. 1–6 in Helen K. Smith (ed.), *Perception and Reading*. Newark, Del.: International Reading Association, 1968.

———. "The Perceptual Basis for Learning," pp. 25–43 in H. Alan Robinson (ed.), *Meeting Individual Differences in Reading*. Chicago: University of Chicago Press, 1964.

Wiseman, D. E. "A Classroom Procedure for Identifying and Remediating Language Problems." *Mental Retardation* 3 (1965): 20–34.

Ysseldyke, James E., and John Salvia. "Diagnostic-Prescriptive Teaching: Two Models." *Exceptional Children* 41 (November 1974): 181–186.

Zigmond, Naomi. *Auditory Learning*. San Rafael, Calif.: Dimensions Publishing, 1968.

10. Languages

THEORY

Language is a wondrous thing — it has been said that language is what makes man Man. It follows that a language deficit may make man less than a man. A language disorder is a non-visible entity. It cannot be seen in the same manner that a crippling defect of the body can be seen. Yet its effects often are more pervasive and insidious than other acute organic defects.

... the greatest prevalence of learning disabilities are those in which language is involved. Because the processes of language have remained an enigma, the methods for training by necessity have been intuitive and empirical. They remain largely at this stage today, although perhaps at a sophisticated level of pragmatism. As the psychological and neurological [and linguistic] factors become more specifically identified, our competencies in the area of education and rehabilitation will increase proportionately.

This statement by McGrady (1968, p. 228) expresses perceptively the idea that language plays a vital role in learning, and that consequently an intimate relationship exists between learning disabilities and deficits in language development.

Language has been recognized as one of the greatest human achievements — more important than all the physical tools invented in the last two thousand years. The acquisition of language is unique to human beings. Although lower animals have developed communication systems, only humans have attained the most highly developed system of communication — speech.

Language fulfills several functions: it provides the individual with a means to communicate and socialize with other human beings; it enables the culture to be transmitted from generation to generation; and it becomes a vehicle of thought. Langer (1958) describes these qualities of language well:

> Language is ... the most momentous and at the same time the most mysterious product of the human mind. Between the clearest animal call of love or warning of danger and man's least trivial *word*, there lies a whole day of Creation — or in modern phrase, a whole chapter of evolution. In language we have the free accomplished use of symbolism, the record of articulate conceptual thinking; without language there seems to be nothing like explicit thought whatever.

In spite of our awareness of its importance to humanity, language remains mysterious and relatively little is known about it. How is it acquired by the child? What is the connection between language and the thinking process? What is the interrelationship between symbolic language and other components of human development, such as motor, perceptual, conceptual, and social learnings? What is the relationship between language development and learning disabilities? What are the universals among the various languages of our world? These questions are among the areas of concern and study for a number of language-related professions, including the fields of linguistics, language pathology, language arts and communications specialties, and psycholinguistics.

LANGUAGE AND LEARNING

Many kinds of learning are dependent on language development and the individual's facility with verbal symbols. The ability to grasp the abstract appears to be highly related to one's mastery of language. Two examples of learning that is limited by language differences or deficiencies appear in research studies of inner-city children and of deaf children.

The language of the inner-city child is significantly different from the standard English spoken by middle-class children. Differences have been noted in vocabulary, dialect, and grammatical structures. Nonstandard language should be viewed as a different but equal language system. Inner-city children have a fully developed language that is functionally adequate and structurally systematic (Carroll 1973). While the language of the inner-city child reflects a language difference rather than a language deficiency, there frequently is a mismatch between the child's language and the language used by teachers in school. The language of the inner-city child has been analyzed as a "restricted code," one that impedes school learning (Bernstein 1964). Consequently, the child is not verbally equipped for the kind of language proficiency required in the classroom.

In a reading test recently administered to inner-city pupils in a major city, fifth-grade pupils scored at the 18th to 20th percentile, while eighth-grade inner-city pupils scored at the 13th to 16th percentile. The norm for the city as a whole was at about the 50th percentile (Black 1967). It should be noted that such tests may be culturally biased in that they reflect middle-class language and values. However, such studies do indicate that one consequence of a language mismatch is that children with such problems fall further and further behind. Two solutions have been proposed. One is to help such students secure a broad oral language base before introducing them to more complex language skills such as reading. The other is to change the learning media and materials for children with different language. Baratz (1973) suggests teaching inner-city children to read by using their own language as the basis for initial readers. In other words, first teach reading, then teach standard English.

The other vivid illustration of the relationship of language to learning is that of deaf children, who are unable to develop speech and language through the avenues of casual hearing or listening. As a consequence of their language deficit, their ability to develop concepts is substantially affected. Research reveals that the educational achievement level of the deaf child is three or four years below that of the hearing child. As a result of the deficiency in development of verbal language functions, the intelligence quotient of the average deaf child is about 10 points lower than that of the hearing child (Pinter, Eisenson, and Stanton 1945).

The role of language in thinking has been examined by such scholars as Vygotsky (1962), Piaget (1952), and Luria (1961); yet the relationship is still not fully understood. Even so, we do know that as language develops, it plays an increasingly important part in thinking processes. Words become the symbols for objects and classes of objects, and for ideas. Language permits us to speak of things unseen, of the past, and of the future. It is a tool that helps us learn, retain, recall, and transmit information, and control our environment.

One of the most dramatic illustrations of the dependency of language on thought is the experience of Helen Keller as she became aware that things have symbolic names that represent them. The impact of this discovery, made at age seven, changed her behavior from that of an intractable, undisciplined animal to that of a language-oriented human being. Her teacher Anne Sullivan described the events (Keller 1961, pp. 273–274):

> I made Helen hold her mug under the spout while I pumped. As the cold water gushed forth, filling the mug, I spelled "w-a-t-e-r" in Helen's free hand. The word coming so close upon the sensation of cold water rushing over her hand seemed to startle her. She dropped the mug and stood as one transfixed. A new light came into her face. She spelled "water" several times. Then she dropped to the ground and asked for its name and pointed to the pump and the trellis and suddenly turning around she asked for my name. . . . All the way back to the house she was highly excited, and learned the name of every object she touched, so that in a few hours she had added thirty new words to her vocabulary.

Helen Keller also described the transformation caused by her own awareness of language as follows (Keller 1961, p. 34):

> As the cool water gushed over one hand she spelled into the other the word *water,* first slowly, then rapidly. I stood still, my whole attention fixed upon the motion of her fingers.
> Suddenly I felt a misty consciousness as of something forgotten — a thrill of returning thought; and somehow the mystery of language was revealed to me. I knew then that "w-a-t-e-r" meant the wonderful, cool something that was flowing over my hand. That living word awakened my soul, gave it light, hope, joy, set it free. . . . I left the wellhouse eager to learn. Everything had a name, and each name gave birth to a new thought.

Helen Keller had learned that a word can be used to signify objects and to order the events, ideas, and meaning of the world about her. Language had become a tool for her to use.

One other dramatic illustration of the effects of the lack of language development is the case of Victor, the "wild boy of Aveyron" (Itard 1962). Victor was captured in southern France in 1800 at about the age of 12, after living alone as an animal in the forest of Aveyron. He had no concept of language and his behavior was totally uncontrolled and animal like. Itard, a physician and one of the early workers interested in special education, tried to humanize Victor by teaching him language skills. Although some minimal learning took place after Itard had worked with him for five years, Victor was never able to develop language skills and did not reach a level of behavior that could be termed "human." Many explanations of Victor's inability to learn have been suggested, but the lack of language acquisition undoubtedly was an important element.

It is interesting to note that much of our knowledge of language development comes through the observation of exceptional children and their language deviations. The balance of this section looks at language from the viewpoints of four different language professionals: the language arts specialist, the language pathologist, the linguist, and the psycholinguist.

LANGUAGE ARTS

Within the school setting, language arts specialists are concerned with all curriculum areas related to language: listening, oral language, reading, writing, and spelling. Their responsibilities include materials, methods, and the organization of these curriculum areas for all children in the school. Although concerned primarily with the developmental language arts program of the entire school, the language arts specialist also has rich contributions to make to the understanding of children with language and learning disabilities and to the development of programs for the atypical child. Analysis of the relationship of the various areas of the language arts is one such contribution.

ELEMENTS OF LANGUAGE

The *language arts* encompass the curriculum activities that utilize language — listening, speaking, reading, and writing. Some writers also add the communication elements of gesturing to this list. An examination of the interrelations of these elements of the language arts has many implications for teaching children with learning disabilities.

For most human beings the acquisition of these skills follows a hierarchy of development: (1) listening, (2) speaking, (3) reading, and (4) writing (Mackintosh 1964). A firm foundation is required at each level before the next skill level can be effectively added or integrated. In the historical development of communication skills, the oral language skills of listening and speaking were developed hundreds of thousands of years before the development of the written skills of reading and writing. The written form of language is relatively recent, and many civilizations, even today, have only a spoken language and no written form. Kellogg (1967) illustrated the hierarchical relationship between the elements of the language arts in the diagram shown in Figure 10.1.

Since people develop the *oral* language skills of listening and speaking first, these skills are referred to as the primary language system; reading and writing are referred to as a secondary language system. In reading, we are dealing with a symbol of a symbol. While the spoken word is a symbol of an idea, the written word is a symbol of the spoken word. Helen Keller is said to have considered finger spelling as her primary language system because she learned it first, and Braille as a secondary system.

Two of the four elements of the language arts can be categorized as *input* or *receptive* skills, while the other two elements are *output* or *expressive* skills. Listening and reading are input or receptive skills, feeding data into the central nervous system. Speaking and writing, which are output or expressive skills, originate data in the brain and send it out.

One implication of these categories for teaching is that a large quantity of input experience and information is necessary before output skills can be effectively executed. This principle has been concisely stated by Dawson (1963) as "*intake* before *outgo*" or input precedes output. Language arts

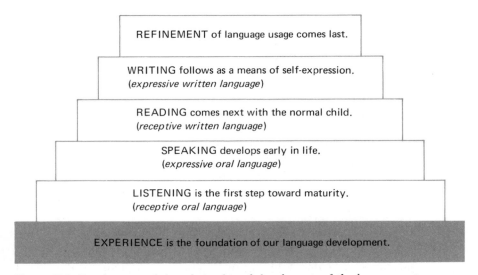

Figure 10.1 Development of the relationship of the elements of the language arts

From Ralph E. Kellogg. "Listening," in Pose Lamb (ed.) *Guiding Children's Language Learning.* Dubuque. Iowa: William C. Brown, 1971, p. 118.

specialists warn against assigning children to produce output, such as a written theme, before they have been exposed to adequate input experiences — such as discussions, field trips, reading, and other media. These experiences will enhance the productivity of the output, the written composition. The integrating mechanism between the input and output is the brain or central nervous system. The integrating process is often referred to as "the black box." The relationship between input and output skills is diagrammed in Figure 10.2.

COMMUNICATION PROCESS

In terms of a communication model, as shown in Figure 10.3, the skills of listening and reading are described as *decoding* functions, whereas speaking and writing are seen as *encoding* functions. In the model, individual A is transmitting an idea to individual B. Individual A must convert her idea into language symbols. She puts it into a coded form; that is, she *encodes* the message into sound symbols (speaking) or visual graphic symbols

Figure 10.2 Relationship of the four elements of language

(writing). Individual B, who receives the message, must then convert the symbols back into an idea. He *decodes* the sound symbols (listening), or decodes the visual symbols (reading).

The implications of this communication model for language and learning disorders are great. A breakdown could occur anywhere in this process. For example, in the encoding portion of the communication process, the impairment could be in the stage of formulating the idea, in encoding it into spoken and written language symbols, in the memory of sequences of previous symbolic experiences, in the brain signals to the motor mechanism used in speaking or writing. In the decoding portion of the communication process, the impairment could be in the reception and perception of the symbols through the eye or the ear, in the integration of these stimuli in the brain, or in the recall or memory as it affects the ability to translate the sensory images into an idea.

The focus of the language arts specialist, then, is upon the normal language development of the child and the language curriculum of the school. The purpose of analyzing the relationship of various elements of the language arts and communication is to enhance the language arts program and language development in the regular curriculum for all the children in the school.

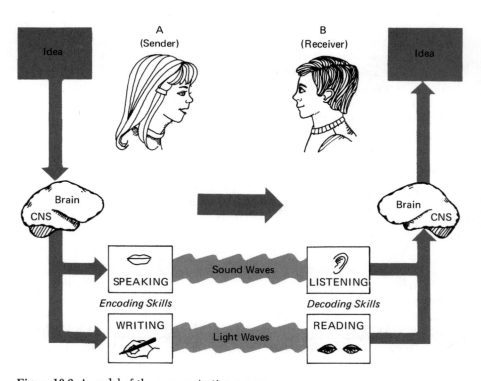

Figure 10.3 A model of the communication process

LANGUAGE PATHOLOGY

The language pathologist is concerned with atypical language development. _Language pathology_ is the study of the causes and treatment of disorders of symbolic verbal behavior (McGrady 1968).

It is important to differentiate between a speech disorder and a language disorder. A _speech disorder_ refers to abnormalities of speech, such as articulation, voice, or fluency difficulties. The child who lisps, or cannot pronounce the "r" sound, or stutters has a speech disorder. A _language disorder_ is much broader, encompassing disorders of the entire spectrum of communication and verbal behavior, including problems such as delayed speech, disorders of vocabulary, word meanings or concept formations, the misapplication of grammatical rules, and poor language comprehension. Because the experience and education of language pathologists are likely to be rooted in the field of speech, their areas of expertise also include knowledge of normal developmental speech, the kinds and degrees of hearing and speech disorders, the pathology of the ear and speech organs, and the fields of acoustics and phonetics.

Humans have developed two forms of communication through language symbols: oral language and written language. The chief interest of the language pathologist is disorders of oral language. The term _developmental aphasia_ is sometimes used to describe the child who has severe difficulty in acquiring oral language, implying that the disorder is caused by a central nervous system dysfunction (Eisenson 1968). Many authorities, however, prefer the term _language disorders_ to describe a variety of language problems, such as delayed speech, paucity of vocabulary, and syntax abnormalities.

The language pathologist warns that many children in our schools probably suffer from some form of language disorder. The problem of some children is in receiving symbolic auditory information or in listening; others have difficulty using auditory verbal symbols or speaking; and others have difficulty reading or writing language. The three-year-old who does not appear to understand simple directions, the four-year-old who has not yet learned to speak, or the ten-year-old who cannot read or write may have a language disorder. There is growing evidence that auditory and language deficiencies are extremely important factors in learning difficulties, and these factors have been neglected in comparison to the emphasis given to visual aspects of learning.

A number of writers have suggested that a useful way to categorize auditory language development is as _inner language, receptive language, and expressive language._ Such an arrangement has been found useful for discussion of language deficits by McCarthy (1964), Schiefelbusch et al. (1967), Wood (1964), and Myklebust (1965). A language disorder can occur in any of these developmental stages of auditory language development.

Inner language disorders. The first level of linguistic learning refers to the preverbal ability to internalize and organize experiences, the antecedents of language and speaking. This process has been referred to as "inner speech" by Vygotsky (1962), "preoperational thought" by Piaget (1952), "inner symbolic manipulation of reality" by Flavell et al. (1963), "central language" by Richardson (1967), and "inner language" by Myklebust (1964). A disorder at this level refers to the inability to assimilate experiences. For example, the child may not be able to organize doll furniture or doll families into a meaningful play situation or may be unable to associate the sound of a bark with a dog. A disorder at this level is the most severe form of language disturbance.

Receptive language disorders. The process of understanding verbal symbols is called *receptive language* (Spradlin 1967), and a disorder of this process may be termed *receptive aphasia* (Kleffner 1964, McGrady 1968). It is thought that language reception is a prerequisite for the development of expressive language.

A child may be deficient in any of the subskills of receptive language. Spradlin (1967) suggests that some children are unable to discriminate between the pitch levels of two tones (tone discrimination), and others cannot discriminate or blend isolated single letter sounds (phonemic discrimination). Another type of receptive language skill that some children lack is the ability to discriminate small word parts within a sentence (morphemic discrimination) — such as the "z" sound difference between "the cows ate grass" and "the cow ate grass."

Some children are unable to understand the meaning of even a single word. Others have difficulty with more complex units of speech, such as sentences or longer speech units. A child with receptive language problems may be able to understand single words such as *sit, chair, eat, candy;* but the child has difficulty understanding sentences using those words, for example, "Sit on the chair after you eat the candy." Some children understand a word in one context but are unable to relate it to another context. The word *run* may be understood as a method of locomotion; but the child may not get the meaning when it is used in reference to something in baseball, a faucet, a lady's stocking, or a river. *Echolalia,* the behavior of repeating words or sentences in parrot-like fashion, without understanding the meaning, is another form of a receptive language disorder.

Expressive language disorders. The process of producing spoken language is called *expressive language* (Spradlin 1967), and a disorder in this process may be called *expressive aphasia* (Kleffner 1964, Johnson and Myklebust 1967). Children with this disorder depend on pointing and gesturing to make their wants known. The child with an expressive language disorder can understand speech and language, does not have a muscular paralysis that prevents speaking, and even may do well on nonverbal tasks; yet this child is poor in the skill of speaking.

There are a number of clinical conditions of expressive language that concern language pathologists. *Dysnomia* refers to a deficiency in remembering and expressing words. A child with dysnomia may substitute a word like *thing* for every object he cannot remember, or he may attempt to use other expressions to talk around the subject. For example, when asked to list the foods she ate for lunch, one 10-year-old girl used circumlocution in describing a "round red thing that rhymed with potato," but she was unable to remember the word *tomato*. Some children remember the sound of the word, but they cannot at will move or manipulate their speech musculature to make the appropriate sounds, even though they do not have a paralysis. The condition is described as a type of *apraxia*. In another type of expressive aphasia, a child is able to speak single words or short phrases but has difficulty formulating complete sentences. Many of the children in our schools who speak in single words or short phrases are not recognized as having a language disorder.

Language pathologists study the nature, causes, and treatment of all language disorders in both children and adults. They analyze normal language development in order to better understand and treat abnormalities in language function.

LINGUISTICS

Another group of scientists, the linguists, study the problem of language from a different perspective. *Linguistics* can be defined as the scientific study of the nature and function of language. Concepts from the field of linguistics are being applied to every area of the language arts. The impact of the application of linguistics on the teaching of listening, speaking, reading, writing, spelling, grammar, and usage may rival the revolution we have witnessed in the mathematics curriculum. Linguists are primarily interested in the study of aspects of language itself. Their prime concern is *not* in education or teaching, nor is it in the application of linguistic findings to the school curriculum. Therefore, educators who wish to incorporate linguistics in educational programs must be knowledgeable in both linguistics and education in order to design and implement workable programs. It seems axiomatic that any professional concerned with language learning or disorders must be well acquainted with the discipline of the science of language.

Linguists use the methodology and objectivity of the scientist in their investigation and analysis of linguistic phenomena. Early linguists were anthropologists who found that to make an intensive study of a particular culture they needed to understand the language of that culture. The anthropological linguists devised systems such as the International Phonetic Alphabet (IPA) to permit phonetic transcriptions of languages under investigation. Historical and comparative linguists played important roles in the study of language by tracing the historical development of language and by comparing common elements of various languages.

Later, American linguists directed their attention toward the scientific study of American English. Using the tools and technology of earlier linguistic scholars, they developed a framework to describe the structure of the American English language. *Structural linguists* have focused on problems of usage and dialectology. Two groups of linguists concerned with understanding the underlying rules of the American English language are the *structural linguists* and the *generative-transformational linguists*.

Linguistics, then, is the study of the patterns of language systems, the nature of language, its development, its function, and the way it is manipulated. One cannot look at linguistics as a method of teaching, but rather as a scientific approach to the understanding of all language in all its forms.

ATTITUDES TOWARD LANGUAGE

For the teachers of children with learning disabilities a number of linguistic attitudes and perspectives are pertinent. The linguist urges that teachers develop a fresh attitude toward language. Language should be viewed as a dynamic, living, changing tool, responsive to the needs and circumstances of the people using it, rather than as a static, unchanging, prescribed set of rules. The American branch of the English language, which our children use, has many variations. The linguist encourages a new respect for various dialects and an acceptance of a variety of language forms. A child's own language is one of the most important links with the outside world. The importance of the child's own language can be appreciated when we realize that it provides one of the the few starting points in the educative process. Linguistic science is forcing us to question many of our traditional values and assumptions about language and the teaching of language — assumptions held for so long that they have been placed in the category of principles, truths, and rules.

LINGUISTIC CONCEPTS

A few basic linguistic concepts and terms are essential for today's teacher of language. Linguists have thought of language as having a number of systems: *phonology, morphology, syntax, semantics,* and *intonation.*

Phonology is the system of speech sounds in a language. The smallest unit of sound is a *phoneme.* Different languages and dialects utilize different phonemes. For example, the word *cat* contains three phonemes: k / ae / t. Phoneme recognition is important in learning to read as well as in oral language. The recognition, analysis, and synthesis of phoneme elements in written words, often referred to as *phonics,* is difficult for some children.

Morphology is the system of meaning units in a language. The smallest unit of meaning is a *morpheme.* Different languages indicate meaning changes through different morphological forms. In standard English, for example, the word *boy* is one morpheme or meaning unit; and the word *boys* contains two morphemes or meaning units (*boy* plus plurality). The child who does not internalize the morphemic structure of standard English might say, "There are three boy."

Children who are unaware of exceptions to morphemic rules may over-generalize. For example, the past tense form of *fight* and *go* might be for-mulated as *fighted* and *goed*. Berko (1958) surmised that normal preschool and first-grade children have well-established rules of morphology. In a study she conducted, children applied their morphological rules to nonsense words. For example, she showed each child a drawing of a birdlike creature and said, "This is a *wug*." Next she pointed to a drawing with two of these creatures and asked the child to complete the sentence, "There are two _____." The application of the morphological rule for plurals gives the answer of *wugs* by adding the phoneme /z/.

Syntax refers to the grammar system of language — the way the words are strung together to form sentences. Different languages have developed different syntactic or grammatical systems. In the English language (unlike some other languages), word order is extremely important to convey mean-ing. Thus, "John pushes a car" has a different meaning from "A car pushes John." A child with a syntactic language disorder may not have learned how to order words in a sentence. Further, in English we can transform the order of the words — still keeping the same subject — to generate a new meaning: the sentence "Mother is working" can be transformed to generate "Is Mother working?" The child with a syntactic language disorder may be unable to generate such sentence transformations. In one research study (Spradlin 1967), when children with language disorders were asked to repeat the question form of "Is the boy running?" many repeated the simple declara-tive form, "The boy is running."

When first graders were shown two pictures, one of a cat chasing a dog and the other of a dog chasing a cat, and were asked to point to the picture called "The cat is chased by the dog," many children chose the incorrect picture. At their developmental level, they did not understand the meaning of the passive form of the sentence (J. Gleason 1969).

Gleason (1965) categorizes ways of analyzing grammar into three groups: traditional grammar, structural grammar, and generative-transformationalist grammar. Each has different implications for teaching language.

The generative-transformational approach differentiates two ways of con-sidering the structure of sentences: *surface structure* and *deep structure*. Surface structure refers to the actual string of words that is heard or read, which provides a superficial view of the sentence. Deep structure refers to the underlying basic elements and relationships that are embedded in a sentence, even though these concepts are not actually represented by words. Deep structure is the underlying meaning of the sentence; surface structure is the form of the sentence as it is used in communication. To fully compre-hend the language, the listener or reader must understand both the surface structure and the deep structure and be able to relate one to the other.

Semantics is the system of meaning in language. It is the most recent area of language to be studied by the linguists and perhaps the least understood. Children with meager vocabulary understanding or usage and youngsters who have difficulty relating a string of words to a meaningful association may have a semantic language disorder. Unlike the morphology, phonology, and syntax systems, which normally become firmly established when the child is very young, the development of vocabulary or the semantic system continues throughout life.

The intonation system refers to sound patterns of the language, including *pitch* (melody), *stress* (accent), and *juncture* (pauses) of a spoken language. The intonation system of each language is different. An example of international differences is the contrast between the sound of "White House cat" (a certain cat who lives in the residence of the president of the United States) and "white house-cat" (a domesticated cat with white fur). Children who have been unable to capture the intonation system of English may speak in a monotone and without expression.

When listening to the intonation pattern of infants, it is impossible to distinguish the babbling of a three-month-old Chinese child from that of a Dutch baby or an American baby. By the age of six months, however, the intonation of the babbling is similar to the intonation of the language in the infant's immediate environment; the babbling is in Chinese, Dutch, English. Experimental evidence indicates that the "native language" of a six-month-old baby can be identified through tape recordings of the baby's babbling (Smith 1972). The baby is demonstrating the acquisition of rules for intonation patterns and has begun to produce phonemes of the native language.

Two other major concepts of linguistic activity within the field of transformational grammar are *language competence* and *language performance*. Language *competence* refers to the speaker's or listener's internalization of the underlying rules of language — that is, knowledge of language. Performance refers to how the speaker actually produces sentences. In many respects the linguist's competence is similar to receptive language, while language performance is similar to expressive language.

The study of linguistics has brought a better understanding of the nature of language and a useful framework for analyzing language deviations found in children with learning disabilities.

PSYCHOLINGUISTICS

Psycholinguistics, as the name implies, is a field of study that blends aspects of two disciplines: psychology and linguistics. In a sense these two disciplines view opposite ends of the language or communication process. Whereas the linguist studies the *output* of the process, the language itself, the psychologist is interested in the *input,* the factors causing the speaker to say certain words at a particular time. Psycholinguistics is a field of study that attempts to look at the total picture of the language process, rather than only one facet of it.

Gleason (1965, p. 61) forecasts that this cross-fertilization between linguistics and psychology will have important implications for understanding language learning in children. Neither discipline by itself has been able to develop a complete perspective of the language learning process.

> The recent reseach of child-language specialists has shown that both views were seriously oversimplified. The process of learning a language is far more complex than either had imagined. The educator has erred, basically, in assuming a far too simple notion of language; the linguists underestimated the complexity of the learning process; the layman, of course, failed at both points.

Because psycholinguistics encompasses many points of view, it serves as a discipline that brings together the many segmented fields studying various aspects of language and learning. The goal of psycholinguistics is to develop an understanding and explanation of language processing. Several promising developments in psycholinguistics that are related to learning disabilities are discussed in this section.

CHILD LANGUAGE DEVELOPMENT

There are several competing explanations of language learning. One school of thought representing behavioral learning theorists argues that language is learned according to the same principles that hold true for the learning of other kinds of behavior (Skinner 1957). The infant begins with no knowledge of language but gradually acquires language skills, largely through reinforced imitation of models. Thus the parents are likely to show delight (reinforcement) when the baby's vocalizations resemble adult speech; the child is thought to have said the first word. The infant likes the attention and, with such reinforcement, tends to repeat those sounds. Language is learned through imitation and reinforcement.

The psycholinguistic approach is an alternative to imitation and reinforcement as the basic mechanism of language development. The biological and genetic foundations of language as proposed by Lenneberg (1967) become the basis for the psycholinguistic explanation of language development. The child is predisposed biologically both to learn and to use language. Chomsky (1959) argues that the human being has developed an innate capacity for dealing with the linguistic universals common to all languages. What is learned is not a string of words but transformational rules that enable the speaker to generate an infinite variety of novel sentences and enable a listener to understand the infinite variety of sentences heard.

Psycholinguists have recently focused attention on the mystery of the acquisition of language. The work of the generative-transformationalists (Chomsky 1965) has touched on topics that also concern specialists in learning disabilities. Two important problems for the generative-transformationalists are: What is it about language that enables a child to learn it, internalize it, and use it? and, What is it about a child that permits him to learn the language? In the words of Noam Chomsky (1965, p. 27):

> What are the initial assumptions concerning the nature of language that the child brings to language learning, and how detailed

and specific is the innate scheme (the general definition of "grammar") that gradually becomes more explicit and differentiated as the child learns the language?

In the process of learning a language, the child has a limited number of primary linguistic experiences. At a rather young age the child hears speech and begins to understand and repeat certain words and sentences. These definite and limited experiences produce an ability to understand and produce new sentences that may never have been heard before. To add to this mystery, children in all cultures have the ability to perform this feat in their native language at about the same chronological and developmental stage. When it is time to enter school, the child who has developed along a normal linguistic pattern uses language relatively as well as the adults in the immediate environment, using and understanding almost all the common sentence patterns. Carroll (1966, p. 577) notes this fascinating characteristic of language learning:

> The process by which children learn their native language is in many respects a mystery.... The "average" or "normal" child who is reared in a sufficiently rich linguistic environment has usually mastered all the essential parts of the system by the time he is six or seven. The fact that he is able to utter and comprehend thousands of sentences that he has never heard before is evidence of this accomplishment.

As the psycholinguist views language acquisition, the child learning a language does not merely learn a set of sentences but, rather, has learned to internalize the total language system in understanding and making new sentences. The task of the psycholinguist is to analyze the process of language learning and producing. Such knowledge should be of great value to the learning disabilities specialist.

Chomsky suggests that the transition in language learning from the simple stages of comprehension and expression to the stage at which the child uses a complex mechanism of language is so rapid that accurate notation of the child's language acquisition and development by observation alone is virtually impossible; and the little that can be observed is not very enlightening. In that brief period of transition, the child suddenly learns to use the mechanisms of grammar. According to Chomsky, the task of learning human language is so complex that some important aspects of language cannot be learned but are innate within the brain. This theory views language learning as similar to learning to walk; rather than being completely acquired, some aspects of spoken language "unfold" or "flower" under appropriate developmental and environmental circumstances.

Significant research on the acquisition and development of language by children has emerged from the Chomsky and generative-transformational theories of linguistics (Menyuk 1969, Berko 1958, Bellugi and Brown 1964, Brown, Cazden, and Bellugi-Klima 1971). As psycholinguists investigate child language development, they try to understand what the child already knows. Children without language problems learn to understand the verbalization of others and to respond in a meaningful way by internalizing these language systems before they reach school age. Research techniques devised to analyze language development provide valuable data concerning the language of children who develop in a normal fashion as well as information about children who develop language in a deviant manner. Such knowledge should be invaluable to the learning disabilities specialist.

IMPLICATIONS OF PSYCHOLINGUISTICS FOR ORAL AND WRITTEN LANGUAGE DISORDERS

Learning disabilities specialists are becoming cognizant that language deficits of one form or another are the basis for many learning disabilities. A language disorder may take the form of an oral language problem, particularly in preschool children in the form of delayed speech, a disorder of grammar or syntax, as a vocabulary deficiency, or as poor understanding of oral language. It may also take the form of written language disorders in reading, writing, or spelling. The learning disabilities teacher attends to both problems — children with oral language problems and youngsters with written language disorders. Young children who have oral language disorders as preschoolers may eventually learn to speak in a normal fashion, but they may manifest their language disorders several years later as a reading disability. Research indicates that many children with severe reading problems have underlying disabilities in oral language (Vogel 1974).

Perhaps it is strange that the process of language learning has been largely taken for granted until the present and that serious research in language acquisition began only in the last decade. However, only as the tools of linguistic analysis were developed did they permit the psycholinguist to study language learning in normal children. Such study, in turn, enabled the language pathologist to analyze the child with language disorders in light of normative data. Psycholinguistic information also has been the impetus for new ways to view reading and the reading process. Specific implications for teaching oral language are presented in this chapter under "Teaching Strategies." Because language and thinking are inseparable, the application of psycholinguistic procedures to reading is described in greater detail in Chapter 11, under the topic "Reading Comprehension."

TEACHING STRATEGIES: ORAL LANGUAGE

The normal sequence of the development of language skills is: (1) listening, (2) speaking, (3) reading, and (4) writing. Spelling and handwriting can be considered part of writing. Teaching strategies for the development of the oral language skills of listening and speaking are presented in the following section. A discussion of the written language skill of reading is presented in the next section, and the written language skills of writing and spelling are presented in the final section of this chapter.

To parallel the term *literacy* for the skills of reading and writing, the term *oracy* has been coined to refer to the skills of listening and speaking (Wilkinson 1968). Oral language, or oracy, has two contrasting sides: understanding oral language, or input, and producing oral language, or output. The two functions may be referred to by the language arts specialists as listening and speaking; by the language pathologist as receptive language and expressive language; and by the psycholinguist as auditory decoding and verbal encoding. Disorders of these functions are referred to by the language pathologist as receptive aphasia and expressive aphasia. The child with "delayed speech" is one who has not developed language and speech skills at the appropriate chronological stage. This child could have a problem in either or both aspects of oral language — in reception or in expression. Although it is often impossible to draw a definite line between experiences in listening and speaking, ability to listen and understand is generally considered a basis for speaking (Mackintosh 1964).

LISTENING

Until recently, the input side of oracy, listening, as an element of the language arts and as a specific language skill has been neglected. While special concern for the instruction of speaking and reading is common, the child is typically expected to acquire the ability to listen without special instruction. The fact is that many children do not acquire functional skills in listening by themselves. According to medical ear specialists, over half the cases referred to them for suspected deafness do not have any defect in hearing acuity or any organic pathology causing their seeming deafness.

The child's ability to listen, it seems, has been taken for granted. We are finally beginning to realize that listening is a basic skill that can be improved through teaching and practice. Compared to the quantity of research in reading, the research and study that has been conducted in listening is miniscule; in fact, most of the reports that were available a few years ago were contained in a single bibliographic volume (Duker 1964). One explanation for poor listening skills is that children of today are so bombarded with constant sound that many have actually learned to "tune out" what they do not wish to hear, and many children have become skillful at *not* listening. It is the task of the teacher, particularly the teacher of children with learning disabilities, to help those who have learned not to listen to become auditorily perceptive and to "tune in."

Some children have a learning problem that stems from their inability to comprehend speech. Such a condition is often termed a receptive language disorder, and the child with such a condition may avoid language activities because listening is so painful.

Listening differs from hearing, which is a physiological process that does not involve interpretation. One can hear a foreign language with good auditory acuity but be unable to listen to what is being said. In contrast to hearing, listening demands that one select appropriate meanings and organize ideas according to their relationships. In addition, listening calls for evaluation, acceptance or rejection, internalization, and at times appreciation of the ideas expressed. Listening is the foundation of all language growth, and the child with a deficit in listening skills has a handicap in all the communication skills.

RELATIONSHIP BETWEEN LISTENING AND READING

The two language modes of receiving information and ideas from others are listening and reading. There are many similarities between these two modes of decoding symbolic language. Both require sensory stimulation, one to the eye and one to the ear. Both require the ability to receive, make sense out of, and organize the sensory stimuli. Both need a memory bank of vocabulary to relate the words that are read or heard. Both need a grasp of the various linguistic systems of the language being used, that is, phonology, morphology, syntax, and semantics. Both require an attentive attitude, for without close attention, half-listening or half-reading results. Finally, both demand the application of specific thinking skills, for comprehension of the ideas being listened to or read. It is not surprising, therefore, that research studies show a high correlation between the receptive language skills of listening and reading and that instruction in listening comprehension is likely to result in improvement in reading comprehension.

There are, however, important differences between listening and reading. The reader can reread and study the material, while the listener can hear the material only once and then it is gone. Of course, the use of a tape recorder modifies that difference somewhat, but a tape recorder can be used in relatively few of the situations that demand careful listening. Readers can regulate their speed, going slower or faster as their purpose and the difficulty of the material dictate, while the listener's speed of listening is set by the speaker. The listener has additional clues of voice, gesture, appearance, and emphasis of the speaker, while the reader cannot derive such supporting information from the printed page. In the listener-speaker combination, there is more opportunity for feedback, questioning, and for a two-way discussion than in reading.

The term *reading* implies comprehension in the reading act; thus Russell (1957) suggests that the term *auding* be used to refer to comprehension in the listening act. In reading, it is useful to classify skills at the level of decoding skills and at the level of comprehension skills; so, too, in listening

Table 10.1 Similarities between the levels of listening and reading

Receptive language skills	Reading (visual)	Listening (auditory)
Sensory stimulation	Seeing (eyes)	Hearing (ears)
Decoding skills	Visual perception	Auditory perception
	Recognition of words in print	Recognition of words and sounds heard
Comprehension	Reading	Listening (auding)

one can speak of a level of decoding or perception of sounds and words and a level of comprehending what is heard, or auding. Table 10.1 illustrates the similarities between the levels of the two receptive language skills of listening and reading.

When teachers ask children "to listen," they do not mean they should simply *hear,* nor do they mean they should just recognize the words being spoken. When children are directed to listen, they are expected to comprehend, or audit, the communication message being sent. Just as reading is made up of many substrata abilities, so listening contains many component abilities and skills.

ACTIVITIES FOR TEACHING LISTENING

The following paragraphs suggest some techniques that have been used to develop, train, and strengthen the subabilities of listening. The optimal sequence of teaching listening or auditory receptive skills has not as yet been clearly specified by research. Therefore, the techniques presented are a collection of methods from authorities in a number of language-related fields.

Listening skills can be categorized into successive levels that require increasingly complex abilities. The following sequence is adapted from Wilt (1964):

1. auditory perception of non-language sounds
2. auditory perception and discrimination of isolated single language sounds
3. understanding of words and concepts, and building of a listening vocabulary
4. understanding sentences and other linguistic elements of language
5. auditory memory
6. auding or listening comprehension:
   a. following directions
   b. understanding a sequence of events through listening
   c. recalling details
   d. getting the main idea

e. making inferences and drawing conclusions

f. critical listening

Following are some suggested strategies for each of these levels of listening.

Auditory Perception of Nonlanguage Sounds

These sounds are the environmental sounds that are around us. Many of the techniques for teaching auditory perception are included in Chapter 9, in "Auditory Perception Activities." The child is helped to be aware of sounds, to contrast sounds, to locate the direction of sounds, and to associate sounds with objects.

Auditory Perception and Discrimination of Language Sounds

An important factor in reading readiness is the ability to perceive and recognize the phoneme sounds of our language. Without such a skill, the learning of phonics is impossible (Liberman 1973).

1. *Initial consonants — auditory recognition.* Use real objects or pictures of objects. Say the name of the object and ask the child to tell which pictures or objects begin with the same sound. The child may group those objects whose names have the same initial sound in one place; may put all objects whose names begin with that sound in one container; or may paste pictures of these objects on a chart. For example, the initial consonant "m" may be presented with "milk, money, missile, moon, man, monkey."

2. *Sound boxes.* A box, approximately the size of a shoe box, can be used for each sound being taught. Put the letter representing the sound on the front, and collect toys, pictures, and other objects for the children to place in the appropriate box.

3. *Initial consonants — same or different.* Say three words, two of which have the same initial consonant. Ask the child to identify the word that begins with a different sound. For example: car — dog — cat.

4. *Consonant blend bingo.* Make bingo cards with consonant blends and consonant digraphs in the squares. Read words and ask the child to cover the blend that begins each word.

5. *Hear and write.* Read words that begin with initial consonants, consonant blends, or consonant digraphs. Ask the child to listen and write the blend that begins each word.

6. *Substitutions.* Help the child learn to substitute one initial sound for another to make a new word. For example: "Take the end of the word *book* and put in the beginning of the word, *hand,* and get something you hang coats on" (hook).

7. *Auditory blending game.* Have the child identify objects or answer questions when you speak the name of an object by separating the individual phonemes. For example: "p-e-n" or "b-a-ll." "What is your n-ā-m?"

8. *Hearing vowels.* Vowels are more difficult than consonants for many children to hear. Begin by listening for and identifying the short vowels. The use of key words for the child to refer to is helpful. For the short

"a" for example, use a picture of an astronaut. After the child recognizes the short vowel, you can help by identifying the long vowel sound. Then contrast the sound of the short vowel with that of the long vowel. The techniques used for the initial consonants and consonant blends may be adapted for the vowel sounds.

9. *Riddle rhymes.* Make up riddle rhymes and encourage the children to make up others. For example: "I rhyme with *look.* You read me. What am I?"

10. *Awareness of rhyming sounds.* Have the child listen to a series of three words and tell which two of the words rhyme: ball — sit — wall; hit — pie — tie.

11. *Same or different.* Say pairs of words or pairs of nonsense words and ask the child to determine if they are the same or different. For example: tag — tack; big — beg; singing — sinking; shin — chin; lup — lub.

12. *Hearing syllables.* Have the child listen to the pronunciation of multi-syllabic words and determine the number of syllables in each word. Clapping or identifying the vowel sounds heard helps the children determine the number of syllables.

Understanding of Words

The development of a listening vocabulary is a basic requirement in listening. Children must understand the names of objects, the names of actions, the names of qualities, and the names of more abstract concepts. It is easier to teach what linguists call form class words, those that carry primary lexical meaning (such as nouns, verbs, adjectives, adverbs), than to teach the structure or function words that indicate relationships within sentences.

13. *Names of objects.* To help a child understand names, use actual objects, such as a ball, pencil, doll. Sometimes exaggeration and gesture is needed to help the child who has a severe receptive disorder understand the meaning of the word that symbolizes the object.

14. *Verb meanings.* It is more difficult to teach the concept of a verb than the name of an object. Verbs such as hop, sit, walk, can be illustrated with the performance of the activity.

15. *Pictures.* Pictures are useful in reinforcing and reviewing the vocabulary that has been taught.

16. *Concepts of attributes.* Words that describe the attributes of objects can be taught by providing contrasting sets of experiences that illustrate the attributes. For example: rough — smooth; pretty — ugly; little — big; hot — cold. Both concrete objects and pictures are useful in teaching attributes.

17. *Development of concepts.* By combining experiences with particular objects, the child is helped to understand the concept beyond the object itself. For example, in learning about the concept of a chair, the child is shown a kitchen chair, an upholstered chair, a folding chair, a lawn chair, a doll chair, and a rocking chair. Through experiences with many objects, the child develops the concept of chair.

18. *Classes of objects.* An even broader classification of objects must be made and labeled with a word. For example, the word *food* refers not to any single type of food but to all foods. Children, therefore, could be taught objects that "are food" and could be asked to remove from a display any objects "that are not food."

Understanding Sentences and Other Linguistic Units

Individuals are expected to comprehend language within the linguistic structure of the sentence rather than in single words. As the linguists and educators develop methods to help children learn the linguistic systems of the American English language, these methods should also prove useful to the teacher who helps children with language disabilities. Some children with a receptive language difficulty need structured practice in understanding sentences.

19. *Directions.* Simple directions given in sentences can give the child needed experiences in understanding sentences. For example, "Give me the blue truck," or "Put the book on the table" are directions that could be given.

20. *Find the picture.* Line up several pictures. Give a sentence about one picture and ask the child to point to the correct picture. This exercise can be made harder by adding more sentences to describe the picture.

21. *Function words.* Linguists refer to function or structure words as the words that show structural relationship between parts of a sentence and grammatical meaning. They include noun determiners, auxiliary verbal forms, subordinators, prepositions, connectors, and question words. These words cannot be taught in isolation; they must be taught within a sentence or phrase. For example, words such as *on, over, under, behind, in front of, beneath, inside, in,* can be taught by placing objects *in* a box or *under* a chair while saying the entire phrase to convey the meaning.

22. *Riddles.* Have the child listen to the sentence and fill in the word that fits. For example: "I am thinking of a word that tells what you use to go down a snowy hill" (sled).

Auditory Memory

The child must not only listen and hear but also must store auditory experiences and be able to retrieve them and relate them when desired. Several teaching strategies for improving auditory memory were presented in Chapter 9.

Listening Comprehension

This skill is similar to what has been called reading comprehension; however, intake is through hearing language rather than reading it. Auding combines listening skills with thinking skills.

23. *Listening for details.* Read a story to the child and ask questions about the story that are detailed in nature: true-false, who, what, when, where, and how questions. In another type of detail exercise, a manual on

a subject such as how to take care of a new pet is read to the child, and the child is asked to list all the things to do.

24. *Sequence of events.* Read a story and ask the child to picture the different events in the order that they happened. The use of a pictorial series, such as a comic strip, to illustrate the events of the story is helpful; the pictures are mixed and the child is asked to place the series in the proper chronological order.

25. *Following directions.* Read directions on making something. Have the materials ready and ask the child to follow the directions step by step.

26. *Getting the main idea.* Read a short but unfamiliar story and ask the child to make up a good title for the story. Read a story and ask the child to choose the main idea from three choices.

27. *Making inferences and drawing conclusions.* Read a part of a story that the child does not know. Stop at an exciting point and ask the child to guess what happens next. In another approach, the teacher reads a story that another child started and explains that the author did not know how to finish it. Now that the dog, Red, is in trouble, can the child suggest an ending?

Critical Listening

Good listening means not only understanding what is said but also the ability to listen critically, to make judgments and evaluations of what is being said.

28. *Recognizing absurdities.* Tell a short story with a word or phrase that does not fit the story. Ask the child to discover what is funny or foolish about the story. For example: "It rained all night in the middle of the day," or "The sun was shining brightly in the middle of the night."

29. *Listening to advertisements.* Have the child listen to advertisements and determine *how* the advertiser is trying to get the listener to buy the products. The mature child enjoys detecting propaganda techniques.

30. *Correct me.* Use flannel board figures while telling a story. Plan obvious errors through discrepancies between what is said and what is placed on the board. Have the child listen for and correct the mistakes.

Additional suggestions for teaching strategies to develop and improve listening skills can be found in numerous sources. Among them: *Learning Disabilities: Educational Principles and Practices* (Johnson and Myklebust 1967); *Listening Aids Through the Grades* (Russell and Russell 1959); *Let's Teach Listening* (Wilt 1957); *Listening Bibliography* (Duker 1964); and *Language and Learning Disorders of the Pre-Academic Child* (Bangs 1969).

Listening Tests

Relatively few listening tests are available to evaluate a child's development in receptive oral language skills — compared to the tests that are available in the field of reading. Among the tests of listening are: *Peabody Picture Vocabulary Test,* the *Ammons Full Range Vocabulary Test, Van*

Wagenen Listening Vocabulary Scales, Listening Comprehension Test (a portion of the *Sequential Tests of Educational Progress*), *Brown-Carlsen Listening Comprehension Test, Durrell Listening-Reading Test*, the *Auditory Reception* and *Auditory Memory* tests (subtests of the *Illinois Test of Psycholinguistic Abilities*), the receptive language portion of the *Northwestern Syntax Screening Test* and the Carrow *Test for Auditory Comprehension of Language*. Descriptive information concerning these tests can be found in Appendix C.

SPEAKING

Oral language, including listening and speaking, is identified as the primary form of language; written language is only a secondary form. In spite of the recognition and acceptance of the primacy of oral language, instructional practices observed in both regular classrooms and remedial work do not always reflect this relationship between oral and written language. Except for the work of speech and language pathologists, emphasis in teaching is too frequently focused on the written forms of communication — reading and writing.

Perhaps one reason for the neglect of oral language in teaching is that there are so many gaps in our knowledge of oral language, i.e., how it develops in the child, what comprises language disorders and delayed language development, and how specifically to go about teaching oral language skills.

Since speaking and language cut across so many disciplines and affect so many aspects of growth and learning, a number of quite diverse perspectives of oral language have evolved. The language pathologist, the language arts specialist, the linguist, the psychologist, the neurologist, and the psycholinguist are all concerned with language behavior. Each discipline has a contribution to make to the formulation of teaching strategies.

Developmental Approach to Language Acquisition

A general overview of the child's language development may provide a perspective for viewing language abnormalities. The child's first attempt to use vocal mechanisms is the birth cry. Through longitudinal and behavioral studies, researchers have observed and categorized the stages that the individual goes through in the short span of time from the birth cry to the full acquisition of speech (McCarthy 1954).

Vocalization during the first nine months of life is called *babbling*. During this stage children produce many sounds, those in their native language as well as many sounds that are found in other languages. Infants derive pleasure from hearing the sounds they make and such sound making gives them the opportunity to use the tongue, larynx, and other vocal apparatus and to respond orally to others. Deaf children have been observed to begin the babbling stages, but because they receive no feedback or satisfaction from hearing the sounds, they soon stop. Some children with language

disorders are reported by parents not to have engaged in activities of babbling, gurgling, or blowing bubbles. Encouragement of such oral play becomes one technique by which the teacher can help these children recapitu-
late the normal stages of language acquisition.

By about nine months, the babbling softens and becomes what is called
jargon. Children retain the phoneme sounds that are used in the language
they hear. The rhythm and melody of oral speaking patterns of others
around them are reflected in their vocalizations. Although intonational patterns may be similar to those of adults, children do not yet use words. It is
as though they are pretending to talk. Chinese children, for example, have
been observed to have mastery of basic Chinese intonation patterns by 20
months of age, a feat that is very difficult for an English-speaking adult
to master. The parents of children who are diagnosed as having language disabilities often report that their children had missed this stage
of development.

Single words, such as *mama* and *dadda,* normally develop between 12 and
18 months of age. The ability to *imitate* is evident at this stage, and children
may well imitate sounds or words that they hear others say or that they
themselves produce. Children with language disabilities are frequently reported not to have engaged in verbal imitation and repetition activities.

Two- and three-word sentences follow the use of single words, for example: *Baby eat, Daddy home, Coat off.* Once children begin to use language,
their skill in speech increases at a remarkably rapid pace. Between 18
months, when a baby first produces a two-word utterance, and age 3, many
children learn the essentials of English grammar and can produce all linguistic types of sentences (Strickland 1969). The child's oral language development at age 3 appears to be almost abrupt; the child has an extensive vocabulary and uses rather complex sentence structures. During this
stage, reports become rather hazy — partly because things develop so rapidly and partly because, as observers, we do not understand the underlying
mechanism of language acquisition. By the time children enter school at
age six, they are said to have completely learned the grammar of their
native language, and their understanding vocabulary is estimated to be as
high as 24,000 words (Seashore 1948). Speaking vocabulary is, of course,
smaller.

As noted in the preceding section of this chapter on linguistics and
child development, it appears to be impossible to observe accurately the
development in language from the beginning simple stages to the quickly
following stage at which children use a complex mechanism of language
(Chomsky 1967). It is in that brief period that children who are developing normally in language suddenly learn to use the mechanisms of grammar — the syntax of their native language: they are able to formulate sentences.

As our knowledge of normal language acquisition accrues, we are discovering that many children with learning disabilities do not follow a normal
developmental language pattern. While language for the normal child seems

to be acquired in a relatively natural and easy manner, without a need for the direct teaching of talking, some children have difficulty in acquiring one or several properties of language. Some have difficulty with the phonology of language — in differentiating and producing the appropriate sounds; others have difficulty in remembering words or in structuring morphological rules; some children have difficulty with grammar or syntax of the language and in putting words together to formulate sentences; still others have a semantic difficulty in vocabulary development.

Experiences in listening (the input or receptive side of language) precede speaking (the output or expressive side of language). Listening alone does not produce the ability to speak, but a looping or feedback process must be created in which the child both listens and speaks. The interrelationship of input and output activities provides immediate reinforcement that shapes speaking behavior. For example, teachers have noted that listening to television does not seem to have an impact on the basic language patterns of the viewer. Although the speech on television may be a good model of standard American English, the speech patterns of viewers reflect that of their home and peer group rather than that of television performers.

ACTIVITIES FOR TEACHING SPEAKING

Below are listed a number of activities to improve skills in verbal expression. These techniques are not intended to be inclusive, but merely representative of activities designed to improve the child's skills in speaking.

Building a Speaking Vocabulary

Some children with language disorders have an extremely limited vocabulary and a very specific, narrow, and concrete sense of the meaning of words. Throughout their lives, people have a much larger listening vocabulary than speaking vocabulary. Young children are able to understand words long before they are able to produce and use them. A child with a language disorder may be able to recognize words when they are spoken but cannot initiate the use of those words. Adults with known brain injuries may lose their ability to remember words easily as a result of damage to the language area of the brain. Such a condition is referred to as *dysnomia*, meaning the inability to remember the names of objects. Children may substitute another referent like "thing" or "whatsit" or "that" or a gesture or pantomime for the word they cannot bring to mind. The following are suggested as ways to help the child use words and build an accessible speaking vocabulary.

1. *Naming.* Have the child name common objects in the room or outside (chair, door, table, tree, stone). Have a collection of objects in a box or bag. As each is removed, have the child name them. Have the child name colors, animals, shapes, etc. Use pictures of objects. A collection or a file of good pictures provides excellent teaching material. Pictures can be made more durable and washable by backing them with cardboard and covering them with a self-adhesive transparent material.

2. *Department store.* The game of department store (or hardware store, supermarket, restaurant, shoe store, etc.) gives the child the opportunity to use naming words. One child plays the role of the customer and gives orders to another child who is the clerk. The clerk collects pictures of the items ordered and gives the orders to his customer while naming them.

3. *Rapid naming.* Give the child a specified length of time (one minute) to name all the objects in the room. Keep a record of the number of words named to note improvement. Pictures can be used, having the child name objects in the pictures. Another variation could be related to sports, the outdoors, pets, etc.

4. *Missing words.* Have the child say the word that finishes a riddle. Who delivers the mail? (mailman). I bounce a _____ (ball). Read a story to the children, pausing at certain places leaving out words; the child is to supply the missing word. The use of pictures helps in recall and naming of the object.

5. *Word combinations.* Some words can best be learned as part of a group. When one member of the group is named, the child may be helped to remember the second. For example: paper and pencil, boy and girl, hat and coat, cats and dogs. Series may also be learned in this fashion: days of the week, months of the year.

6. The teacher should be alert for troublesome words. It may be possible to have an immediate lesson when such a word is noted, then plan for future exercises using that word.

Producing Speech Sounds

Some children have difficulty in initiating the motor movements required to produce speech. Such children may be able to remember the words, but cannot activate the appropriate speech musculature, although they do not have a paralysis. Such a condition has been referred to as a speech *apraxia.* The techniques of the speech specialist in working with problems of articulation may be helpful in this condition.

7. *Exercising speech muscles and organs.* The child is encouraged to use the various muscles used in speaking for nonspeech activities: smiling, chewing, swallowing, whistling, yawning, blowing, laughing, and various tongue movements are exercised.

8. *Feeling vibrations and observing sounds.* As the teacher makes sounds, the child feels the vibrations of the sounds by touching the teacher's face or throat and observing the mouth movements and shaping during the production of sounds. The use of a mirror is helpful to enable a child to observe herself in producing sounds.

Learning Linguistic Patterns

9. *Morphological generalizations.* Some children have difficulty learning to internalize and use the morphological structure of the language. For example, one must make generalizations concerning the system of forming plurals, showing past tense, forming possessives. One must also learn the

exceptions where generalizations do not hold true. For example, the phoneme /s/ or /z/ is usually added to a word in English to show plurality: "three cats" or "two dogs." In some cases the sound of /ez/ is added as in "two dresses," or the root word is changed as in "two men." In a few cases the word is not changed, as in "four fish." For the child unable to formulate such generalizations, games in making plurals can be helpful. It is interesting to note that the morphemic rules of standard American English do not always hold in dialectical variations. The morphemic generalization in inner-city or ghetto dialect (as well as in certain other languages) is to use the appropriate quantitative adjective but not pluralize the noun: *"That cost two dollar."*

10. *Use pictures to build morphological generalizations.*

Picture 1 shows: The boy is painting a picture.
Picture 2 shows: The picture is now *(painted)*.

Point to the picture that describes each sentence.
Picture 1: The dog is running.
Picture 2: The dogs are running.

Formulating Sentences

Some children are able to use single words or short phrases but are ineffective in generating longer syntactic units or sentences. Linguists hypothesize that children, in acquiring language, must learn to internalize sentence patterns so that they can "generate" new sentences. Some linguists have said that the child becomes a sentence-producing machine. To achieve this state, many skills are required — including the ability to understand language, to remember word sequences, and to formulate complex rules of grammar.

11. *Plan experiences with many kinds of sentences.* Start with the basic kernel sentence and help the child to generate transformations on the kernel sentence. For example, two kernel sentences can be combined in various ways:

Kernel sentence:	The children play games.
Kernel sentence:	The children are tired.
Transformation:	The children who are tired play games.
	The children who play games are tired.

Sentence pattern variations:

Statements	*Questions*
Children play games.	Do children play games?
Games are played by children.	Are games played by children?
Children do not play games.	Don't children play games?
Children do play games.	

12. *Structure words.* These are the function words that show the relationship between parts of the sentence. Words such as *on, in, under, who,* are

best taught within the sentence. Close observation reveals that many children have hazy concepts of the meaning of such words. Children can be asked to put blocks *in, on,* or *under* a table or chair, and then to explain what they did. Words such as *yet, but, never, which* often need clarification. The teacher can give a sentence with only the key or class words and then ask the child to add the structure words. For example: "Jack — went — school — sweater."

13. *Substitution to form sentences.* Form new sentences by substituting a single word in an existing kernel sentence. "I took my *coat* off. I took my *boots* off." "The child is *reading.* The child is *running.* The child is *jumping.*"

14. *Detective game.* To help in formulating questions, have the child ask questions concerning the location of a hidden object until it is found.

Practicing Oral Language Skills

Reading specialists assert that much practice is needed in using and stabilizing newly learned reading skills; they frequently say, "You learn to read by reading." Practice is needed, too, for children with a deficiency in verbal expression skills, who need much opportunity in using words and in formulating sentences. For these children, plans must be made to enable them to practice their speaking skills.

15. *Oral language activities.* A number of activities can be used to promote practice in the use of oral language and speaking. These include: conversations; discussions; radio or television broadcasts; show and tell sessions; puppetry; dramatic play; telephoning; choral speaking; reporting; interviewing; telling stories, riddles, or jokes; book reports; and role playing.

16. *Discussion of objects.* Help the child tell about attributes of an object. (The ITPA attributes of the *Verbal Expression* test — such as label, category, color, size, shape, composition, major parts, number, and comparison — are useful areas for discussion.)

17. *Categories.* Place items that can be grouped to teach categories in a box. For example: toys, meat, people, animals, vehicles, furniture, fruit. Ask the child to find the ones that go together and tell what they are. Or teachers can name the category while the children find and name the items. Put items together and ask which do not belong.

18. *Comprehension.* Ask questions that require children to think and formulate responses. What would you be if you dressed funny and were in a circus? Why is it easier to make a dress shorter than it is to make it longer? Why should you put a goldfish in a bowl of water?

19. *Tell me how* . . . you brush your teeth, go to school, etc. Also, tell me why . . . . Tell me where do we . . . .

20. *Finishing stories.* Begin a story and let the child finish it. For example: Betty went to visit her aunt in a strange city. When the plane landed, Betty could not see her aunt at the airport . . . .

21. *Peabody Language Kits* (Dunn et al. 1966, 1967, 1968). These kits

are boxes containing puppets, pictures, and language lessons, all designed to develop oral language abilities.

Additional suggestions for teaching expressive oral language skills can be found in Berry (1969), Lee et al. (1975), Bush and Giles (1969), Wallace and Kauffman (1973), Chappell (1972), Bangs (1968), Johnson and Myklebust (1967), and Hammill and Bartel (1975).

Oral Language Tests

Several methods are used to assess language development. One way is to give the child a *standardized normed test,* wherein the child is presented with a stimulus and asked to answer with a word. A second is to obtain a *language sample* and analyze that sample using techniques of linguistic analysis.

Most of the oral language tests are standardized normed tests. In these tests a definite structure is used and the child is scored according to the number of correct answers. For example, in the *Grammatic Closure* test of the ITPA, the child is asked to supply the appropriate grammatical form: "Here is a bed. Here are two _____."

Some oral language tests of the standardized normed type include the *Verbal Expression* and *Grammatic Closure* tests (subtests of the *Illinois Test of Psycholinguistic Abilities*), the *Vocabulary* test (subtest of the WISC-R), and *Verbal Opposites* and *Free Associations* (of the *Detroit Tests for Learning Aptitude*). Other tests that assess language are the *Houston Test of Language Development,* the *Mecham Verbal Language Development Scale,* the *Northwestern Syntax Screening Test,* and the *Utah Tests of Language Development.* The *Peabody Picture Vocabulary Test,* while designed as an intelligence test, also yields useful information on receptive language development.

Descriptive information concerning these tests can be found in Appendix C.

The analysis of a language sample approach is used in the *Developmental Sentence Analysis* (DDS) (Lee 1974), which is based on a transformational-generative grammar analysis. The DDS technique scores a corpus of 50 sentences that are obtained by presenting stimulus materials such as interesting pictures to encourage the child to produce language. The language sample produced is put on tape. The child's language is reviewed and scored on eight categories of grammatical forms: (1) indefinite pronouns or noun modifiers, (2) personal pronouns, (3) main verbs, (4) secondary verbs, (5) negatives, (6) conjunctions, (7) interrogative reversals, and (8) "wh" questions. Scores for ages two to seven are given in the scoring tables. A follow-up to this assessment method for teaching language through storytelling is presented by Lee et al. (1975). Other examples of the language sample approach to testing are Gottsleben et al. (1974) and the *Carrow Elicited Language Inventory.*

A type of language sample is also used by DeHirsch (1966), who counted the number of words used in a story as an informal measure of oral language development. This measure proved to be a significant predictor of reading failure. In this test kindergarten children were asked to tell the story of *The Three Bears,* and the total number of words used by the child constituted the score. Scores ranged from 54 to 594 words, with 226 words marking the critical score level that gave maximum differentiation between the children who later failed in reading in the first grade and those who did not.

TEACHING STRATEGIES: READING

Children with learning disabilities may have difficulties in any area of learning and development, but poor reading skills are the handicap of the greatest number of children in learning disabilities educational programs (Kirk and Elkins 1974). The teaching of reading has historically been a prime responsibility of the schools. The process of learning to read can be divided into two phases: (1) word-recognition skills, with emphasis on the beginning stages of learning to read; and (2) reading comprehension, with emphasis on the later stages of reading. This section concentrates on the first phase of learning to read. The second phase, reading comprehension, is discussed in Chapter 11.

IMPORTANCE OF READING

It is true, as McLuhan (1964) has so forcefully stated, that in today's world increasing quantities of sensory data and information come to us through nonreadable media, and the global environment of television has replaced the world of print in many ways. In fact, it has been suggested that a "bookless curriculum" be established in our schools, which would offer instruction through the use of nonprinted media designed to relate information and to create appropriate learning experiences (Silberberg and Silberberg 1969).

Even so, it is interesting to note that, in spite of the fact that millions of Americans viewed such events on television as the tragic assassinations, the demonstrations in Chicago during the 1968 Democratic convention, the "moon walk," and the Watergate investigation, people were eager to read the newspapers the next day to make the events they viewed more coherent and to place them in context. In spite of the new role that nonprinted media play in providing a message, illiteracy is a more debilitating handicap than ever.

A few generations ago, people managed to get along quite well in the business and social world without the ability to read, but this is no longer true. Longer periods of compulsory education, the requirement of diplomas and degrees for jobs, more comprehensive school testing programs, the necessity of filling out application forms and taking licensing examinations — all make life for the nonreader uncomfortable and full of closed doors. Reading teachers have an aphorism: "Children must learn to read so that they can later read to learn." Indeed, reading is the basic tool for all subjects in school, and failure in a school subject is frequently due to inadequate reading skills.

With the increase of automation and computerized technology, there is a demand for trained people. Old jobs have become obsolete, and it is predicted that all individuals in every occupational area will have to retrain themselves to prepare for new jobs many times during their work careers. Reading is a key tool for retraining and maintaining employable skills. Recent sociological research revealed that even the crime syndicate has gone through an innovative stage and upgraded requirements. One study of crime organizations concluded that "as criminal jobs become increasingly complex" there will be "no place in the higher levels of organized crime for high-school dropouts" (*Chicago Tribune*, May 15, 1967).

Many of the ills of our society have been related to reading disabilities. The ranks of the unemployed, school dropouts, juvenile delinquents, and criminals tend to have very poor reading skills. Examinations of the problems of our schools, of poverty, of the concerns of troubled parents, as well as of most learning disorders, seem to show some association with poor reading. It is not surprising that a large percentage of our current government-sponsored education and poverty programs feature some aspect of reading improvement. The National Advisory Committee on Dyslexia and Related Disorders (1969) concluded that the problem of reading failure was "the most serious educational problem confronting the nation." The U.S. Office of Education has established the "right to read" as a national goal.

The two disciplines concerned with children who have difficulty in learning to read are the fields of reading (particularly the area of remedial reading) and learning disabilities. While there are certain differences in perspectives between the two fields, operationally they are often quite similar (Lerner 1975, 1975[a]).

DEVELOPMENT OF READING SKILLS

The teacher of children with reading problems should have an understanding of developmental reading programs and normal reading growth. The sequence of stages that the child normally goes through in acquiring reading skills is commonly divided as: (1) development of reading readiness, (2) the initial stage in learning how to read, (3) rapid development of reading skills, (4) the stage of wide reading, and (5) refinement of reading skills (Harris 1970).

Stage 1: Development of reading readiness. This stage begins at birth and continues through the beginning stages of reading. It encompasses the development of language skills of listening and speaking, of motor development, of auditory and visual discrimination, of concept and cognitive thinking, and of the ability to attend to and concentrate on activities. The role of kindergarten has traditionally been to build such reading readiness skills, sometimes referred to as *prerequisites* of reading.

Stage 2: Initial stage of learning to read. This stage, the start of the formal reading program, has traditionally occurred in first grade; but reading may begin in kindergarten, second grade, or even later. This beginning-to-read stage is the stage of reading that has been the most researched, and the greatest number of innovations and changes has been for children first beginning to read.

Great controversies about the teaching of reading have also revolved about the beginning stage of reading instruction. Chall's (1967) widely reviewed and controversial investigation of differing approaches to beginning reading, reported in *Learning to Read: The Great Debate*, concluded that beginning reading is primarily a decoding process and that code-emphasis methods at this stage produce the best results. Another comprehensive investigation of beginning reading, the *Cooperative Research Program in First-Grade Reading Instruction* (Bond and Dykstra 1967), came to somewhat different conclusions. This large-scale cooperative research, using 20,000 pupils and 27 individual first-grade projects, generated data on the following beginning-to-read methods: basal reading, basal plus phonics, initial teaching alphabet, linguistic, language-experience method, and phonic/linguistic approaches. A major conclusion of this extensive research study was that no one method was so outstanding that it should be used to the exclusion of the others (Bond 1966). Two peripheral findings were: (1) that in almost every instance the experimental population made significantly greater gains than the control population (Stauffer 1966), and (2) that there was greater variation between the teachers within a method than there was between the methods.

A variety of methods are used for the initial stage of reading. Some children begin reading with the language-experience approach; some begin with the first preprimer of the basal reader; some start with a phonics method; and some begin with the new materials or methods, such as linguistics, programed reading, or i.t.a. At this stage, children typically begin to develop a sight vocabulary, start to associate sound with the visual symbol of the letter, and learn to follow a line of print from left to right across a page. Much of the reading at this stage is oral, and children realize that reading is "talk written down."

Stage 3: Rapid development of reading skills. This phase normally takes place in the second and third grades. It is an extension, refinement, and amplification of the previous stage. The child proceeding normally in reading now rapidly develops advanced word-recognition skills, builds a substantial sight vocabulary, becomes adept at using various types of context clues, and establishes the techniques of phonic and structural analysis. The bulk of the phonics program is presented by the end of third grade. This implies that the child developing normally has learned phonic generalizations and makes effective application of them by the end of the primary years. This stage lays the foundation for later reading development.

Stage 4: Stage of wide reading. The program of the intermediate grades emphasizes wide reading and extends and enriches the child's reading experiences. The basic skills of the primary grades are improved and strengthened. Now the child progressing normally can read for pleasure. Voluntary reading reaches a peak in these years. Librarians find more enthusiasm for reading among children at this period than perhaps at any other. This is the age of reading series books. During this period children discover *Dr. Dolittle* books, the *American Heritage* series, *All-of-a-Kind Family* books, the *Bobbsey Twins* and the *Nancy Drew* series, or a favorite author like Marguerite Henry, Lois Lenski, Robert McCloskey, or Beverly Cleary. During this stage, too, children share the discovery of a good book, and a list of children in the classroom are soon waiting to read the new favorite of one of their classmates. Book clubs are popular at this age, and librarians report that the middle graders will want to read a book that has been shown on television. At this stage children developing normally in reading enjoy it, but they need help in developing skills in reading factual materials.

Stage 5: Refinement of reading. Schools are beginning to realize that reading development is not completed by the end of elementary school, even for students who do not have special reading problems. During junior high school and senior high school, students need continued guidance for effective reading growth. In fact, reading skills are never completely perfected; even into college and adult life one is still developing advanced reading skills. The development of more advanced comprehension skills, the attainment of study skills, an increase in reading rate, and the achievement of a flexibility in reading for different purposes are the responsibility of secondary schools. It is at this point, when longer periods of concentrated reading are required, that many children begin to fail in reading. The reading problem at this stage is quite a different one from that of the child who is unable to learn to decode a graphic symbol at the beginning stage of reading.

READING METHODS AND MATERIALS

Many innovations have appeared in recent years to help teach reading. Some of these new approaches use fragments of older methods or combine elements of several methods; some of the new approaches have modified the sequence of presentation in an attempt to simplify the initial learning experiences; and some new approaches represent attempts to operationalize recent learning theories. This section reviews the major methods and materials currently being used in reading instruction. Each of these methods may be useful for the child with learning disabilities, but the teacher must be aware of the attributes and limitations of the method or material.

"Decoding" Approaches to Beginning Reading

Decoding refers to the ability to master the relationship between the sound and the letter symbol. Many reading authorities speak of this skill as the ability to "break the code." To decode a word in reading, the learner must become aware of the phonemic segment within the word. Liberman (1973) has found that children with reading disabilities find it difficult to analyze the phonemic structure of the word and match it with the phonemic structure of the spoken word they already know.

The written form of English has an inconsistent phoneme-grapheme relationship, that is, the relationship between the letter and its sound equivalent is not always predictable. Some authorities feel that printed English is difficult for many children to decipher because of the irregular spelling pattern of the English language. The letter "a," for example, is given a different sound in each of the following typical first-grade words: *at, Jane, ball, father, was, saw, are.* Another way to view this complexity is to observe that the phoneme of long "i" has a different spelling pattern in each of the following words: *aisle, aye, I, eye, ice, tie, high, choir, buy, sky, rye, pine, type.* To further complicate the problem of learning to read English, many of the most frequently used sight words in first-grade books have irregular spelling patterns. A few of these words are shown in column *A* of Table 10.2, and the way they would be spelled with a dependable phoneme-grapheme relationship, so that readers could "sound them out," is shown in column *B*.

There are two ways to attack this problem of an undependable written form of English: (1) Simplify the initial learning phase by choosing only those words having a consistent sound-symbol spelling relationship. This is the solution of the various phonics approaches and some "linguistic" approaches to reading. (2) Change the written grapheme symbol by modify-

Table 10.2 Typical first-grade sight words

A. *English spelling*	B. *Phonic spelling*
of	uv
laugh	laf
was	wuz
is	iz
come	kum
said	sed
what	wut
from	frum
one	wun
night	niet
know	noe
they	thai

ing the written code or the alphabet. This is the approach of the initial teaching alphabet (i.t.a.). Both of these solutions delay some of the more complex aspects of our written language system for later teaching. In effect, children are kept from learning the "awful truth about spelling" until second grade or later.

The most significant reading programs having special emphasis on decoding are: (a) phonics approaches, (b) linguistic approaches, (c) early letter approaches, and (d) modified-alphabet approaches. Children who learn poorly through the auditory modality are likely to have difficulty in learning through decoding approaches.

Phonics Methods

Phonics systems and phonics books have been on the market for over 40 years. The availability of multimedia has enabled "old wine to be put into new bottles." Old phonics materials are being produced as transparencies, preprinted carbon masters for duplication, filmstrips charts, recordings, tapes, and computers. The phonics method is typically synthetic, rather than analytic. First, isolated letters and their sound equivalents are taught; then these individual elements are blended or synthesized into whole words. Some of the widely used phonics programs are:

The Economy Program: Phonetic Keys to Reading (Economy Company)
Phonovisual Program (Phonovisual Products, Inc.)
Building Reading Skills (McCormick-Mathers Publishing)
New Phonics Skilltexts (Charles E. Merrill)
Phonics We Use (Lyons and Carnahan)
Eye and Ear Fun (Webster Publishing)
Learning About Words Series (Bureau of Publications, Teachers College, Columbia University)
Speech-to-Print Phonics (Harcourt Brace & World)
Wordland Series (Continental Press)
Conquests in Reading (Webster Publishing)
Individualized Phonics (Teachers Publishing)
Remedial Reading Drills (Hegge, Kirk, Kirk) (George Wahr Publishing)
Basic Word-Study Skills for Middle Grades (Ginn & Company)
Additional programs are included in Appendix B.

Two basal readers that feature an initial phonics approach are: *Basic Reading* (J. B. Lippincott) and *Open Court Basic Readers* (Open Court Publishing).

Typical exercises in phonics materials are similar to those on page 240.

Teachers of reading and phonics. Recent studies have revealed that many teachers of reading are not well grounded in phonics and phonic generalizations (Lerner and List 1970). Some teachers do not remember learning phonics when they learned to read, and many teachers have not received phonics instruction in their preservice teacher education. The reader may wish to take the *Foniks Kwiz*, Appendix A. A brief review of phonic generalizations follows the quiz.

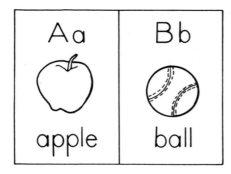 

Linguistic Approach

The linguistic approach to reading, stemming from the Bloomfield-Fries (Fries 1963) framework, defines learning to read as essentially a decoding process. This view assumes that children coming to school have already mastered oral language; their reading task is learning to break the coded relationship between the written letter and the phoneme sound in order to respond to the printed marks with the appropriate sounds of speech. Reading, then, within this framework, is decoding the phoneme-grapheme relationship. The linguistic approach emphasizes phonology, or the sound system of the English language, while the linguistic systems of morphology, syntax, and semantics are not emphasized (Lerner 1968).

The developers of the linguistic approach to reading reason that children who have already learned to make generalizations about the phonemes or sound elements of oral language should, in a similar way, learn to make generalizations about the written letter symbols that represent speech sounds. Reading is introduced by carefully selecting for the initial reading experiences only those words having a consistent and regular spelling pattern. Words that use a consonant-vowel-consonant (CVC) pattern are presented as whole words, and children are expected to learn the code by making generalizations through minimal contrasts of sounds in the words selected. For example, the child is to make a generalization concerning the short "a" sound by learning words in print such as:

can	Nan	van
fan	Dan	pan
man	tan	ran

These carefully selected, regularly spelled words are then strung together to make sentences. For example: (Bloomfield and Barnhart 1963, p. 22)

> Nan can fan Dan.
> Can Dan fan Nan?
> Dan can fan Nan.
> Nan, fan Dan.
> Dan, fan Nan.

This linguistic approach differs from the phonics method in that the letters and sound equivalents are not present in isolation to be blended into whole words, but the letters are embedded in words with regular spelling patterns so that the learner can make generalizations about minimal contrast elements (Fries 1965). Some materials based on this linguistic approach are:

Merrill Linguistic Readers (Charles E. Merrill)
SRA Basic Reading Series (Science Research Associates)
Visual-Linguistic Basic Reading Series (Educational Services Press)
The Structural Reading Series (L. W. Singer)
Miami Linguistic Readers (D. C. Heath)
Linguistic Readers (Harper & Row)
Let's Read (Clarence L. Barnhart)

Another linguistic approach to the teaching of reading, emphasizing other linguistic systems, is proposed by Lefevre (1964). This approach involves the development of comprehension in reading by building the skill of "sentence sense." Sentence sense means the ability to translate the secondary written language back into its primary form, spoken English, so that the child will understand the meaning of the sentence. The linguistic tool for accomplishing this is called *intonation,* which consists of pitch, stress, and juncture.

Early Letter Emphasis

There is a trend in many commercial reading programs to emphasize early letter learning, that is, learning the names of the letters of the alphabet as a prereading skill. A number of studies show that knowledge of letters has a high correlation to success in learning to read (Barrett 1965). Because of the high predictive value of letter knowledge to reading achievement, a number of readiness and basal reading programs are now teaching names of letters as a prereading skill.

MODIFIED ALPHABETS

One procedure for simplifying initial reading instruction is to change the alphabet so that a regular correspondence between sound and symbol can be assured. The modified alphabet approaches described in this section include: (1) the initial teaching alphabet (i.t.a.), (2) words in color, (3) REBUS, and (4) DISTAR. Other modified alphabet systems to teach reading are UNIFON (Western Publishing, 1968) and the *Diacritical Marking System* (Fry 1964).

Initial Teaching Alphabet (i.t.a.)

The initial teaching alphabet is an attempt to provide a medium that will make spelling as regular as possible. The i.t.a. alphabet consists of 44 characters, each representing a different phoneme. The symbols of the conventional alphabet have been augmented for those phonemes having no letters of their own in traditional orthography, for example, *sh, ch, th.* Certain

"whot ſhωd wee næm mie
nue bruther?" hal askt.
"ie nœ a gωd næm,"
maggi sed. "mie dog's næm
is spot. næm yωr bæby spot."

"spot is a gωd næm
for a dog," ted sed.
"it's not a gωd næm
for a bæby," sed hal.

letters of the alphabet, such as *q* and *x*, have been eliminated because they have sound equivalents represented by other letters. Capital letters or uppercase letters have been eliminated to reduce confusion (Tanyzer and Mazurkiewicz 1967). A sample selection written in i.t.a. is shown above.

With normal reading growth, the transition to the conventional alphabet (traditional orthography, or t.o.) is planned for the beginning of the second year in the i.t.a. basal series.

Words in Color (Gattegno 1962)

Words in Color is an attempt to make initial reading easier and more regular through the use of color, without changing the alphabet or the spelling. A single phoneme sound is always represented by one color regardless of its spelling. The children learn the sound of the "white one," the color of short "a." Whether the spelling is *a, au,* or *ai* as in *pat, laugh,* or *plaid,* it is written in white and pronounced with the short "a." The short "u" as in *up* is yellow, and short "i" as in *if* is pink, and so on.

The Rebus Approach

Another attempt to simplify the initial stages of learning to read is through the use of rebus symbols for beginning reading. A rebus is a picture or a symbol of a printed word, and it is used in the reading material instead of certain printed words. For example, in the Peabody Rebus Reading Program (Woodcock 1969), the printed word "be" is represented by a picture of a

THE   DOG   CAT TABLE   BOX   ON   IN   UNDER IS

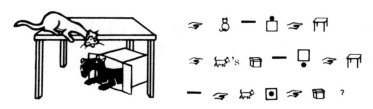

Sample Rebus vocabulary and passage from *Peabody Rebus Reading Program*. Circle Pines, Minn.: American Guidance Services, Inc.

bumblebee. An illustration from the Peabody Reading Program is shown above.

DISTAR Reading System

One program that uses some modification of the traditional print, as well as emphasizing early letter recognition, is the *DISTAR Reading System* (Engelmann and Bruner 1969). The materials and method also make use of a behavioral approach to teaching and specify the teacher's wording and actions. The steps to be followed in this approach include:

1. *Symbol-action games* are used to teach skills such as left-to-right orientation and linear sequence.
2. *Blending* tasks are used to teach children to spell words by sounds (say it slow) and to blend quickly (say it fast).
3. *Rhyming tasks* are used to teach children to recognize the relationship between sounds and words.

The system is a highly structured step-by-step program with emphasis on "code-cracking" skills. Directions for the teacher are precisely specified to meet the educational objectives set for the materials. A sample DISTAR lesson is shown on page 244.

LANGUAGE-EXPERIENCE APPROACH TO READING

The language-experience method views reading as an integrated extension of the facets of language arts (Lee and Allen 1963). The development of reading skills is interrelated with the development of the skills of listening, speaking, and writing. The raw materials are the experiences and language of the child. The child begins by dictating stories to the teacher. These are written down by the teacher, and they become the basis of the child's first reading experiences. According to Allen (1968), the language-experience approach to reading permits the child to conceptualize the following about written material:

What I can think about, I can talk about.
What I can say, I can write (or someone can write for me).
What I can write, I can read.
I can read what others write for me to read.

There is no predetermined, rigid control over vocabulary, syntax, or content, and the teacher uses the raw materials of the reading matter that the child composes to develop reading skills. This approach to reading has a vitality and immediacy, as well as an element of creativity, that have proven useful both in the beginning-to-read stage with young children and in corrective work with older pupils. Although the interest of the child is high, this approach is initially very dependent on the visual modality and visual memory for words. The emphasis is on reading material that grows out of the child's experiences and the child's natural language in expressing these experiences. A systematic structured system of teaching phonological skills is de-emphasized within this approach.

MULTISENSORY APPROACHES TO READING

Several methods of teaching reading are built upon the premise that stimulation of several avenues of sensory input reinforces learning. In these methods, kinesthetic and tactile stimulation is emphasized along with the auditory and visual modalities. These methods utilize tracing in teaching and are often referred to as VAKT (visual-auditory-kinesthetic-tactual) methods. The tracing is usually performed by having the child trace a word or letter that has been written on a strip of paper in large cursive and manuscript writing. To teach a word, a strip of about 4 inches by 10 inches could be used. The child traces the word with a finger in contact with the paper. To increase the tactile and kinesthetic sensation, sandpaper letters, sand or clay trays, or fingerpaints could be used for tracing activities.

In learning a word in the VAKT technique, the child (1) sees the word, (2) hears the teacher say the word, (3) says the word himself, (4) hears himself say the word, (5) feels the muscle movement as he traces the word, (6) feels the tactile surface under his fingertips, (7) sees his hand move as he traces, and (8) hears himself say the word as he traces it (Harris 1970, p. 355).

Two methods of teaching reading that emphasize the tactile and kinesthetic modalities are the *Fernald method* (1943) and the *Gillingham and Stillman method* (1966). Although both of these methods stress tracing, they are quite different in their approach to teaching. In the Fernald method the child learns a word as a total pattern, tracing the entire word, and thereby strengthening her memory and visualization of the entire word. The steps of the Fernald method are described in the next section, on spelling (p. 265). The Gillingham-Stillman method, in contrast, uses the tracing technique to teach individual letters.

The Gillingham-Stillman method is an outgrowth of the Orton theory of reading disability (S. Orton 1937, J. Orton 1966). It is a highly structured approach requiring five lessons a week for a minimum of two years. The initial activities are concerned with the learning of individual letter sounds and blending. The child uses a tracing technique to learn single letters and their sound equivalents. These single sounds are later blended into larger groupings and then blended into short words. Simultaneous spelling tasks are also part of this technique; while writing the letters, the child says both the sounds of the letters in sequence and the letter names. The method emphasizes phonics and a highly structured sequence of learning. Independent reading is delayed until the major part of the phonics program has been covered.

The *neurological impress method* is a relatively new approach to the teaching of reading for students with severe reading disabilities (Heckelman 1969, Langford et al. 1974). It is a system of unison reading by the student and the instructor at a rapid pace. The student sits slightly in front of the instructor and both read together, the voice of the instructor being directed into the ear of the student at a fairly close range. The student or teacher uses a finger as a locator as the words are read, and the finger should be at the location of the spoken word. At times the instructor may be louder and faster than the student and at other times the instructor may read softer than the reading voice of the student who may lag slightly behind. No preliminary preparations are made with the reading material before the student sees it. The object is simply to cover as many pages of reading material as possible within the time available without causing fatigue to the student. The theory underlying the method is that the auditory process of feedback from the reader's own voice and the voice of someone else reading the same material establishes a new learning process.

INDIVIDUALIZED READING

The goal of the individualized reading program is to assure that each child within the classroom is reading in books that are suited to individual needs. No one set of instructional material is likely to be suitable for an entire class or even for all members of a reading group within a class. With this method, each child selects his or her personal interests and level and has the opportunity to read at the appropriate rate (Veatch 1959).

An important feature of this method is the individual conference between the child and the teacher. At this conference the child reads aloud and discusses the book with the teacher. Records concerning the child's reading material, level of performance, and strengths and weaknesses in reading skills are kept by the teacher from information gathered at the conference. The teacher can then plan activities to build and develop the skills the child is lacking.

Individualized reading builds upon the child's own interests and enthusiasm. This method has proved to be particularly successful with those who do not do well in a group situation, as it breaks an undesirable lockstep of some reading practices and promotes an unmeasurable, but highly desirable, positive attitude toward reading.

Paperback books programs. In addition to reading library books and trade books in individualized reading programs, buying one's own paperback books and membership in paperback book clubs have both proved to be fruitful approaches to individualized reading programs. Fader (1966) described one such program, in which paperback books were used to bring the pleasures of reading to delinquent boys.

PROGRAMED READING INSTRUCTION

A few programed materials are available for teaching reading. These materials are designed to be self-instructional and self-corrective. The concept behind the programed materials is that the learning process is enhanced because the material is individualized and self-teaching, and provides instant reinforcement. The subject matter is presented in small, discrete, sequential steps or "frames" containing a single question or instruction. The student responds to the question and then checks the answer to see if it is correct before proceeding to the next frame. Programed reading series include *Sullivan Reading* (Behavioral Reading Laboratories) and *Programmed Reading* (Webster/McGraw-Hill).

BASAL READING SERIES

Basal readers are a sequential and interrelated set of books and supportive materials intended to provide the basic material for the development of fundamental reading skills. A basal reading series consists of graded readers that gradually increase in difficulty, typically beginning with very simple readiness and first-grade books and going through the sixth- or eighth-grade level. The books increase in difficulty in vocabulary, story content, and skill development. Most basal reading series assume an eclectic approach to the teaching of reading, incorporating *many* procedures to teach readiness, vocabulary, word recognition, comprehension, and the enjoyment of literature.

The basal reader, as the major tool of reading instruction for the past 40 years, has been the target of continual criticism from diverse groups, including professors of education, scholars from other academic disciplines, the popular press, parent groups, political observers, moralists, and, most recently, women's liberation groups. Critics have scoffed at and satirized the language, phonics presentation, story content, class appeal, pictures, qualities and environment of the characters of the basal reader. In spite of this highly vocal and severe criticism of the basal reader, its acceptance in the classroom has been widespread. Surveys have found the basal reader to be the major tool for reading instruction in 90 to 95 percent of the elementary classrooms throughout the country (Austin and Coleman 1963).

The eclectic nature of the basal reader permits changes to occur readily. Modifications are continually being made as publishers respond to the demands of the times and their consumer market. Recent trends in basal readers are: to introduce phonics earlier and to make the teaching of phonics more obvious; to introduce formal reading earlier; to have readiness and kindergarten books introduce more formal aspects of the reading program than they once did — such as letters and sight words; to make stories longer and more sophisticated; and to have the stories tell about many ethnic groups and ways of life.

One of the most notable trends at present is the introduction of multiracial and urban-centered materials. Some of the basal series especially designed for disadvantaged, urban, multiracial groups are:

City Schools Reading Program (Follett Publishing)
The Bank Street Readers (Macmillan)
Multi-media Chandler Reading Program (Chandler Publishing)

BEHAVIOR MODIFICATION APPROACHES TO READING

Recent interest in behavior modification as a technique in teaching educational skills has been directed to the teaching of reading. The conceptual framework behind such an approach requires the setting of specified, observable, and measurable behavioral objectives. The environmental stimuli are then structured so that they will bring about a change in the child's behavior and produce the desired objective. A description of case studies in which behavior-modification techniques were used to improve reading is presented by Wark (1969) and Haring and Hauch (1969). Lovitt and Hurlburt (1974) experimented with a behavior-modification technique for teaching reading skills and found it a useful way to teach phonics and thereby improve oral reading.

Some commercial materials incorporate elements of the behavioral approach, e.g., DISTAR, discussed in this section, and the *criterion-referenced systems,* discussed in greater detail in Chapter 11, under "Reading Comprehension." Specific procedures for using the behavior-modification approach as a teaching strategy for reading are presented in Chapter 12.

The *Edmark Reading Program* (Edmark Associates) is based on a stimulus-response-reinforcement approach to learning. The program teaches a 150-word vocabulary and provides varied student activities. Four kinds of carefully sequenced activities are used in 227 lessons: word recognition, direction books, practice/phrase matching, and storybook. This program is designed for students with extremely limited skills and is reported to be successful with children with low IQ scores.

TECHNOLOGICAL INNOVATIONS IN READING

Various kinds of machines are being used to teach reading. The *talking typewriter* developed by O. K. Moore (Johnson 1969) features a typewriter that speaks the name of the letter as the child types it while pictures representing words are flashed on a screen.

Computer-Assisted Instruction (CAI) is a program that uses a computer to teach initial reading. It was implemented in the Stanford Project, an experiment in Palo Alto, California (Atkinson and Fletcher 1972). Wearing earphones, the child observes images on a television screen and touches certain of the screen images with a light-projecting pen. If she touches the right image a voice says, "Good." If she is incorrect a voice says "No" and then repeats the instruction. If several consecutive mistakes are made, the computer sets up a signal that calls the teacher for more help.

Teaching machines combine the audio and visual presentation with coordinated tapes and film strips to teach reading. Some of these machines have branch programs; that is, the correct response to a question will trigger the next step of a teaching lesson, while an incorrect response will trigger a review or a remedial lesson. *Systems 80* (Borg Warner) is such a machine.

Machines used to improve reading rate include *tachistoscopes* and *accelerating devices*. The tachistoscope exposes numbers, letters, or whole words for short periods of time, ranging from 1/100 to 1½ seconds. The purpose of the short exposure is to increase the speed of visual perception. The accelerating devices provide rate training. There are a number of different types of machines to pace reading. With some, materials are exposed at a predetermined rate on a screen; other machines expose reading material in a book at a predetermined rate. The first regulates eye movement at a far-point distance; the latter at near point. The purpose of such devices is to reduce fixations and regressions, develop better attention and concentration, and require more rapid thinking. Films are also available for this purpose. The ability of the reader to transfer skills from a machine-regulated application to reading a book is a controversial topic in the field of reading.

READING LABORATORIES

Some reading programs, particularly in secondary schools, have developed special-purpose reading laboratory rooms with small carrels to be used by individual students. These individual learning carrels are designed for many types of audiovisual equipment and reading machines, as well as for use of books and workbooks. Individual reading programs that utilize the multimedia approach are developed and designed to meet the requirements of each student. Electrical and mechanical devices, as well as some of the more conventional materials, appear to be well suited to such an approach.

SYSTEMS APPROACHES TO READING

The term *systems* has appeared in the name of a number of recent reading programs. The Scott, Foresman *Reading System* consists of components that make up the sets of interrelated parts. The components include a variety of multimedia materials such as pupils' books, study books, teachers' read-aloud books, practice sheets, tests, linguistic blocks, games, puzzles, cassettes, and special practice books. The teacher is to create a subsystem using these component parts to design a program to meet the specific needs of each child.

The term *system* is also used to designate instructional management systems. In this context it is a business term used to imply *product control*. The product being controlled here is the child learning to read. These programs use a step-by-step process, providing materials and directions for managing children toward meeting specified goals. Each child uses the same materials, but at varying rates to gain the specified skill. Such system approaches include *Curriculum Management System* (Harcourt Brace Jovanovich), *Ginn Management System — Reading 360* (Ginn and Co.) and *Power Reading System* (Winston Press).

The enormous number of reading materials, reading approaches, and reading methods is almost bewildering. The publishers of materials and designers of specific methods exude confidence that their approaches will be able to accomplish what others have failed to do. Cumulative reading research seems to indicate that the most important variable in successful reading programs is not the material, method, or approach, but rather the teacher who is interacting with the child.

To select appropriate reading materials or methods prudently, the learning disabilities specialist must develop competencies in the following: (1) analyzing the nature of the task to be performed with the reading material or method under consideration, (2) analyzing the mental processes and learning styles of the child who is to be helped, and (3) matching the appropriate types of materials to the disabilities and abilities of the child.

DYSLEXIA

The term *dyslexia* is commonly used in the field of learning disabilities to identify children who have difficulty in learning to read. Since professionals in the field of learning disabilities are so frequently questioned about dyslexia, it seems appropriate to devote a portion of this section on reading to various views of the dyslexic child and to clarify certain questions. What is dyslexia? Have scholars in the field of reading been aware of dyslexia as a factor in reading failure? What theoretical frameworks led some diagnosticians to use the term *dyslexia* and others to prefer the term *reading disability*? (Lerner 1971, 1975).

Although there may be agreement that dyslexia has something to do with children's difficulty in reading, there are great differences among more precise definitions of dyslexia. A review of the literature reveals that the word *dyslexia* is currently being used in a variety of ways by different authors. Its diverse definitions cover a wide range and include (a) evidence of an etiology of brain damage, (b) the observation of behavioral manifestations of central nervous system dysfunction, (c) the indication of a genetic or inherited cause of the reading problem, (d) the presence of a syndrome of maturational lag, (e) use as a synonym for reading retardation, and (f) use to describe a child who has been unable to learn to read through the regular classroom methods.

The literature consists of two almost entirely separate strands of thought concerning dyslexia. The two views are (1) the medical perspective, and (2) the educational perspective. The first group views dyslexia as an inability to read due to brain damage or central nervous system dysfunction. This view is largely medically oriented and much of the research originated in Europe. At the opposite pole, another group of authorities views dyslexia as a reading disability and says that it "simply means there is something wrong with the person's reading" or that dyslexics are "children who are of average or better intelligence who are finding it difficult to learn to read." This view stems largely from educators, psychologists, and reading specialists, and it originated largely in the United States.

The term *dyslexia* has its roots in the term *alexia*, which describes a loss of ability to read because of an injury to the brain, such as a cerebral stroke. The condition of alexia, also called "acquired word blindness," occurs in an adult who had already learned to read. Children who did not learn to read normally were presumed to have brain lesions similar to those found in cases of alexia in adults. Since the condition of adults who lose the ability to read was called *acquired alexia*, children who failed to learn to read were assumed to have *developmental alexia* or *dyslexia*.

TWO PERSPECTIVES ON DYSLEXIA: MEDICAL AND EDUCATIONAL

Literature on the medical perspective first appeared in England with an article written by a physician (Morgan 1896). Since that time many other investigators have attempted to find medical explanations for poor reading or dyslexia, including Hinshelwood (1917), Schmitt (1918), Orton (1937), Hallgren (1950), Hermann (1961), Critchley (1964), Money (1966), and Johnson and Myklebust (1967). In the past 70 years, over 20,000 books, articles, and papers have been published on the subject; they have sought a common behavior pattern among all dyslexic children and clearcut evidence of a neurological etiology (Eichenwald 1967). The difficulty in finding empirical evidence to support the medical perspective is that it is almost impossible, even at present, to directly examine the brain of the child. Therefore, evidence of dyslexia owing to brain damage or dysfunction is most difficult to establish diagnostically and is necessarily presumptive in nature.

Educators, reading specialists, and psychologists generally have a different view of dyslexia from that of the medically oriented scholars. The early studies of children who could not read (Monroe 1932, Robinson 1946) investigated the causes of reading failure, including the neurological factor; but these investigators concluded that the neurological theories of causation had not been strongly established. Vernon (1957) concluded that the term dyslexia was unacceptable because the condition is not comparable to alexia. Bond and Tinker (1967) also maintained that it is impossible to distinguish dyslexia from a severe reading disability and that "the clinical worker may question the value of the term."

IMPLICATIONS OF THE MEDICAL AND EDUCATIONAL PERSPECTIVES ON DYSLEXIA

What are some of the implications of the differences in these two perspectives? For purposes of discussion, the two frameworks will be called the *medical perspective* and the *educational perspective*.

1. While the scholars working within the medical perspective search for a single etiological factor as causal, the scholars in the educational perspective seek a combination of causes, stressing that it is not likely that a single factor can be shown to be causal.

2. The educators are likely to place greater emphasis on the developmental sequence of reading skills, making an intensive search for the child's break with the developmental reading pattern. The medically oriented investigator is likely to place greater emphasis on the language-related areas, such as speech and oral language skills, as well as on other related disabilities, such as arithmetic skills, perception, motor development, and social skills.

3. For the educator, alexia, or the loss of reading skill in the case of an adult, is different from the inability to learn to read in the case of a child. Therefore, the term dyslexia is not generally used among this group. They emphasize the necessity of differentiating "maturational lag" from central nervous system dysfunction.

4. Educators see the diagnosis of dyslexia as lacking operationality in that

it does not lead to appropriate teaching strategies. After the diagnosis of dyslexia is made, one must still investigate what reading skills are lacking, how the child best learns, what are the appropriate materials to overcome the problem, and so on. The diagnosis of dyslexia alone provides few clues to the appropriate treatment and remedial measures.

5. While medically oriented clinicians are likely to focus solely on the disabled child and to emphasize individual treatment, educators are likely to perceive a broader role and function within the school and to devote a portion of their time and energy to the developmental reading program of the entire school in seeking preventive measures.

In conclusion, two strands of thinking concerning dyslexia have been developed by two separate fields of study: (a) the medical perspective and (b) the educational perspective. The review of the literature on dyslexia does not lead to conclusive evidence for or against the approach of either discipline. Researchers and scholars must and should study the reading problem of children in terms of their own training, experience, and framework. Each discipline has built a substantial body of literature, but neither is benefiting sufficiently from the work and foundation that has already been made by the other. If children who cannot read are to be helped, disciplines must forget labels and begin to work together.

The *National Advisory Committee on Dyslexia and Related Reading Disorders* was created by the Secretary of Health, Education and Welfare in 1968 to investigate, clarify, and resolve the controversial issues surrounding dyslexia. The Committee report, released by HEW in August 1969, reported the following statement about dyslexia: "In view of these divergencies of opinion the Committee believes that the use of the term 'dyslexia' serves no useful purpose" (National Advisory Committee on Dyslexia and Related Reading Disorders 1969, p. 38). Perhaps more important, however, the Report recommended to the Secretary of the Department of HEW several vital steps to improve the reading of students within our nation who experience difficulty in learning to read. One of the key recommendations was the creation of an Office of Reading Disorders within an appropriate agency of the Department of Health, Education and Welfare.

TEACHING STRATEGIES: WRITTEN LANGUAGE

This section deals with learning disabilities in the expressive communication areas of written language; specifically, handwriting, spelling, and written expression.

It is common knowledge that many people dislike writing. Hook (1967) illustrates this disdainful attitude toward writing with the story of the New York City taxicab driver who skillfully guided his cab past a pedestrian. In explaining to his passenger why he was so careful, the cabbie said, "I always try to avoid hittin' 'em because every time ya hit one, ya gotta write out a long report about it."

The written form of language is the highest and most complex form of communication. In the hierarchy of language skills, it is the last to be learned. Prerequisite to writing is a foundation of previous learnings and experiences in listening, speaking, and reading. In addition to an adequate basis of auditory language skills, proficiency in using written language requires many other skills. The ability to keep one idea in mind, to formulate the idea in words and appropriate syntactic patterns, to plan the correct graphic form for each letter and word, to correctly manipulate the writing instrument to produce the letter shapes, to integrate complex eye-hand relationships, and to have sufficient visual and motor memory — all are required for the act of writing.

The three areas of written language discussed in this section are (1) handwriting, (2) spelling, and (3) written expression.

HANDWRITING

Handwriting is the most concrete of the communication skills. The child's handwriting can be directly observed, evaluated, and preserved. It differs from the receptive skill of reading in that the measurement of the reading comprehension skill must necessarily be indirect, through the asking of questions; children must verbalize in some way to let you know what they have read. Handwriting also differs from the expressive skill of speaking since it provides a permanent record of the output and since it requires visual and motor skills.

Difficulty in handwriting, sometimes referred to as *dysgraphia*, may reflect the underlying presence of many other deficits. Children with handwriting problems may be unable to execute efficiently the motor movements required to write or to copy written letters or forms; they may be unable to transfer the input of visual information to the output of fine motor movement; they may be poor in other visual-motor functions and in activities requiring motor and spatial judgments. Hildreth (1947) has commented on the intricacy of the psychomotor process involved in handwriting.

> Learning to write is not a mechanical, lower-level reflex response, but a thinking process, entailing activity of the cortical nerve areas. Smooth motor coordination of eye and hand, control of arm, hand, and finger muscles are acquired in the process of learning to write and are needed for legible results. Learning to write also requires maturity adequate for accurate perception of the symbol patterns. Writing from memory demands the retention of visual and kinesthetic images of forms, not present to the senses, for future recall. ... The capacity for graphic representation, such as writing requires, depends on the motor function of the eye and its coordination with eye movements.

Hildreth suggests that some of the underlying shortcomings that interfere with the child's handwriting performance are: (a) poor motor skills, (b) unstable and erratic temperament, (c) faulty visual perception of letters and words, and (d) difficulty in retaining visual impressions. In addition, the child's difficulty may be in cross-modal transfer from the visual to motor modalities. Left-handedness provides an additional obstacle to learning to write. Another cause of poor writing is poor instruction in handwriting skills.

Figure 10.4 illustrates the attempts of two 10-year-old boys with handwriting disorders to copy some writing materials. Difficulties of this type are sometimes referred to as *dysgraphia*.

Handwriting of Mike: 10 years old

Handwriting of Allen: 10 years old

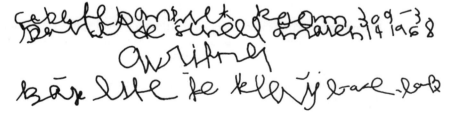

Figure 10.4 Illustrations of the handwriting of two 10-year-old boys with handwriting disabilities (In both cases the boys were asked to copy from a sample.)

CURSIVE VS. MANUSCRIPT HANDWRITING

There is some difference of opinion as to whether writing instruction for children with learning disabilities should begin with manuscript or cursive writing. The developmental handwriting curriculum in most schools begins with manuscript writing (sometimes called *printing*) in first grade; the transfer to cursive writing (sometimes called *script*) is typically made somewhere in the third grade.

The arguments for beginning with cursive writing are that it minimizes spatial judgment problems for the child and that there is a rhythmic continuity and wholeness that is missing from manuscript writing. Further, errors of reversals are virtually eliminated with cursive writing; and by beginning with the cursive form in initial instruction, the need to transfer from one form to another is eliminated. Many children with learning disabilities find it difficult to make the transfer to cursive writing if they have first learned manuscript writing.

The advantages of manuscript writing are: it is easier to learn since it consists of only circles and straight lines; the manuscript letter form is closer to the printed form used in reading; and some educators feel it is not important for a child to transfer to cursive writing at all since the manuscript form is legal, legible, and thought by some to be just as rapid.

Good results have been obtained with instruction in both symbolic forms. Reinforcing the system the child is using in the classroom seems to be a wise strategy, if all other things are equal. For young children this is likely to be the manuscript form; and for children in the intermediate grades the cursive form is likely to be used. Samples of manuscript and cursive letters are shown in Figure 10.5 on page 256.

THE LEFT-HANDED CHILD

Left-handed children present a special problem since their natural tendency is to write from right to left on the page. In writing from left to right, left-handers have difficulty seeing what they have written because the hand covers it up, and there is a tendency to smudge the writing as the left hand moves. To avoid the smudging, some left-handed children begin "hooking" the hand in writing when they begin using ball-point pens.

Left-handedness today is accepted as natural for some children. The child who has not yet stabilized handedness should be encouraged to write with the right hand. However, the child with a strong preference for the left hand should be permitted to write as a "lefty," even though this creates some special problems in writing and requires special instruction.

For manuscript writing, the paper should be placed directly in front of the left-handed child, without a slant. However, for cursive writing the top of the paper should be slanted north-northeast, opposite to the slant used by the right-handed child. The pencil should be long, gripped about one inch from the tip, with the eraser pointing to the left shoulder. The position of

ABCDEFGHIJKLMNOPQR
STUVWXYZabcdefghijklm
nopqrstuvwxyz 1234567891o

*Aa Bb Cc Dd Ee Ff
Gg Hh Ii Jj Kk Ll
Mm Nn Oo Pp Qq Rr
Ss Tt Uu Vv Ww Xx
Yy Zz 1 2 3 4 5 6 7 8 9 10*

Figure 10.5

From the *Sample Manuscript Alphabet*, Grade 3, and the *Sample Cursive Alphabet*, Grade 3. Columbus: Zaner-Bloser, 1958.

the hand is curved, with the weight resting on the outside of the little finger, and "hooking" should be avoided. Research shows that left-handers can learn to write just as fast as right-handers.

TYPEWRITING

Children with severe problems of dysgraphia who do not make progress with clinical instruction, or children who write very slowly, may find a typewriter a more effective means of written communication. The electric typewriter has proved to be useful for children with severe motor difficulty. Special instruction in typing will be required to help the child learn to use the typewriter. A handbook for teaching typewriting skills to learning-disabled children gives directions for making teacher-prepared materials, for developing teaching procedures, and for modifying the basic typing program to meet special needs (Davis 1971). Not only can children with handwriting problems learn to type reasonably well, but as they learn to type, they appear to develop a better awareness of the sequences of letters in words.

ACTIVITIES FOR TEACHING HANDWRITING

The following activities are representative of methods that have been useful in helping children learn to write.

1. *Chalkboard activities.* These provide a practice before beginning writing instruction. Circles, lines, geometric shapes, letters, and numbers can be made with large free movements using the muscles of the shoulders, arms, hands, and fingers. For additional suggestions see Chapter 8, "chalkboard activities," in the section on fine motor activities.

2. *Other materials for writing movement practice.* Fingerpainting, or writing in a clay pan or a sand tray, gives the child practice in writing movements. Put a layer of sand, cornmeal, salt, or nondrying clay on a cookie sheet. Use commercial or homemade fingerpaints for the painting practice. The finger or a pointed stick can be used to practice writing shapes, forms, letters, and numbers. A small wet sponge could be used on a chalkboard to draw shapes.

3. *Position.* To prepare for writing, have the child sit in a comfortable chair, have the table at the proper height, feet flat on the floor, both forearms on the writing surface. The nonwriting hand should hold the paper at the top.

4. *Paper.* For manuscript writing the paper should be placed without a slant, parallel with the lower edge of the desk. For cursive writing the paper is tilted at an angle approximately 60 degrees from vertical — to the left for right-handed children and to the right for left-handed children. To help the child remember the correct slant, a strip of tape to parallel the top of the paper may be placed at the top of the desk. To keep the paper from sliding, it may be necessary to attach the paper to the desk with masking tape.

5. *Holding the pencil.* Many children with writing disorders do not know how, or are unable, to hold a pencil properly between the thumb and middle finger with the index finger riding the pencil. The pencil should be grasped above the sharpened point. A piece of tape or a rubber band can be placed around the pencil to help the child hold it at the right place.

For the child who has difficulty with the grasp, Larson (1968) suggests putting the pencil through a practice golf ball (the kind with many holes). Have the child place the middle finger and thumb around the ball to practice the right grip. Large primary-size pencils, large crayons, and felt-tip pens are useful for the beginning stages of writing. Clay might be placed around the pencil to help the child grasp it. Short pencils should be avoided, as it is impossible to grip them correctly.

6. *Stencils and templates.* Geometric forms (squares, circles, etc.), letters, and numbers can be represented in stencils made from cardboard or plastic. Clip the stencil to the paper to prevent it from moving. Have the child trace the form with a finger or with a pencil or crayon. Then remove the stencil and reveal the figure that has been made. The stencil can be made so that the hole creates the shape, or, in reverse, a cutout of the shape itself where the outer edges of the stencil create the shape. Discarded hospital X-ray films and packaged-meat trays have proved to be useful materials for making templates.

7. *Tracing.* Make heavy black figures on white paper and clip a sheet of onionskin paper over the letters. Have the child trace the forms and letters. Start with diagonal lines and circles, then horizontal and vertical lines, geometric shapes, and finally use letters and numbers. The child may also trace with a crayon or felt-tip pen over a black letter on paper, or may use a transparent sheet. Another idea is to put letters on transparencies and project the image with an overhead projector onto a chalkboard or a large sheet of paper. The child can then trace over the image.

8. *Drawing between the lines.* Have the child practice making "roads" between double lines in a variety of widths and shapes. Then the child can write letters by going between the double lines of outlined letters. Use arrows and numbers to show direction and sequence of the lines.

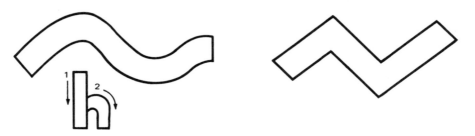

9. *Dot-dot.* Draw a complete figure and then an outline of the same figure using dots. Ask the child to make the figure by connecting the dots.

10. *Tracing with reducing cues.* Write the complete letter or word and

have the child trace it; then write the first part of the letter or word and have the child trace your part and then complete the letter. Finally, reduce the cue to only the upstroke and have the child write the entire letter or word.

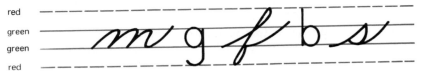

11. *Lined paper.* Begin by using unlined paper. Paper with wide lines may be used later to help the child determine placement of letters. Larson (1968) suggests use of specially lined paper that is color cued to aid in letter placement. Regular lined paper can also be color cued to help the child in making letters. Paper of this type is marketed by Developmental Learning Materials (Appendix E).

red	
green	*m g f b s*
green	
red	

12. *Template lines.* For children who need additional help in stopping at lines, tape can be placed at bottom and top lines. Windows can be cut out of shirt cardboard to give further guidance to the child for spacing letters. Below is a picture of a cardboard with three window slots for 1-line, 2-line, and 3-line letters.

1-line window

2-line window

3-line window

One-line letters are those that fit in a single-line space: a, c, e, i, m, n. Two-line letters are considered to be those with ascenders only: b, d, h, k, l, t. And three-line letters are those with descenders: f, g, j, p, q, z, y.

13. *Letter difficulty.* Larson (1968) suggests teaching the cursive letters in the following order: beginning letters — m, n, t, i, u, w, r, s, l, e; more difficult letters — x, z, y, j, p, h, b, k, f, g, q; and combinations of letters — me, be, go, it, no, etc.

14. *Auditory reinforcement.* Some children are helped in the motor act of writing by hearing the directions, for example, "down-up-and-around." Care must be taken when using this technique that the child is not distracted by these verbal instructions.

15. *Words and sentences.* After the child learns to write single letters, instruction should proceed to the writing of words and sentences. Spacing, size, slant are additional factors to be considered.

These activities are representative of handwriting techniques suggested by many authors for helping the child with learning disabilities. Additional suggestions can be obtained in Larson (1968), *Academic Therapy Quarterly* (1968), Otto, McMenemy, and Smith (1973), Wallace and Kauffman (1973), Frostig and Maslow (1973), and Hammill and Bartel (1975).

There are several handwriting scales for evaluating a child's skill, such as *Ayres Measuring Scale for Handwriting* (Educational Testing Service), and the *Freeman Evaluation Scale for Guiding Growth in Handwriting* (Zaner-Bloser).

The goal of handwriting instruction is to help the child develop a useful communication tool. The child should develop a skill in writing legibly and be able to accomplish writing with ease.

SPELLING

The ability to spell well, someone once quipped, is "a gift from God." Spelling is one curriculum area in which neither creativity nor divergent thinking is encouraged; only one pattern or arrangement of letters can be accepted as correct. The written form or orthography of the English language has an inconsistent pattern; that is, it does not have a complete one-to-one correspondence with the oral or spoken sounds of English. Therefore, spelling is not an easy task, even for children who are not afflicted with learning disabilities. Spelling a word is much more difficult than reading a word. Recognizing a word in print is a decoding task, and in a reading situation there are many clues to aid the reader in word recognition, including context, phonics, structural analysis, and configuration. Reproducing a word, however, is an encoding task and the opportunity to draw upon peripheral clues is greatly reduced. Many children who are poor in the ability to reproduce words in spelling are skilled in the ability to recognize them in reading. However, the child who is poor in decoding words in reading is almost always poor in spelling as well.

Examples of the irregular relationship between phonemes (the spoken sound) and graphemes (the written symbol) are easy to cite. George Bernard Shaw, an advocate of spelling reform, is attributed with the suggestion that the word "fish" be spelled *ghoti: gh* as in "cough"; *o* as in "women"; *ti* as in "nation." Following phonic generalizations, the word *natural* could be spelled *pnatchurile*. The many inconsistencies that exist in English spelling are illustrated in the following limericks.*

> A king, on assuming his reign,
> Exclaimed with a feeling of peign:
> "Tho I'm legally heir
> No one here seems to ceir
> That I haven't been born with a breign."

> A merchant addressing a debtor,
> Remarked in the course of his lebtor
> That he chose to suppose
> A man knose what he ose
> And the sooner he pays it, the bedtor!

> A young lady crossing the ocean
> Grew ill from the ship's dizzy mocean,
> She called with a sigh
> And a tear in her eigh,
> For the doctor to give her a pocean.

> And now our brief lesson is through —
> I trust you'll agree it was trough;
> For it's chiefly designed
> To impress on your migned
> What wonders our spelling can dough!

* Reprinted by special permission of Dr. Emmett Albert Betts, *Phonemic Spelling Council*, Reading Research Laboratories, University of Miami, Coral Gables, Florida 33124.

Horn (1957) found pupils' spelling of the word "awful" was varied, including: *offul, awful, offel,* and *offle*. Each is an accurate phonetic transcription of the oral sounds of the word. With the orthography of English, a child could conceivably think of the following rules to spell the word "post": *p* as in *psychology, o* as in *Ouija Board, s* as in *sugar,* and *t* as in *themselves*.

Effect of Linguistics on Spelling

In spite of the seemingly numerous exceptions to the rules, recent research in linguistics has indicated that there are predictable spelling patterns and an underlying system of phonological and morphological regularity. Hanna and others (1967) reported that an in-depth analysis of 17,000 words showed that the correct spelling pattern can be predicted for a phoneme sound 90 percent of the time when the main phonological facts of position in syllables, syllable stress, and internal constraints underlying the orthography are taken into consideration. A linguistic approach to the teaching of spelling capitalizes on the underlying regularity that exists between phonological and morphological elements in the oral language and their graphemic representation in orthography.

What is suggested by linguists is that children be helped to discover the underlying linguistic patterns and that words for spelling instruction be selected on the basis of demonstrating the underlying linguistic patterns. Linguists maintain that the spelling curriculum should be organized to encourage such linguistic discovery. When teaching a spelling pattern of the phoneme "oy," for example, the teacher should include in the spelling lesson words like: *boy, joy, Roy,* and *toy,* to help children form a linguistic or phonological generalization.

Similar proposals have been made by authorities in other fields. Durrell (1956), for instance, suggests that spelling programs be merged with phonics instruction. He argues that the phonics and word-analysis skills be practiced, not in the reading class but during the spelling class. Durrell believes that children make greater progress in spelling through word-analysis practice in reading than through daily instruction in spelling. This view received support in a research study of phonics training and spelling achievement conducted by Cramer (1969).

Visual Sequential Memory

In addition to phonological generalizations, the ability to spell appears to be related to visual sequential memory. The child who is unable to remember or visualize the letters and order of the letters in words will be poor in spelling. Many of the techniques that have been successful in teaching spelling have, in effect, been ways to strengthen visual sequential memory. Fernald (1943), for example, developed a tracing technique to teach spelling which reinforced the visual image of the word by using the tactile and kinesthetic modalities (p. 265). To spell a word correctly, the individual must not only have stored the word in memory, but also be able to retrieve it completely. Unlike recognizing a word in reading, there are no visual clues.

TRADITIONAL APPROACH TO SPELLING

The traditional spelling programs have selected words for spelling instruction on the basis of "frequency-of-use" word lists rather than on the basis of "linguistic patterns." A common core of spelling words that are most frequently used in writing was determined through extensive investigations of the writing done by children and adults. Spelling programs that select words on the basis of their utility in writing use the studies of writing vocabularies conducted by spelling authorities such as Fitzgerald (1951). A relatively small number of words do most of the work. The following estimate of needed spelling words is given by Rinsland (1945):

100 words make up more than 60% of elementary children's writing;
500 words make up more than 82% of elementary children's writing;

1,000 words make up more than 89% of elementary children's writing; 2,000 words make up more than 95% of elementary children's writing.

Fitzgerald (1955) suggests that 2,650 words and their repetitions in derivative forms make up about 95 percent of the writing of elementary school children. He recommends a basic list of 3,500 words for children in elementary school. The criteria for word selection in the traditional spelling curriculum, then, are frequency of use, permanency, and utility.

PROBLEMS RELATED TO SPELLING

There are many subskills and abilities demanded in the act of spelling. Individuals must be able, initially, to read the word; they must be knowledgeable and skillful in certain relationships of phonics and structural analysis; they must be able to apply appropriate phonic generalizations; they must be able to visualize the appearance of the word; and, finally, they need to have the motor facility to write the word. Difficulties in spelling may be due to a deficit in any or a combination of the above skills.

If visual memory is diagnosed as the major problem factor, activities to help the child strengthen and reinforce visual memory are suggested. If a deficit in auditory perception of letter sounds appears to be a factor, or if auditory memory is unable to hold sounds or syllables in mind, the teaching plan would have to take these factors into account. Motor memory is also a factor in spelling, for the speller must remember how the word "felt" when it was previously written. In addition, intersensory transfer probably plays a crucial role in developing efficient spelling ability. A crossing and integrating of visual, auditory, and kinesthetic modalities are needed before the spelling of a word becomes a subconscious, automatic process.

Some recent work on a behavioral approach to spelling is based on the need to develop intersensory transfer for efficient spelling behavior. According to Personke and Yee (1966, p. 284):

> No one channel is correct for spelling a particular word each time it is met. Reinforcement of correct responses enlarges the store of the memory drum. The internal inputs, particularly of the immature speller, are subject to constant change. This shifting from one channel to another is perhaps the best indication of the complementarity of the channels.

Using this model, Brothers and Holsclaw (1969) suggest a spelling program designed to fuse five spelling behaviors: (1) copying, (2) proofreading, (3) rewriting, (4) writing from memory consciously, and (5) spelling automatically without conscious thought.

DIAGNOSIS OF SPELLING DIFFICULTIES

Many survey tests of spelling are available as part of a comprehensive academic achievement battery. These tests yield a grade-level score, but an analysis of the errors made will give greater diagnostic information. A diagnostic test of spelling, the *Gates-Russell Spelling Diagnostic Test* (1937), contains nine subtests and gives information on the following areas: spelling words orally, word pronunciation, giving letter-for-letter sounds, spelling one or more syllables, reversals, methods of word attack and word study, auditory discrimination, and a measure of the effectiveness of visual, kinesthetic, or combined methods of study.

An informal diagnostic test of spelling ability was suggested by Watson (1935) for classroom use. An adaptation of this test can be made for individual diagnosis. The essentials of this method are:

1. Select a list of 30 to 50 words based on any graded list of the grade level of the child or the class.
2. Administer the spelling test.
3. Score the test and tabulate the results. If used with a class, note the lowest 20 percent.
4. Have the pupils define words they misspelled. Omit words that are not known since they are not in the child's vocabulary.
5. Have pupils spell any remaining words orally. Keep a record of the spelling, note the syllabication, phonic use, and speech or hearing difficulties.
6. Compare the original spelling to note differences in oral and written responses.
7. Ask the children to study words missed (for about 10 minutes) and observe their method of study.
8. Analyze errors and incorporate information from the data obtained from other sources.
9. Draw conclusions as to the nature of the spelling problem. Plan educational strategies to overcome the difficulties.
10. Discuss the analysis and teaching plan with the pupil. Provide for pupils to see progress.

ACTIVITIES FOR TEACHING SPELLING

1. *Auditory perception and memory of letter sounds.* Provide practice in auditory perception of letter sounds, strengthen knowledge of phonics and structural analysis, and develop skills in applying phonic generalizations. See Chapter 9 for specific techniques.

2. *Visual perception and memory of letters.* Help the child strengthen visual perception and memory so that the visual image of the word can be retained. Materials should be clear and concise, and the child should be helped to focus attention on the activity. Letting the child use a pocket flashlight might be helpful as an aid in focusing attention. To develop speed of visual recognition, a tachistoscope can be used to expose material from 1½ seconds to 1/100 second. Flash cards can also be used as an aid in developing speed. See Chapter 9 for specific methods to develop visual perception and memory.

3. *Multisensory methods in spelling.* When children are asked to study

spelling lessons, they are frequently at a loss as to what to do. The following five steps are suggested by Fitzgerald (1955) as a multisensory approach that utilizes the visual, auditory, kinesthetic, and tactile modalities.

a. *Meaning and pronunciation.* Have the child look at the word, pronounce it correctly, and use it in a sentence.

b. *Imagery.* Ask the child to "see" the word and say the word. Have the child say each syllable of the word, say the word syllable by syllable, spell the word orally, and then trace the word in the air, or over the word itself, with a finger.

c. *Recall.* Ask the child to look at the word and then close his eyes and see the word in his mind's eye. Have him spell the word orally. Ask him to open his eyes to see if he was correct. (If an error is made he should repeat the process.)

d. *Writing the word.* The child writes the word correctly from memory, checks the spelling against the original to see if it was correct, and then checks the writing, too, to make sure every letter is legible.

e. *Mastery.* The child covers the word and writes it. If she is correct, she should cover and write it two more times.

4. *The Fernald Method* (Fernald 1943). This method is a multisensory approach to teaching reading and writing as well as spelling. Very briefly, the following steps are involved:

a. The child is told he is going to learn words in a new way that has proved to be very successful. He is encouraged to select a word that he wishes to learn.

b. The teacher writes that word on a piece of paper, 4 inches by 10 inches, as the child watches and as the teacher says the word.

c. The child traces the word, saying it several times, then writes the word on a separate piece of paper, while saying it.

d. The word is then written from memory without looking at the original copy. If it is incorrect, the tracing and saying steps are repeated. If the word is correct, it is put in a file box. The words in the file box are used later in stories.

e. At later stages this painstaking tracing method for learning words is not needed. Now the child learns a word by *looking* as the teacher writes it, *saying* it, and *writing* it. At a still later stage, the child can learn by only looking at a word in print and writing it, and, finally, by merely looking at it.

5. *The "Test-Study-Test" vs. the "Study-Test" method.* In teaching spelling to a classroom, there are two common approaches: the "test-study-test" and the "study-test" plans. The test-study-test method uses a pretest, which is usually given at the beginning of the week. The child then studies only those words that were missed on the pretest. This method is better for older children who have fairly good spelling abilities since there is no need to study words they already know. The study-test method is better for the young child and the child with poor spelling abilities. Since too many words

would be missed on a pretest, this method permits the study of a few well-selected words before the test is given.

6. *Spelling words on the filmstrip projector.* Put spelling words on transparencies. Cut strips to widths to fit into the projector. Push the strip through to show spelling words on the screen. Cover and show quickly for tachistoscopic use. Words can also be written with certain letters left out, to be completed by the child (Lerner and Vaver 1970).

7. *Listening centers and tapes.* Spelling lessons can easily be put on tape. After the child has advanced to a level that would enable working by oneself, spelling lessons can be completed in a listening laboratory. The use of earphones allows for individualization of instruction, and for many children the earphones provide an aid to block out distracting auditory stimuli.

8. *Programed spelling.* Some of the new materials in spelling are designed as programed materials. The material is given in small steps, immediate reinforcement is provided, and the programs are designed to be self-instructional.

9. The *Bad Speller's Dictionary* (Krevisky and Linfield 1963) is useful for poor spellers. Words are arranged alphabetically according to their common misspellings.

These methods are merely representative of techniques designed to teach spelling. Additional methods can be found in *Building Spelling Skills (Academic Therapy Quarterly* 1967), *Corrective and Remedial Teaching* (Otto, McMenemy, and Smith 1973), *Guiding Language Learning* (Dawson 1963), *Learning Disabilities* (Johnson and Myklebust 1967), *Teaching Children with Learning Problems* (Wallace and Kauffman 1973), and *Teaching Children with Learning and Behavior Problems* (Hammill and Bartel 1975).

WRITTEN EXPRESSION

Poor facility in expressing thoughts through written language is probably the most prevalent disability of the communication skills. Many adults, as well as children, are unable to communicate effectively and to share ideas through writing. The ability to write down ideas requires many underlying prerequisite skills: facility in oral language, ability to read, some skill in spelling, a legible handwriting, some knowledge of the rules of written usage.

PROBLEMS RELATED TO WRITING

In addition to the preceding requirements, the child must have something to write about. Writing is a means of producing an output of ideas; obviously, there can be little output without an abundance of input. Because a strong relationship exists between the quantity of input experiences and the quality of output in the form of writing, the teacher must provide rich input experiences, such as trips, stories, discussions, and oral language activities. A written assignment that is given without first supplying a receptive buildup (such as, "Write a 500-word theme on Spring") is not likely to yield rich written productions. Writing needs prior sufficient input experiences to create and stimulate ideas the child can write about.

Another possible detriment to writing is the teacher's response to the child's writing, if it takes the form of excessive correction. Children can be discouraged from trying if they attempt to express ideas and then have their papers returned full of grammatical, spelling, punctuation, and handwriting corrections in red ink with heavy penalties for mistakes. As one child remarked, "An 'F' looks so much worse in red ink." From the behavior modification viewpoint, the child is receiving negative reinforcement. Such children soon learn to beat the game by limiting their writing vocabulary to words they know how to spell, by keeping their sentences simple, by avoiding complex and creative ideas, and by keeping their compositions short.

ACTIVITIES FOR TEACHING WRITTEN EXPRESSION

A number of methods have been used to avoid such discouragement. Teachers may grade only ideas, not the technical form, for some assignments. Or two grades can be given: one for ideas and one for technical skills. For the child who makes errors in many areas, only one skill at a time might be selected for correction, such as capitalization. It is useful to make a differentiation between *personal* writing lessons and *functional* writing lessons. In personal writing, the goal is to develop ideas and express them in written form. The *process* rather than the output itself is important, and there is less need for technical perfection. In contrast, the goal of functional writing is learning the form of the output. In this case the final product, such as a business letter, is to be read by another individual and certain standards and forms are essential. By separating the goals of these two types of lessons, different kinds of writing skills can be developed in each.

Dawson (1963) has suggested a developmental sequence in teaching writing:

1. *Composing and dictating to the teacher.* Before children begin to write by themselves, they can develop skills in organizing ideas through language by dictating compositions. The teacher writes the story down; the child gets the idea that thoughts can be expressed in oral language and written down. These experiences are then permanent, and they can be reviewed by the child and read by other people. The child also sees how capital letters, spelling, and punctuation are used to clarify the thoughts expressed.

2. *Copying.* The next step in learning to write is to copy the ideas the teacher has put in written form. Now the child needs the visual-motor skills and handwriting skills. Copying may be very tiring for some children, and it needs close supervision to be of value.

3. *Dictation.* After studying an experience story that the child has written and copied, the teacher helps the child recall the story and then the teacher dictates the entire story or parts of the story for the child to write. At first

the child will need to study the story carefully, but later the child will be able to write as the teacher dictates, without previous study.

4. *Rewriting.* Have the child rewrite the story independently without the dictation by the teacher.

5. *Practice.* Like any other skill, much practice is needed in learning to write. Give the child many experiences in writing. Difficult spelling words can be anticipated and listed on the board, or the child may simply ask for the spelling of difficult words. Fader (1966) found that the assignment of a certain number of pages per week in a personal journal that was uncorrected, and even unread, by the teacher was an excellent technique to provide the needed practice and to improve the quality of writing.

Among the few available tests to measure written language expression are the *Sequential Tests of Educational Progress* (STEP), and the *Picture Story Language Test* (Myklebust 1965). Additional teaching methods to help children learn to write are suggested by Ferris (1967), "Teaching Children to Write" in *Guiding Children's Language Learning* (Dawson 1963), *They All Want to Write* (Burrows et al. 1965), *From Thoughts to Words* (Glaus 1965), *Slithery Snakes and Other Aids to Children's Writing* (Petty and Bowen 1967) and *Invitations to Speaking and Writing Creatively* (Meyers and Torrance 1965).

SUMMARY

This chapter has presented *theories* of language, language development, and language deviations in children, and it has reviewed *teaching strategies* for helping children learn various oral and written language skills. The theory section approached learning disabilities from the perspectives of four language-related professions: the language arts specialty, language pathology, linguistics, and psycholinguistics. Language plays a vital role in the learning process. Further, language disorders almost always result in a learning disability.

The language arts specialist is concerned with the development of language as it affects academic work. Four elements of language — listening, speaking, reading, and writing — were analyzed and their relationship discussed. The dependency of written language communication skills (reading and writing) on a sound and firm foundation of oral language development (listening and speaking) was emphasized.

The language pathologist studies the causes and treatment of disorders of symbolic verbal behavior. This subsection discussed the kinds of language disorders that are found in children with learning disabilities.

Linguistics is the scientific study of the nature of language. Several basic linguistic concepts were discussed. Professionals who propose to teach language or treat language disorders should know something about the nature of language — the field of linguistics.

The psycholinguist is interested in the complete communication process — the underlying psychology of language as well as the nature of language itself. Psycholinguists are developing ways of analyzing the thinking processes underlying language and are studying language acquisition.

In spite of the differences within these professions, there is much agreement in their analyses of the language problem. By studying the problems of language and learning from the framework of the other fields, professionals from each can develop unique contributions to the field of learning disabilities.

The "Teaching Strategies" section discussed the oral language skills of *listening* and *speaking* and the written language skills of *reading, handwriting, spelling,* and *written expression.*

Listening is the first mode in which the child uses to learn language. Understanding language becomes the basis for all further language learning. Methods of building listening skills were suggested.

Speaking, or producing oral language, is a problem for many learning-disabled children. The oral language disorder may be one of delayed speech, deficient vocabulary, or of disordered sentence formulation. Ways of helping children develop more adequate oral language production were reviewed.

Reading becomes one of the major academic difficulties of children with learning disabilities. There is a developmental sequence of reading skills: reading readiness, initial stage of learning to read, rapid development of reading skills, and refinement of reading. Reading can be divided into two major kinds of learning: word recognition and reading comprehension. Alternative approaches to the teaching of reading were considered: decoding methods (phonics, linguistics, modified alphabets, the early letter emphasis approach), the language-experience approach, multisensory approaches, individualized reading programs, programed reading, basal reading series, technological assistance, reading laboratories, and systems approaches.

The issue of dyslexia in learning disabilities and reading was discussed, and two major viewpoints of dyslexia were presented — the medical and educational perspectives.

The final section discussed handwriting, spelling, and written expression. Handwriting is difficult for many children with learning disabilities. This disability may be related to visual-motor disturbances, poor motor development, a deficit in spatial relationships, or a deficit in voluntary motor movement. Teaching strategies that have been useful in helping such children learn handwriting were presented.

Even children who are successful in reading can find spelling difficult to master. Linguistic factors such as the phonological system and visual sequential memory were discussed in relation to spelling. The rationale of the traditional approach to spelling was presented. Many characteristics of the child with learning disabilities combine to make spelling very difficult. Some techniques for teaching spelling were suggested.

Written expression is another troublesome area for the child with learning disabilities. The many elements that have to be integrated and combined for the child to write makes this task difficult. Several ways to develop skills in written expression were suggested.

Written language skills are the last of the language skills to be learned. It is important that the child have a sound foundation in oral language skills as a base for the addition of the most difficult of the language skills.

REFERENCES

Academic Therapy Quarterly. "Building Handwriting Skills." San Rafael, Calif.: Academic Therapy Publications 4 (Fall 1968): entire issue.

Academic Therapy Quarterly. "Building Spelling Skills." San Rafael, Calif.: Academic Therapy Publications 3 (Fall 1968): entire issue.

Allen, Roach Van. "How a Language Experience Program Works," pp. 1–8 in Elaine C. Vilscek (ed.), *Decade of Innovations: Approaches to Beginning Reading.* Newark, Del.: International Reading Association, 1968.

Atkinson, Richard C., and John D. Fletcher. "Teaching Children to Read with Computers." *Reading Teacher* 25 (January 1972): 319–327.

Austin, Mary C., and Coleman Morrison. *The First R: The Harvard Report on Reading in Elementary Schools.* New York: Macmillan, 1963.

Austin, Mary C., et al. *The Torch Lighters: Tomorrow's Teachers of Reading.* Cambridge, Mass.: Harvard University Press, 1961.

Ayres Measuring Scale for Handwriting. Princeton, N.J.: Cooperative Test Division of Educational Testing Services, 1912.

Bangs, Tina E. *Language and Learning Disorders of the Pre-Academic Child.* New York: Appleton-Century-Crofts, 1968.

Baratz, Joan C. "The Relationship of Black English to Reading," pp. 101–113 in J. Laffey and R. Shuy (eds.), *Language Differences: Do They Interfere?* Newark, Del.: International Reading Association, 1973.

Barrett, Thomas C. "Visual Discrimination Tasks as Predictors of First Grade Reading Achievement." *Reading Teacher* 18 (January 1965): 276–282.

Bellugi, U., and R. W. Brown, eds. *The Acquisition of Language.* Monographs of the Society for Research in Child Development 29 (1964).

Berko, Jean. "The Child's Learning of English Morphology." *Word* 14 (1958): 150–177.

Bernstein, Basil. "Elaborated and Restricted Codes: Their Social Origins and Some Consequences." *American Anthropologist* 66, Part 2 (1964): 55–69.

Berry, Mildred. *Language Disorders in Children.* New York: Appleton-Century-Crofts, 1969.

Black, Millard H. "To What End?," pp. 25–28 in James K. Kerfoot (ed.), *Reading for the Disadvantaged.* Newark, Del.: International Reading Association, 1967.

Bloomfield, Leonard, and Clarence L. Barnhart. *Let's Read,* Part I. Bronxville, N.Y.: C. L. Barnhart, 1963.

Bond, Guy L. "First-Grade Reading Studies: An Overview." *Elementary English* 43 (May 1966): 464–470.

Bond, Guy L., and Robert Dykstra. "The Cooperative Research Program in First-Grade Reading Instruction." *Reading Research Quarterly* 2 (Summer 1967): entire issue.

Bond, Guy L., and Miles A. Tinker. *Reading Difficulties: Their Diagnosis and Correction,* 2nd ed. New York: Appleton-Century-Crofts, 1967.

Brothers, Aileen, and Cora Holsclaw. "Fusing Behaviors into Spelling." *Elementary English* 46 (January 1969): 32–37.

Brown, Roger, Courtney Cazden, and Ursula Bellugi-Klima. "The Child's Grammar from I and III," pp. 382–411 in A. Bar-Adon and W. Leopold (eds.), *Child Language: A Book of Readings*. Englewood Cliffs, N.J.: Prentice-Hall, 1971.

Burrows, Alvina Treut, et al. *They All Want to Write*. New York: Holt, Rinehart & Winston, 1965.

Bush, W. C., and Giles, M. T. *Aids to Psycholinguistic Teaching*. Columbus: Merrill, 1969.

Carroll, John. "Language and Cognition: Current Perspectives from Linguistics and Psychology," pp. 174–185 in J. Laffey and R. Shuy (eds.), *Language Differences: Do They Interfere?* Newark, Del.: International Reading Association, 1973.

———. "Some Neglected Relationships in Reading and Language Learning." *Elementary English* 43 (October 1966): 576–579.

Chall, Jeanne. *Learning to Read: The Great Debate*. New York: McGraw-Hill, 1967.

Chappell, Gerald. "Learning Disabilities and the Learning Clinician." *Journal of Learning Disabilities* 5 (December 1972): 611–619.

Chomsky, Noam. *Aspects of the Theory of Syntax*. Cambridge, Mass.: MIT Press, 1965.

———. "A Review of B. F. Skinner's Verbal Behavior." *Language* 35 (1959): 26–58.

Cramer, Ronald L. "The Influence of Phonic Instruction on Spelling Achievement." *Reading Teacher* 22 (March 1969): 499–503.

Critchley, MacDonald. *Developmental Dyslexia*. Springfield, Ill.: Charles C. Thomas, 1964.

Davis, Maetta. *Typing Keys for the Remediation of Reading and Spelling*. San Rafael, Calif.: Academic Therapy Publications, 1971.

Dawson, Mildred, et al. *Guiding Language Learning*. New York: Harcourt, Brace and World, 1963.

DeHirsch, Katrina, et al. *Predicting Reading Failure*. New York: Harper & Row, 1966.

Duker, Sam. *Listening Bibliography*. New York: Scarecrow Press, 1964.

Dunn, L. M., and J. O. Smith. *Peabody Language Development Kit*. Circle Pines, Minn.: American Guidance Services, 1965.

Durrell, Donald. *Improving Reading Instruction*. New York: Harcourt, Brace & World, 1956.

Eichenwald, Heinz F. "The Pathology of Reading Disorders: Psychophysiological Factors," in M. Johnson and R. Kress (eds.), *Corrective Reading in the Elementary Classroom*. Newark, Del.: International Reading Association, 1967.

Eisenson, John. "Developmental Aphasia: A Speculative View with Therapeutic Implications." *Journal of Speech and Hearing Disorders* 33 (February 1968): 3–13.

Engelmann, Siegfried, and Elaine C. Bruner. *Distar Reading I and II: An Instructional System*. Chicago: Science Research Associates, 1969.

Fader, Daniel N., and M. Schaevitz. *Hooked on Books*. New York: Berkley Publishing, 1966.

Fernald, Grace. *Remedial Techniques in Basic School Subjects*. New York: McGraw-Hill, 1943.

Ferris, Donald R. "Teaching Children to Write," Chapter 6 in Pose Lamb (ed.), *Guiding Children's Language Learning*. Dubuque, Iowa: William C. Brown, 1967.

Fitzgerald, James A. *A Basic Life Spelling Vocabulary*. Milwaukee: Bruce Publishing, 1951.

————. "Children's Experiences in Spelling," Chapter 11 in V. Herrick and L. Jacobs (eds.), *Children and the Language Arts*. Englewood Cliffs, N.J.: Prentice-Hall, 1955.

Flavell, J. H., D. R. Beach, and J. M. Chinsky. "Spontaneous Verbal Rehearsal in a Memory Task as a Function of Age," *Child Development* 37 (1963): 283–300.

Freeman Evaluation Scale for Guiding Growth in Handwriting. Columbus: Zaner-Bloser, 1958.

Fries, Charles C. *Linguistics and Reading*. New York: Holt, Rinehart & Winston, 1963.

————. "Linguistic Approaches," in James Kerfoot (ed.), *First Grade Reading Programs*. Newark, Del.: International Reading Association, 1965.

Frostig, Marianne, and Phyllis Maslow. *Learning Problems in the Classroom*. New York: Grune & Stratton, 1973.

Fry, Edward. "A Diacritical Marking System to Aid Beginning Reading Instruction." *Elementary English* 41 (May 1964).

Gates-Russell Spelling Diagnostic Test. New York: Teachers College, Columbia University, 1937.

Gattegno, Caleb. *Words in Color*. Chicago: Learning Materials, Inc., Encyclopaedia Britannica, 1962.

Gillingham, Anna, and Bessie W. Stillman. *Remedial Training for Children with Specific Difficulty in Reading, Spelling, and Penmanship*, 7th ed. Cambridge, Mass.: Educators Publishing Service, 1966.

Glaus, Marlene, *From Thoughts to Words*. Champaign, Ill.: National Council of Teachers of English, 1965.

Gleason, Jean Berko. "Language Development in Early Childhood," pp. 15–31 in James Walden (ed.), *Oral Language and Reading*. Champaign, Ill.: National Council of Teachers of English, 1969.

Gleason, H. A., Jr. *Linguistics and English Grammar*. New York: Holt, Rinehart & Winston, 1965.

Gottsleben, R., G. Bushini, and D. Tyack. "Linguistically Based Training Programs." *Journal of Learning Disabilities* 7 (April 1972): 197–203.

Hallgren, B. "Specific Dyslexia: A Clinical and Genetic Study." *Acta Psychiatrica Neurologica,* Supplement 65 (1950): 1–287.

Hammill, Donald, and Nettie Bartel. *Teaching Children with Learning and Behavior Problems*. Boston: Allyn & Bacon, 1975.

Hanna, Paul R., et al. "A Summary: Linguistic Cues for Spelling Improvement." *Elementary English* 44 (December 1967): 862–865.

Haring, Norris G., and Mary Ann Hauch. "Improving Learning Conditions in the Establishment of Reading Skills with Disabled Readers." *Exceptional Children* 35 (January 1969): 341–352.

Harris, Albert. *How to Increase Reading Ability*, 5th ed. New York: David McKay, 1970.

Heckelman, R. G. "A Neurological Impress Method of Remedial Reading Instruction." *Academic Therapy* 4 (Summer 1969): 277–282.

Hermann, Knud. *Reading Disability: A Medical Study of Word-Blindness and Related Handicaps*. Springfield, Ill.: Charles C. Thomas, 1959.

Hildreth, Gertrude. Chapters 19–21 in *Learning the Three R's*. Minneapolis: Educational Test Bureau, 1947.

Hinshelwood, James. *Congenital Word-Blindness*. London: H. K. Lewis, 1917.

Hook, J. N. "So What Good Is English?" Distinguished Lecture for National Council of Teachers of English, 1967.

Horn, Ernst. "Phonetics and Spelling." *Elementary School Journal* 57 (May 1957): 424–432.

Itard, J. M. *The Wild Boy of Aveyron*. New York: Appleton-Century-Crofts, 1962.

Johnson, Doris, and Helmer Myklebust. *Learning Disabilities: Educational Principles and Practices*. New York: Grune & Stratton, 1967.

Johnson, Dorothy K. "The O. K. Moore Typewriter Procedure," pp. 511–516 in A. R. Binter, et al. (eds.), *Readings on Reading*. Scranton, Pa.: International Textbook, 1969.

Karnes, M. B. *Helping Young Children Develop Language Skills: A Book of Activities*. Washington, D. C.: Council for Exceptional Children, 1968.

Keller, Helen. *The Story of My Life*. New York: Dell, 1961.

Kellogg, Ralph E. "Listening," pp. 107–134 in Pose Lamb (ed.), *Guiding Children's Language Learning*. Dubuque, Iowa: William C. Brown, 1971.

Kirk, Samuel A., and John Elkins. *Characteristics of Children Enrolled in Child Service Demonstration Centers*. Leadership Training Institute in Learning Disabilities, University of Arizona. Project no. H 12–7145B; Grant OEG–714425. U.S. Office of Education, Bureau of Education for the Handicapped, June 1974.

Kirk, Samuel A., James P. McCarthy, and Winifred D. Kirk. *The Illinois Test of Psycholinguistic Abilities*, rev. ed. Urbana, Ill.: University of Illinois Press, 1968.

Kleffner, Frank R. "Teaching Aphasic Children," pp. 330–337 in J. Magary and J. Eichorn (eds.), *The Exceptional Child*. New York: Holt, Rinehart & Winston, 1964.

Krevisky, J., and J. Linfield. *The Bad Speller's Dictionary*. New York: Random House, 1963.

Langer, Suzanne K. *Philosophy in a New Key*. New York: Mentor Books, New American Library, 1958.

Langford, Kenneth, K. Slade, and A. Barnett. "An Explanation of Impress Techniques in Remedial Reading." *Academic Therapy* 9 (Spring 1974): 309–319.

Larson, Charlotte. "Teaching Beginning Writing." *Academic Therapy Quarterly* 4 (Fall 1968): 61–66.

Lee, Dorris M., and Roach Van Allen. *Learning to Read Through Experience*, 2nd ed. New York: Appleton-Century-Crofts, 1963.

Lee, Laura L. *Developmental Sentence Analysis*. Evanston, Ill.: Northwestern University Press, 1974.

Lee, Laura, R. Koenigsknecht, and S. Mulhern. *Interactive Language Development Teaching: The Clinical Presentation of Grammatical Structure*. Evanston, Ill.: Northwestern University Press, 1975.

Lefevre, Carl. *Linguistics and the Teaching of Reading*. New York: McGraw-Hill, 1964.

Lenneberg, E. H. *Biological Foundations of Language*. New York: Wiley, 1967.

Lerner, Janet W. "A Global Theory of Reading — and Linguistics." *Reading Teacher* 21 (February 1968): 416–421.

———. "A New Focus for Reading Research — The Decision-Making Process." *Elementary English* 44 (March 1967): 236–242.

———. "Remedial Reading and Learning Disabilities: Are They the Same or Different?" *Journal of Special Education* 9 (Summer 1975): 119–132.

———. "Two Perspectives: Reading and Learning Disabilities," pp. 271–285 in S. Kirk and J. McCarthy (eds.), *Learning Disabilities: Selected ACLD Papers*. Boston: Houghton Mifflin, 1975(a).

———. "A Thorn by Any Name: Dyslexia or Reading Disability." *Elementary English* 48, January 1971.

Lerner, Janet W., and Lynne List. "The Phonics Knowledge of Prospective

Teachers, Experienced Teachers, and Elementary Pupils." *Illinois School Research* 7 (Fall 1970): 39–42.

Lerner, Janet W., and Gerald A. Vaver. "Filmstrips in Learning." *Academic Therapy Quarterly* 4 (Summer 1970): 320–325.

Liberman, Isabelle Y. "Segmentation of the Spoken Word and Reading Acquisition." *Bulletin of the Orton Society* 23, 1973, reprint no. 54.

Lovitt, Thomas C., and Mary Hurlburt. "Using Behavior-Analysis Techniques to Assess the Relationship Between Phonics Instruction and Oral Reading." *Journal of Special Education* 8 (Spring 1974): 57–72.

Luria, A. R. *Speech and the Regulation of Behavior.* New York: Liveright, 1961.

Mackintosh, Helen K., ed. *Children and Oral Language.* Joint publication of the Association for Childhood Education International, Association for Supervision and Curriculum Development, International Reading Association, National Council of Teachers of English, 1964.

McCarthy, Dorothea. "Language Development in Children," pp. 476–581 in Leonard Carmichael (ed.), *A Manual of Child Psychology.* New York: Wiley, 1954.

McCarthy, J. "Research of the Linguistic Problems of the Mentally Retarded." *Mental Retardation Abstracts* 2 (1964): 90–96.

McGrady, Harold J. "Language Pathology and Learning Disabilities," pp. 199–233 in H. Myklebust (ed.), *Progress in Learning Disorders,* Vol. I. New York: Grune & Stratton, 1968.

McLuhan, Marshall. *Understanding Media: The Extensions of Man,* 2nd ed. New York: Signet, New American Library, 1964.

Menyuk, Paula. *Sentences Children Use.* Cambridge, Mass.: MIT Press, 1969.

Meyers, R. E., and Paul Torrance. *Invitations to Speaking and Writing Creatively.* Boston: Ginn, 1965.

Money, John, ed. *The Disabled Reader: Education of the Dyslexic Child.* Baltimore: Johns Hopkins Press, 1966.

Monroe, Marion. *Children Who Cannot Read.* Chicago: University of Chicago Press, 1932.

Morgan, W. P. "A Case of Congenital Word-Blindness." *British Medical Journal* 2 (November 1896): 1378.

Myklebust, Helmer. *Picture Story Language Test. The Development and Disorders of Written Language,* Vol. 1. New York: Grune & Stratton, 1965.
———. *The Psychology of Deafness,* 2nd ed. New York: Grune & Stratton, 1964.

National Advisory Committee on Dyslexia and Related Disorders. *Report to the Secretary of the Department of Health, Education and Welfare,* August 1969.

Orton, June L. "The Orton-Gillingham Approach," pp. 119–146 in John Money (ed.), *The Disabled Reader.*

Orton, Samuel T. *Reading, Writing and Speech Problems in Children.* New York: W. W. Norton, 1937.

Otto, Wayne, Richard A. McMenemy, and R. Smith. *Corrective and Remedial Teaching: Principles and Practices.* Boston: Houghton Mifflin, 1973.

Personke, Carl, and Albert H. Yee. "A Model for the Analysis of Spelling Behavior," *Elementary English* 43 (March 1966): 278–284.

Petty, Walter, and Mary Bowen. *Slithery Snakes and Other Aids to Children's Writing.* New York: Appleton-Century-Crofts, 1967.

Piaget, J. *The Origins of Intelligence in Children.* M. Cook, trans. New York: International University Press, 1952.

Pinter, Rudolph, John Eisenson, and Mildred Stanton. Chapter 5 in *The Psychology of the Physically Handicapped.* New York: Appleton-Century-Crofts, 1945.

Reger, Roger, W. Schroeder, and K. Uschold. *Special Education.* New York: Oxford University Press, 1968.

Richardson, Sylvia O. "Language Training for Mentally Retarded Children," pp. 146–161 in R. Schiefelbusch et al. (eds.), *Language and Mental Retardation.* New York: Holt, Rinehart & Winston, 1967.

Rinsland, Henry D. *A Basic Vocabulary of Elementary School Children.* New York: Macmillan, 1945.

Robinson, Helen M. *Why Pupils Fail in Reading.* Chicago: University of Chicago, 1946.

Russell, David H., and Elizabeth F. Russell. *Listening Aids Through the Grades.* New York: Teachers College, Columbia University, 1959.

Schiefelbusch, Richard, Ross H. Copeland, and James O. Smith. *Language and Mental Retardation.* New York: Holt, Rinehart & Winston, 1967.

Schmitt, Clara. "Developmental Alexia," *Elementary School Journal* 18 (May 1918): 680–700, 757–769.

Seashore, Robert H. "The Importance of Vocabulary in Learning Language Skills," *Elementary English* 25 (March 1948): 137–152.

Sequential Tests of Educational Progress. Princeton, N.J.: Cooperative Test Division, Educational Testing Service.

Silberberg, N., and E. Silberberg. "The Bookless Curriculum: An Educational Alternative." *Journal of Learning Disabilities* 2 (June 1969): 302–307.

Skinner, B. F. *Verbal Behavior.* New York: Appleton-Century-Crofts, 1957.

Smith, Frank. "The Learner and His Language," pp. 35–42 in R. Hodges and E. Rudorf (eds.), *Language and Learning to Read.* Boston: Houghton Mifflin, 1972.

Spradlin, Joseph. "Procedures for Evaluating Processes Associated with Receptive and Expressive Language," pp. 118–136 in R. Schiefelbusch, R. Copeland, and J. Smith (eds.), *Language and Mental Retardation.* New York: Holt, Rinehart & Winston, 1967.

Stauffer, Russell G. "The Verdict: Speculative Controversy." *Reading Teacher* 19 (May 1966): 563.

Strickland, Ruth. "Building on What We Know," pp. 55–62 in J. Allen Figurel (ed.), *Reading and Realism,* Newark, Del.: International Reading Association, 1969.

Tanyzer, Harold J., and Albert J. Mazurkiewicz. *Early-to-Read i/t/a Program Book 2.* New York: i/t/a Publications, 1967.

UNIFON Reading Program. Racine, Wis.: Western Publishing Educational Services, 1966.

Veatch, Jeanette. *Individualize Your Reading Program.* New York: G. P. Putnam & Sons, 1959.

Vernon, M. *Backwardness in Reading.* London: Cambridge University Press, 1957.

Vogel, Susan A. "Syntactic Abilities in Normal and Dyslexic Children." *Journal of Learning Disabilities* 7 (February 1974): 103–109.

Vygotsky, L. S. *Thought and Language.* Cambridge, Mass.: MIT Press, 1962.

Wallace, G., and James M. Kauffman. *Teaching Children with Learning Problems.* Columbus: Merrill, 1973.

Wark, David M. "Case Studies in Behavior Modification," pp. 217–228 in G. Schick and M. May (eds.), *The Psychology of Reading Behavior.* Milwaukee: National Reading Conference, 1969.

Watson, A. E. *Experimental Studies in the Psychology and Teaching of Spelling.* Contributions to Education, no. 638. New York: Teachers College, Columbia University, 1935.

Wilkinson, Andrew. "Oracy in English Teaching," *Elementary English* 45 (October 1968): 743–748.

Wilt, Miriam E. "Let's Teach Listening." Creative Ways in Teaching the Language Arts, Leaflet 4. Champaign, Ill.: National Council of Teachers of English, 1957.

――――. "The Teaching of Listening and Why," in V. Anderson et al. (eds.), *Readings in the Language Arts.* New York: Macmillan, 1964.

Wood, Nancy. *Delayed Speech and Language Development.* Englewood Cliffs, N.J.: Prentice-Hall, 1964.

――――. *Verbal Learning.* San Rafael, Calif.: Dimensions Publishing Co., 1969.

Woodcock, Richard W., and Charlotte R. Clark. *Peabody Rebus Reading Program.* Circle Pines, Minn.: American Guidance Service, 1969.

11. Cognitive Development

THEORY

The abilities to think, to conceptualize, to use abstractions, to reason, to criticize, and to be creative are essential human functions. This chapter examines some aspects of cognition and its relationship to disturbances in learning: (a) cognitive abilities, (b) approaches to studying cognitive development, (c) learning disabilities related to cognitive development, and (d) theories of teaching cognition. Two curriculum areas that exemplify cognitive skills, arithmetic and reading comprehension, are discussed in the "Teaching Strategies" section.

COGNITIVE ABILITIES

The term *cognitive skills* refers to a collection of mental abilities that enable one to know and to be aware. Cognition refers to the manner in which humans acquire, interpret, organize, store, retrieve, and employ knowledge. Neisser (1967) defined cognition as the process by which sensory input is transferred, reduced, elaborated, stored, recovered, and used. Cognitive abilities develop at all stages of the child's life. For example, when the young child plays at putting pots and pans inside each other, certain cognitive skills are developing. It is difficult to examine cognition apart from other kinds of learning due to the fact that the growth of cognitive ability cannot be separated from the basic growth of the individual, which includes all of the areas of motor, perceptual, memory, language, and social learning.

A disturbance in the thinking process no doubt is an important factor for many children with learning disabilities. Further, a disturbance or inadequate development in other areas of learning is likely to affect adversely the development of the higher cognitive abilities. In discussing the development of cognitive structures in children with learning problems, Gardner (1955, pp. 145–146) states:

> It is known that even mild brain damage may have severe effects upon concept formation. . . . Impairments of the capacity to categorize and abstract effectively are sometimes among the most easily observed sequelae of brain damage. . . .
>
> In the school situation, the combination of difficulties affecting concept formation may have some traumatic effects. It may be difficult for even the mildly brain-damaged child to understand, and especially to remember relationships among superficially dissimilar ideas. He may adopt a piecemeal approach to concept formation in which some abstract relationships (in which a capacity for concrete association can be substituted for true abstraction) with remarkable ease but fail to grasp other relationships that appear superficially to be equally simple.

APPROACHES TO STUDYING COGNITIVE DEVELOPMENT

Two of the approaches that psychologists use to study cognitive abilities are: (1) those that identify the various components of cognition and (2) those that analyze the sequential development of cognitive abilities in human beings, particularly in the young child.

COMPONENTS OF MENTAL FUNCTIONING

Ideas concerning the makeup of intellectual functioning have changed in the last 50 years. While the early scholars viewed intelligence as a global or general entity (the "g" factor), the tendency in more recent years has been to view intelligence as consisting of many subskills of mental functioning. Spearman (1927) measured two factors, a general factor and a specific factor unique to a particular test. The *Stanford-Binet Intelligence Scale* (Terman and Merrill 1937) yielded a single overall score to indicate IQ. The 1960 revision of this test continues the single overall score approach.

The SRA *Primary Mental Abilities tests* (Thurstone and Thurstone 1947) broke intelligence into seven components; but in the 1962 revision of the PMA tests, separate scores are obtained in five areas: verbal meaning, number facility, reasoning, perceptual speed, and spatial relations. The 1949 *Wechsler Intelligence Scale for Children* (WISC) and the 1974 revision called WISC-R (Wechsler 1949, 1974) divide intelligence into two areas: verbal and performance. The test yields a separate Verbal IQ and a Performance IQ, as well as a Full IQ. In addition, each area is broken into 6 subtests, giving 12 subcomponent scores. Anastasi (1968) advises caution in overinterpreting individual subtest scores on the WISC for purposes of a differential diagnosis.

The *Illinois Test of Psycholinguistic Abilities* (Kirk, McCarthy, and Kirk 1968) divides mental function into 12 subabilities, each designed to measure a discrete component of mental function. A comparison of intraindividual differences among the specific subtests guides the diagnosis and treatment for learning disabilities. A study by Newcomer, Hare, and Hammill (1974) suggests that with some exceptions the ITPA subtests appear to measure discrete independent abilities. Sedlak and Weener (1973) reviewed studies with the ITPA and concluded that it is still premature to judge if the ITPA gives a measurement of differential abilities.

Guilford (1967) suggests in his *Structure of the Intellect* that there are as many as 120 different factors of intellectual abilities, of which about 80 are known. Guilford's three-dimensional model of the structure of the intellect (Figure 11.1) classifies intellectual abilities into three categories, each of which cuts across the others: (1) operations, (2) content, and (3) products. The model was developed through factor-analytic research.

1. *Operations.* These are the processes involved in thinking. The Guilford

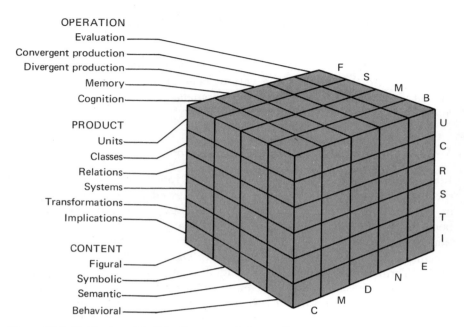

Figure 11.1 Guilford model of the Structure of the Intellect

From *The Nature of Human Intelligence* by J. P. Guilford, p. 63. Copyright © 1967 by McGraw-Hill Book Company. Used with permission of McGraw-Hill Book Company.

model has five categories of operations: cognition, memory, convergent thinking, divergent thinking, and evaluation.

a. *Cognition* refers to ways of understanding or comprehension. The group of cognitive abilities has to do with discovery and recognition of information.

b. *Memory* refers to the operations of retention and reproduction of information.

c. *Convergent thinking* is the bringing together of known facts or associations that result in one definite, predictable outcome. The conclusion is determined by the given information, and there is a recognition of the best of the conventional conclusions.

d. *Divergent thinking* is the utilization of knowledge in new ways to produce one or many novel solutions or a variety of ideas. This ability may be referred to as creative thinking.

e. *Evaluation* requires the establishment of a value system against which to weigh various alternative actions or results. The ability is sometimes called critical thinking.

2. *Content.* Content can be of various types: figural, semantic, symbolic, behavioral. This completely different way of classifying abilities cuts across operations. Content is concerned with the nature of the material or information. Information that is concrete — that can be seen, heard or felt — is

called "figural." Information in the abstract form of symbols (such as letters, numbers, or words) is "symbolic" content. "Semantic" content refers to the ideas or meanings that the symbols represent. "Behavioral" content refers to information about the behavior of ourselves and others — including thoughts, desires, feelings, and intentions.

3. *Products.* This term refers to the levels of intellectual activities: units, classes, relations, systems, transformations, implications. This third classification is concerned with the products of information, the form of the relationships or groupings of information. Each level of activity is more complex, requiring a higher degree of mental functioning and a more sophisticated way of relating information.

Figure 11.1 shows Guilford's three-dimensional model of the structure of the intellect. When the three cross-classifications are combined, the intersection of a certain kind of *operation,* a certain kind of *content,* and a certain kind of *product,* is represented by a single cell. There are 120 separate cells in the structure of the intellect as represented in the model.

Meeker (1969) extended Guilford's *Structure of the Intellect* (SOI) model by designing applications for education. She attempted to interpret this complex psychological model of the intellect for use within the framework of the school curriculum by specifying tasks to teach cognitive skills. Meeker's book presents a method of interpreting *WISC* and *Stanford-Binet* responses in light of Guildford's SOI model. By plotting scores according to the SOI model, the diagnostician is able to also make specific teaching recommendations for cognitive skill development.

In a followup publication, Meeker et al. (1970) present and illustrate specific teaching tasks. These learning tasks are prescribed for specific cells in the three-dimensional Guilford SOI model. For example, for the cell created in the model by the intersection of the three dimensions of *cognition, figural,* and *implications* (CFI), a specific maze-tracing task is prescribed to develop the cognitive ability tapped by this cell. Underlying Meeker's application of this model is the presumption that components of the intellect can be trained and that better scholarship will follow.

Each of these psychological frameworks, then, is an attempt to identify the components that make up mental functioning.

DEVELOPMENTAL HIERARCHY OF COGNITIVE ABILITIES

A second way that psychologists analyze thinking is by studying the development of cognitive abilities in children. These frameworks suggest a progressive development of cognitive abilities under certain conditions.

Piaget, a Swiss psychologist, has spent his life studying the intellectual development of children (Flavell 1963). There are many facets to Piaget's theories of child development. His concepts of maturational stages of logical thinking are discussed in Chapter 12, but the idea that cognitive growth occurs via a series of invariant and interdependent stages is also pertinent in this context. At each stage the child is capable of learning only certain cognitive tasks.

In another facet of Piaget's theories, he suggests that the child adapts to the environment and structures knowledge in two complementary ways: assimilation and accommodation. In assimilation children incorporate new experiences into their already existing schemata or cognitive structures. In accommodation, they focus on the new features of the situation and may change their schemata or cognitive structures accordingly. A young child, in picking up a ball, will assimilate the grasping techniques already mastered, but will also accommodate the new features of the ball by changing the schemata. In accommodation there is a slight expansion of the cognitive structure. Cognitive development consists of a succession of changes in these structures.

Another important facet of Piaget's theories is the child's developing concept of conservation, which illustrates the sequential development of cognitive ability. In one of these experiments, two balls of clay equal in size are placed on a scale to show the child that they are equal. One ball of clay is then flattened. The eight-year-old is likely to predict that they are still the same weight, while the four-year-old states that the flattened ball of clay weighs more. In another experiment, an equal amount of liquid is poured into two identical glasses. When the liquid from one glass is emptied into a tall thin container, the five-year-old is convinced that the tall thin glass contains more liquid. The seven-year-old knows that there is no difference in volume. The concept of conservation is an example of a developmental hierarchy of cognitive ability.

Bloom et al. (1965) developed a taxonomy, or a sequential classification system, of all the types of learning in the cognitive domain. Under intellectual abilities and skills, he listed comprehension, application, analysis, synthesis, and evaluation.

Gagné (1970), who believes that learning is in part genetically and in part environmentally determined, provides a hierarchy of eight progressively complex types of cognitive learning: (1) signal learning, (2) stimulus-response learning, (3) chaining, (4) verbal association, (5) discrimination learning, (6) concept learning, (7) rule learning, and (8) problem solving. The prerequisite for any one type of learning is that learning at the previous level in the progression already be established.

Each of these psychological frameworks attempts to examine the sequential development of progressively complex cognitive tasks in the growing child.

LEARNING DISABILITIES RELATED TO COGNITIVE DEVELOPMENT

The theories of cognition and mental functioning have implications for understanding children with learning disabilities. The significance in terms of

(1) developmental imbalances, (2) inadequate cognitive structures, (3) problems in concept development, and (4) disorders in nonverbal and verbal thinking are discussed in this section.

DEVELOPMENTAL IMBALANCES

The components of the mental-functioning approach to studying cognition identify multidimensional abilities (and consequent disabilities) of mental functioning. One implication of this approach is that some of the abilities function or dysfunction somewhat apart from the others. As testing instruments are developed to measure the subabilities, the diagnostician is able to compare performance in various subskills and note disparities. Moreover, along with the diagnostic tools to identify subareas of mental function, methods of teaching to build these areas are generated.

Some theorists of learning disabilities focus on the many component parts of the intellect contributing to the learning process; they hypothesize that an uneven development among the various skills has a positive relationship to learning disturbances. According to Gallagher (1966), an observed key difference between children with special learning problems and children without learning problems is that children who find learning difficult exhibit a large disparity in the developmental patterns of intelligence subskills that are important to school success. The normal child without a learning disorder exhibits a relatively uniform pattern among subskills, with small differences between best and worst performances in various mental abilities.

Similarly, school-age mentally retarded children also show a relatively consistent pattern, although they exhibit a low function level over *all* areas of abilities and skills in comparison to the norm for their chronological age. Neither the normal child nor the mentally retarded child shows substantial variations among the various mental abilities; however, the child with learning disabilities exhibits significant differences in abilities among various mental factors.

To illustrate such a characteristic, a first-grade child with developmental imbalances may show the general language development of a six-year-old, while the child's perceptual-motor skill may be at a two- or three-year-old level.

Gallagher (1966, p. 28) defines developmental imbalances as follows:

> Children with developmental imbalances are those who reveal a developmental disparity in psychological processes related to education of such a degree (often four years or more) as to require the instructional programming of developmental tasks appropriate to the nature and level of the deviant developmental process.

To determine abilities (or strengths and weaknesses) of a child, it is necessary to break down general intellectual functioning into its various contributing component parts and to measure the functioning level of each. A profile of the subskill scores obtained on a diagnostic test designed for this purpose can indicate if a child with a learning problem has developmental imbalances. Although we lack evidence to show how much disparity in pattern represents a range within normal limits, Gallagher suggests that a deviation of four years or more between the best and worst skills is beyond the normal range.

The *Illinois Test for Psycholinguistic Abilities* (Kirk, McCarthy, and Kirk 1968), previously discussed in Chapter 5, is one test designed to show a patterning of abilities for diagnostic interpretation. Figure 11.2 shows a profile obtained on a student as a result of performance on the ITPA. The composite score of the child's Psycholinguistic Abilities Age (PLA) was 5 years 9 months. The figure shows the child's performance in the 12 subtests expressed in scaled scores. The mean or average scaled score was 35. The profile shows that some scores were more than one standard deviation above the mean score, while some scores were more than one standard deviation below the mean score. The performance of this student on the ITPA shows a disparity of 4 standard deviations between the high score on the Verbal Expression subtest and the low score on the Manual Expression subtest. Similarly, when these scores are translated into age-scores (not shown on the graph), they reveal a disparity of over five years between the high and low scores. The gap between scores higher than one standard deviation above the mean and scores lower than one standard deviation below the mean suggests that this child has a significant developmental imbalance, as does the disparity of more than five years between high and low age scores. Further analysis reveals that these intraindividual differences are statistically significant. In addition, such a profile of performance in component abilities permits the location of specific abilities and disabilities that can aid in both diagnosis and the planning of teaching strategies. For example, in the case shown in Figure 11.2, the subject performed substantially better on the auditory-vocal subtests than on the visual-motor subtests, suggesting strength in the auditory-vocal channels and a deficit in the visual-motor channel functions.

INADEQUATE COGNITIVE STRUCTURES

The psychological theories that focus on the developmental hierarchy of cognitive function suggest that we must structure learning experiences to enhance the development of cognitive structures. Cognitive abilities of the child are qualitatively different from those of the adult, and the child's thinking skills change in form through maturation. Further, these cognitive structures develop in a sequential fashion that cannot be altered.

The implication of these theories for understanding learning problems is that the environment may be hindering instead of assisting the child's cognitive growth. If the school makes cognitive demands that depend on cognitive structures that the child has not yet developed, learning problems may result. Moreover, the curriculum of the school may not be designed to enhance the development of cognitive structures.

Furth (1970), who has interpreted Piaget's theories for teachers, concludes

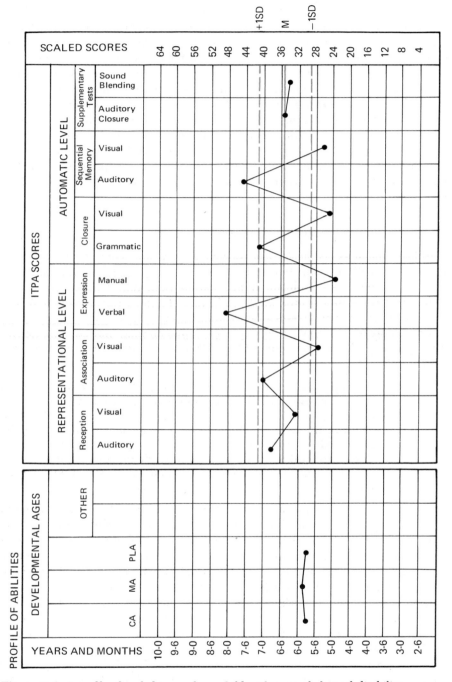

Figure 11.2 A profile of scaled scores for a child with a visual channel disability

From Samuel A. Kirk and Winifred D. Kirk, *Psycholinguistic Learning Disabilities: Diagnosis and Remediation.* Urbana, Ill.: University of Illinois Press, 1971.

that the first job of our schools should be to strengthen the thinking foundation on which further learning is grounded. He emphasizes that a school which in the earliest grades focuses primarily on reading cannot focus on thinking. The school chooses to foster one or the other. The droll tale of the seven-year-old child who asks a classmate to meet for discussion of their homework in differential calculus when the big hand is on the four and the little hand is on the two illustrates the educational implication. The point is that surface learning, which does not affect the child's cognitive structure and for which the child is not ready, is illusory learning.

The developmental hierarchy of the cognitive abilities approach to learning disabilities is closely related to the maturational approach. A further discussion of the implications is located in the section "Maturational Perspectives" in Chapter 12.

FAULTY CONCEPT DEVELOPMENT

The learning of concepts is now regarded as an important objective in all areas of education. Contributing to this belief are such eminent scholars as Bruner (1956, 1966), Guilford (1967), Piaget (Flavell 1963), Hunt (1961), Skinner (1953), and Gagné (1970). All agree to the general statement that the learning of concepts is an important objective. The difficulty comes in operationalizing the goal of concept development into methods of learning and teaching. Klausmeier and Miller (1968, p. 1) point out three reasons for this difficulty:

1. Concepts have not been clearly defined. As a result teachers and others do not know precisely what to teach as concepts.
2. Learning theorists have not come up with a clear explanation of concept learning. The course of concept learning cannot be predicted or controlled well, based on learning theory.
3. The considerable knowledge from empirical research about concept learning has not been translated into instructional guidelines.

Concepts are commonly explained as the thinking process, ideas, cognition, or abstractions. A typical illustration of a concept is a *chair, dog,* or *man*. These terms refer to an idea, an abstraction, or a symbol of concrete experiences. A person's experiences may have included exposure to a specific rocking chair, an upholstered chair, and a baby's high chair; but the concept *chair* symbolizes a set of attributes about "chairness"; the person makes an inference about new experiences with chairs, such as a lawn chair, observed for the first time. The symbol itself does not have an empirical reference point. The Greeks searched for an understanding of concepts which Plato, in the *Republic*, equated with knowing the "essence" of things.

Although it is possible to form concepts without words, language plays an important role in concept development; and a child's language disorder is likely to be reflected in faulty conceptual abilities.

At a higher level of conceptualization, the ideas are still further removed from concrete referents. The concept *chair* is part of a higher concept of *furniture*. Concepts even more removed from the sensory world are ideas such as *democracy, loyalty, fairness,* or *freedom.* A "generalization" is broader than a concept and is formed by relating at least two concepts. The following statement may be considered a generalization: "Man makes adaptations to his environment."

The Now Society

© Chronicle Publishing Co. 1974   5-22

It burn. It bright. I call it "wheel."

What happens when concepts have not been well built? What are the consequences to learning if concepts are meager, lacking in preciseness, inaccurate, or isolated strands?

Children may have learning problems at any of the levels of conceptualization. Some children confuse one attribute of an object with the concept of the object. For example, one child could not understand the circular concept of the roundness of a plate. When told that the plate was round and asked to feel the circle along its edges, the child said, "That's not round; that's a dish." Some children confuse the concept of an object with its name. When one girl was asked if the moon could be called by another name, such as "cow," she responded, "No, because the moon doesn't give milk."

Multiple meanings of words also cause confusion. The confusion of multiple meanings in our language is well illustrated by Smith (1963) who gave as an example the many meanings of the word, "note": (1) In music, *note* means the elliptical character in a certain position on the music staff. (2) In arithmetic or business, a *note* might mean a written promise to pay. (3) In English or study hall a *note* might refer to an informal written communication. (4) In social studies a *note* might refer to a formal communique between the heads of two nations. (5) In science one might be able to *note* results of an experiment, meaning to observe it. (6) In English class, the selection in literature might discuss an individual who was a person of great *note* in the community. (7) In any lesson, the student could be asked to make *note* of an examination date, meaning to remember it. (8) The teacher could make a *note* in the margin of the paper, meaning to make a remark. (9) In material on England, paper money may be called a *bank note*. The child who could not hold the various concepts of this word in mind would have trouble understanding many areas of the curriculum.

The following serves to illustrate the consequences of the misunderstanding of a symbol with multiple concepts: Nine-year-old Susie came home from school in tears with a medical form from the school nurse advising her parents to take their daughter for an eye examination. The child sobbed that the cause of her anguish was not that she needed eye-glasses, but that the blank next to the word *SEX* on the examination form had been filled in by the nurse with an "F." That symbol "F" conveyed the concept of a grade, and Susie feared she had failed sex.

A further confusion in school learning is related to the fact that important concepts are presented as technical terms in school subjects: *plateau, continental divide, density of population, pollution, the law of gravity, monopoly.* Problems in reading in the content areas are frequently due not to the difficulty of the words, but to the concentration and compactness of the presentation of the concepts.

If the pupil fails to read a word he does not know, it may change the meaning of the entire passage. One high school student thought the school was using pornographic material because the people described in the following passage were nude: "The pilgrims did not wear gaudy clothes." Since the boy did not know the meaning of the word *gaudy*, he simply eliminated it from the sentence. Another high school student, misinterpreting a concept because of a word with multiple meanings, filled in an exercise in the following manner. "One swallow does not make a (drunk)."

An implication for teaching to remedy this confusion between concepts and words and faulty conceptualizations is that children need experiences that will equip them for building appropriate concepts. A first step in building a concept is that of having primary experiences. A further aid to concept development is helping children develop the skill of drawing conclusions from the experiences. A more advanced stage is learning to classify, summarize, and generalize conclusions from several experiences.

Disorders in Nonverbal and Verbal Thinking

Two different kinds of cognitive processing can be observed — those that are independent of language formulations and linguistic meanings and those thinking skills that are part of the language process. *Nonverbal thinking skills* include visual skills, performance skills, spatial abilities, and certain aspects of social skills. Children with disabilities in nonverbal areas have difficulty in observing and interpreting gestures and facial expressions, in putting puzzles together, in remembering visual forms and shapes, in visualizing spatial relationships, in thinking numerically, and in certain aspects of arithmetic.

Verbal thinking skills are related to language, which cannot be separated from the cognitive and thinking process. Both the receptive language skills of listening and reading and the expressive language skills of speaking and writing can be viewed as elements of cognition. Language becomes a vehicle for thinking by helping to organize and assimilate input data and by helping to formulate and develop the output. At the same time, the development of cognitive strategies strengthen and enhance language development.

Because of the commonality in the thinking processes underlying all areas of language, the improvement of language skill in one area is likely to result in the improvement of language in other areas. For example, improvement in the skill of listening is likely to produce a concomitant improvement in the area of reading comprehension. Further, many children with severe basic language disabilities, such as severely delayed language acquisition, have been observed to deteriorate in all areas of intellectual function as they get older. The absence of functional language seems to adversely affect nonverbal cognitive abilities.

A specific academic problem may reflect a disorder in nonverbal thinking, or verbal thinking, or both. The *Teaching Strategies* section of this chapter discusses *arithmetic* as an example of a nonverbal cognitive skill and *reading comprehension* as an example of a verbal cognitive skill.

THEORIES OF TEACHING COGNITION

It is helpful to identify two contrasting theories of cognitive learning. They are (a) the stimulus-response approach, and (b) the hypothesis-testing approach. Each theory leads to quite different methods of teaching.

Stimulus-Response Theory of Learning

In the stimulus-response framework, learning proceeds as a result of conditioned and mechanical connections between environmental events and the response of an individual to those events. Associations are formed as a function of external stimulus conditions. An assumption of this view is that cognitive learning of complex processes is similar to the learning of simple skills. Further, this view assumes that explanations of simpler kinds of learning provide adequate explanations of concept learning and cognition.

Basically, the sequence to be considered in teaching is (a) stimulation, (b) response, and (c) reward. By manipulating and structuring the stimulation and reward, the teacher can achieve certain desired responses or behaviors on the part of the subject. Structure, over-learning, reinforcement, and drill are important elements of this approach. The beginning work within this approach to learning is generally attributed to Skinner (1953).

A program to teach the cognitive skills within the stimulus-response framework must specify precisely what skill is to be learned, and then design a program to stimulate and reward the desired response. One teaching method that results from this theory of learning is behavior modification, which is described in greater detail in Chapter 12. Another outgrowth of this view is programed instruction.

The development of *programed instructional materials* evolved from the stimulus-response theory of learning. Such materials are designed to teach many areas of the curriculum, including reading and arithmetic. The essential principles of programed instruction are:

1. to break down the subject to be taught to an ordered sequence of steps or stimulus items
2. to provide a means for the students to respond in a specified way to each item or stimulus and to record the response
3. to reinforce the student's response by providing immediate knowledge of the results
4. to make each sequential step very small to ensure that the student will make few errors and practice mostly correct responses
5. to move the student step by step, from what is known to what should be learned

The program must identify as precisely as possible the objectives set for the student. Further, a successful program must ascertain continually that the student working through the program is learning each task identified by the program.

In summary, the stimulus-response approach to cognitive learning postulates that the educator can design teaching materials and manipulate the environment in such a fashion that specific cognitive skills will be learned. Examples of materials designed from this point of view include: *Distar* programs in reading, arithmetic and language by Engelmann and others (Science Research Associates), *Write and See* by Skinner and others (Lyons and Carnahan), and *Programmed Reading* by Sullivan Associates (McGraw-Hill). Reported research studies based on the stimulus-response theory of teaching reading include the "Stanford Computer-Assisted Instruction" (Atkinson and Hanson 1966) and "Programmed Tutoring" (Ellson et al. 1965).

HYPOTHESIS-TESTING THEORY OF LEARNING

In contrast to the stimulus-response view of cognitive learning is the hypothesis-testing theory. This view presumes cognitive learning to be a highly active process of "seeking" behavior rather than a passive process of "responding" behavior. In this view, cognitive learning can be approached as a kind of decision-making process. Individuals observe data, propose their own problems, construct hypotheses to solve the problems, seek to reaffirm their hypotheses, and, finally, formulate their own generalizations. Curriculum plans that have evolved from such a viewpoint have been referred to as the "inquiry method," "discovery-learning," "creativity approaches," and "problem-solving techniques." One curriculum designer who works from this theory is Suchman (1960).

The hypothesis-testing approach to the teaching of cognitive skills in the area of reading is suggested by Stauffer (1969). He believes that children need to be taught to read in such a way that the child is free to develop cognitive and thinking skills. The child, not the teacher, must gather the data, make predictions, propose the problems, ask questions, and, finally, find solutions. Teachers' questions about the content are used as an occasional testing device, rather than as a conditioning mechanism.

Reading comprehension is approached as a process of inquiry (Stauffer 1967). The task of the teacher is to set up an environment that is conducive to the thinking process while the child is reading. The student is helped to (1) raise questions, (2) build hypotheses, (3) read and process data, and (4) test findings to determine validity. While the teacher plays an important guiding role, the initiative and structure come from the student. This approach to the teaching of reading is described in greater detail in the teaching strategies section under "Reading Comprehension."

INSTRUCTIONAL IMPLICATIONS

Henderson (1969, pp. 89–90) contrasts the hypothesis-testing and the stimulus-response approaches to teaching cognitive skills. The following differences are emphasized.

1. In the stimulus-response approach, the responsible agent is the teacher (or the material); but in the hypothesis-testing approach, the responsible agent is the student. In the first, what the teacher (or material) does to the pupil is significant; while in the latter, what the student does to the material is significant.

2. In the hypothesis-testing approach, the student takes the initiative, selecting what is to be acted upon. In the stimulus-response approach, the teacher selects the material to be acted upon.

3. The hypothesis-testing approach analyzes the thinking and cognitive skills while the stimulus-response approach analyzes the content to be learned. Teaching that evolves from the hypothesis-testing framework emphasizes the selection and exercise of cognitive skills, not a mastery of particular content.

In this discussion, the two approaches to teaching cognition — the stimulus-response approach and the hypothesis-testing approach — have been presented as diametrically opposed extremes. Probably there is a role to be played by each approach. Individuals undoubtedly acquire some learning according to stimulus-response principles and some according to hypothesis-testing principles. Individuals are both passive responders and active searchers. Teaching methods, therefore, should reflect both kinds of learning. The *Teaching Strategies* section of this chapter discusses two academic areas of cognitive processing — *arithmetic* and *reading comprehension.* Arithmetic encompasses nonverbal thinking, while reading comprehension depends on verbal and language-related thinking.

TEACHING STRATEGIES

Cognitive abilities are needed in every area of the school curriculum as well as in most other areas of learning. In spite of the obvious importance of cognitive skills, the guidelines for implementing the teaching of thinking skills are still rather hazy. Theories of cognitive development are still in the process of formulation and modification; the dimensions and components of cognition have not as yet been precisely defined; nor have the relationships among these components been operationally determined. As a consequence, the development of curricula and teaching strategies to promote cognitive skills along the lines of theoretical cognitive models is still in its infant stages. Even so, current models of cognitive development do suggest certain desirable goals and some means of reaching these goals.

The child who has a deficit in cognition is likely to perform poorly in many school subjects. In this section, only two areas of functioning will be considered in relation to cognitive skills: (1) arithmetic, as a school subject requiring quantitative thinking; and (2) reading comprehension, as a school subject requiring a language-type of thinking. These two areas of functioning provide a useful vehicle for the discussion of cognitive skills. Arithmetic and reading are basic school subjects that children with learning disabilities frequently fail, and these subjects represent two sectors of cognitive functioning — nonverbal and verbal. Activities for teaching arithmetic and reading comprehension are also presented in this section.

ARITHMETIC

Arithmetic is an academic area that requires nonverbal thinking. While nonverbal processing is crucial to mathematical learning, language also plays an important role in certain operations of arithmetic. Both language and nonverbal thinking appear to contribute to arithmetic functioning.

Arithmetic has been called a universal language. It is a symbolic language that enables human beings to think about, record, and communicate ideas concerning the elements and the relationships of quantity. The field of mathematics includes counting, measurement, arithmetic, calculation, geometry, and algebra. The focus of the "new mathematics" is on helping children gain insight into the structure and application of our number system.

CHARACTERISTICS OF THE CHILD WITH AN ARITHMETIC DISABILITY

The subject of remedial arithmetic has received much less attention than other areas of remedial education. Yet for many youngsters with learning disabilities, arithmetic is the specific area of difficulty — at both the elementary and the secondary levels. A learning disability in the area of arithmetic comprehension and related conceptual disturbances in learning about quantitative elements has been referred to as *dyscalculia* (Cohn 1961). Not all children with learning disabilities have difficulty with number concepts. In fact, many children with severe reading disability have been observed to be strong in arithmetic skills. Nevertheless, arithmetic is a school subject that very frequently is a problem area for children with learning disabilities.

Kaliski (1967) has noted that many of the symptoms that identify children with learning disabilities can be related to arithmetic difficulties. Disturbances in spatial relationships, visual perception abnormalities, perseveration, difficulty with symbols, and cognitive disturbances all have obvious implications for number learning. Some of the characteristics of children identified as dyscalculic are discussed in the following subsections. It must be remembered, however, that each child is unique and not all children with an arithmetic disability possess all of the deficiencies described.

For some children, difficulty with numerical relationships begins at an early age. The ability to count, to understand the one-to-one correspondence, to match, to sort, and to compare are dependent upon the child's experiences in manipulating objects. The child with a short attention span, with poor perception, or with poor motor development may not have had appropriate experiences with activities of manipulation — experiences that would prepare the child to build understandings of space, form, order, time, distance, and quantity.

A child's early concepts of quantity are evidenced in early language in such phrases as, "all gone," "that's all," "more," "big," and "little." The young child plays with pots and pans and with boxes that fit into each other; the child puts objects into containers. All these activities aid the development of a sense of space, sequence, and order. The child with an arithmetic learning disability may have missed these essential experiences as an infant. Parents often report that children with such disorders had not enjoyed or engaged in play with blocks, puzzles, models, or construction-type toys (Johnson and Myklebust 1967).

Disturbances of Spatial Relationships

Concepts of spatial relationships are normally acquired at the preschool level. Kaliski (1967) reports that the child with an arithmetic disability often confuses spatial relationships such as: up-down, over-under, top-bottom, high-low, near-far, front-back, beginning-end, and across. Strauss and Lehtinen (1947) found that a disturbance in spatial perception interferes with the visualization of the entire number system. The child may be unable to perceive distances between numbers, and may not know if the number *3* is closer to *4* or *6*.

Disturbances of Visual-Perception and Visual-Motor Association

Children with arithmetic disabilities have been observed to have difficulty with activities that require visual perception and visual-motor association. Strauss (1951) noted that some brain-injured children are unable to count objects in a series by pointing to each of them and saying, "One, two, three, four, five." Such children must first learn to count by grasping and physically manipulating objects. Grasping the objects appears to be an earlier development in the neuromotor and perceptual developmental hierarchy than pointing to objects.

Many children with a basic arithmetic disability are unable to see objects in groups or sets — an ability that enables others to quickly identify the number of objects in a group. Even when adding a group or set of three with a set of four objects, some children with an arithmetic disability must begin by counting the objects one by one to determine the total number in the sets.

Some children are unable to visually perceive a geometric shape as an entire entity. For these children, a square may not appear as a square shape but as four unrelated lines, as a hexagon, or even as a circle.

Other children have difficulty in learning to visually perceive number symbols. Strauss (1951) noted that some children confuse the vertical stroke of the number *1* and the number *4*, or they may confuse the upper half of the number *2* and portions of the number *3*.

Children with poor arithmetic abilities frequently perform inadequately in visual-motor tasks. Because they cannot capture the gestalt of a shape and because they have a disturbance in perceiving spatial relationships and in making spatial judgments, they may not be able to copy geometric forms, shapes, numbers, or letters adequately. Consequently, such children are likely to be very poor in handwriting as well as arithmetic.

Other Characteristics

Children with poor number sense have been observed to have an inaccurate or imprecise notion of body image. These children may be unable to understand the basic relationship of the body parts. When asked to draw a picture of a human figure, the child may draw the body parts as completely unrelated or misplaced, or with stick legs coming from the head, or with no body at all.

In addition, children with an arithmetic disability often have a poor sense of direction and time. They become lost easily and cannot find their way to a friend's house or home from school. They often forget if it is morning or afternoon and may go home during the recess period thinking the school day has ended. They have difficulty estimating the time span of an hour, a minute, several hours, or a week; and they cannot guess how long a task will take.

An understanding of the underlying number system is important to success in mathematics, but of equal importance is the development of skills in the computational operations or arithmetic. For efficient learning in arithmetic, these computational skills of adding, subtracting, multiplying, and dividing must become automatic. Often the child with a severe memory deficit understands the underlying number system, but is unable to remember the number facts. Such a child may find it necessary to do repeated addition for each multiplication problem.

Scores on social maturity and social perception have been found to be low among many children with poor arithmetic abilities. Johnson and Myklebust (1967) describe a research project that showed that the mean social quotient of a group of dyscalculic children was substantially below their mean verbal intelligence quotient. Further, the performance scores on an intelligence test for this group were far below the scores obtained on the verbal portions of the test.

Finally, it has been noted that some children with an arithmetic disability have good verbal and auditory abilities. Such children are highly verbal and may even be excellent readers. However, the problems of other children with an arithmetic disability are compounded by handicaps in reading. The child who cannot read and understand the arithmetic problem will obviously be unable to perform the mathematical tasks required.

In their summary of a study of research on the basic cognitive processes underlying the attainment of quantitative concepts, Chalfant and Scheffelin (1969, Chap. 10) grouped factors related to a quantitative disability into five categories: (1) intelligence, (2) spatial ability, (3) verbal ability, (4) problem-solving ability, and (5) neurophysiological correlates. The child's arithmetic disability may be due to a verbal, spatial, perceptual, or memory deficiency. If so, it may be necessary to provide special remedial procedures to ameliorate the basic disorder in the learning processes.

MODERN MATH

In most schools today, the arithmetic curriculum follows a modern mathematics program. The modern mathematics curriculum assumes an hypothesis-testing approach to learning. The goal of the "modern math" program is to help the child develop an understanding of the basic structure of our number system rather than rote performance and rote learning of isolated skills and facts. The emphasis is on teaching the *why*, as well as the *how*, of arithmetic. The mathematics program leads pupils to knowledge through the processes of *discovery* and *exploration;* the program emphasizes the comprehension, formulation, and practical application of new concepts and skills.

These goals appear to be desirable ones for the child with learning disabilities. However, the question to be asked is, "How does the modern mathematics approach affect children with a learning disability in numbers and mathematics?" It is difficult to answer this question at present because little research is available to clarify the issue. Virtually nothing has been written on remedial methods for teaching the new mathematics. Indeed, the problem faced by children who have failed after exposure to the modern mathematics curriculum seem similar to those faced by children who failed in the traditional mathematics programs. After more than a decade of experience with the modern math curriculum in our schools, many children continue to have problems mastering this inherently difficult subject (Otto, McMenemy, and Smith 1973).

TEACHING THE CHILD WITH AN ARITHMETIC DISABILITY

Before deciding on the techniques for teaching arithmetic, the teacher must understand the *child* as well as the *subject matter* of arithmetic. In addition to knowing whether the child is successful at certain levels and certain operations in arithmetic, it is necessary to probe into the strengths and weaknesses of learning which the child brings to the arithmetic situation. How do the child's adaptations of deficiencies affect the child's approach? What other tasks does the child approach in this way? How far back is it necessary to go to insure a firm foundation in number concepts? What techniques appear to be most appropriate?

Chalfant and Schefflin (1969, Chapter 10) suggest that it is useful to investigate the following areas in assessing psychological and neurological correlates to learning disabilities in quantitative thinking:

1. Determine if the child has *comprehension of number structure and arithmetic operations*. Is the child able to understand the meaning of spoken numbers? Can the child read and write numbers? Do basic arithmetic operations? Tell which is larger and which is smaller?

2. Determine the child's skills in *spatial orientation*. Has the child established a left-right directionality or shown evidence of spatial disorientation?

3. Does the child have difficulty with *finger localization*? Can the child name or designate the fingers of each hand in response to oral command or the fingers that are touched when eyes are closed?

4. To what extent does *language ability* affect to contribute to problems in arithmetic?

Bereiter (1968) points out that arithmetic problems are created because arithmetic is not taught in a way that insures that the concept will remain available for use. Bereiter suggests that the following principles be adhered to in developing general mathematical intelligence:

1. The emphasis in arithmetic instruction should be on *finding out* answers to questions, rather than toward merely doing something.

2. Whatever is learned should be *generalized* to many different kinds of applications and experiences with different ways of handling the problem.

3. Beginning mathematics should be made *coherent,* instead of a collection of unrelated topics and tricks (as is sometimes true of modern math instruction).

4. Instruction must be *thorough* so that children have the needed practice. In some modern math programs insufficient time is devoted to practice.

5. The mathematics program should be taught so that the child gains *confidence* in mathematics ability. Adults often become alarmed and defensive when faced with a mathematical problem because they lost confidence during their early arithmetic instruction.

Freidus (1966) stresses the importance of checking far enough back into the previously acquired number learnings to insure readiness for what the child now needs to learn. Time and effort invested in building a firm foundation can prevent many of the difficulties that children experience as they try to move on to more advanced and more abstract arithmetic processes. Freidus (1966, pp. 116–120) suggests consideration of the following levels in assessing the child's development of number concepts:

1. Sets and Matching (concept of the "same" and grouping of objects).
2. Relationship concepts (comparing and relating objects).
3. Measuring and Pairing (estimating, fitting objects, one-to-one correspondence).
4. Counting (matching numerals to objects).
5. Sequential values (arranging like objects in order by quantitative differences).
6. Relationships of parts to whole and parts to each other (experimentation with self-correcting materials to discover numerical relationships).
7. Operations (manipulation of number facts without reference to concrete objects — number facts up to ten).
8. The Decimal System (learning of the system of numeration and notation beyond ten and upon the base ten).

Activities for Teaching Arithmetic

The following section presents a collection of techniques and methods for teaching the child with an arithmetic disability.

1. *Basic computational skills.* Learning disabilities teachers report that many problems in arithmetic are due to deficiencies in basic computational skills. Each child's problem should be evaluated with reference to underlying deficits in learning processes, verbal, spatial, perceptual, or memory factors. In addition, however, the learning of basic computational skills that the child is lacking must be considered, including addition, subtraction, multiplication, division, fractions, decimals, and percentages. May (1974) provides excellent suggestions for teaching computational skills.

2. *Addition.* Knowledge of addition facts provides the foundation for all other computational skills in arithmetic. Addition is a short method of counting, and pupils should know that they can resort to counting when all else fails. Addition can be thought of as *part plus part equals whole.* Important symbols to learn are: + (plus or "put together") and = (equals or "the same as"). As with the other areas, first use concrete objects; then use cards with sets that represent numbers; and, finally, use the number sentence with the numbers alone: $3 + 2 = \square$. From this the child can also learn: $3 + 2 = \square$; $\square + 2 = 5$; and $3 + \square = 5$.

Addition using sums between 10 and 20 is more difficult. May (1974) suggests several approaches. It is easier to start with doubles, such as $8 + 8 = 16$. Then ask, how much is $9 + 8$? One more than 16.

Another way is to "make a 10." For example in $7 + 5$, the pupil takes 3 of the 5, and adds it to the 7 to make 10. Now the pupil can see that $10 +$ the remaining $2 = 12$. Use movable disks so that the child can actually experience the process.

$$10 + 2 = 12$$
$$7 + 5 = 12$$

The number line provides another way to teach addition. (See activity number 17.)

3. *Subtraction.* After a good start on addition, subtraction is introduced. An important new symbol is − (minus or "take away"). The pupil places a set of objects on the desk and then takes away a certain object. How many are left? $6 - 2 = \square$. Then use cards with sets on them. Find 6 by using a card with a set of 2 and a card with a set of 4. Tell the child you have a set of 6 when the cards are joined. Take away the set of 2 and ask the child what is left.

Another way of illustrating subtraction is using rods, such as Cuisenaire Rods. Start with the rod that represents a total sum. Place on top a type of rod that represents part of the sum. Ask the pupil to find the rod that fills the empty space.

The number line is useful in subtraction as well as addition. (See activity number 17.)

4. *Multiplication.* Very frequently the child with an arithmetic disability does not know multiplication tables. If this is so, division will also be impossible to learn.

Multiplication is a short method of adding. Instead of adding $2 + 2 + 2 + 2$, the pupil can learn $2 \times 4 = 8$. May (1974) points out that subtraction is *not* a prerequisite of multiplication, and a student having difficulty with subtraction might do better with multiplication. The symbol to learn is × (times).

May suggests that there are a number of ways of explaining multiplication. One way is the *multiplication sentence.* How much are 3 sets of 2? Using sets of objects, the student can find the total either by counting objects, or by adding equal addends.

The concept of communicative property can be introduced. The sentence $3 \times 5 = \square$ does not change in the form $5 \times 3 = \square$.

In the *equal addend approach*, ask the student to show that

$$3 \times 5 = 5 + 5 + 5, \text{ or } 15.$$

In the *number line* approach, pupils who can use number lines for addition will probably do well in using them for multiplication. The child adds a unit of 5, 3 times on the line, to end up at the 15 on the number line.

The *rectangular array approach* contains an equal number of objects in each row: 3×5 is shown as:
  0 0 0 0 0
  0 0 0 0 0
  0 0 0 0 0

5. *Division.* This computational skill is considered the most difficult to learn and teach. Basic division facts come from knowledge of multiplication facts. Long division requires many operations, and students must be able to do all the steps before they put them together. The new symbol is $\div$ (divide).

May (1974) suggests a number of ways to approach division. *Using sets,* $6 \div 3 = \square$. Draw a set of 6 and enclose 3 equal sets. The missing factor is seen as 2:

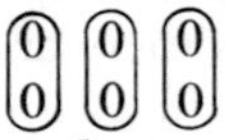

How many subsets are there? How many objects are there in each set?

The *number line* can also be used. By jumping back a unit of 3, how many jumps are needed?

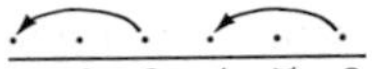

The *missing factors* approach uses known multiplication facts and reverses the process: $3 \times \square = 12$. Then change to a division sentence: $12 \div 3 = \square$.

6. *Fractions.* Geometric shapes are usually used to introduce fractional numbers. The new symbol is:

$\dfrac{1}{2}$ $\begin{array}{l} 1 \to \text{number of special parts} \\ 2 \to \text{total number of equal parts} \end{array}$

Start with halves, followed by quarters and then eighths. Cut shapes out of flannel board or paper plates. Wallace and Kauffman (1973) suggest this chart:

½		½	
¼	¼	¼	¼
⅛ ⅛	⅛ ⅛	⅛ ⅛	⅛ ⅛

7. *Learning the computational facts.* Once the concepts behind the facts are known, the pupil must memorize the facts themselves. To do this

it is necessary to write them, say them, play games with facts, take speed tests, etc. Helpful also are flash cards, rolling dice, playing cards, or even learning a fact a day. A wide variety of methods should be used (May 1974).

To learn fractions, as well as other computational skills, the child with an arithmetic disability requires much experience with concrete and manipulative materials before moving to the abstract and symbolic level of numbers. Objects and materials that can be physically taken apart and put back together help the child to visually observe the relationship of the fractional parts of the whole.

There are 56 basic number facts to be mastered in each mode of arithmetic computation (addition, subtraction, multiplication, and division), if the facts involving the 1's $(3 + 1 = 4)$ and doubles $(3 \times 3 = 9)$ are not included (Otto, McMenemy, and Smith 1973). Examples of number facts are: $3 + 4 = 7$; $9 - 5 = 4$; $3 \times 7 = 21$; $18 \div 6 = 3$. In the computational skill of addition, for example, there are eighty-one separate facts involved in the span from $1 + 1 = 2$ to $9 + 9 = 18$. Few pupils have trouble with the 1's $(5 + 1 = 6)$ or with the doubles $(2 + 2 = 4)$. Therefore, if these facts are omitted, there are 56 basic addition facts to be mastered. Similarly with the other calculation processes, without the 1's and doubles there are 56 facts to be mastered in each of the other computation areas — subtraction, multiplication, and division.

8. *Workspace.* A large table with equipment that can help in performing number tasks is helpful. Counting materials, an abacus, beans, sticks, play money, rulers, measuring instruments are among the items the child might use.

9. *Matching and sorting.* A first step in the development of number concepts is the ability to focus upon and recognize a single object or shape. Have the child search through a collection of assorted objects to find a particular type of object. For example, the child might look in a box of colored beads or blocks for a red one, search through a collection of various kinds of nuts for all the almonds, choose the forks from a box of silverware, look in a box of buttons for the oval ones, sort a bagful of cardboard shapes to pick out the circles, or look in a container of nuts and bolts for the square pieces.

10. *Puzzles, peg boards, formboards.* These are useful to help the child focus on shapes and spatial relations. For the child who has difficulty finding and fitting the missing piece, auditory cues and verbalization may be helpful. Discuss the shape being sought and ask the child to feel the edges for tactile cues.

11. *Relationship between concepts of size and length.* Have the child compare and contrast objects of different size, formulating concepts of smaller, bigger, taller, shorter. Make cardboard objects such as circles, trees, houses, etc., or collect objects like washers, paper clips, screws, etc. Have the child arrange them by size. Have the child estimate the size of objects by guessing whether certain objects would fit into certain spaces.

12. *Pairing and one-to-one correspondence.* To provide a foundation for counting, the child must have a concept of one-to-one relationships. Activities designed to match or align one object with another are useful. Have the child arrange a row of pegs to match a prearranged row in a pegboard. Have the child set a table and place one cookie on each dish. Have the child plan the allocation of materials to the group so that each person receives one object.

13. *Counting.* Some children learn to count verbally, but without attaining the concept that each number corresponds to one object. Such children are helped by making a strong motor and tactile response along with the counting. Visual stimuli or pointing to the object may not be enough because such children will count erratically, skipping objects or saying two numbers for one object. Motor activities to help such a child establish the counting principle include placing a peg in a hole, clipping clothespins on a line, and stringing beads onto a pipe cleaner. The auditory modality can be used to reinforce visual counting by having the child listen to the counts of a drum beat with eyes closed. The child may make a mark for each sound and then count the marks. Have the child establish the counting principle through motor activities, e.g., clap three times, jump four times, tap on the table two times.

14. *Recognition of sets of objects.* Cards with colored discs, domino games, playing cards, concrete objects, felt boards, magnetic boards, mathematics workbooks — all provide excellent materials for developing concepts of sets.

15. *Serial order and relationships.* While learning to count, ask the child to tell the number that comes after 6, or before 5, or between 2 and 4. Also, ask the child to indicate the first, last or third of a series of objects. Other measured quantities can be arranged by other dimensions, such as size, weight, intensity, color, volume, pitch of sound, etc.

16. *Visual recognition of numbers.* Children must learn to recognize the printed numbers, *7, 8, 3,* and the words, *seven, eight, three*; and they must learn to integrate the written forms with the spoken symbol. For the child who confuses one number with another, color cues may be used: make the top of the 3 green and the bottom red. Have the child match the correct number with the correct set of objects; felt, cardboard, sandpaper symbols, and sets of objects can be used.

17. *Number lines.* Number lines and number blocks to walk on are helpful in understanding the symbols and their relationships to each other.

$$\begin{array}{ccccccc} \cdot & \cdot & \cdot & \cdot & \cdot & \cdot \\ \hline 0 & 1 & 2 & 3 & 4 & 5 & 6 \end{array}$$

18. *Measuring.* Pouring sand, water, or beans from a container of one shape or size to a different container helps the child develop concepts of measurement. Estimating quantities, the use of measuring cups, and the introduction of fractions can be emphasized in such activities.

19. *Rate of perception.* The use of a tachistoscope or flashcards is a way to increase the rate of recognition of sets of objects, of number symbols,

and of answers to number facts. A teacher-made tachistoscope can be improvised by putting information on transparencies, then cutting the transparencies into strips and inserting them in a filmstrip projector. By covering the lens with a sheet of cardboard and exposing the material for a short period of time, the teacher uses the projector as a tachistoscope (Lerner and Vaver 1970).

20. *Playing cards.* A deck of ordinary cards becomes a versatile tool for teaching number concepts. Arranging suits in sequential order by number, matching sets, adding and subtracting the individual cards, and quick recognition of the number in a set are some activities to be accomplished with a deck of cards.

21. *Puzzle cards of combinations.* Make cardboard cards on which problems of addition, subtraction, multiplication, and division are worked. Cut each card in two so that the problem is on one part and the answer is on the other. Each card must be cut uniquely, so that when the student tries to assemble the puzzle, only the correct answer will fit.

22. *Tap out combinations.* Tap out combinations of numbers on a table or have the child tap out the combinations. This reinforces the number learning with the kinesthetic and auditory modality.

23. *Reinforcement of auditory expression.* Some children find it helpful to talk aloud as they relate the number sequences and facts.

24. *Counting cups.* Make a set of containers, such as cups, with a numeral to designate each container. Have the child fill the container with the correct number of objects, using items such as bottle caps, chips, buttons, screws, or washers.

25. *Number stamp.* Using a stamp pad and a stamp (the eraser on the end of a pencil will serve very well), the child can make a set of numerals with matching dots. Two children can play the classic card game "War" with one standard deck of cards and one deck made with stamped dots; the first child to recognize and claim matching cards can take them.

26. *Parking lot.* Draw a parking lot on a poster, numbering parking spaces with dots instead of numerals. Paint numerals on small cars and have the child park the car in the correct parking space.

27. *Other areas related to arithmetic.* Children with arithmetic disabilities are likely to have difficulty with concepts in related areas. Specific lessons and plans will be needed to develop concepts of time and of directions, map reading, reading of graphs and charts, and concepts of money.

28. *Directions in space.* This activity is designed to help the child understand the concepts of north, east, south, and west on a map. Draw a large circle on the floor. Place the directions N, S, E, W on the appropriate spots on the circle. The child in the center of the circle is asked to turn in different directions in response to the teacher.

29. *Time.* Time is a difficult dimension for many children with learning disabilities to grasp. Such children may require planned remediation to learn to tell time. Real clocks or teacher-made clocks are needed to teach this skill. A teacher-made clock can be created by using a paper plate and

cardboard hands attached with a paper fastener. A sequence for teaching time might be to teach: (1) the hour (1:00 o'clock); (2) the half-hour (4:30 o'clock); (3) the quarter hour (7:15 o'clock); (4) five-minute intervals (2:25 o'clock); (5) before and after the hour; (6) minute intervals; and (7) seconds. Use television schedules of programs or classroom activities and relate them to clock time.

30. *Money.* The use of real money and lifelike situations is an effective way to teach number facts to some children: playing store; making change; ordering a meal from a restaurant menu, then adding up the cost and paying for it. All these situations provide concrete and meaningful practice for learning arithmetic.

31. *Measurement.* Actual containers and measurement objects should be used to introduce the idea of measurement. Containers for pints, quarts, half-gallons, gallons, pounds, and half-pounds provide the opportunity to teach measurement and to demonstrate relationships of measurement.

Many of the materials for teaching arithmetic concepts and skills have to be teacher made. However, some commercial materials are useful. Among them are the Cuisenaire Rods (Cuisenaire Company), Stern *Structural Arithmetic Program* (Houghton Mifflin), Montessori materials, various materials from other commercial firms (Teaching Resources, Developmental Learning Materials). Additional materials for teaching arithmetic are listed in Appendix B. Materials should be considered to be tools that are useful when they are appropriate to the child, the disability, the diagnosis, and the teaching plan. The materials, themselves, should not be permitted to direct the teaching program.

Additional suggestions for teaching strategies in arithmetic can be found in *Corrective and Remedial Teaching* (Otto, McMenemy, and Smith 1973); *Learning Disabilities* (Johnson and Myklebust 1967); *Psychopathology and Education of the Brain-Injured Child* (Strauss and Lehtinen 1947); *PLUS* (Educational Services); *Teaching Children with Learning Problems* (Wallace and Kauffman 1973); *Teaching Mathematics in the Elementary School* (May 1974); *Building Number Skills in Learning-Disabled Children* (Arena 1970); *Learning Problems in the Classroom* (Frostig and Maslow 1973); *Clinical Teaching* (Smith 1974); *These Kids Don't Count* (Sharp 1971); *Temporal Learning* (Bateman 1968); *Arithmetic and Mathematics* (Bereiter 1968); and *Teaching Children with Learning and Behavior Problems* (Hammill and Bartel 1975).

READING COMPREHENSION

Learning to read can be viewed as a two-stage process: (1) the decoding stage, and (2) the meaning-getting stage. In the initial phase of learning to read, learning to decode the printed symbols is very important. The child must learn to decode words by associating sound with the printed or graphic equivalent. This stage of reading was discussed in Chapter 10. In the later stage of learning to read, the emphasis shifts to the skills of obtaining meaning from the printed page, reading comprehension. Getting meaning is the heart of the reading act. Decoding and recognizing words are valuable only as they make comprehension possible.

Most of the attention and debate concerning reading methods have been directed to the decoding stage of reading; yet the problems related to teaching reading comprehension are far more important. Disabilities with the comprehension area of reading affect many more children than disabilities in decoding. Further, reading comprehension is much more difficult to teach.

For many children with learning disabilities who have difficulty in reading, the problem is not in decoding words but in understanding the meaning of what is read. The difficulty may be associated with language disability, with poor attending capacity, or with a deficit in cognitive and conceptual functioning. Reading comprehension is placed in this chapter because it reflects verbal thinking.

Reading scholars are still plagued by the question "What is reading?" Reading can be seen as many things. For instance, does reading mean those skills that enable one to decode the black squiggles called print? Is reading a symbol of spoken language or talk written down? Is it a visual receptive form of language? Is it the process of integrating visual and auditory stimuli? Is reading a visual process, determined by certain kinds of eye movements? Is reading a mental procedure entailing the processing of psycholinguistic data? Is it a form of verbal comprehension? Is reading thinking? Is it a means of enjoyment, escape, and vicarious experience? Is it a tool of learning? Is reading a subject to be taught in school? Is it a way of bridging time and space? For the reading scholar, reading is likely to be all of this and more (Lerner 1972).

Several models of reading that have evolved from studies and examinations of reading comprehension are discussed in this section: *cognitive models, psycholinguistic models,* and *specific skills models.* The section concludes with ways of teaching reading comprehension.

READING AS A COGNITIVE PROCESS

Thorndike (1917) likened the cognitive process used in mathematics to that of reading comprehension. Although mathematics is considered a nonverbal operation, while reading is considered a verbal one, both were ascertained to have similar underlying cognitive processes (Thorndike 1917, p. 329).

> ... understanding a paragraph is like solving a problem in mathematics. It consists in selecting the right elements of the situation and putting them together in the right relations, and also with the right amount of weight or influence or force for each.... all under the influence of the right mental set or purpose or demand.

There is a parallel between reading comprehension skills and cognitive or thinking skills. Stauffer (1970), for example, defines reading as cognitive functioning. Moreover, there is a similarity between the comprehension skills needed for reading and the comprehension skills needed for listening to oral language. In both of these modes of verbal comprehension, the skill depends upon the individual's capacity to use and understand language, familiarity with the content of the material, and ability to attend to and actively interact with the ideas and concepts of the writer or speaker. It is not surprising, therefore, to find that practice in listening skills results in improvement in reading.

Stauffer views reading comprehension as something akin to problem solving. As in problem solving, the reader must employ concepts, develop hypotheses, test them out, and modify those concepts. In this way, reading comprehension is a mode of inquiry, and methods that employ discovery techniques should be used in the teaching of reading.

Serafica and Sigel (1970) found a difference in cognitive styles between good readers and disabled readers. These researchers detected a dysfunction in cognition in the poor readers, particularly in their ability to reach a conceptual synthesis and in their skills of categorization.

The key to teaching from this approach is to guide students to set up their own questions and purposes for reading. Students read to solve problems that they have set for themselves. For example, the child guesses what will happen in the story and reads to determine the accuracy of those speculations. This approach is described in teaching strategy number 8 (*Directed Reading-Thinking Activity*) in "Activities for Teaching Reading Comprehension."

Another way to categorize thought getting in reading is in terms of depth of understanding of the material. These levels have been referred to as: (1) literal comprehension, (2) interpretation, (3) critical reading, and (4) creative reading. Each level requires increasingly complex cognitive functioning (N. Smith 1972).

Literal comprehension refers to the skills at the bottom of the reading comprehension ladder. It is the ability to recognize and understand the direct, stated ideas of the author. It is sometimes referred to as "reading the lines" of print.

The *interpretation* level refers to the kind of reading needed to gather not only the meanings directly stated by the text, but also the meanings that are implied. The reader must think of more than the words and symbols themselves to supply the meanings intended. This level of reading has also been referred to as "reading between the lines."

The *critical* level is the third level of reading, and it refers to the kind of reading that requires personal judgment and evaluation. At this level, the reader forms generalizations, draws conclusions, compares, analyzes and applies ideas gained in reading. This level is often referred to as "reading beyond the lines."

The *creative* level of reading is considered the highest of mental processes, involving the development of new thoughts, fresh ideas, and imaginative insights as a result of the reading experience.

There are times when effective reading requires the reader to perform at all of these levels when reading a single selection. Such an occasion is aptly described by Adler (1956, p. 14) in *How to Read a Book:*

> When [people] are in love and are reading a love letter, they read for all they are worth. They read every word three ways: they read the whole in terms of the parts, and each part in terms of the whole; they grow sensitive to context and ambiguity, to insinuation and implication; they perceive the color of words, the order of phrases, and the weight of sentences. They may even take punctuation into account. Then, if never before or after, they read.

In this context, however, the focus is that reading at the higher levels is closely related to the thinking processes. Good teaching of reading necessitates the development of thinking during the reading process; and, further, training in the thinking process facilitates reading comprehension.

READING AS A PSYCHOLINGUISTIC PROCESS

From the psycholinguistic perspective, reading is considered an extension of natural language development. Consequently, if reading is viewed as a language process, then a reading disability can be analyzed as a language disorder. The framework of *generative transformational linguistics* is used to analyze the language functions underlying reading. The analysis of reading within a psycholinguistic framework necessitates asking questions such as: What is the language process that occurs during reading? How does the language process mold and shape reading performance? Such inquiries are deliberated by Athey (1971), who provides an extensive review of language models as they relate to the reading process, and by reading scholars who have analyzed the relationship of psycholinguistic processes to reading (Smith 1971, 1973, Goodman and Fleming 1969, Hodges and Rudoff 1972, and Walden 1969).

Reading and speaking are obviously two vastly different language modes. One difference noted by Goodman (1969) is the unit of the word. The word as a unit of language assumes greater importance in written language than in the oral form. In fact, beginning readers are often confused by single words because the oral language does not sound the way the written form looks. One child could not comprehend the meaning when he read the individual words of the sentence, "I want to go to the store." He did not hear each of those individual words as discrete entities when the sentence was spoken orally. The linguist's concern is primarily the study of *oral* language. Words are conventional units of written language separated by white space, but they do not really exist separately in speech. This discrepancy proves to be a problem for at least some children who have difficulty bridging the gap between the written language and the auditory form that they know.

Another difference between reading and speaking is that reading is a way of receiving or decoding the language of others, whereas speaking is a way of encoding or expressing ideas through language. It is much easier to observe what is happening when people speak than when they read. Although a child who is reading may be asked comprehension questions, the examiner finds it difficult to determine from only the responses how the child is actually processing language while reading. Certain psycholinguistic procedures appear to be useful ways of getting at the language processing that underlies reading. Initially the psycholinguist's interest in reading was with questions of a linguistic nature, such as how the grammatical structure of sentences is learned. Later, however, this interest shifted to cognitive matters of meaning and comprehension (Smith 1973).

Smith (1971, 1973) contends that the task of the beginning reader is to construct a set of rules to translate the surface structure of written language (the visual symbols on the page) into meaning (the deep structure). Smith further contends that reading is *not* primarily a visual process. While some information is visual information (from the printed page), other information is nonvisual — what we already know about reading, language, and the word, what we bring to the printed page. According to Smith, the more nonvisual information the reader has, the less visual information is needed to identify letters and words. Further, there is a severe limit to the amount of information the visual system can process through the eye. The reader who concentrates on words, Smith observes (1971, p. 221), is unlikely to get much meaning from the passage:

> The more difficulty a reader has with reading, the more he relies on the visual information; this statement applies to both the fluent reader and the beginner. In each case, the cause of the difficulty is inability to make full use of syntactic and semantic redundancy, of nonvisual sources of information.

Fluent readers take advantage of the redundancy of our language and ignore the occasional word *not* in their sight vocabulary; many words can be skipped with little effect on overall comprehension.

Smith (1973, p. 8) summarizes his psycholinguistic perspective with three themes:

1. Only a small part of information necessary for reading comprehension comes from the printed page.
2. Comprehension must precede the identification of individual words (reading is not primarily visual).
3. Reading is *not* decoding to sound.

In regard to reading instruction, Smith draws a clear distinction between *understanding* the reading process and what should go on in the classroom. The job of the psycholinguist, according to Smith, is to help the teacher understand reading — not to help teach it.

"Miscue" Analysis of Oral Reading

Goodman and his associates view reading as a psycholinguistic guessing game (Goodman 1967, 1969, Burke and Goodman, 1970), that is, the reader's thought and language ability interact in anticipating what is to come. The reader must develop skill in selecting the fewest and most productive cues necessary to provide guesses about the words. Therefore, an analysis of the errors (or miscues) gives insight into the ongoing psycholinguistic process of reading.

The miscue analysis research shows that while more proficient readers do not tend to make fewer errors than other children, their errors (or miscues) are of a different kind. The errors of less proficient readers typically reflect errors of graphic information (*want* for *what*) but make little sense in the context of the passage as a whole. More accomplished readers tend to make errors that appear quite gross visually (*car* for *automobile*) but retain the underlying meaning of the passage.

The role of the teacher, according to Goodman (1972) is to make reading an extension of natural language learning. He contends that this will happen if teachers understand the language processes underlying reading.

Deighton (1968) observed that, during the reading process, the reader cannot complete the thought until the final word or phrase. For example, in the two phrases "the little white pebble" and "the little understood theory," the word *little* connotes something quite different in each phrase. The reader cannot know the meaning of the word, or sometimes even the pronunciation, until the end of the phrase or sentence. In English the meaning of the beginning is dependent on the end. The flow of thought in English is not left to right, but in many cases circular. Although the eye goes from left to right, the mind does not. Certain ideas and words must be held until some part of the sentence permits the completion of the thought. For example, "When *Lee* looked at the *note* again, she realized that she should have played a sharp." The meaning of *note* and the gender of *Lee* must be kept in abeyance until the end of the sentence provides the clarification. In the following example, a decision about pronunciation cannot be made until the end of the sentence: "John had *tears* in his shirt."

An interesting study of the psycholinguistic processes underlying reading was made by Beaver (1968). In this study children were given material to read orally and their errors in reading were carefully noted. Psycholinguistic analysis of the errors revealed that many were not phonic or phonological shortcomings. Most of the errors (about four-fifths of his sample) were other kinds of linguistic errors, such as morphological or syntactic errors. Beaver reasoned that the process going on when a person reads is not only decoding, but also a kind of retroactive encoding. A reader scans the syntactic structure of the sentence, passes the whole back through his own grammar or language rules, and then interprets it within his own grammar or language system. However, his own language system may not correspond to the actual syntactic system of the text. Examples of such errors are:

> Text: I am Tiphia, servant *to* Mighty Gwump.
> Reader: I am Tiphia, servant *of* Mighty Gwump.

> Text: Now he had been *caught.*
> Reader: Now he had been *catched.*

> Text: Bobby's team *was* the Wildcats.
> Reader: Bobby's team *were* the Wildcats.

> Text: I *have taken* the book.
> Reader: I *has took* the book.

Such studies suggest that a reader not only must decode the words and language of the writer, but also *recode* the ideas into his own language pattern to get meaning. The errors are not in decoding the author's language but in recoding it into the reader's linguistic patterns. Any system of teaching reading that is oblivious to underlying psycholinguistic processes is missing an essential element of reading.

Cloze Procedure

A technique called the "cloze procedure" has been used by some reading researchers to discover the psycholinguistic processes underlying the reading act (Jongsma 1971, Bormuth 1968). The cloze procedure is based on the Gestalt idea of closure — the impulse to complete a structure and make it whole by supplying a missing element. The procedure is applied to the reading process as follows: every "nth" word in a printed passage is omitted and the reader is asked to make closure by supplying the missing words. Because words are deleted at random, both *lexical* words and *structural* words are omitted. In the linguistic framework, lexical words carry primary meaning and are roughly similar to the verbs, nouns, adjectives, and adverbs. The structural words consist of those words which indicate relationships, such as articles, prepositions, conjunctions, and auxiliary verbs. Thus, reader's closure must bridge gaps in both language and thought; what the reader supplies gives clues to his underlying psycholinguistic processes.

Although this technique has thus far been used by only a small group of reading specialists, it has unexplored possibilities for language research, diagnosis, and instruction. The procedure has been used successfully as a test of reading comprehension, as a measure of readability or assessment of the difficulty level of a reading selection, and as a method of improving reading. Bormuth (1968, p. 435) described the following steps for the cloze procedure in measuring readability of a reading selection:

1. Passages are selected from the material which is being evaluated.
2. Every fifth word in the passage is deleted and replaced by an underlined blank of a standard length.
3. The tests are duplicated and given, without time limits, to students who have *not* read the passages from which the tests were made.
4. The students are instructed to write in each blank the word they think was deleted.
5. Responses are scored correct when they exactly match the words deleted (minor misspellings are disregarded).

This technique has been reported to be a valid means of measuring the readability level (comprehension difficulty) of passages as well as a reliable measure of reading comprehension. One advantage of the cloze test over the conventional reading test or other fill in the blank tests is that the words deleted are randomly selected; therefore, they may represent either lexical words or structural words.

The cloze procedure may have possibilities in probing other psycholinguistic abilities. An analysis of why an individual fails to supply the missing words may be used to measure listening ability, to analyze the role of reasoning in reading, to diagnose the student's skills with both structural and lexical linguistic components, to gather information on cognitive styles, and to supply information on the human brain as an information storage and retrieval system.

A sample selection of a cloze passage is shown in teaching strategy number 9 in "Activities for Teaching Reading Comprehension."

READING COMPREHENSION AS SPECIFIC SKILLS

The specific-skills approach to reading comprehension is based on the contention that there are many contributing subabilities or skills that comprise reading comprehension. Reading scholars have delineated the multifaceted nature of reading comprehension and specified individual tasks that appear to be required for comprehension. N. Smith (1963), for example, stresses that "comprehension" as such cannot be taught because it is a blanket term covering an entire composite of thought-getting processes in reading. It is necessary to determine specific comprehension skills and to distinguish one from another in terms of the function involved.

In this approach, then, it is necessary to identify each skill to be taught. Many such lists have been offered. Each basal series, for example, has its own list of comprehension skills. The list developed by Fareed (1971) is typical:

1. Noting clearly stated facts and important details.
2. Grasping the main ideas.
3. Following a sequence of events or steps.
4. Drawing inferences and reaching conclusions.
5. Organizing ideas and relationships.
6. Applying what is read to solve problems and verify statements.
7. Evaluating material for bias, relevancy, and consistency.

These comprehension skills, as well as teaching strategies to help children learn these skills, are discussed in greater detail later in this section.

A type of skills approach to reading that has recently gained much interest is the *criterion-referenced testing* (CRT) approach. Proger and Mann (1973) forecast that this approach will prove to be a useful one for children with learning disabilities. It is intended to enable the teacher to pinpoint which reading subskills children do not know and when they ultimately learn them (Rude 1974).

In the CRT framework, the authors of the material establish a specific sequence of reading skills. The child is tested for each skill; if achievement does not reach a pre-established criterion of success, teaching is provided specifically for that skill. When the skill is learned according to the established criterion the child goes on to the next subskill in the hierarchy. For example, when Frank learns skill number 25 (the "bl" blend) at a 90 percent level of proficiency, he moves on to skill number 26. The number of specified skills identified in these programs ranges up to 450 (Thompson and Dziuban 1973).

The CRT (criterion-referenced testing) approach has been proposed as an alternative to the NRT (norm-referenced testing) approach. Using NRT, for example, Frank's reading is assessed by his grade-level score of 2.7 on a standardized reading test. CRT is used to identify an individual student's performance in a very specific behavior in order to make a very specific decision. In contrast, NRT is used to identify an individual's performance with respect to the performance of others on the same test — the standardization population. The measurement system in CRT tells you that Marty has the skills to swim a mile or that Jackie has achieved an acceptable criterion level of 85 percent in reading skill number 12. The NRT measurement system tells you that Marty is an average swimmer for her age or that Jackie has reached a reading level of 3.6.

The CRT approach in reading deals with both word-analysis skills and reading-comprehension skills. CRT has been compared to climbing a ladder; each rung must be touched or the child will fall off. Reading is viewed as a collection of sequential skills. Accordingly, when every skill has been learned, the child should be able to read. Several available criterion-referenced materials for reading are: *Read On* (Random House), *Fountain Valley Teacher Support System in Reading* (Richard L. Zweig), *Croft In-service Reading Program* (Croft Educational Services), *Wisconsin Design for Reading Skills Development* (National Computer Systems), *Individual Pupil Monitoring System–Reading* (Houghton Mifflin), *Prescriptive Reading Inventory* (CTB, McGraw-Hill), and *Skills Monitoring System–Reading* (Harcourt Brace Jovanovich).

ACTIVITIES FOR TEACHING READING COMPREHENSION

1. *Noting clearly stated facts and important details of a selection.* This skill is considered one of the easiest comprehension skills. Most of the questions asked on reading tests and by teachers are questions of detail. For example: "What color was Jane's new dress?" "What is the largest city in Montana?" "In what year was the treaty signed?" This skill requires memory; if the detail can be related to a main idea, it is easier to remember.

2. *Grasping the main idea.* This skill entails the reader's ability to get the nucleus of the idea presented or to capture the core of the information. It is much harder than finding details, and many children are unable to see through the details to get the central thought of a selection. Teachers can help children develop this skill by asking them to select the best title of a selection from several alternatives, by having them make up a title for a selection, or by asking them to state in one sentence what a short selection is about.

3. *Following a sequence of events or steps.* This skill is one of organizing — being able to see the steps of a process or the events in a story. Seeing such order is important to thinking, understanding language, and reading. To provide practice with this skill, the teacher can give the events in scrambled order and ask the child to sort them into the correct order. The ability to follow printed directions is closely allied to this skill, and the reader proceeds step by step to carry out some project. The *Boy Scout Handbook,* model plane directions, a cookbook, or directions for playing a game provide practical material for teaching this skill.

4. *Drawing inferences and reaching conclusions.* This skill requires great emphasis on thoughtful reading and interpretation. Here the reader must go beyond the lines and the facts that are given in order to reach a conclusion. Questions such as "What does the author mean?" or "Can you predict or anticipate what will happen next?" are geared to encourage such thinking. The reader who can do this is thinking along with the author.

5. *Organizing ideas.* This skill refers to the ability to see interrelationships among the ideas of a reading selection. It involves sensing cause and effect, comparing and contrasting relationships, and seeing the author's general plan for structuring the material. Studying the table of contents, looking at topic headings, and outlining are techniques to help the student see how the ideas are organized.

6. *Applying what is read to solve problems and verify statements.* If reading is to be a functional skill, the material must be adapted to new situations and integrated with previous experiences. The ability to transfer and integrate the knowledge and skills gained in reading is a difficult skill for many children to acquire. Information gained through reading a story about a boy in Mexico might be applied to a lesson in social studies. Or a problem can be formulated and the answer found through reading a selection.

7. *Evaluating materials for bias, relevancy, and consistency.* This skill is sometimes referred to as critical reading. The ability to make judgments about the author's bias, to compare several sources of information, to detect propaganda techniques, and to determine the logic of an argument or approach are all included in this skill. Even children who are able readers are likely to need help with this comprehension skill. Children enjoy the critical examination of advertisements for the detection of propaganda techniques. The comparing of editorials on the same subject or of two news reports of a single event provides good material for developing this skill.

8. *The Directed Reading-Thinking Activity Plan.* Stauffer (1969) urges that the cognitive processes in reading are best taught through the directed reading-thinking activity (DR-TA). Pointing to the many similarities between reading and thinking, he concludes that reading should be taught as a thinking activity. Both reading and thinking require a context to be read or thought about, both embody the dynamics of discovery, and both entail a systematic examination of ideas.

> Reading, like thinking is in continual change. At every turning of a page, or even a phrase, the reader has to take into account the context — its parts, its problems, its perplexities. From these he must be able to follow the threads of a plot that point the way toward the plot end. Or, he must follow the course of ideas in nonfiction that lead to an outcome or solution. He must assess what he finds, weigh it, accept or reject it, or alter his objectives.
>
> It is apparent, therefore, that both reading and thinking start with a state of doubt or of desire. It is apparent also that the process of reconstruction goes on as inquiry or discovery, until the doubt is resolved, the perplexity settled, or the pleasure attained (Stauffer 1969, p. 38).

Within such an approach, teaching reading becomes a way of teaching thinking. Important questions the teacher asks in directing the process are: "What do you think?" "Why do you think so?" and "Can you prove it?" The emphasis in the DR-TA is on pupil thinking. The goals are to teach pupils:

(1) to examine, (2) to hypothesize, (3) to find proof, (4) to suspend judgment, and (5) to make decisions.

9. *The cloze procedure.* This approach can be used for teaching reading comprehension, as well as for judging the difficulty of reading material. Exercises such as the one below can be devised. In this case the reading material was retyped with every tenth word deleted and replaced by a standard-sized line. The child supplies the missing words.

Farming in Switzerland

Switzerland is a country of very high, steep mountains _____ narrow valleys. In the valleys are the farms where _____ farmers raise much of the food they need for _____ and their animals. Because the valleys are tiny, the _____ are small. There is no room on them for _____ grassland that is needed for pasturing cows or goats _____ sheep during the summer.

(Answers: and, the, themselves, farms, the, or)

From P. McKee, M. Harrison, A. McCowen, and E. Lehr, *High Roads,* fourth-grade reader (Boston: Houghton Mifflin, 1962), p. 34.

10. *Questioning strategies.* The type of questions teachers ask stimulate the various types of thinking that children employ during reading. A study by Guzak (1972) revealed that many of the questions teachers use demand recall of details. Questions that provoke conjecture, explanation, evaluation, and judgment must also be planned. N. Smith (1972, p. 219) illustrates four types of comprehension questions:

Literal comprehension: What did little brother want to eat?
Interpretation: Why was the cooky jar kept on the basement steps?
Critical Reading: Did mother do the right thing in leaving the children alone?
Creative Thinking: How would you have solved this problem?

11. *Materials for teaching reading comprehension.* Some materials that are designed to help the child develop comprehension skills are listed in Appendix B. A few of the commonly used materials include:

Standard Test Lessons in Reading by W. A. McCall & L. M. Crabbs (Teachers College Press, Columbia University), grades 2–12

Gates-Peardon Practice Reading Exercises (Teachers College Press, Columbia University), grades 3–6

E D L Study Skills Library (Educational Developmental Laboratories), grades 4–9

Barnell Loft Specific Skill Series (Barnell Loft, Ltd.), grades 1–6

New Practice Readers (Webster Division; McGraw-Hill), grades 2–8

Effective Reading (Globe Book Co.), grades 4–8

Reading for Meaning Series (J. B. Lippincott Co.), grades 4–12

Reader's Digest Reading Skill Builders (Reader's Digest Services, Inc.), grades 1–8

Study Exercises for Developing Reading Skills (Laidlaw Brothers), grades 4–8

Developmental Reading Text-Workbooks (Bobbs-Merrill Co.), grades 1–6

Be A Better Reader Series (Prentice-Hall), grades 4–12

Additional materials for teaching reading comprehension are listed in Appendix B, part 3

SUMMARY

This chapter has reviewed cognitive skills and their relation to learning disabilities. It has discussed the teaching of cognitive skills in two academic areas — arithmetic and reading comprehension.

Cognitive skills refer to a collection of mental abilities. Two approaches to studying cognitive development are (1) the components of mental functioning and (2) the developmental hierarchy of cognitive abilities. Several psychological theories were examined under each approach. The implications for learning disabilities include (1) developmental imbalances, (2) inadequate cognitive structures, (3) problems in concept development, and (4) disorders in nonverbal and verbal thinking. Finally, two theories of teaching cognition were reviewed: the stimulus-response theory and the hypothesis-testing theory.

Two areas of the curriculum, arithmetic and reading comprehension, were selected as vehicles for a discussion of teaching cognitive skills. The arithmetic section dealt with the relationship between arithmetic and learning disabilities and with problems of teaching the child with arithmetic disabilities. The reading comprehension section reviewed the question of what is reading; discussed reading as a cognitive process, reading as a psycholinguistic process, and reading comprehension as specific skills; and, finally, presented teaching strategies for teaching reading comprehension.

REFERENCES

Adler, Mortimer J. *How to Read a Book.* New York: Simon & Schuster, 1956.

Anastasi, Anne. *Psychological Testing.* New York: Macmillan, 1968.

Arena, John, ed. *Building Number Skills in Learning-Disabled Children.* San Rafael, Calif.: Academic Therapy Press, 1970.

Athey, Irene J. "Language Models and Reading." *Reading Research Quarterly* 7 (Fall 1971): 16–111.

Atkinson, R. C., and D. N. Hansen. "Computer-Assisted Instruction in Initial Reading: The Stanford Project." *Reading Research Quarterly* 2 (Fall 1966): 5–26.

Bateman, B. *Temporal Learning.* San Rafael, Calif.: Dimensions Publishing, 1968.

Beaver, Joseph C. "Transformational Grammar and the Teaching of Reading." *Research in the Teaching of English* 2 (Fall 1968): 161–171.

Bereiter, Carl. *Arithmetic and Mathematics.* San Rafael, Calif.: Dimensions Publishing, 1968.

Bloom, Benjamin S., et al., eds. *Taxonomy of Educational Objectives, Handbook I: Cognitive Domain.* New York: David McKay, 1956.

Bormuth, John R. "The Cloze Readability Procedure." *Elementary English* 45 (April 1968): 429–436.

Bruner, J. S. *Toward a Theory of Instruction.* Cambridge, Mass.: Harvard University Press, 1966.

Bruner, J. S., J. J. Goodnow, and G. A. Austin. *A Study of Thinking.* New York: Wiley, 1956.

Burke, Carolyn, and K. Goodman. "What a Child Reads: A Psycholinguistic Analysis." *Elementary English* 47 (January 1970): 121–130.

Chalfant, James C., and Margaret A. Scheffelin. *Central Processing Dysfunction in Children: A Review of Research.* NINDS monograph no. 9. Bethesda Md.: U.S. Department of Health, Education and Welfare, 1969.

Cohn, Robert. "Dyscalculia." *Archives of Neurology* 4 (1961): 301–307.

Deighton, Lee C. "Flow of Thought Through an English Sentence," pp. 73–76 in M. Dawson (ed.), *Developing Comprehension Including Critical Reading.* Newark, Del.: International Reading Association, 1968.

Ellson, D. G., Larry Barber, T. L. Engle, and Leonard Kampwerth. "Programmed Tutoring: A Teaching Aid and a Research Tool." *Reading Research Quarterly* 1 (Fall 1965): 77–127.

Engelmann, Siegfried. *Conceptual Learning.* San Rafael, Calif.: Dimensions, 1969.

Engelmann, Siegfried, and Elaine Bruner. *Distar Reading I and II.* Chicago: Science Research Associates, 1969.

Engelmann, Siegfried, and Doug Carnine. *Distar Arithmetic I and II.* Chicago: Science Research Associates, 1970.

Engelmann, Siegfried, Jean Osborn, and Therese Engelmann. *Distar Language I and II.* Chicago: Science Research Associates, 1970.

Fareed, Ahmed. "Interpretive Responses in Reading History and Biology: An Exploratory Study." *Reading Research Quarterly* 6 (Summer 1971): 493–532.

Flavell, John H. *The Developmental Psychology of Jean Piaget.* Princeton, N.J.: Van Nostrand, 1963.

Freidus, Elizabeth S. "The Needs of Teachers for Special Information on Number Concepts," Chapter 7 in W. Cruickshank (ed.), *The Teacher of Brain-Injured Children.* Syracuse, N.Y.: Syracuse University Press, 1966.

Frostig, M., and P. Maslow. *Learning Problems in the Classroom.* New York: Grune & Stratton, 1973.

Furth, Hans G. *Piaget for Teachers.* Englewood Cliffs, N.J.: Prentice-Hall, 1970.

Gagné, Robert M. *The Conditions of Learning,* 2nd ed. New York: Holt, Rinehart & Winston, 1970.

Gallagher, James. "Children with Developmental Imbalances: A Psychoeducational Definition," Chapter 2 in William Cruickshank (ed.), *The Teacher of Brain-Injured Children.* Syracuse, N.Y.: Syracuse University Press, 1966.

Gardner, Riley W. "The Needs of Teachers for Specialized Information on the Development of Cognitive Structures," pp. 137–150 in William Cruickshank (ed.), *The Teacher of Brain-Injured Children.* Syracuse, N.Y.: Syracuse University Press, 1966.

Goodman, Kenneth. "Analysis of Oral Reading Miscues: Applied Psycholinguistics." *Reading Research Quarterly* 2 (February 1969): 9–30.

————. "Reading: A Psycholinguistic Guessing Game." *Journal of the Reading Specialist* 6 (May 1967): 126–133.

————. "Reading: The Key Is in Children's Language." *Reading Teacher* 25 (March 1972): 505–508.

————. "Words and Morphemes in Reading," pp. 25–33 in K. Goodman and J. Fleming (eds.), *Psycholinguistics and the Teaching of Reading.* Newark, Del.: International Reading Association, 1969.

Goodman, K., and J. Fleming, eds. *Psycholinguistics and the Teaching of Reading.* Newark, Del.: International Reading Association, 1969.

Guilford, J. P. *The Nature of Human Intelligence.* New York: McGraw-Hill, 1967.

Guszak, F. "Questioning Strategies of Elementary Teaching in Relation to Comprehension," pp. 221–390 in L. Harris and C. Smith (eds.), *Individualizing Reading Instruction: A Reader.* New York: Holt, Rinehart & Winston, 1972.

Hammill, D., and N. Bartel. *Teaching Children with Learning and Behavior Problems.* Boston: Allyn and Bacon, 1975.

Henderson, Edmund H. "Do We Apply What We Know About Comprehension?" pp. 85–96 in Nila B. Smith (ed.), *Current Issues in Reading.* Newark, Del.: International Reading Association, 1969.

Hodges, Richard, and E. Rudorf. *Language and Learning to Read.* Boston: Houghton Mifflin, 1972.

Hunt, J. McV. *Intelligence and Experience.* New York: Ronald Press, 1961.

Johnson, Doris, and H. Myklebust. *Learning Disabilities: Educational Principles and Practices.* New York: Grune & Stratton, 1967.

Jongsma, E. *The Cloze Procedure as a Teaching Technique.* Newark, Del.: International Reading Association, 1971.

Kaliski, Lotte. "Arithmetic and the Brain-Injured Child," pp. 458–466 in Edward Frierson and Walter Barbe (eds.), *Educating Children with Learning Disabilities: Selected Readings.* New York: Appleton-Century-Crofts, 1967.

Kirk, Samuel A., and Winifred D. Kirk. *Psycholinguistic Learning Disabilities: Diagnosis and Remediation.* Urbana, Ill.: University of Illinois Press, 1971.

Kirk, Samuel A., James J. McCarthy, and Winifred D. Kirk. *Illinois Test of Psycholinguistic Abilities,* rev. ed. Urbana, Ill.: University of Illinois Press, 1968.

Klausmeier, Herbert J., and Gerald Miller. "Concept Learning," pp. 1–14 in Russell G. Stauffer (ed.), *Reading and Concept Attainment.* Newark, Del.: International Reading Association, 1968.

Lerner, Janet W. "Reading Disability as a Language Disorder." *Acta Symbolica* 3 (Spring 1972): 39–45.

Lerner, Janet W., and Gerald A. Vaver. "Filmstrips in Learning." *Academic Therapy Quarterly* 5 (Summer 1970): 320–324.

May, Lola J. *Teaching Mathematics in the Elementary School,* 2nd ed. New York: Free Press, 1974.

Meeker, Mary N. *The Structure of the Intellect: Its Interpretation and Uses.* Columbus: Merrill, 1969.

Meeker, Mary N., K. Sexton, and M. Richardson. *SOI Abilities Workbook.* Los Angeles: Loyola Marymount University, 1970.

Montessori, M. *The Montessori Method,* translated by Anne E. George. Cambridge, Mass.: Bentley, 1964.

Myers, P., and D. Hammill. *Methods for Learning Disorders.* New York: Wiley, 1969.

Neisser, U. *Cognitive Psychology.* New York: Appleton-Century-Crofts, 1967.

Newcomer, Phyllis, Betty Hare, and Donald Hammill. "Construct Validity of the ITPA." *Exceptional Children* 40 (April 1974): 509–512.

Otto, Wayne, R. McMenemy, and R. Smith. *Corrective and Remedial Teaching.* Boston: Houghton Mifflin, 1973.

Plato. *The Republic,* translated by B. Jowett. New York: Modern Library.

PLUS (Arithmetic Ideas). Stensville, Mich.: Educational Services, 1964.

Proger, B., and L. Mann, "The Criterion-Referenced Measurement: The World of Gray Versus Black and White." *Journal of Learning Disabilities* 6 (February 1973): 37–84.

Rude, Robert. "Objective-Based Reading Systems: An Evaluation." *Reading Teacher* 28 (November 1974): 169–175.

Sedlak, R. A., and P. Weener. "Review of Research on the Illinois Test of Psycholinguistic Abilities," pp. 113–164 in L. Mann and D. Sabatino (eds.), *The First Review of Special Education,* Vol. 1. Philadelphia: JSE Press, 1973.

Serafica, F., and I. Siegel. "Styles of Categorization and Reading Disability." *Journal of Reading Behavior* 2 (Spring 1970): 105–115.

Sharp, F. *These Kids Don't Count.* San Rafael, Calif.: Academic Therapy Press, 1971.

Skinner, B. F. *Science and Human Behavior.* New York: Macmillan, 1968.

Skinner, B. F., et al. *Write and See.* Chicago: Lyons & Carnahan, 1968.

Smith, Frank. *Understanding Reading.* New York: Holt, Rinehart & Winston, 1971.

———, ed. *Psycholinguistics and Reading.* New York: Holt, Rinehart & Winston, 1973.

Smith, Nila B. "The Many Faces of Reading Comprehension," pp. 209–220 in L. Harris and C. Smith (eds.), *Individualizing Reading Instruction: A Reader.* New York: Holt, Rinehart & Winston, 1972.

———. *Reading Instruction for Today's Children.* New York: Prentice-Hall, 1963.

Smith, R. M. *Clinical Teaching: Methods of Instruction for the Mentally Retarded.* New York: McGraw-Hill, 1974.

Spearman, C. *The Abilities of Man.* New York: Macmillan, 1927.

Stauffer, Russell G. "Reading as Experience in Inquiry." *Educational Leadership* 24 (February 1967): 407–412.

———. *Directing Reading Maturity as a Cognitive Process.* New York: Harper & Row, 1969.

———. "Reading as Cognitive Functioning," pp. 124–147 in Harry Singer and Robert Ruddell (eds.), *Theoretical Models and Processes of Reading.* Newark, Del.: International Reading Association, 1970.

Stern, Catharine. *Structural Arithmetic Program.* Boston: Houghton Mifflin, 1952.

Strauss, A. A. "The Education of the Brain-Injured Child." *American Journal of Mental Deficiency* 56 (January 1951): 712–718.

Strauss, A. A., and L. Lehtinen. *Psychopathology and Education of the Brain-Injured Child.* New York: Grune & Stratton, 1947.

Suchman, J. Richard. "Inquiry Training in the Elementary School." *Science Teacher* 27 (1960): 42–47.

Sullivan Associates. *Programmed Reading.* St. Louis: Webster-McGraw-Hill, 1969.

Teaching Resources Program and materials. Boston: Educational Services of the *New York Times* Teaching Resources Corp.

Terman, L., and M. Merrill. *The Stanford-Binet Intelligence Scale.* Boston: Houghton Mifflin, 1937 (revised 1960).

Thompson, R., and C. Dziuban. "Criterion-Referenced Reading Tests in Perspective." *Reading Teacher* 27 (December 1973): 292–294.

Thorndike, Edward L. "Reading as Reasoning: A Study of Mistakes in Paragraph Reading." *Journal of Educational Psychology* 8 (June 1917): 323–332.

Thurstone, L. L., and T. C. Thurstone. *SRA Primary Mental Abilities*. Chicago: Science Research Associates, 1947.

Walden, James, ed. *Oral Language and Reading*. Champaign, Ill.: National Council for Teachers of English, 1969.

Wallace, G., and J. Kauffman. *Teaching Children with Learning Problems*. Columbus: Merrill, 1973.

Wechsler, David. *The Wechsler Intelligence Scale for Children*. New York: Psychological Corp., 1949. (WISC-R revised, 1974).

12. Maturational, Social, and Psychological Views

THEORY

This chapter discusses children with learning disabilities from the following perspectives: maturational, psychological, and social. The chapter concludes with suggested teaching strategies for strengthening the child's self-concept and emotional well-being, for helping the child overcome social deficits, and for using behavior modification techniques.

MATURATIONAL PERSPECTIVES

Piaget, the famous Swiss developmental psychologist, is purported to have remarked: "Every time I describe a maturational sequence in the United States, an American asks, 'How can you speed it up?' "

The maturational perspective implies that attempts to speed up or bypass the developmental process may actually create problems. Knowledge of maturation and the normal developmental process of children provides a framework for understanding children with learning problems. This section deals with concepts of how the child's maturational status affects the ability to learn.

MATURATIONAL LAG

Bender (1957) was an early researcher of the concept of maturational lag, or a slowness in certain specialized aspects of neurological development. This point of view acknowledges that each individual has a preset rate of development and maturation of the various factors of human growth, including intelligence. Children who show discrepancies among various subabilities do not necessarily suffer from central nervous system dysfunction or brain damage; rather, the discrepancies show that various abilities are maturing at different rates. Proponents of the maturational-lag viewpoint hypothesize that children with learning disorders are not so different from children without them. It is more a matter of *timing* than an actual difference in abilities. They assume a temporary developmental lag in the maturation of certain skills and abilities.

The concept of maturational lag, according to Ames (1968), leads to a belief that the majority of learning disabilities need not occur but are actually created because children are pushed by society into attempting performances before they are ready. The educator compounds the distortion by introducing experiences beyond the readiness or capacity of the child at a given stage of development. Ames (pp. 72–73) concludes that:

> The outstanding cause of school difficulty in our experience is immaturity. The majority of children experiencing learning problem as seen by our clinical service have been overplaced in school. This presents a serious hazard since overplacement or lack of readiness not only aggravates learning problems when they exist, but causes problems in cases where there is potential for good performance. Many children's normal or superior intelligence has led to great academic expectations on the part of parents and schools; however, they have been immature for the work of the grade in which age placed them. Thus, instead of being often labeled "underachievers," these children actually performed remarkably well considering that too much was being expected of them. . . . In final summary, it may be suspected that we create a high percentage of the learning problems encountered in the elementary schools.

Koppitz (1973), in a five-year follow-up study of 177 special-class pupils with learning disabilities, found that "slow maturation" described most of these children. She concluded that children with learning disabilities are more immature and more poorly integrated than most and that they need more time to learn and to grow up. Many children with learning disabilities need extra time in order to compensate for neurological malfunction — usually requiring one or two more years than other pupils to complete their schooling. Moreover, the Koppitz study indicated that when given this extra time and some help, these children often do well academically.

The maturational-lag point of view also receives support from the findings of a study conducted by Silver and Hagin (1966). This study was of children who had been diagnosed and treated for reading disabilities at Bellevue Hospital Mental Hygiene Clinic. A number of years later, when the subjects were young adults of 16 to 24 years of age, they were called back for a follow-up evaluation. At that time, they did not show difficulty in spatial orientation of symbols, auditory discrimination, or left-right discrimination, although they had manifested such problems as children. Through the process of maturation, many of these problems had apparently disappeared.

In an extensive study aimed at finding factors that best predicted reading failure in kindergarten children, deHirsch et al. (1966) found that tests that were most sensitive to differences in maturation were the ones that best predicted reading and spelling achievement in second grade. Of the tests grouped under the category "Maturation-Sensitive Tests," 76 percent were significantly correlated with grade achievement, compared to only 17 percent of the "Non-maturation-Sensitive Tests." DeHirsch contended that the data generated by the study supported the theory that maturational status is the crucial factor in forecasting subsequent reading achievement.

Wepman (1967) also supports a maturational-lag point of view, contending that a diagnosis of brain injury from observation of behavior is untenable and that a more useful concept is failure of neural development or *agenesis*. He states that there is greater evidence to support the concept of cerebral agenesis, or a lag in neural development, for the majority of nonphysically handicapped children with learning disorders, than there is for the concept of neurological damage.

Primary Reading Retardation

A closely related view is taken by Rabinovitch (1962), a physician whose work at the North Hawthorne Center in Northville, Michigan, led to a categorization of three kinds of diagnostic groupings of reading retardation: (1) brain injury with resultant reading retardation; (2) secondary reading retardation (cases with exogenous causative factors, such as emotional problems or lack of opportunity); and (3) primary reading retardation (no definite brain damage suggested in the history or in the neurological examination). The concept of primary reading retardation can be compared to the theories of maturational lag, or a lag in neural development. Primary reading retardation involves severe impairment of capacity to learn to read, where there is no evident brain damage or other causative factors.

Avoidance of Difficult Processing Skills

Another view of the impact of maturation on the child with learning abilities is proposed by Kirk (1967), who sets forth the hypothesis that during the growing stages the child normally tends to perform in those functions that are comfortable while avoiding activities and functions that are uncomfortable. Since certain processes have lagged in maturation and are not functioning adequately for the child with learning disabilities, that child avoids and withdraws from activities requiring that process. As a result, that function fails to develop and the deficit area is thereby intensified and exaggerated. The purpose of remedial teaching is to build and develop these deficit areas so the child can reverse this behavior and development.

MATURATIONAL STAGES OF LOGICAL THINKING: PIAGET

The child's ability to think and learn changes with age, that is, with passage through a series of maturational or developmental stages. The quantity, quality, depth, and breadth of the learning that occurs is a function of the stage during which it takes place. Piaget (Flavell 1963) provides a schematic description of the normal child's stages of development.

1. The child's first two years of life are called the *sensorimotor* period. During this time the child learns through senses and movements and by interacting with the physical environment. By moving, touching, hitting, biting, and so on, and by physically manipulating objects, the child learns about the properties of space, time, location, permanence, and causality. A discussion of sensorimotor learning was presented in Chapter 8.

2. Piaget calls the next five years of life, ages 2 to 7, the *preoperational* stage. During this stage the child makes intuitive judgments about relationships and also begins to think with symbols. Language now becomes increasingly important, and the child learns to use symbols to represent the concrete world. He begins to learn about the properties and attributes of the world about him. His thinking is dominated largely by the world of perception. The subject of perception was the concern of Chapter 9.

3. The period occurring between ages 7 to 11 is called the *concrete operations* stage. The child is now able to think through relationships, to perceive consequences of acts, and to group entities in a logical fashion. She is better able to systematize and organize her thoughts. Her thoughts, however, are shaped in large measure by previous experiences and dependent on concrete objects that she has manipulated or understood through the senses.

4. The fourth stage, that of *formal operations*, commences at about age 11 and reflects a major transition in the thinking process. At this stage, instead of observations directing thought, thought now directs observations. The child now has the capacity to work with abstractions, theories, and logical

relationships without having to refer to the concrete. The formal operations period provides a generalized orientation toward problem-solving activity.

The transition from one level to the next involves maturation. According to Piaget, the stages are sequential and hierarchal, and it is essential that a child be given opportunities to stabilize behavior and thought at each stage of development.

Yet, the school curriculum frequently requires the child to develop abstract and logical conceptualizations in a given area without providing sufficient opportunity to go through preliminary levels of understanding. Attempts to teach abstract, logical concepts divorced from any real experiential understanding on the part of the child may lead to inadequate and insecure learning. The teacher may think the child is learning true concept development, but it may be only surface verbal responses.

Illustrations of young children who have surface verbal skills without an in-depth understanding of concepts are frequently amusing. One first-grade pupil, who was being exposed to "modern math" in school, watched his mother unpack the oranges from a grocery bag and remarked, "I see you have a set of objects equivalent to the numeral six." Several hours later the same child was observed doing his arithmetic homework with his shoes and socks off. His simple explanation was that the answer was "eleven" and he had run out of fingers. One wonders if he truly had captured the concept of numbers and sets.

Another kindergarten child explained with seemingly verbal proficiency the scientific technicalities of a space ship being shot into orbit. Her seemingly precocious explanation ended with: "and now for the blast-off ... 10 — 3 — 8 — 5 — 6 — 1!"

The maturation of the cognitive ability to categorize objects was apparent when each of three children, ages 7, 9, and 11, was asked to pack clothes for a trip in two suitcases. The 11-year-old was adultlike in her thinking, packing day clothes in one case and night clothes in another. The 7-year-old had no organizational arrangement and proceeded to randomly stuff one suitcase with as much as it would hold and then to stuff the second with the remainder. The 9-year-old girl made an organizational plan that called for clothes above the waist to go in one suitcase and clothes below the waist to go in the second. The top parts of pajamas and a two-piece bathing suit were placed in one suitcase and the bottoms in the other. Each child had categorized in a manner appropriate to the individual's maturational stage.

Schools sometimes neglect the need for prelogical experiences and learnings in their attempts to meet the current trend to teach abstract concepts and logical thinking in the primary grades. In instituting a modern mathematics program in one district's kindergarten, the teachers were advised that an understanding of the one-to-one correspondence was a higher and more important cognitive level than other kinds of number learning. Special learnings of numbers taught through games like "Ten Little Indians" and other counting experiences were unfortunately dropped from the kindergarten curriculum because these activities did not develop "logical thinking."

In interpreting Piaget for teachers, Furth (1970) pleads for schooling that allows for the development of a foundation of natural experience, rather than demanding learning at stages for which the child is not ready. A further discussion of Piaget's ideas appears in Chapter 11.

In summary, the maturational point of view expresses the belief that all individuals have a natural development and time for the maturation of various skills. What is sometimes thought to be a learning problem in a child may be merely a lag in the maturation of certain processes. It is important for those who have the responsibility of providing the educational environment for the child to be aware of the child's stage of maturation and of any lags in maturation that may be present. It has been noted, ironically, that with all our attempts to be "scientific" about decisions made in education, one of the most important — when to teach a child to read — is based on the science of *astrology*. The star under which the child is born, the birth date, is the key determining factor of this crucial decision because this determines when the child begins formal school learning.

SOCIAL PERCEPTION PERSPECTIVES

DEFICITS IN SOCIAL PERCEPTION

Learning social skills, though not strictly in the realm of academic achievement, is nevertheless a vital area of learning. Some authorities view children who are unable to perform social activities in keeping with their chronological age and intelligence as handicapped by deficiencies in social perception (Johnson and Myklebust 1967). These authors hypothesize that a child's deficit in social perception is a neurological dysfunction that can be related to certain areas of the brain. Such children may be average or even high in areas of learning such as verbal intelligence, but they have difficulty in the basic social demands of everyday life.

CHARACTERISTICS OF THE CHILD WITH A SOCIAL DISABILITY

What are the observable characteristics related to a deficit in social perception of the child with learning disabilities? Such a child has been described in general as (1) performing poorly in independent activities expected of children of the same chronological age, (2) poor in judging moods and attitudes of people, (3) insensitive to the general atmosphere of a social situation, and (4) continually doing or saying the inappropriate thing. Strauss and Lehtenin (1947) observed an emotional shallowness in the brain-injured children enrolled in their schools. They observed that their feelings lacked the enduring quality of normal emotions. Benton (1962) noted a lack of affective bonds between the brain-injured child and other people. Baer (1961) reported that these children frequently have impaired interpersonal relations. Lewis (1960) stated that the mechanism that organizes behavior and enables the child to perceive social situations and develop awareness of social attitudes fails to operate properly. Similarly, Bryan (1974), who conducted a study of the peer popularity of learning-disabled children by using a sociometric technique, found that learning-disabled children suffered significantly more social rejection by their classmates than those without learning problems. These writers view the social deficits as part of a syndrome of many other characteristics. Johnson and Myklebust (1967), however, suggest that the socially imperceptive child may have a wholly separate learning disability. These authors see the child with such a handicap as having characteristics that are different from those of other types of learning disabilities. Consequently, children with a social disability require a different kind of therapy.

A 12-year-old girl with a social disability is described by Nall (1971, p. 71), who predicted that she would not be able to get along in a secondary school because of her social imperception.

> She read well. She did math well. She wrote well. She just could not get along with others. She was too impulsive. What she thought, she said. She scratched where it itched. She went where she happened to look. When she finally was academically ready to enter high school, she could not be sent. She would not have lasted there a day.

Another example of a child with a social disability is six-year-old Sally, who was judged by the psychologist to have an IQ in the high superior range. She was able to read simple stories by the time she entered first grade. However, Sally's mother was frequently called for parent-teacher conferences because of her daughter's highly disruptive social disability. The kindergarten teacher reported that Sally was bossy, turned other children away from her, and had been a social problem all year. The first-grade teacher said that Sally found it difficult to accept a "no" answer, stamped her feet, cried frequently, pushed others to be first in line, and alienated the other children by kissing and hugging them to gain affection.

Sally's mother also described her daughter's behavior at home as intolerable; sitting still for even a few minutes seemed to be impossible, and she ate so rapidly that she stuffed half of a sandwich in her mouth all at once. Sally would invite a classmate to her house to play and would be so excited that she couldn't do much but run around. The friend would soon tearfully beg Sally's mother to go home, and Sally would also be in tears because of the frustration of trying so hard and not knowing what went wrong. Several other incidents typical of such children were reported by the mother. Once, for example, when a neighbor arrived to play with Sally, Sally exclaimed to the girl, "My, but you are fat." The would-be friend left in tears, while Sally could not understand what she had done wrong. On another occasion, when Sally was invited to a birthday party, her behavior was so disturbing that the mother of the birthday girl called to ask that Sally be taken home.

Another illustration of the behavior of the child with poor social perception is Laura, a 13-year-old with high average intelligence, who was rejected from a summer camp program because she failed the intake interview. When asked by the camp counselor why she would be attending camp, Laura replied that her parents wanted to go to Europe and that was the only way to get rid of her. With such a response, the interviewer decided that Laura was not a good candidate for the camp. In contrast, Laura's younger brother, at age 9, was a socially perceptive youngster whose answer to the interviewer was, "I want to go to camp because it's healthy and I love the great outdoors."

Laura's social imperception problems continued in high school. In her freshman year, her mother was informed by her science teacher that Laura would receive a grade of "B." Although her numerical scores in the course entitled her to a grade of "A," the science teacher explained that Laura's extremely poor perception of appropriate social behavior caused her to be a disturbing element in the science class and forced him to lower her grade.

Such students often go unrecognized as children with a learning disability, for their deficits may not prevent them from using verbal language with fluency or from learning to read or write. Further, at present there are few formal procedures for identifying these children. There is some evidence that the social quotient as measured by the *Vineland Social Maturity Scale* (Doll 1953) is likely to be substantially lower than the verbal ability measured by intelligence test performance (Johnson and Myklebust 1967). Other traits that appear to correlate with a social disability are poor self-perception and immature concepts of body image. The *Goodenough-Harris Drawing Test* (Harris 1963) yields indications of the child's development in these areas.

Since a deficit of social skills implies a lack of sensitivity to people and a poor perception of social situations, the deficit affects almost every area of the child's life. This is probably the most debilitating learning problem the child can have. Methods for helping a child to become more socially perceptive are discussed in the "Teaching Strategies" section of this chapter.

PSYCHOLOGICAL PERSPECTIVES

Two approaches from the discipline of psychology to analyze and treat the child with learning disabilities are discussed in this section. The first represents a psychodynamic framework; the second framework is from behavioral psychology.

PSYCHODYNAMIC VIEW: EMOTIONAL STATUS

Psychodynamic development, personality structure, and ego functioning have important implications for understanding the child with learning problems.

Among the scholars who have concentrated on the psychological and emotional aspects of learning disabilities are Giffin (1968), Rappaport (1966), and Eisenberg (1967). While the previous views of the child with learning disorders emphasized the motor, perceptual, language, or cognitive learnings of the child, those professionals who view the child from a personality or psychiatric perspective ask the question: "How does the child with learning disabilities *feel?*" (Giffin 1968).

Rappaport (1966) contrasts the ego development of the normal child with that of the child with learning disabilities. The normal child, who has a central nervous system that is intact and maturing in an even and normal manner, has the opportunity to develop important basic ego functions. The normally developing child has hundreds of opportunities for self-satisfaction, as well as the satisfaction of pleasing others. The parent-child relationship is mutually satisfying because normal accomplishments stimulate parental responses of approval and encouragement.

Normal children, as a result of both their inner feelings about their accomplishments and their awareness of the approval of those around them, develop feelings of self-worth and prideful identity. Their feelings about their experiences in the world are positive, for they establish healthy identifications with their mothers, fathers, and other key figures in their lives. Ego functions, such as frustration tolerance and consideration for others, are developed in a normal manner. They learn to interact successfully with other people in their environment.

In contrast, the personality development of children with learning disabilities does not follow such a pattern, according to Rappaport (1966). Ego functions are adversely affected if the central nervous system is not intact and is not maturing in a normal and even manner. A disturbance in such functions as motility and perception leads to an inadequate development of ego functions. Attempts at mastery of tasks lead to feelings of frustration, rather than feelings of accomplishment. Instead of building up self-esteem, the child's activities produce an attitude of self-derision and do not stimulate the parent's normal responses of pride; instead they cause the parents to experience feelings of anxiety and frustration, which finally result in rejection or overprotection.

For learning-disabled children, then, the feelings within themselves and the feedback from the outside environment mold a concept of an insecure and threatening world and a concept of themselves as inept persons without identity. Such a child does not receive the normal satisfaction of recognition, achievement, or affection.

The battering of the child's developing personality continues and increases in school. Donald, a nine-year-old who was failing in school and had virtually no opportunities for success, was losing his self-concept and the belief that he was indeed a person with an individual identity. In response to a class assignment to write a biographical sketch, he poignantly revealed, "My name is Donald Turner. I am average."

Giffin (1968) suspects that pupils who manifest learning problems when beginning academic work in school probably have been handicapped by learning disabilities in preschool life. The school may be a place where they face a situation that makes no allowances for their shortcomings and where those directing the learning are unable to comprehend the difficulties.

Ironically, the characteristic inconsistency and unpredictability of children with learning disabilities may account for an occasional academic breakthrough when they perform well, and such random moments of achievement may serve to make matters worse for the child. Now the school may be convinced that "he could do it if he just tried harder." Failure now may be viewed purely on terms of behavior and poor attitude. Eisenberg (1967) notes that increased impatience and an attitude of blame on the part of the teacher intensifies the child's anxiety, frustration, and confusion, which brings disastrous consequences to the ego.

There appears to be no common characteristic of personality development for children with learning disabilities. The child's emotional reaction to academic failure will depend in large part on individual attitudes and beliefs about success and failure (Dreikurs et al. 1971, Ellis 1972). Each child has a unique way of handling feelings, deficiencies, and environment. As Eisenberg (1967, p. 171) puts it: "The patient is a psychobiological entity, subject both to biological and to social influences in manifesting a psychological continuity of his own."

Emotional problems, thus, are often found in the learning-disabled child.

Indeed, many clinics report that the majority of learning and reading disability cases have accompanying emotional maladjustment problems. Moreover, children often are referred for psychiatric counseling primarily because they manifest academic failures (Nichol 1974). Harris (1970) notes the following forms of emotional reactions to learning problems: (1) conscious refusal to learn, (2) overt hostility, (3) negative conditioning to learning, (4) displacement of hostility, (5) resistance to pressure, (6) clinging to dependency, (7) quick discouragement, (8) the attitude that success is dangerous, (9) extreme distractability or restlessness, and (10) absorption in a private world.

talking — about "me, I myself."

Time and effort spent in trying to determine if the learning failure or the emotional problem is the primary precipitating factor may have little value (Aylward 1971). A more constructive approach is to help the child accomplish an educational task so that feelings of self-worth are oriented in a positive direction. This, in turn, will reinforce ego function, thereby increasing the child's capability to learn. The beginning of this mutual reinforcement cycle is also the beginning of effective treatment.

In summary, the child's feelings must be taken into consideration in an analysis of learning disabilities, for the psychodynamics and emotional status of the child have an impact on the learning process. The important questions from this point of view are: How does the child feel? Are the child's needs being satisfied? What is the child's emotional status? Emotional well-being and a favorable attitude are essential prerequisites before effective learning can take place.

Teaching strategies to build self-concept and to enhance a healthy mental attitude are presented in the "Teaching Strategies" section of this chapter and in Chapter 6 under "Establishing Therapeutic Relationships in Clinical Teaching."

BEHAVIORAL PSYCHOLOGY VIEW: BEHAVIOR MODIFICATION

The study of the behavior of the child, in contrast to the study of the child's emotional status, reflects a field of psychology called behavioral psychology. A key interest of behavioral psychologists is behavior modification, a method of modifying human activity that includes academic as well as social learning activity. Behavior modification can be described as a systematic arrangement of environmental events to produce a specific change in observable behavior (Krasner and Ullman 1965, Wallace and Kauffman 1973, Poteet 1973, Hall 1971, Haring and Phillips 1972).

The behavior modification approach to studying human behavior is an outgrowth of the concept of operant conditioning developed by learning theorists such as Skinner (1963). The early experiments, conducted with animals, revealed that pigeons and rats would persist in behaviors (such as pressing a bar) if a positive reinforcement (such as a food pellet) were

given immediately following the activity. The use of reinforcements conditioned the desired behavior.

When the concepts and procedures of operant conditioning and reinforcement theory were applied to human beings, it was called behavior
modification. Researchers observed that these methods can be used to
modify and shape the child's behavior and learning pattern. The technique
has been used more often with children whose primary problem is unacceptable social behavior than it has with the learning-disabled child. Nevertheless, the theory and implications for teaching are important for academic
as well as social learning.

Behavior modification procedures require the investigator to (1) carefully
and systematically observe and tabulate the occurrence of specific events
that precede the behavior of interest and the specific events that follow the
behavior of interest and (2) manipulate those events to effect a desired
change in the subject's behavior. The event preceding the behavior of interest is called the *antecedent event* or *stimulus*, while the event immediately following the behavior in question is called the *subsequent event* or
reinforcement. For example, when John is asked to read, he begins to disturb
others in the classroom by hitting them. The stimulus or antecedent event
that precedes John's hitting behavior is the request that John read. When
Betty reads five pages, she receives two tokens that are exchangeable for
toys. The subsequent event of reinforcement following reading behavior is
the receipt of the tokens.

The investigator working in this tradition observes the effects of various
reinforcements or rewards on the individual behavior of a particular child
and then analyzes the observations to determine patterns of response to
rewards. Finally, the investigator attempts to construct a reward system
that will promote the desired behavior.

Research suggests that reinforcements that are positive and immediate
are most effective in promoting the desired behavior. Examples of positive
reinforcers include candy, tokens, points earned, praise, flashing lights, or
simply the satisfaction of knowing that the answer is correct. For example,
in teaching reading, the desired behavior could be having the child say the
sound equivalent of the letter "a" every time a stimulus card with the letter
"a" is shown. For each correct response the child may immediately receive
a positive reinforcement, such as a piece of candy, some frosted cereal, stars,
points, or money.

The behavior modification approach requires that the teacher determine
a behavioral goal to be accomplished by the child. This goal must be specific rather than broad; moreover, evidence of learning should be observable
instead of only being inferred. For example, the goal of teaching a child
to be sociable is too broad and too difficult to observe; however, the behavior of saying "thank you" when the child is offered food is specific and
observable.

Unlike some other theories of learning disabilities, the teacher using
behavior modification techniques does not seek to discover the underlying

causes of inappropriate behavior but tries to change the behavior by manipulating the environment of the learner. For example, the hyperkinetic child might be encouraged to modify hyperactive behavior if there is a positive reinforcement for a behavior of sitting quietly for a period of five minutes. The highly distractable child could be encouraged to modify behavior by receiving a positive reinforcement for reading a certain number of words, or pages or reading for a certain period of time.

Within this approach, the behaviors that interfere with learning a task are first identified; then plans are made to manipulate the environment to shape a desired behavior. As an illustration, Marion's hyperactivity and constant movement in the room during the reading lesson interfered with her learning to read. A desired behavior was to have Marion remain in her seat during the lesson. This behavior was shaped through a system of positive reinforcements. Each time Marion remained in her seat for a period of five minutes during the reading lesson, she was reinforced with a small piece of candy. As her attentive behavior was shaped by the candy reinforcer, she stayed in her seat for longer periods of time and her ability to attend improved.

Key Concepts in Behavior Modification

The literature and research in the area of behavior modification in general and its specific application to overcoming learning problems have mushroomed in the past few years. A number of concepts essential for comprehending the work in behavior modification are discussed below.

REINFORCEMENT. A reinforcer is an event occurring after a person makes a response; it has the effect of controlling or modifying the person's response behavior. There are two types of reinforcers: positive and negative.

A *positive reinforcer* is a pleasurable event that follows the response and increases the likelihood that the person will make a similar response in similar situations in the future. For example, if Jim, who usually shouts out answers, is recognized by the teacher as soon as he raises his hand, he will tend to raise his hand in the future. If four-year-old Trudy, who has delayed speech, is given a piece of candy after she says a word, she is likely to emit another response of saying a word.

A *negative reinforcer* is an unpleasurable event following an unwanted response and has the effect of increasing desirable response behavior. In this case the person tries to escape the negative reinforcer or unpleasant situation by selecting an alternative mode of behavior — the desired behavior. For example, Joe's mother nags him to do his homework; Joe does his homework to avoid the negative reinforcer — his mother's nagging. Negative reinforcers may also take the form of withdrawal of positive reinforcement. Thus, if Alan gets out of his seat, two tokens are taken away from him. Alan stays in his seat to avoid losing his tokens. Negative reinforcement is different from punishment, which is used to suppress undesirable behavior but provides no alternative behavior for the child to select. An example of punishment is arbitrarily spanking the child for misbehaving.

EXTINCTION. This is the removing of sources of reinforcement that have been following a behavior so that behavior will decrease in strength and eventually cease. Inappropriate classroom behavior is often unknowingly being reinforced by the teacher who gives the child attention in the form of reprimands or reminders. For example, every time Sam talks out in class, he becomes the center of attention as the teacher tells him how disturbing his actions are. The extinction concept implies that if Sam's behavior (that of a child who makes noises in the classroom) is ignored instead of being reinforced by verbal comments, Sam's noise-making behavior will lessen and eventually be extinguished.

SCHEDULES OF REINFORCEMENT. The schedule of reinforcement is the plan of conditions under which reinforcement will occur. The plan of reinforcement is also called *contingencies*, that is, the arrangement of the relationship between the desired behavior and the occurrence of the reinforcement. The schedule of reinforcement may be either continuous or intermittent. *Continuous reinforcement* is the arrangement of reinforcing the desired behavior every time it occurs. For example, every time Joan completes an arithmetic problem, she receives a star.

Intermittent reinforcement means that reinforcement will be given every *nth* time rather than each time. For example, Joan is not given a star for each problem but for each page, then for two pages, five pages, etc. There are two kinds of intermittent reinforcement schedules: *interval* (based on reinforcements given at certain times) and *ratio* (based upon reinforcements given after so many responses). The interval schedule can be either on a *fixed schedule* (reinforcement given after a predetermined time period, such as five minutes) or a *variable schedule* (reinforcement given somewhat randomly but with the time period varying around a certain average). The ratio schedule can be either a *fixed ratio* (reinforcement given after a fixed number of behaviors, such as after every fifth word read correctly) or a *variable ratio* (reinforcement given somewhat randomly but varying around a certain average).

SHAPING BEHAVIOR. This term refers to the concept of breaking the desired goal into a sequence of ordered steps or tasks, then reinforcing a behavior that the child already emits and gradually increasing the requirement for reinforcement. This approach is sometimes referred to as *successive approximations*. For example, the eventual behavioral goal is to have Patty sit at her desk for a 20-minute period. Patty's behavior may be shaped by reinforcing the following steps or successive approximations: first she is reinforced for standing near her desk for a few seconds, then for touching her desk, then for kneeling on her desk, then for sitting at her desk for a few seconds, then for sitting two minutes, etc. (Wallace and Kauffman 1973).

CONTINGENCY MANAGEMENT. The concept that something desirable can be used to reinforce something the child does not wish to do is the essence of contingency management. What is known as the *Premack Principle* states that preferred activities can be used to reinforce less preferred activities

(Premack 1959). This contingency relationship is also referred to as "Grandma's Rule" because grandmothers are alleged to promise, "If you finish your plate, then you can have dessert." For example, if Willie prefers constructing models to reading, the opportunity to work on a model would be contingent upon completing a certain reading assignment. Or Dave can play ball after he finishes his spelling work.

Contingency contracting is a technique used to make more formal arrangements. In such cases a written agreement is negotiated so that the child agrees to do something the teacher desires and the teacher agrees to provide something the child wants in return. For example, Karen writes an agreement that after she completes 20 arithmetic problems, she will be given an extra free period. The contract must be signed by both parties.

TOKEN REINFORCEMENTS. In this method the reinforcers are accumulated to be exchanged at a later time for a more meaningful "back-up" reinforcer. For example, the token reinforcer could be poker chips or plastic objects, which are saved to be exchanged for a more valuable object of the child's selection, such as toys, gum, comic books, candy, etc. Time must be scheduled for exchanges, and information about exchange rates must be made available. In some programs a total token economy is built into the project.

PRECISION TEACHING. This is a variation of behavior modification, a relatively new procedure in special education. It offers a standardized system of monitoring behavior and charting daily improvement and change (Lindsley 1974, Starlin 1971, Bates and Bates 1971). Bradfield (1971) specifies four components of precision teaching: (1) a specific system of recording and charting data using a standardized six-cycle daily behavior chart (p. 343), (2) a precise defining of behaviors to be changed, (3) an emphasis on the total learning process rather than on the reinforcements to be used, and (4) an organized attempt to collect and distribute projects that have used the precision teaching system.

In precision teaching, improvement is viewed as acceleration of the desired behavior; performance is measured, therefore, as frequency of occurrence (or rate). If a child begins to do something more frequently, then performance is improving. A pupil's performance rate is measured on the standardized six-cycle recording system. Methods of using precision teaching are described in greater detail in the "Teaching Strategies" section of this chapter.

A Hierarchy of Behavioral Levels

A goal of the behavior modification approach is to gradually reduce the need for immediate extrinsic reinforcers so that the individual can eventually achieve such behavior without outside motivation. Hewett (1967, 1968) developed a seven-level hierarchy of behavior that reflects the dependency on outside reinforcers. Moving from level to level, the individual moves from complete dependency on immediate extrinsic reinforcement to complete independence and self-motivation in learning situations.

At the *primary* level children will modify their behavior only to receive the primary reinforcement that gratifies basic desires. For example, a child may learn appropriate behaviors to receive candy reinforcements. At the *acceptance* level the teacher is able to communicate complete acceptance of the child and the child will now work on a one-to-one basis without the need for constant direct reinforcement. At the *order* level, the teacher is able to hold the child for more appropriate behavior and the child will accept certain conditions for learning, including structure, routine, and definite limits in the learning situation. In the *exploratory* level of the behavioral hierarchy, the child is ready to investigate the world through motor activity, sensory and perceptual exploration, and concrete experiences. At the *relationship* level of this hierarchy the child is concerned with the teacher's approval and recognition; and this interpersonal relationship takes on value as a social reinforcer. At the *mastery* level the child is finally ready for academic learning and now learns the basic skills of reading, writing, and arithmetic. Finally, at the *achievement* level the child consistently reflects self-motivating behavior, achieving up to his potential, eager for new learning experiences, and no longer needing outside reinforcers to motivate learning.

While this hierarchy has been used extensively to view the emotionally disturbed child, many applications can be made to the child with learning disabilities.

In summary, it is important to remember that behavior modification places great emphasis on the precise definition of the behavior of interest; on the careful observation, measurement, and recording of that behavior; and on an analysis of the environmental events surrounding the behavior.

Studies reporting the use of behavior modification for teaching children with learning disabilities are increasing (Bradfield 1971, Lovitt 1967, Lovitt et al. 1968, Haring and Hauck 1969, Novy et al. 1974, Fauke et al. 1974). Specific methods and techniques for behavior modification are presented in the "Teaching Strategies" section of this chapter.

TEACHING STRATEGIES

This section of the chapter presents teaching strategies for (1) building self-concept and establishing healthy emotional attitudes, (2) developing social perception skills, and (3) using behavior modification procedures.

BUILDING SELF-CONCEPT
AND EMOTIONAL ATTITUDES

The child whose failure to learn is accompanied by emotional problems may be the victim of a continuous cycle of failure to learn and emotional reaction to the failure. In this cycle the failure to learn leads to adverse emotional responses — feelings of self-derision, poor ego perception, and anxiety, which augment the failure to learn syndrome. Remediation must find a way to reverse this cycle — to build feelings of self-worth, to increase confidence and self-concept, and to experience success. Teaching strategies, thus, are designed to redirect this cycle of failure.

1. *Psychiatric and psychological services.* For the most severely affected child, it may be necessary to provide psychiatric or psychological treatment before or during educational treatment. If so, appropriate referrals should be made.

2. *Building a psychotherapeutic relationship.* For most children the learning disabilities clinician can provide a type of psychotherapeutic therapy through skilled and sensitive clinical teaching. Specific techniques for building such a relationship were discussed in Chapter 6, "Establishing Therapeutic Relationships in Clinical Teaching."

3. *Bibliotherapy.* This is an approach to helping youngsters understand themselves and their problems through books in which the characters learn to cope with problems similar to those faced by the child. By identifying with a character and working out the problem with the character, children are helped with their own problems (Moody 1971, Riggs 1971). Books designed to explain the learning problem to the child are also useful (Hayes 1974).

4. *Magic Circle.* This is a human development approach in which children learn to communicate with other members of their group and learn to understand each other and themselves. Bessell and Palomares (1971) have a manual describing this approach. The children and their teacher, who serves as a catalyst, verbally explore themselves and each other through group interaction in activities related to specific goals. A daily 20-minute session is held with participants seated in a circle. Children are encouraged to share their feelings, to learn to listen, and to observe others. The program seeks to promote active listening, to focus on feelings, to give recognition to each child, and to promote greater understanding. Sample circle topics are:

> It made me feel good when I....
> I made someone feel bad when I....
> Something I do very well is....
> What can I do for you....

Current programs are available for prekindergarten to grade six.

5. *Mutual Story-Telling Technique.* Gardner (1974) describes this approach as follows. A self-created story is elicited from the child. The therapist surmises its psychodynamic meanings and creates a story with the same characters in a similar setting but introducing a healthier adaptation than that revealed in the child's story.

6. *Transactional analysis.* This technique is an adaptation of TA (transactional analysis) techniques (Harris 1968) for use with children (Freed 1971).

7. *Use of Creative Media.* Teachers can use art, dance, and music as therapy techniques for promoting the emotional involvement of children with learning disabilities (Long, Morse, and Newman 1971, pp. 213–239).

8. *Materials.* The DUSO (Developing Understanding of Self and Others) presents programs of activities with accompanying kits of materials designed to stimulate social and emotional development (American Guidance Service, Inc.). The kits are designed for grades K through four, and they focus on lessons such as learning to talk about feelings, accepting one's self-identity, making responsible choices, and friendship. The TAD (Toward Affective Development) program consists of group activities, lessons, and materials designed to stimulate psychological and affective development for children in grades three to six (American Guidance Services, Inc.).

9. *Counseling.* The child's reaction to failure and to success depends in part on attitude, emotional status, and beliefs and expectations. Healthier emotional attitudes can be developed through counseling, both individually and in groups. Direction for working with children in groups toward this end is provided by Dreikurs (1971), Ellis (1972), and Ohlsen (1973).

DEVELOPING SOCIAL
PERCEPTION SKILLS

While the normal child is able to learn social skills through daily living and observation, the child with a deficit in social skills needs conscious effort and specific teaching to learn about the social world, its nuances, and its silent language. Just as we teach children to do schoolwork — to read, write, spell, do arithmetic, pass tests — we can teach them to learn to live with and around other people in a normal manner. Just as we must use different methods to teach school subjects, so we have to use different methods to teach children how to get along with others (Nall 1971).

The activities presented in this section represent ways that have been used to help children develop social skills. The activities are divided into the following categories: (a) body image and self-perception, (b) sensitivity to other people, (c) social situations, and (d) social maturity.

Body Image and Self-Perception

1. See Chapter 8, the section on body image, for suggested motor activities for the development of concepts of body image.

2. Have the child locate parts of the body on a doll, on another child, and finally on himself. Discuss the function of each part of the body.

3. Make a cardboard man with moveable limbs. Put the man in various positions and have the child duplicate the positions. For example, put the left leg and right arm out.

4. Make a puzzle from a picture of a person, and have the child assemble the pieces. Cut the puzzle so that each major part is easily identifiable.

5. Have the child complete a partially drawn figure or tell what is missing in an incomplete picture.

6. Help the child put together a scrapbook about himself. Include pictures of him at different stages of growth, pictures of his family and his pets, a list of his likes and dislikes, anecdotes of his past, accounts of trips, awards he has won, and so on.

Sensitivity to Other People

The concept that the spoken language is but one means of communication and that people "talk" to each other without the use of words was presented by Hall in *The Silent Language* (1961). The child with a social deficit, however, needs help in learning how to decode the communication messages involved in this "silent language." For example, these children often fail to understand the meaning implied in facial expression and gesture.

7. Draw pictures of faces or collect pictures of faces and have the child ascertain if the face conveys the emotion of happiness or sadness. Other emotions to be shown include anger, surprise, pain, love, etc. Dimitrovsky (1964) suggests pictures that can be used for such an activity.

8. Discuss the meanings of various gestures, such as waving goodbye, shaking a finger for "no," shrugging a shoulder, turning away, tapping of a finger or foot in impatience, outstretched arms in gestures of welcome.

9. Find pictures, short filmed sequences, or story situations where the social implications of gesture, space, and time are presented.

10. Help the child learn to recognize implications in human voice beyond the words themselves. Have a child listen to a voice on a tape recorder to determine the mood of the speaker and to decipher the communication beyond the words.

Social Situations

Children with disabilities in this area have been called "children with social imperceptions" or "social cripples" by professionals, while members of their peer group may label them "weirdos," "queers," or "out of it." Such children appear unable to make the appropriate response in social situations without direct teaching.

11. Read or tell the child an incomplete story that involves social judgment. Have the child anticipate the ending or supply the completion of the story. A short film of a social situation provides an opportunity to critically discuss the activities of the people in the film. For example, discuss the consequences of a child's rudeness when an acquaintance tries to begin a conversation; or of a child's making a face when asked by her mother's friend if she likes her new dress; or of hitting someone at a party; and so on.

12. A series of pictures can be arranged to tell a story involving a social situation. Have the child arrange the pictures and explain the story. Comics, readiness books, beginning readers, and magazine advertising all provide good source materials for such activities. These series can also be pictures on transparencies.

13. Use transparency overlays on an overhead projector to create a fairly

complex social situation. Discuss the social situation as it develops. Start with a basic simple form and add additional concepts with each transparency overlay. The complete picture might show activities on a school playground, for example.

14. Space and directional concepts are often imprecise. Specific activities to help a child read maps, to practice following directions to reach specific places, and to estimate distances are helpful.

15. Time concepts are often faulty. Learning to tell time; discussing appropriate activities for morning, afternoon, and evening; estimating time needed to accomplish various activities may all be helpful.

16. Help the child learn to differentiate between real and make-believe situations. What could happen in real life and what could happen only in the world of make-believe?

Social Maturity

Social development involves growing from immaturity to maturity. At the time of birth the human infant, among all species of animal life, is perhaps the most dependent upon others for sheer survival. The road from complete dependency to relative independency is the long and gradual growth toward social maturity.

Behavior can be observed and recorded to indicate a level of social growth. Areas of social maturity include the recognition of rights and responsibilities of self and others, making friends, cooperating with a group, following procedures agreed upon by others, making moral and ethical judgments, gaining independence in going places, etc. The *Vineland Social Maturity Scale* is an instrument designed to measure social maturity. The scale is a standardized developmental schedule extending from birth to adulthood. Social maturation is divided into six categories: (1) self-help, (2) locomotion, (3) occupation, (4) communication, (5) self-direction, and (6) socialization. The scale indicates for example, that a 6-year-old should be able to go to school alone; a 10-year-old should be able to get about her home town freely; a 12-year-old should begin to buy some of his own articles for personal use; a 15-year-old should be able to manage an allowance; and an 18-year-old should be able to make arrangements for a trip to a distant point.

17. *Anticipating consequences of social acts.* Role playing, creative play, stories, and discussions can help the child to see what happens if rules of the game or rules of manners are broken.

18. *Establishing independence.* Encourage the child to go places alone. Make simple maps with directions to follow, talk about the various steps to take in getting to the desired location. Use a walking map, if necessary. Plan activities so that the child makes simple purchases alone. Plan activities that provide opportunities to talk to other people, ask directions, interview others, etc.

19. *Ethical judgments.* Help the child learn cultural mores and learn to

make value judgments. *Unfinished Stories For Use in the Classroom* (National Education Association 1968) provides good material for discussing judgments of right and wrong.

20. *Planning and implementing.* Have the child make plans for a trip, activity, party, picnic, meeting, etc. Then help the child successfully implement the plan to gain a feeling of independence and maturity.

21. The *"Weekend Problem."* As a consequence of a disability in social perception, some children have difficulty in making friends. Parents frequently complain of a "weekend problem" when their child appears to have nothing to do. Without companions and friends, summers and vacations often prove to be difficult periods for such youngsters. The initiative and cooperation of parent groups and community organizations will be needed to help develop solutions to such problems.

USING BEHAVIOR MODIFICATION TECHNIQUES

Behavior modification techniques can be used with children with learning disabilities both for managing behavior and for teaching academic skills. The techniques focus on the child's actual behavior rather than its underlying cause. While many teachers recognize that behavior modification is similar to procedures they have intuitively used in the past, precise application of the theory of behavior modification requires that procedures be systematic, that the behaviors in question be observable, and that the techniques be very specific. Haphazard applications, including those which consider unobservable changes, are not considered to be within the realm of behavior modification. Certain concepts of behavior modification, such as positive reinforcement, negative reinforcement, extinction, schedules of reinforcement, shaping, contingency management, and token reinforcement, were discussed in the theory section of this chapter. Specific procedures are presented below. Additional methods can be found in Wallace and Kauffman, Chapters 2 and 6 (1973), Poteet (1973), Gearhart, Chapter 11 (1973), and Frostig and Maslow, Chapter 5 (1973).

Basic Decisions

Lovitt and others (1971) note that the following basic decisions must be made if a behavior modification framework is to be effective:

1. Discover a consequence or reinforcement event that will accelerate a child's rate of performance on a specific task.
2. Change the program of instructional materials so that the correct performance is facilitated.
3. When the child's performance is accurate, increase the reinforcer; and when the child makes an error decrease the reinforcer.
4. Eventually, have the child make independent instructional decisions, such as corrections and establishment of reinforcement values.

Precise and accurate data describing the child's performance must be collected to form the basis for making decisions and planning the methods for modifying behavior.

Monitoring Behavior

Behavior modification stresses the importance of an objective record of the child's behavior as the basis for judging whether or not the desired change has occurred. A graph or chart is used to record daily observations. On a typical graph (Figure 12.1), the vertical axis shows countable behaviors, such as the number of times the behavior occurred, the percent of correct responses, the rate or speed of behavior, the duration of behavior, or problems completed. The horizontal axis represents the successive days on which the behavior was recorded. Typically, the graph is also divided into periods. The graph in Figure 12.1 shows four time periods in which the child's behavior was observed: A, B, A', B'. The first period (A) provides a *base line*, observations of the child's behavior before reinforcement; the second

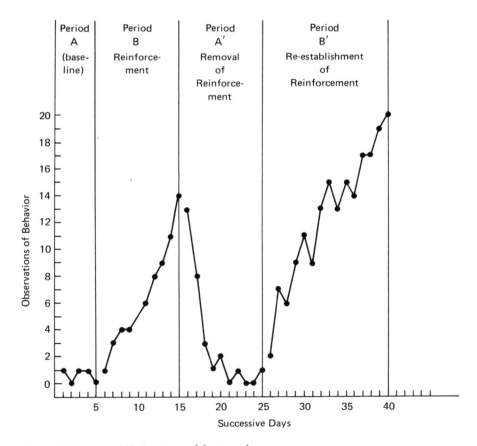

Figure 12.1 A sample behavior modification chart

period (B) shows behavior with reinforcement; the third period (A') shows behavior when reinforcement is removed; and period 4 (B') indicates behavior when reinforcement is re-established. Figure 12.1 suggests that the reinforcement in this case was effective in increasing the desired behavior. Many other kinds of schedules are used in behavior modification procedures.

Finding Reinforcers

It is important to find the appropriate reinforcer. What is seen as desirable by one student may have little interest for another. Poteet (1973) suggests that there are several ways to find the appropriate reinforcer: observe the child to see what she chooses for free time, ask her, and ask her parents. Reinforcers can be extrinsic — something external, such as candy or toys — or they can be intrinsic — something internal, such as the joy of mastering a task. The reinforcement can be social, such as praise or approval from teacher or parent. It can be a token to be exchanged for a later reinforcement, or it can take the form of a privilege. A good reinforcement for each child is simply the one that works.

Several suggested reinforcements are:

Foods: gum, candy, sugared cereal, peanuts, popcorn, raisins.

Play material: toy animals, cars, marbles, jump ropes, gliders, crayons, coloring books, clay, dolls, kits, balls, puzzles, comic books, balloons, games, yoyos.

Tokens: marks on the blackboard, marks on the child's paper, gold or silver stars, marbles in a jar, plastic chips on a ring, poker chips, tickets, washers on a string.

Activities or privileges: presenting at "show and tell," going first, running errands, free time, helping with cleanup, taking the class pet home for the weekend, leading the songs, seeing a film strip, listening to music, doing artwork, having a longer recess period.

Modeling

Modeling, or demonstration of appropriate behavior, can be used for both academic behavior and nonacademic behavior. Since children constantly observe the behavior of their peers and their teacher, this behavior can serve as an example that the child will tend to follow. When exemplary behavior in others is reinforced, it provides such a model for the child, who receives vicarious reinforcement. For example, a model is provided for Kathy when the teacher says, "I like the way Roger is studying." Ignoring the poorly behaved student while focusing attention on the well behaved has proven to be an effective management technique. Teachers should be aware that their behavior also provides a model for children. The children observe teacher behaviors, such as reading for pleasure, searching for information, or trying to discover solutions to problems, as models to be emulated.

Precision Teaching

As noted earlier, precision teaching, like behavior modification, evolved from theories of operant conditioning. It emphasizes rate of improvement or frequency of occurrence. To implement precision teaching, a standardized recording system is used. This chart, designed to simplify and standardize the recording of behavior, measures the frequency of occurrence and determines the rate of change of improvement. The Standard Behavior Chart developed to record such data is shown in Figure 12.2 (Lindsley 1974, Bates and Bates 1971, Starlin 1971, *Teaching Exceptional Children* 1971, Alper and White 1971, Alper et al. 1974).

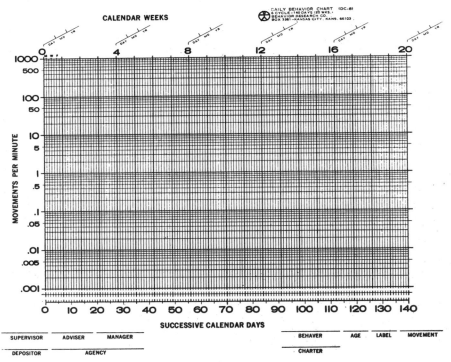

Figure 12.2 Standard behavior chart

The chart has a six-cycle design to provide an adequate range of behaviors. Behaviors that occur once a day as well as those that occur as frequently as 1,000 times per minute can be charted. The Standard Behavior Chart is also designed to insure that the types of behavior teachers would tend to measure are not biased by the nature of the chart. It also has the advantage of helping teachers who are familiar with the procedures of precision teaching to communicate about behaviors recorded without preliminary explanations of the kind of graph used.

The numbers across the bottom of the chart indicate time by days and weeks. Thus, day lines go up and down the chart. The numbers up the left side of the chart indicate movements per minute or how many times a child does something. The lines going across the chart are thus frequency lines.

Since equal percent gains get equal distance on the Standard Behavior Chart, one can project the future course of behavior by drawing a straight line through the middle of the day frequencies previously charted. The direction of this line shows whether the frequency of performance is increasing, decreasing, or remaining the same. The developers of precision teaching claim that charting is very simple and that teachers are easily trained in the mechanics of it.

While both behavior modification and precision teaching stem from work in operant conditioning, they differ in important ways, according to Lindsley (1974). Behavior modification focuses on use of extrinsic rewards or reinforcement with tokens or candy to bring about change; precision teaching relies on more traditional change procedures. Rather than using synthetic rewards, precision teaching tries to get children to do more successful classroom work by making curricular changes that involve them in the learning process. In behavior modification, measurement tends to be used to determine whether the reward system was effective or should be altered. In precision teaching, the daily recording of frequencies of differing classroom performance on the Standard Behavior Chart permits teachers and students to project the outcome of procedures they are currently using.

Finally, precision teaching is not viewed by its developers as a different approach but as a tool designed to improve and refine current teaching methods and materials. It is viewed simply as a way to present methods and a way to provide a more precise measurement instrument of present teaching.

SUMMARY

This final chapter of Part Three has discussed theories of maturational, psychological, and social abnormalities of children with learning disabilities. Representative teaching strategies to help children learn social skills were suggested.

The maturation theories describe the normal developmental patterns of children and emphasize that each stage of development requires stabilization before the subsequent stage can be successfuly added. The development of abstract thinking is one of the last stages to evolve, and it must build upon many other previous learnings. A maturational lag in a specific area of development may be the cause of poor academic achievement in some cases of learning disabilities.

Problems in social perception were discussed and characteristics of the child with a social disability were reviewed. Two psychological theories also were reviewed. The first, a psychodynamic approach, analyzed the emotions and feelings of the child with learning disabilities. This view suggests that a child's failures at home and school result in poor ego development. In turn, this has further implications for a worsened learning situation. The second psychological theory, a behavioral view, discussed an approach to helping the child learn by modifying learning behavior through behavior modification techniques.

Teaching strategies for building a child's self-concept and establishing emotional well-being, for improving social perception, and for using behavior modification procedures were suggested.

REVIEW OF PART THREE

The purpose of Part Three, within the plan of this book, was to review the many approaches, frameworks, and theories of children with learning disabilities. An additional purpose was to describe representative teaching strategies that evolve from each of the theories or approaches. Each of these theories concentrates on an in-depth analysis of one aspect of the child. It is essential to understand as fully as possible each of these elements, since each of the views has an important contribution to make. Still, the problem of integrating the many views and factors remains a difficult one. The child is more than a sum of many different parts; therefore, to most effectively help a child, a comprehensive and integrative view is needed. The problem is that each of the factors must be understood separately, yet the interrelationships of the many factors must also be clarified and seen as a whole.

The problem of implementing a workable teaching program in an institutional setting is discussed in Part Four.

REFERENCES

Alper, A., L. Nowlin, K. Lemoine, M. Perine, and B. Bettencourt. "The Rated Assessment of Academic Skills." *Academic Therapy* IX (Winter 1973–1974): 151–164.

Alper, Theodore G., and Owen R. White. "Precision Teaching: a Tool for the School Psychologist and Teacher." *Journal of School Psychology* 9 (No. 4, 1971): 445–455.

Ames, Louise Bates. "Learning Disabilities: The Developmental Point of View," pp. 39–76 in H. Myklebust (ed.), *Progress in Learning Disabilities,* Vol. 1. New York: Grune & Stratton, 1968.

Aylward, John L. "The Role of the Learning Disability Specialist in Educating Emotionally Disturbed Children." *Journal of Learning Disabilities* 4 (May 1971): 277–279.

Baer, Paul E. "Problems in the Differential Diagnosis of Brain Damage and Childhood Schizophrenia." *American Journal of Orthopsychiatry* 31 (1961): 728–737.

Bates, S., and D. Bates. " '. . . and a Child Shall Lead Them': Stephanie's Chart Story." *Teaching Exceptional Children* 3 (Spring 1971): 111–113.

Bender, Loretta. "Specific Reading Disability as a Maturational Lag." *Bulletin of the Orton Society* 7 (1957): 9–18.

Benton, A. L. "Behavioral Indices of Brain Injury in School Children." *Child Development* 33 (1962): 199–208.

Bessell, H., and U. Palomares. *Methods in Human Development: Theory Manual.* San Diego: Human Development Training Institute, 1971.

Bradfield, Robert H. "Precision Teaching: A Useful Technology for Special Education Teachers," pp. 31–39 in H. Bradfield (ed.), *Behavior Modification of Learning Disabilities*. San Rafael, Calif.: Academic Therapy Publications, 1971.

Bradfield, Robert H., ed. *Behavior Modification of Learning Disabilities*. San Rafael, Calif.: Academic Therapy Publications, 1971.

Bryan, Tanis H. "Peer Popularity of Learning-Disabled Children." *Journal of Learning Disabilities* 10 (December 1974): 621–625.

deHirsch, Katrina, Jeanette J. Jansky, and William S. Langford. *Predicting Reading Failure*. New York: Harper & Row, 1966.

Dimitrovsky, L. "The Ability to Identify the Emotional Meanings of Vocal Expressions at Successive Age Levels," pp. 69–89 in J. R. Davitz (ed.), *The Communication of Emotional Meaning*. New York: McGraw-Hill, 1964.

Doll, E. *The Measurement of Social Competence: Manual for the Vineland Social Maturity Scale*. Minneapolis: Educational Test Bureau, 1953.

Dreikurs, R., B. Greenwald, and F. Pepper. *Maintaining Sanity in the Classroom*. New York: Harper & Row, 1971.

Eisenberg, Leon. "Psychiatric Implications of Brain Damage in Children," pp. 171–187 in E. Frierson and W. Barbe (eds.), *Educating Children with Learning Disabilities*. New York: Appleton-Century-Crofts, 1967.

Ellis, A., *How to Raise an Emotionally Healthy, Happy Child*. N. Hollywood, Calif.: Wilshire Books, 1972.

Fauke, J., J. Burnett, M. Powers, and B. Sulzer-Azaroff. "Improvement of Handwriting and Letter Recognition Skills: A Behavior Modification Procedure." *Journal of Learning Disabilities* 6 (May 1973): 296–300.

Flavell, John H. *The Developmental Psychology of Jean Piaget*. Princeton, N.J.: Van Nostrand, 1963.

Freed, Alvyn, *TA for Kids*. Sacramento: Alvyn M. Freed, 1971.

Frostig, M., and P. Maslow. *Learning Problems in the Classroom: Prevention and Remediation*. New York: Grune & Stratton, 1973.

Furth, Hans G. *Piaget for Teachers*. Englewood Cliffs, N.J.: Prentice-Hall, 1970.

Gardner, Richard A. "Mutual Storytelling Technique in the Treatment of Psychogenic Problems Secondary to Minimal Brain Dysfunction." *Journal of Learning Disabilities* 7 (March 1974): 135–143.

Gearhart, B. R. *Learning Disabilities: Educational Strategies*. St. Louis: C. V. Mosby, 1973.

Giffin, Mary. "The Role of Child Psychiatry in Learning Disabilities," pp. 75–98 in H. Myklebust (ed.), *Progress in Learning Disabilities*, Vol. 1. New York: Grune & Stratton, 1968.

Hall, Edward T. *The Silent Language*. Greenwich, Conn.: Premier Book, Fawcett, 1961.

Hall, R. Vance. "Responsive Teaching: Focus on Measurement and Research in the Classroom and the Home." *Focus on Exceptional Children* 7 (December 1971): 1–7.

Haring, Norris G., and Mary Ann Hauck. "Improving Learning Conditions in the Establishment of Reading Skills with Disabled Readers." *Exceptional Children* 35 (January 1969): 341–352.

Haring, Norris G., and E. L. Phillips. *Analysis and Modification of Classroom Behavior*. Englewood Cliffs, N.J.: Prentice-Hall, 1972.

Harris, Albert. *How to Increase Reading Ability*, 5th ed. New York: Basic Books, 1970.

Harris, Dale. *Children's Drawings as a Measure of Intellectual Maturity*. New York: Harcourt, Brace & World, 1963.

Harris, Thomas A. *I'm OK — You're OK.* New York: Avon Books, 1969.

Hayes, Marnell L. *The Tuned-In, Turned-On Book About Learning Problems.* San Rafael, Calif.: Academic Therapy Publications, 1974.

Hewett, Frank M. "A Hierarchy of Educational Tasks for Children with Learning Disorders," pp. 342–352 in E. Frierson and W. Barbe (eds.), *Educating Children with Learning Disabilities.* New York: Appleton-Century-Crofts, 1967.

————. *The Emotionally Disturbed Child in the Classroom.* Boston: Allyn & Bacon, 1968.

Johnson, Doris, and H. Myklebust. *Learning Disabilities: Educational Principles and Practices.* New York: Grune & Stratton, 1967.

Kirk, Samuel. "Amelioration of Mental Abilities Through Psychodiagnostic and Remedial Procedures," pp. 186–219 in George A. Jervis (ed.), *Mental Retardation.* Springfield, Ill.: Charles C. Thomas, 1967.

Koppitz, Elizabeth M. "Special Class Pupils with Learning Disabilities: A Five-Year Follow-up Study." *Academic Therapy* 8 (Winter 1972–1973): 133–139.

Krasner, Leonard, and Leonard Ullman, eds. *Research in Behavior Modification: New Developments and Implications.* New York: Holt, Rinehart & Winston, 1965.

Lewis, R., S. Strauss, and L. Lehtinen. *The Other Child.* New York: Grune & Stratton, 1960.

Lindsley, Ogden R. "Precision Teaching in Perspective," pp. 477–482 in S. Kirk and F. Lord (eds.), *Exceptional Children: Educational Resources and Perspectives.* Boston: Houghton Mifflin, 1974.

Long, N., W. Morse, and R. Newman. *Conflict in the Classroom: Education of Children with Problems.* Belmont, Calif.: Wadsworth Publishing, 1971.

Lovitt, Thomas C. "Assessment of Children with Learning Disabilities." *Exceptional Children* 34 (December 1967): 233–239.

Lovitt, Thomas C., Harold P. Kunzelmann, P. Nolen, and W. Hulten. "The Dimensions of Classroom Data." *Journal of Learning Disabilities* 1 (December 1968): 710–721.

Moody, Mildred T. *Bibliotherapy: Methods and Materials.* Chicago: American Library Association, 1971.

Nall, Angie. "Prescriptive Living," pp. 69–74 in J. Arena (ed.), *The Child with Learning Disabilities: His Right to Learn.* San Rafael, Calif.: Academic Therapy Publications, 1971.

Nichol, Hamish. "Children with Learning Disabilities Referred to Psychiatrists: A Follow-up Study." *Journal of Learning Disabilities* 7 (February 1974): 118–122.

Novy, P., J. Burnett, M. Power, and B. Sulzer-Azaroff. "Modifying Attending-to-Work Behavior of a Learning-Disabled Child." *Journal of Learning Disabilities* 6 (April 1973): 217–222.

Ohlsen, M., ed. *Counseling Children in Groups.* New York: Holt, Rinehart & Winston, 1973.

Poteet, James A. *Behavior Modification: A Practical Guide for Teachers.* Minneapolis: Burgess Publishing, 1973.

Premack, D. "Toward Empirical Behavior Law I, Positive Reinforcement." *Psychological Review* 66 (1959): 219–233.

Rabinovitch, Ralph D. "Dyslexia: Psychiatric Considerations," Chapter 5 in John Money (ed.), *Reading Disability: Progress and Research Needs in Dyslexia.* Baltimore: Johns Hopkins, 1962.

Rappaport, Sheldon R. "Personality Factors Teachers Need for Relationship Structure," pp. 45–56 in W. Cruickshank (ed.), *The Teacher of Brain-*

Injured Children: A Discussion of the Bases of Competency. Syracuse, N.Y.: Syracuse University Press, 1966.

Riggs, Corinne. *Bibliotherapy.* Newark, Del.: International Reading Association, 1971.

Silver, Archie A., and Rosa A. Hagin, "Maturation of Perceptual Functions in Children with Specific Reading Disabilities." *The Reading Teacher* 19 (January 1966): 253–259.

Skinner, B. F. "Operant Behavior." *American Psychologist* 18 (1963): 503–515.

Starlin, Clay. "Evaluating Progress Toward Reading Proficiency," pp. 389–465 in B. Bateman (ed.), *Learning Disorders: Reading*, Vol. 4. Seattle: Special Child Publications, 1971.

Strauss, Alfred, and Laura Lehtinen. *Psychopathology and Education of Brain-Injured Children.* New York: Grune & Stratton, 1974.

Teaching Exceptional Children 3 (Spring 1971): entire issue.

Unfinished Stories for Use in the Classroom. Stock no. 381–11766. Washington, D. C.: National Education Association, 1968.

Wallace, Gerald, and James H. Kauffman. *Teaching Children with Learning Disabilities.* Columbus: Merrill, 1973.

Wepman, Joseph M. "Neurological Approaches to Mental Retardation," Chapter 7 in R. Schiefelbusch, R. Copeland, and J. Smith (eds.), *Language and Mental Retardation.* New York: Holt, Rinehart & Winston, 1967.

FOUR

Organization and Management of Learning Disabilities Programs

 13. Delivering Educational Services

The implementation of a program for children with learning disabilities generally takes place within some organizational setting, such as a school, clinic, hospital, or child guidance center. Many systems of educational services within an organization are possible, and each system provides a different learning environment for the child. Both the service system selected and the organizational setting itself will have a direct and strong impact on the child, the teacher, and the success of the program.

This chapter discusses (1) the various systems of educational services and organizational facilities and settings and (2) some representative, innovative, and experimental ongoing programs in various parts of the country.

EDUCATIONAL SERVICE SYSTEMS

An array of service systems and placement facilities has been developed for diagnosing and treating children with learning problems (Deno 1970). As a particular child progresses in learning, changes in the setting may be necessary; new patterns may prove to be better suited to new educational needs. Therefore, flexible arrangements and a range of educational services are needed to provide for the diverse and changing educational needs of children. Factors to be considered in placement include the child's educational level and chronological age, the individualization of instruction offered in the regular classroom of the school, and the child's level of schooling (primary, intermediate, secondary).

Among the systems of educational services developed for teaching children with learning disabilities in schools are residential schools, special day schools, self-contained classrooms, itinerant programs, resource rooms, and mainstreaming programs. Other organizational settings for serving learning-disabled children include community agencies, child guidance clinics, hospital clinics, university clinics, mental health centers, and private clinics.

Deno's "Cascade system" of special education (Figure 13.1, p. 352) represents the continuum of educational services. The tapered design indicates considerable differences in the number of children involved at different levels. The more specialized facilities serve fewer children. However, services provided at these facilities are more intensive.

RESIDENTIAL SCHOOLS

Residential schools provide full-time placement for children away from their homes. Relatively few children have handicaps severe enough to warrant such placement. However, if the community lacks adequate alternative facilities, if the behavioral manifestations are extremely severe, and if the emotional reaction among other members of the family is debilitating, residential placement on a twenty-four-hour basis may be the only solution for both the child and the family.

Although residential schools are the oldest provision for dealing with exceptional children, they have many disadvantages. Removal of the child from home and neighborhood, emphasis on the handicap, rigidity of institutional life, and lack of opportunity for normal social experiences are among the shortcomings of the residential school. As the public and private schools

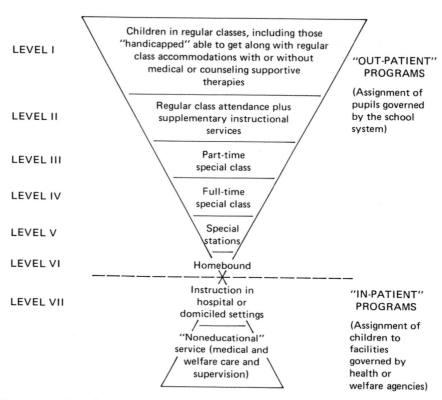

LEVEL I — Children in regular classes, including those "handicapped" able to get along with regular class accommodations with or without medical or counseling supportive therapies

LEVEL II — Regular class attendance plus supplementary instructional services

LEVEL III — Part-time special class

LEVEL IV — Full-time special class

LEVEL V — Special stations

LEVEL VI — Homebound

LEVEL VII — Instruction in hospital or domiciled settings

"Noneducational" service (medical and welfare care and supervision)

"OUT-PATIENT" PROGRAMS

(Assignment of pupils governed by the school system)

"IN-PATIENT" PROGRAMS

(Assignment of children to facilities governed by health or welfare agencies)

Figure 13.1 Cascade system of special education services

From Evelyn Deno, "Special Education as Developmental Capital," *Exceptional Children* 37 (November 1970), p. 235.

and other community agencies develop more services, the need decreases for residential placement for most children with learning disabilities.

SPECIAL DAY SCHOOLS

Special day schools are separate school facilities established specifically for children with a special handicap — in this case, learning disabilities. These schools are usually private and, historically, have been established when the public was either unaware of or unwilling to recognize the learning problem. Some children attend the special school full time; others attend for a half-day and may attend the public school for the balance of the school day.

The disadvantages of such programs include the high expense to parents, the traveling distance required, and the lack of opportunity to be with normal children for some portion of the school day. These schools have served well, however, as pilot programs for later classes in public schools.

SELF-CONTAINED SPECIAL CLASSES

The designation of special classrooms within the public school was one of the first approaches of the public school system to the education of children with learning disabilities. Classes were established that contained 6 to 10 children diagnosed as having brain damage, perceptual handicaps, minimal brain dysfunction, or other related problems. A wide variety of materials and environmental arrangements were available to the teacher. Often the classes were begun with one or two children, and additional pupils were enrolled one at a time to permit the establishment of classroom routine before each new child was added to the class.

Cruickshank et al. (1961) provided a detailed description of special classes for brain-injured and hyperactive children that became a prototype for many self-contained special classes. The classroom researched by Cruickshank had specially equipped rooms designed to reduce environmental distractions, and the teaching techniques were highly structured and exacting. In many of the early special-class public school programs, criteria for admittance included medical evidence of a neurological abnormality.

The goal of special classes is to help children organize themselves for increased independent learning so that they will be able to eventually return to regular classes. Usually the children begin the transition by attending a selected subject within the regular classroom, gradually increasing participation until they attend regular classes on a full-time basis. If the transition is to be effective, a good working relationship must be maintained between the teacher of the class and the teacher of the regular classes.

ITINERANT PROGRAMS

For those children whose handicap is not severe enough to warrant a special class, the itinerant teacher can provide teaching services. The itinerant learning disabilities teacher travels to several schools, serving children in many classrooms by providing educational treatment. Children are scheduled to leave their regular classroom at a specified time for work with the itinerant teacher. They may come individually or in small groups of two to five. Sessions may be held daily or several times a week, generally lasting from 30 minutes to an hour. Care must be taken in scheduling. For example, if the pupil enjoys physical education, the teacher should avoid preempting this period for the teaching session. In addition, the classroom teacher should be consulted about the optimum time for the child to leave the classroom. If the learning disabilities teacher intends to work on reading, the regular classroom reading time may provide a convenient time for scheduling the special therapy session. Some schools use a revolving time schedule so that the child misses a different subject for each session with the itinerant teacher.

The rooms used by the itinerant teacher should be pleasant and have an abundant supply of materials. Since the child often has a short attention span, it is wise to plan for a number of different activities during the teaching session; these should provide for a change of pace.

RESOURCE ROOMS

A current trend in the field of learning disabilities is toward the development of resource rooms for children with learning disabilities. This room is served by a highly trained professional who is capable of diagnosing the child, of planning a teaching program on the basis of this diagnosis, and of implementing the teaching plan. The position of the resource teacher may include many responsibilities. In addition to diagnosing and teaching, the resource teacher may be a consultant, aiding the classroom teacher in interpreting the diagnostic findings and in operationalizing the diagnosis in terms of teaching methods, approaches, and materials. The resource teacher may help the classroom teacher plan the classroom instruction for the child with learning disabilities. Moreover, the resource teacher may be responsible for in-service sessions, demonstration lessons, and continuous evaluation of the progress of the children.

The learning disabilities resource teacher may also serve as a liaison between the school's various specialists, such as the psychologist, speech teacher, physical education teacher, nurse, and administrators, as well as nonschool participants, such as the parents, physicians, and representatives of community agencies. These duties require a person who not only is an expert in the field of learning disabilities but also has the capacity to work well with other professionals by gaining their confidence and respect. The successful resource teacher must have that extra spark of enthusiasm needed for work with children who find learning difficult and must be able to transmit this enthusiasm and spirit to others. Dynamic human relations and an understanding of the entire school organization is required of the person serving in the role of resource teacher. The resource room is discussed more fully in Chapter 14.

MAINSTREAMING PROGRAMS

Mainstreaming involves integrating children with learning disabilities, as well as children with other exceptionalities, within the general education program of the school (Beery 1972, 1974; Birch 1974; Chaffin 1974; Grosnick 1971; Yates 1973; Christopolos 1973). Placement in these programs is in the regular classroom, and the classroom teacher takes on much of the responsibility for supplying appropriate teaching. In order to implement such a program successfully, the learning disabilities specialist takes on the role of a consultant to the classroom teacher, so that learning disabled children can remain in the regular classroom yet receive supportive services.

According to Kauffman et al. (1975), a mainstreaming program requires integration, careful educational planning, and clarification of responsibilities. Its implementation can lead to ideological and organizational conflicts. For these reasons, mainstreaming represents one of the most complex educational service innovations undertaken to date.

The theory behind the development of mainstreaming services is discussed in Chapter 3, and the impact of mainstreaming practices on the role of the learning disabilities specialist is discussed in Chapter 14.

Preschool Programs

Preschool programs for children between the ages of three and five are beginning to be established for early identification of children with potential learning disorders. By identifying these children at an early age, programs of prevention can be implemented and later school failure may thereby be avoided or lessened. These programs involve screening, intensive diagnosis, and developmental disabilities-type classes. Preschool programs are discussed more fully in Chapter 3.

Secondary School Programs

Most of the help for children with learning disabilities has been at the elementary levels, but junior and senior high schools are beginning to provide services for the pupil with learning disabilities. The problems increase at the high school level. High school staff members are likely to be primarily interested in their own specialty areas. Their concern and perspective tend to be content oriented rather than child oriented. Consequently, it becomes more difficult to convince the high school staff that accommodations are needed and that flexibility is required to help these students. Scheduling, too, becomes a difficult problem because students cannot easily miss scheduled classes. Free periods, a second English period, release from music or art classes have provided the needed time in some secondary programs.

Further difficulties at the secondary school level are due to the increased frustration and emotional problems that accompany the learning disabilities of a student who has reached the high school level. High school students generally need direct help in finding ways to attack their content subjects.

In some high school programs students attend their regular classes, which may be modified, but they also report to a "resource room" for several periods a week. Diagnosis and planning of programs may be made by a multidisciplinary team consisting of the school psychologist, social worker, guidance counselor, and learning disabilities teacher. However, implementation and teaching are the responsibility of the learning disabilities specialist. Many students participating in such a program may have been previously diagnosed as having other kinds of exceptionality or other causes of school failure. Secondary programs and college facilities are more fully discussed in Chapter 3.

This portion of the chapter has presented an overview of the major systems of educational services and organizational settings. Within these systems there have been a number of innovative, experimental, and cooperative projects. Some specific programs are described in the following portion of this chapter.

REPRESENTATIVE ONGOING PROGRAMS

The ongoing programs for children with learning disabilities described in this section represent the many programs that have been implemented in various parts of the country. The diversity found among the programs illustrates that there are many ways to help these children. Differences in programs are due to institutional variations, personnel available, and theoretical perspectives of the program developers.

Diagnostic and treatment services for children with learning disabilities are offered not only in school settings, but also by child guidance clinics, hospital clinics, and university clinics. In such nonschool settings, children usually report for therapy sessions after school, on Saturdays, or during the summer. In some cases they are released from school for therapy sessions at the agencies. Such settings often have the advantage of having a staff of varied professionals who can provide interdisciplinary services, such as medical specialists, social workers, or guidance counselors. Individual schools and school districts have developed innovative organizational arrangements for helping children with learning disabilities. Like the children themselves, each school environment is unique. Therefore, a pattern or structure that has been successful in one school environment cannot completely be adapted to another without modification.

MODEL CENTERS PROGRAMS FOR LEARNING-DISABLED CHILDREN

Model centers called the Child Service Demonstration Program (CSDP) were established by the Bureau for the Education of the Handicapped (BEH), Office of Education, through funds created by the Learning Disabilities Act of 1969. This act was incorporated into the Elementary and Secondary Education Act of 1970 as Title VI G. By 1975 CSDP programs were in operation in almost every state. These model centers provide a variety of systems of educational services covering a range of ages from preschool through secondary levels. The model programs offer opportunities for observation and replication.

Senf (1974) provides an overview of the 41 model centers in operation in 1974. He notes that selection of children for the model programs followed one of two procedures: teacher referral or some form of mass screening. Remediation in the programs varied considerably, but the majority of programs utilized a diagnostic-prescriptive approach. Some used a resource room approach; others used a consultation model; others a combination. In addition to child services, in-service training for classroom teachers was a major component of the program. Typically, monthly or semimonthly in-service workshops were given. A number of the projects stressed parent involvement and created handbooks to help parents understand their children and aid in their education. A wide variety of diagnostic tests and remedial procedures was used in the projects.

The Bureau of Education for the Handicapped viewed these model centers as opportunities to try out learning disabilities programs. An intended outcome of the bureau's support was that successful programs would spread throughout the state and would be financed by state and local funds.

STATEWIDE PROGRAMS

Many of the states have recently passed legislation mandating special education for any child in the state who requires such help. In Texas such legislation evolved into a statewide program known as "Plan A," which is described as a dynamic new system in special education, capable of providing comprehensive service to every handicapped boy and girl in the state. The plan includes all handicapped individuals from ages 3 through 21. Three significant recommendations of the plan are (*Comprehensive Special Education in Texas* 1972, p. 5):

—Discontinue labeling and categorizing children. (Do not label one child as brain injured, another as emotionally disturbed, a third as mentally retarded, etc.)

—Shift the emphasis from the handicapping condition to the education needs of each child. (Discontinue emphasizing the fact that a given child is crippled. Instead assess his individual needs and program his education accordingly.)

—Shift the emphasis from the self-contained special class to mainstream or regular education facilities. Where a handicapped child can achieve, provide him with an education in the regular school program with modifications and support as needed.

The preschool program is one important component of the Texas plan. Plan A calls for: screening all children as young as age three for handicaps that might impede learning; provision of special early childhood programs with remedial emphasis for children identified as needing help; special training for regular classroom teachers and development of a corps of special education teachers to make possible the education of handicapped children in public school classrooms; and the creation of learning centers in each Plan A school where teachers and students can be helped by specialists skilled in diagnostic teaching and the use of specialized materials and techniques (*ACLD Newsbriefs* 1974).

The *California Master Plan for Special Education* is a comprehensive plan for "individuals with exceptional needs." While a major concept of the plan is decategorization of students, subclassifications for reporting purposes are: communicatively handicapped, physically handicapped, learning handicapped, and severely handicapped (Mayer and Scheffelin 1975).

Some school systems have implemented a plan that calls for the division of diagnostic and teaching responsibilities between two or more staff members. The *psychoeducational diagnostician* provides the diagnosis through testing and consultation with other professionals who examine the child. A broad teaching plan is developed from the diagnosis. The *educational therapist* implements that plan and does the actual teaching. Continuous communication is required between these persons because plans must be modified as additional information is acquired through the teaching process.

Jacobson (1969) describes such a program in Skokie, Illinois, in which responsibilities are divided between a *diagnostic teacher* and a *remedial teacher*. The diagnostic teacher is responsible for: (1) screening the school population to identify children with learning disabilities; (2) giving diagnostic tests to identify and diagnose children with learning disabilities; (3) requesting special services, such as psychological or medical aid, when necessary; (4) evaluating the child; and (5) formulating educational prescriptions or a teaching plan. The duties of the remedial teacher are to implement the educational prescription by teaching the child. The remedial teacher meets the child several times a week in a small group or individually. The educational prescriptions are designed to be sufficiently clear and detailed to be carried out by faculty who are not learning disabilities specialists but are classroom teachers by training and experience. Another feature of this program is a file consisting of number-coded cards categorized by academic subjects and psychological correlates to learning. Remedial plans usually include references to numbered-coded file cards that will provide the teacher with specific activities relevant to the skill being taught. In this way, the remedial teacher learns while teaching.

The *psychoeducational diagnostician* is the heart of the learning disabilities program in Schaumberg Township, Illinois (McCarthy 1969). A primary aim of the person in this role is to bridge the gap between diagnosis and teaching — between the psychologist who has never taught and the teacher who does not understand psychological jargon. The duties of the psychoeducational diagnostician in this program include providing intensive diagnosis, clinical teaching, and consultation with the classroom teacher. In addition, this school system developed an early identification screening program, self-contained classrooms, itinerant teaching programs, and resource rooms.

The *master teacher* serves in a liaison role for the schools in the Las Cruces, New Mexico area (New Mexico State University 1970). Within the Regional Resource Center for the Improvement of the Education of Handicapped Children, which is a project of New Mexico State University at Las Cruces and the public schools, the master teacher is responsible for helping classroom teachers in regular and special classrooms to implement teaching prescriptions that have been formulated by the diagnostic-prescription team at the Regional Resource Center. The following stages of implementation concern the master teacher:

1. A child is recommended by the public school principal and the Regional Resource Center staff.
2. The public school teacher agrees to attempt to implement individual recommended prescriptions.
3. An assessment of the child is made by the staff at the Regional Resource Center, and a master teacher is assigned to the case.
4. Teacher conferences are held every four weeks to evaluate progress and provide the next set of educational objectives to be carried out in the succeeding four-week period.
5. The master teacher demonstrates within the classroom the first step of each four-week teaching plan agreed upon at the conference.

A *placement specialist* is used in a public school program in Memphis, Tennessee (Perry and Morris 1969). The responsibility of the placement specialist is to translate technical and clinical information into workable terms. This specialist formulates a psychoeducational profile from information derived from psychologists and others and interprets it to parents, administrators, and special class teachers. The specialist also helps make appropriate placement for pupils and aids the special teacher in implementing the findings of the diagnosis.

A *child-oriented resource room* in Buffalo, New York, is described by Reger and Koppman (1974) as an evaluation center in which teachers perform the diagnostic functions. Parents are encouraged to participate in the evaluation process. These resource rooms, located in both elementary and secondary schools, each handle up to 15 students.

Many schools have a *multiplan* arrangement that utilizes several educational delivery systems within a single school. Thus the self-contained classroom, the itinerant teacher, and the resource room could all be found within one school or district. The severity of the child's problem would determine the appropriate placement. Such arrangements also have the advantage of providing alternative placement facilities as the child progresses and the needs change.

Area Learning Centers

Area regional learning centers provide a team approach to attacking the problems involved in the diagnosis, prescriptions, materials, and follow-up (Huizinga and Smalligan 1968). In one such program in Grand Rapids, Michigan, a classroom teacher may call on the area learning center for help. The child in question is observed and tested by the consultant, who also provides the classroom teacher with information about the child's problem and with suggestions for teaching the child within the regular classroom. If further diagnosis is deemed necessary, the child is brought to the learning center for further testing by the team staff, which includes reading experts, psychologists, psychiatrists, pediatricians, and others. An educational plan is made and a conference is held with the classroom teacher.

A good example of an area clinic is the Public School Reading Clinic of the St. Louis public schools, described by Stubblefield (1966). Each of the seven well-equipped clinics in St. Louis services the schools in the administrative district in which it is located. The staff of each clinic includes four full-time teachers and a secretary; part-time services of a physician, nurse, and a social worker are also available to the clinic. Students are excused from their home schools to attend a session at the clinic that lasts for about an hour. The St. Louis clinics also fulfill an important function as a teacher training institution because classroom teachers work in the clinics for a period of time and then return to their positions in the classroom.

Gold (1969) describes a Regional Learning Disability Center in Binghamton, New York. Fifteen public and two private school districts, located in three counties, established a diagnostic and treatment center under Title III. Pupils referred to the area center were screened with informal tests to determine eligibility for the program. In addition to diagnostic and treatment facilities for children in the cooperating school districts, the center housed a professional library, developed a curriculum resource center, sponsored in-service training programs, offered consultation services to school districts, and developed research papers to provide schools with information.

The operation of a learning disabilities area learning center for 29 elementary schools of Waterford, Michigan, is described by Heckerl and Webb (1969). A multidisciplinary staff at the school district's Learning Improvement Center first identifies and then diagnoses children in the district who are likely to benefit from a learning disabilities program. Educational procedures are subsequently planned for children accepted into the program. Groups limited to six children meet four times a week for 45-minute sessions with a teacher from the Learning Improvement Center. The center also provides supportive help and special materials for the classroom teacher to use with the child in the regular classroom; it provides in-service training sessions for the classroom teachers in the district; it offers a clinical training session for teachers; and it offers an educational program for children during the summer.

SCHOOL LEARNING CENTERS

The Madison School Plan in Santa Monica, California (Taylor et al. 1972), was designed to eliminate the traditional categorical disability groupings and self-contained classrooms. In addition to serving the learning-disabled child, the Madison plan included other categories of exceptionality.

Children were organized according to their learning deficit in regard to regular classroom functions. Four groups were specified: Preacademic I, Preacademic II, Academic I, and Academic II. In Preacademic I, children worked in self-contained units with a teacher or an aid on activities such as paying attention, responding, following directions, and taking part verbally. In Preacademic II, six to eight children worked on beginning academic skills and were integrated into the regular classroom for a few minutes each day. In Academic I, the special class simulated a regular classroom setting. This classroom setting dealt with 12 to 25 children with primary academic problems, and the children spent increasing amounts of time in regular classrooms. Academic II was the regular classroom in the school. The child who reached this stage could be placed in the regular classroom within the school.

PRESCHOOL PROGRAMS

Framke (1975) describes a preschool program in Maine Township, Illinois, called *Project Pre-Dict*. Children who reside in the district are accepted for screening on a referral basis from parents, medical personnel, schools, or other agencies. If screening indicates a developmental problem, such as delay in language, motor development, or social behavior, the child is then eligible for more intensive diagnostic testing. A classroom program for teaching children found to be in need of a preschool program is available. The purposes of Project Pre-Dict are: (1) to identify and to examine those children who show signs or symptoms of developmental delay or deviation, (2) to initiate a program of compensatory in-service education that will enable parents to help their own child, and (3) to provide special services to children prior to the time they enter school and at the time of school entry.

SECONDARY PROGRAMS

A high school program for students with learning disabilities in Old Tappan, New Jersey, is described by Russell (1974). In this program high school students identified as learning disabled, who are considered socially adequate and intellectually average, are offered a choice of 14 courses to be taken throughout their four years of high school. They attend a regular homeroom and participate in all minor and extracurricular activities. These students are admitted only to special courses in areas of their deficits while they enroll in the mainstream courses in areas of strength.

COOPERATIVE SCHOOL DISTRICT ARRANGEMENTS

Many small school districts have found it advantageous to merge their efforts in building programs for children with learning disabilities. One such cooperative enterprise combined the efforts of six school systems, public and parochial, from three counties in Kentucky (Pollack 1969). Four multidisciplinary teams were organized — each composed of a psychologist, a psychometrist, a psychiatric social worker, and an educational specialist; these teams served four geographical areas in the three-county region. The teams assumed responsibility for conferring and consulting, as well as for the evaluation and treatment of children with learning disabilities.

HOSPITAL SETTINGS

Clinics for children with learning disabilities are located in some hospital settings. Whitsell and Whitsell (1968) describe one such clinic at the University of California Medical Center, Department of Pediatrics, in San Francisco. This hospital clinic accepts children between the ages of 5 and 16, providing, among other services, a treatment facility for children who are having difficulty in learning school subjects. In addition, the clinic assists in the evaluation of children brought to the Hospital Child Study Unit who are encountering school and learning problems. After an interdisciplinary diagnosis is made, the child reports to the clinic two or three times a week for instruction individually or in small groups of not more than five.

The reporters of this hospital program conclude that the hospital environment has advantages for medical personnel, clinical teachers, the child, and the community. Medical students, interns, and residents all help in the diagnosis; they communicate freely with teachers and become aware of the problems encountered in the instructional situations. The clinical teachers interact daily with the medical staff and thereby gain confidence in their roles as members of an interdisciplinary team. Whitsell and Whitsell also suggest that the medical setting provides a better understanding and appreciation of the problem by the child and the parents. In addition to an indirect psychotherapeutic benefit, the hospital setting provides auxiliary services the child may need. The advantage to the community is that this type of clinic provides a facility for training medical students, physicians, nurses, social workers, psychologists, and other paramedical personnel.

COMMUNITY MENTAL HEALTH CENTERS AND CHILD GUIDANCE CENTERS

Mental health centers and child guidance clinics are other settings for programs for children with learning disabilities. A description of one such program, the Child Guidance Center in Marathon County, Wisconsin, is reported by Kline and others (1968). In this center children receive therapy for one-hour sessions, four to five times per week. The program makes extensive use of nonprofessional volunteers who work on a part-time basis. Orientation courses, periods of observation, and consultation with an orthopsychiatric team help train these nonprofessionals to provide the educational therapy.

COMPUTER-RELATED PROGRAMS

A few learning disabilities programs utilize computer facilities to provide educational services. Computer-managed instruction programs described by Cartwright and Hall (1974) are located in Florida, Ohio, Utah, and New York. In these programs the computer becomes an aid for planning the pupils' instructional program. One of the model centers programs in

New Jersey uses a computer-based instructional and diagnostic information retrieval network (Gearhart 1973). Using teletype terminals, the computer gives the user instructional methods and materials to meet the needs of a specific student with various learning characteristics. Ways of using the computer as a simulation method for training learning disabilities specialists are described by Cartwright and Hall (1974) and Lerner and Schuyler (1974, 1975).

SUMMER PROGRAMS

Schools and camps provide special programs during the summer for children with learning disabilities. Rochford and others (1969) describe one summer program in Erie County, New York. In this four-week summer session, children received instruction in academic areas, perceptual skills, art, physical education, and swimming. Sabatino and Hayden (1970) describe a six-week summer program in La Plata, Maryland, which emphasized unisensory perceptual training. The use of language cues as a technique for strengthening perceptual deficits was another feature of this program.

The summer season provides an ideal opportunity to develop sensori-motor and perceptual-motor skills, such as those described by Kephart (1971). Some summer programs for the child with learning disabilities, such as the Achievement Center for Children at Purdue University and a camp in Ft. Collins, Colorado, have combined camping and academic activities. Stetler and Turner (1969) describe a combined camping-academic program in Monmouth County, New Jersey. An integrated camping and academic summer program located at a children's camp serves as a teacher-training practicum for Northeastern Illinois University (Lerner et al. 1971).

Educators who have had experience with summer programs underscore the importance of creating an atmosphere that is very different from that of the academic year so that the child does not feel penalized by attending school during the summer months. Moreover, summer programs provide a practical way to lengthen the school year.

INTERDISCIPLINARY TEAM APPROACH

An underlying aim of many programs for children with learning disabilities is the integration of the professional skills of contributing disciplines. An interdisciplinary team approach to both diagnosing and treating learning difficulties has been a goal of the Pupil Appraisal Center of North Texas at the North Texas State University (Landreth et al. 1969). The developers of this team approach found that children are likely to have a complex, multi-faceted cluster of learning disabilities rather than a single difficulty in isolation. They therefore concluded that a multifaceted diagnosis, as well as a multifaceted therapeutic teaching arrangement, was necessary.

In actual practice, team approaches are often interdisciplinary in name only; certain team members or disciplines are not accorded equal status in diagnosis, and the teamwork is not carried through in therapy. As a result, the teaching is isolated, scattered, and without interdisciplinary contact. To assure that the work of the members of the team in both diagnosis and therapy is unified and integrated, developers of the Pupil Appraisal Center caution that the following elements are essential:

1. Members of the team should have a commitment to the belief that learning disabilities do not occur in isolation. Because there are many factors involved in the learning problem, each discipline has an essential contribution to make.
2. Team cohesiveness requires freedom from professional prejudices. Interdisciplinary rivalries can easily be transformed into personality conflicts that prevent interdisciplinary cooperation.
3. Familiarity among the team members as to their colleagues' ideas, perspectives, and ways of talking about their fields is important in the formation of a successful team. Without such familiarity and frequent communication, common perceptions cannot be established; and without common perceptions, effective communication is not possible.
4. Sufficient time, free from other pressures, is needed by team members with diverse backgrounds to develop quality interaction.
5. Personal acceptance of each other's professional competencies is necessary for effective team functioning. The freedom to admit errors or inadequacies without fear of losing professional or personal status may lead to higher levels of group processes.
6. Physical proximity is conducive to an effective team relationship. A physical facility that provides team members the opportunity for frequent face-to-face contact strongly reinforces communication.

SUMMARY

This chapter has presented the array of systems for delivering educational services and the various organizational settings for helping the child with learning problems. The chapter also described some representative ongoing programs.

The basic delivery systems in school programs are: (1) *self-contained classrooms,* which provide a separate classroom setting for 6 to 10 children with learning disabilities; (2) the *itinerant teacher,* who travels to several schools and teaches children individually or in small groups; (3) the *resource room,* which is the center for servicing the children with learning disabilities within a school (the resource room contains a variety of teaching materials and equipment, and the specialist who is responsible for it is likely to have many responsibilities, including diagnosing children, planning teaching programs, implementing teaching programs, consulting with classroom teachers, and coordinating the efforts of others); and (4) *mainstreaming* programs, in which the learning disabilities specialist provides consultation to the regular classroom teacher, so that the child may remain in the regular classroom with adjustments made to the child's special needs. In each succeeding type of educational service the learning disabilities specialist serves a greater number of children but does so with less intensity.

In addition, special programs are being developed at the preschool level and at the high school level. Resources for learning-disabled children are also located in nonschool settings, including mental health centers, hospital clinics, child guidance centers, university clinics, and private clinics.

The goal is not to find the *one* best model for the delivery of educational service but, rather, to increase instructional options so that a variety of systems are available to meet the needs of each particular child. While one youngster may do well if the teacher makes a slight alteration within the regular classroom, another may need the environmental conditions of a self-contained special classroom. In general, children with mild problems need different models than those who are severely affected. A range of educational delivery systems is needed to provide comprehensive service for children with all types of learning disabilities.

REFERENCES

ACLD Newsbriefs no. 90 (May 1974).

Beery, Keith. "Mainstreaming: A Problem and an Opportunity for General Education." *Focus on Exceptional Children* 6 (November 1974): 1–7.

————. *Models of Mainstreaming.* San Rafael, Calif.: Dimensions Publishing, 1972.

Birch, Jack W. *Mainstreaming: Educable Mentally Retarded Children in Regular Classes.* Reston, Va.: Council for Exceptional Children, 1974.

Cartwright, G. P., and K. A. Hall. "A Review of Computer Uses in Special Education," pp. 307–350 in L. Mann and D. Sabatino (eds.), *Second Review of Special Education.* Philadelphia: Journal of Special Education Press, 1974.

Chaffin, Jerry D. "Will the Real 'Mainstreaming' Program Please Stand Up! (or . . . Should Dunn Have Done It?)" *Focus on Exceptional Children* 6 (October 1974): 1–18.

Christopolos, Florence. "Keeping Exceptional Children in Regular Classes." *Exceptional Children* 39 (April 1973): 569–572.

Comprehensive Special Education in Texas: An Overview of a Dynamic New Education Program Termed "Plan A." Austin, Tex.: Department of Special Education and Special Schools, Texas Education Agency, 1972.

Cruickshank, William M., et al. *A Teaching Method for Brain-Injured and Hyperactive Children.* Syracuse, N.Y.: Syracuse University Press, 1961.

Deno, Evelyn. "Special Education as Developmental Capital." *Exceptional Children* 37 (November 1970): 229–237.

Framke, Richard W., Project Director. *Development Guidelines; Title III, ESEA. Project PRE-DICT: A Model Early Intervention Pre-Kindergarten Program.* Park Ridge, Illinois: Maine Township Special Education Program, Maine Township High School District 207, 1975.

Gearhart, B. R. *Learning Disabilities: Educational Strategies.* St. Louis: C. V. Mosby, 1973.

Gold, Laurence. "The Implementation of a Regional Learning Disability Center for Treatment of Pupils Who Manifest the Dyslexic Syndrome," pp.

82–94 in George D. Spache (ed.), *Reading Disability and Perception.* Newark, Del.: International Reading Association, 1969.

Grosnick, Judith K. "Integration of Exceptional Children in Regular Classes: Research and Procedure." *Focus on Exceptional Children* 3 (October 1971): 1–11.

Heckerl, John R., and Susan M. Webb. "An Educational Approach to the Treatment of Children with Learning Disabilities." *Journal of Learning Disabilities* 2 (April 1969): 199–204.

Huizinga, Raleigh J., and Donald H. Smalligan, "The Area Learning Center — A Regional Program for School Children with Learning Disabilities." *Journal of Learning Disabilities* (September 1968): 502–506.

Jacobson, Anita M. "Systemwide Identification and Instructional Practices," pp. 103–112 in J. Arena (ed.), *Successful Programing: Many Points of View.* San Rafael, Calif.: Academic Therapy Publications, 1969.

Kauffman, M., J. Gottlieb, J. Agard, and M. Kukic. "Mainstreaming: Toward an Explication of the Construct." *Focus on Exceptional Children* 7 (May 1975): 1–12.

Kephart, Newell C. *The Slow Learner in the Classroom.* Columbus: Merrill, 1971.

Kline, Carl L., et al. "The Treatment of Specific Dyslexia in a Community Mental Health Center." *Journal of Learning Disabilities* 1 (August 1968): 456–466.

Landreth, Gary L., Willard S. Jacquet, and Louise Allen. "A Team Approach to Disabilities." *Journal of Learning Disabilities* 2 (February 1969): 24–29.

Lerner, Janet W., Dorothy Bernstein, Lillian Stevenson, and Anne Rubin. "Bridging the Gap in Teacher Training: A Camping-Academic Program for Children with School Learning Disorders." *Academic Therapy Quarterly* 6 (Summer 1971): 367–374.

Lerner, Janet W., and James A. Schuyler. "Computer Simulation: A Method of Training Learning Disabilities Diagnosticians." *Journal of Learning Disabilities* 7 (October 1974): 471–479.

Lerner, Janet W., and James A. Schuyler. *Computer Applications in Learning Disabilities: Final Report.* Microfiche and Hard copy. ED096974. Arlington, Va.: ERIC Document Reproduction Service, February, 1975.

Mayer, C. Lamar, and Margaret Scheffelin. "State-wide Planning for Special Education in California." *Journal of Learning Disabilities* 8 (April 1975): 238–242.

McCarthy, Jeanne McRae. "Providing Services in the Public Schools for Children with Learning Disabilities," pp. 43–52 in John Arena (ed.), *Management of the Child with Learning Disabilities.* San Rafael, Calif.: Academic Therapy Publications, 1969.

New Mexico State University, Las Cruces, N.M. Regional Resource Center. *Job Specifications,* description for Master Teacher, 1970.

Perry, Harold W., and Thann E. Morris. "The Role of the Educational Diagnostician," pp. 128–130 in J. Arena (ed.), *Successful Programing: Many Points of View.* San Rafael, Calif.: Academic Therapy Publications, 1969.

Pollack, John S. "Opportunities for Learning Disabilities, Title III, ESEA," pp. 149–152 in J. Arena (ed.), *Successful Programing: Many Points of View.* San Rafael, Calif.: Academic Therapy Publications, 1969.

Reger, R., and M. Koppman. "The Child-Oriented Resource Room Program," pp. 272–276 in S. Kirk and F. Lord (eds.), *Exceptional Children: Educational Resources and Perspectives.* Boston: Houghton Mifflin, 1974.

Rochford, Timothy, Wendy Schroder, and Roger Reger. "A Summer Program for Children with Learning Disabilities," pp. 333–339 in J. Arena (ed.), *Successful Programing: Many Points of View.* San Rafael, Calif.: Academic Therapy Publications, 1969.

Russell, R. W. "The Dilemma of the Handicapped Adolescent," pp. 155–172 in R. Weber (ed.), *Handbook of Learning Disabilities.* Englewood Cliffs, N.J.: Prentice-Hall, 1974.

Sabatino, David A., and David L. Hayden. "Prescriptive Teaching in a Summer Learning Disabilities Program." *Journal of Learning Disabilities* 3 (April 1970): 220–227.

Senf, Gerald. *Model Centers Program for Learning Disabled Children: Historical Perspective.* Preview Series. Tucson, Ariz.: Leadership Training Institute for Learning Disabilities. University of Arizona, 1974.

Stetler, Margaret, and Dolores Turner. "Summer Workshops and Recreation Programs for the Learning Disabled," pp. 340–355 in J. Arena (ed.), *Successful Programing: Many Points of View.* San Rafael, Calif.: Academic Therapy Publications, 1969.

Stubblefield, Caroline. "The Public School Reading Clinic as a Training Center," pp. 16–23 in *Some Administrative Problems of Reading Clinics.* Newark, Del.: International Reading Association, 1965.

Taylor, Frank, A. Artuso, M. Solowy, F. Hewett, H. Quay, and R. Stillwell. "A Learning Center Plan for Special Education." *Focus on Exceptional Children,* 4 (May 1972): 1–7.

Whitsell, Alice J., and Leon J. Whitsell. "Remedial Reading in a Medical Center." *The Reading Teacher* 21 (May 1968): 707–711.

Yates, James R. "Model for Preparing Regular Classroom Teachers for 'Mainstreaming,'" *Exceptional Children* 39 (March 1973): 471–472.

14. Administering the Learning Disabilities Program

THE LEARNING DISABILITIES SPECIALIST
    Technical Role
    Managerial Role

THE RESOURCE ROOM

PARENTS
    Parent Reactions to Handicapped Children
    Parent Counseling and Conferences
    Suggestions for Parents

SUMMARY

This chapter deals with the administration of the learning disabilities program within the school. As noted in the previous chapter, no one system of educational services is *the* best. A continuum of services is needed so that various options are available to meet the diverse needs of learning-disabled children. As new trends within the field emerge and as new concepts develop, the responsibilities of the learning disabilities specialist undergo transformation. Several concerns related to administering a program are discussed in this chapter: the role of the learning disabilities specialist, the resource room, and working with parents.

THE LEARNING DISABILITIES SPECIALIST

The teacher of children with learning disabilities plays many roles. Among the jobs performed, either as an individual or as part of a team, are: (1) setting up programs for identifying, diagnosing, and instructing children with learning disabilities; (2) finding or screening the children within the school who are handicapped by learning disabilities; (3) consulting with professionals from contributing disciplines and interpreting their reports; (4) testing and diagnosing individual children; (5) planning prescriptive educational programs; (6) implementing the educational plan through teaching and creating or locating appropriate materials and methods; (7) interviewing and consulting with parents; (8) helping the classroom teacher and other school personnel to understand the child and providing teachers with ways to help the child; and (9) perhaps most important, helping the child to develop self-understanding and to gain the hope and confidence necessary to cope with and start to overcome the handicap.

Defining the role of the learning disabilities specialist is a difficult task because the functions of the position are in transition. It is important, therefore, to be alert to emerging concepts, ideas, and problems, and to be able to adapt to change. Two dimensions of the tasks of this position should be considered: (1) the technical role and (2) the managerial role.

TECHNICAL ROLE

Learning disabilities specialists must, of course, be highly competent in all of the technical aspects of their areas of specialization, which includes underlying knowledge of pertinent conceptual frameworks and familiarity with important related literature. They must also know a variety of screening and testing instruments and be able to administer and interpret widely used tests. The ability to conduct interviews and gather case history information, to use observational techniques and informal methods to gather information are also required technical skills. The capacity to formulate a diagnosis and to communicate such information to others is essential. Specialists must be skilled in developing teaching plans and must be familiar with specific remediation strategies, methods, and materials. Competencies in reading and evaluating research are also needed.

The title *diagnostic-remedial specialist* has been used by Kirk (1971) to describe the complex technical role and responsibilities. This individual is highly trained in the diagnostic-teaching process and knowledgeable in the field of learning disabilities and other related areas. The specialist serves as the responsible agent for the child, pulling together the findings of other specialists in order to diagnose and assess the child, plan the appropriate teaching procedures, and implement the teaching. In sum, the specialist in learning disabilities is an expert in helping the learning-disabled child find the elusive key to learning. Since the normal pathways for learning may not be open to this child, new roads must be found, and some avenues must be cleared so that linguistic, academic, and behavioral goals can be reached.

Most of the chapters in this book deal with the technical dimensions of the role.

MANAGERIAL ROLE

The second and growing dimension of the role of the learning disabilities specialist is the managerial role. This requires working with other people: other specialists, the classroom teacher, paraprofessionals, and administrators. When the self-contained classroom was the predominant type of delivery service, there was relatively little need for interaction with other school personnel and little interdependence of functions. As the systems for delivering educational services enlarged to itinerant, resource, mainstreaming, and consulting models, the need for interdependence increased. Interaction, communication, and development of common goals became strategies for integrating the various components of the system. Objectives of a program can only be met if all the persons within the system function in an integrated fashion, and managerial skills are needed to integrate these functions into a coordinated working system.

Working with Other Specialists

As the scope of the responsibilities of the learning disabilities teacher expands, the common boundaries of interest with other specialists increase. Work with various specialists in closely related disciplines, such as psychology, reading, speech, counseling, school nursing, etc., derives from areas of common interests.

These commonalities of interest, or areas of interface, also may lead to territorial conflicts. Questions of primary responsibility for a specific area may arise. Who, for example, should work with the child who has a severe reading problem? Several specialists lay claim to this child: the learning disabilities specialist, the reading specialist (Lerner 1975, 1975a), and the speech and language pathologist, who may perceive their expertise as encompassing the entire realm of language problems, including reading (McGrady 1974). The child with a language disorder could be served by the speech clinician or by the learning disabilities specialist. Diagnostic functions could be within the jurisdiction of the school psychologist or the learning disabilities specialist.

Such interface relationships may be the most delicate and demanding aspects of the job. The role responsibilities as perceived by the learning disabilities specialist may not mesh with the perceptions of other specialists on the staff. Coping with such differences in role perception requires both sensitivity and astute political savvy.

Working with Classroom Teachers

The importance of the classroom teacher in helping the learning-disabled child is becoming increasingly evident. Under a resource room delivery system, the classroom teacher must coordinate efforts with the learning that occurs in the resource room. Under a mainstreaming model, the teacher must learn to work as a member of a team. At times the learning disabilities specialist may work with the child in the regular classroom; at times an aide or paraprofessional will work with the child in the classroom; at other times the teacher will be responsible for the instructional program of the child.

Mainstreaming has created a number of unanticipated problems. Classroom teachers are often untrained in special education and unprepared to handle problems of the atypical child. They may be fearful of the responsibility and in some cases reluctant to accept this additional task. Successful integration of the learning-disabled child into the regular classroom needs careful thought, planning, and supervision. Managerial efforts have to be geared to gaining the classroom teacher's acceptance of the goals of the program and willingness to coordinate efforts to help the child.

Shaw and Shaw (1972) suggest that persons responsible for working with the classroom teacher be called "classroom specialists," whose duties would include arranging in-service learning experiences and working with classroom teachers to modify classroom problem situations referred by classroom teachers. The specialist should be competent in diagnosis and evaluation, instructional techniques, classroom organization and arrangement, and behavior management and also should be knowledgeable in curricula materials, practices, and independent learning activities. All of these are technical competencies, but, according to Shaw, the most important skill is the ability to relate and communicate with peer professionals. Overall, the combination of professional technical competences and interpersonal skills characterizes this individual.

Working with Paraprofessionals

Many of the delivery systems make extensive use of paraprofessionals or aides (paid and volunteer nonprofessional persons who undertake the task of assisting teachers) (Reid and Reid 1974). These individuals should be given very structured, limited, and specific assignments in working with children. Their duties must be carefully planned and supervised by either the learning disabilities specialist or by the classroom teacher. Instruction should be clear, and material should be easy to use. The precise educational responsibilities of the paraprofessional must be clear to everyone involved. At the same time, it is essential that paraprofessionals perceive themselves as working parts of the system and view their work as significant and worthwhile.

Working with Administrators

It is clear from research reported in organizational theory that if changes are to be made in the system there must be support from administrators (March and Simon 1961). Without the understanding and support of the principal of the school and superintendent of the system, it is virtually impossible to implement a successful learning disabilities program and reach established goals. Change in an organization comes from the top, and the start must be made with the top management.

To illustrate a difference in role perception by administrators and learning disabilities personnel, Ms. Baily, a newly graduated learning disabilities teacher, accepted her first teaching position in Parkside School District. Her rather naïve view of the educational world, gained in part from her university training, was that learning disabilities is the center with many other disciplines contributing to the field. When she expectantly asked the superintendent for the administrative staff and line chart, she discovered to her dismay that learning disabilities was not the focal point of the chart; in fact, it was not even on the chart. The superintendent kindly suggested that one box in the bottom left-hand corner of the chart might be considered a related learning disabilities component. The perception of the role of learning disabilities on the part of the new graduate was vastly different from the perception shown on the administrative chart. Such a discrepancy, sometimes called *cognitive dissonance* (Festinger 1964), requires a certain amount of adjustment. Part of the managerial function is to develop common perceptions among all persons involved; certainly the administrator must be part of the communication and planning system.

Change-Agent Mission

Reger (1973) views the mission of the learning disabilities specialist to be developing more understanding attitudes within the entire school toward children in general and those with learning disabilities in particular. In short, the learning disabilities specialist becomes a change agent — a catalyst to instigate fresh approaches to teaching and learning. It is a very delicate role and Reger observes that learning disabilities specialists who are

> . . . teachers with a mission to change the schools cannot approach the task with any display of zealousness. They do not accomplish their mission by direct confrontation. They work toward their mission by example and subtle persuasion. It may take several years of skillful work before any change becomes noticeable. The mission is an idea and need not be practical. (Reger 1973, p. 610)

With such a mission the overall goal is to integrate or imbed special education into regular education.

A note of caution, however, should be voiced concerning the dangers that are possible in this direction. Research in organizational theory suggests that as programs become merged into the larger system, they sometimes lose their identity and are eventually discarded (March and Simon 1961), that is, the goals of the subunit become restricted to conform to the existing goals of the larger organization. The inference of this principle of organizational process is that by integrating into general education, special education may lose visibility and viability. As a result, its goals eventually would be submerged and supplanted. If this happens, it is likely that learning disabilities will become poorly conceptualized, underfinanced, and poorly managed in the classroom of an already burdened teacher. Another danger under a completely integrated system is that the child will lose advocates within the school, a function often assumed by the learning disabilities teacher. It is essential to keep the concepts and objectives of the field of learning disabilities alive — a task that requires visibility, constant monitoring, involvement, and decision making.

Working as a Consultant

Perhaps the most difficult task of the learning disabilities specialist is that of consulting. While consulting with the classroom teacher is of paramount importance, this function should be envisioned in terms of the entire school system. Unless all elements within the system operate in a coordinated fashion, the objectives and goals of the learning disabilities program will not be satisfactorily met. This implies that the concept of consulting must include administrators, paraprofessionals, the school board, other specialists, and parents, as well as the classroom teacher. While all the delivery systems need the consultative function to work effectively, the more other persons are involved in the delivery system, the greater will be the need for effective consultation.

Several managerial principles of the consulting function in regard to the school as a system are:

1. *Common goals.* It is essential that there be a common perception of the goals and objectives of the learning disabilities program among the various persons involved. All must know the purpose of the program. If individuals are working toward different purposes, there is likely to be conflict and dissatisfaction. Common goals must be perceived by classroom teachers, administrators, paraprofessionals, other specialists, and other individuals who may be involved.

2. *Open and clear communication.* A planned communication system is needed to serve several purposes. It will help to establish common perceptual bases among the members involved in a project and will provide a scheduled opportunity to clear up questions as soon as they occur. If problems continue without opportunity for face-to-face communication, dissatisfaction increases and misunderstanding develops.

3. *Clarification of responsibilities.* It is important to clarify responsibilities of all persons involved — to avoid both conflicts and gaps in functions.

4. *Resolution of conflicts.* When problems do arise, methods of resolving them should be developed. They should not be ignored, but neither should decisions be forced by use of power. Instead, problem-solving strategies should be developed. All information should be placed out in the open and the problem attacked by all individuals involved.

5. *Adequate time and facilities.* Unless time is set aside for the functions of planning, communicating, and evaluating, there will be insufficient time in the crowded school day for these purposes. Space, time, and assurance of uninterrupted sessions are needed for productive work.

Reger (1973) has several specific management suggestions. He believes that a specific amount of time, 10 to 15 percent, should be set aside for consultation with other teachers and for making classroom observations. It is also important that classroom teachers be provided time to participate in staffings that concern children in their rooms. Some arrangements for aides or substitutes may be necessary to free classroom teachers for staffings. Time should be provided for in-service training as well. Reger feels that this is especially important for first-year teachers and recommends a half-day each week for this purpose.

Several specific strategies are useful in building consulting services.

1. *In-service education.* To acquaint all persons involved in the system with the field of learning disabilities, it is essential to think of in-service for all — classroom teachers, as well as administrators, paraprofessionals, other specialists, etc.

2. *Demonstration of methods and materials.* Materials, methods, techniques, tests can be shown, demonstrated, or used in trial periods with children in the classroom, etc. Publishers' consultants — films, tapes, etc. — can also be used for this purpose. Teachers are usually interested in knowing about new and useful items.

3. *Case discussions.* An in-depth discussion of a particular case can be used to present certain concepts and principles. Emphasis may be on diagnosis, remediation, or other aspects of the case. Computer simulation games have been used for this purpose (Lerner and Schuyler 1974, 1975). Getting participants involved in the case under discussion can be an effective way to make a point or to teach a concept.

4. *Clinical experiences.* It may be possible to give classroom teachers and others actual clinical experiences in both diagnosis and teaching. Opportunities to participate in clinics in various settings would give teachers a better understanding of the child with learning disabilities.

5. *Guest speakers and attendance at conferences.* New ideas, new approaches, and fresh perspectives can be gained by inviting guest speakers to speak to the group. Attendance at local, state, and national meetings also provides a renewal of energy, interest, and ideas.

6. *Newsletter.* A regular written communication for participants in the system on a semiweekly, monthly, or quarterly basis can be developed by the learning disabilities personnel to keep system members up on ideas, materials, and happenings in the field.

In summary, organizational factors that affect the direction of a learning disabilities program include the administration of the institution, the working and personal relationship among staff members, the goals and ambitions of the organization, and the role and status of the learning disabilities specialist within the organization.

THE RESOURCE ROOM

The resource room as one type of delivery system was briefly discussed in Chapter 13. While there is little research data to indicate the superiority of this type of educational service over the others, it appears to be the most prevalent type at present (Wiederholt 1974; Sabatino 1972; Reger 1972, 1973; Hammill and Wiederholt 1972). For this reason the resource room is discussed in greater detail in this section. Wiederholt (1974, p. 1) defines the resource room:

> A resource room is basically any special education instructional setting to which a child comes for specific periods of time on a regularly scheduled basis for remedial instruction. . . . The child attends the resource room only on a part-time basis, remaining for at least a portion of the day in his regular classroom.

Many managerial functions can be met by having the learning disabilities teacher working within a resource room setting. Reger (1973) observes that the resource room specialist, a teacher in action in a single school setting, is readily accepted as part of that building and gets to know the teachers, the administrators, and the children there. The resource room teacher is not tied to one classroom and therefore is able to share responsibilities for children with all the teachers in the building who have children in the program. The specialist's time is flexible, permitting acceptance of many varied responsibilities.

When the field of learning disabilities began, the organizational pattern typically followed was the self-contained classroom model, the organizational pattern used in other areas of special education. The hope was that by placing the child in a separate classroom designed especially for children with learning disabilities and taught by a highly trained specialist, the child's problem would be eliminated and return to the regular classroom would soon be possible. Experience showed, however, that additional services were needed. With the self-contained classroom only a few children could be selected for help, the cost per child was high, the child had limited contact with normal children, and the integration back into the regular classroom was difficult. Alternative ways to serve the child were needed. The resource room, headed by a learning disabilities specialist, was one such alternative.

The advantage of the resource room over the self-contained classroom as an administrative arrangement is that services can be offered to more children, particularly mildly handicapped children. (Both types of settings, however, are needed to serve children with varying degrees of handicaps.) Another advantage of the resource room is that it has the flexibility of providing services without attaching a stigmatizing label. Therefore, some resource rooms are designed according to *noncategorical* models, while others are *categorical* rooms, admitting only those youngsters identified as learning disabled. Wiederholt (1974, p. 6) summarizes the advantages:

1. Mildly handicapped pupils can benefit from specific resource room training while remaining integrated with their friends and agemates in school.
2. Pupils have the advantages of a *total remedial program*, which is prepared by the resource teacher but may be implemented in cooperation with the regular class teacher.

3. Resource rooms are *less expensive* as the teachers are able to serve a greater number of children than special class programs.
4. More children's needs can be served under the resource room arrangement than can be served [through the self-contained classroom].
5. Since the resource teacher is assigned to a particular school, he is less likely to be viewed as an "outsider" by the other teachers in the school. In addition, he probably better understands the programing problems in a particular school.
6. Because young children with mild though developing problems can be accommodated, later severe disorders may be prevented.

A highly competent and personable individual is needed to meet the responsibilities of the resource room teacher. Wiederholt specifies these qualities as: (1) the ability to work closely and harmoniously with other teachers and the ancillary staff, (2) the ability to make educational and behavioral diagnosis, and (3) the ability to design and implement individualized instruction for children referred to the resource room. The first item reflects a managerial skill, while the other two are technical skills.

Some specific recommendations for the resource room are made by Wiederholt. Since the child is in the regular classroom for a large part of the day, both diagnosis and remediation must be related to the child's needs in the regular classroom. In planning the schedule of the resource room teacher, time should be allotted for periods of assessment, for remediation, and for consultation. Teacher aides, including paraprofessionals, parent volunteers, or older pupils, are useful in enhancing the services afforded by the resource room. Many kinds of equipment and materials are needed to insure flexibility and variety. The resource room teacher might take the initiative in developing a resource team. Such an approach would give school personnel the opportunity to interact and to develop a communication flow. Finally, it is of paramount importance that the room be an attractive and well-organized place for children to live and learn.

Sufficient funds are needed to purchase supplies, equipment, and materials for the resource room. Reger (1973) suggests that to equip a newly established resource room a minimum of $1,500 to $2,000 should be available. In addition, an annual budget of $1,000 is needed to maintain the program.

In summary, a resource room is simply an administrative arrangement. Its success depends upon many factors, including the competence of the resource teacher, the support and cooperation of all levels of administration, and the availability of adequate space and materials.

PARENTS

Too often, the parent is the most forgotten element in the entire complex. We forget that he has the same problems we have but he has them in greatly magnified intensity. Whereas we have this child for a few hours a day in a limited and controlled situation, he has him twenty-four hours in all kinds of situations and all types of demands.

Much valuable information can be gained from parents and much valuable aid in the child's handling can be obtained from them if one can only learn to communicate.... When a parent understands the problem, he need no longer be afraid of a technical term, he can attack his own problem. He need no longer be frustrated by unrecognizable behavior. He need no longer frustrate the child by simple but, for him, impossible demands. He can aid the child in the achievement of increasingly complex accomplishments. (Kephart 1972, p. vi)

There has been an awakening of concern for the problem of parents of exceptional children. There are several reasons for this: (1) parent groups have been the major impetus for much of the special education legislation and the establishment of many programs; (2) recent legislation has given parents a variety of rights in regard to the handicapped child, such as the right to obtain complete psychoeducational data on their child and the right to have the final say on educational placement recommended by the school; (3) we are realizing the important role that parents can play in helping the child; and (4) we are beginning to perceive the significant effect a child's handicap has on the parents.

PARENT REACTIONS TO HANDICAPPED CHILDREN

A study by Wetter (1972) indicated that the attitude of parents who have a child with a learning disorder is very different from that of parents of a youngster who does not present such a problem. Parents of learning-disabled children exhibit attitudes of greater overindulgence and overprotection. Bryant (1971) noted three frequent attitudes on the part of mothers toward their handicapped children. The first attitude is reflected by mothers who reject their child or are unable to accept the child as a handicapped person. Complex love-hate and acceptance-rejection relationships are found among this group. Rejected children not only have problems in adjusting to themselves and their disabilities, but they also have to contend with disturbed family relationships and emotional insecurity. Unfortunately, such children receive even less encouragement than the normal child and have to absorb more criticism of their behavior.

A second relationship involves mothers who overcompensate in their reactions to their child and the disorder. They tend to be unrealistic, rigid, and overprotective. Often such parents try to compensate by being overzealous, giving continuous instruction and training in the hope of establishing superior ability.

The third group consists of mothers who accept their children along with their disorders. These mothers have gained the ability to provide for the special needs of their handicapped children while continuing to live a normal life and tending to family, home, civic, and social obligations. The child's chances are best with parents who have accepted both their child and the defects.

Psychiatric or psychological help is often needed by the parents of children with learning disabilities. Giffin (1968) indicated that psychiatrists are becoming increasingly aware that the presence of a handicapping problem must be faced by both child and other members of the family. In addition to an honest acceptance of the problem, there must be recognition that improvement is often a slow process. Giffin has found that the reaction of parents is often one of denial, followed by anger, then by a search for other diagnoses. Sometimes parents also need help of a psychotherapeutic nature in accepting the problem, in developing empathy for their child, and in providing a beneficial home environment. Guidance counselors and social workers play important roles in providing such help.

PARENT COUNSELING AND CONFERENCES

Establishing healthy parental attitudes and parent-teacher cooperation are, of course, desirable goals. Two procedures to meet these goals are parent counseling and parent-teacher conferences.

In *parent counseling* parents meet regularly in groups, under the guidance of a professional counselor or educator, to discuss common problems. The opportunity to meet with other parents whose children are encountering similar problems tends to reduce the parents' sense of isolation. Further, such parent groups have been useful in alerting the community, school personnel, other professionals, and legislative bodies to the plight of their children.

Often the first step in parent counseling is helping the parents get over initial feelings about their handicapped child. According to Buscaglia (1975), the initial period of reaction may be one of mourning, misunderstanding, guilt, depreciation of self, and even a sense of shame. Parents may react to these feelings by turning away in confusion, or they may overreact, become aggressive, and try to break down doors to get things done. Buscaglia believes that these aggressive parents are much needed in our profession for they are the ones who keep the educators moving. Educators should empathize with parents to help them get over the initial period of reaction.

During the course of one parent counseling program described by McPhail (1972), the topics of discipline, communication skills, behavior modification, contingency contracting, and developing responsibilities were discussed.

Barsch (1967, pp. 150–151), after a seven-year experiment in group counseling of parents of brain-damaged children, reached the following conclusions:

> 1. A counseling technique to help parents develop experimental approaches to behavior organization in the brain-injured child is ego-strengthening, supportive, and practically helpful.

2. These parents experience a homogeneity of anxieties stemming from apprehension regarding the psychological and educational development of their children. Only on a secondary basis do they appear to concern themselves with factors in physical development.

3. A selection process is necessary to determine whether the needs of a particular parent might best be served in a group or individual counseling setting, or whether referral for psychotherapy might be more profitable.

4. The parent of the brain-injured child must be considered an integral part of the organization of the child's behavior.

5. Parents can be taught to perceive their children differently and learn to deal with their child's problems more effectively.

6. Comments of the mothers consistently reflect changed response patterns in relation to problems represented by their children; they learn to apply a technique. There is some restoration of feelings of competency and self-worth.

7. The mothers learn to recognize their unique responsibility in developing organized response patterns in their children.

8. The number of mothers (10) selected for each group on an arbitrary basis has proven an effective and workable figure.

Although this study was specifically designed for parents of brain-damaged children, it appears to have applicability for effective counseling of parents of children with all learning disabilities.

Parent-teacher conferences can serve to establish a bridge between the home and school. Both parents and teachers tend to shy away from conferences, parents fearing what they will hear and teachers fearing that parents will react negatively. Yet the conferences should be viewed as an opportunity to help the child. By coordinating efforts, the child's life in school and at home can work together to enhance progress. If they are compartmentalized, they may be working at cross purposes, making the child's life even more difficult.

Dodd and Dodd (1972) believe that in setting up a conference teachers should try to reassure parents that they are going to communicate with another human being — not a cog in an impersonal system. The teacher should communicate a sincere interest in the child and respect for the parents, as well as conveying a sense of confidence without being arrogant. The problem should be discussed in a calm manner, avoiding technical jargon. Parents want to understand the nature of the problem and therefore diagnostic data and current teaching approaches should be interpreted and explained. The parents must also be helped to become sensitive to the nature of the child's learning difficulties and to those tasks that are difficult.

In addition, parents usually want to know what they can do at home. Most specialists believe that at home parents should involve the children in domestic responsibilities and not try to help them with schoolwork. Since academic learning is the area of most difficulty, children being taught academic skills by their parents might be failing consistently in front of the most meaningful adults in their lives. Moreover, parents find that helping children in academic areas can be formidable and frustrating. Even well-trained learning disabilities specialists who perform outstandingly well professionally often fail miserably when trying to deal with learning disabilities in their own children. Too often when parents try to help their children in academic areas, it results in harm to the child, to the parents, and to their relationship. The pressures and demands of the academic learning situation interfere with the role of the parents in developing a good self-image. Instead, suggestions for parent involvement should be related to home living (Brown 1969, Miller 1973, Cruickshank 1967). When the parent undertakes the task of tutoring, the child too often loses a parent while gaining a mediocre teacher (Brutten et al. 1973).

Child-teacher conferences are also important to help children understand their problems. Children are often worried, frightened, and confused; they need to have their evaluation and teaching plan explained in words they can understand. Such a conference can help in clearing up confusion and alleviating concern. A delightful short book designed to explain learning disabilities to a child is *The Tuned-In, Turned-On Book About Learning Problems* (Hayes 1974).

SUGGESTIONS FOR PARENTS

A book designed to acquaint parents of learning-disabled children with an overview of the field, *Something's Wrong with My Child* (Brutten, Richardson, and Mangel 1973), offers a number of suggestions to help parents make life at home easier.

1. Don't lose outside interests. Try to relinquish your child's care to a competent baby-sitter periodically. Parents need time off for independence and morale boosting.

2. Don't push your child into activities for which the child is not ready. The child can react by trying halfheartedly to please you, may rebel either actively or passively, or may just quit or withdraw into a world of daydreams. By forcing the child to meet arbitrary and inappropriate standards imposed by the adult world, learning becomes painful rather than pleasurable.

3. Be alert to any hint that your child is good at *something*. By discovering an unimpaired area or native talent, give your child a new chance for success. The tasks may be small, such as folding napkins or helping with specific kitchen chores.

4. Match tasks to the child's level of functioning. For example, have easy-to-wipe surfaces and breakproof containers to reduce spills when the child uses these materials. Think about the child's problem and figure out a way to help. As an illustration, Brutten et al. suggest drawing an outline of the child's shoes on the closet floor to indicate left and right.

5. Be direct and positive in talking to your child. Try not to criticize but to be supportive and directive. For example, if the child has trouble follow-

ing directions, ask him to look at you while you speak and then to repeat what you have said.

6. Keep the child's room simple and in a quiet part of the house — a place to relax and retreat.

7. Simplify family routine. For example, mealtime for some children can be an extremely complex and stimulating situation. Your child may be unable to cope with the many sounds, sights, smells, etc. It may be necessary to have the child eat earlier at first and gradually join the family meal — perhaps starting with dessert.

8. Help the child learn that she must live with other children in a world that doesn't revolve around her. Because some learning-disabled children do not play well with other children, parents have to go out of their way to plan and guide such social experiences. This may mean inviting a single child to play for a short period of time, arranging with parents of other learning-disabled children for joint social activities, or volunteering to be a den mother or a Brownie leader.

9. Above all, Brutten et al. advise that all children need to learn that they are significant. They must be treated with respect and allowed to do their own work. They should learn that being a responsible and contributing member of the family is important — probably more important than learning the academic skills demanded by the school.

Teachers may wish to recommend reading materials for parents to help them become better acquainted with the problem of learning disabilities and ways of helping their children. Several such books for parents are:

Becker, W., and J. Becker. *Successful Parenthood.* Chicago: Follett, 1974.

Brutten, Milton, Sylvia O. Richardson, and Charles Mangel. *Something's Wrong with My Child: A Parents' Book About Children with Learning Disabilities.* New York: Harcourt Brace Jovanovich, 1973.

Cruickshank, William M. *The Brain-Injured Child in Home, School, and Community.* Syracuse, N.Y.: Syracuse University Press, 1967.

Hart, Jane, and Beverly Jones. *Where's Hannah? A Handbook for Parents and Teachers of Learning Disorders.* New York: Hart, 1968.

Kronick, Doreen, ed. *They Too Can Succeed: A Practical Guide for Parents of Learning Disabled Children.* San Rafael, Calif.: Academic Therapy Publications, 1969.

Levy, Harold B. *Square Pegs, Round Holes.* Boston: Little, Brown, 1973.

Miller, Julano. *Helping Your L.D. Child at Home.* San Rafael, Calif.: Academic Therapy Publications, 1973.

Siegel, Ernest. *Helping the Brain-Injured Child: A Handbook for Parents.* New York: New York Association for Brain-Injured Children, 1962.

Valett, Robert E. *Modifying Children's Behavior: A Guide for Parents and Professionals.* Palo Alto, Calif.: Fearon, 1971.

Williams, Beverly. *Your Child Has a Learning Disability: What Is It?* Chicago: National Easter Seal, 1970.

SUMMARY

This chapter has discussed a number of facets of administering the learning disabilities program. The role of the learning disabilities specialist was discussed from two perspectives: the technical dimension and the managerial dimension. Within the managerial dimension, the problems of working with other specialists, classroom teachers, paraprofessionals, and administrators present special challenges. In addition, the learning disabilities specialist may function as a change-agent or consultant.

The resource room serves as one system for delivering educational services. The need, advantages, and functions of the resource room were discussed.

Finally, the chapter dealt with the issue of working with parents. Parent reactions to their child's handicap, ways of conducting parent counseling sessions and parent-teacher conferences, and some suggestions for parents to use were presented.

REFERENCES

Barsch, Ray. "Counseling the Parent of the Brain-Damaged Child," pp. 145–151 in E. Frierson and W. Barbe (eds.), *Educating Children with Learning Disabilities.* New York: Appleton-Century-Crofts, 1967.

Brown, George. "Suggestions for Parents." *Academic Therapy* 7 (Spring 1972): 277–284.

Brutten, Milton, Sylvia O. Richardson, and Charles Mangel. *Something's Wrong with My Child.* New York: Harcourt Brace Jovanovich, 1973.

Bryant, John E. "Parent-Child Relationships: Their Effect on Rehabilitation." *Journal of Learning Disabilities* 4 (June 1971): 325–332.

Buscaglia, Leo F. "Parents Need to Know: Parents and Teachers Work Together," pp. 365–377 in S. Kirk and J. McCarthy (eds.), *Learning Disabilities: Selected ACLD Papers.* Boston: Houghton Mifflin, 1975.

Cruickshank, William M. *The Brain-Injured Child in Home, School, and Community.* Syracuse, N.Y.: Syracuse University Press, 1967.

Dodd, John, and Nancy Dodd. "Communication with Parents." *Academic Therapy* 7 (Spring 1972): 277–284.

Festinger, Leon. *Conflict, Decision, and Dissonance.* Stanford, Calif.: Stanford University Press, 1964.

Giffin, Mary. "The Role of Child Psychiatry in Learning Disabilities," pp. 75–98 in H. Myklebust (ed.), *Progress in Learning Disabilities,* Vol. 1. New York: Grune & Stratton, 1968.

Hammill, D. D. and J. L. Wiederholt. *The Resource Room: Rationale and Implementation.* Ft. Washington, Pa.: Journal of Special Education Press, 1972.

Hayes, Marnell. *The Tuned-in, Turned-on Book About Learning Problems.* San Rafael, Calif.: Academic Therapy Publications, 1974.

Kephart, Newell C. Introduction to D. Woodward and N. Biondo. *Living Around the Now Child.* Columbus: Merrill, 1972.

Kirk, Samuel A. "Learning Disabilities: The View from Here," pp. 20–25 in D. Hammill and N. Bartel (eds.), *Educational Perspectives in Learning Disabilities.* New York: Wiley, 1971.

Lerner, Janet W. "Remedial Reading and Learning Disabilities: Are They the Same or Different?" *Journal of Special Education* 9 (Summer 1975): 119–132.

Lerner, Janet W. "Two Perspectives: Reading and Learning Disabilities," pp. 271–285 in S. Kirk and J. McCarthy (eds.), *Learning Disabilities: Selected ACLD Papers.* Boston: Houghton Mifflin, 1975.

Lerner, Janet W., and James A. Schuyler. "Computer Simulation: A Method for Training Educational Diagnosticians." *Journal of Learning Disabilities* 7 (October 1974): 471–478.

Lerner, Janet W., and James A. Schuyler. *Computer Applications in Learning Disabilities.* Microfiche and Hard Copy. ED096974. Arlington, Va.: ERIC Document Reproduction Service, February, 1975.

March, James G., and Herbert A. Simon. *Organizations.* New York: Wiley, 1961.

McGrady, Harold. Report in "Minutes of the Division of Children with Learning Disabilities." *Division for Children with Learning Disabilities Newsletter* 4 (Spring 1974): 9–12.

McPhail, Gail. "Getting Parents Involved." *Academicy Therapy* 7 (Spring 1972): 271–275.

Miller, Julano. *Helping Your L.D. Child at Home.* San Rafael, Calif.: Academic Therapy Publications, 1973.

Reger, Roger. "Resource Rooms: Change Agents or Guardians of the Status Quo?" *Journal of Special Education* 6 (Winter 1972): 377–382.

———."What Is a Resource Room Program?" *Journal of Learning Disabilities* 6 (December 1973): 609–614.

Reid, Barbara, and William Reid. "Role Expectations of Paraprofessionals in Special Education." *Focus on Exceptional Children* 6 (December 1974): 1–14.

Sabatino, David. "Resource Rooms: The Renaissance in Special Education." *Journal of Special Education* 6 (Winter 1972): 335–348.

Shaw, Stan F., and Wilma K. Shaw. "The In-Service Experience Plan, or Changing the Bath without Losing the Baby." *Journal of Special Education* 6 (Summer 1972): 121–126.

Wetter, Jack. "Parent Attitudes Toward Learning Disability." *Exceptional Children* 38 (February 1972): 490–491.

Wiederholt, J. Lee. "Planning Resource Rooms for the Mildly Handicapped." *Focus on Exceptional Children* 5 (January 1974): 1–10.

Appendixes

APPENDIX A PHONICS

This appendix has two sections. The first part is a short phonics quiz to assess the teacher's knowledge of this subject area. The second part is a brief review of some phonic generalizations.

Ǝ FŎN′ ĬKS KWĬZ (A PHONICS QUIZ)

The purpose of the phonics quiz is to give teachers the opportunity to evaluate their knowledge of phonics, structural or morphemic analysis, and phonic generalizations. Even among advocates of conflicting approaches to the teaching of reading, there is agreement that skills in word recognition and phonics are essential for effective reading. And all reading authorities agree that teachers of reading and language arts have the responsibility to help children acquire the skills that will enable them to unlock unknown words. Without phonics, most children cannot become self-reliant, discriminating, efficient readers.

In spite of this strong and united stand taken by the reading experts, many teachers and prospective teachers are not knowledgeable in this content area (Lerner and List 1970). *The Torch Lighters* (Austin 1961), an intensive and broad study of tomorrow's teachers of reading, supported by the Carnegie Corporation, revealed that many prospective teachers do not know techniques or generalizations of phonics. A major recommendation resulting from the study was that college instructors take responsibility in making certain that their students who will be teaching reading master the principles of phonics. Phonics and structural or morphemic analysis, then, should be part of the content area for the teacher of reading, language arts, and English.

It should be noted that recent research on the utility of phonic generalizations reveals that these rules have many exceptions. In fact, some are applicable less than half the time. Therefore certain generalizations may have a limited utility value (Clymer 1963, Emans 1967, Bailey 1967, Burmeister 1968, Lerner 1969, Winkley 1966). Nevertheless, these generalizations do provide a helpful start in analyzing unknown words.

Although knowledge of rules and facts concerning phonics is part of the content area for the teacher, this is not presented as a recommended way to teach phonics to a child. The strategies selected to teach a child the skill of unlocking words will depend upon many factors.

To check your knowledge of phonics, select the correct answer for each of the following 50 questions. Compare your choices with the correct answers printed at the end of the Phonics Quiz. Score two points for each correct answer. Check the table below the answers for your rating and classification.

CHOOSE THE CORRECT ANSWER

Consonants

1. Which of the following words ends with a consonant sound?
   a) piano   b) baby   c) relay   d) pencil   e) below

2. A combination of 2 or 3 consonants pronounced so that each letter keeps its own identity is called a
   a) silent consonant   b) consonant digraph   c) diphthong
   d) schwa   e) consonant blend

3. A word with a consonant digraph is
   a) stop   b) blue   c) bend   d) stripe   e) none of the above

4. A word with a consonant blend is
   a) chair   b) ties   c) thing   d) strict   e) where

5. A soft "c" is in the word
   a) city   b) cat   c) chair   d) Chicago   e) none of the above

6. A soft "g" is in the word
   a) great   b) go   c) ghost   d) rig   e) none of the above

7. A hard "c" is sounded in pronouncing which of the following nonsense words?
   a) cadur   b) ceiter   c) cymling   d) ciblent   e) chodly

8. A hard "g" would be likely to be found in which of the following nonsense words?
   a) gyfing   b) gesturn   c) gailing   d) gimber   e) geit

9. A *voiced* consonant digraph is in the word
   a) think   b) ship   c) whip   d) the   e) photo

10. An *unvoiced* consonant digraph is in the word
    a) those   b) thirteen   c) that   d) bridge   e) these

Vowels

11. Which of the following words contains a long vowel sound?
    a) paste   b) stem   c) urge   d) ball   e) off

12. Which of the following words contain a short vowel sound?

        a) treat b) start c) slip d) paw e) father

13. If "tife" were a word, the letter "i" would probably sound like the "i" in

        a) if b) beautiful c) find d) ceiling e) sing
        Why?

14. If "aik" were a word, the letter "a" would probably sound like the "a" in

        a) pack b) ball c) about d) boat e) cake
        Why?

15. If "ne" were a word, the letter "e" would probably sound like the "e" in

        a) fed b) seat c) batter d) friend e) weight
        Why?

16. A vowel sound represented by the alphabet letter name of that vowel is a

        a) short vowel b) long vowel c) diphthong d) digraph
        e) schwa

17. An example of the schwa sound is found in

        a) cotton b) phoneme c) stopping d) preview e) grouping

18. A diphthong is in the word

        a) coat b) boy c) battle d) retarded e) slow

19. Which of the following words contains a vowel digraph?

        a) toil b) amazing c) happy d) cape e) coat

Syllables

Indicate the correct way to divide the following nonsense words into syllables:

20. l i d b e r

        a) li–dber b) lidb–er c) lid–ber d) none of the above
        Why?

21. s e f u m

        a) se–fum b) sef–um c) s–efum d) sefu–m e) none
        Why?

22. s k e b l e

        a) skeb–le b) ske–ble c) sk–eble d) none of these
        Why?

23. g o p h u l

        a) gop–hul b) go–phul c) goph–ul d) none
        Why?

24. r e p a i n l y

        a) rep–ain–ly b) re–pai–nly c) re–pain–ly
        d) none of the above
        Why?

25. How many syllables are in the word "barked"?

        a) one b) two c) three d) four e) five

26. How many syllables are in the word "generalizations"?
       a) four b) five c) six d) seven e) eight
27. A word with an open syllable is
       a) pike b) go c) bend d) butter e) if
28. A word with a closed syllable is
       a) throw b) see c) why d) cow e) win

Accent

29. If "trigler" were a word, which syllable would probably be accented?
       a) trig b) ler c) neither d) both
       Why?
30. If "tronition" were a word, which syllable would probably be accented?
       a) tro b) ni c) tion d) none
       Why?
31. If "pretaineringly" were a word, which syllable would probably be accented?
       a) pre b) tain c) er d) ing e) ly
       Why?

Sound of Letter "y"

32. If "gly" were a word, the letter "y" would probably sound like
       a) the "e" in *eel* b) the "e" in *pet* c) the "i" in *isle*
       d) the "i" in *if* e) the "y" in *happy*
       Why?
33. If "agby" were a word, the letter "y" would probably sound like
       a) the "e" in *eel* b) the "e" in egg c) the "i" in *ice*
       d) the "i" in *if* e) the "y" in *cry*
       Why?

Silent Letters

34. *No* silent letters are found in which of the following nonsense words?
       a) knip b) gine c) camb d) wron e) shan
35. *No* silent letters are in
       a) nade b) fruting c) kettin d) foat e) pnam

Terminology

36. A printed symbol made up of two letters representing one single phoneme or speech sound is a
       a) schwa b) consonant blend c) phonetic
       d) digraph e) diphthong
37. The smallest sound bearing unit or a basic sound of speech is a
       a) phoneme b) morpheme c) grapheme
       d) silent consonant e) schwa

38. A study of all the speech sounds in language and how these sounds are produced is
   a) phonics   b) semantics   c) orthography   d) etymology
   e) phonetics

39. The application of speech sounds applied to the teaching of reading letters or groups of letters is called
   a) phonics   b) phonemics   c) orthography   d) etymology
   e) phonetics

40. The study of the nature and function of human language utilizing the methodology and objectivity of the scientist is
   a) phonetics   b) phonology   c) linguistics   d) morphology
   e) semantics

41. The approach to beginning reading which selects words that have a consistent sound-symbol relationship (CVC) is the
   a) basal reader approach   b) phonics approach
   c) linguistics approach   d) language-experience approach
   e) initial teaching alphabet approach

42. The approach to beginning reading which uses a more simple, reliable alphabet to make the decoding of English phonemes less complex is the
   a) basal reader approach   b) phonetic approach
   c) linguistic approach   d) language-experience approach
   e) initial teaching alphabet approach

43. A *phonic element* is similar to which word in linguistic terminology?
   a) syntax   b) phoneme   c) morpheme
   d) grapheme   e) intonation

44. The study of structural analysis is similar to what element of linguistics?
   a) syntax   b) phonology   c) morphology
   d) graphology   e) intonation

The Utility of Phonic Generalizations

In examining both words that are exceptions to the rules and words that conform to the rules, researchers have found a varying percent of utility to the generalizations in items 45–48. How frequently does each hold true?

45. When there are two vowels side by side, the long sound of the first one is heard and the second is usually silent.
   a) 25%   b) 45%   c) 75%   d) 90%   e) 100% of the time

46. When there are two vowels, one of which is final *e*, the first vowel is long and the *e* is silent.
   a) 30%   b) 60%   c) 75%   d) 90%   e) 100%

47. When a vowel is in the middle of a one-syllable word, the vowel is short.
   a) 30%   b) 50%   c) 70%   d) 90%   e) 100%

48. When a word begins with *kn*, the *k* is silent.
   a) 30%   b) 50%   c) 70%   d) 90%   e) 100%

49. The first American educator to advocate the teaching of phonics as an aid to word recognition and pronunciation was
  a) Noah Webster in *The American Blueback Spelling Book*, 1790
  b) William McGuffey in *McGuffey's Readers*, 1879
  c) Leonard Bloomfield, *Language*, 1933
  d) Rudolph Flesch in *Why Johnny Can't Read*, 1955
  e) Charles Fries, *Linguistics and Reading*, 1963

50. Most reading authorities agree that
  a) the sight word method is the best way to teach reading
  b) the phonics method is the best way to teach reading
  c) structural or morphemic analysis is the best way to teach reading
  d) there is no *one* best way to teach reading

Read the following nonsense words applying phonic generalizations to determine their appropriate pronunciations.

bongtrike	crangle
plignel	magsletting
abcealter	phister
conborvement	flabinstate
gingabution	craipthrusher
recentively	wonaprint
fudder	knidderflicing
gentropher	

ANSWERS TO PHONICS QUIZ

1. d
2. e
3. e
4. d
5. a
6. e
7. a
8. c
9. d
10. b
11. a
12. c
13. c: long vowel with silent "e"
14. e: with 2 vowels, first is long, second is silent
15. b: one-syllable ending in vowel is long
16. b
17. a
18. b
19. e
20. c: divide between 2 consonants
21. a: vowel, consonant, vowel
22. b: words ending in "le"— consonant precedes the "le"
23. b: consonant digraphs are not divided
24. c: prefix and suffix are separate syllables
25. a
26. c
27. b
28. e
29. a: accent first of two syllables
30. b: accent syllables before "tion" ending
31. b: accent syllable with two adjacent vowels
32. c: "y" at end of one syllable word has a long "i" sound
33. a: "y" at end of multisyllable word has long "e" sound
34. e
35. b
36. d
37. a
38. e
39. a
40. c
41. c
42. e
43. b
44. c
45. b
46. b
47. c
48. e
49. a
50. d

Score	Rating
92–100	EXCELLENT Congratulations! You do know your phonics.
84–92	GOOD A brief refresher will help, though.
76–84	FAIR Study with your favorite third grader.
68–76	POOR You could be a case of "the blind leading the blind."

A REVIEW OF COMMON PHONIC GENERALIZATIONS

CONSONANTS

Consonants are the letters in the alphabet that are not vowels. Consonant speech sounds are formed by modifying or altering or obstructing the stream of vocal sound with the organs of speech. These obstructions may be stops, fricatives, or resonants. Consonant sounds are relatively consistent and have a regular grapheme-phoneme relationship. They include: b, d, f, h, j, k, l, m, n, p, r, s, t, v, w, y (initial position).

Consonants "c" and "g"

Hard "c" pronounced like "k" when followed by a, o, u (cup, cat).
Soft "c" pronounced like "s" when followed by i, e, y (city, cent).
Hard "g" when followed by *a, o, u* (go, gay).
Soft "g" when followed by *i, e, y,* sounds like "j" (gentle, gyp).

Consonant Blends

A combination of two or three consonant letters blended in such a way that each letter in the blend keeps its own identity: bl, sl, cl, fl, gl, pl, br, cr, dr, fr, gr, pr, tr, sc, sk, sl, sw, sn, sp, sm, spl, spr, str, scr, ng, nk, tw, dw.

Consonant Digraphs

A combination of two consonant letters representing one phoneme or speech sound that is not a blend of the two letters: sh, ch, wh, ck, ph, gh, th.

Silent Consonants

Silent consonants are those consonants which, when combined with specific other letters, are not pronounced. In the examples below, the silent conso-nants are the ones enclosed in parentheses, and the letters shown with them are the specific letters that cause them to be silent in combination. (There are exceptions, however.)

i(gh)	sight, bright
m(b)	comb, lamb
(w)r	wren, wrong

(1)k	talk, walk
(k)n	knew, knife
s(t)	listen, hasten
f(t)	often, soften

VOWELS

The vowels of the alphabet are the letters *a, e, i, o, u,* and sometimes *y.* The vowel speech sounds are produced in the resonance chamber formed by the stream of air passing through in the oral cavity.

Short vowels: a, e, i, o, u, (sometimes y). A single vowel in a medial position usually has the short vowel sound: consonant, vowel, consonant (CVC). A diacritical mark called a "breve" ˘ may indicate the short vowel: păt, săd, lĕd, sĭt, pŏt, cŭp, gўp.

Long vowels: a, e, i, o, u, (sometimes y). The long vowel sounds the same as the alphabet letter name of the vowel. It is indicated with the diacritical mark ē called a macron: gō, cāke, ēel, īce, nō, ūniform, crȳ.

Double Vowels: Vowel Digraph

Frequently, when two vowels are adjacent, the first vowel has the long sound while the second is silent. Recent research has shown this generalization to hold true about 45% of the time: tie, coat, rain, eat, pay.

Final "e"

In words with a vowel-consonant-e pattern (VCe), the vowel frequently has the long sound while the "e" is silent. Research has shown this generalization to hold true about 60% of the time: make, Pete, slide, hope, cube.

Vowels Modified by "r"

Vowels followed by the letter "r" are neither long nor short, but the sound is modified by the letter "r." This holds true about 85% of the time: star, her, stir, horn, fur.

Diphthongs

Two adjacent printed symbols representing two vowels, each of which contributes to a blended speech sound: joy, toil, cow, house, few.

Schwa Sound

This is the vowel sound in an unaccented syllable and is indicated with the symbol ə: balloon, eaten, beautify, button, circus

SYLLABICATION

Number of Syllables

There are as many syllables in a word as there are vowel sounds heard: bruise (1 syllable), beautiful (3 syllables).

Two Consonants (VC-CV)

If the initial vowel is followed by two consonants, divide the word between the two consonants. This rule holds true about 80% of the time: con-tact, let-ter, mar-ket.

Single Consonant (V-CV)

If the initial vowel is followed by one consonant, the consonant usually begins the second syllable. There are many exceptions to this rule. The generalization holds true about 50% of the time: mo-tor, na-tion, stu-dent.

Consonant-Le (C-le) Endings

If a word ends in "le," the consonant preceding the "le" begins the last syllable. This generalization holds true about 95% of the time: ta-ble, pur-ple, han-dle.

Consonant Blends and Consonant Digraphs

Consonant blends and digraphs are not divided in separating a word into syllables. This holds true 100% of the time: teach-er, graph-ic, de-scribe.

Prefixes and Suffixes

Prefixes and suffixes usually form a separate syllable: re-plac-ing, dis-appoint-ment.

Suffix "ed"

If the suffix "ed" is preceded by "d" or "t," it does form a separate syllable and is pronounced "ed." If the suffix "ed" is not preceded by a "d" or "t," it does not form a separate syllable. It is pronounced like "t" when it follows an unvoiced consonant, and it is pronounced like "d" when it follows a voiced consonant: sanded (ed), patted (ed), asked (t), pushed (t), tamed (d), crazed (d).

Open and Closed Syllables

Syllables that end with a consonant are closed syllables and the vowel is short: *can*-vass.

Syllables that end with a vowel are open syllables and the vowel is long: *ba*-by.

The "y" Sound in One-Syllable Words and Multisyllable words

When the "y" is the final sound in a one-syllable word, it usually has the sound of a long "i": cry, my, ply.

When the "y" is the final sound of a multisyllable word, it usually has the long "e" sound: funny, lady.

ACCENT

When there is no other clue in a two-syllable word, the accent frequently falls on the first syllable. This generalization is true about 80% of the time: pen'cil, sau'cer.

In inflected or derived forms of words, the primary accent usually falls on or within the root word: fix'es, un touched'.

Two vowels together in the last syllable of a word gives a clue to an accented final syllable: re main', re peal'.

If two identical consonants are in a word, the syllable before the double consonant is usually accented: big'ger, hal'low ed.

The primary accent usually falls on the syllable preceding the suffixes ion, ity, ic, ical, ian, ial, ious: at ten' tion, hys ter' ical, bar bar' ian, bil' ious.

REFERENCES

Austin, Mary C. *The Torch Lighters: Tomorrow's Teachers of Reading.* Cambridge, Mass.: Harvard University Press, 1961.

Bailey, Mildred H. "The Utility of Phonic Generalizations in Grades One Through Six," *Reading Teacher* 20 (1967): 413–418.

Burmeister, Lou E. "Usefulness of Phonic Generalizations," *Reading Teacher* 21 (1968): 349–356.

Clymer, Theodore L. "The Utility of Phonic Generalizations in the Primary Grades," *Reading Teacher* 16 (1963): 252–258.

Emans, Robert. "When Two Vowels Go Walking and Other Such Things," *Reading Teacher* 21 (1967): 262–269.

Lerner, Janet W. "The Utility of Phonic Generalizations—A Modification," *The Journal of the Reading Specialist* 8 (March 1969): 117–118.

Lerner, Janet W. and Lynne List. "The Phonics Knowledge of Prospective Teachers, Experienced Teachers, and Elementary Pupils," *Illinois School Research* 7 (Fall 1970): 39–42.

Winkley, Carol K. "Which Accent Generalizations Are Worth Teaching?" *Reading Teacher* 20 (1966): 219–224.

APPENDIX B   MATERIALS

Many commercial materials are available on the market that may prove useful in planning teaching programs for children with learning disabilities. The materials should be viewed as tools to be used as needed to teach a particular child. The learning disabilities specialist, not the author of the set of materials, should direct the program and make the decisions concerning the focus and direction of the teaching process. Some of the commercial materials available are listed in this appendix. Since new items are constantly being introduced, this listing cannot be complete. The listing of materials in this section does not imply recommendation. The lists are meant to serve as a convenient reference of materials for educators as they implement learning disabilities programs. The items should be carefully evaluated or catalog descriptions should be examined before materials are selected. The complete names and addresses of publishers and companies that manufacture this material are included in Appendix E.

The materials are divided into the following sections:

1. Materials for teaching the young child: readiness, perception, language, number concepts, emotional and social development
2. Materials for teaching beginning reading: phonics and word analysis, and reading comprehension skills
3. Materials for the secondary level student: language reading, spelling, writing, mathematics, social studies, and other areas
4. Multimedia equipment and machines for teaching

MATERIALS FOR TEACHING THE YOUNG CHILD

This section is divided into (a) general materials, (b) arithmetic materials, (c) handbooks, and (d) publishers.

GENERAL MATERIALS

Academic Games Development Program. Motivational Research. Games for learning.

Auditory Discrimination Training. Learning Through Seeing, Inc. A program for prereading and beginning reading.

Auditory Perception Training. Developmental Learning Materials. A multimedia kit (cassette, spirit masters, etc.) for teaching auditory perception.

Dandy Dog's Early Learning Program. American Book Company. A readiness program.

Detect. Science Research Association. A sensorimotor approach to visual discrimination.

Developing Learning Readiness Program. Webster. A motor and perceptual development program.

Children's World. Holt, Rinehart and Winston, Inc. A kit of multisensory materials for early childhood and readiness.

Concept Builders with Write and See. New Century.

DISTAR Language I and II. Science Research Association. A highly structured program designed to teach basic language concepts and build vocabulary and communication skills, (preschool and primary).

DUSO (Developing Understanding of Self and Others). American Guidance Services. A kit of activities and materials to facilitate social and emotional development, (K-4).

Early Childhood Discovery Materials. Macmillan. A readiness program.

Early Learning. McGraw-Hill/Early Learning. Materials for readiness, beginning reading, and language.

Goldman-Lynch Sounds & Symbols Kit. American Guidance Services. To stimulate production of speech.

The Fitzhugh PLUS program. Allied Education Council. Perceptual training, spatial organization books for reading and arithmetic.

The Frostig Program for the Development of Visual Perception. Follett. Workbooks for training visual perception.

I Can Do It. Mafex Associates. Visual-motor activities.

Inquisitive. Science Research Associates. Games for exploring numbers and space.

The Language and Thinking Program. Follett. Materials to develop language and cognitive skills, (ages 3–7).

Learning Aids for Young Children in Accordance with Montessori. Teaching Aids. Materials and equipment for readiness, perception, and motor development.

The MWM Program for Developing Language Abilities. Educational Performance Associates. A kit of remedial materials based on language disabilities as diagnosed by the ITPA, (ages 3–11).

Matrix Games Package. Appleton-Century-Crofts. Games for readiness.

Michigan Successive Discrimination Program. Ann Arbor Press. Symbol tracking, visual tracking, word tracking.

Montessori-type Teaching Aids. Educational Teaching Aids. Materials patterned after the Montessori program.

Peabody Language Developmental Kits. American Guidance Services. Kits of puppets, pictures, and lesson plans to develop oral language skills.

Try Experiences for Young Children. Noble & Noble. Visual perceptual tasks.

TAD (Toward Affective Development). American Guidance Services. Group activities and materials to stimulate psychological and affective development, (3–6).

MATERIALS DESIGNED TO TEACH ARITHMETIC CONCEPTS

Arithmetic Step by Step. Continental Press. Boxed preprinted duplicating masters for ten units in arithmetic, (readiness–3).

Count Down. Economy Co. Use of paces (audio-tape player) and pacetapes (tape recordings), books for individualized mathematics program, (1–3).

DISTAR Arithmetic I and II. Science Research Associates. Structured program to teach basic number concepts, (K–2).

Mathematics in Action Series. American Book Co. Series of eight books designed for students with arithmetic difficulties.

Mathematics materials. A. Daigger & Co., Educational Teaching Aids Division. Manipulative and concrete materials for teaching number concepts.

Mathematics materials. Edukaid of Ridgewood. Equipment and materials for teaching arithmetic.

Mathematics materials. The Judy Co. Concrete materials to enhance the teaching of number concepts.

Mathematics materials. Teaching Resources Corp. Number relationships, time concepts, games, and manipulative materials.

Math Lab. Benefic Press. A kit of boxed cards with activities to teach mathematics concepts, (primary–junior high school).

Pacemaker Arithmetic Readiness. Fearon. Primary level special education pre-arithmetic skills.

PLUS. Educational Services, Inc. Teacher's handbook of games, ideas, and activities to teach arithmetic.

The Sensorithmetic Program. Developmental Learning Materials. Teaching basic number and arithmetic concepts through the use of sensory reinforcement materials.

Stern Structural Arithmetic. Houghton Mifflin. A kit of manipulative objects, (K–3).

Handbooks and Manuals

The following are organized resource collections of methods and materials for remediation.

Adapt Handbook I: A Mainstream Approach to Identification, Assessment, and Amelioration of Learning Disabilities (by Robert R. Ferrald and Robert G. Schambers). Adapt Press, Inc.

Educational Therapy Materials from the Ashlock Learning Center (by Patrick Ashlock and Sister Marie Grant). Charles C. Thomas.

Handbook in Diagnostic Teaching: A Learning Disabilities Approach (by Phillip Mann and Patricia Suiter). Allyn and Bacon.

The Remediation of Learning Disabilities: A Handbook of Psychoeducational Resource Programs (by Robert E. Valett). Fearon.

Workjobs. Addison-Wesley. A manual of ideas and suggestions for teacher-made materials and equipment for early childhood readiness and remediation.

Publishers and Manufacturers of Materials

Beckley-Cardy
Continental Press

Creative Playthings, Inc.
Developmental Learning Materials
Dick-Blick
Educational Teaching Aids
Garrard Publishing Co.
J. L. Hammet Co.
Houghton Mifflin Co.
Ideal School Supply Co.
Instructo Corp.
The Judy Co.
Kenworth Educational Service
Mafex Association
Milton Bradley Company
F. A. Owen Publishing Co.
J. A. Preston Corp.
Teachers Publishing Corp.
Teaching Resources Corp.

MATERIALS FOR TEACHING BEGINNING READING

PHONICS AND WORD ANALYSIS

Conquests in Reading. Webster. Review of phonics and word attack skills, (4–6).

Decoding for Reading. Macmillan. Audiovisual program for older nonreaders.

Developmental and Remedial Reading Materials. Educator's Publishing Service.

DISTAR Reading I and II. Science Research Associates. Program to teach beginning reading; emphasis on cracking the code, (K–2).

Dr. Spello. Webster Division, McGraw-Hill. Phonics and spelling book, (4–8).

Durrell-Murphy Phonics Practice Program. Harcourt Brace Jovanovich. Self-directing phonics picture cards.

Edmark Reading Program. Edmark Associates. A programed approach designed for students with extremely limited skills; teaches a 150-word vocabulary.

First Experiences with Consonants. First Experiences with Vowels. Instructo Corp. Materials to teach consonants and vowels.

Get Set Games. Houghton Mifflin. Games to teach decoding skills.

Ginn Word Enrichment Program. Ginn. Seven workbooks for word recognition skills.

Intersensory Reading Method. Book-Lab, Inc. Beginning phonics: books, cards, materials.

i/t/a Early-to-Read Program revised. Initial Teaching Alphabet. Uses i/t/a as a medium for beginning reading.

The Landon Phonics Program. Chandler. A phonics series.

Language Experiences in Reading Program. Encyclopaedia Britannica Education Corp. Language experience approach to beginning reading.

Lift-Off to Reading. Science Research Associates. A programed beginning reading approach.

Macmillan Reading Spectrum. Macmillan. Six levels of word analysis, (4–6).

Merrill Linguistic Readers. Merrill. A linguistic-approach basal reader.

Michigan Language Program. Learning Research Associates. Individualized program for beginning reading books for listening, reading words, word attack and comprehension.

Mott Basic Language Skills Program. Allied Education Council. Reading program for adolescents. Levels 1–3, levels 4–6. Text-workbooks.

Open Court Correlated Language Arts Program. Open Court Publishing Co. Basal reader series stressing phonics.

The Palo Alto Reading Program: Sequential Steps in Reading. Harcourt Brace Jovanovich. A programed and linguistic approach to beginning reading.

Peabody Rebus Reading Program. American Guidance Service. The use of rebus pictures for teaching beginning reading.

Phonetic Keys to Reading. Economy Company. A phonic approach to beginning reading. Books, cards, charts, (1–4).

Phonics Skill Builders. McCormick-Mathers. Set of six workbooks for teaching phonics skills, (1–6).

Phonics We Use. Lyons and Carnahan. A series of phonics workbooks, (1–8).

The Phonovisual Method. Phonovisual Products. A series of books, charts, manuals, and cards for teaching phonics, (primary).

Programmed Reading. McGraw Hill. Twenty-one books of programed instruction in reading.

The Reading Experience and Development Series (READ). American Book Co.

Reading Helper Books. Book-Lab, Inc. Five activities books for beginning reading, (K–2).

Reading in High Gear. Science Research Associates. A programed reading program for adolescent non-readers.

Reading with Phonics. Lippincott. Workbooks and phonics cards for teaching phonics skills, (primary).

Remedial Reading Drills (Hegge, Kirk, Kirk). George Wahr Publishing Co. Exercises to develop skills in phonics and word recognition, (1–3).

Speech-to-Print Phonics. Harcourt Brace Jovanovich. Cards and manual for developing phonics skills.

SRA Reading Program. Science Research Associates. A basal reading series with a linguistic emphasis, (1–6).

Structural Reading Program. L. W. Singer Co. A structured basal program with emphasis on phonics, (prereading–2).

Sullivan Remedial Reading Program. Behavioral Research Laboratories. Series of programed workbooks.

Weekly Reading Practice Books. American Guidance Service. Beginning Reading phonics program.

Wenkart Phonics Readers. Wenkart Publishing Co. A set of readers with a phonics emphasis.

Word Attack Series. Teaching College Press. Three workbooks to teach word-analysis skills.

Wordland Series. Continental Press. A phonics program on reprinted ditto masters.

Words in Color. Xerox Education Division. Use of color to teach initial reading.

Write and See. Appleton-Century-Crofts, New Century Publications. Self-correcting phonics materials with reappearing ink process, (1–4).

Additional materials for the older student are in "Materials for the Secondary Level Student," on page 402.

READING COMPREHENSION

Be a Better Reader, Foundations. Prentice-Hall. Designed for practice in reading in content areas, (4–6).

Developmental Reading Text-Workbooks. Bobbs-Merrill Co. Six workbooks to give training and practice in several programs in reading, (K–6).

Diagnostic Reading Workbooks Series. Charles E. Merrill. Workbooks designed for developmental or remedial programs in reading, (K–6).

Gates-Peardon Reading Exercises. Teachers College Press. Reading exercises to develop the ability to read for general significance, to predict outcomes, to understand directions, to note details.

New Practice Readers. Webster Division/McGraw-Hill. Reading selections and questions designed to improve comprehension skills in reading, (2–8).

New Reading Skilltext Series. Charles E. Merrill. Reading comprehension workbooks, (1–6).

Reading Skills Builders. Reader's Digest Services. Magazine format with short reading selections and accompanying comprehension skills, (1–8).

Reading Success Series. My Weekly Reader. Six booklets of high-interest level to teach basic reading skills.

Reading Thinking Skills. Continental Press. Preprinted masters for liquid duplicating, (PP–6).

Specific Skills Series. Barnell-Loft. Exercises booklets designed for practice in specific reading comprehension skills: locating the answer, following directions, using the context, getting the facts, working with sound, drawing conclusions, getting the main idea, (1–8).

SRA Reading Laboratory. Science Research Associates. Boxed materials consisting of multilevel and color-cued reading matter and answer keys. Reading rate and comprehension, (1–12).

Standard Test Lessons in Reading (McCall-Crabbs). Teachers College Press. Paperback booklets with short reading selections and comprehension questions, (3–7).

Additional materials for the older student are in "Materials for the Secondary Level Student," on page 402.

MATERIALS FOR THE SECONDARY LEVEL STUDENT

LANGUAGE

CFC (Concepts for Communication). Developmental Learning Materials. A kit to teach language using multimedia language, listening concepts.

Communication Series (by Turner and Livingstone). Follett.

Language Training for Adolescents. Educators Publishing Services. Reading and language program for adolescents with special language disabilities.

READING

Action Reading System and *Double Action.* Scholastic Book Services. Reading levels 2.0–5.0. Kit of reading material for secondary school students who are seriously behind in reading.

Activity-Concept English (ACE). Scott, Foresman. A kit of many reading components for students deficient in language skills.

Activities of Reading Improvement. Steck-Vaughn. Three workbooks of specific reading skills for junior high students.

Advanced Reading Skills. Reader's Digest. Magazine format of short stories, (R.L. 4–8).

Basic Reading Skills for Junior High School Use. Scott, Foresman. Workbook for developing reading skills. Designed for remedial reading pupils at junior high level.

Be a Better Reader. Prentice-Hall. Reading improvement in the content areas, (4–6 and junior high).

Breakthrough. Allyn and Bacon. Stories especially designed for the problem reader; stories of mature interest but low reading level.

Building Reading Skills in the Content Areas. Educational Activities. Cassettes for subject areas of geography, history, science, and mathematics, (R.L. 2–6).

Classroom Reading Clinic. McGraw-Hill/Webster Division. A variety of reading materials. Elementary reading level. Skill building and high-interest, low-vocabulary books.

Contact. Scholastic. Series of anthologies for secondary students at the 4–6 reading level. Designed to motivate the hard-to-reach student.

Developing Reading Efficiency. Burgess. A workbook for junior high level containing lessons for a variety of reading skills.

Developmental Reading Text Workbooks. Bobbs Merrill, (R.L. 1–6).

Diagnostic Reading Workbooks Series. Charles E. Merrill. R.L. 1–6 for remedial reading programs.

Directions. Houghton Mifflin. Short anthologies, reading skill booklets, for the reluctant reader.

Effective Reading. Globe Book. Exercises and materials for levels 4–8.

Gaining Independence in Reading. Charles E. Merrill. Three hard-covered textbooks, (4–12).

Gates-Peardon Reading Exercises. Teachers College Press. Reading exercises to develop the ability to read for general significance, to predict outcomes, to understand directions, and to note details, (3–6).

Improve Your Reading Ability. Charles E. Merrill. Text-workbook for developing comprehension skills and rate. Intermediate difficulty level.

McCall-Crabbs Standard Test Lessons in Reading. Teachers College Press. Paperback booklets with short reading selections and comprehension questions, (3–7).

New Goals in Reading. Steck-Vaughn. Reading workbooks, (4–6).

New Practice Readers. Webster Division/McGraw-Hill. Reading selections and questions designed to improve comprehension skills in reading, (2–8).

Open Highways Program. Scott Foresman. Basal reading series for poor readers at secondary level, reading 3–4 years below grade level.

Reading Developmental Kits. Addison-Wesley. Boxed kits of cards that can be used for junior and senior high levels, (primary–10).

Reading Essential Series. Steck-Vaughn, (1–8).

Reading for Concepts A-H. McGraw-Hill. Series of books for reading for concepts, (R.L. 1.6–8.9).

Reading for Meaning Series. J. B. Lippincott. A series of workbooks designed to improve comprehension skills, vocabulary, central thought, details, organization, and summarization, (4–6 and 7–10).

Reading for Understanding. Science Research Associates. Boxed multilevel selections graduated in difficulty. Designed to develop comprehension skills, (5–12).

Reading Improvement Material. Reader's Digest Services. Workbooks for reading improvement at advanced levels, (7–10).

Reading Skills Builders. Reader's Digest. Magazine format with short reading selections and accompanying comprehension questions, (1–8).

The Reading Skills Lab Program. Houghton Mifflin. Nine workbooks to teach specific comprehension skills, (4–6).

Reading Spectrum. Macmillan. Variety of individualized supplementary materials for skills and recreational reading, (junior high).

Read-Understand-Remember Books. Allied Education Council. For developing understanding and retention. Self-correction, (R.L. 2.7–7.2).

Remediation Reading (RR). Modern Curriculum Press. Word-recognition skills workbook designed for older student.

SCOPE/Skills and SCOPE/Visuals. Scholastic. Series of high-interest/low-reading-level skills workbooks, 4–6.

SCORE. Scholastic. Weekly news magazine for grades 8–12, (R.L. 4–6).

Specific Reading Skills. Jones-Kenilworth. Wordbuilding, comprehension, critical and creative reading, (PP–8.5).

Specific Skills Series. Barnell-Loft. Exercise books designed for practice in specific reading comprehension skills, locating the answer, following directions, using the context, getting the facts, working with sound, drawing conclusions, getting the main idea, (1–8).

SRA Reading Laboratory. Science Research Associates. Boxed materials consisting of multilevel reading matter. Comprehension questions and rate improvement materials, (1–12; kit 3a for 7–9).

Step Up Your Reading Power. Webster/McGraw Hill. Five workbooks for remedial secondary school level; six fact questions and two thought questions after each selection.

Study Skills Library. Educational Developmental Laboratories, Division of McGraw-Hill. Reading skills focusing on content subjects. Material is boxed by subject area and difficulty level, (4–9).

Study Type Reading Exercises. Teachers College Press. Reading exercises at the secondary level, (high school).

The Thinking Box. Benefic Press. Designed to develop critical thinking skills. Boxed material, individualized to teach twelve thinking skills, (upper intermediate to junior high).

PUBLISHERS OF HIGH-INTEREST, EASY-READING-LEVEL BOOKS

Descriptive material on easy-reading-level books with mature interest can be obtained from these publishers.

Beckley-Cardy Co.
The Bobbs-Merrill Co.
Bowmar Publishing Co.
The Children's Press
Doubleday & Co.
Fearon Publishers
Field Enterprises
Garrard Publishing Co.
Globe Book Co.
Harper & Row
D. C. Heath and Co.
Holt, Rinehart and Winston
Houghton Mifflin Co.
The Macmillan Co.
William Morrow & Co.
G. P. Putnam's Sons
Random House
Reader's Digest
Scholastic Book Services
Science Research Associates
Scott, Foresman and Co.
Webster Publishing Co.
Wheeler Publishing Co.

SPELLING

Dr. Spello. Webster Division/McGraw-Hill. Reinforcement for spelling skills, (4–9).

Lippincott's Basic Spelling Books. J. B. Lippincott. Ungraded series of ten books.

Michigan Spelling Series. Ann Arbor Publishers.

Programmed Spelling. Ann Arbor Publishers. Programed spelling workbook for junior and senior high school students; contains commonly misspelled words.

Spellbound. Educator's Publishing Service. Text for poor spellers in junior and senior high school.

Spelling Patterns of Sound. McGraw-Hill. Developmental text-tape program based on contemporary linguistic research of English spelling patterns. Text on fourteen 60-minute cassette tapes.

Spelling Reference Book. Developmental Learning Materials. Basically a dictionary (spelling only) of most misspelled words, (2–4).

Spelling Word Power Lab Series. Science Research Associates. Kit to teach spelling on an individualized, comprehensive basis for junior high school students.

A Spelling Workbook Emphasizing Rules and Generalizations for Corrective Drill. Educator's Publishing Service. For students with spelling and reading difficulties, (7–12).

The Spell of Words. Educator's Publishing Service. For high school students with spelling problems.

Sullivan's Programmed Spelling. Behavioral Research Laboratories. Individualized programed workbooks for teaching spelling, (1–8).

WRITING

Activity-Concept-English (ACE). Scott, Foresman. Writing and reading workbooks for secondary students with severe language skill handicaps.

Composition in Action. Science Research Associates. Workbooks for teaching composition techniques, (junior and senior high school).

Everyday Reading and Writing. New Readers Press.

The Write Thing. Houghton Mifflin. To stimulate composition with multimedia materials, (7–12).

Writing Aids Through the Grades. Teachers College Press. One-hundred-and-eighty-six ideas to teach writing.

MATHEMATICS

Activities in Mathematics. Scott, Foresman. For students who have been unsuccessful in math. First course—patterns, numbers, measurement, and probability. Second course—graphs, statistics, proportions, and geometry.

Aftermath Series. Creative Publications. Enrichment books for practice.

Applications in Math. Scott, Foresman. Course A and B for the general math student (9–12).

Arithmetic Workbook. Dick Blick. Spirit master with activities for extra practice, (6–10).

Basic Algebra. Merrill. Individualized cassettes teaching program.

Basic Mathematics. Merrill. Spirit masters math program for low achievers.

The Bucknell Mathematics Self-Study System I. Webster/McGraw-Hill. Independent self-study for underachievers.

Coins and Bills. Developmental Learning Materials. Simulated money for teaching monetary transactions.

Consumer Related Mathematics. Holt, Rinehart and Winston. Practical mathematics. Tests and individualized study units in arithmetic, (3–12).

Cues and Signals in Math I and II. Ann Arbor Publishers. Two books to give additional practice, designed to accompany a basic math program.

E.T.A. Curriculum Enrichment Material. Education Teaching Aids. Cards for remedial practice.

Foundation Mathematics. Webster Division/McGraw-Hill. Programed mathematics.

Fractions. Ann Arbor Publishers. Designed for adolescents.

I.D.E.A.S. Merrill. Individually diagnosed error analysis system; spirit masters for basic computation.

Improving Your Ability in Mathematics. Harcourt Brace Jovanovich. Duplicating masters for basic computation.

Individualized Arithmetic Instruction. Love Publishing. Spirit masters for multi-level arithmetic drill sheets.

Individualized Computational Skills. Houghton Mifflin, (1–12).

Mathematics One and Two: Discovery and Practice. Harcourt Brace Jovanovich. Math program for lower track high school: basic operations, algebra, geometry, and trigonometry.

Math Lab. Benefic Press. Uses cards for a variety of math activities.

Math Study-Scope. Benefic Press. Program uses plastic cylinder to present one problem at a time.

Merrill Mathematics Skill Tapes. Merrill. Cassettes, studybooks, whole numbers, fractions, decimals.

Michigan Arithmetic Program. Ann Arbor Publishers. Uses listening, fluency, and games for group or individual work.

Pacemaker Practical Arithmetic Series. Fearon. Practice in arithmetic skills with a strong vocational slant.

Programmed Mathematics, Series II. Webster Division/McGraw-Hill. Individualized programed books for high school mathematics; designed for the reluctant reader.

Scott Geoboards. Creative Publications. Geoboards for using geoboard activity cards; sets of cards for using boards.

Synchromath Experiences. Rand McNally. Remedial mathematics for junior and senior high school.

Tangle Table. Creative Publications. Remedial practice in computation.

Tangramath. Creative Publications. Teaches concepts of physical shapes (1–10).

SOCIAL STUDIES

American History (by Jack Abramowitz). Follett.

Global Culture Series. McCormick-Mathers. World history.

Government by the People. New Readers Press. Federal government.

Life Near and Far, Life in Different Lands. Steck-Vaughn Co. World history.

The People Power. New Readers Press. Concept of democracy.

Spectra Program: Promise of America. Scott, Foresman. American history.

Study Techniques for Academic Subjects. Baldridge Reading Instructional Materials. Techniques for reading, history, mathematics, science, language, and literature, (7–13).

World History (by Jack Abramowitz). Follett.

SPECIAL SUBJECTS

Basic Driver Education. Interstate Printers. Lessons in driver education.

Be Informed Series. New Readers Press. Booklets on practical living: Buying an Auto, Finding a Job, etc.

Career Guidance Series (by Turner and Livingstone). Follett.

Studying for a Driver's License. New Readers Press.

MULTIMEDIA EQUIPMENT AND MACHINES FOR TEACHING

Audio-Visual Research. Reading ratometer. AVR Eye-Span Trainer, AVR Flash-tachment. Machines for improvement of reading rate.

Bell and Howell. Language Master. An audio-tape system for teaching language, phonics, vocabulary.

Benefic Press. Reading multimedia kits. A multimedia reading program for adolescents.

Borg-Warner Educational Systems. System 80. An individualized audiovisual programed approach to teaching beginning reading.

Bowmar. Coordinated books, photographs, sound filmstrips, and records for the readiness level.

Bowmar. Reading Incentive Program. Books, records, and filmstrips, junior high school interest level.

Craig Corp. Craig Reader: machines for reading-rate improvement. Multitrack recording tape equipment.

Educational Developmental Laboratories. Audiovisual reading improvement equipment; tapes and workbooks for listening skills.

Educational Projections Corp. Self-instructional reading readiness program; film lessons for reading readiness; multichoice viewer.

Electronic Future, Inc. Wireless Reading Systems, Audio Flashcard system.

General Learning Corp. Phono-viewer system. Combination filmslide record units; designed to be self-instructional for young children.

Hoffman Information Systems. Audiovisual reading improvement program.

Imperial International Learning. Audiovisual equipment. Spelling, reading, speech, and mathematics programs.

Keystone View Co. Overhead projector, tachistoscope.

PAL System. Industrial Industries, Inc. Uses filmstrips in a teaching machine. Perceptual training, perceptual thinking, and language-reading.

Perceptual Development Laboratories. Reading-rate improvement equipment.

Psychotechnics. Remedial reading filmstrips, tachistoscope, reading laboratories, shadowscope reading pacer.

Reader's Digest. Young Pegasus Packet. Related storybook and games for readiness.

Reading Institute. Hand tachistoscope, manually operated.

Rheem Califone. Multimedia reading program with tape lessons, books, and manuals.

Scholastic Magazine. Multimedia kit of posters, records, paperbacks for reading improvement. (Reading levels, 2–4; interest, junior high).

Science Research Associates. Reading accelerator, pacer for improvement of reading rate.

Teaching Technology Corp. Multimedia reading program, filmstrips, tapes, records, magnetic cords, manuals, books.

Viking Press. Viking Sound Filmstrips. Coordinated record, filmstrip and user's guide for presentation of literature to children.

APPENDIX C TESTS

This appendix provides an alphabetical listing of some tests that are useful in formulating a diagnosis. This list includes tests that have been mentioned elsewhere in this book, as well as tests not discussed previously. The descriptive material about each test is brief and is not designed to be evaluative. Since tests are frequently revised and new forms of manuals are issued, it is desirable to obtain a current catalog from the publisher before placing an order. Detailed descriptions and critical evaluation of tests can be obtained from the Mental Measurement Yearbook, O. K. Buros, Editor, Gryphon Press (see Appendix E for address). Buros is available in reference libraries. The test publisher appears after the test name; each publisher's address is in Appendix E.

Ammons Full-Range Picture Vocabulary Test. Psychological Test Specialists. Forms A and B, preschool to adult. An individually administered test of receptive language vocabulary.

Basic School Skills Inventory. Follett. Identifies areas of difficulty in school performance (ages 4–7).

Bender-Gestalt Test. Western Psychological Services. An individually administered test of a child's performance in copying designs. The Koppitz Scoring (*The Bender Gestalt Test for Young Children:* E. Koppitz. N.Y.: Grune & Stratton, 1963) provides a developmental scoring system for young children to age 10.

Benton Visual Retention Test, Revised. Psychological Corp. Individually administered test of ability to draw designs from memory.

Boehm Test of Basic Concepts. Psychological Corp. Diagnostic group test of understanding of concepts, 35 minutes, (ages 5–6).

Botel Reading Inventory. Follett. A group of tests to determine a variety of reading skills, (levels 1–12).

Brown-Carlsen Listening Comprehension Test. Harcourt Brace Jovanovich. A receptive language test designed for group use to determine ability to understand spoken English, (grades 9–13).

California Achievement Tests. California Test Bureau. A battery of group tests to assess several areas of academic achievement, levels 1–college. Also *California Reading Tests* (levels 1–college).

Carrow Elicited Language Inventory. Learning Concepts. Indicates language problems, (ages 3–8).

(Carrow) Test for Auditory Comprehension of Language. Learning Concepts. Assesses the child's understanding of language structure, using forms in Spanish and English, (ages 3–10 and 6–11).

CIRCUS: Comprehensive Assessment in Nursery School and Kindergarten. Educational Testing Service. A screening instrument for preschool-age children with potential learning problems.

Classroom Reading Inventory. William C. Brown. A reading inventory that can be administered to individuals or groups.

Detroit Tests of Learning Aptitude. Bobbs-Merrill. An individual test of mental functioning, ages 4–adult. There are nineteen subtests measuring various elements of mental processing. In addition to an overall mental age score, each subtest yields a separate mental age score, allowing a flexible choice of tests for diagnostic purposes.

Developmental Test of Visual-Motor Integration. Follett. A visual-motor test of the subject's abilities in copying designs, (ages 5–20).

Devereau Behavior Rating Scale. Devereau Foundation. A rating scale for behavior with separate forms for adolescents, children, and elementary school.

Diagnostic Tests and Self-Help in Arithmetic. California Test Bureau. Test designed to determine a diagnosis of arithmetic difficulties.

DIAL (Developmental Indicators for the Assessment of Learning). DIAL, Inc. A prekindergarten screening test for identifying children with learning problems.

Doren Diagnostic Reading Test of Word Recognition Skills. American Guidance Services. Group or individually administered word skills test, (grades 1–6).

Durrell Analysis of Reading Difficulty. Harcourt Brace Jovanovich. A battery of diagnostic tests designed to help in the analysis and evaluation of specific reading difficulties.

Durrell Reading-Listening Series. Harcourt Brace Jovanovich. Primary (grades 1–3.5); intermediate (grades 3.5–6); advanced (grades 7–9). Group tests of listening and reading ability that permit a comparison of these two language skills.

Early Detection Inventory. Follett. Fifteen-minute individual screening test for preschool, (ages 3–6).

Early Identification and Treatment of Learning Disabilities. Westinghouse Learning Corp. Screening and teaching for preschool-age children.

Evanston Early Identification Scale. Follett. One-hour group or individual assessment, ages 5–6.

First Grade Screening Test. American Guidance Services. Group test to identify potential learning problems.

Follett Individual Reading Test. Follett. Placement inventory for individual test for reading placement.

Frostig Developmental Test of Visual Perception. Consulting Psychologists Press. This test measures abilities in five separate areas of visual perception.

Gates-MacGinitie Reading Tests. Teachers College Press. A general test of silent reading designed for group administration, with five forms (for grades 1–9).

Gates-McKillop Reading Diagnostic Tests. Teachers College Press. Battery of tests for individual administration, designed to give diagnostic information about a child's reading skills.

Gilmore Oral Reading Test. Harcourt Brace Jovanovich. An oral reading test, individually administered; gives information about word accuracy, rate, and comprehension, (grades 1–8).

Goldman-Fristoe-Woodcock Auditory Skills Test Battery. American Guidance Services. Twelve tests of auditory skills.

Goldman-Fristoe Test of Articulation. American Guidance Services. Thirty-minute test for children over two years of age. Articulation of words and sentences.

Goldman-Fristoe-Woodcock Test of Auditory Discrimination. American Guidance Services. Tests auditory discrimination of phonemes against a quiet background and against a noisy background, (ages 4 and up).

Goodenough-Harris Drawing Test. Harcourt Brace Jovanovich. Provides a score cf nonverbal intelligence obtained through an objective scoring of a child's drawing of a human figure.

Gray Oral Reading Tests. Bobbs-Merrill. An individually administered oral reading test that combines rate and accuracy to obtain grade level score. Comprehension questions available but not scored.

Harris Tests of Lateral Dominance. Psychological Corp. Tests to show right or left preference with hand, eye, foot.

Heath Railwalking Test. A quick test of balance and motor ability while walking across a rail or balance beam. (See C. Goetzinger, "A Reevaluation of the Heath Railwalking Test," *Journal of Educational Research* 54, 1960, pp. 187–191; S. Heath, "Railwalking performance as related to mental age and etiological type among the mentally retarded," *American Journal of Psychology* 55 (April 1942): 240. H. G. Seashore, "The development of a beam walking test and its use in measuring development of balance in children," *American Association for Health, Physical Education and Recreation, Research Quarterly* 18 (December 1947): 246.

Houston Test of Language Development. Houston Press. Part I (18 months–36 months); Part 2 (3–6 years). Assesses several areas of general language development.

Illinois Test of Pscholinguistic Abilities, Revised. University of Illinois Press. Individually administered test containing twelve subtests of dimensions of mental processes. Scores obtained on subtests can be used for diagnostic purposes.

Iowa Every-Pupil Tests of Basic Skills. Houghton Mifflin. Group tests of several academic areas: reading, arithmetic, language, workstudy skills, (ages 3–9).

Key Math Diagnostic Arithmetic Test. American Guidance Services. Thirty-minute measure of fourteen arithmetic subskills, individually administered, four levels of evaluation, (preschool–grade 6).

Keystone Visual Survey Service for Schools. Keystone View Co. Individually administered visual screening device to determine the need for further referral for a visual examination.

Lincoln-Oseretsky Motor Development Scale. Western Psychological Services. Individual tests of a variety of motor skills, (ages 6–14).

McCullough Word Analysis Tests. Ginn. Group tests of word analysis skills, (grades 4–8).

Mecham Verbal Language Development Scale. American Guidance Service. An evaluation of language development obtained through an interview with an informant, usually a parent.

The Meeting Street School Screening Test. Crippled Children and Adults of

Rhode Island. Early identification of children with learning disabilities; individually administered screening and diagnostic instrument; 30 minutes, (ages 4½–6).

Metropolitan Achievement Tests. Harcourt Brace Jovanovich. Battery of tests. Group administration. Measures several areas of academic achievement: reading, spelling, arithmetic, (grades 5–8).

Monroe Reading Aptitude Tests. Houghton Mifflin. Group-administered test to measure readiness for reading. Non-reading test that assesses several areas of mental functioning, (ages 6–9).

Motor-free Test of Visual Perception. Academic Therapy. Ten-minute test of visual perception that does not require a motor component, (ages 4–8).

Nebraska Test of Learning Aptitude. Marshall A. Hiskey. An individual test of intellectual potential, used widely with the deaf or hard-of-hearing.

Nelson-Denny Reading Test. Houghton Mifflin. Group or individual general reading assessment, grade 9–adult level).

Northwestern Syntax Screening Test. Northwestern University Press. Individually administered test of receptive and expressive language, (ages 3–7).

Oseretsky Tests of Motor Proficiency. American Guidance Services. Individual test of motor development, 20–30 minutes, (ages 4–16).

Ortho-rater. Bausch & Lomb. Individual visual screening test.

Otis-Lennon Mental Ability Test. Harcourt Brace Jovanovich. Group test of general mental ability and scholastic aptitude, (K–12).

Peabody Individual Achievement Test (PIAT). American Guidance Services. Individually administered test including five subjects: mathematics, reading recognition, reading comprehension, spelling, and general information, 30–40 minutes, (kindergarten to adult).

Peabody Picture Vocabulary Test. American Guidance Services. An individually administered test of receptive language vocabulary and intelligence, (ages 2–8).

Picture Story Language Test. Grune & Stratton. An individually administered test of the child's achievement in written language.

Pupil Rating Scale. Grune & Stratton. A rating scale for elementary level students to be filled out by teacher.

Purdue Perceptual Survey. Charles E. Merrill. A series of tests for assessing motor development and motor skills, (ages 4–10).

Roswell-Chall Auditory Blending Test. Essay Press. Individually administered short tests to assess ability to hear and blend sounds to say the word.

Roswell-Chall Diagnostic Reading Test. Essay Press. Individually administered short test to assess child's phonic abilities.

Screening Test of Auditory Perception (STAP). Academic Therapy Publications. Group and individual test of auditory perception. Assesses ability to differentiate vowel sounds, initial consonants, and blends; to recognize and remember rhymes and rhythmic patterns; to discriminate same or different pairs of words.

Sequential Tests of Educational Progress. Educational Testing Service. A battery of achievement tests, including tests of reading comprehension and listening comprehension, (grades 4–12).

(Slingerland) Screening Tests for Identifying Children with Specific Language Disability. Educator's Publishing Services. Three sets of screening tests for early grades. Group administered. Informal scoring.

Slosson Intelligence Test. Slosson Educational Publications. A short individual screening test of intelligence, for use by teachers and other professional persons for a quick estimate of mental ability.

Southern California Test Battery for Assessment of Dysfunction. Western Psychological Services, (ages 3–10). A battery containing the following separate tests: *Southern California Kinesthesia and Tactile Perception Tests; Southern California Figure-Ground Visual Perception Test; Southern California Motor Accuracy Test; Southern California Perceptual-Motor Tests;* and the *Ayers Space Test.*

Spache Diagnostic Reading Scales. California Test Bureau. Individually administered battery of tests to diagnose reading difficulties, (grades 1 and up).

SRA Achievement Scales. Science Research Associates. Group tests of several areas of academic achievement, including reading, (grades 1–9).

SRA Primary Mental Abilities Tests. Science Research Associates. Group intelligence test designed to measure several subabilities of mental functioning. MA and IQ scores for verbal meaning, number facility, reasoning, perceptual speed, and spatial relations, (grades K–adult).

Stanford Achievement Test. Harcourt Brace Jovanovich. Group tests of academic achievement, including reading.

Stanford-Binet Intelligence Scale, revised Form L-M Norms edition. Houghton Mifflin. Individual test of general intelligence, yielding MA and IQ scores; to be administered by trained psychological examiners, (ages 2–adult).

Stanford Diagnostic Arithmetic Test. Harcourt Brace Jovanovich. Group test to diagnose nature of arithmetic difficulties.

Stanford Diagnostic Reading Test. Harcourt Brace Jovanovich. Group test to diagnose nature of reading difficulties; measures performance in comprehension, vocabulary, syllabication, auditory skills, phonetic analysis, and reading rate, (grades 2.5–8.5).

Templin-Darley Tests of Articulation. University of Iowa Bureau of Research and Service. Individual test of the articulation of speech sounds.

Test of Auditory Perception (TAP), in D. Sabatino, "The Construction and Assessment of an Experimental Test of Auditory Perception," *Exceptional Children* 36 (1969): 729–737. Six subtests of auditory processing.

Utah Test of Language Development. Communication Research Association. Thirty-minute test of language ability and skills, (ages 4–8).

Valett Developmental Survey of Basic Learning Abilities. Fearon Publishers. A survey of skill development in several areas of growth, (ages 2–7).

Van Wagenen Listening Vocabulary Scales. Van Wagenen Psycho-educational Research Laboratories. A listening or receptive test of words, (grades 2–6).

Vineland Social Maturity Scale. American Guidance Service. Individual measure of social maturity and independence; information derived by interview with an informant, usually a parent, (birth–adult).

Wechsler Adult Intelligence Scale. Psychological Corp. An individual intelligence test for subjects over age 15, yielding verbal, performance, and full-scale scores; to be administered by trained psychological examiners.

Wechsler Preschool and Primary Scale of Intelligence (WPSI). Psychological Corp. Individual intelligence test similar to the WISC for preschool children, yielding verbal, performance, and full-scale scores; to be administered by trained psychological examiners; (ages 4–6.5).

Wepman Test of Auditory Discrimination. Language Research Associates. Individual test of auditory discrimination of phoneme sounds, (ages 5–9).

Wide Range Achievement Test, Revised Edition (1965). Guidance Associates. A brief individual test of word recognition, spelling, and arithmetic computation, (ages 5–adult).

WISC-R revised edition of the *Wechsler Intelligence Scale for Children (WISC).* Psychological Corp. Individual intelligence test that yields verbal and performance scores as well as full-scale MA and IQ scores; to be administered by trained psychological examiner, (ages 5–15).

Woodcock Reading Mastery Tests. American Guidance Services. Individual tests for identification of words, word attack, word comprehension, and passage comprehension, 20–30 minutes, (K–12). CRT and NRT interpretation.

APPENDIX D   SUPPORTIVE INFORMATION

FILMS AND FILMSTRIPS

Some films and filmstrips that are useful for teacher training or community education are listed in this section. They present theories, diagnosis, and teaching strategies for learning disabilities.

Adolescence and Learning Disabilities. Describes the tasks of adolescence and relates them to the learning-disabled adolescent. Color/sound, 40 minutes. Lawren Productions, Inc., P.O. Box 1542, Burlingame, Calif. 94010.

Anyone Can. Teacher training guide for a program of motor development. Sound/color, 30 minutes. Bradley Wright Films, 309 N. Duane Ave., San Gabriel, Calif. 91775.

Bright Boy: Bad Scholar. Illustrates the diagnosis and treatment of children with learning disabilities. Sound/black and white, 28 minutes. Contemporary Films, McGraw-Hill, 330 W. 42nd St., New York, N.Y. 10036.

Early Recognition of Learning Disabilities. Shows children with learning disabilities in their early school years. Interviews with parents and teachers. Sound/color, 30 minutes. For free loan, write to: National Medical Audiovisual Center (Annex), Station K, Atlanta, Ga. 30324. For purchase: National Audiovisual Center, National Archives and Records Service, Washington, D.C. 20409.

Help in Auditory Perception. Overview of problems in auditory perception, and description of materials and tasks assigned to students for independent study. Sound/black and white, 36 minutes. New York State Education Department, Division for Handicapped Children, Special Education Instructional Materials Center, 800 North Pearl Street, Albany, N.Y. 12204.

Help in Visual Perception. Presents the activities involved in increasing visual memory in a child whose "eyes play tricks" on him. Sound/black and white, 30 minutes. New York State Education Department, Division for Handicapped Children, Special Education Instructional Materials Center, 800 North Pearl Street, Albany, N.Y. 12204.

If A Boy Can't Learn. Deals with a seventeen-year-old high school student with a learning disability. Sound/color, 28 minutes. Lawren Productions, Inc., P.O. Box 1542, Burlingame, Calif. 94010.

I'm Not Too Famous At It. Shows the importance of knowing what children can and cannot do and exhibits the many and varied behavioral problems associated with learning disabilities. Sound/black and white, 28 minutes. Contemporary Films, McGraw-Hill, 330 W. 42nd St., New York, N.Y. 10036.

I'm Really Trying. A segment of the "Marcus Welby, M.D.," television show about a learning disabled boy. Sound/color, 52 minutes. ACLD, 220 Bownsville Rd., Pittsburgh, Pa. 15210.

The Learning Series. Four films showing graphic episodes of children attempting to cope with life tasks for which they are not ready. Sound/black and white, 28 minutes. Contemporary Films, McGraw-Hill, 330 W. 42nd St., New York, N.Y. 10036.

Motor Development I. Deals with the early development of motor sequences in children. Sound/black and white, 51 minutes. N. C. Kephart, Film Coordinator, Special Education Section, Purdue University, SCAX, Lafayette, Ind. 47907.

Motor Development II. Continuation of Motor Development I showing examples of differentiation, mostly abnormal, with comparisons in movement. Sound/black and white, 50 minutes. (Same source as Motor Development I.)

Movement Exploration. Demonstrates the techniques of various motor skills. Sound/color, 22 minutes. Documental Films, 3217 Trout Gulch Rd., Aptos, Calif. 95003.

A Movigenic Curriculum. Explains an experimental motor curriculum. Shows exercise for various areas of motor development. Sound/black and white, 41 minutes. Ray Barsch, SEIMC, 55 Elk St., Albany, N.Y. 12224.

Public School Program for Learning Disabilities. Film of a self-contained classroom of young children with various neurological learning disorders. Sound/color, 16 minutes. Office of Educational Service Region of Cook County, 33 W. Grand Ave., Chicago, Ill. 60610.

Revised Illinois Test of Psycholinguistic Abilities. A demonstration of the administration of the various subtests of the revised Illinois Test of Psycholinguistic Abilities. Sound/black and white, 43 minutes. University of Illinois Visual Aids Services, Urbana, Ill. 61820.

The School Daze of the Learning Disability Child. Explores and explains the basic handicaps of the learning-disabled child, how they create interpersonal problems at home and school, and what might be done to overcome their effects. Film sound strip, two part, 45 minutes. Alpern Communications, 220 Gulph Hills Rd., Radnor, Pa. 19087.

The Sensitoric Readiness Program. Illustrates the academic implications of training in motor skills. Sound/black and white, 22 minutes. Pathway School Resource Center, Box 181, Norristown, Pa. 19404.

Thursday's Children. Presents three major areas: (1) characteristics (especially sensory-motor problems), (2) diagnostic evaluation, and (3) educational programing. Sound/color, 32 minutes. Swank Motion Pictures, Inc., 201 South Jefferson Ave., St. Louis, Mo. 63166.

Visual Perception and Failure to Learn. Uses the Frostig Test of Visual Perception to demonstrate the relationship between disabilities in visual perception and various difficulties in learning and behavior. Sound/black and white, 20 minutes. Churchill Films, 662 North Robertson Blvd., Los Angeles, Calif. 90069.

A Walk in Another Pair of Shoes. Narrator Tennessee Ernie Ford explains to children some of the problems encountered by learning-disabled children. Sound/color filmstrip, 18½ minutes. CANHC Film Distribution, P.O. Box 1526, Vista, Calif. 92083.

Why Billy Couldn't Learn. Demonstrates problems, diagnosis, and education of children with neurological handicaps. Sound/color, 40 minutes. California Association for Neurologically Handicapped Children, 6742 Will Rogers St., Los Angeles, Calif. 96405.

JOURNALS AND PERIODICALS

The list below includes some journals and periodicals that contain articles; research; program descriptions; reviews of books, tests, and materials; news of professional organization activities; and other information that may be useful to the learning disabilities specialist.

Academic Therapy. 1539 Fourth St., San Rafael, Calif. 94901.

Asha, A Journal of the American Speech and Hearing Association. 9030 Old Georgetown Rd., Washington, D.C. 20014.

Elementary English. Official journal of the Elementary Section of the National Council of Teachers of English. 111 Kenyon Rd., Urbana, Ill. 61801.

Exceptional Children. Publication of the Council for Exceptional Children. 1920 Association Dr., Reston, Va. 22091.

The Exceptional Parent. P.O. Box 101, Boston, Mass. 02117.

Focus on Exceptional Children. 6635 E. Villanova Place, Denver, Colo. 80222.

Journal of Learning Disabilities. 101 E. Ontario, Chicago, Ill. 60611.

Journal of Reading. Published for secondary teachers by the International Reading Association. 800 Barksdale Rd., Newark, Del. 19711.

The Journal of Special Education. 1115 5th Ave., New York, N.Y. 10003.

Reading Research Quarterly. Publication of the International Reading Association, devoted to complete research studies. 800 Barksdale Rd., Newark, Del. 19711.

The Reading Teacher. Publication of the International Reading Association. 800 Barksdale Rd., Newark, Del. 19711.

Teaching Exceptional Children. Publication of the Council for Exceptional Children. 1920 Association Dr., Reston, Va. 22091.

COLLEGES FOR STUDENTS WITH LEARNING DISABILITIES

Finding the appropriate post-high school education is an important and difficult task. The high school guidance counselor can be an extremely helpful source. Descriptive data in the annual *Barron's Guide to Colleges and Universities* and the *Barron's Guide to Two-Year Colleges* (Barron's Educational Series, Inc.) is available in most high school guidance offices and in many public libraries.

A *National Directory of Four Year Colleges, Two Year Colleges and Post-High School Training Programs for Young People with Learning Disabilities* (Moss 1971, 1975) compiled by members of the Department of Special Education at East Texas State University for the Association for Children with Learning Disabilities, gives results of a national survey. Using the 1971 *Directory,* Wells (1973) sent a questionnaire to heads of English departments of 387 four-year and two-year colleges that indicated they would admit students with learning disabilities. Of the 153 responses received by Wells, the following 20 schools answered that they had staff persons with special training in learning disabilities.

College	Enrollment (approximate)
Agriculture and Technical College, Morrisville, N.Y.	2,500
Arkansas Polytechnical, Russeville, Ark.	2,492
College of the Redwoods, Eureka, Calif.	4,313
Cuyahoga Community College, Cleveland, Ohio	16,313
Fulton-Montgomery Community College, Johnstown, N.Y.	1,039
Grand Canyon College, Phoenix, Ariz.	851
Gulf Coast Community College, Panama City, Fla.	2,000
Harford Junior College, Bel Air, Md.	2,000
Idaho State University, Pocatello, Idaho	8,400
Loyola University of L.A., Los Angeles, Calif.	1,840
Kansas State College, Pittsburg, Kans.	5,720
Milwaukee Technical College, Milwaukee, Wisc.	23,000
Northeastern Junior College, Sterling, Colo.	1,400
Quinsigamond Community College, Worcester, Mass.	1,400
Southeastern Community College, Whitesville, N.Y.	1,158
Southwest Texas College, Uvalde, Tex.	1,325
St. Mary's College of O'Fallon, O'Fallon, Mo.	294
St. Phillip's College, San Antonio, Tex.	2,400
Treasure Valley Community College, Ontario, Oreg.	856
Westmar College, LeMars, Iowa	1,100

Other colleges with programs for students with learning disabilities are College of the Ozarks, Clarksville, Ark. 72830 and Curry College, Milton, Mass. 02186.

Special provisions for College Board admission testing can be made for handicapped students (College Entrance Examination Board and Educational Testing Service, 1974). Information about this testing program can be obtained from ATP for Handicapped Students, College Entrance Examination Board, Box 592, Princeton, N.J. 08540.

REFERENCES

College Entrance Examination Board and Educational Testing Service. *College Admissions Testing Program for Handicapped Students*. Princeton, N.J.: 1974.

Moss, John R. (Chairman). *A National Directory of Four Year Colleges, Two Year Colleges and Post-High School Training Programs for Young People with Learning Disabilities*. Commerce, Tex.: East Texas State University 1971, 1975. Commerce is also headquarters for the Association for Children with Learning Disabilities.

Wells, Lorraine Rosemary S. *Writing Disorders in the Learning Disabilities Student in the College Classroom*. Unpublished doctoral dissertation, Northwestern University, Evanston, Ill. August 1973. (See Appendix A, p. 192.)

APPENDIX E   ADDRESSES OF PUBLISHERS

The following list contains, in alphabetical order, the names and addresses of the publishers and manufacturers of materials mentioned elsewhere in this book, as well as some entries of producers of materials that were not mentioned. The purpose of this listing is to serve as a convenient directory for the reader. The rapidity of changes in names and addresses makes it inevitable that some of the entries below will become out of date during the life of this textbook.

Academic Therapy Publications, 1539 Fourth St., San Rafael, Calif. 94901.
Adapt Press, Inc., 808 West Avenue North, Sioux Falls, S.D. 57104.
Addison-Wesley Publishing Co., 2725 Sand Hill Rd., Menlo Park, Calif. 94025
Allied Education Council, P.O. Box 78, Galien, Mich. 49113
Allyn & Bacon, 470 Atlantic Ave., Boston, Mass. 02210
American Book Co., 450 W. 33 St., New York, N.Y. 10001
American Education Publications, 245 Long Hill Rd., Middletown, Conn. 06457
American Guidance Associates, 1526 Gilpin Ave., Wilmington, Del.
American Guidance Service, Inc. (AGS), Publishers' Building, Circle Pines, Minn. 55014
American Speech and Hearing Association, 9030 Old Georgetown Rd., Washington, D.C. 20014
Ann Arbor Publishers, P.O. Box 338, Worthington, Ohio 43085
Appleton-Century-Crofts, 440 Park Avenue South, New York, N.Y. 10016
Arrow Book Club (Scholastic Book Services), 50 West 44 St., New York, N.Y. 10036
Association for Childhood International, 3615 Wisconsin Ave. N.W., Washington, D.C. 20036.
Baldridge Reading Instructional Materials, 14 Grigg St., Greenwich, Conn. 06830
Bantam Books, Inc., 666 Fifth Ave., New York, N.Y. 10019
Barnell-Loft, 958 Church St., Baldwin, N.Y. 11510
Basic Books, Inc., 10 E. 53 St., New York, N.Y. 10022
Bausch & Lomb Optical Co., Rochester, N.Y. 14602
Beckley-Cardy, 1900 N. Narragansett, Chicago, Ill. 60639
Behavioral Research Laboratories, P.O. Box 577, Palo Alto, Calif. 94302
Bell and Howell, 7100 McCormick Rd., Chicago, Ill. 60645
Benefic Press, 10300 W. Roosevelt Rd., Westchester, Ill. 60153
The Bobbs-Merrill Co., 4300 W. 62 St., Indianapolis, Ind. 46206
Book-Lab, Inc., 1449 37 St., Brooklyn, N.Y. 11218
Borg-Warner Educational Systems, 7450 N. Natchez Ave., Niles, Ill. 60648
Bowmar, Box 3623, Glendale, Calif. 91201
William C. Brown Co., 2460 Kerper Blvd., Dubuque, Iowa 52001
Burgess Publishing, 7108 Olms Lane, Minneapolis, Minn. 55435

California Test Bureau, A Division of McGraw-Hill, Del Monte Research Park, Monterey, Calif. 93940

Center for Applied Linguistics, 1717 Massachusetts Ave. N.W., Washington, D.C. 20036

Children's Press, 1224 West Van Buren St., Chicago, Ill. 60607

Communication Research Associates, P.O. Box 110012, Salt Lake City, Utah

Consulting Psychologists Press, 577 College Ave., Palo Alto, Calif. 94306

Continental Press, Inc., Elizabethtown, Pa. 17022

Council for Exceptional Children, 1920 Association Dr., Reston, Va. 22091

Craig Corp., 921 W. Artesia Blvd., Compton, Calif. 90220

Creative Playthings, Inc., Edinburg Rd., Cranbury, N.J. 08540

Creative Publications, P.O. Box 10328, Palo Alto, Calif. 94303

Crippled Children and Adults of Rhode Island, The Meeting Street School, 33 Grotto Ave., Providence, R.I.

Cuisenaire Company of America, Inc., 12 Church St., New Rochelle, N.Y. 10885

Developmental Learning Materials, 7440 N. Natchez Ave., Niles, Ill. 60648

Devereau Foundation, Devon, Pa.

Dexter & Westbrook, Ltd., 958 Church St., Rockville Centre, N.Y. 11510

DIAL, Inc., Box 911, Highland Park, Ill. 60035

Doubleday & Co., Garden City, N.Y. 11530

The Economy Company, 1901 N. Walnut Ave., Oklahoma City, Okla. 74103

Edmark Associates, 655 S. Orcas St., Seattle, Wash. 98108

Educational Activities, Inc., 1937 Grand Ave., Baldwin, N.Y. 11520

Educational Development Laboratories, A Division of McGraw-Hill, 1121 Avenue of the Americas, New York, N.Y. 10020

Educational Performance Associates, 563 Westview Ave., Ridgefield, N.J. 07657

Educational Service, Inc., P.O. Box 219, Stevensville, Mich. 49127

Educational Teaching Aids Division, A. Daigger & Co., 159 W. Kinzie St., Chicago, Ill. 60610

Educational Testing Service, Princeton, N.J. 08540

Educator's Publishing Service, 75 Moulton St., Cambridge, Mass. 02138

Edukaid of Ridgewood, 1250 E. Ridgewood Ave., Ridgewood, N.J. 07450

Electronic Future, Inc., 57 Dodge Ave., North Haven, Conn. 06473

Encyclopaedia Britannica Educational Corp., 425 N. Michigan Ave., Chicago, Ill. 60611

Essay Press, Box 5, Planetarium Station, New York, N.Y. 10024

Fearon Publishers, 6 Davis Dr., Belmont, Calif. 94002

Field Educational Publications, Inc., 2400 Hanover St., Palo Alto, Calif. 94002

Follett Educational Corp., 1010 W. Washington Blvd., Chicago, Ill. 60607

Alvyn M. Freed, 391 Munroe St., Sacramento, Calif. 95825

Garrard Publishing Co., 1607 N. Market St., Champaign, Ill. 61820

General Learning Corp., 250 James St., Morristown, N.J. 07960

Ginn & Co., 191 Spring St., Lexington, Mass. 02173

Globe Book Co., 175 Fifth Ave., New York, N.Y. 10010

Grune & Stratton, 111 Fifth Ave., New York, N.Y. 10003

Gryphon Press, 220 Montgomery St., Highland Park, N.J. 08904

Guidance Associates, 1526 Gilpin Ave., Wilmington, Del. 19800

E. M. Hale & Co., 1201 S. Hastings Way, Eau Claire, Wisc. 54701

C. S. Hammond & Co., 515 Valley St., Maplewood, N.J. 07040

Harcourt Brace Jovanovich, Inc., 757 Third Ave., New York, N.Y. 10017

Harper & Row Publishers, Inc., 10 East 53 St., New York, N.Y. 10022
D. C. Heath & Co., 125 Spring St., Lexington, Mass. 02173
Marshall S. Hiskey, 5640 Baldwin, Lincoln, Neb. 68507
Hoffman Information Systems, Inc., 5632 Peck Rd., Arcadia, Calif. 91006
Holt, Rinehart and Winston, Inc., 383 Madison Ave., New York, N.Y. 10017
Houghton Mifflin Co., One Beacon St., Boston, Mass. 02107
Houston Press, University of Houston, Houston, Tex. 77000
Ideal School Supply Co., 11000 South Lavergne, Oak Lawn, Ill. 60453
Initial Teaching Alphabet Publications, Inc., 6 E. 43 St., New York, N.Y. 10017
Instructional Industries, Inc., Executive Park, Ballston Lake, N.Y. 12019
Instructo Corp., 200 Cedar Hollow Rd., Paoli, Pa. 19301
The Instructor Publications, 7 Bank St., Dansville, N.Y. 14437
International Reading Association, 800 Barksdale Rd., Newark, Del. 19711
Jones-Kenilworth Co., 8301 Ambassador Row, Dallas, Tex. 75247
Journal of Learning Disabilities, 101 East Ontario St., Chicago, Ill. 60611
Journal of Special Education, 433 S. Gulph Rd., King of Prussia, Pa. 19406
The Judy Co., 310 N. Second St., Minneapolis, Minn. 55401
Kenworthy Educational Service, P.O. Box 3031, 138 Allen St., Buffalo, N.Y. 14201
Keystone View Co., 2212 E. 12 St., Davenport, Iowa 52803
Laidlaw Bros., Thatcher & Madison Sts., River Forest, Ill. 60305
Language Research Associates, Box 95, 950 E. 59 St., Chicago, Ill. 60637
Learning Concepts, 2501 N. Lamar, Austin, Tex. 78705
Learning Corporation of America, 1350 Avenue of the Americas, New York, N.Y.
    10019
Learning Research Associates, 1501 Broadway, New York, N.Y. 10036
Learning Resource Division, EDL, 202 Miriam Dr., Lakeland, Fla. 33803
Learning Through Seeing, LTS Bldg., Box 368, Sunland, Calif. 91040
J. P. Lippincott Co., E. Washington Square, Philadelphia, Pa. 19105
Love Publishing Co., 6635 E. Villanova Pl., Denver, Colo. 80222
Lyons and Carnahan Educational Publishers, 407 E. 25 St., Chicago, Ill. 60616
The Macmillan Co., 866 Third Ave., New York, N.Y. 10022
Mafex Associates, Inc., 111 Barron Ave., Johnstown, Pa. 16906
McCormick-Mathers Publishing Co., 450 W. 33rd St., New York, N.Y. 10001
McGraw-Hill Book Co., 1221 Avenue of the Americas, New York, N.Y. 10020
McGraw Hill/Early Learning, Paoli, Pa. 19301
David McKay Co., 750 Third Ave., New York, N.Y. 10017
Charles E. Merrill, 1300 Alum Creek Dr., Columbus, Ohio 43216
Milton Bradley Co., 74 Park St., Springfield, Mass. 01101
Modern Curriculum Press, 13900 Prospect Rd., Cleveland, Ohio 44136
William C. Morrow, 105 Madison Ave., New York, N.Y. 10016
The C. V. Mosby Co., 11830 Westline Industrial Dr., St. Louis, Mo. 63141
Motivational Research Inc., P.O. Box 140, McLean, Va. 22101
National Council of Teachers of English, 1111 Kenyon Rd., Urbana, Ill. 61801
National Education Association Publications, 1201 16 St., N.W., Washington,
    D.C. 20036
National Reading Conference, Inc., Reading Center, Marquette University, Mil-
    waukee, Wisc. 53233
New Readers Press, Box 131, Syracuse, N.Y. 13210
New York Association for Brain Injured Children, 305 Broadway, New York,
    N.Y. 10007

Noble & Noble, Publishers, 1 Dag Hammarskjold Plaza, New York, N.Y. 10017
Northwestern University Press, 1735 Benson Ave., Evanston, Ill. 60201
Open Court Publishing Co., Box 599, 1039 Eighth St., LaSalle, Ill. 61301
Orton Society, 8415 Bellona Lane, Towson, Md. 21204
F. A. Owen Publishing Co., 7 Bank St., Dansville, N.Y. 14437
Peek Publications, P.O. Box 11065, Palo Alto, Calif. 94303
Perceptual Development Laboratories, 6767 Southwest Ave., St. Louis, Mo. 63143
Phonovisual Products, 12216 Parklawn Dr., Rockville, Md. 20852
Prentice-Hall, Inc., Englewood Cliffs, N.J. 07632
J. A. Preston Corp., 71 Fifth Ave., New York, N.Y. 10003
Priority Innovations, P.O. Box 792, Skokie, Ill. 60076
The Psychological Corp., 304 E. 45 St., New York, N.Y. 10017
Psychological Test Specialists, Box 1441, Missoula, Mont. 59801
Psychotechnics, 1900 Pickwick Ave., Glenview, Ill. 60025
G. P. Putnam Sons, 200 Madison Ave., New York, N.Y. 10016
Rand McNally & Co., P.O. Box 7600, Chicago, Ill. 60680
Random House, 201 E. 50 St., New York, N.Y. 10022
Reader's Digest Services, Educational Division, Pleasantville, N.Y. 10570
Rheem Califone, 5922 Bancroft St., Los Angeles, Calif. 90016
Scholastic Magazine and Book Services, 50 W. 44 St., New York, N.Y. 10036
Science Research Associates, 259 E. Erie St., Chicago, Ill. 60611
Scott, Foresman and Co., 1900 East Lake Ave., Glenview, Ill. 60025
Silver Burdett Co., A Division of General Learning Corp., 250 James St., Morris-
    town, N.J. 07960
The L. W. Singer Co., A Division of Random House, 201 E. 50 St., New York,
    N.Y. 10022
Slosson Educational Publications, 140 Pine St., East Aurora, N.Y. 14052
Society for Visual Education, 1356 Diversey Parkway, Chicago, Ill. 60614
Special Child Publications, 4635 Union Bay Place N.E., Seattle, Wash. 98105
Steck-Vaughn Co., Box 2028, Austin, Tex. 78767
C. H. Stoelting Co., 424 N. Homan Ave., Chicago, Ill. 60624
Teachers College Press, Teachers College, Columbia University, 1234 Amsterdam
    Ave., New York, N.Y. 10027
Teachers Publishing Corp., 22 W. Putnam Ave., Greenwich, Conn. 06830
Teaching Aids, 159 W. Kinzie St., Chicago, Ill. 60610
Teaching Resources Corp., 100 Boylston St., Boston, Mass. 02116
Teaching Technology Corp., 7471 Greenbush Ave., North Hollywood, Calif. 91609
Charles C. Thomas Publisher, 301–27 E. Lawrence Ave., Springfield, Ill. 62717
3 M Visual Products, 3 M Center, St. Paul, Minn. 55101
Tweedy Transparencies, 207 Hollywood Ave., East Orange, N.J. 07018
United States Department of Health, Education and Welfare, Washington, D.C.
    20025
United States Government Printing Office, Superintendent of Documents, Wash-
    ington, D.C. 20025
University of Chicago Press, 5801 Ellis Ave., Chicago, Ill. 60637
University of Illinois Press, Urbana, Ill. 61801
George Wahr Publishing Co., 316 State St., Ann Arbor, Mich. 41808
Webster Division, McGraw-Hill, Manchester Rd., Manchester, Mo. 63011
Weekly Reader Paperback Book Club, American Education Publications, A Xerox
    Company, 55 High St., Middletown, Conn. 06457

Wenkart Publishing Co., 4 Shady Hill Square, Cambridge, Mass. 02138
Western Psychological Services, 12031 Wilshire Blvd., Los Angeles, Calif. 90025
Western Publishing Education Services, 1220 Mound Ave., Racine, Wisc. 53404
Westinghouse Learning Corp., P.O. Box 30, Iowa City, Iowa 52240
Wheeler Publishing Co., 10 E. 53 St., New York, N.Y. 10022
John Wiley & Sons, 605 Third Ave., New York, N.Y. 10016
Winston Press, Inc., 25 Groveland Terrace, Minneapolis, Minn. 55403
Winter Haven Lions Research Foundation, Box 1112, Winter Haven, Fla. 33880
Xerox Education Publications, Education Center, Columbus, Ohio 43216
Zaner-Bloser Co., 612 North Park St., Columbus, Ohio 43215
Richard L. Zweig Associates, 20800 Beach Blvd., Huntington Beach, Calif. 92648

APPENDIX F GLOSSARY

Agnosia The inability to obtain information through one of the input channels or senses, despite the fact that the receiving organ itself is not impaired. The medical term is associated with a neurological abnormality of the central nervous system.

Alexia The loss of ability to read because of some brain damage, such as a cerebral stroke. The term also refers to the complete failure to *acquire* reading skills as well as to a partial or complete loss of these skills through brain damage.

Anomia (dysnomia) Difficulty in recalling or remembering words or the names of objects.

Aphasia Impairment of the ability to use or understand oral language. It is usually associated with an injury or abnormality of the speech centers of the brain. Several classifications are used, including expressive and receptive, congenital, and acquired aphasia.

Apraxia Difficulty in motor output or in performing purposeful motor movements. This medical term reflects an abnormality of the central nervous system.

Auding A level of auditory reception that involves comprehension as well as hearing and listening.

Auditory blending The ability to synthesize the phonemes of a word, when they are pronounced with separations between phonemes, so that the word can be recognized as a whole.

Auditory perception The ability to interpret or organize the sensory data received through the ear.

Basal reader approach A method of teaching reading in which instruction is given through the use of a series of basal readers. Sequence of skills, content, vocabulary, and activities are determined by the authors of the series. Teacher's manuals and children's activity books accompany the basal reading series.

Behavior modification A technique of changing human behavior based on the theory of operant behavior and conditioning. Careful observation of events preceding and following the behavior in question is required. The environment is manipulated to reinforce the desired responses, thereby bringing about the desired change in behavior.

Bibliotherapy The use of reading, particularly the use of characters in books with whom the child identifies, for therapeutic purposes.

Binocular difficulties A visual impairment due to the inability of the two eyes to function together.

Body image An awareness of one's own body and the relationship of the body parts to each other and to the outside environment.

Brain-injured child A child who before, during, or after birth has received an injury to or suffered an infection of the brain. As a result of such organic impairment, there are disturbances that prevent or impede the normal learning process.

Cerebral dominance The control of activities by the brain, with one hemisphere usually considered consistently dominant over the other. In most individuals, the left side of the brain controls language function, and the left side is considered the dominant hemisphere.

Clinical teaching An approach to teaching that attempts to tailor-make learning experiences for the unique needs of a particular child. Consideration is given to the child's individualistic ways of learning and processing information.

Closure The ability to recognize a whole or Gestalt, especially when one or more parts of the whole are missing or when the continuity is interrupted by gaps.

Cloze procedure A technique used in testing, teaching reading comprehension, and determining readability. It involves deletion of words from the text and leaving blank spaces. Measurement is made by rating the number of blanks that can be correctly filled.

Cognition The act or process of knowing; the various thinking skills and processes are considered cognitive skills.

Concept An abstract idea generalized from particular instances.

Conceptual disorders A disturbance in the thinking process and in cognitive activities, or a disturbance in the ability to formulate concepts.

Content words (class words or lexical words) Words in a language that have referential meaning, as opposed to words or morphemes with relational value (function or structure words). Content words are roughly similar to verbs, nouns, adjectives, and adverbs.

Cross-modality perception The neurological process of converting information received through one input modality to another system within the brain. The process is also referred to as "intersensory transfer," "intermodal transfer," and "transducing."

Delivery systems The various ways of offering educational services to children, e.g., self-contained classes, resource rooms, regular classrooms, etc.

Developmental imbalance A disparity in the developmental patterns of intellectual skills.

Developmental reading The pattern and sequence of normal reading growth and development in a child in the learning-to-read process.

Dyscalculia Lack of ability to perform mathematical functions, usually associated with neurological dysfunction or brain damage.

Dysgraphia Extremely poor handwriting or the inability to perform the motor movements required for handwriting. The condition is often associated with neurological dysfunction.

Dyslexia A disorder of children who, despite conventional classroom experience, fail to attain the skills of reading. The term is frequently used when neurological dysfunction is suspected as the cause of the reading disability.

Dysnomia See *Anomia*.

Echolalia The parrot-like repetition of words, phrases, or sentences spoken by another person, without understanding the meaning of the language.

Educational therapist A teacher who teaches or treats a child who has difficulty in learning. Specialized materials and methods are used.

Electroencephalograph An instrument for graphically recording and measuring electrical energy generated by the cerebral cortex during brain functioning. It is often abbreviated as EEG.

Endogenous A condition or defect based on hereditary or genetic factors is labeled an endogenous condition.

Etiology The cause or origin of a condition.

Exogenous A condition or defect resulting from other than heredity or genetic factors (such as environment or trauma) is labeled an exogenous condition.

Expressive language skills Skills required to produce language for communication with other individuals. Speaking and writing are expressive language skills.

Figure-ground distortion An inability to focus on an object itself without having the background or setting interfere with perception.

Figure-ground perception The ability to attend to one aspect of the visual field while perceiving it in relation to the rest of the field.

Function words See *Structure words*.

Grapheme A written language symbol that represents an oral language code.

Homologous This term refers to body structures that have the same origin in different species; e.g., the arm of a man and the wing of a bird. It is also used to refer to crawling by moving the two arms together and then the two legs together.

Hyperkinesis Constant and excessive movement and motor activity.

Hypokinesis The absence of a normal amount of bodily movement and motor activity. Extreme lack of movement or listlessness.

Impulsivity The behavioral characteristic of acting upon impulse without consideration of the consequences of an action.

Individualized reading The method of teaching reading that utilizes the child's interest; learning is structured through the child's own reading selections, using a variety of books. The teacher acts as a consultant, aid, and counselor.

Innate response system The unlearned motor responses that the child has within him at birth.

Inner language The process of internalizing and organizing experiences without the use of linguistic symbols.

Intonation system The linguistic system within any particular language that has to do with the pitch (melody), stress (accent), and juncture (pauses) of the spoken language.

Itinerant teacher A teacher who moves about a school district to several schools and schedules children for teaching periods. Children leave their regular classrooms to work with the itinerant teacher.

Language arts School curricular activities that utilize language, namely: listening, speaking, reading, writing, handwriting, and spelling.

Language-experience approach to reading A method of teaching reading and other language skills, based on the experiences of children. The method frequently involves the generation of experienced-based materials that are dictated by the child, written down by the teacher, then used in class as the material for teaching reading.

Language pathology The study of the causes and treatment of disorders of symbolic behavior.

Lateral confusion See *Mixed laterality.*

Laterality Involves the awareness of the two sides of one's body and the ability to identify them as left or right correctly.

Learning disabilities (Based on definition provided by the National Advisory Committee on Handicapped Children, U.S. Dept. of Health, Education and Welfare, 1968.) A learning disability refers to one or more significant deficits in essential learning processes requiring special educational techniques for its remediation. Children with learning disabilities generally demonstrate a discrepancy between expected and actual achievement in one or more areas, such as spoken, read, or written language, mathematics, and spatial orientation. The learning disability referred to is not primarily the result of sensory, motor, intellectual, or emotional handicap, or lack of opportunity to learn. Deficits are to be defined in terms of accepted diagnostic procedures in education and psychology. Essential learning processes are those currently referred to in behavioral science as perception, integration, and expression, either verbal or nonverbal. Special education techniques for remediation require educational planning based on the diagnostic procedures and findings.

Lexical words See *Structure words.*

Linguistics The scientific study of the nature and function of human language.

Mainstreaming Placing of children with handicaps within the regular education system of the school, particularly in the regular classroom.

Maturational lag A slowness in certain specialized aspects of neurological development.

Memory The ability to store and retrieve upon demand previously experienced sensations and perceptions, even when the stimulus that originally evoked them is no longer present. Also referred to as "imagery" and "recall."

Minimal brain dysfunction A mild or minimal neurological abnormality that causes learning difficulties in the child with near-average intelligence.

Mixed laterality or lateral confusion Tendency to perform some acts with a right side preference and others with a left, or the shifting from right to left for certain activities.

Modality The pathways through which an individual receives information and thereby learns. The "modality concept" postulates that some individuals learn better through one modality than through another. For example, a child may receive data better through the visual modality than the auditory modality.

Morpheme The smallest meaning-bearing unit in a language.

Morphology The linguistic system of meaning units in any particular language.

Noncategorical Refers to a system of grouping handicapped children together within reference to a particular label or category of exceptionality.

Ocular pursuit Eye movement that is the result of visually following a moving target.

Oracy The communication skills of oral language: listening and speaking.

Perception The process of organizing or interpreting the raw data obtained through the senses.

Perception of position The perception of the size and movement of an object in relation to the observer.

Perception of spatial relationship The perception of the positions of two or more objects in relation to each other.

Perceptual constancy The ability to accurately perceive the invariant properties of objects — such as shape, position, size, etc. — in spite of the variability of the impression these objects make on the senses of the observer.

Perceptual disorder A disturbance in the awareness of objects, relations, or qualities, involving the interpretation of sensory stimulation.

Perceptually handicapped A term applied to the person who has difficulty in learning because of a disturbance in perception of sensory stimuli.

Perceptual-motor A term describing the interaction of the various channels of perception with motor activity. The channels of perception include visual, auditory, tactual, and kinesthetic.

Perceptual-motor match The process of comparing and collating the input data received through the motor system and the input data received through perception.

Perseveration The tendency to continue an activity once it has been started and to be unable to modify or stop the activity even though it is acknowledged to have become inappropriate.

Phoneme The smallest unit of sound in any particular language.

Phonetics A study of all the speech sounds in language and how these sounds are produced.

Phonics The application of portions of phonetics to the teaching of reading, particularly the teaching of reading in English. The establishment of the sound (or phoneme) of the language with the equivalent written symbol (or grapheme).

Phonology The linguistic system of speech sounds in a particular language.

Primary reading retardation The capacity to learn to read is impaired and no definite brain damage is suggested in the history or neurological examination. Further, there is no evidence of secondary reading retardation (that due to exogenous causes such as emotional disturbances or lack of opportunity). The problem seems to reflect a lack of neurological organization.

Programed reading A method of teaching reading that uses programed self-instructional and self-corrective materials.

Psychoeducational diagnostician A specialist who diagnoses and evaluates a child who is having difficulty in learning. A variety of psychological and educational testing instruments are used.

Psycholinguistics The field of study that blends aspects of two disciplines — psychology and linguistics — to examine the total picture of the language process.

Readability level An indication of the difficulty of reading material in terms of the grade level at which it might be expected to be read successfully.

Receptive language Language that is spoken or written by others and received by the individual. The receptive language skills are listening and reading.

Resource teacher A specialist who works with children with learning disabilities and acts as a consultant to other teachers, providing materials and methods to help children who are having difficulty within the regular classroom. The resource teacher works from a centralized resource room within a school where appropriate materials are housed.

Semantics A lingustic term referring to the meaning system in language.

Semi-autonomous systems concept of brain function A theory of brain function suggesting that at times a given modality functions semi-independently and at other times the modality functions in a supplementary way with another modality system; at still other times, all the modality systems function together as a unit.

Sensory-motor A term applied to the combination of the input of sensations and the output of motor activity. The motor activity reflects what is happening to the sensory organs such as the visual, auditory, tactual, and kinesthetic sensations.

Social perception The ability to interpret stimuli in the social environment and appropriately relate such interpretations to the social situation.

Soft neurological signs Neurological abnormalities that are mild or slight and difficult to detect, as contrasted with the gross or obvious neurological abnormalities.

Strauss Syndrome A collection of behavioral characteristics describing the child who has difficulty in learning.

Strephosymbolia Perception of visual stimuli, especially words, in reversed or twisted order. The condition may be explained as "twisted symbols."

Structure words (function words, lexical words) Linguistic referents for words of a sentence that show the relationship between parts of the sentence, as opposed to content words. Structure words include these elements of traditional grammar: prepositions, conjunctions, modal and auxiliary verbs, and articles.

Syntax The grammar system of a language. The linguistic rules of word order and the function of words in a sentence.

Tachistoscope A machine that exposes written material for a short period of time. Practice with such machines is designed to improve rate and span of visual perception of words.

Tactile perception The ability to interpret and give meaning to sensory stimuli that are experienced through the sense of touch.

Task analysis The technique of carefully examining a particular task to discover the elements it comprises and the processes required to perform it.

Trial lessons A diagnostic technique to discover how a child best learns. Short lessons are given through the visual, auditory, tactual, and combination approaches. Evaluations of the child's performance on each provides information concerning his learning style.

Visual-motor coordination The ability to coordinate vision with the movements of the body or parts of the body.

Visual perception The identification, organization, and interpretation of sensory data received by the individual through the eye.

Index